Cost–Benefit Analysis

Concepts and Practice

Fifth edition

Cost–Benefit Analysis provides accessible, comprehensive, authoritative, and practical treatments of the protocols for assessing the relative efficiency of public policies. Its review of essential concepts from microeconomics and its sophisticated treatment of important topics with minimal use of mathematics helps students from a variety of backgrounds to build solid conceptual foundations. It provides thorough treatments of time discounting; dealing with contingent uncertainty using expected surpluses and option prices; taking account of parameter uncertainties using Monte Carlo simulation and other types of sensitivity analyses; revealed preference approaches; stated preference methods including contingent valuation; and other related methods.

Updated to cover contemporary research, this edition is considerably reorganized to aid in student and practitioner understanding, and includes eight new cases to demonstrate the actual practice of cost–benefit analysis. Widely cited, it is recognized as an authoritative source on cost–benefit analysis. Illustrations, exhibits, chapter exercises, and case studies help students to master concepts and develop craft skills.

Anthony E. Boardman is a Professor Emeritus at the University of British Columbia. With colleagues, he has won the Peter Larkin Award, the Alan Blizzard Award, the John Vanderkamp prize, and the J.E. Hodgetts Award. He has also been a consultant to many leading public-sector and private-sector organizations, including the Government of Canada and the Inter-American Development Bank. He served two terms on the Patented Medicine Prices Review Board and is currently on the Board of the Institute for Health System Transformation and Sustainability.

David H. Greenberg is Professor Emeritus of economics at the University of Maryland, Baltimore County (UMBC). He is a labor economist and cost–benefit analyst who received his PhD at MIT. Before coming to UMBC, he worked for the Rand Corporation, SRI International, and the US Department of Health and Human Services. He has taught courses in cost–benefit analysis at the University of Wisconsin-Madison, George Washington University, Budapest University of Economic Science, and Central European University. He is a long-time consultant to MDRC, Abt Associates and other research organizations.

Aidan R. Vining is the CNABS Professor of Business and Government Relations at Simon Fraser University in Vancouver. With co-authors, he is a winner of the John Vanderkamp prize (Canadian Economics Association) and the J.E. Hodgetts Award (Institute of Public Administration of Canada). With David Weimer, he is the co-author of *Policy Analysis; Concepts and Practice*.

David L. Weimer is the Edwin E. Witte Professor of Political Economy at the University of Wisconsin-Madison. He was president of the Association for Public Policy Analysis and Management in 2006 and president of the Society for Benefit–Cost Analysis in 2013. He is a past editor of the *Journal of Policy Analysis and Management* and currently serves on many editorial boards. He is also a Fellow of the National Academy of Public Administration.

Cost–Benefit Analysis

Concepts and Practice

Fifth edition

Anthony E. Boardman
University of British Columbia, Vancouver

David H. Greenberg
University of Maryland, Baltimore County

Aidan R. Vining
Simon Fraser University, British Columbia

David L. Weimer
University of Wisconsin–Madison

CAMBRIDGE
UNIVERSITY PRESS

CAMBRIDGE
UNIVERSITY PRESS

University Printing House, Cambridge CB2 8BS, United Kingdom

One Liberty Plaza, 20th Floor, New York, NY 10006, USA

477 Williamstown Road, Port Melbourne, VIC 3207, Australia

314–321, 3rd Floor, Plot 3, Splendor Forum, Jasola District Centre, New Delhi – 110025, India

79 Anson Road, #06–04/06, Singapore 079906

Cambridge University Press is part of the University of Cambridge.

It furthers the University's mission by disseminating knowledge in the pursuit of
education, learning, and research at the highest international levels of excellence.

www.cambridge.org
Information on this title: www.cambridge.org/9781108415996
DOI: 10.1017/9781108235594

First, second, third, fourth edition © Pearson Education, Inc., 1996, 2001, 2006, 2011

Fourth edition © Anthony E. Boardman, David H. Greenberg, Aidan R. Vining, and David L.Weimer 2018

Fifth edition © Anthony E. Boardman, David H. Greenberg, Aidan R. Vining, and David L.Weimer 2018

First edition 1996
Second edition 2001
Third edition 2006
Fourth edition 2011 & 2018
Fifth edition 2018

Printed in the United States of America by Sheridan Books, Inc., 2018

A catalogue record for this publication is available from the British Library

Library of Congress Cataloging-in-Publication Data
Names: Boardman, Anthony E., author.
Title: Cost–benefit analysis : concepts and practice / Anthony E. Boardman,
University of British Columbia, Vancouver, [and three others].
Description: Fifth edition. | Cambridge, United Kingdom ; New York, NY :
Cambridge University Press, [2018]
Identifiers: LCCN 2017056020 | ISBN 9781108415996
Subjects: LCSH: Cost effectiveness.
Classification: LCC HD47.4 .C669 2018 | DDC 658.15/54–dc23
LC record available at https://lccn.loc.gov/2017056020

ISBN 978-1-108-41599-6 Hardback
ISBN 978-1-108-40129-6 Paperback

Additional resources for this publication at www.cambridge.org/Boardman5ed

Contents

Preface

Collaborative academic projects often take longer than originally anticipated, not just because of the normal delays of coordinating the efforts of busy people, but also because initially modest goals can become more ambitious as participants delve into their subject. We confess to both these sins with respect to preparing the first edition of this text. Our goal was to produce a book that would be conceptually sound, practically oriented, and easily accessible to both students and practitioners. Although our final product was far different in form and content than we initially planned, we believe that our first edition was such a book.

Our plans evolved for a number of reasons. Perhaps most importantly, through our teaching of undergraduate and graduate students in different countries, as well as our experiences training government employees in different jurisdictions, we realized that many topics demanded extended treatment if the essential basics were to be conveyed effectively and if solid foundations were to be laid for further learning of advanced topics. We also decided that integrating illustrations and examples with concepts and methods is useful in addition to presenting independent cases. The result is a series of chapters that develop conceptual foundations, methods of application, and extensions of cost–benefit analysis (CBA) through numerous practical examples and illustrations.

Our own use of the book in teaching, as well as comments from other teachers and students, have helped us identify several areas for incremental improvement in subsequent editions. With this current edition, however, we decided to take a fresh look at both organization and content. With respect to organization, we interlace the chapters providing the theoretical foundations with those showing how to implement them. For example, the chapter introducing the basics of measuring social surplus changes in markets is followed immediately with the chapter on estimating demand schedules. With respect to content, we added a number of cases that show the application of concepts in policy analyses. For example, following the chapter on estimating demand schedules, we provide cases presenting the use, and misuse, of social surplus as a benefit measure in regulatory impact analyses. Other cases illustrate using evidence from multiple sources to arrive at net benefits, conducting Monte Carlo simulation to assess uncertainty in net benefits, estimating costs and benefits from social experiments, using contingent valuation methods to assess the benefits of non-market goods, developing a shadow price from multiple data sources, and weighting costs and benefits to incorporate distributional values.

In overview, this new fifth edition provides the following:

- Updated content and references

- Rearrangement of chapters to facilitate better integration of theory and craft

- Addition of six cases providing extended illustrations of CBA craft

As with the earlier editions, answers to chapter problems, including spreadsheets that can be provided to students, are available for instructors.

Acknowledgments

Our project over the years has been made more productive and enjoyable by our many colleagues and students who gave us advice, comments, encouragement, or information. We thank here just a few people who were particularly helpful: Marcus Berliant, Edward Bird, James Brander, Stanley Engerman, Eric Hanushek, Robert Havemen, Doug Landin, Walter Oi, William G. Waters II, and Michael Wolkoff. We thank Roy I. Gobin, George T. Fuller, Ruth Shen, and Larry Karp, who wrote thoughtful reviews of the first edition for the publisher; Ian Davis, John DeWald, Tim Gindling, and Laurie T. Johnson, who offered valuable comments during preparation of the second edition; Terri Sexton and Nachum Sicherman, who offered valuable comments during preparation of the third edition; Thomas Hopkins and M. Leslie Shiell, who offered valuable comments during preparation of the fourth edition; and John Janmaat, Farhad Sabetan, and Gideon Yaniv, who offered valuable comments during preparation of the fifth edition. Haynes Goddard kindly provided helpful suggestions for both the second and third editions. We especially thank Mark Moore, whose joint work with us helped us substantially improve our discussion of the social discount rate, and Roger Noll, who made extremely valuable suggestions that prompted many other substantial revisions. Of course, they are not responsible for any errors that remain.

We also thank Robert Dreesen and the editorial team at Cambridge University Press for encouraging us to take the time to do a substantial revision. We hope that teachers and students find the new edition to be both authoritative and pedagogically effective.

List of Cases

1 Introduction to Cost–Benefit Analysis

In the Affair of so much Importance to you, wherein you ask my Advice, I cannot for want of sufficient Premises, advise you what to determine, but if you please I will tell you how. When those difficult Cases occur, they are difficult, chiefly because while we have them under Consideration, all the Reasons pro and con are not present to the Mind at the same time; but sometimes one Set present themselves, and at other times another, the first being out of Sight. Hence the various Purposes or Inclinations that alternately prevail, and the Uncertainty that perplexes us.

To get over this, my Way is, to divide half a Sheet of Paper by a Line into two Columns; writing over the one Pro, and over the other Con. Then during three or four Days Consideration, I put down under the different Heads short Hints of the different Motives, that at different Times occur to me, for or against the Measure. When I have thus got them all together in one View, I endeavor to estimate their respective Weights; and where I find two, one on each side, that seem equal, I strike them both out. If I find a Reason pro equal to some two Reasons con, I strike out the three. If I judge some two Reasons con, equal to some three Reasons pro, I strike out the five; and thus proceeding I find at length where the Balance lies; and if after a Day or two of farther consideration, nothing new that is of Importance occurs on either side, I come to a Determination accordingly. And, tho' the Weight of Reasons cannot be taken with the Precision of Algebraic Quantities, yet, when each is thus considered, separately and comparatively, and the whole lies before me, I think I can judge better, and am less liable to make a rash Step; and in fact I have found great Advantage from this kind of Equation, in what may be called Moral or Prudential Algebra.

B. Franklin, London, September 19, 1772[1]

1.1 Individual Versus Social Costs and Benefits

Benjamin Franklin's advice about how to make decisions illustrates many of the important features of cost–benefit analysis (CBA). These include a systematic cataloguing of impacts as benefits (pros) and costs (cons), valuing the impacts in dollars (assigning weights), and then determining the *net benefit* of the proposal relative to the current policy (net benefit equal incremental benefits minus incremental costs).

When we as individuals talk of costs and benefits, we naturally tend to consider our *own* costs and benefits, generally choosing among alternative courses of action according to whichever has the largest net benefit from our perspective. Similarly, in evaluating various investment alternatives, a firm tends to consider only those costs (expenditures) and benefits (revenues) that accrue to it. In CBA we try to consider *all of the costs and benefits to society as a whole*, that is, the *social costs* and the *social benefits*. For this reason, some analysts refer to CBA as *social* cost–benefit analysis.

CBA is a policy assessment method that quantifies in monetary terms the value of all consequences of a policy to all members of society. Throughout this book we use the terms *policy* and *project* interchangeably. More generally, CBA applies to policies, programs, projects, regulations, demonstrations, and other government interventions. *The broad purpose of CBA is to help social decision-making and to increase social value or, more technically, to improve allocative efficiency.*

CBA analysts focus on social costs and social benefits, and conduct social cost–benefit analysis. However, it is tedious to keep including the word "social". We usually drop it and simply refer to costs, benefits, and cost–benefit analysis. Thus, B denotes the social benefits (the aggregate benefits to all members of society) of a policy, and C denotes the social costs (the aggregate costs to all members of society) of the policy. The aggregate value of a policy is measured by its *net social benefit*, sometimes simply referred to as the net benefit, and usually denoted *NSB*:

$$NSB = B - C \qquad\qquad (1.1)$$

The term social is usually retained in the expression net social benefit to emphasize that CBA does concern the impacts on society as a whole.

Implicitly, the benefits, costs, and net social benefit of a policy are relative to some "benchmark." Usually, the "benchmark" is the status quo policy, that is, no change in the current policy. Generally, the benefits, costs, and net social benefit of a policy measure incremental changes relative to the status quo policy.

Stated at this level of abstraction, it is unlikely that many people would disagree with doing CBA from an ethical perspective. In practice, however, there are two types of disagreements. First, social critics, including some political economists, philosophers, libertarians, and socialists, have disputed the fundamental utilitarian assumptions of CBA that the sum of individual utilities should be maximized and that it is possible to trade off utility gains for some people against utility losses for others. These critics are not prepared to make trade-offs between one person's benefits and another person's costs. Second, participants in the public policy-making process (analysts, bureaucrats, and politicians) may disagree about such practical issues as what impacts will actually occur over time, how to monetize (attach value to them), and how to make trade-offs between the present and the future.

In this chapter we provide a non-technical but reasonably comprehensive overview of CBA. Although we introduce a number of key concepts, we do so informally, returning to discuss them thoroughly in subsequent chapters. Therefore, this chapter is best read without great concern about definitions and technical details.

1.2   Types of CBA Analyses

CBA may be conducted at different times in the project or policy life cycle. One type of CBA is called *ex ante* or prospective CBA. *Ex ante* literally means "before." Thus, *ex ante* CBA is conducted before the decision is made to undertake or implement a project or policy. The policy may or may not be under consideration by a government agency. If it is, then *ex ante* CBA informs the decision about whether resources should be allocated to that specific project or policy or not. Basically, *ex ante* CBA attempts to answer the question: *would* this policy or project be a good idea, that is, would it have a positive net social benefit?

Another type of CBA is called *ex post* or *retrospective CBA. Ex post* literally means "after." Thus, strictly speaking, *ex post* CBA is conducted after a policy or project is completed. It addresses the question: *was* this policy or project a good idea? Because *ex post* analysis is conducted at the end of the project, it is obviously too late to reverse resource allocation decisions with respect to that particular project. However, this type of analysis provides information not only about a specific intervention, but also about the "class" of similar interventions. In other words, it contributes to learning by government managers, politicians, and academics about the costs and benefits of future projects and whether they are likely to be worthwhile. Such learning can be incorporated into future *ex ante* CBAs. The potential benefit, however, depends on the similarity between the future project and the project previously analyzed. For example, *ex post* CBAs of experiments involving the efficacy of new surgical procedures or new pharmaceutical products can usually be generalized to larger populations. However, if the proposed intervention is much bigger than the experiment, there may be unknown scale effects. Also, if the proposed program has a more extended time frame than the experiment, behavioral responses may affect costs or benefits unpredictably.

Most projects take many years to "complete." The impacts of a highway or subway system, for example, often continue for many decades (even centuries) after initial construction. In such cases, and, in fact, for any ongoing policy or project, prudent government analysts might well wish to conduct a CBA sometime after the policy or project has begun but before it is complete. To clarify that such an analysis applies to a still ongoing project, such studies are sometimes called *in medias res* CBAs (to maintain our fancy use of Latin). They attempt to answer the question: is continuation of this policy or project a good idea? An *in medias res* CBA can be conducted any time after the decision to undertake a project has been made (but before it is complete). Such studies are also called *post-decision analyses.*

An *in medias res* CBA might recommend the termination or modification of a particular policy or project. In practice, CBAs of infrastructure projects with large sunk costs are unlikely to recommend discontinuation of a project that is near to completion or even just after completion, but it does happen occasionally. Interestingly the Tennessee Valley Authority decided to complete the Tellico Dam when it was 90 percent complete, even though the incremental social costs exceeded the incremental social benefits.[2] Also, a Canadian Environmental Assessment panel recommended decommissioning a just-completed dam on the basis of an *in medias res* analysis which showed that, with use, future environmental costs would exceed future benefits.[3]

Many businesses and critics of government complain about the burden of existing regulations and of too much "red tape." *In medias res* CBAs of some regulations might find that the critics are correct and they should be scrapped or changed for the benefit of society as a whole. In fact, *in medias res* CBAs conducted during the 1960s and 1970s of industry-specific economic regulations showed that the costs of regulation often exceeded the benefits, thereby paving the way for deregulation initiatives in the trucking, airline, and telecommunications industries.[4] These decisions were made both economically and politically easier by the reality that, unlike many physical infrastructure projects, regulatory projects usually have significant ongoing costs, rather than sunk, up-front costs. The same point also applies to ongoing social programs, such as government-funded training programs.

In practice, the term *in medias res* CBA is not used often: such CBAs are referred to as *ex post*, retrospective, hindsight, or post-decision analyses. It is particularly important if this is the case, therefore, to be clear when an *ex post* CBA is conducted: it might be any time after the decision to implement a new policy has been made.

There is also a fourth type of CBA – one that compares an *ex ante* CBA with an *ex post* CBA or an *in medias res* CBA *of the same project*.[5] Considerable research has found, for example, that the costs of large government infrastructure projects are often underestimated.[6] In contrast, another study that assessed the accuracy of US regulatory cost estimates found that these costs tend to be overestimated.[7] This comparative type of CBA helps to identify past errors, understand the reasons for them, and avoid them in the future.

1.3   The Basic Steps of CBA: Coquihalla Highway Example

CBA may look quite intimidating and complex. To make the process of conducting a CBA more manageable, we break it down into 10 basic steps, which are listed in Table 1.1. We describe and illustrate these steps using a relatively straightforward example: the proposed construction of a new highway. For each step, we also point out some practical difficulties. The conceptual and practical issues that we broach are the focus of the rest of this book. Do not worry if the concepts are unfamiliar to you; this is a dry run. Subsequent chapters fully explain them.

Suppose that in 1986 a cost–benefit analyst, who worked for the Province of British Columbia, Canada, was asked to perform an *ex ante* CBA of a proposed four-lane highway between the town of Hope in the south-central part of the province and Merritt, which is north of Hope. This highway would pass through an area called the Coquihalla (an indigenous name) and would be called the Coquihalla Highway. A summary of the analyst's *ex ante* CBA is presented in Table 1.2. The original numbers were present values as of 1986, which have now been converted to 2016 dollars to make them

Table 1.1 *The Major Steps in CBA*

1. Explain the purpose of the CBA
2. Specify the set of alternative projects
3. Decide whose benefits and costs count (specify standing)
4. Identify the impact categories, catalogue them, and select metrics
5. Predict the impacts quantitatively over the life of the project
6. Monetize (attach dollar values to) all impacts
7. Discount benefits and costs to obtain present values
8. Compute the net present value of each alternative
9. Perform sensitivity analysis
10. Make a recommendation

Table 1.2 *Coquihalla Highway CBA (2016 $ Million)*

	No tolls		With tolls	
	Global perspective (A)	Provincial perspective (B)	Global perspective (C)	Provincial perspective (D)
Social benefits:				
Time and operating cost savings	763.0	572.1	568.4	426.3
Safety benefits	70.5	52.8	49.3	37.0
New users	1.6	1.2	0.6	0.4
Alternate route benefits	28.6	21.3	18.4	13.9
Toll revenues	–	–	–	73.2
Terminal value of hwy.	104.3	104.3	104.3	104.3
Total social benefits	968.0	751.7	741.0	655.1
Social costs:				
Construction	661.8	661.8	661.8	661.8
Maintenance	14.9	14.9	14.9	14.9
Toll collection	–	–	16.4	16.4
Toll booth construction	–	–	0.6	0.6
Total social costs	676.6	676.7	693.7	693.7
Net social benefit	291.2	75.2	47.3	–38.6

Source: Adapted from Anthony Boardman, Aidan Vining, and W. G. Waters II, "Costs and Benefits through Bureaucratic Lenses: Example of a Highway Project," *Journal of Policy Analysis and Management*, 12(3), 1993, 532–55, table 1, p. 537.

easier to interpret. How did the analyst obtain these numbers? What were the difficulties? We go through each of the 10 steps in turn.

1.3.1   *Explain the Purpose of the CBA*

Step 1 requires the analyst to explain why she is conducting a CBA. She should answer the question: *what is the rationale for considering a change in policy*, in this case, building a new highway? Stated broadly, the goal of CBA is to improve social welfare. More specifically, CBA attempts to maximize allocative efficiency, which we discuss in Chapter 3. That chapter argues that, where markets work well, individual self-interest leads to an efficient allocation of resources and, therefore, there should be no government intervention. *Prima facie* rationales for CBAs are *market failure* or *government failure*.[8] Where there is market failure, analysts use CBA to assess whether a particular intervention is more allocatively efficient than no intervention (or some other alternatives). Sometimes there is government failure: a government policy or project is currently in effect, but this policy appears to be less allocatively efficient than no intervention or some other alternative policy. In either of these situations CBA attempts to ascertain whether a new policy or program is more allocatively efficient than the existing policy. The analyst should explain the market failure or government failure that provides a purpose for the study.

In 1986, the existing routes to the interior of northern British Columbia were highly congested, dangerous (with many traffic accidents), and would not have the capacity to handle anticipated increases in traffic volumes. For political reasons, the government was unwilling to impose tolls on the existing routes. Widening the main road would have been prohibitively expensive because much of it was in a river canyon. The focus of the study was, therefore, on whether to build a new highway between Hope and Merritt in an alternative location, specifically in the Coquihalla Valley, which follows the Coldwater River.

1.3.2   *Specify the Set of Alternative Projects*

Step 2 requires the analyst to specify the set of alternative projects. In this example, there were only two feasible alternative highway projects: one built with tolls and one without. The provincial department of transportation decided that the toll, if applied, would be $78.3 for large trucks and $15.7 for cars (in 2016 dollars). Thus, the analyst had a tractable set of only two alternatives to analyze.

In practice, there are often difficulties even at this stage because the number of potential alternatives is often quite large. Even restricting the analysis to a highway in the Coquihalla valley, it could vary on many dimensions including, for example, the road surface (either bitumen or concrete), routing (it could take somewhat different routes), size (it could have more or fewer lanes), toll level (could be higher or lower), wild animal friendliness (the highway could be built with or without "elk tunnels"), or timing (it could be delayed until a later date). Resource and cognitive constraints mean that analysts typically analyze only a few alternatives.[9]

CBA compares one or more potential projects with a project that would be displaced (i.e., not undertaken) if the project(s) under evaluation were to proceed. The displaced project is often called the *counterfactual.* Usually, the counterfactual is the status quo policy or no change in government policy. It does not mean "do nothing." It means that government continues to do what it has been doing: while there would be no new highway, the existing highway would continue to be maintained. Table 1.2 presents the social benefits, social costs, and net social benefit if the highway were built (with or without tolls) relative to what the social benefits, social costs, and net social benefit would be if the highway were not built (the status quo). Thus, one can interpret these social benefits, social costs, and net social benefit as *incremental* amounts. *In practice, as in this example, the term incremental is often omitted for convenience, but it is implicit.*

Sometimes the status quo policy is not a viable alternative. *If a project would displace a specific alternative, then it should be evaluated relative to the specific displaced alternative.* If, for example, the government has committed resources to either (1) constructing a new highway project and maintaining the alternative routes) or (2) not constructing a new highway but expanding the capacity of the existing routes, and there is no possibility of maintaining the status quo, then the new highway project should be compared with the expansion of the capacity of existing routes, rather than with the status quo policy.

This CBA example pertains to a specific proposed highway. There is no attempt to compare this project to alternative highway projects in the rest of British Columbia, although one could do so. Rarely do analysts compare a project in one substantive arena of government, such as transportation, to projects in other arenas, such as health care or national defense. The limited nature of these kinds of comparisons sometimes frustrates politicians and decision-makers who imagine that CBA is a *deus ex machina* that will rank *all* policy alternatives. On the other hand, CBA evidence from different arenas can allow decision-makers to rank potential projects in terms of their net social benefit.

1.3.3 *Decide Whose Benefits and Costs Count (Standing)*

Next, the analyst must decide who has *standing*; that is, whose benefits and costs should be included and counted. In this example, the analyst conducted the CBA from the provincial perspective because taxpayers living there would pay for it, but thought that it was important to also take a global perspective. A CBA from the provincial perspective considers only the impacts (i.e., benefits and costs) that affect British Columbian residents, including costs and benefits borne by the British Columbian government. The global perspective considers the benefits and costs that affect anyone, irrespective of where they reside. Thus, it includes benefits and costs to Americans, Albertans, and even tourists using the highway from the United Kingdom or China. Including these two perspectives on standing with the no-tolls and with-tolls alternatives gives the four columns in Table 1.2 labeled A through D and effectively means there are four distinct perspectives on costs and benefits.

The issue of standing is quite often contentious. While national governments usually take only national (i.e., domestic) costs and benefits into account, critics argue that issues that have significant negative impacts on residents of other countries should be analyzed from a global perspective. Environmental issues that fall into this category include ozone depletion, global climate change, and acid rain. At the other extreme, local governments typically want to consider only benefits and costs to local residents and to ignore costs and benefits borne by residents of adjacent municipalities or higher levels of government. Our highway example deals with this issue by analyzing costs and benefits from both the subnational British Columbian perspective and the global perspective. Note that it does not adopt or measure the usual default perspective of the nation. Although these perspectives are not technically alternatives, they function as such in this example because they result in different estimates of costs, benefits, and net benefit.

1.3.4   *Identify the Impact Categories, Catalogue Them, and Select Metrics*

Step 4 requires the analyst to identify the impacts of the proposed alternative(s), catalogue them as benefits or costs, and specify the metric for each impact category. We use the term *impacts* broadly to include both inputs (resources employed) and outputs (predominantly benefits). A list of the relevant impact categories is referred to as an *impact inventory*. Preferably, analysts will construct an *impact matrix*, which describes or summarizes the impact of each policy alternative (or the impacts of one policy alternative on different groups) on each impact category.[10] Sometimes the impacts are referred to as "ingredients" and steps 4 and 5 are labeled the "*ingredients method*," although this terminology makes more intuitive sense for inputs than for outputs.

Different groups of residents will benefit from the highway. First, consider the users who currently travel on existing routes between Merritt and Hope, but will switch to the new highway. They will benefit from time saved (initially measured in hours), reduced vehicle operating costs (measured in dollars), and safety benefits due to a shorter, safer highway (initially measured in lives saved and the reduction in the number of accidents). Anticipation of these benefits is likely to attract some new users to travel this route (initially measured in number of vehicle trips). In the transportation literature, these new users are referred to as *generated traffic*. A third group consists of current users of the alternative routes who will continue to use these routes and will benefit from reduced congestion time on those routes (again initially measured in hours), because many other travelers will switch to the new highway. A fourth group is government, which may benefit from toll revenues (measured in dollars). A final benefit category for this project is the *terminal value* (sometimes called the *horizon value*) of the highway (measured in dollars). In practice, this highway will be in place for many years, but the analyst chose to predict and monetize the benefits and costs for only 20 years because no major refurbishment was expected to occur during that period. Sometimes we refer to such a period as the "life of the project." The terminal value reflects the present value of the net social benefit of the highway for all subsequent years. The cost impact categories are construction costs, maintenance and snow removal, toll collection, and toll booth construction and maintenance (all measured in dollars).

Although this list of impacts appears comprehensive, critics might argue that some important impacts were omitted. These include several externalities that spill beyond the use of the highway for transportation, including health impacts from reduced automobile emissions, environmental impacts on the elk population and other wildlife, and changes in scenic beauty. Also, the social cost of the land (the *opportunity cost*) should have been included.

It is important to try to include the full range of consequences of each project. However, from a practical perspective, analysts can consider only a manageable number of important impacts. Impacts associated with sunk costs should be ignored, although the analyst must be careful because recognizing economic sunkness is not simple. For example, when the Tellico Dam was being considered, the Tennessee Valley Authority argued incorrectly that "since the farm land behind the dam had already been purchased, the value of this land should be considered a sunk cost, even though the land has yet to be flooded and could be resold as farm land if the project was not completed."[11] Who owns the land or has paid for it is often irrelevant. If, in fact, the land did have an alternative use, then there was an opportunity cost and land should have been included as an impact category.

Furthermore, as we discuss in Chapter 7, it is often incorrect to include secondary or "knock-on" effects. Such effects are often redistributional. For example, one might think that hotel businesses and gas stations in Hope, near the southern end of the highway, might suffer negative effects because the new highway would bypass the town. However, highway users would stay elsewhere and buy their gas elsewhere, in Merritt, for example. Thus, while business-owner residents of Hope might be worse off, other business-owner residents in the province would be better off. The effects cancel out, resulting in a net effect of zero. Therefore, they can be ignored in many circumstances.

From a CBA perspective, analysts are interested only in project impacts that affect the utility of individuals who have standing. (The caveat is that this applies only where human beings have the relevant knowledge and information to make rational decisions.) Impacts that do not have any positive or negative utility to human beings are not counted. Suppose, for example, the highway project would decimate the population of a particular avian species. Birds do not have standing. This impact should only be included if some humans regard it as a cost.

Politicians often state the benefits of some projects in very general terms. For example, they might say that a project will promote "community capacity building." Similarly, they tend to regard "growth" and "regional development" as beneficial impacts, possibly because it might lead to increased tax revenue for their jurisdictions. In contrast, CBA requires analysts to identify explicitly the ways in which the project would make some individuals in the province better off through, for example, improved skills, better education, or higher incomes.

Analysts should also be on the lookout for impacts that different groups of people view in opposing directions. Consider, for example, land that periodically floods but would not do so if a proposed project is implemented. Residents on the flood plain generally view these periodic floods as a cost because they damage homes, while duck hunters regard them as a benefit because they attract ducks. Even though opposing valuations of the same impact could be aggregated in one category, it is usually more informative to have two impact categories – one for damaged homes, and another for recreation benefits.

In this example, the impact metrics are straightforward – hours of time saved, dollar value of operating and construction costs, for example. If environmental impacts had been included, however, the choice of metrics would not have been as straightforward.

For example, if the change in automobile emissions was included as an impact, the analyst might measure it by tons of various pollutants or the resultant health effects (e.g., changes in mortality or morbidity). The choice of metric often depends on data availability and the ease of monetization. For example, an analyst may wish to measure the number of crimes avoided due to a policy intervention, but may not have any way to estimate this impact. However, she may have access to changes in arrest rates or changes in conviction rates and may be able to use one or both of these measures to estimate changes in crime.[12] Bear in mind, however, that all surrogate indicators involve some loss of information. For example, the conviction rate might be increasing while there is no change in the actual crime rate.

1.3.5   *Predict the Impacts Quantitatively Over the Life of the Project*

The proposed highway project, like almost all public projects, has impacts that extend over time. The fifth task is to predict all of the impacts in each year during the discount period (the life of the project) for each alternative. More specifically, the analyst has to predict the *incremental impacts* of the highway relative to the current policy for the no-tolls and the with-tolls alternatives, and from the provincial and global perspectives. Obviously, there is considerable uncertainty in making these predictions. Analysts may determine the "most likely" impact in each time period or the expected impact in each period. In this initial case example, for simplicity, we ignore uncertainty in the predictions.

There were three different types of road user on the Coquihalla: truck drivers, drivers or passengers in cars on business, and drivers or passenger in cars on vacation. As we see in subsequent chapters, road users were partitioned in this way because their benefits vary quite a bit. For each of these three user groups, the analyst predicted for each alternative for each year: the number of vehicle-trips on the new highway, the number of vehicle-trips on the old roads (alternative routes), and the proportion of travelers that reside in British Columbia. With these estimates, knowing that the highway is 195 kilometers long, and with other information, the analyst could estimate for each year the following incremental benefits: the total vehicle-kilometers saved, the number of accidents reduced, and the number of lives saved.

The analyst predicted that the new highway would save 6.5 lives each year. Lives would be saved for two reasons. First, the new highway would be shorter than the alternative routes. As a result, the analyst expected that travelers would avoid 130 million vehicle-kilometers (vkms) of driving each year, and evidence suggests that, on average, there are 0.027 deaths per million vkms. The shorter distance would, therefore, save 3.5 lives per year (130 vkms × 0.027 lives lost per vkm) on the basis of less distance driven. The new highway was also predicted to be safer per kilometer because it would be a divided highway. It was expected that 313 million vkms would be driven each year on the new highway. Based on previous traffic engineering evidence, the analyst estimated that the new highway would lower the fatal accident rate by one-third. Consequently, the new highway was expected to save 3.0 lives per year due to being safer (313 vkms × 0.027 lives lost per vkm × 0.33). Combining the two components suggests 6.5 lives would be saved each year.

In order to treat something as an impact, an analyst has to know there is a cause–effect relationship between some physical outcome of the project and the utility of human beings with standing. For some impacts the expected cause–effect relationships are reasonably well established, for instance, for the causal relationship between motor vehicle usage and motor vehicle accidents. For other impacts, however, the causal relationships are less obvious. What, if any, is the impact of exhaust fumes from additional vehicle usage on residents' morbidity and mortality? Would this be offset by fewer airplane flights? Demonstrating and estimating such cause–effect relationships often requires an extensive review of scientific and social science research. Sometimes the evidence may be inconclusive. For example, controversy surrounds the effect of chlorinated organic compounds in bleached pulp mill effluent on wildlife. Although a Swedish study found such a link, a later Canadian study found none.[13] In practice, predicting impacts can be difficult and contentious.

In order to predict impacts over future time periods, analysts often assume a particular growth rate and apply it to all future time periods. However, some impacts might increase at an increasing or decreasing rate. For example, the number of statistical lives saved in a year might increase not only because of more drivers using the safer route but also because, without the new route, there would be significantly more congestion on the old routes, leading to proportionately more fatal accidents. Analogously, the cost of highway maintenance might be relatively constant for some years and then increase due to vintage (age) or more users.

Prediction is especially difficult where projects are unique, have long time horizons, or relationships among relevant variables are complex. Many of the realities associated with doing steps 4 and 5 are brilliantly summarized by Kenneth Boulding's poem on dam building, presented in Exhibit 1.1. Many of his points deal with the omission of impact categories due to misunderstanding or ignorance of cause-effect relationships and to the accuracy of estimations. He also makes points about the distributional impacts of costs and benefits, which we discuss later.

Exhibit 1.1 A Ballad of Ecological Awareness

The cost of building dams is always underestimated,
There's erosion of the delta that the river has created,
There's fertile soil below the dam that's likely to be looted,
And the tangled mat of forest that has got to be uprooted.

There's the breaking up of cultures with old haunts' and habits' loss,
There's the education programme that just doesn't come across,
And the wasted fruits of progress that are seldom much enjoyed
By expelled subsistence farmers who are urban unemployed.

There's disappointing yield of fish, beyond the first explosion;
There's silting up, and drawing down, and watershed erosion.
Above the dam the water's lost by sheer evaporation;
Below, the river scours, and suffers dangerous alteration.

For engineers, however good, are likely to be guilty
Of quietly forgetting that a river can be silty,
While the irrigation people too are frequently forgetting
That water poured upon the land is likely to be wetting.

Then the water in the lake, and what the lake releases,
Is crawling with infected snails and water-borne diseases.
There's a hideous locust breeding ground when water level's low,
And a million ecologic facts we really do not know.

There are benefits, of course, which may be countable, but which
Have a tendency to fall into the pockets of the rich,
While the costs are apt to fall upon the shoulders of the poor.
So cost–benefit analysis is nearly always sure
To justify the building of a solid concrete fact,
While the Ecologic Truth is left behind in the Abstract.

— Kenneth E. Boulding
(Reprinted with the kind permission of Mrs. Boulding)

1.3.6   *Monetize (Attach Dollar Values to) All Impacts*

The analyst next has to monetize each and every impact. To *monetize* means to value in dollars. In this example, the analyst monetized the following categories of time saved: leisure time saved per vehicle (25 percent of the gross wage in the region times the average number of passengers) = $13.1 per vehicle-hour; business time saved per vehicle = $23.5 per vehicle-hour; and truck drivers' time saved per vehicle = $27.4 per vehicle-hour. One of the most important impacts to monetize in transportation and health CBAs is the value of a statistical life saved, the VSL. The term "statistical life" is used to imply that the reference is not to a specific person's life. In this *ex ante* study, conducted in 1986, the VSL used was $978,685 in 2016 dollars based on the literature at that time. A large body of recent research suggests that the VSL is much higher than that, as we discuss in Chapter 17.

Sometimes, the most intuitively important impacts are difficult to value in monetary terms. In CBA, the value of a benefit is typically measured in terms of "willingness to pay." As we discuss in Chapter 3, where markets exist and work well, willingness to pay can be determined from the appropriate market demand curve. Naturally, problems arise where markets do not exist or do not work well. For example, scholars have spent many person-years trying to determine the appropriate VSL. Valuing negative environmental impacts is especially contentious. In practice, most CBA analysts do not reinvent these wheels, but instead draw upon previous research: they use best-practice "plug-in" values whenever possible. Although catalogues of impact values are not comprehensive, considerable progress has been made in coming up with reasonable plug-ins as we show in Chapter 17.

If no person is willing to pay for some impact or to avoid it, then that impact would have zero value in a CBA. For example, if construction of a dam would lead to the extermination of a species of small fish, but no person with standing is willing to pay a positive amount to save that species, then the extermination of this fish would have zero cost in a CBA of the dam.

Some government agencies and critics of CBA are unwilling to attach a monetary value to life or to some other impact. This forces them to use an alternative method of analysis, such as *cost–effectiveness analysis, qualitative cost–benefit analysis* or *multi-goal analysis*, which are described in Chapter 3.

1.3.7 *Discount Benefits and Costs to Obtain Present Values*

For a project that has impacts that occur over years, we need a way to aggregate the benefits and costs that arise in different years. In CBA, future benefits and costs are *discounted* relative to present benefits and costs in order to obtain their *present values* (PV). The need to discount arises for two main reasons. First, there is an *opportunity cost* to the resources used in a project: they could earn a positive return elsewhere. Second, most people prefer to consume now rather than later. Discounting has nothing to do with inflation per se, although inflation must be taken into account.

A cost or benefit that occurs in year t is converted to its present value by dividing it by $(1 + s)^t$, where s is the social discount rate. Suppose a project has a life of n years and let B_t and C_t denote the social benefits and social costs in year t, respectively. The present value of the social benefits, $PV(B)$, and the present value of the social costs, $PV(C)$, of the project are, respectively:

$$PV(B) = \sum_{t=0}^{n} \frac{B_t}{(1+s)^t} \tag{1.2}$$

$$PV(C) = \sum_{t=0}^{n} \frac{C_t}{(1+s)^t} \tag{1.3}$$

In the Coquihalla Highway example, the analyst used a real (inflation-adjusted) social discount rate of 7.5 percent. As we discuss in Chapter 10, the choice of the appropriate social discount rate can be contentious and is, therefore, a good candidate for sensitivity analysis. For government analysts, the discount rate to be used is usually mandated by a government agency with authority (e.g., the Office of Management and Budget, or the General Accountability Office in the USA, or the Ministry of Finance or the Treasury Board in Canada). However, as we demonstrate in Chapter 10, those rates are generally too high. For projects that do not have impacts beyond 50 years (that is *intra-generational* projects), we recommend a real social discount rate of 3.5 percent. If the project is *inter-generational*, then we recommend time-declining discount rates.[14]

1.3.8 *Compute the Net Present Value of Each Alternative*

At the beginning of this chapter we stated that the net social benefit of a project equals the difference between the (incremental) social benefits and the (incremental) social costs, as in Equation (1.1). By definition, the *net present value* (*NPV*) of a policy alternative equals the difference between the *PV* of its (incremental) social benefits and the *PV* of its (incremental) social costs:

$$NPV = PV(B) - PV(C) \qquad (1.4)$$

Thus, the *NPV* of a project or policy is identical to the *present value of the (incremental) net social benefit*:

$$NPV = PV(NSB) \qquad (1.5)$$

The basic decision rule for a single alternative project (relative to the status quo policy) is simple: *adopt the project if its NPV is positive.* In short, the analyst should recommend proceeding with the proposed project if its $NPV = PV(B) - PV(C) > 0$; that is, if its (incremental) benefits exceed its (incremental) costs:

$$PV(B) > PV(C)$$

When there is more than one alternative to the status quo policy being analyzed and all the alternatives are mutually exclusive, then the rule is: *select the project with the largest NPV.* This rule assumes implicitly that at least one *NPV* is positive. If no *NPV* is positive, then none of the specified alternatives are superior to the current policy, which should remain in place.

1.3.9   *Perform Sensitivity Analysis*

It should be clear that the PVs and NPVs discussed above are *predicted values*, based on certain assumptions. As the foregoing discussion emphasizes, however, there will be uncertainty about the assumptions – both the predicted impacts and the appropriate monetary valuation of each unit of each impact. For example, the analyst may be uncertain about the predicted number of lives saved and about the appropriate dollar value to place on a statistical life saved. The analyst may also be uncertain about the appropriate social discount rate. In order to get a handle on these uncertainties, the analyst might conduct sensitivity analysis which, with only one alternative, shows the values of a parameter that would change the recommendation from "go" to "no go," or vice versa. Also, analysts might examine different scenarios, with for example, "most likely," "optimistic," and "pessimistic" assumptions. Or analysts might construct decision trees or perform Monte Carlo analysis, as we discuss in Chapter 11. The purpose is to obtain a better understanding of the distribution of the estimated NPV.

1.3.10   *Make a Recommendation*

Suppose that one is only faced with two alternatives, A and B, one of which may or may not be the status quo policy. Alternative A has a higher expected NPV and lower risk (smaller variance) than alternative B. In this situation, the analyst would unambiguously recommend alternative A. Now suppose, however, that Alternative A has a higher expected NPV but has more risk than alternative B. In this situation, it is not so obvious what the analyst should recommend. One might think that the analyst should present the analysis, point out the trade-offs, and turn the decision-making over to the decision-maker. If so, a risk adverse decision-maker might choose alternative B. However, as we explain in Chapter 12, the *analyst can usually act as if society is risk-neutral and should therefore recommend the alternative with the largest expected NPV*.

In fact, there is some confusion about the appropriate decision rule. Both the *internal rate of return* and the *benefit–cost ratio* have also been proposed as alternative decision rules. This is one area where there is a right answer and wrong answers. The *appropriate criterion to use is the NPV rule*. As explained in Chapters 3 and 9, the other rules sometimes give incorrect answers; the *NPV* rule does not.

While the *NPV* criterion results in a *more efficient* allocation of resources, it does not necessarily recommend *the most efficient* allocation of resources because the most efficient alternative might not have been actually considered by the analyst or might not have been feasible because of budget constraints, political concerns, or other reasons. This point is illustrated in Figure 1.1. Consider a set of proposed projects that vary according to the amount of output (Q), which in turn depends on the scale of the project. The benefits and costs associated with alternative scales are represented by the functions $B(Q)$ and $C(Q)$, respectively. The benefits increase as the scale increases, but at a decreasing rate. In contrast, costs increase at an increasing rate. A small-scale project (for example, Q_1) has positive net benefit relative to the status quo policy, Q_0. As the scale increases, the net benefit increases up to the optimal scale, Q^*.[15] As the scale increases beyond Q^*, the net benefit decreases. The net benefit is positive as long as the benefit curve is above the cost curve, it is zero where the cost curve and benefit curve intersect, and it is negative for yet larger-scale projects.

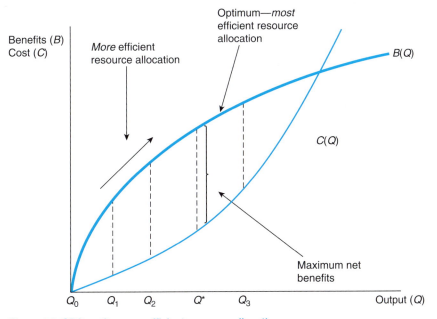

Figure 1.1 CBA seeks more efficient resource allocation.

Suppose that the analyst actually evaluates only two alternative projects, those with output levels, Q_1 and Q_2. Clearly, output level Q_2 is preferred to output level Q_1, which, in turn, is preferred to the status quo output level, Q_0. The analyst would therefore recommend Q_2. However, as the figure shows, the net social benefit is maximized at output level Q^*. The analyst could not recommend this optimal output level because it was not among the set of alternatives evaluated. As this example illustrates, use of the NPV criterion leads to a more efficient outcome than the status quo, but not necessarily the most efficient outcome.

In the highway example, three of the four alternative projects had positive expected *NPV*s and one had a negative expected *NPV*. The latter indicates that from the British Columbian perspective it would be more efficient to maintain the status quo and not build the Coquihalla highway than to build it and charge tolls. As discussed earlier, both the no-tolls alternatives were superior to the with-tolls alternatives. This result gives a flavor of the possibly counterintuitive recommendations that CBA can support. In this case, tolls lower the expected *NPV* of the tolled alternatives because they deter some people from using the highway, and so fewer people enjoy benefits; this reduces total benefits.[16]

Finally, as this discussion emphasizes, analysts almost always make recommendations, not decisions. CBA concerns how resources *should* be allocated; it is *normative*. It does not claim to be a *positive* (i.e., descriptive) theory of how resource-allocation decisions are actually made. Such decisions are made in political and bureaucratic arenas where politicians or administrators may have goals that are not totally congruent with allocative efficiency. CBA is only one input to this political decision-making process – one that attempts to push it toward more efficient resource allocation. CBA does not always drive choice between alternatives. Politicians are often not persuaded by economic efficiency arguments. Indeed, the Coquihalla highway was built with tolls, although they were removed in 2008, mainly for political reasons as far as we can determine.

1.4   Bureaucratic and Political "Lenses"[17]

CBA concerns how resources should be allocated. In practice, however, when bureaucrats or politicians conduct analysis, they have a tendency to *see* "costs" and "benefits" differently. Most of them have not taken formal courses in CBA. Although they may think they know what CBA is, they may be mistaken. Bureaucrats' roles have a strong influence on what they think CBA is, or should be, about. Specifically, their perceptions of what constitutes "benefits" and "costs" are based on whether they are *analysts, spenders*, or *guardians*.[18] These labels are indicative of three different perspectives (lenses) bureaucrats bring to project evaluation. We assume the analysts' perspective is standard CBA, which we have just illustrated. Guardians and spenders have quite different perspectives.

This section describes both perspectives and shows how they differ from CBA. This helps clarify what CBA actually is, in contrast to what some decision-makers or politicians may think it is. This section also identifies many of the common mistakes in CBA, which often vary systematically according to an individual's background and experiences. Even those trained in CBA may subconsciously modify their orientation toward those of guardians or spenders as a consequence of the immediacy of their daily bureaucratic roles. If you are in a government job, then you should make sure that you do not unconsciously drift into a guardian or spender perspective. We also hope that by understanding these different perspectives, analysts may be better able to communicate with guardians and spenders about how to conduct CBA appropriately. It might also help guardians and spenders be better able to communicate with each other about the "biases" inherent in their perspectives. Finally, this section should help students understand better why project decisions are often not consistent with CBA – they are often made by guardians or spenders, not analysts.

These three lenses are only archetypes. In practice, an individual engaged in the analytic or decision-making process may not exhibit all of the attitudes associated with a particular lens. Some bureaucrats may be conflicted, sometimes adopting one cognitive perspective, sometimes another. Guardians in line agencies can be prone to cognitive dissonance because they have dual allegiances. They may veer between being guardians, spenders, or both. In practice, though, most bureaucrats recognize what their tendency is.

1.4.1   *Guardians*

Guardians are most often found in central budgetary agencies, such as the US Office of Management and Budget, or in controllership or accounting functions within line agencies. They naturally tend to have a bottom-line budgetary orientation. They often equate benefits with revenue inflows to their agency or other governmental coffers (at the same jurisdictional level) and to equate costs with revenue outflows from their agency or other governmental coffers (at the same level). Thus, they engage in *budget impact analysis*, also called *cash flow analysis* or *revenue-expenditure analysis*.[19] Guardians tend to regard actual CBA as naive, impractical, and, worst of all in their eyes, a tool whereby spenders can justify whatever it is they want to do.

The conceptual lens of "pure" provincial-based guardians is illustrated by the way they look at the costs and benefits of the Coquihalla Highway, as shown in Table 1.3. These evaluations of the no-tolls and with-tolls alternatives can be compared to the analyst's evaluations that appear in columns B and D of Table 1.2, respectively.

To guardians, all toll revenues are regarded as benefits, whether paid by the jurisdiction's residents (in this case, the province) or by non-residents. Construction costs are treated as a cost because they require a financial expenditure by the provincial government. Because guardians seek to minimize net budgetary expenditures, their preference, not surprisingly, is for the with-tolls alternative. Indeed, their gut reaction is to consider raising tolls to generate larger revenues, irrespective of its effect on levels of use or its impact on social benefits.

How does the guardian's perspective differ from the CBA perspective? Most importantly, guardians ignore impacts valued by consumers and producers such as time and lives saved. In this example they ignore social benefits that amount to $751.8 million for the no-tolls alternative and $581.9 million for the with-tolls alternative, both from the provincial perspective. When guardians are in control of a government service, it is easy to understand why one has to wait so long for the service. Neither your time nor anyone else's figures into their calculations! Similarly, guardians tend to ignore non-governmental social costs, such as congestion and pollution.

In the Coquihalla Highway example, all social costs happen to represent governmental budgetary costs, and so there is no difference between the CBA cost figures and the guardians' cost figures. In other situations, however, there might be a considerable difference between the two. For example, guardians treat the full cost of labor in a job-creation program as a cost, while CBA analysts consider only the opportunity cost (such as the lost leisure time of newly employed workers). Another manifestation of the same mistake concerns the treatment of resources currently owned by the government, such as offices or land. Guardians tend to treat these resources as free (i.e., having no opportunity cost) because using them for a project does not entail additional budgetary outlay.

Similarly, guardians treat all toll revenues as a benefit and ignore the losses suffered by citizens from paying tolls. From the CBA analyst's perspective, these toll payments are a transfer from residents to the government: the offsetting costs and benefits result in zero net benefit. On the other hand, provincial guardians treat subsidies from the federal government as a benefit because they are revenue inflows to their level of government. However, if the federal government has earmarked a certain amount of money to transfer to British Columbia, and if funds used for one purpose reduce the

Table 1.3 *Coquihalla Highway from a Provincial Guardian's Perspective (2016 $ Million)*

	No tolls	With tolls
Revenues ("benefits"):		
Tolls from BC residents	0	219.4
Tolls from non-BC residents	0	73.2
Total "benefits"	0	292.6
Expenditures ("costs"):		
Construction	661.8	661.8
Maintenance	14.9	14.9
Toll collection		16.4
Toll booth construction		0.6
Total "costs"	676.6	693.7
Guardian's net "benefit"	–676.6	–401.1

Source: Adapted from Anthony Boardman, Aidan Vining, and W. G. Waters II, "Costs and Benefits through Bureaucratic Lenses: Example of a Highway Project," *Journal of Policy Analysis and Management*, 12(3), 1993, 532–55, table 2, p. 539.

amount available for other purposes, then federal funds for this highway should not be treated as a benefit from the provincial perspective.

Finally, guardians generally want to use a high social discount rate. Because of their financial background or their agency's culture, they naturally prefer to use a financial market rate, which is generally higher than the social discount rate. They also know that using a high discount rate will make it more difficult to justify most infrastructure projects because costs occur earlier than benefits. Thus, they can limit spenders who, in their view, overestimate benefits, underestimate costs, and generally use money less efficiently than the private sector.

1.4.2	*Spenders*

Spenders are usually employed within service or line departments. Some service departments, such as transportation, are involved with physical projects, while social service departments, such as those dealing with health, welfare, or education, make human capital investments. Other service departments, such as housing, make both types of expenditures. The views of spenders are somewhat more varied than those of guardians because the constituencies of particular agencies are more varied. Nevertheless, there are several commonalities.

Spenders tend to deliver government-mandated services to particular groups in society. They see their purpose as helping these groups and other members of society. Therefore, we characterize them as primarily engaging in *constituency-support analysis.* Most importantly, spenders tend to regard government expenditures on constituents as benefits rather than as costs. Thus, they typically see expenditures on labor (jobs) as a benefit rather than a cost. The conceptual lens of "pure" provincial-based spenders can be illustrated by the way they would look at the costs and benefits of the Coquihalla Highway, which is shown in Table 1.4.

Table 1.4 *Coquihalla Highway from a Provincial Spender's Perspective (2016 $ Million)*

	No tolls	With tolls
Constituency "benefits":		
Project costs (from CBA)	676.6	693.7
Project benefits (from CBA)	751.8	655.1
Total constituency "benefits"	1,428.4	1,348.8
Constituency "costs":		
Tolls from BC residents	0	219.4
Total constituency "costs"	0	219.4
Spender's "net benefit"	1,428.4	1,129.4

Source: Adapted from Anthony Boardman, Aidan Vining, and W. G. Waters II, "Costs and Benefits through Bureaucratic Lenses: Example of a Highway Project," *Journal of Policy Analysis and Management*, 12(3), 1993, 532–55, table 3, p. 542.

Spenders treat social benefits and monetary payments received by their constituents (residents of British Columbia in this example) as benefits. Thus, time saved, lives saved, and vehicle-operating costs saved by residents of British Columbia are benefits. However, they also regard wages received by construction workers who build the highway as a benefit. Thus, spenders tend to think of both project benefits *and* project costs as being benefits. With this kind of accounting lens, each of the with-tolls and no-tolls highway alternatives generates net constituency benefits. In general, spenders tend to support *any* of the four alternatives rather than the status quo (no project). Also, because spenders tend to think of social costs as benefits, they are likely to want to finish partially completed projects, regardless of whether the incremental social costs exceed the incremental social benefits. Thus, the mistrust of spenders by guardians is perfectly understandable. Guardians and spenders almost always oppose one another in terms of alternative ranking of projects with fees or tolls.

Spenders view monetary outlays by British Columbia residents (i.e., constituents) as costs; so tolls paid by them are a cost. There is no other cost borne by spenders' constituents.

Table 1.4 illustrates that spenders favor the no-toll alternative primarily because a toll would impose a cost on their constituents. Indeed, spenders normally do not favor any user fees unless a large percentage of the payers are not constituents. If spenders could collect and keep the toll revenue within their own budget, then they would face a dilemma: tolls would reduce constituency benefits, but would increase the agency's ability to provide services to its constituents. Thus, they would face a trade-off between constituency-support maximization and agency budget maximization.[20]

In general, as Robert Haveman and others have pointed out, politicians prefer projects that concentrate benefits on particular interest groups and camouflage costs or diffuse them widely over the population.[21] Spenders have similar tendencies. They tend to weight each impact category by the strength of the connection that constituents make between the impact and their agency. They focus on impacts for which their constituents will give them a lot of credit. Because people almost always notice expenditures on themselves, such as construction jobs, such "benefits" are invariably weighted more heavily than are diffuse social benefits.[22]

The perspective of spenders concerning market efficiency has a bearing on the way they view many aspects of CBA. To spenders, markets are almost always inefficient. Spenders act as if unemployment is high in all labor markets. They believe that hiring someone to work on a government project will reduce unemployment. Even if some workers switch from other employment, these workers' vacated jobs will be filled by unemployed workers. Thus, even if the job created did not go directly to an unemployed worker, there would eventually be a job created somewhere in the economy for an unemployed worker. Spenders do not recognize that project resources are diverted from other potentially productive uses that might also create jobs.

Spenders have much in common with proponents of *economic impact analysis*, which measures the impact of some project or policy on the economy as a whole. It is often used by politicians and others to justify expensive "events," such as hosting the Olympics, song contests, world fairs (e.g., Expos), or the like. It is important to recognize that such studies estimate economic activity, not social welfare. Economic impact analysis draws on *input–output analysis*. These analyses often include multiplier effects, which reflect interdependencies among sectors. For example, a project might hire a construction worker to work on a stadium who then spends his money as he sees fit and then those paid by the construction worker spend the money they receive on something else, and so on. All of these expenditures increase economic activity. In the extreme, "super-spenders" have a "Midas touch" view of project evaluation: first declare the expenditures (which are really a social cost) to be a "benefit" and then power up these benefits by a multiplier. Inevitably, these spenders see any government project as producing benefits greater than costs.

Spenders generally favor using a low (even zero) social discount rate. For some, this is because they are not familiar with the concept of discounting. For others, they know a low discount rate tends to raise the project's *NPV* and, therefore, the probability of its adoption. Other ways spenders generate support for their projects is to choose a poorly performing counterfactual (a straw man), to lowball cost projections, or to overestimate project usage.[23]

1.5   The Origins and Demand for CBA

1.5.1   *Origins*

Some scholars trace the origin of CBA to Sir William Petty, author of *Political Arithmetick*, who argued that the British government should have paid to transport people out of London in 1665 to avoid the plague and thus save lives. He suggested that the value of a statistical life for a resident of England was £90 (at that time) and that, after taking account of transporting people out of London and caring for them, every pound spent would have yielded a return of £84. Petty, a doctor and founding member of The Royal Society, further argued in 1676 that the state should intervene to provide better medicine.[24]

1.5.2   *Government*

The US Army Corps of Engineers, which designed and built canals, dams, harbors, and other water projects, was an early user and developer of CBA. The Flood Control Act of 1936 explicitly required the US Army Corps of Engineers to conduct CBA. Later, the Bureau of the Budget's Circular A-47 of 1952 and academic work by Otto Eckstein, John Krutilla, and others encouraged the use of CBA in other areas.[25] In the mid-1960s Barbara Castle, then Minister of Transport in the United Kingdom, promoted CBA for the evaluation of transportation projects. By the end of the 1960s CBA had spread around the world and was used in developed and developing countries for many different projects. Government agencies in many countries now require CBA of regulatory changes. Currently, the World Bank and other multilateral development banks require CBA or cost–effectiveness analysis for appraisal of all projects. Other actual or potential uses of CBA include the courts, various progressive interest groups, and private corporations.

In the United States, executive orders have expanded the use of CBA by federal agencies over time. Presidents Nixon, Ford, and Carter introduced requirements that improved agency project evaluation. Most importantly, in Executive Order 12291, issued in early 1981, President Reagan required the use of *regulatory impact analysis* (RIA) by executive branch agencies for every major regulatory initiative, specifically those that would have an annual effect on the economy of $100 million or more in terms of costs, benefits, or transfers. (A well-conducted RIA attempts to assess whether a regulation would improve social welfare through cost–benefit analysis, and would address all of the steps in Table 1.1.[26] In practice, however, RIAs are often not well conducted and do not necessarily monetize all of the relevant impacts.[27]) Subsequently, President Clinton (Executive Order 12866 in 1993) more clearly specified the rules for conducting RIA and set up the Office of Information and Regulatory Affairs (OIRA) within the Office of Management and Budget (OMB). The OMB provides guidance to agencies and reviews individual regulations, including agencies' RIAs. Two orders introduced by President Obama (Executive Order 13563 in 2011 and Executive Order 13610 in 2012) are important for promoting "retrospective analyses" of existing rules, that is, *in medias res* CBAs.[28] In a recent attempt to reduce the regulatory burden on business, especially small businesses, President Trump (Executive Order 13771 in 2017) required each agency seeking to introduce a new regulation to identify two regulations for repeal with *compliance costs* (not social costs) that are at least as high as the new one it would like to introduce.

Government agencies in most major developed countries have produced comprehensive guides or guidelines for conducting CBA. Individual agencies have produced guides focused on specific policy areas, such as transportation, the environment, or waste management, or are about specific topics, such as the value of the social discount rate. International agencies, such as the European Commission (EC), the World Bank and the Inter-American Development Bank (IDB), also provide comprehensive guides or guides on specific topics. While some guides are up to date, others are not.[29]

1.5.3   *The Courts*

Courts of law use CBA and CBA methods in a variety of ways. Perhaps the most well-known example is the use of CBA in the assessment of damages in the *Exxon Valdez* disaster. Quantitative valuation of the costs of the environmental impacts relied heavily on contingent valuation analysis, a CBA method discussed in detail in Chapter 16. Lawsuits continued many years after the disaster itself.

CBA is also used in antitrust cases. The Canadian Competition Act generally disallows proposed mergers if they result in a "significant lessening of competition." However, in a horizontal merger, production costs might fall due to economies of scale. In a classic article, Oliver Williamson argued that "a rational treatment of the merger" requires an analysis of the "trade-off" of the two effects.[30] Currently, Section 9b of the Canadian Competition Act explicitly prohibits the Competition Tribunal from intervening in a merger if the efficiency gains to the merging firms are greater than the potential anticompetitive effect. In effect, this requires determining whether the merger is allocatively efficient (i.e., has positive net social benefit).

1.5.4   *CBA, Sustainability, Corporate Social Responsibility, and the Triple Bottom Line*

Most private-sector corporations are now paying attention to *sustainability* or their "*triple bottom line*" (i.e., their social, economic, and environmental impacts), and are being more transparent about such impacts. For a longer time, companies have been concerned about *corporate social responsibility* (CSR). These terms are not well-defined, but overlap considerably. Basically, they mean that firms consider their impacts on current members of society (broadly defined) and on future generations. In practice, however, there is no common measure of sustainability or CSR. Firms might measure and report their carbon footprint, their emissions of carbon and other gases, or their recycling efforts, or they might obtain a LEED (Leadership in Energy and Environmental Design) building rating. Different firms might measure different impacts. However, the basic goal of sustainability and CSR is to improve the welfare of society as a whole, similar to CBA. This similarity has led some authors to argue that corporations should use CBA to measure their sustainability efforts or CSR.[31] Firms would likely analyze specific projects, rather than report measures on an annual basis, but it would require the application of a consistent set of principles, instead of the current ad hoc approach.

In practice, many environmentalists and other progressive groups prefer to make their arguments on emotional and ethical grounds and are reluctant to conduct CBAs. Richard Revesz and Michael Livermore argue that such groups will be more effective if they do not "give up on rationality" and perform CBAs. The authors argue that this is necessary if we truly want to protect our natural environment.[32]

1.6   The Cost of Doing CBA

There are literally thousands of RIAs conducted each year. Some RIAs are not particularly expensive. However, others are. For example, Thomas Hopkins reported in 1992 that a CBA of reducing lead in gasoline cost the Environmental Protection Agency (EPA) roughly $1 million.[33] On average, in the 1980s, the EPA spent approximately $700,000 for each CBA of projects with annual compliance costs in excess of $100 million.[34] Large-scale evaluations of welfare-to-work programs, of which CBA is one component, often run into millions of dollars. CBA of projects that are large, complex, and have unique features can be particularly expensive.

1.6.1   *Readers of This Book*

This book is primarily for those, whether student, consultant, or government analyst, who want to know how to do CBA. It is also for people who want to know how to interpret CBA – in other words, for clients of CBA. Clients can be helped in two ways. In the narrow sense, clients should be well-enough informed to judge whether a specific CBA has been conducted well. Evidence suggests that, even with extensive budgets, US federal agencies have difficulty performing CBA well.[35] This is certainly true for other governments with less analytic capacity and smaller budgets. Also, clients need to be well-enough informed to avoid endorsing flawed analysis because there is a growing trend for oversight agencies and external critics to point out and publicize analytic errors.

1.7   Conclusion

This chapter provides a broad overview of many of the most important issues in CBA. We deal with these issues in detail in subsequent chapters. At this point, do not worry if you can only see CBA "through the glass, darkly." Do not worry if you cannot entirely follow the highway analysis. Our aim is to give you a taste of the practical realities. We think that it is important to provide readers with a sense of these realities before dealing with the technical issues.

CBA is often taught in a way that is completely divorced from political reality. We wish to avoid this mistake. Politicians, especially those feeling financially constrained, frequently want a budget impact analysis, rather than a CBA. CBA is a normative tool, not a description of how political and bureaucratic decision-makers actually make decisions. It is an input to decision-making. Because CBA disregards the demands of politicians, spenders, guardians, and interest groups, it is not surprising that there are tremendous pressures to ignore it or, alternatively, to adapt it to the desires of various constituencies or interest groups. In practice, correct CBA is no more than a voice for rational decision-making.

Exercises for Chapter 1

1. Imagine that you live in a city that currently does not require bicycle riders to wear helmets. Furthermore, imagine that you enjoy riding your bicycle without wearing a helmet.

    a. From your perspective, what are the major costs and benefits of a proposed city ordinance that would require all bicycle riders to wear helmets?

    b. What are the categories of costs and benefits from society's perspective?

2. The effects of a tariff on imported kumquats can be divided into the following categories: tariff revenues received by the treasury ($8 million), increased use of resources to produce more kumquats domestically ($6 million), the value of reduced consumption by domestic consumers ($13 million), and increased profits received by domestic kumquat growers ($4 million). A CBA from the national perspective would find costs of the tariff equal to $19 million – the sum of the costs of increased domestic production and forgone domestic consumption ($6 million + $13 million). The increased profits received by domestic kumquat growers and the

tariff revenues received by the treasury simply reflect higher prices paid by domestic consumers on the kumquats that they continue to consume and, hence, count as neither benefits nor costs. Thus, the net benefit of the tariff is negative (−$19 million). Consequently, the CBA would recommend against adoption of the tariff.

a. Assuming the Agriculture Department views kumquat growers as its primary constituency, how would it calculate the net benefit if it behaves as if it is a spender?

b. Assuming the Treasury Department behaves as if it is a guardian, how would it calculate the net benefit if it believes that domestic growers pay profit taxes at an average rate of 20 percent?

3. (Spreadsheet recommended) Your municipality is considering building a public swimming pool. Analysts have estimated the present values of the following effects over the expected useful life of the pool:

	PV (million dollars)
National government grant	2.2
Construction and maintenance costs	12.5
Personnel costs	8.2
Revenue from municipal residents	8.6
Revenue from non-residents	2.2
Use value benefit to municipal residents	16.6
Use value benefit to non-residents	3.1
Scrap value	0.8

The national government grant is only available for this purpose. Also, the construction and maintenance will have to be done by a non-municipal firm.

a. Assuming national-level standing, what is the net social benefit of the project?

b. Assuming municipal-level standing, what is the net social benefit of the project?

c. How would a guardian in the municipal budget office calculate the net benefit?

d. How would a spender in the municipal recreation department calculate the net benefit?

Notes

1. "Letter to Joseph Priestley", in *Benjamin Franklin: Representative Selections, with Introduction, Bibliography and Notes*, Frank Luther Mott and Chester E. Jorgenson (New York, NY: American Book Company, 1936), pp. 348–49.

2. R. K. Davis, "Lessons in Politics and Economics from the Snail Darter," in Vernon K. Smith, editor, *Environmental Resources and Applied Welfare Economics: Essays in Honor of John V. Krutilla* (Washington, DC: Resources for the Future, 1988), 211–36.

3. Federal Environmental Assessment Review Office, Oldman River Dam: Report of the Environmental Assessment Panel, Ottawa, Ontario, May 1992.

4. See Robert Hahn and John A. Hird, "The Costs and Benefits of Regulation: Review and Synthesis." *Yale Journal of Regulation*, 8(1), 1991, 233–78.

5. Anthony E. Boardman, Wendy L. Mallery, and Aidan R. Vining, "Learning from *Ex Ante/Ex Post* Cost–Benefit Comparisons: The Coquihalla Highway Example." *Socio-Economic Planning Sciences*, 28(2), 1994, 69–84.

6. Bent Flyvbjerg, "What You Should Know about Megaprojects and Why: An Overview." *Project Management Journal*, 45(2), 2014, 6–19.

7. Winston Harrington, Richard D. Morgenstern, and Peter Nelson, "On the Accuracy of Regulatory Cost Estimates." *Journal of Policy Analysis and Management*, 19(2), 2000, 297–322. See also Henry J. Aaron, "Seeing Through the Fog: Policymaking with Uncertain Forecasts." *Journal of Policy Analysis and Management*, 19(2), 2000, 193–206.

8. David L. Weimer and Aidan R. Vining, *Policy Analysis: Concepts and Practice*, 6th edn (New York, NY: Routledge, 2017).

9. In practice, individuals can only focus on approximately four to seven alternatives, at best. G. A. Miller, "The Magical Number Seven, Plus or Minus Two: Some Limits on Our Capacity for Processing Information." *Psychological Review*, 65(1), 1956, 81–97.

10. See, for example, table 1 in David Long, Charles D. Mallar, and Craig V. Thornton, "Evaluating the Benefits and Costs of the Jobs Corps." *Journal of Policy Analysis and Management*, 1(1), 1981, 55–76.

11. Robert D. Behn, "Policy Analysis and Policy Politics." *Policy Analysis*, 7(2), 1981, 199–226, at 213, n. 27.

12. Remember that valuation of the impact at step 6 should be consistent with the chosen measurement indicator. For example, the valuation of an arrest should be lower than the valuation of a conviction so that the analyst would obtain similar estimates of the benefits of reduced crime from using either indicator.

13. These studies are discussed by Robert Williamson, "Pulp Cleanup May Be Waste of Money." *Toronto Globe and Mail*, December 23, 1992, pp. A1, A6.

14. These values are based on those laid out in Mark A. Moore, Anthony E. Boardman, Aidan R. Vining, David L. Weimer, and David H. Greenberg, "Just Give Me a Number! Practical Values for the Social Discount Rate." *Journal of Policy Analysis and Management*, 23(4), 2004, 789–812.

15. Note that at the optimum output level, marginal benefits equal marginal costs: $\frac{dB}{dQ} = \frac{dC}{dQ}$. One can see that the slope of the benefit curve at Q^* equals the slope of the cost curve at Q^*.

16. In contrast, tolls on *congested* highways generally increase the net social benefit.

17. This section draws heavily from Anthony Boardman, Aidan Vining, and W. G. Waters II, "Costs and Benefits through Bureaucratic Lenses: Example of a Highway Project." *Journal of Policy Analysis and Management*, 12(3), 1993, 532–55.

18. This terminology was introduced by Sanford Borins and David A. Good, "Spenders, Guardians and Policy Analysts: A Game of Budgeting Under the Policy and Expenditure Management System." Toronto, Case Program in Canadian Administration, Institute of Public Administration of Canada, 1987 (revised 1989).

19. Such analysis is very helpful for certain purposes, but a problem arises when an analyst does this type of analysis while thinking that he or she is performing CBA.

20. See, for example, William A. Niskanen, "Bureaucrats and Politicians." *Journal of Law and Economics*, 18(3), 1975, 617–43; and André Blais and Stéphane Dion, editors, *The Budget-Maximizing Bureaucrat: Appraisals and Evidence* (Pittsburgh, PA: University of Pittsburgh Press, 1991). For various reasons, senior spenders may be more interested in the discretionary budget or "budget shaping" than in budget maximizing; see Patrick Dunleavy, *Democracy, Bureaucracy and Public Choice* (Englewood Cliffs, NJ: Prentice Hall, 1992). They may, therefore, be willing to support projects that involve considerable "contracting out" and other activities that may not be budget maximizing per se.

21. Robert H. Haveman, "Policy Analysis and the Congress: An Economist's View." *Policy Analysis*, 2(2), 1976, 235–50.

22. Barry R. Weingast et al. refer to this phenomenon as the "Robert Moses effect" after the famous New Yorker who

exploited it so effectively. See Barry R. Weingast, Kenneth A. Shepsle, and Christopher Johnsen, "The Political Economy of Benefits and Costs: A Neoclassical Approach to Distributive Politics." *Journal of Political Economy*, 89(4), 1981, 642–64, at 648.

23. See, for example, Bent Flyvbjerg, Mette Skamris Holm, and Soren Buhl, "Underestimating Costs in Public Works Projects: Error or Lie?" *Journal of the American Planning Association*, 68(3), 2002, 279–93; and Linda R. Cohen and Roger G. Noll, editors, *The Technology Pork Barrel* (Washington, DC: The Brookings Institution, 1991).

24. Rashi Fein, "Petty's Cash Ledger," letter to *The Economist*, Jan. 11 2014, accessed from www.economist.com/news/letters/21593391-france-hotels-heathrow-iran-william-petty-films-our-country-year on April 1, 2017.

25. For a very brief discussion of the origins of CBA, see D. W. Pearce, *Cost–Benefit Analysis* (London: MacMillan, 1971).

26. Many countries have guidelines for conducting RIA. See www.oecd.org/gov/regulatory-policy/ria.htm, accessed April 3, 2017.

27. See Robert W. Hahn, Jason K. Burnett, Yee-Ho I. Chin, Elizabeth A. Mader, and Petrea R. Moyle, "Assessing Regulatory Impact Analyses: The Failure of Agencies to Comply with Executive Order 12,866." *Harvard Journal of Law & Public Policy*, 23(3), 2000, 859–85. This study found that, in a sample of 48 major RIAs conducted from mid-1960 to mid-199, only 29 percent quantified the net benefit.

28. On retrospective regulatory review, see Randall Lutter, "Regulatory Policy: What Role for Retrospective Analysis and Review?" *Journal of Benefit–Cost Analysis*, 4(1), 2013, 17–38.

29. See, for example, Office of the Management and Budget (OMB), *Circular A-94: Guidelines and Discount Rates for BenefitCost Analysis of Federal Programs* (Washington, DC: OMB, 1992); Office of the Management and Budget (OMB) (Washington, DC: OMB, 2003); HM Treasury, *The Green Book: Appraisal and Evaluation in Central Government* (London: The Stationary Office, 2003 (updated 2011)); Treasury Board of Canada Secretariat (TBS), *Canadian Cost–Benefit Analysis Guide: Regulatory Proposals (interim)* (Ottawa, Ontario: TBS, 2007); European Commission, *Guide to Cost–Benefit Analysis of Investment Projects* (Brussels: European Commission, 2015); Australian Government, *Guidance Note: Cost–Benefit Analysis* (Office of Best Practice Regulation, 2016).

30. Oliver Williamson, "Economies as an Antitrust Defense: The Welfare Tradeoffs." *American Economic Review*, 58(1), 1968, 18–36.

31. Anthony E. Boardman, "Using Social Cost–Benefit Analysis to Measure Corporate Social Responsibility." *Infogas*, 5(15), 2009, 6–13 (in Spanish).

32. Richard Revesz and Michael Livermore, *Retaking Rationality: How Cost Benefit Analysis Can Better Protect the Environment and Our Health* (New York, NY: Oxford University Press, 2008).

33. Thomas D. Hopkins, "Economic Analysis Requirements as a Tool of Regulatory Reform: Experience in the United States." Statement presented to the Sub-Committee on Regulations and Competitiveness Standing Committee on Finance, House of Commons, Ottawa, September 15, 1992, p. 10.

34. US Environmental Protection Agency, EPA's Use of Benefit–Cost Analysis: 1981–1986, EPA-230–05-87–028, Office of Policy, Planning and Evaluation, August 1987, pp. 1–3.

35. Robert W. Hahn and Patrick M. Dudley, "How Well Does the US Government Do Benefit–Cost Analysis?" *Review of Environmental Economics and Policy*, 1(2), 2007, 192–211.

2 Conceptual Foundations of Cost–Benefit Analysis

It seems only natural to think about the alternative courses of action we face as individuals in terms of their costs and benefits. Is it appropriate to evaluate public policy alternatives in the same way? The CBA of the highway sketched in Chapter 1 identifies some of the practical difficulties analysts typically encounter in measuring costs and benefits. Yet, even if analysts can measure costs and benefits satisfactorily, evaluating alternatives solely in terms of their net benefits may not always be appropriate. An understanding of the conceptual foundations of CBA provides a basis for determining when CBA can be appropriately used as a decision rule, when it can usefully be part of a broader analysis, and when it should be avoided.

The goal of *allocative*, or *Pareto*, *efficiency* provides the conceptual basis for CBA. In this chapter, we provide a non-technical introduction to Pareto efficiency. We then explain its relationship to *potential Pareto efficiency*, which provides the practical basis for actually doing CBA. Our exploration of the roles of Pareto efficiency and potential Pareto efficiency in CBA provides a basis for distinguishing it from other analytical frameworks. It also provides a basis for understanding the various philosophical objections commonly made against the use of CBA for decision-making.

2.1 CBA as a Framework for Assessing Efficiency

CBA can be thought of as providing a framework for assessing the relative efficiency of policy alternatives.[1] Although we develop a more formal definition of efficiency in the following section, it can be thought of as a situation in which resources, such as land, labor, and capital, are deployed in their highest-valued uses in terms of the goods and services they create. In situations in which decision-makers care only about efficiency, CBA provides a method for making direct comparisons among alternative policies. Even when goals other than efficiency are important, CBA serves as a yardstick that can be used to provide information about the relative efficiency of alternative policies. Indeed, analysts rarely encounter situations in which efficiency is not one of the relevant goals. Critical evaluation of these assertions requires a more precise definition of efficiency.

2.1.1 *Pareto Efficiency*

A simple and intuitively appealing definition of efficiency, referred to as *Pareto efficiency*, underlies modern welfare economics and CBA. *An allocation of goods is Pareto-efficient if no alternative allocation can make at least one person better off without making anyone else worse off.* An allocation of goods is inefficient, therefore, if an alternative allocation can be found that would make at least one person better off without making anyone else worse off. One would have to be malevolent not to want to achieve Pareto efficiency – why forgo gains to persons that would not inflict losses on others?

Figure 2.1 illustrates the concept of Pareto efficiency in the simple allocation of a fixed amount of money between two persons. Imagine that the two persons will receive any total amount of money of up to $100 if they agree on how to split it between themselves. Assume that if they do not agree, then each person receives just $25. The vertical axis measures the amount of money received by person 1, and the horizontal axis measures the amount of money received by person 2. The point labeled $100 on the vertical axis represents the outcome in which person 1 receives the entire $100. Similarly, the point labeled $100 on the horizontal axis represents the outcome in which person 2 receives the entire $100. The line connecting these two extreme points, which we call the *potential Pareto frontier*, represents all the feasible splits between the two persons that allocate the entire $100. Splits involving less than $100 lie within the triangle formed by the potential Pareto frontier and the axes. The one labeled ($25, $25) is such a point. This point represents the status quo in the sense that it gives the amounts the two persons receive if they do not reach an agreement about splitting the $100. The segment of the potential Pareto frontier that gives each person at least as much as the status quo is called the *Pareto frontier*.

The shaded triangle formed by the lines through the status quo point and the Pareto frontier represents all the alternative allocations that would make at least one of the persons better off than the status quo without making the other worse off. The

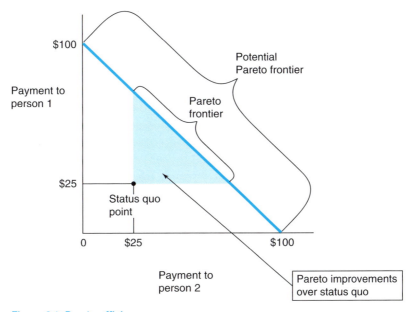

Figure 2.1 Pareto efficiency.

existence of these points, which are feasible alternatives to the status quo that make at least one person better off without making the other worse off, means that the status quo is not Pareto-efficient. Movement to any one of these points is called a *Pareto improvement*. Any Pareto improvement that does not lie on the potential Pareto frontier would leave open the possibility of further Pareto improvements and thus not provide a Pareto-efficient allocation. Only on the potential Pareto frontier is it impossible to make a feasible reallocation that makes one person better off without making the other person worse off.

It should be clear that the segment of the potential Pareto frontier that guarantees at least $25 to each person represents all the Pareto-efficient allocations relative to the status quo. Each of these points makes a Pareto improvement over the status quo and leaves no opportunity for further improvements. The segment of the potential Pareto frontier that represents actual Pareto improvements depends upon the status quo. In other words, implicit in the concept of Pareto efficiency are the initial starting positions of the members of society. We return later to the significance of the difference between the potential and actual Pareto frontiers in our discussion of criticisms of CBA.

2.1.2   *Net Benefits and Pareto Efficiency*

The link between positive net social benefits (henceforth, net benefits) and Pareto efficiency is straightforward: *if a policy has positive net benefits, then it is possible to find a set of transfers, or side payments, that makes at least one person better off without making anyone else worse off.* A full understanding of this link requires some reflection on how one measures the benefits and costs of the incremental impacts of a policy alternative.

The overall guiding principle for valuation is willingness to pay (WTP), the amount that each person would be willing to pay to obtain the impacts of the policy taking account of all the changes in the person's consumption that would result. In practice, however, it is customary and convenient to divide impacts into the outcomes produced by the policy and the inputs required to implement it. As illustrated in Figure 2.2, assessing benefits and costs requires one to employ WTP as the method for valuing the outcomes of a policy and opportunity cost as the method for valuing the resources required to obtain those outcomes through implementation of the policy. Although we develop

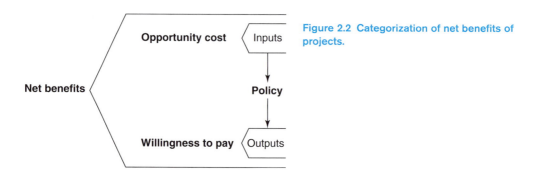

Figure 2.2 Categorization of net benefits of projects.

these important concepts more fully in Chapters 3, 5, 6, and 7 in the context of market exchange, the simple introductions that follow provide the basis for understanding the link between net benefits and Pareto efficiency.

Willingness to Pay. Consider a proposed policy that would produce outputs of relevance to three people. Assume that these people make honest revelations of their assessments of the values of the outputs. Through a series of questions, we elicit the payments that each person would have to make or receive under the policy so that he or she would be indifferent between the status quo and the policy with the payments. So, for example, imagine that person 1 honestly reveals that she would be indifferent between the status quo and paying $100 to have the policy implemented. Similarly, person 2 might say that he is indifferent between the status quo and paying $200 to have the policy implemented. These values are the WTP of persons 1 and 2 for the policy. Unlike persons 1 and 2, assume that person 3 does not like the outcomes of the proposed policy and would have to receive a payment of $250 if the policy were implemented to feel just as well off as he did under the status quo; this $250 is the amount that would have to be given to the person in conjunction with the proposed policy so that he is indifferent between it and the status quo. The negative of this amount (−$250) would be the WTP of person 3 for the policy. As the policy in effect takes something away from person 3, the amount is called the person's *willingness to accept* (WTA).[2]

The algebraic sum of these WTP values is the appropriate measure of the net benefits of the outcomes of the policy. In this example, the WTP amounts can be divided into $300 of benefits ($100 + $200) accruing to persons 1 and 2 and $250 of costs (−$250) accruing to person 3. The net benefits are thus positive and equal to $50. If these were the only three persons affected by the policy, and if the policy required no resources to implement, then the $50 would be the appropriate measure of net benefits from the perspective of CBA. Simple implementation of the policy would not be Pareto-efficient because person 3 would be made worse off with respect to the status quo policy. Yet, we can easily imagine altering the policy so that it would be Pareto-efficient. For example, imagine that person 3 receives $75 from person 1 and $175 from person 2 as part of the policy. Now person 1 is better off than the status quo ($100 of benefits minus $75 given to person 3), person 2 is better off ($200 of benefits minus $175 given to person 3), and person 3 is no worse off ($250 of costs from the policy minus $250 of benefits in the form of compensation from persons 1 and 2). The key point is that if, and only if, the aggregate net benefits of the policy as measured by the WTP of all affected individuals are positive, then there exist sets of contributions and payments that would make the policy a Pareto improvement over the status quo.

Opportunity Cost. The implementation of policies almost always requires the use of some inputs that could be used to produce other things of value. For example, implementing a policy to build a bridge across a river would require the use of labor, steel, concrete, construction machinery, and land that could be used to produce other things of value to people. The concept of opportunity cost is used in CBA to place a dollar value on the inputs required to implement policies. *The opportunity cost of using an input to implement a policy is its value in its best alternative use.* Opportunity cost measures the value of what society must forgo to use the input to implement the policy.

Return to the example of the three persons whose aggregate WTP for the policy was $50. Imagine that the policy requires inputs that have an opportunity cost of $75. That is, if the policy were implemented, then some other members of society would have to give up goods valued at $75. In this case, the policy does not generate enough net benefits to the three persons to allow them to compensate those who must forgo the $75 of goods – the net benefits to society as a whole are negative $25 ($50 of net benefits to the three persons minus $75 in opportunity costs to the rest of society). Thus, the policy could not be made Pareto-efficient because it does not produce enough benefits to permit all those who bear costs to be compensated fully. If the opportunity cost were only $20 instead of $75, then net benefits to society would be $30 and it would be possible to compensate all those who bear costs so that no one is made worse off, and some people are made better off, by the policy. In general, if the net benefits of a policy are positive, then it is potentially Pareto-improving.

2.2   Using CBA for Decision-Making

The connection between net benefits and Pareto efficiency should now be clear. *As long as analysts value all outcomes in terms of willingness to pay (or willingness to accept) and value all required inputs in terms of opportunity costs, then the sign of the net benefits indicates whether it would be possible to compensate those who bear costs sufficiently so that no one is made worse off and at least one person is better off.* Positive net benefits indicate the potential for compensation to make the policy Pareto-efficient; negative net benefits indicate the absence of this potential.

One could imagine the following decision rule for CBA: adopt only policies that are actually Pareto-efficient. In other words, only policies that yield positive benefits after providing full compensation to all those who bear costs would be adopted so that there would be at least some winners and no losers. Although conceptually this is appealing, such a rule would be extremely difficult to apply in practice for a number of reasons. First, it would place great informational burdens on analysts not just to measure aggregate costs and benefits, which can often be inferred from observing prices and quantities in markets, but also to measure costs and benefits for each person, a task that would generally render CBA too costly to use. Second, once the distribution of costs and benefits at the individual level were known, the administrative costs of actually making specific transfers for each government policy would almost certainly be high. Third, it is difficult to operate a practical system of compensation payments that does not distort the investment and work behavior of households. Fourth, the requirement that everyone be fully compensated would create a strong incentive for people to find ways to overstate the costs and understate the benefits that they expect to receive from policies, complicating the already difficult task of inferring how much each person is willing to pay for the impacts produced by the policy. The "actual Pareto efficiency" principle in practice would thus result in society forgoing many policies that offer positive net benefits and the diversion of much effort toward the seeking of unjustified compensation.

2.2.1   *Potential Pareto Efficiency*

CBA utilizes an alternative decision rule with somewhat less conceptual appeal, but much greater feasibility, than the actual Pareto efficiency rule. It is based on what is known as the *Kaldor–Hicks criterion*: a policy should be adopted if and only if those who will gain could fully compensate those who will lose and still be better off.[3] The Kaldor–Hicks criterion provides the basis for the *potential Pareto efficiency rule*, or, more commonly, the *net benefits criterion: adopt only policies that have positive net benefits.* As long as net benefits are positive, it is possible that losers could be compensated so that the policy potentially could be Pareto improving. In terms of Figure 2.1, any point on the potential Pareto frontier would pass the potential Pareto efficiency rule, while only those points on the potential Pareto frontier that guarantee at least $25 to each person (the labeled interior segment of the potential Pareto frontier) pass the actual Pareto efficiency rule.

In practice, the assessment of whether a particular policy would increase efficiency depends on whether it offers a *potential Pareto improvement.* That is, does the policy provide sufficient net gains so that all losers *could* be compensated? Potential Pareto efficiency is achieved only when all potential Pareto improvements have been exhausted.

Several justifications, aside from feasibility, are commonly offered in defense of the potential Pareto efficiency rule. First, by always choosing policies with positive net benefits, society maximizes aggregate wealth. This indirectly helps those who are worse off because richer societies have greater capability for helping their poorest members and, if redistribution is a normal good (that is, other things being equal, people want more of it as their wealth increases), members of society have a greater willingness to help.[4] Second, it is likely that different policies will have different sets of winners and losers. Thus, if the rule is consistently applied to government activity, then costs and benefits will tend to average out across people so that each person is likely to realize positive net benefits from the full collection of policies. Third, as we discuss later in this chapter, the rule stands in contrast to the incentives in representative political systems to give too much weight to costs and benefits that accrue to organized groups and too little weight to costs and benefits that accrue to unorganized interests. Its use in public discourse may thereby reduce the chances that Pareto-inefficient policies will be adopted. Fourth, if a more equal distribution of wealth or income is an important goal, then it is possible to address it directly through transfers after a large number of efficiency-enhancing policies have been adopted. In other words, redistribution, at least in theory, can be done "wholesale" with a single redistribution program rather than "retail" in each particular program.

2.2.2   *Application of the Decision Rule in Practice*

Two polices can be thought of as independent if the adoption of one does not influence the costs and benefits of the other. When all relevant projects are independent, the CBA decision rule is simple: *adopt all policies that have positive net benefits.* A more general version of the rule applies in situations involving multiple policies that may enhance or interfere with each other: *choose the combination of policies that maximizes net benefits.* Physical, budgetary, and other constraints may limit the combinations of policies that are feasible.

Table 2.1 *Choosing Efficient Projects and the Use of Net Benefits versus Benefit–Cost Ratios*

	Costs relative to no project (millions of dollars)	Benefits relative to no project (millions of dollars)	Net benefits (millions of dollars)	Benefits/ costs
Project A	1	10	9	10
Project B	10	30	20	3
Project C	4	8	4	2
Project D	3	5	2	1.7
Projects C and D	7	21	14	3
Project E	10	8	−2	0.8

(1) No constraints: Choose A, B, and combination C and D (net benefits equal $43 million).
(2) All projects mutually exclusive: Choose B (net benefits equal $20 million).
(3) Total costs cannot exceed $10 million: Choose A and combination C and D (net benefits equal $23 million).
Source: Adapted from David L. Weimer and Aidan R. Vining, *Policy Analysis: Concepts and Practice*, 6th ed. (New York, NY: Routledge, 2017), figure 16.2.

Consider the list of projects in Table 2.1. Interpret the costs and benefits as being expressed in terms of present values, so that they can be directly compared with dollars of current consumption. Note that projects C and D are shown as synergistic. That is, the net benefits from adopting both together exceed the sum of the net benefits from adopting each one independently. Such might be the case if project C were a dam that created a reservoir that could be used for recreation as well as hydroelectric power and D were a road that increased access to the reservoir. Of course, projects can also interfere with each other; for instance, the dam might reduce the benefits of a downstream recreation project. The important point is that care must be taken to determine interactions among projects so that the combinations of projects providing the greatest net benefits in aggregate can be readily identified.

Suppose we could choose any combination of projects; then we should simply choose all those with positive net benefits – namely, projects A, B, and combination C and D.

Suppose now the policies are mutually exclusive. For example, we cannot drain a swamp to create agricultural land and simultaneously preserve it as a wildlife refuge. When all the available policies are mutually exclusive, efficiency is maximized by choosing the one with the largest net positive benefits – project B, with net benefits of $20 million. Assume, however, that all projects are mutually exclusive, except C and D, which can be built together to obtain synergistic gains. By taking the combination of C and D to be a separate project, we can consider all the projects on the list to be mutually exclusive. Looking down the column labeled "Net benefits," we see that project B still offers the largest net benefits and therefore should be the one selected, but the combination of C and D offers the next highest net benefits.

Analysts often compare programs in terms of *benefit–cost ratios.* Note that project B, which offers the largest net benefits, does not have the largest ratio of benefits to costs. Project A has a benefit–cost ratio of 10, while project B has a benefit–cost ratio of only 3. Nevertheless, project B should be selected because it offers larger net benefits than project A. This comparison shows how the benefit–cost ratio can sometimes confuse the choice process when the projects under consideration are of different scale (that is, project B involves substantially higher costs than project A). Furthermore, the benefit–cost ratio is sensitive to whether negative WTP (willingness to accept) amounts are subtracted from benefits or added to costs. For example, imagine that the cost of $10 million for project B was opportunity costs and the benefits of $30 million consisted of $40 million for one group and −$10 million for another. Treating the negative WTP as a cost rather than as a negative benefit would leave the net benefits unchanged but lower the benefit–cost ratio from 3 to 2. Thus, benefit–cost ratios are subject to manipulation. For these reasons, *we recommend that analysts avoid using benefit–cost ratios to rank policies and rely instead on net benefits.*

Return to Table 2.1 and interpret the listed costs as public expenditures exactly equal to opportunity costs and the listed benefits as the WTP values for all project effects. Now assume that, while none of the projects are mutually exclusive in a physical sense, total public expenditures (costs) cannot exceed $10 million because of a budget constraint that is binding for political reasons. If project B is selected, then the budget constraint is met, and net benefits of $20 million result. If project A and the combination of projects C and D are selected instead, then the budget constraint is also met, but net benefits of $23 million result. No other feasible combination offers larger net benefits. Thus, under the budget constraint, net benefits are maximized by choosing projects A and the combination of C and D.

2.3   Fundamental Issues Related to Willingness to Pay

Three sets of fundamental issues arise with respect to the interpretation of WTP as a measure of benefits in the assessment of the efficiency of policies. First, a theoretical limitation in the aggregation of willingness-to-pay amounts across individuals opens the possibility that the net benefits criterion will not lead to fully satisfactory rankings of policies. Second, normative issues arise because of the dependence of WTP on the distribution of wealth in society. Third, normative issues also arise with respect to the issue of *standing*, which concerns whose WTP counts in the aggregation of benefits.

2.3.1   *Theoretical Limitation of WTP as the Basis for Social Orderings*

Although using net benefits as a basis for choosing efficient public policies is intuitively appealing, its implementation through the aggregation of the willingness-to-pay amounts of the members of society confronts a fundamental theoretical limitation: ranking policies in terms of net benefits does not guarantee a transitive social ordering of the policies.

A *transitive* ordering requires that if X is preferred to Y, and Y is preferred to Z, then X is preferred to Z. The logic of transitivity seems so clear that it is usually taken as an axiom of rationality in the preferences of individuals. We would certainly be skeptical about the mental state of someone who tells us she prefers apples to oranges, and she prefers oranges to peaches, but she prefers peaches to apples. This violation of transitivity implies a cyclical, and therefore ambiguous, ordering of the alternatives. Clearly, transitivity is a desirable property of any preference ordering.

If every member of a society has transitive preferences, then do reasonable procedures for aggregating their preferences always produce a transitive social ordering? An example makes clear that the answer is no. Consider a common aggregation procedure: majority rule voting over pairs of alternatives. Imagine that society consists of three voters who have preferences over three alternatives, X, Y, and Z, as displayed in Table 2.2. Specifically, voter 1 prefers X to Y to Z, voter 2 prefers Z to X to Y, and voter 3 prefers Y to Z to X. If the voters express their sincere preferences in each round of voting, then we would find that given the choice between X and Y, voters 1 and 2 (a majority) would vote for X because they each prefer it to Y. Similarly, given the choice between Y and Z, a majority would vote for Y. Yet in a choice between X and Z, a majority would vote for Z. Thus, the implied social ordering is intransitive because X is preferred to Y, Y is preferred to Z, but Z is preferred to X!

Is the possibility of obtaining an intransitive social ordering peculiar to the use of pairwise majority rule voting to produce rankings of alternatives? Surprisingly, it can result from any rule for creating a social ordering that satisfies certain minimal requirements. We cannot expect any rule for creating a social ranking of policy alternatives to be fully satisfactory. As CBA is a social choice rule, it must either not satisfy one or more of the minimal requirements or risk producing an intransitive ordering of alternatives.

In 1951, Kenneth Arrow proved that any *social choice rule* that satisfies a basic set of fairness conditions can produce intransitive social orderings.[5] *Arrow's theorem* applies to any rule for ranking alternatives in which two or more persons must rank three or more alternatives. It requires any such scheme to satisfy at least the following conditions to be considered fair: First, each person is allowed to have any transitive preferences

Table 2.2 *Cyclical Social Preferences under Pairwise Majority Rule Voting*

Preference ordering	Voter 1	Voter 2	Voter 3
First choice	X	Z	Y
Second choice	Y	X	Z
Third choice	Z	Y	X

(1) Pairwise voting outcomes: X versus Y, X wins; Y versus Z, Y wins; X versus Z, Z wins.
(2) Implied social ordering: X is preferred to Y, Y is preferred to Z, but Z is preferred to X!

over the possible policy alternatives (*axiom of unrestricted domain*). Second, if one alternative is unanimously preferred to a second, then the rule for choice will not select the second (*axiom of Pareto choice*). Third, the ranking of any two alternatives should not depend on what other alternatives are available (*axiom of independence*). Fourth, the rule must not allow any person dictatorial power to impose his or her preferences as the social ordering (*axiom of non-dictatorship*). Arrow's theorem states that any fair rule for choice (one that satisfies the four previous axioms) will not guarantee a transitive *social ordering* of policy alternatives. That is, it is possible that individual preferences are such that the social ordering will be intransitive and produce cyclical rankings, such as A is preferred to B and B is preferred to C but C is preferred to A! Thus, unless the net benefit rule, which is a social choice rule, violates one of the axioms, it cannot guarantee a transitive social ordering of policies.

In order to ensure that the use of WTP in the implementation of the net benefit rule will produce a transitive social ordering of policies, some restrictions, violating the axiom of unrestricted domain, must be placed on the preferences that individuals are allowed to hold.[6] Economic models commonly assume that individual preferences are represented by utility functions (numerical representations of preference orderings) that exhibit positive but declining marginal utility; that is, other things equal, incremental consumption of any good increases utility but not by as much as the previous incremental unit. Unfortunately, this relatively weak restriction of the domain of preferences (it rules out preferences that cannot be represented by such utility functions) is not enough to guarantee that the net benefit rule based on WTP will *always* produce a transitive social ordering. Two additional restrictions are required for such a guarantee: (1) the utility functions of individuals must be such that the individual demand curves that they imply can be aggregated into a market demand curve with the sum of individual incomes as an argument, and (2) all individuals must face the same set of prices.[7] The first restriction is quite strong in that it requires each individual's demand for each good to increase linearly with increasing income and to have the same rate of increase for each individual. The second restriction, generally satisfied when all goods are traded in markets, may be violated when policies allocate quantities of goods to individuals who cannot resell them in markets.

The necessity of restricting the allowed preferences of individuals to guarantee a transitive social ordering from the use of WTP in the implementation of the net benefits criterion makes clear that it is an imperfect criterion for assessing the relative efficiency of alternative policies.[8] Of course, analysts can avoid this theoretical problem by assuming that the preferences of individual consumers conform to restrictive assumptions consistent with the existence of an appropriate aggregate demand function. Alternatively, analysts can avoid it by assuming that policies affect the price of only a single good. Indeed, as discussed in the next five chapters, analysts seeking to estimate WTP typically work with an aggregate, or market, demand schedule for a single good, implicitly assuming away price effects in the markets for other goods.

Despite its theoretical imperfection as a measure of efficiency, WTP is an intuitively appealing and practical concept for guiding the implementation of the net benefits criterion. As discussed next, however, its dependence on the distribution of wealth raises a serious normative concern about its use.

Dependence of WTP on the Distribution of Wealth

The willingness of a person to pay to obtain a desired policy impact will tend to be higher the greater the wealth that she or he has available. Consequently, the sum of the willingness of persons to pay, the benefit measure in CBA, depends on their levels of wealth. If the distribution of wealth in society were to be changed, then it would be likely that the sum of individuals' willingness-to-pay amounts would change as well, perhaps altering the ranking of alternative policies in terms of their net benefits.

The dependence of net benefits on the distribution of wealth would not pose a conceptual problem if losers from adopted policies were *actually* compensated so that the adopted polices would produce actual, rather than potential, Pareto improvements. From a utilitarian perspective, Pareto improvement guarantees that the sum of utilities of individuals in society increases. In application of the potential Pareto principle, however, it is possible that an adopted policy could actually lower the sum of utilities if people with different levels of wealth had different *marginal utilities of money.*[9]

As an illustration, consider a policy that gives $10 of benefits to a person with high wealth and inflicts $9 of costs on a person with low wealth. If the low-wealth person's marginal utility of money is higher than that of the high-wealth person, then it is possible that the utility loss of the low-wealth person could outweigh the utility gain of the high-wealth person. Thus, while the Pareto principle allows us to avoid interpersonal utility comparisons by guaranteeing increases in aggregate utility for policies with positive net benefits, the potential Pareto principle does not do so.

The implication of the dependence of WTP on wealth is that the justification for the potential Pareto principle weakens for policies that concentrate costs and benefits on different wealth groups. Policies with positive net benefits that concentrate costs on low-wealth groups may not increase aggregate utility; moreover, policies with negative net benefits that concentrate benefits on low-wealth groups may not decrease aggregate utility. However, if the potential Pareto principle is consistently applied and adopted, then policies do not produce consistent losers or winners. Consequently, the overall effects of the policies taken together will tend to make everyone better off. Hence, concerns about reductions in aggregate utility would be unfounded.

Critics of CBA sometimes question the validity of the concept of Pareto efficiency itself because it depends on the status quo distribution of wealth. In Figure 2.1, note that the location of the Pareto frontier would change if the location of the status quo point were changed. Some have advocated the formulation of a social welfare function that maps the utility, wealth, or consumption of all individuals in society into an index that ranks alternative distributions of goods.[10] In this broader framework incorporating distributional values, an efficient policy is one that maximizes the value of the social welfare function. But how does society determine the social welfare function? Unfortunately, Arrow's theorem, as well as practical difficulties in obtaining needed information, precludes the formulation of a social welfare function through any fair collective choice procedure.[11] In practice, it must therefore be provided subjectively by the analyst.[12] We believe that it is usually better to keep the subjective distributional values of analysts explicit by comparing policies both in terms of efficiency and the selected distributional criteria, as illustrated in the discussion of multigoal analysis and distributionally weighted CBA later in this chapter. As an alternative, analysts can report net benefits by wealth or income group, as well as for society as a whole.

2.3.3   *Dependence of Net Benefits on Assumptions about Standing*

The question of whose WTP should count in the aggregation of net benefits has come to be known as the issue of standing.[13] It has immediate practical importance in at least three contexts: the jurisdictional definition of society and its membership, the exclusion of socially unacceptable preferences, and the inclusion of the preferences of future generations. Recognition of social constraints, rights, and duties often helps answer the question of standing.

Jurisdictional Definition of Society. The most inclusive definition of society encompasses all people, no matter where they live or to which government they owe allegiance. Analysts working for the United Nations or some other international organization might very well adopt such a universalistic, or global, perspective. Yet for purposes of CBA, most analysts define society at the national level. The basis for this restriction in jurisdiction is the notion that the citizens of a country share a common constitution, formal or informal, that sets out fundamental values and rules for making collective choices. In a sense, they consent to being a society and recognize that citizens of other countries have their own constitutions that make them distinct polities. Furthermore, these rules include fiscal and monetary policies that shape a national economy in which resources and goods are allocated.

The distinction between universal and national jurisdiction becomes relevant in the evaluation of policies whose impacts spill over national borders. For example, if US analysts adopt the national-level jurisdiction as defining society, then they would not attempt to measure the willingness of Canadian residents to pay to avoid pollution originating in the United States that exacerbates acid rain in Canada. Of course, the willingness of US citizens to pay to reduce acid rain in Canada should be included in the CBA, although in practice, it would be very difficult to measure.

As in the highway example discussed in Chapter 1, a similar issue arises with respect to subnational units of government. As an illustration, consider a city that is deciding whether to build a bike path. Assume that a CBA from the national perspective (giving standing to everyone in the country) predicts that the project will generate $1 million in benefits (which all accrue to city residents) and $2 million in costs (which are also borne by city residents), thereby resulting in negative $1 million in net benefits (or $1 million in net costs). Also assume, however, that through an intergovernmental grants program the national government will repay the city's $2 million of costs resulting from this particular project. The grant appears to the city residents as a $2 million benefit offsetting $2 million in local costs. Thus, from the perspective of the city, the bike path generates $1 million in net benefits rather than $1 million in net costs.

One can make an argument that the city should treat its residents as the relevant society and, hence, should not give standing to non-residents. The city government has a charter to promote the welfare of its residents. The city by itself can do relatively little to affect national policy – even if it does not take advantage of all the opportunities offered by the national government, other cities probably will. Furthermore, analysts who do not adopt the city's perspective but instead employ only the broader national perspective risk losing influence, a possibility of special concern to analysts who earn their living by giving advice to the city.

Adopting the subnational perspective, however, makes CBA a less-valuable decision rule for public policy. We believe that *analysts should ideally conduct CBA from the national perspective.* They may, of course, also conduct a parallel CBA from the subnational perspective as a response to the narrower interests of their clients. If major impacts spill over national borders, then the CBA should be done from the global as well as the national perspective.

Jurisdictional Membership. Deciding the jurisdictional definition of society leaves open a number of questions about who should be counted as members of the jurisdiction. For example, almost all analysts agree that citizens of their country, whether living domestically or abroad, should have standing. With respect to non-citizens in their country, most analysts would probably give standing to those who were in the country legally. No consensus exists with respect to the standing of other categories of people: Should illegal aliens have standing? What about the children of illegal aliens?

One source of guidance for answering these types of questions is the system of legally defined rights.[14] For example, a ruling by the courts that the children of illegal aliens are entitled to access publicly funded education suggests that analysts give these children standing in CBA. Reliance on legally defined rights to determine standing, however, is not always morally acceptable. It would not have been right to deny standing in CBA to slaves in the antebellum United States, non-whites in apartheid South Africa, or Jews in Nazi Germany simply because they lacked legal rights. Therefore, legal rights alone cannot fully resolve the issue of standing in CBA. They provide a presumption, but one that analysts may sometimes have an ethical responsibility to challenge. Democratic regimes usually provide mechanisms for challenging such presumptions, but often with personal cost to individual analysts.

One other issue of membership deserves brief mention. CBA is anthropocentric. *Only the WTP of people counts.* Neither flora nor fauna have standing. That is not to say that their "interests" have no representation. Many people are willing to pay to preserve a species, and some are even willing to pay to preserve individual animals or plants. As discussed in Chapter 13, it is conceptually correct within the CBA framework to take account of these WTP amounts, although doing so effectively is often beyond our analytical reach.

Exclusion of Socially Unacceptable Preferences. People sometimes hold preferences that society seeks to suppress through widely supported legal sanctions. For instance, although some people would be willing to pay for the opportunity to have sexual relations with children, most countries attempt to thwart the expression of such preferences through strict criminal penalties. Should such socially unacceptable preferences be given standing in CBA? Common sense suggests that the answer should be no. One approach to answering this question conceptually adds duties and prohibitions to legal rights as sources of guidance about social values. Together they can be thought of as social constraints that should be taken into account in CBA just as the analyst takes into account physical and budgetary constraints.[15] Clear and widely accepted legal sanctions may help identify preferences that should not have standing.

An important application arises in estimating the net benefits of policies that are intended to reduce the amount of criminal behavior in society. In early applications, some analysts counted reductions in the monetary returns to crime as a cost borne by criminals, offsetting the benefits of reduced criminal activity enjoyed by their victims.[16] As the returns from crime are illegal and widely viewed as wrong, however, the social constraint perspective argues against treating them in this manner.

The issue of the standing of preferences can be especially difficult for analysts to resolve when they are dealing with foreign cultures. Consider, for instance, the CBA of a program to bring water to poor communities in Haiti.[17] Analysts found that husbands had negative WTP amounts for the time that their wives saved from easier access to water. By contemporary standards in most urban settings, people would generally regard these preferences as unworthy. Yet in the cultural context of rural Haiti at the time, they were consistent with prevailing norms. Should these preferences of husbands have standing? In practice, lack of data to estimate WTP amounts for this sort of impact usually spares analysts from having to answer such difficult questions.

Inclusion of the Preferences of Future Generations. Some policies adopted today, such as disposal of nuclear wastes or preservation of wetlands, may have impacts on people not yet born. Although we believe that these people should have standing in CBA, there is no way to measure their WTP directly because they are not yet here to express it.[18] How serious a problem does this pose for CBA?

The absence of direct measures of the willingness of future generations to pay for policy impacts generally poses few problems for two reasons. First, because few policies involve impacts that appear only in the far future, the WTP of people alive today for the effects during their lifetimes can be used to some extent to predict how future generations will value them. Second, as most people alive today care about the well-being of their children, grandchildren, and great-grandchildren, whether born or yet to be born, they are likely to include the interests of these generations to some extent in their own valuations of impacts. Indeed, because people cannot predict with certainty the place that their future offspring will hold in society, they are likely to take a very broad view of future impacts.

In Chapters 10 and 13, we return to the question of the standing of future generations when we discuss the social discount rate and existence value, respectively.

2.4   Concerns about the Role of CBA in the Political Process

The most vocal critics of CBA fear that it subverts democratic values. Some see the monetizing of impacts as a profane attempt to place a price on everything. Others see CBA as undermining democracy. Although these fears are largely unfounded, they deserve explicit consideration by advocates of CBA.

2.4.1   *Does CBA Debase the Terms of Public Discourse?*

A number of objections have been raised to the effort made in CBA to value all policy impacts in terms of dollars: Pricing goods not normally traded in markets – for example, life itself – decreases their perceived value by implying that they can be compared to goods that are traded in markets; pricing such goods reduces their perceived value by weakening the claim that they should not be for sale in any circumstance; and pricing all goods undercuts the claim that some goods are "priceless."[19] The language and conceptual frameworks that people use almost certainly affect the nature of debate to some extent. It is not clear, however, how influential the technical concepts of economics are in actually shaping public discourse. In any event, the correct interpretation of how non-market goods are monetized largely undercuts the charge that CBA debases public discourse.

Consider the issue of the monetization of the value of life. On the surface it may appear that economists are implying that a price can be put on someone's life. A closer look, which we provide in Chapters 15 and 17, shows that the value of life estimated by economists is based on the implicit value people place on their own lives in making decisions that involve trade-offs between money or something else of value, and mortality risks. It is thus the value of a *statistical life*, the WTP to avoid risks that will result in one less death in a population. Although it may not be appropriate to place a dollar value on the life of any particular person, it is appropriate to use the value of a statistical life in assessing proposed policies that change the risks of death that people face.

Exhibit 2.1

Does wealth produce happiness? Surveys conducted within countries consistently find that rich people (say those in the top quarter of the income distribution) on average report being happier than poorer people (say those in the bottom quarter of the income distribution). Yet, if one looks at either of these groups over time, one discovers that its absolute level of happiness is roughly constant despite the fact that economic growth has made them richer. Similarly, comparing the happiness of the rich (or poor) across countries generally shows similar levels of happiness despite substantial differences in the overall levels of wealth between the countries. What explains this puzzle? Richard Layard suggests two psychological effects that move up the norm to which people compare their own circumstances as societies become wealthier: habituation and rivalry. Habituation involves getting used to things we have – an initial feeling of happiness from acquisition tends to evaporate as we get used to having the goods. Rivalry involves comparing one's situation to those in a reference group – happiness depends on one's relative position.

These phenomena raise concerns about interpreting changes in income as changes in aggregate happiness. A policy that increased everyone's income would certainly pass the net benefits test. Yet extreme habituation might quickly return everyone to their initial levels of utility, or extreme rivalry would result in no utility gains at all because no one's relative position changes!

Source: Adapted from Richard Layard, "Happiness: Has Social Science a Clue?" Lionel Robbins Memorial Lectures, London School of Economics, Lecture 1: Income and Happiness: Rethinking Economic Policy, March 3, 4 and 5, 2003.

Every day, people voluntarily make trade-offs between changes in the risk of death and other values: driving faster to save time increases the risk of being involved in a fatal traffic accident; eating fatty foods is pleasurable but increases the risk of fatal heart disease; skiing is exhilarating but risks fatal injury. Is it inappropriate to take account of these preferences in valuing the impacts of public policies? Most economists would answer no. Indeed, valuing statistical lives seems less problematic than attempting to place a dollar value on a specific person by estimating the person's forgone future earnings, the procedure often employed by courts in cases of wrongful death.

2.4.2   *Does CBA Undermine Democracy?*

Some critics of CBA charge that it undermines democracy by imposing a single goal, efficiency, in the assessment of public policies. Their charge would be justified if the appropriate comparison were between a world in which public policy is determined solely through democratic processes that gave weight to all interests and a world in which public policy is determined strictly through the application of CBA. However, this is an inappropriate comparison for two reasons. First, actual governmental processes fall far short of "ideal democracy." Second, at most, CBA has modest influence in public policy-making.[20]

The interests of vocal constituencies, often those who can organize themselves in anticipation of obtaining concentrated benefits or avoiding concentrated costs, typically receive great attention from those in representative governments who wish to be re-elected or advance to higher office. Less-vocal constituencies usually have their interests represented less well. The interests of many of these less-vocal constituencies are often better reflected in CBA. For example, CBA takes account of the individually small, but in aggregate, large costs borne by consumers because of government price-support programs that raise prices to the benefit of a small number of well-organized agricultural producers. But CBA rarely serves as the decisive decision rule for public policy. Indeed, it is difficult to identify important public policies selected *solely* on the basis of CBA.

A realistic assessment of representative democracy and the current influence of CBA should allay concerns that the latter is subverting the former. To the extent that CBA is influential, it probably contributes to more democratic public policy by drawing attention to diffuse interests typically underrepresented in a representative democracy. It would have to become much more influential before it could possibly be viewed as undermining democratic processes. Despite our hopes that the readers of this book will help make the use of CBA more prevalent, we have no concerns about it being overly influential in the near future.

2.5 Limitations of CBA: Other Analytical Approaches

It is important for analysts to realize the limitations of CBA. Two types of circumstances make the net benefits criterion an inappropriate decision rule for public policy. First, technical limitations may make it impossible to quantify and then monetize all relevant impacts as costs and benefits. Second, goals other than efficiency are relevant to the policy. For example, some policies are intended to affect the equality of outcomes or opportunity. Nevertheless, even when the net benefits criterion is not appropriate as a decision rule, CBA usually provides a useful yardstick for comparing alternative policies in terms of efficiency along with other goals.

2.5.1 *Technical Limitations to CBA*

CBA in its pure form requires that all impacts relevant to efficiency be quantified and made commensurate through monetization. Only when all the costs and benefits are expressed in dollars can the potential Pareto principle be applied through the calculation of net benefits. Limitations in theory, data, or analytical resources, however, may make it impossible for the analyst to monetize all the impacts of a policy. Nonetheless, it may still be desirable to do a qualitative cost–benefit analysis or, if all but one important effect can be monetized, to switch from CBA to cost–effectiveness analysis. A brief description of each of these alternative approaches follows.

Qualitative CBA. The advice given by Benjamin Franklin at the beginning of Chapter 1 can be thought of as a prescription for qualitative CBA. In conducting qualitative CBA, the analyst typically monetizes as many of the impacts as possible and then makes qualitative estimates of the relative importance of the remaining costs and benefits. Consider, for instance, a program to plant trees along an urban highway. The cost of the program, which consists only of the expenditures that must be made to hire a contractor to plant and to maintain the trees, can be directly monetized. The benefits, however, include a number of effects that are likely to be difficult to monetize: the visual pleasure the trees give to motorists, the reduction of noise in adjoining neighborhoods, and the filtering of pollutants from the air. With sufficient resources, the analyst would be able to monetize these benefits through a variety of techniques such as surveys of motorists and comparisons with monetary estimates of the effects of other noise-reduction programs on property values. However, because the program involves relatively small costs, it is unlikely that such efforts would be justified. Instead, a reasonable approach would be to list these benefits with rough estimates of their order of magnitude.

Analysts who lack the time, data, or other resources needed to value all relevant impacts directly may be able to make use of estimates found in other cost–benefit analyses or economic research. For example, most analysts doing CBA do not directly estimate people's WTP for reductions in mortality risk. Instead, as discussed in Chapters 4, 16, and 17, they rely on econometric studies investigating how people trade such things as changes in wages for changes in levels of risk.

When possible, analysts should quantify the impacts of the policy; that is, they should estimate the numeric values of the non-monetized impacts. For example, consider analysis of a proposed regulation to restrict commercial fishing practices so that fewer dolphins will be killed per ton of tuna harvested. The regulation produces a benefit because some people have a positive WTP for dolphin deaths avoided. Actually monetizing, that is, measuring the WTP, is a difficult task that might not be feasible for the analyst conducting the CBA. Even if monetization is infeasible, however, it is useful to attempt to predict the number of dolphins saved by the regulation. Doing so increases the usefulness of the qualitative CBA for others by conveying the magnitude of the impact of the regulation. Additionally, the client or other users of the analysis may be able to provide estimates of the willingness of people to pay for each dolphin saved so that (fully monetized) CBA becomes feasible.

Analysts often face a more complicated choice than simply whether to quantify a category of costs or benefits. Empirical measures can have varying degrees of accuracy, ranging from precise estimates in which we have great confidence to imprecise estimates in which we have little confidence. The decision to quantify, and with what degree of effort, should reflect the value of the increased precision that can be obtained and the costs of obtaining it. In other words, we should make such decisions within a CBA framework!

Cost–Effectiveness Analysis. Analysts can often quantify impacts but not monetize them all. If analysts are unable or unwilling to monetize the major benefit, then cost–effectiveness analysis may be appropriate. Because not all of the impacts can be monetized, it is not possible to estimate net benefits. The analysts can, however, construct a ratio involving the quantitative, but non-monetized, benefit and the total dollar costs. A comparison allows the analyst to rank policies in terms of the cost–effectiveness criterion. However, unlike the net benefits criterion of CBA, it does not directly allow the analysts to conclude that the highest-ranked policy contributes to greater efficiency.

Return to the qualitative CBA of the fishing regulation discussed earlier. Suppose that, except for the benefit from avoided dolphin deaths, all the impacts could be monetized, resulting in an estimate of net cost of c dollars. If the number of deaths of dolphin avoided is n_d, then the analyst could construct an effectiveness–cost ratio for the regulation, n_d/c, which can be interpreted as the average number of dolphins saved per dollar of cost borne. (Alternatively, the analyst could construct the cost–effectiveness ratio as c/n_d, which can be interpreted as the average dollar cost per dolphin saved.) Now imagine a number of alternative regulations, each of which involves different net costs and a different number of dolphins saved. A cost–effectiveness ratio can be calculated for each of these programs to facilitate comparison across alternative regulations.

Using cost–effectiveness analysis for decision-making usually requires that some additional information be brought to bear. If the objective is to save as many dolphins as possible at a net cost of no more than c^*, then the analyst should select the most effective regulation from among those with net costs of less than c^*. Alternatively, if the objective is to save at least n_d^* dolphins, then the analyst should select the regulation with the lowest cost from among those regulations saving at least n_d^*. This is not necessarily the alternative with the best cost–effectiveness ratio. For example, if $n_d^* = 1000$, one would choose a regulation that saved 1000 dolphins at a cost of \$1 million (\$1000 per dolphin saved) over an alternative regulation that saved 500 dolphins at a cost of \$50,000 (\$100 per dolphin saved).

Analysts often encounter situations in which they or their clients are unable or unwilling to monetize impacts such as human lives saved, injuries avoided, or the acres of old-growth forest preserved. Because cost–effectiveness analysis may be useful in these situations, we consider its uses and limitations in greater depth in Chapter 18.

2.5.2   *Relevance of CBA when Goals Other than Efficiency Matter*

One goal, efficiency, underlies CBA. The general public, politicians, and even economists, however, very often consider goals reflecting other values to be relevant to the evaluation of public policies proposed to solve social problems. Although efficiency almost always is one of the relevant goals in policy analysis, other goals, such as equality of opportunity, equality of outcome, expenditure constraints, political feasibility, and national security, for instance, may be as, or even more, important. Indeed, the spenders and guardians we met in Chapter 1 behave as if they are responding to goals other than efficiency. When goals in addition to efficiency are relevant, as well as when efficiency is the only goal, but relevant impacts cannot be confidently monetized, *multigoal analysis* provides the appropriate framework. In the special case in which efficiency and equality of outcome are the only relevant goals, *distributionally weighted* CBA may be an appropriate technique.

Multigoal Analysis. The most general analytical framework is multigoal analysis. At the heart of multigoal analysis lies the notion that all policy alternatives should be compared in terms of all the relevant goals. Although multigoal analysis can be prescribed as a number of distinct steps,[21] three of its aspects are especially important. First, the analyst must move from relevant social values to general goals to specific impact categories that can be used as yardsticks for evaluating alternative policies. For example, the value of human dignity may imply a goal of improving equality of opportunity, which might be expressed as quantifiable impacts such as increasing participation in higher education and expanding workforce participation. Second, the analyst must evaluate each alternative policy, including current policy, in terms of each of the impacts. Third, as no policy alternative is likely to dominate the others in terms of progress toward all the goals, the analyst usually can only make a recommendation to adopt one of the alternatives by carefully considering and making a subjective judgment concerning the trade-offs in the achievement of goals it offers relative to the other alternatives.

As a simple example, consider a multigoal analysis of alternative income transfer policies intended to help poor families. The analyst might construct the worksheet shown in Table 2.3 as a checklist for keeping track of the relevant goals. Increasing efficiency and improving the quality of life of poor families are both appropriate substantive goals. The former captures the aggregate gain or loss to society from transfers; the latter captures that portion of the gain or loss accruing to the poorest families. The goal of achieving political feasibility might be added to take account of the likely lack of consensus on the relative importance of the substantive goals among politicians. In this example, it can be thought of as an instrumental goal that is valuable not for its own sake but because it helps achieve the substantive goals.

The major efficiency impacts are likely to be changes in earnings and increases in investment in human capital for the recipients of aid and the incremental real resource costs of administering the aid policy. In practice, these impacts would be measured relative to current policy. Consequently, the predicted impacts would be zero for current policy. If both of the efficiency-related impacts could be monetized, then the criterion for assessing efficiency would simply be the sum of the net benefits of these three impacts as measured in CBA – positive net benefits would indicate an increase in efficiency over current policy. However, if either of these impacts could not be monetized, then efficiency would be assessed in terms of the two categories. The goal of improving the quality of life of poor families would probably be expressed in terms of such impacts as reducing the number of families below the poverty line, reducing the number of one-parent families, and increasing the educational achievement of family members. The impact associated with the additional goal of political feasibility might be the change in the probability of passage of legislation required to implement the policy.

Before selecting among the alternative policies, the analyst should fill in all the cells of a matrix like the one shown in Table 2.3. Each cell would contain a prediction of the effect of a particular policy in terms of a particular impact category. By filling in all

Table 2.3 *Evaluation Matrix Worksheet for Alternative Family Aid Policies*

		Policy alternatives		
Goals	Impact vategories	Policy A (current policy)	Policy B	Policy C
Efficiency	Changes in labor earnings			
	Increased investment in human capital			
	Incremental administrative costs			
Quality of life of poorest families	Number of families below poverty line			
	Number of one-parent families			
	Educational achievement of family members			
Political feasibility	Probability of adoption of required legislation			

the cells, the analyst seeks to gain a comprehensive comparison of the alternatives across all the impact categories, and hence across their related goals.

Note that one can think of CBA, qualitative CBA, and cost–effectiveness analysis as special cases of multigoal analysis. In the case of CBA, there is one goal (efficiency) with one criterion (net benefits) so that the evaluation matrix has only one row, and the choice among alternatives is trivial (simply select the policy with the largest net benefits) – as impacts of the alternatives to current policy would be assessed relative to current policy, there would be no explicit column for current policy and the decision rule would be to select one of the alternatives only if it has positive net benefits. In the case of qualitative CBA, there is also one goal, but because all relevant impacts cannot be monetized, it corresponds to several criteria, one for each impact. In the case of cost–effectiveness analysis, the goal of efficiency is often combined with some other goal such as satisfying a constraint on monetary costs or achieving some target level of reduction in the quantified but non-monetized impact.

Distributionally Weighted CBA. If both efficiency and equality of income are relevant goals and their relative importance can be quantified, then distributionally weighted CBA provides an alternative decision rule to the maximization of net benefits. Instead of considering aggregate net benefits as in standard CBA, net benefits are calculated for each of several relevant groups distinguished by income, wealth, or some similar characteristic of relevance to a distributional concern. As discussed in more detail in Chapter 19, the net benefits of each group are multiplied by a weighting factor, selected by the analyst to reflect some distributional goal, and then summed to arrive at a number that can be used to rank alternative policies.

The major problem that analysts encounter in doing distributionally weighted CBA is arriving at an appropriate and acceptable set of weights. A general approach, which takes as a desirable social goal increasing equality of wealth, involves making the weights inversely proportional to wealth (or income) to favor policies that tend to equalize wealth (or income) in the population.[22] This approach, like others that place more weight on costs and benefits received by those with lower wealth, is consistent with the social goal of raising the position of the least advantaged in society. As reasonable arguments can be made in support of each of these approaches, the absence of a consensus about appropriate weights is not surprising.[23]

Obviously, developing weights that allow a single quantitative criterion for ranking alternative policies makes the choice among policy alternatives easier. Yet this ease is achieved only by making an assumption that forces efficiency and equality of outcomes to be fully commensurate. Dissatisfaction with the strong assumption required to do this has led a number of analysts to suggest that distributionally weighted CBA should always be done in conjunction with standard CBA to make clearer the efficiency implications of the selected weights.[24] In doing so, the study becomes, in effect, a multigoal analysis, raising the question of whether an explicit treatment of efficiency and equality as separate goals might not be a more appropriate framework when both efficiency and distributional concerns are important. Cost–effectiveness analysis might also provide a more reasonable approach than distributionally weighted CBA by posing the question in terms of achieving the most desirable redistribution possible for some fixed level of net cost.[25]

Exhibit 2.2

A study by the Congressional Budget Office to assess three alternatives for reducing US consumption of gasoline listed the following criteria:

This study weighs the relative merits of tightening CAFE standards, raising the federal gasoline tax, and creating a cap-and-trade program against several major criteria:

Cost-effectiveness. Reducing gasoline consumption would impose costs (both monetary and nonmonetary) on various producers and consumers. A cost-effective policy would keep those costs to a minimum.

Predictability of gasoline savings. How reliably would the policy bring about the desired reduction in gasoline consumption?

Effects on safety. How would the policy alter the number and severity of traffic accidents?

Effects on other external costs related to driving. Reducing gasoline consumption would affect not only the United States' energy security and carbon emissions but other driving-related external costs (ones whose full weight is borne by society at large rather than by an individual). Those external costs include traffic congestion, the need for highway construction and maintenance, and emissions of air pollutants besides carbon dioxide.

In addition to those factors, the three policy options would have other implications that policy-makers may care about, such as their effects on people at different income levels and in different parts of the country and their impact on the amount of revenue collected by the federal government. (Summary, p. 1.)

One could imagine turning the analysis into a CBA by monetizing the effects on safety and the effects on other external costs related to driving and treating predictability of gasoline savings through sensitivity analysis. As monetizing the distributional concerns would be difficult, a multigoal analysis with the CBA assessing efficiency and a separate treatment of distributional impacts could be useful.

Source: Adapted from Congressional Budget Office, *Reducing Gasoline Consumption: Three Policy Options*, November 2002 (www.cbo.gov/ftpdocs/39xx/doc3991/11–21–GasolineStudy.pdf).

2.6   Conclusion

CBA is a method for determining if proposed policies could potentially be Pareto-improving: positive net benefits make this possible, in the sense of creating wealth sufficient to compensate those who bear costs so that some people are made better off without making anyone else worse off. Willingness to pay and opportunity cost are the guiding principles for measuring costs and benefits. Much of the rest of this book deals with how to make use of the concepts in practice.

Exercises for Chapter 2

1. Many experts claim that, although VHS came to dominate the video recorder market, Betamax was a superior technology. Assume that these experts are correct, so that, all other things equal, a world in which all video recorders were Betamax technology would be Pareto-superior to a world in which all video recorders were VHS technology. Yet it seems implausible that a policy that forced a switch in technologies would be even potentially Pareto-improving. Explain.

2. Let's explore the concept of willingness to pay with a thought experiment. Imagine a specific sporting, entertainment, or cultural event that you would very much like to attend – perhaps a World Cup match, the seventh game of the World Series, a Bruce Springstein concert, or an opera starring Renée Fleming.

    a. What is the most you would be willing to pay for a ticket to the event?

    b. Imagine that you won a ticket to the event in a lottery. What is the minimum amount of money that you would be willing to accept to give up the ticket?

    c. Imagine that you had an income 50 percent higher than it is now, but that you didn't win a ticket to the event. What is the most you would be willing to pay for a ticket?

    d. Do you know anyone who would sufficiently dislike the event that they would not use a free ticket unless they were paid to do so?

    e. Do your answers suggest any possible generalizations about willingness to pay?

3. How closely do government expenditures measure opportunity cost for each of the following program inputs?

    a. Time of jurors in a criminal justice program that requires more trials.

    b. Land to be used for a nuclear waste storage facility that is owned by the government and located on a military base.

    c. Labor for a reforestation program in a small rural community with high unemployment.

    d. Labor of current government employees who are required to administer a new program.

    e. Concrete that was previously poured as part of a bridge foundation.

4. Three mutually exclusive projects are being considered for a remote river valley: Project R, a recreational facility, has estimated benefits of $20 million and costs of $16 million; project F, a forest preserve with some recreational facilities, has estimated benefits of $26 million and costs of $20 million; project W, a wilderness area with restricted public access, has estimated benefits of $10 million and costs of $2 million. In addition, a road could be built for a cost of $8 million that would increase the benefits of project R by $16 million, increase the benefits of project F by $10 million, and reduce the benefits of project W by $2 million. Even in the absence of any of the other projects, the road has estimated benefits of $4 million.

    a. Calculate the benefit–cost ratio and net benefits for each possible alternative to the status quo. Note that there are seven possible alternatives to the status quo: R, F, and W, both with and without the road, and the road alone.

    b. If only one of the seven alternatives can be selected, which should be selected according to the CBA decision rule?

5. An analyst for the US Navy was asked to evaluate alternatives for forward-basing a destroyer flotilla. He decided to do the evaluation as a CBA. The major categories of costs were related to obtaining and maintaining the facilities. The major category of benefit was reduced sailing time to patrol routes. The analyst recommended the forward base with the largest net benefits. The admiral, his client, rejected the recommendation because the CBA did not include the risks to the forward bases from surprise attack and the risks of being unexpectedly ejected from the bases because of changes in political regimes of the host countries. Was the analyst's work wasted?

6. Because of a recent wave of jewelry store robberies, a city increases police surveillance of jewelry stores. The increased surveillance costs the city an extra $500,000 per year, but as a result, the amount of jewelry that is stolen falls. Specifically, without the increase in surveillance, jewelry with a retail value of $900,000 million would have been stolen. This stolen jewelry would have been fenced by the jewelry thieves for $600,000. What is the net social benefit resulting from the police surveillance program?

7. (Spreadsheet recommended.) Excessive and improper use of antibiotics is contributing to the resistance of many diseases to existing antibiotics. Consider a regulatory program in the United States that would monitor antibiotic prescribing by physicians. Analysts estimate the direct costs of enforcement to be $40 million, the time costs to doctors and health professionals to be $220 million, and the convenience costs to patients

to be $180 million (all annually). The annual benefits of the program are estimated to be $350 million in avoided resistance costs in the United States, $70 million in health benefits in the United States from better compliance with prescriptions, and $280 million in avoided resistance costs in the rest of the world. Does the program have positive net benefits from the national perspective? If not, what fraction of benefits accruing in the rest of the world would have to be counted for the program to have positive net benefits?

Notes

1. Unless otherwise stated, we intend efficiency to mean *allocative efficiency*, as defined in this section. A broader interpretation of efficiency, which we discuss in a later section, is the maximization of a specific social welfare function that explicitly ranks alternative allocations.

2. In this stylized example, the distinction between willingness to pay and willingness to accept is purely semantic. However, the distinction has substantive importance when one actually seeks to measure WTP through survey methods, because, as discussed in Chapter 16, people often demand larger payments to accept small decrements in some good than they are willing to pay to obtain small increments of exactly the same size. For now, we use WTP inclusively, assuming that its elicitation appropriately takes account of whether people perceive policies as giving them something or as taking away something.

3. Nicholas Kaldor, "Welfare Propositions of Economics and Interpersonal Comparisons of Utility." *Economic Journal*, 49(195), 1939, 549–52; and John R. Hicks, "The Valuation of the Social Income." *Economica*, 7(26), 1940, 105–24. The principle can also be stated as suggested by Hicks: Adopt a policy if and only if it would not be in the self-interest of those who will lose to bribe those who will gain not to adopt it. Technically, a potential Pareto improvement can be guaranteed only when it shows positive sums of compensating and equivalent variation (concepts introduced in Chapter 4).

4. Those who are worse off in society may or may not have been the ones who have borne the net costs of public policies. This argument thus shifts the focus from fairness with respect to particular policies to the relative position of those in society who are worse off for whatever reason.

5. Kenneth Arrow, *Social Choice and Individual Values*, 2nd edn (New Haven, CT: Yale University Press, 1963). For a treatment that can be followed with minimal mathematics, see Julian H. Blau, "A Direct Proof of Arrow's Theorem." *Econometrica*, 40(1), 1972, 61–67.

6. For an overview, see Charles Blackorby and David Donaldson, "A Review Article: The Case Against the Use of the Sum of Compensating Variation in Cost–Benefit Analysis." *Canadian Journal of Economics*, 23(3), 1990, 471–94.

7. Charles Blackorby and David Donaldson, "Consumers' Surpluses and Consistent Cost–Benefit Tests." *Social Choice and Welfare*, 1(4), 1985, 251–62.

8. Even if one does not demand that the potential Pareto principle always produces a transitive social ordering of policies, the most commonly used measure of WTP, *compensating variation*, can produce what are called *Scitovsky reversals* (Tibor Scitovsky, "A Note on Welfare Propositions in Economics." *Review of Economic Studies*, 41(1), 1941, 77–88). Compensating variation, which is discussed in Appendix 3A, is the change in income that would be needed to make the consumer indifferent between the new policy with the income change and the old policy without it. For example, if the price of a good increases, it is the amount of income needed to compensate consumers so that they would be indifferent between the original price and the new price with the compensation. A Scitovsky reversal results when the sum of compensating variations for a group of individuals is positive for a move from one Pareto-efficient policy to another *and* is also positive for a move from the new policy back to the original policy! More generally, the sum of compensating variations can be positive for moves among Pareto-efficient allocations, so that it being positive is a necessary but not a sufficient condition for a potential Pareto improvement (Blackorby and Donaldson, "A Review Article: The Case Against the Use of the Sum of Compensating Variation in Cost–Benefit Analysis," 471–94).

9. The marginal utility of money is how much a person's utility changes for a small increase in the person's wealth. Economists generally assume declining marginal utility of money. That is, as a person's wealth increases, each additional dollar produces smaller increases in utility.

10. Abram Bergson [as Burk], "A Reformulation of Certain Aspects of Welfare Economics." *Quarterly Journal of Economics*, 52(2), 1938, 310–34.

11. Tibor Scitovsky, "The State of Welfare Economics." *American Economic Review*, 51(3), 1951, 301–15; and Kenneth Arrow, *Social Choice and Individual Values*, 2nd edn (New Haven, CT: Yale University Press, 1963).

12. One could imagine asking a sample of members of society to value alternative states of the world resulting from alternative policies, including the situations of other people. In this way, their WTP would include the value they place on the distributional impacts of policies. Unfortunately, implementing such surveys is very difficult.

13. The seminal work is Dale Whittington and Duncan MacRae Jr., "The Issue of Standing in Cost–Benefit Analysis." *Journal of Policy Analysis and Management*, 5(4), 1986, 665–82.

14. Richard O. Zerbe Jr., "Comment: Does Benefit Cost Analysis Stand Alone? Rights and Standing." *Journal of Policy Analysis and Management*, 10(1), 1991, 96–105.

15. For a development of the notion of social constraints in CBA, see William N. Trumbull, "Who Has Standing in Cost–Benefit Analysis?" *Journal of Policy Analysis and Management*, 9(2), 1990, 201–18; and Richard O. Zerbe Jr., "Is Cost–Benefit Analysis Legal? Three Rules." *Journal of Policy Analysis and Management*, 17(3), 1998, 419–56. For

a more general treatment of institutional constraints and social welfare, see Daniel W. Bromley, *Economic Interests and Institutions: The Conceptual Foundations of Public Policy* (New York, NY: Basil Blackwell, 1989).

16. David A. Long, Charles D. Mallar, and Craig V. D. Thornton, "Evaluating the Benefits and Costs of the Job Corps." *Journal of Policy Analysis and Management*, 1(1), 1981, 55–76.

17. For a discussion of this case from the perspective of a number of issues of standing of preferences, see Duncan MacRae Jr. and Dale Whittington, "Assessing Preferences in Cost–Benefit Analysis: Reflections on Rural Water Supply Evaluation in Haiti." *Journal of Policy Analysis and Management*, 7(2), 1988, 246–63.

18. See Daniel W. Bromley, "Entitlements, Missing Markets, and Environmental Uncertainty." *Journal of Environmental Economics and Management*, 17(2), 1989, 181–94.

19. Steven Kelman, "Cost–Benefit Analysis: An Ethical Critique." *Regulation*, January/February 1981, 33–40.

20. Alan Williams, "Cost–Benefit Analysis: Bastard Science? And/Or Insidious Poison in the Body Politick?" *Journal of Public Economics*, 1(2), 1972, 199–226; and Aidan R. Vining and David L. Weimer, "Welfare Economics as the Foundation for Public Policy Analysis: Incomplete and Flawed but Nevertheless Desirable." *Journal of Socio-Economics*, 21(1), 1992, 25–37.

21. For a detailed presentation of multigoal analysis, see David L. Weimer and Aidan R. Vining, *Policy Analysis: Concepts and Practice*, 6th edn (New York, NY: Routledge, 2017), chapter 15.

22. For a demonstration of the application of various measures of vertical and horizontal equality, see Marcus C. Berliant and Robert P. Strauss, "The Horizontal and Vertical Equity Characteristics of the Federal Individual Income Tax," in Martin David and Timothy Smeeding, editors, *Horizontal Equity, Uncertainty, and Economic Well-Being* (Chicago, IL: University of Chicago Press, 1985), 179–211.

23. The fact that people routinely donate to charities suggests that, other things equal, most people would be willing to pay something to obtain a distribution of wealth that is more favorable to the currently poor. Ironically, CBA provides a conceptual way to place a dollar value on alternative distributions of wealth: the sum of the willingness of the individual members of society to pay for moving from the status quo distribution of wealth to an alternative one. Unfortunately, it is usually impractical to elicit WTP amounts of this sort.

24. For example, Harberger proposes that a dual test be applied: The policy should have positive weighted and unweighted net benefits. Arnold C. Harberger, "On the Use of Distributional Weights in Social Cost–Benefit Analysis." *Journal of Political Economy*, 86(2, part 2), 1978, S87–120.

25. For an excellent development of this approach, see Edward M. Gramlich and Michael Wolkoff, "A Procedure for Evaluating Income Distribution Policies." *Journal of Human Resources*, 14(3), 1979, 319–50.

3 Microeconomic Foundations of Cost–Benefit Analysis

Microeconomic theory provides the foundations for CBA. This chapter begins with a review of the major concepts of microeconomic theory that are relevant to the measurement of social costs and benefits. Most of them should be somewhat familiar from your previous exposure to economics. After that, the chapter moves to welfare economics, which concerns the normative evaluation of markets and of policies. This part of the chapter is particularly concerned with the treatment in CBA of the taxes required to fund government projects.

We assume the presence of perfect competition throughout this chapter. Specifically, we assume the following: that there are so many buyers and sellers in the market that no one can individually affect prices, that buyers and sellers can easily enter and exit the market, that the goods sold are homogeneous (i.e., identical), that there is an absence of transaction costs, that information is perfect, and that private costs and benefits are identical to social costs and benefits (i.e., there are no externalities). Chapters 5, 6, and 7 consider how to measure benefits and costs when some of these assumptions are relaxed; that is, various forms of market failure are present.

3.1 Demand Curves

An individual's *ordinary demand curve* (schedule) indicates the quantities of a good that the individual wishes to purchase at various prices. The market demand curve is the horizontal sum of all individual demand curves. It indicates the aggregate quantities of a good that all individuals in the market wish to purchase at various prices.

In contrast, a market *inverse demand curve*, which is illustrated by line D in Figure 3.1, has price as a function of quantity. The vertical axis (labeled Price) can be interpreted as the highest price someone is willing to pay for an additional unit of the good. A standard assumption in economics is that demand curves slope downward. The rationale for this assumption is based on the principle of *diminishing marginal utility*; each additional unit of the good is valued slightly less by each consumer than the preceding unit. For that reason, each consumer is willing to pay less for an additional unit than for the preceding unit. Indeed, at some point, each consumer might be unwilling to pay anything for an additional unit; his or her demand would be sated.

In Figure 3.1 a member of society is willing to pay a price of P_1 for one unit of good X. Also, there is a person (possibly the same person who is willing to pay P_1 for the first unit) who would pay P_2 for a second unit of good X, and there is someone who would

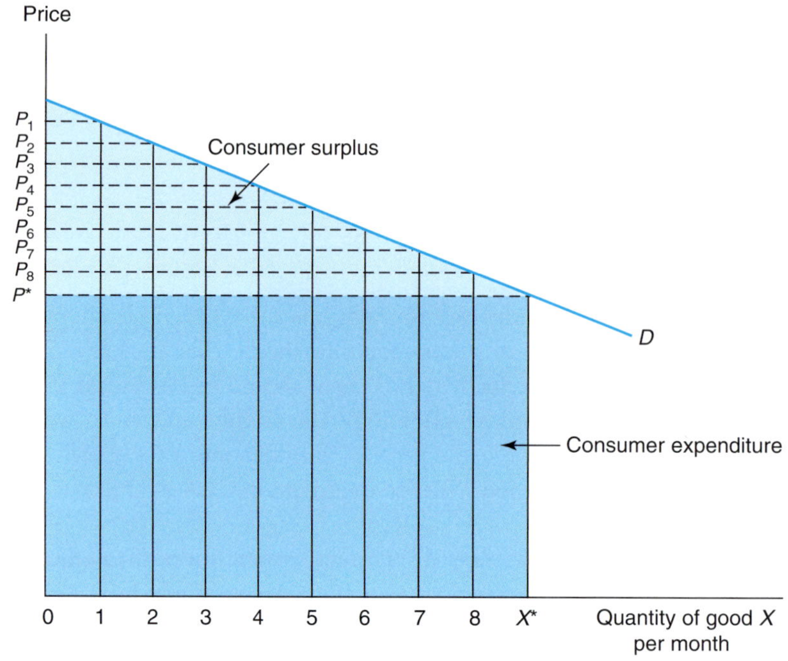

Figure 3.1 Consumers' total benefits and consumer surplus.

pay P_3 for a third unit of X, and so forth.[1] Each additional unit is valued at an amount given by the height of the inverse demand curve. The sum of these willingness-to-pay amounts equals the total willingness to pay (WTP) for the good by all the members of society. For X^* units, total WTP equals the area under the inverse demand curve from the origin to X^*, which is represented by the sum of the light and dark shaded areas.

As stated in Chapter 2, WTP is an appropriate measure of the benefit of a good or service. Because P_1 measures the marginal benefit of the first unit, P_2 measures the marginal benefit of the second unit, and so on, the sum of X^* marginal benefits measures the *total benefits* (B) all members of society would obtain from consuming X^* units of good X.[2] Thus, the area under the demand curve, which consists of the sum of the lightly and darkly shaded areas, measures the *total benefits* (B) society would receive from consuming X^* units of good X – its total willingness to pay for the X^* units.

3.1.1   *Consumer Surplus and Changes in Consumers' Surplus*

In a competitive market consumers pay the market price, which we denote as P^*. Thus, consumers spend P^*X^*, represented by the darkly shaded area, to consume X^* units. The *net benefit* to consumers equals the total benefits (B) minus consumers' actual expenditures (P^*X^*). This lightly shaded area, which equals the area below the demand curve but above the price line, is called *consumer surplus (CS):*

$$CS = B - P^*X^* \tag{3.1}$$

Consumer surplus (sometimes called *consumers' surplus*) is a basic concept used in CBA. Under most circumstances, changes in consumer surplus can be used as a reasonable measure of the benefits to consumers of a policy change. In the appendix to this chapter, we examine the circumstances under which changes in consumer surplus do provide close approximations to WTP values and those where they do not. In most instances, such approximations are sufficiently accurate for CBA purposes.

To see how the concept of consumer surplus can be used in CBA, suppose that initially the price and quantity consumed are given by P^* and Q^*, respectively, and then consider a policy that results in a price change. For example, as shown in Figure 3.2(a), a policy that reduces the price of good X from P^* to P_1 would result in a benefit to consumers (an increase in consumer surplus) equal to the area of the shaded area P^*ABP_1. This consumer benefit occurs because existing consumers pay a lower price for the X^* units they previously purchased, and some consumers gain from the consumption of $X_1 - X^*$ additional units. Similarly, as shown in Figure 3.2(b), a policy that increases the price of good X from P^* to P_2 would impose a "cost" on consumers (a loss in consumer surplus) equal to the area of the shaded area P_2ABP^*.

Suppose that a policy results in a price decrease, as in Figure 3.2(a). Let $\Delta P = P_1 - P^* < 0$ denote the change in price and let $\Delta X = X_1 - X^* > 0$ denote the change in the quantity of good X consumed. If the demand curve is linear, then the change in consumer surplus, ΔCS, can be computed by using the formula:

$$\Delta CS = -(\Delta P)(X^*) - \frac{1}{2}(\Delta X)(\Delta P) \tag{3.2}$$

If the demand curve is linear, Equation (3.2) also gives the change in consumer surplus due to a price increase. In this situation, which is shown in Figure 3.2(b), $\Delta P = P_2 - P^* > 0$, $\Delta X = X_2 - X^* < 0$, and $\Delta CS < 0$. Note that for Equation (3.2) to yield the correct

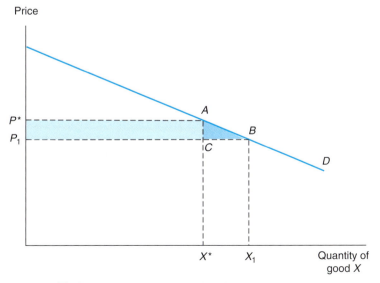

Figure 3.2(a) Change in consumer surplus due to a price decrease.

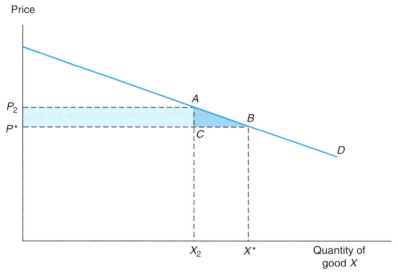

Figure 3.2(b) Change in consumer surplus due to a price increase.

answer for either a price increase or a price decrease one must begin with the initial price and quantity, P^* and Q^*, and measure changes, positive or negative, from these starting points. In fact, this formula usually provides a good approximation to the change in consumer surplus even if the demand curve is not linear as long as the changes in price and quantity demanded are small.

Sometimes the analyst may not know the shape of the demand curve and, therefore, may not know directly how many units will be demanded after a price change, but she may know the (own) *price elasticity of demand, E_d.* The price elasticity of demand is defined as the percentage change in quantity demanded that results from a 1 percent increase in price. Formally:[3]

$$E_d = \frac{P}{X} \frac{dX}{dP} \tag{3.3a}$$

Because demand curves slope downward, $dX/dP < 0$, and the price elasticity of demand is always negative. All else equal, as the slope of the ordinary demand curve *increases* (i.e., becomes steeper – more negative), the elasticity *decreases* (becomes more negative). Because this is not intuitive, we follow the standard practice of talking about an elasticity as if it is positive, in effect taking the absolute value. We say that the elasticity *increases* as the slope of the ordinary demand curve *increases*. Also, the more responsive quantity is to a change in price, we say that demand is more elastic. Non-economists may find this a bit confusing at first, but will soon get used to it.

The demand curves shown in Figures 3.1 and 3.2 are inverse demand curves. Their slopes are given by dP/dX rather than dX/dP. Consequently, while the price elasticity of demand increases (in absolute value) as the slope of the ordinary demand curve increases, the price elasticity of demand decreases (in absolute value) as the slope of the inverse demand curve increases.

Given an initial price and quantity, P^* and X^*, and defining ΔX and ΔP as the changes in quantities and prices relative to the initial price and quantity, then the price elasticity of demand approximately equals:

$$E_d = \frac{P^*}{X^*}\frac{\Delta X}{\Delta P} \qquad\qquad (3.3b)$$

Substituting Equation (3.3b) into Equation (3.2) and rearranging provides the following approximation for the change in consumer surplus due to a price change for a linear demand curve:

$$\Delta CS = -X^*\Delta P - \frac{E_d X^*(\Delta P)^2}{2P^*} \qquad\qquad (3.4)$$

3.1.2   *Taxes*

The analysis of the impact of taxes is very important in CBA because governments have to finance their projects, and taxation is ultimately the main source of financing. Suppose that the price increase from P^* to P_2 shown in Figure 3.2(b) results from the imposition of an excise tax, where each unit of good X is taxed by an amount equal to the difference between the old and the new price ($P_2 - P^*$). In this case, the rectangular part of the trapezoid in Figure 3.2(b), P_2ACP^*, represents the tax revenue collected. It is a *transfer* from consumers of X to the government. It is called a transfer because, from the perspective of society as a whole, its net impact is zero: consumers pay the tax, but this cost is offset by an identical benefit received by the government.[4]

However, the triangular part of the area, ABC, is a real cost of the tax, rather than a transfer. It represents lost consumer surplus for which there is no offsetting benefit accruing to some other part of society. This loss in consumer surplus is an example of *deadweight loss*.[5] It results from a distortion in economic behavior from the competitive equilibrium. The tax causes some consumers to purchase less output than they would in the absence of the tax because, inclusive of the tax, the price now exceeds those consumers' WTP. Those consumers, who in the absence of the tax would collectively have purchased $X^* - X_2$ units of the good, and received the consumer surplus represented by the triangular area, ABC, lose this consumer surplus.

It follows from Equation (3.4) that the deadweight loss resulting from a price change is approximately:

$$\Delta DWL = -\frac{E_d X^*(\Delta P)^2}{2P^*} \qquad\qquad (3.5)$$

If the change in price is due to a unit tax, t, then the deadweight loss is:

$$\Delta DWL = -\frac{E_d X^* t^2}{2P^*} \qquad\qquad (3.6)$$

There will always be a deadweight loss if a government imposes a tax on a good sold in a competitive market. Of particular interest is the amount of the *leakage* or *excess* *tax burden* (ETB), which equals the ratio of the deadweight loss due to the tax to the amount of tax revenue collected. If the price increase in Figure 3.2(b) is due to a tax, the leakage equals the area ABC divided by area P_2ACP^*, which can be computed:

$$Leakage \equiv ETB = -\frac{E_d t}{2P^*\left(1+\dfrac{\Delta X}{X^*}\right)} \tag{3.7}$$

If the change in output is relatively small, then a simple formula provides a slight over-estimate of the leakage:

$$Leakage \equiv ETB = -\frac{E_d t}{2P^*} \tag{3.8}$$

Further consideration of the social cost of taxation can be found later in the chapter.

3.2   Supply Curves

In CBA, as Chapter 2 demonstrated, costs are opportunity costs. Figure 3.3 presents a standard U-shaped *marginal cost* (*MC*) curve for an individual firm, where costs are opportunity costs. This curve pertains to costs in the short run, when at least one factor of production, for example capital, is fixed. Later, we consider the long run where all factors of production can vary. As you know, the *MC* curve passes through the firm's *average variable cost* (*AVC*) curve at its lowest point, as shown in Figure 3.3. The rising part of the *MC* curve reflects *diminishing marginal returns* – the reality that, given at least one fixed factor of production (say, capital), diminishing factor returns must eventually occur. Diminishing returns occur as output expands and increasing amounts of the variable factors of production (say, labor) are used with the fixed factor(s), or it reflects rising opportunity costs of a variable factor of production as more units of that factor are employed.

Just as the demand curve indicates the marginal benefit of each additional unit of a good consumed, the supply curve indicates the marginal cost of each additional unit of the good produced. Thus, the area under the firm's marginal cost curve represents the firm's *total variable cost* (*VC*) of producing a given amount of good X, say X^*.

The upward-sloping segment of the firm's marginal cost curve above the firm's *AVC*, which is heavily darkened, corresponds to the *firm's supply curve* in a competitive market. If the price were lower than the firm's average variable cost, then the firm could not cover its average variable cost and would choose to shut down, rather than produce any output. At a price above average variable cost, however, the upward-sloping segment of the marginal cost curve determines how much output the firm will produce at any given price. For example, at a price of P^*, the firm would maximize profit by producing at X^*. If it produced more output than X^*, it would take in less in additional revenue than the additional cost it would incur. If it produced less output than X^*, it would lose more in revenue than it would save in costs.

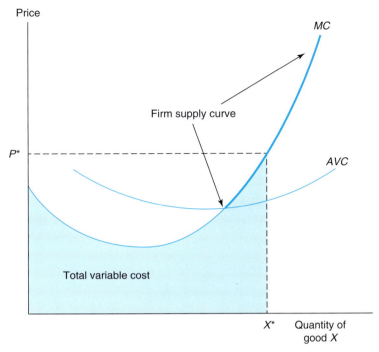

Figure 3.3 Individual firm's supply curve.

Chapter 2 indicated that the concept of opportunity cost is critical to CBA. The cost of a policy or project reflects the opportunity costs incurred by various members of society to implement the policy. Consequently, the cost curve in Figure 3.3 is shown under the assumption that the owners of all the resources the firm uses are paid prices equal to the opportunity costs of the resources. For such factors as capital and entrepreneurship, the opportunity cost includes a *normal return*,[6] reflecting their best alternative use.[7]

3.2.1   *Market Supply Curve*

The *market supply curve* shown in Figure 3.4 is derived by summing horizontally the supply curves of all the individual firms in a market. It indicates the total supply available to the market at each price. For example, at price P_1 firms in aggregate are willing to supply X_1 units. Because individual firm supply curves are based on their marginal cost, the market supply curve also reflects marginal cost. For example, the marginal cost of the X_1th unit is P_1 so the firms are willing to supply X_1 units at price P_1.

As with marginal cost curves for individual firms, the area under the market supply curve represents the total variable cost of producing a given amount of output, say X^*. The area $0abX^*$ is the total variable cost of supplying X^* units. Put another way, it is the minimum total revenue that firms must receive before they would be willing to produce output X^*.

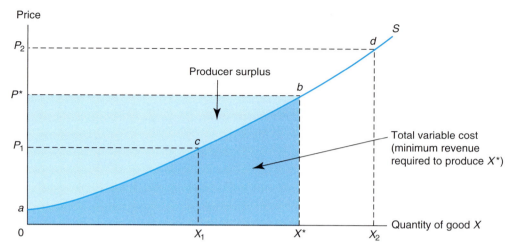

Figure 3.4 Market supply curve.

3.2.2   *Producer Surplus and Changes in Producer Surplus*

Suppose that the market price of a good is P^* and, consequently, firms supply X^* units. Their revenue in dollars would be P^*X^*, which corresponds to the rectangle $0P^*bX^*$ in Figure 3.4. Their total variable cost (TVC) would be $0abX^*$, the darkly shaded area in Figure 3.4. The difference between these two areas, the lightly shaded area aP^*b, is the *producer surplus* (PS):

$$PS = P^*X^* - TVC \tag{3.9}$$

Producer surplus is the benefit going to firms (or their factors of production). It equals the difference between actual revenues and the minimum total revenue that firms in the market represented in Figure 3.4 must receive before they would be willing to produce X^* units at a price of P^*.

Producer surplus is the supply-side equivalent of consumer surplus. Just as changes in prices resulting from government policies have impacts on consumers that can be valued in terms of changes in consumer surplus, price changes also result in impacts on producers that can be valued in terms of changes in producer surplus. For example, in Figure 3.4, a decrease in the market price from P^* to P_1 decreases producer surplus by P^*bcP_1 to P_1ca, and an increase in price from P^* to P_2 increases producer surplus by P_2dbP^* to P_2da.

3.3   Social Surplus and Allocative Efficiency[8]

Let us now look at the market as a whole. In the absence of impacts on government, the sum of consumer surplus and producer surplus is called *social surplus* (SS) (or sometimes *total surplus*). In sum:

$$SS = CS + PS \tag{3.10}$$

Figure 3.5 shows social surplus, depicting both a market demand curve and a market supply curve on the same graph. Once again, Figure 3.5 is drawn assuming perfect competition. Equilibrium occurs at a price of P^* and a quantity of X^*. Consumer surplus is the area caP^*, producer surplus is the area P^*ab, and social surplus is the sum of these two areas, cab.

Net social benefits equals the difference between total consumer benefits and total producer costs. Total consumer benefits equal the area under the demand curve, caX^*0, while total costs equal total variable costs, the area under the supply curve, baX^*0.[9] The total difference is the area cab. This should make it clear that social surplus equals net social benefits.

Keeping in mind that the demand curve reflects marginal benefits (MB) and the supply curve reflects marginal cost (MC), at the competitive equilibrium demand equals supply and marginal benefits equals marginal cost. Net social benefits are maximized.[10] Thus, in the presence of a well-functioning, perfectly competitive market net social benefits and social surplus are maximized. The outcome is *Pareto-efficient*: it is not possible to make someone better off without making someone else worse off. This equilibrium is *allocatively efficient* (or *economically efficient*) because social surplus is maximized. The fact that a competitive equilibrium is economically efficient is referred to as the first fundamental theorem of welfare economics, clearly reflecting its importance.

In a perfectly competitive market, anything that interferes with the competitive process will reduce allocative efficiency. Suppose, for example, government policy restricts output to X_1, due, for example, to output quotas. At least some people will be worse off relative to output level X^*. The loss in social surplus at X_1 would equal the triangular area dae – the area between the demand curve (*MB*) and the supply curve (*MC*) from X_1 to X^*. Similarly, the loss in social surplus at X_2 would equal the triangular area afg – the area between the demand curve and the supply curve from X^* to X_2. These

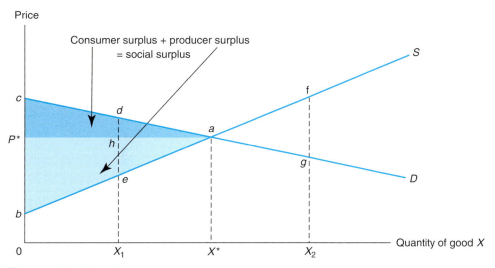

Figure 3.5 Social surplus.

deadweight losses reflect reductions in social surplus relative to the competitive market equilibrium (at X^*). A government policy that moves the market away from the perfectly competitive equilibrium increases deadweight loss and reduces social surplus. Thus, in most circumstances it is only in the presence of market failures that government should consider intervening in a market. The presence of market failure, however, provides only a *prima facie* rationale for intervention. Someone must perform the CBA to decide whether intervention is actually justified. Along the same lines, a proposed government policy that would move a currently distorted market toward the perfectly competitive equilibrium would produce net social benefits by increasing social surplus and reducing deadweight loss.

It is important to note the relationship between price and allocative efficiency. Allocative efficiency is maximized in Figure 3.5 at a price of P^* and a quantity of X^*. At the equilibrium point, a, the price paid by consumers equals the marginal cost of producing the good. *Allocative efficiency is achieved only when the price paid by consumers for a good equals the marginal social cost to society of producing that good.*[11]

3.3.1   *Profits and Factor Surplus*

The formula that measures producer surplus, Equation (3.9), is not always satisfactory because it excludes firms' *fixed costs*. Thus far the analysis has focused on short-term effects where some factors of production are fixed. Some government policies do not change firms' fixed costs, while others do change them. For example, if a government makes a one-time purchase of concrete to build a road extension, the fixed costs of the firms that provide the concrete would probably not change and Equations (3.9) and (3.10) should apply. On the other hand, for large, long-term projects, such as the Three Gorges Dam in China, all the factors of production (including the number of concrete trucks) would be variable. In these situations, changes in fixed costs should be included in the measure of social surplus. We need a way to do this. Note, by the way, if as is usual we focus on annual benefits and annual costs, then the fixed costs may have to be amortized over their useful life or the life of the project. There is also a practical caveat: whether or not we include fixed costs, but especially if we do, it is easier for most people to think about *profits* than producer surplus.

Fortunately, there is an easy way to deal with both concerns. Producer surplus equals *profits* (π) plus *Ricardian rents* going to factors of production, which we call *factor surplus* (*FS*).[12] One example of Ricardian rent is the return going to a particularly productive plot of land in a competitive agricultural market. The person that farms the land may rent this land, in which case the rents go to the landowner from whom he rents it. Or the farmer may own the land, in which case he gets them. To take another example, in a market for labor in the presence of minimum wage laws, rents may go to workers. In both cases, Equation (3.10) should be rewritten as follows:

$$SS = CS + \pi + FS \tag{3.11a}$$

The incremental net social benefit (ΔSS) of a change in policy is then given by:

$$\Delta SS = \Delta CS + \Delta \pi + \Delta FS \tag{3.11b}$$

Much of Canadian competition policy concerns whether proposed mergers should be permitted to go ahead. In these cases, the effect on employees, ΔFS, is usually assumed to be zero, and so the key issue boils down to whether the potential reduction in consumer surplus, ΔCS (because of increased prices), is more than offset by increases in profits, $\Delta\pi$. Firms making this argument in a merger hearing where a government agency is seeking to block the merger on foregone consumer surplus grounds is using the so-called "efficiency defense."[13]

3.3.2   *Government Surplus*

Thus far, the analysis has only considered the effects of policy change on consumers and producers. From a practical standpoint, it is useful to treat government as a distinct actor or sector in society. This is a reality, although society actually only consists of individuals. If we did not treat government as a distinct sector, we would have to trace every incremental change in government revenue or expenditure back to individual investors or consumers. As this is neither practical nor really necessary, impacts on government must also be included. Specifically, the analyst should include the net budget impacts on government, which is normally called *government surplus* (*GS*). Financial inflows to government from taxes increase government surplus, while financial outflows from expenditures decrease government surplus. When there is some change in government surplus, social surplus consists of the following components:

$$SS = CS + PS + GS \qquad (3.12a)$$

The incremental net social benefit (ΔSS) of a change in policy is therefore given by:

$$\Delta SS = \Delta CS + \Delta PS + \Delta GS \qquad (3.12b)$$

In a competitive market, the *net social benefit of a project equals the net change in government revenue plus the resulting change in the sum of consumer surplus and producer surplus.* Often in projects that are subjected to CBA, a government or several governments incur all of the costs of a project, while none of the financial benefits accrue to them. For example, the government may incur all of the costs of building rent-free housing for disabled people. To simplify, and consistent with the assumption of perfect competition, it is reasonable to assume no change in producer surplus in this kind of situation. The benefit of this project is the increase in consumer surplus, the cost is net government expenditure, and the net social benefit equals the benefits minus the costs. That is, $B = \Delta CS$, $C = -\Delta GS$, and $\Delta SS = NSB = B - C$.

Now, in contrast, consider a project where the government builds the same housing but charges a market rent. As before, it is reasonable to assume that there is no change in producer surplus. There are two ways to compute the change in social surplus (or net social benefits). The first way measures the benefit as the change in consumer surplus and the cost as the change in government expenditure (i.e., construction costs plus operating costs), as above. The rent paid is simply a transfer – a cost to consumers, but a benefit to government. *The net effect of a transfer is zero. Thus, it may be ignored in the calculation of net social benefits.* In fact, including the rent paid to government as part of government surplus would be incorrect.

The second way to compute the NSB initially focuses on the gross benefits of the project. The *gross benefit* to consumers (B) equals the area under the inverse demand curve. From Equation (3.1), $B = \Delta CS + $ Rents. The total cost to society equals the sum of the rents paid by consumers and the project expenditures paid by government. Therefore, the net social benefits are given by $NSB = B - C = \Delta CS - $ Construction costs – Operating expenses, which is the same as before.

This example makes it clear that sometimes there are several different ways to calculate net social benefits. In the example, it is possible to measure gross benefits that include consumer expenditures (e.g., rent) if this transfer is also included in the costs. Alternatively, one can focus on changes in consumer surplus, producer surplus and government surplus as expressed in Equation (3.12b).

To illustrate the direct estimation of Equation (3.12b), suppose that initially the perfectly competitive market shown in Figure 3.6 is in equilibrium at a price of P^* and the quantity X^*. Then suppose that a new policy is enacted that guarantees sellers a price of P_T. Such policies have been enacted in otherwise competitive agricultural markets in the United States. Examples include the markets for both corn and cotton. Generically, these are known as *target pricing policies*. At a target price of P_T, sellers desire to sell a quantity of X_T. However, buyers are willing to pay a price of only P_D for this quantity, so this becomes the effective market price. Under target pricing, the gap between P_T and P_D is filled by subsidies paid to sellers by the government. As the marginal cost of producing X_T exceeds marginal benefit for this quantity of good X, a social surplus loss (deadweight loss), corresponding to area *bde*, results from the policy.

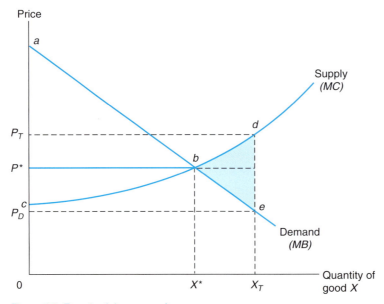

Figure 3.6 Target pricing example.

3.4   Distributional Implications

Target pricing policies affects consumers, producers, and the government differently. The incremental benefit, incremental cost, and change in social surplus (net benefit) to each of the three affected groups, and therefore to society as a whole, can be summarized in a *social accounting ledger* as shown in Table 3.1. Because buyers pay a price of only P_D under the exemplar policy, consumer surplus increases from area abP^* to area aeP_D, a gain of P^*beP_D. Producers (sellers) receive an effective price of P_T, causing producer surplus to increase from area P^*bc to area P_Tdbc, a gain of P_TdbP^*. The government provides subsidies that are represented by the area P_TdeP_D. Subtracting the *GS* cost from the *CS* and *PS* gains, as shown in Equation (3.12), results in a deadweight loss resulting from the policy equal to area *bde*.[14]

As the right-hand column of Table 3.1 shows, the government subsidy (P_TdeP_D) can be broken down into three areas: the consumer surplus gain, the producer surplus gain, and the deadweight loss. While area *bde* represents the net social loss from the policy, the remainder of the subsidy represents transfers from taxpayers (or citizens) to buyers and sellers. Because the benefits and costs associated with transfers are fully offsetting, they have no net impact on the change in social surplus as defined in Equation (3.12b).

Table 3.1 shows the distribution of the benefits and costs of the policy to different groups. The distributional impact of alternative policies is often of interest to government when it is considering a new policy. In particular, governments, which usually face budget constraints, are interested in the budgetary implications of any proposed policy. Thus, they may want to know the effects on government surplus as well as on aggregate social surplus. Such considerations are implicit in the mantra of *"value for money"* and the purported justification for public–private partnerships.[15]

We provide social accounting ledgers throughout this book.[16] Furthermore, Chapter 19 directly discusses the distribution of benefits and costs across various (some disadvantaged) consumer groups. Exhibit 3.1 illustrates the use of such a ledger. It concerns the impacts of three hypothetical alternative proposed pipeline proposals (they are mutually exclusive) on three groups of stakeholders separately (represented as three different companies).

Table 3.1 *Social Accounting Ledger for the Target Pricing Example*

Group	Gains	Losses	Net gains
Consumers	P^*beP_D		P^*beP_D
Producers	P_TdbP^*		P_TdbP^*
Government		P_TdeP_D	$-P_TdeP_D$
Society (NSB)			$-bde$

Exhibit 3.1

This exhibit presents a hypothetical example in which the government is evaluating proposals from three different (national) companies, labelled A, B, and C, for constructing and operating a pipeline that would transport oil from inside the country to customers in another country – say from Northern Canada into the United States. The benefits and costs associated with each proposal are presented in two ways.

The first table exemplifies "traditional" CBA, which ignores distributional considerations. Impacts are categorized as benefits or costs from the perspective of society as a whole. Society would be better off if it adopted the proposals of Company A or Company B, rather than not constructing a pipeline (the NPV of the net social benefits are positive) and would be best off by adopting Company B's proposal. The second table, in contrast, indicates how three different groups would be affected by each proposal. It shows that all firms would enjoy net benefits as their profits (producer surplus) would be positive. Some firms (A and B), however, would enjoy more profits than others (firm C). Government would also benefit as government surplus (tax revenues) would be positive. However, a third party composed of individuals who live near the pipeline would be worse off under all three proposals. (There is no benefit (consumer surplus) from using the oil in this illustration because it is assumed that the oil is exported and foreigners do not have standing.) The second table also indicates that, although net social benefits would be similar under the proposals from Company A and B, there is a trade-off between them because the government would receive greater tax revenues under Company A's proposal, but residents would be better off under the proposal from Company B. Thus, the second table provides richer information than the first one.

Cost–Benefit Analysis of Alternative Pipeline Proposals

	Company A	Company B	Company C
Social benefits			
Revenues	4.00	4.00	4.00
Total benefits	4.00	4.00	4.00
Social costs			
Construction cost	1.88	1.98	2.36
Operating costs	1.20	1.25	1.50
Environmental cost of construction	0.20	0.20	0.20
Subsequent environmental costs	0.29	0.13	0.08
Total costs	3.57	3.56	4.14
Net social benefits	0.43	0.44	−0.14

Cost–Benefit Analysis of Alternative Pipeline Proposals (Net Benefits to Each Affected Group)

	Company A	Company B	Company C
Company impacts			
Benefits			
Revenues	4.00	4.00	4.00
Costs			
Construction cost	1.88	1.98	2.36
Operating costs	1.20	1.25	1.50
Taxes	0.24	0.20	0.05
Firm environmental costs*	0.18	0.08	0.05
Costs	3.50	3.51	3.96
Profit	**0.50**	**0.49**	**0.04**
Residents' costs			
Environmental cost of construction	0.20	0.20	0.20
Subsequent environmental costs	0.15	0.07	0.04
Less compensation received	−0.04	−0.02	−0.01
Net cost to residents	**0.31**	**0.25**	**0.23**
Government revenues (taxes)	**0.24**	**0.20**	**0.05**
Net social benefits	**0.43**	**0.44**	**−0.14**

* Includes compliance costs and compensation paid to residents.

3.5   Incororating the Social Cost of Raising Revenue through Taxation

3.5.1   *Marginal Excess Tax Burden and the Marginal Cost of Public Funds*

Most government policies and projects require government expenditure. This expenditure has to be financed in some way. This chapter has demonstrated that an excise tax on a good usually results in deadweight loss. Income taxes also generally result in a deadweight loss. Indeed, social surplus is usually (but not always) reduced when the government taxes consumers, taxpayers, or producers. In addition, it can occur when the government provides a subsidy, as seen in the target price example.

As there are numerous sources of potential deadweight loss in addition to taxes and subsidies, economists refer to the proportion of each tax or subsidy dollar that results in a deadweight loss as a potential source of *leakage* or *excess tax burden*, terms introduced earlier in the chapter. In the target pricing example, for instance, the leakage or excess tax burden consists of the area $bde/P_T deP_D$. The leakage also includes the administrative costs associated with taxes and subsidies, any inefficient substitution of leisure for work, of barter for legal trade, and the inefficiency resulting from search for tax loopholes.

The increase in deadweight loss resulting from raising an additional dollar of tax revenue is called the *marginal excess tax burden* (METB). The size of the METB depends on the magnitude of behavioral responses to a tax change; for example, the extent to which consumer purchases or work hours change due to a tax on earnings.[17] Usually, these responses vary according to the type of tax that is incrementally changed. In general, the METB is greater when the taxed activity is more demand elastic or when labor is more supply elastic. (For reasons explained below, elasticities mentioned in this section should be viewed as uncompensated, rather than compensated.) Importantly, the METB from income tax is higher than the METB from either property taxes or sales taxes.

Given the pervasiveness of METB, the social cost of raising one dollar of government revenue through taxes equals one dollar that is transferred from tax payers *plus* the resultant deadweight loss, the METB. Thus, the social cost of raising a dollar via taxes equals 1 + METB, which is called the *marginal cost of public funds* (MCPF),[18] that is,

$$MCPF = 1 + METB \tag{3.13}$$

There are numerous empirical estimates of the size of the METB and, in addition, some direct estimates of the MCPF. These estimates vary for a number of reasons including, as mentioned above, the type of tax. With respect to federal projects, it is usually reasonable to view income taxes as the marginal tax source. Thus, hereafter, the focus is on METB and MCPF estimates of income taxes.

The major distortions that are attributable to income taxes imposed on individuals occur in labor markets. Therefore, almost all estimates of the marginal excess tax burden of the income tax utilize estimates of labor supply elasticities. Although most estimates of the METB of the income tax use compensated labor supply elasticities, a few estimates are based instead on uncompensated elasticities. The former compensates individuals for reductions in income or utility caused by income taxes, while the latter do not (see the chapter appendix for a fuller explanation). It can be reasonably argued that unless a policy or program sufficiently benefits those who fund it through their taxes so that they are essentially compensated (not likely to be the case for most projects or programs), an METB based on uncompensated labor supply elasticities should be used in CBA.[19] Moreover, except under limited special circumstances (e.g., when labor supply is completely inelastic), 1 + METB is only equal to the MCPF when the latter is based on uncompensated labor supply elasticities.[20]

Daniel Fujiwara has assembled a number of estimates of the METB based on both compensated and uncompensated labor supply elasticities. The estimates based on uncompensated labor supply elasticities are summarized in the first five rows of Table 3.2.[21] The average of the five mid-point estimates is 23 cents per dollar and the median is 19 cents per dollar. The average of the low estimates is 18 cents per dollar and the average of the high estimates is 28 cents per dollar. The mean for the 20 studies based on compensated labor supply elasticities that Fujiwara collected is 26 cents per dollar, with a range between 21 cents and 32 cents per dollar once the more extreme values are eliminated. The METB estimates based on compensated labor supply elasticities tend to be larger because the reduction in hours worked resulting from a given increase in taxes is greater with a compensated elasticity.

Bev Dahlby has assembled four estimates of the MCPF. These estimates, which have been converted to METB estimates by subtracting one, are shown in the bottom four rows of Table 3.2.[22] Including these four additional estimates, the average of the mid-point estimates is 22.5 cents per dollar and the median is 19 cents per dollar. Considering only the five estimates from the United States, the average of the mid-points is again 23 cents per dollar and the median is 18.5 cents per dollar.

Although an estimate of 19 cents per dollar or 23 cents per dollar provides a reasonable value for the METB for federal projects that are funded by income taxes, these estimates are less appropriate for local government projects that are much more likely to be funded by property taxes. For such projects, a METB of 17 cents per dollar, which was specifically estimate for property tax, should be used.[23]

Exhibit 3.2 presents a hypothetical example that computes the average social cost of taxing higher-income households and redistributing the money to lower-income households. The exhibit illustrates the computation of the marginal excess tax burden and the marginal cost of public funds.[24]

Table 3.2 *Estimates of the Marginal Excess Tax Burden*

Study	Country	METB	Mid-point of METB estimate
Dahlby (1994)	Canada	0.09–0.38	0.235
Stuart (1984)	USA	0.43	0.430
Fullerton and Henderson (1989)	USA	0.06–0.17	0.115
Ballard et al. (1985)	USA	0.12–0.23	0.185
Campbell and Bond (1997)	Australia	0.19	0.190
Ahmad and Croushore (1994)	USA	0.121–0.167	0.144
Gruber and Saez (2002)	USA	0.285	0.285
Kleven and Kreiner (2006)	UK	0.26	0.260
Ruggeri (1999)	Canada	0.18	0.180

Sources: The estimates for the first five rows are from studies using uncompensated labor supply elasticities and are from Daniel Fujiwara, *The Department for Work and Pensions Social Cost–Benefit Analysis Framework: Methodologies for Estimating and Incorporating the Wider Social and Economic Impacts of Work in Cost–Benefit analysis of Employment Programmes*, Working Paper No. 86 (London: Department for Work and Pensions, 2010, table 3.1); the estimates for the bottom four rows are from Bev Dahlby, *The Marginal Cost of Public Funds: Theory and Application* (Cambridge, MA: The MIT Press, 2008, table 5.3).

Exhibit 3.2

The following table, which is adapted from a study by Edgar Browning, is based on a simplified hypothetical society with only five households. The idea is to tax everyone to obtain $1350 in additional revenue and then distribute the $1,350 equally to all five.

It is assumed that all five households initially work 2,000 hours a year and face the same marginal tax rate of 40 percent. Thus, as shown in column 2 of the table appearing below, the gross before-tax hourly wage rate of household A is $5 ($10,000/2,000), but its after-tax net wage rate is only $3 ($5 × 0.6). The gross and net hourly wage rates for the other four households is computed in the same way. It is further assumed that the labor supply elasticity for all of the households is 0.15, that is, a 1 percent change in net wages will cause households to alter their hours worked by 0.15 percent.

Suppose now that the government introduces a separate income tax of 1 percent that increases each household's marginal tax rate from 40 to 41 percent. This reduces their net after-tax wage rate by 1.67 percent (i.e., 0.01/0.60 = 0.0167). Consequently, hours worked fall by 0.25 percent (0.15 × 0.0167 × 0.0025), or 5 hours per year. So, as shown in column 3 of the table, earnings also fall by 0.25 percent.

The net additional tax revenue is shown in column 4. Household A, for example, initially paid taxes of $4,000 ($10,000 × 0.4), while after the imposition of the new income tax, it paid taxes of about $4,090 ($9,975 × 0.41), an increase of approximately $90. The total of $1,350 in additional tax revenue is divided equally, with each household receiving $270. The net transfer (column 5 − column 4) is summarized in column 6.

Column 7 of the table presents the total change in disposable income, the sum of columns 3 and 6. The net incomes of the three richest households is reduced by $570 in aggregate, while the net incomes of the two poorest families is increased by a total of only $195. All five families, however, are now working less and enjoying more leisure. Assuming that the value of additional leisure equals the after-tax net wage rate, household A receives a leisure gain valued at $15 ($3 × 5 hours), household B receives a leisure gain valued at $30 ($6 × 5 hours), and so on. Column 8 summarizes the total change in real income (including the value of the gain in leisure). The real incomes of households A and B increase by $240 in aggregate, while the incomes of households C, D, and E decrease by $390.

Thus, as shown in column 6, $270 is transferred from the two richest households to the two poorest households. As shown in column 8, however, the real incomes of the two poorest households increase by $240 in aggregate, whereas the real incomes of the three richest households decrease by $390. Thus, the example shows that it costs society $390/$240 = $1.63 in lost income for every dollar transferred, ignoring administrative costs. The excess amount of 63 cents is sometimes called *the marginal efficiency cost of redistribution*, the loss to other members of society when low-income persons are made better off by one dollar. The numerator of the marginal excess tax burden is $150 in deadweight loss ($390 – $240, or the amount appearing at the bottom of column 8), while the denominator is $1,350 (the amount of the tax actually collected, which is shown at the bottom of column 4). Thus, in this hypothetical example, the METB is 0.11 and the MCPF is 1.11.

The Marginal Cost of Redistribution

Household (1)	Initial (gross) earnings (2)	Net change in earnings (3)	Additional tax revenue* (4)	Transfer (5)	Net transfer (6)	Change in disposable income (7)	Change in real income (8)
A	10,000	−25	90	270	180	155	170
B	20,000	−50	180	270	90	40	70
C	30,000	−75	270	270	0	−75	−30
D	40,000	−100	360	270	−90	−190	−130
E	50,000	−125	450	270	−180	−305	−230
Total	150,000	−375	1,350	1,350	0	−375	−150

* These figures are rounded to the nearest $10.
Source: Adapted from Edgar K. Browning, "The Marginal Cost of Redistribution," Public Finance Quarterly, 21(1), 1993, 3–32, table 1 at p. 5. Reprinted by permission of Sage Publications, Inc.

3.5.2   *Allocative Efficiency Given the Reality of the MCPF*

A program that requires a government to spend dollars funded out of taxation has a social cost equal to the amount spent multiplied by the MCPF. Symmetrically, a program that yields government revenue (through user fees, for example) allows it to reduce or avoid taxation and therefore benefits society by the MCPF multiplied by the government revenue generated. Taking such efficiency effects into account, Equation (3.12) becomes:

$$SS = CS + PS + (MCPF)GS \tag{3.14a}$$

$$\Delta SS = \Delta CS + \Delta PS + (MCPF)\Delta GS \tag{3.14b}$$

In other words, in order to appropriately measure the allocative efficiency impacts of a project and to compute its net social benefits, government project expenditures and revenues should be multiplied by the marginal cost of public funds.

3.6   Measuring Changes in Welfare

This chapter focuses on allocative efficiency and the measurement of net social benefits. Welfare, however, can be more broadly formulated as concerning allocative efficiency and *equity*. Conceptually, it is straightforward to generalize Equation (3.14b) so that it measures this broader view of changes in welfare:

$$\Delta W = \gamma_c \Delta CS + \gamma_p \Delta \pi + \gamma_f \Delta FS + \gamma_g \Delta GS \tag{3.15}$$

where γ_c, γ_p, γ_f, and γ_g are welfare weights for consumers, producers, factors of production, and government, respectively. This formulation distinguishes between producer surplus that accrues to firms, denoted as $\Delta \pi$, and producer surplus that accrues to factors of production (usually labor), denoted as ΔFS. Some studies have used Equation (3.15) to measure changes in welfare due to privatization as is illustrated in Exhibit 3.3.

If $\gamma_c = \gamma_p = \gamma_f = 1$ and $\gamma_g = \text{MCPF}$ and $\gamma_p \Delta \pi + \gamma_f \Delta FS = \Delta PS$, then Equation (3.15) becomes Equation (3.14b), and it measures net social benefits. This specification evaluates alternatives in terms of allocative efficiency. However, the weights may take on other values because of equity considerations.[25] Furthermore, different weights may be associated with different consumer groups, an issue discussed in detail in Chapter 19.

Exhibit 3.3

Anthony Boardman and his colleagues estimated the welfare gains from the privatization of Canadian National (CN) Railway in 1995. This was one of the largest rail privatizations in history. The authors were able to create a credible counterfactual based on cost data from Canadian Pacific Railway (CP), the privately owned competitor. The authors argued that the benefit to consumers (shippers) was zero because the evidence suggested that privatization had a negligible impact on CN's and CP's prices and output. Thus, the sole factor of production of interest was employees. Employment did decrease at CN following privatization, but the rate of decrease in employment was slower after 1992 than before 1992 (when the privatization was announced). Following the CN privatization, wages and salaries at CN increased faster than at CP. Thus, there is no clear evidence that employees were either better or worse off as a result of privatization. Consequently, analytic attention focused on firms (and their shareholders) and on any impact on the Canadian government. Using their preferred estimate of the counterfactual, the authors estimated that the increase in profits to foreign (non-Canadian) shareholders was $4.46 billion, the increase in profits to Canadian shareholders was $3.69 billion, and the increase in surplus going to the Canadian government was $6.90 billion. Following standard CBA practice in assigning equal welfare weights to profits and governments (i.e., $\gamma_p = \gamma_g = 1$) implies that the net social benefit equals $15.06 billion. Assuming that only Canadians have standing suggests that the net social benefit to Canadians was

$10.59 billion ($6.90 billion + $3.69 billion). As noted in the text, however, there are efficiency arguments for setting $\gamma_g = 1 + \text{METB}$. Boardman and colleagues also argue that there are efficiency arguments for setting $\gamma_p = 1 + $ *shadow price of capital*, a topic that we discuss in detail in Chapter 10. They propose $\gamma_g = 1.4$ and $\gamma_p = 1.16$, implying that the net benefit to Canadians of the privatization of CN equaled $13.94 billion.

Source: Anthony E. Boardman, Claude Laurin, Mark A. Moore, and Aidan R. Vining, "A Cost–Benefit Analysis of the Privatization of Canadian National Railway," *Canadian Public Policy*, 35(1), 2009, 59–83.

3.7   Conclusions

The primary objective of CBA is a more efficient allocation of resources. This chapter has reviewed the major principles from microeconomics and welfare economics that provide the technical foundation for cost–benefit analysis. The key concept is that in conducting a CBA one must estimate the changes in social surplus that result when new policies, programs, or projects are implemented. The change in social surplus provides a measure of the change in allocative efficiency (or net social benefits). Social surplus is often expressed as the sum of consumer surplus, producer surplus, and government surplus. However, projects have to be financed and are often financed by taxes, and all taxes create a deadweight loss. To account for the efficiency impacts of taxes, government inflows or outflows should be multiplied by the MCPF or, equivalently, by 1 + METB.

This chapter assumes that markets are initially perfectly competitive. Chapters 5, 6, and 7 make use of the concepts introduced in this chapter to develop measures of benefits and costs that are conceptually appropriate under numerous different circumstances.

APPENDIX 3A

Consumer Surplus and Willingness to Pay

In this chapter, we asserted that under most circumstances, estimates of changes in consumer surplus, as measured by demand curves, can be used in CBA as reasonable approximations of individuals' WTP to obtain or to avoid the effects of policy changes. In this appendix, we examine the circumstances under which measured changes in consumer surplus do in fact provide a close approximation to WTP and the circumstances under which they do not. For illustrative purposes, the focus is on the link between the amount of money a consumer would be willing to pay to avoid a given price increase and estimates based on the demand curve of the loss in the consumer's surplus resulting from the price increase.

Compensating Variation

The maximum amount of money that consumers would be willing to pay to avoid a price increase is the amount required to return them to the same level of utility that they enjoyed prior to the change in price, an amount called *compensating variation*. If consumers had to spend any more than the value of their compensating variation, then they would be worse off paying to avoid the increase, rather than allowing it to occur. If they could spend any less, then they would be better off paying to avoid the increase, rather than allowing it to occur. Hence, for a loss in consumer surplus resulting from a price increase to equal the consumers' WTP to avoid the price increase, it has to correspond exactly to the compensating variation value associated with the price increase.

These points can be best demonstrated by an indifference curve analysis, as presented in Figure 3A.1(a). This diagram represents a consumer who faces a world that offers only two goods, X and Y. The straight lines in the diagram represent budget constraints. The particular budget constraint that a consumer faces depends upon her income level and on the relative prices of goods X and Y. The greater the consumer's income, the more of X and Y she can afford and, consequently, the greater the distance the budget constraint will be from the origin, 0. Thus, for example, the budget constraint JK represents a higher income level than the budget constraint GI, and the budget constraint GH represents a higher income level than the budget constraint LK. The slope of the consumer's budget constraint indicates how many additional units of Y she can obtain if one less unit of X is purchased. Thus, holding everything else constant, the slope of the budget constraint is negative and depends upon the price of X relative to the price of Y. Consequently, if the price of X rises relative to that of Y, her budget constraint becomes more steeply sloped, changing, for example, from budget constraint GH to budget constraint GI. As a result, a larger number of units of Y can be purchased in exchange for each unit of X that she gives up.

The curved lines in Figure 3A.1(a) are *indifference curves*. All points along a single indifference curve represent combinations of goods X and Y that provide a consumer with equal levels of utility. Thus, the consumer is indifferent between points b and d on U_0 or points a and c on U_1. The further an indifference curve is from the origin, the greater the level of utility. Thus, the consumer would prefer any point on indifference curve U_1 (e.g., point a) to any point on indifference curve U_0 (e.g., point b), as more of both good X and good Y could be consumed at point a than at point b.

The indifference curves in Figure 3A.1(a) are negatively sloped because any movement along an indifference curve by definition represents a situation whereby an increase in the consumption of one good is offset by a sufficient reduction in the consumption of the other good such that the consumer's level of utility is left unchanged.[1] Were an individual to consume either more or less of both goods, the level of utility would obviously change.

The convex shape of the indifference curves (i.e., they bend inward toward the origin) reflects diminishing marginal utility – as the consumer consumes more of one good, she becomes increasingly less willing to give up consumption of an additional unit

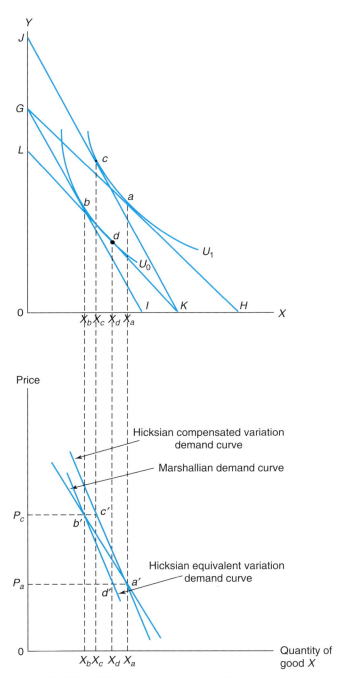

Figure 3A.1(a) Indifference curve analysis of a price change.
Figure 3A.1(b) Demand curve analysis of price change.

of the other good. For example, the convex shape of indifference curve U_0 implies that at point b the consumer would be willing to give up more units of Y in order to consume one additional unit of X than she would at point d.

Now let us assume that good X in Figure 3A.1(a) is a product on which the consumer spends only a small fraction of her total income, for example, movie tickets, and good Y is a composite good on which the consumer spends the rest of her income. Under this assumption, good Y is a reasonable approximation of the consumer's total money income. Consequently, the slope of a budget constraint in the figure would indicate the price of good X, that is, the amount of money income (i.e., good Y) the consumer would have to give up to obtain one more unit of X.

Assume that the consumer initially faces budget constraint GH. She will then choose point a on indifference curve U_1. Point a represents an equilibrium because the consumer cannot increase her utility by moving to any alternative point and, hence, has no incentive to do so.[2] Now assume that as a result of a new government policy, the price of good X is doubled.[3] This changes the consumer's equilibrium to point b on a more steeply sloped budget constraint, GI, and a lower indifference curve, U_0. Thus, her consumption of good X falls from X_a to X_b.[4]

On the other hand, if the consumer were paid a lump sum of money sufficient to compensate her entirely for the price increase in X, then it would shift her budget constraint from GI to JK, thereby allowing her to move back to the original indifference curve, U_1. However, given the new situation, she would now choose point c (rather than a) and would consume X_c of the good (rather than X_a). As the vertical distance between the two parallel budget constraints (i.e., the difference between points G and J on the vertical axis) represents the amount of good Y (that is, money income) that she would have to be paid in order to lose no utility from the price increase, this distance measures the compensating variation associated with the price increase.

In sum, this compensating variation value is the maximum amount that the consumer would be willing to pay to avoid the price increase. To confirm this, suppose that the price increase occurs and that the consumer is fully compensated for it. Then next suppose that if she is willing to pay all the compensation she received – that is, the full value of her compensating variation – the price increase will be revoked. Will she accept or reject this offer? She would, in fact, be indifferent to this revocation. If she accepts it, then she will return to her initial equilibrium at point a on indifference curve U_1; if she rejects it, then she will remain at point c, which is also on U_1. Thus, the compensation value represents the maximum amount the consumer would be willing to pay to avoid the price increase. If she could pay a bit less to revoke the price increase, then she would reject the revocation offer. If she had to pay a bit more, then she would accept it.

Income and Substitution Effects

Given the information contained in Figure 3A.1(a), the total effect of the increase in the price of X on the consumer's demand for good X (i.e., the change from X_a to X_b) can be decomposed into two separate effects: a *compensated substitution effect* and an *income effect.*[5] The compensated substitution effect is represented in Figure 3A.1(a) as the change in demand from X_a to X_c. It allows one to examine the effect of a change in the price of X on the demand for X if someone were exactly compensated for any losses of utility she suffers as a result of the price increase and, as a consequence, remained on indifference curve U_1. The compensated substitution effect always causes the demand for a good to change in the opposite direction to a change in the price of the good. For example, holding the consumer's level of utility constant, an increase in the price of good X causes her to substitute some of the now relatively less expensive good Y for good X. Hence, as shown in the figure, X_c is smaller than X_a.

The income effect is represented in Figure 3A.1(a) as the change in demand from X_c to X_b. It occurs because the increase in the price of good X reduces the consumer's disposable income. If, as the figure implies, X is a *normal good* – that is, if purchases of the good and disposable income are positively related – then the consumer will purchase less of it. Hence, X_b is smaller than X_c. Thus, like the substitution effect, the income effect associated with the price increase will also cause the consumer to reduce her demand for the good.

Demand Curves

The slopes of the budget constraints in Figure 3A.1(a) indicate both the old and the new prices of good X and the points tangent to these budget constraints with indifference curves. They indicate the amount of the good that the consumer wants at each price, so the figure provides information about two points along the consumer's demand curve for X. Indeed, as we know the quantity of output the consumer would demand after the price increase, both whether her utility were held constant or not, we can determine the location of pairs of points along two different demand curves. Figure 3A.1(b) shows these two pairs of points as points a' and c' and as points a' and b', respectively (ignore the third pair of points, d' and b', for the moment.) One can approximate demand curves with straight lines by simply drawing straight lines between the two points in each pair.

The line in Figure 3A.1(b) that connects points a' and b' is a demand schedule of the sort usually shown in textbooks. This demand curve, which is known as a *Marshallian demand curve*, incorporates both the substitution and income effects associated with changes in the price of good X. Statistical efforts by economists to estimate relations between the price of a good and quantities purchased, which are discussed in Chapter 4, are usually attempts to estimate Marshallian demand curves empirically, as this work typically involves trying to hold income, other prices, and other factors constant.

The demand curve in Figure 3A.1(b) that connects points a' and c' keeps utility constant as the price of good X changes. This demand curve, thus, incorporates only the compensated substitution effect associated with price changes. This demand curve is sometimes called the *utility compensated* or the *Hicksian compensated variation demand curve*. Because Hicksian demand curves are unaffected by income effects, they are usually, as is the case illustrated in Figure 3A.1(b), more steeply sloped than Marshallian demand schedules. Unlike Marshallian demand curves, Hicksian demand curves usually cannot be directly estimated using statistical techniques. However, it is often possible to indirectly estimate them by first estimating the Marshallian demand curve and then, in effect, netting out the income effect.[6]

Equivalence of Consumer Surplus and Compensating Variation

Movements up the Hicksian compensated variation demand curve, for example, from P_a to P_c, are equivalent to allowing the price to increase while compensating the consumer with a lump-sum payment of just sufficient size to permit her to remain on her original indifference curve. This lump-sum payment can be measured graphically as either the vertical distance between the two parallel budget constraints in Figure 3A.1(a) (i.e., as the difference between money income at points G and J) or as the change in consumer surplus indicated by the Hicksian compensated variation demand curve in Figure 3A.1(b), that is, the area $P_a a'c'P_c$. Thus, the change in consumer surplus resulting from a price change measured with a Hicksian compensated variation demand schedule exactly equals the consumer's compensating variation; that is, the maximum amount the consumer would be willing to pay to avoid the price increase.

Hence, it is Hicksian compensated variation demand curves that best permit measurement of the compensating variation associated with price changes. To the extent that the two demand curve measures differ, using a Marshallian compensated variation demand curve to measure consumer surplus will result in a biased estimate of compensating variation and, therefore, of WTP. As can be seen from Figure 3A.1(b), each measure does produce different estimates of consumer surplus; they differ by the triangular area $a'b'c'$. For a price increase, the change in consumer surplus is smaller if measured with the Marshallian demand schedule than with a Hicksian compensated variation demand curve; for a price reduction, it is larger.

In summary, the difference between the two types of demand curves is that the Marshallian curve incorporates the income effects associated with price changes, as well as the substitution effects, while the Hicksian curve incorporates only the latter. Thus, the biased estimate of WTP that results from using Marshallian rather than Hicksian demand curves to measure consumer surplus depends upon the size of the income effect associated with a price change. *Usually this income effect and, hence, the bias are small and can be safely ignored in CBA.*[7] This, at least, is the case when the price change is moderate and the good in question accounts for a fairly small part of total consumption. Thus, CBAs of government policies that affect corn, cotton, tobacco, and gasoline prices are not generally much affected by use of Marshallian rather than Hicksian demand curves. However, *the bias can be of some importance for a CBA of a government policy that would result in large price changes in major consumption goods such as housing or automobiles or in large changes in wage rates.* Consequently, except for a few instances when it clearly seems inappropriate to do so, throughout of this book we assume that the income effects associated with various policy changes are sufficiently small that consumer surpluses that are measured by using Marshallian demand schedules provide reasonable approximations of WTP.

Equivalent Variation as an Alternative to Compensating Variation

In situations in which the bias should not be ignored, there is an alternative to compensating variation for measuring the welfare effects of price changes that should be used instead because it has more desirable properties: namely, *equivalent variation.*[8]

In terms of Figure 3A.1(a), equivalent variation is the amount of money, GL, that if paid by the consumer would cause her to lose just as much utility as the price increase. If she could pay a bit less, then she would not be as bad off as the price increase makes her. If she had to pay a bit more, then she would be even worse off.

Using the equivalent variation approach, Figure 3A.1(a) shows the income effect as the change in demand from X_a to X_d, while the substitution effect is shown as the change in demand from X_d to X_b. Note that, as in the case of the compensating variation approach, both effects that result from the price increase cause the quantity of the good demanded to fall as long as the good is a normal good. Also note that the compensating variation approach measures the substitution effect by holding utility constant at its level *before* the price change was made, while the equivalent variation approach measures the substitution effect holding utility constant *after* the price change. In both cases, however, a Hicksian demand curve can be derived because, holding utility constant, the old and the new prices of good X and the quantity demanded at both prices are all known. Thus, the Hicksian compensated variation demand curve is represented in Figure 3A.1(b) by the line that connects points a' and c' and the Hicksian equivalent variation demand curve is represented by the line that connects points d' and b'. Neither of the Hicksian demand curves are affected by income effects; hence, they are more steeply sloped than the Marshallian demand curve. Compensating variation is represented in Figure 3A.1(b) by the area $P_a a' c' P_c$ and equivalent variation by the area $P_a d' b' P_c$.

As indicated by Figure 3A.1(b), the compensating variation that results from the price increase is larger than the change in consumer surplus measured with the Marshallian demand curve by the triangular area $a'b'c'$, while the resulting equivalent variation is smaller by the area $b'd'a'$. The opposite holds in the case of a price decrease. The size of these differences, as previously discussed, depends on the size of the income effect. If it is large, then ideally equivalent variation should be used to measure the change in welfare resulting from a price change, rather than either Marshallian consumer surplus or compensating variation. This is often, but not always, possible if a measure of Marshallian consumer surplus is available.[9]

Exercises for Chapter 3

1. A person's demand for gizmos is given by the following equation:

    $q = 6 - 0.5p + 0.0002I$

    where q is the quantity demanded at price p when the person's income is I. Assume initially that the person's income is $60,000.

    a. At what price will demand fall to zero? (This is sometimes called the choke price because it is the price that chokes off demand.)

    b. If the market price for gizmos is $10, how many will be demanded?

    c. At a price of $10, what is the price elasticity of demand for gizmos?

    d. At a price of $10, what is the consumer surplus?

    e. If price rises to $12, how much consumer surplus is lost?

    f. If income were $80,000, what would be the consumer surplus loss from a price rise from $10 to $12?

2. At the current market equilibrium, the price of a good equals $40 and the quantity equals 10 units. At this equilibrium, the price elasticity of supply is 2.0. Assume that the supply curve is linear.

    a. Use the price elasticity and market equilibrium to find the supply curve. (Hint: the supply curve has the following form: $q = a + (\Delta q/\Delta p)p$. First, find the value of $\Delta q/\Delta p$; then, find the value of a.)

    b. Calculate the producer surplus in the market.

    c. Imagine that a policy results in the price falling from $40 to $34. By how much does producer surplus fall?

    d. What fraction of the lost producer surplus is due to the reduction in the quantity supplied and what fraction is due to the fall in price received per unit sold?

3. (This question pertains to Appendix 3A; instructor-provided spreadsheet recommended.) Imagine a person's utility function over two goods, X and Y, where Y represents dollars. Specifically, assume a Cobb–Douglas utility function:

    $U(X, Y) = X^a Y^{(1-a)}$

    where $0 < a < 1$.

    Let the person's budget be B. The feasible amounts of consumption must satisfy the following equation:

    $B = pX + Y$

where p is the unit price of X and the price of Y is set to 1.

Solving the budget constraint for Y and substituting into the utility function yields:

$U = X^a (B - pX)^{(1-a)}$

Using calculus, it can be shown that utility is maximized by choosing:

$X = aB/p$

Also, it can be shown that the area under the Marshallian demand curve for a price increase from p to q yielding a change in consumption of X from x_p to x_q is given by:

$$\Delta CS = \left[aB \ln(x_q) - px_q \right] - \left[aB \ln(x_p) - px_p \right] - (q - p)x_q$$

When $B = 100$, $a = 0.5$, and $p = .2$, $X = 250$ maximizes utility, which equals 111.80. If price is raised to $p = .3$, X falls to 204.12.

a. Increase B until the utility raises to its initial level. The increase in B needed to return utility to its level before the price increase is the compensating variation for the price increase. (It can be found by guessing values until utility reaches its original level.)

b. Compare ΔCS, as measured with the Marshallian demand curve, to the compensating variation.

Notes

1. One can envision deriving an inverse demand curve through an auction in which bids are taken on the first unit of a good offered for sale, then on the second unit, then the third unit, and so forth, with successively lower bids obtained for each additional unit of the good that is offered. This kind of auction is called a Dutch auction. Although now done electronically, in years past it was common in Holland to have a mechanical "clock" with hands that started at the bid made on the previous unit and swept through successively lower bids until stopped by an individual who wished to make a bid.

2. The total benefit (B) from consuming X^* units can be obtained by integrating under the (inverse) demand curve, $P(x)$, from the origin to X^*:

$$B = \int_0^{X^*} P(x)\,dx$$

Because the inverse demand curve measures marginal benefits, MB, we can also write:

$$B = \int_0^{X^*} MB(x)\,dx$$

3. If the absolute value of E_d is greater than 1 and, hence, the percentage change in quantity demanded is greater than the percentage change in price, then demand is said to be *elastic*. On the other hand, if the absolute value of E_d is less than 1 and, hence, the percentage change in quantity demanded is smaller than the percentage change in price, then demand is said to be *inelastic*. If the value approaches infinity (i.e., the demand curve is horizontal), then demand is said to be *perfectly elastic*, while if the value is 0 (the demand curve is vertical), then demand is said to be *completely inelastic*. The use of elasticity estimates in conducting CBAs is further described in Chapter 4.

4. The government is not, of course, the ultimate beneficiary of the tax revenues. However, if it simply returned this revenue to consumers, then consumers in aggregate would be compensated for their greater expenditures on the units of the good that they continue to purchase.

5. More generally, with a downward-sloping demand (marginal benefit) curve, $MB(x)$, and an upward-sloping supply (marginal cost) curve, $MC(x)$, the deadweight loss (DWL) may be defined more formally:

$$DWL = \int_{x^*}^{x_1} (MB(x) - MC(x))\,dx, \text{ if } x^* < x_1$$

$$DWL = \int_{x_2}^{x^*} (MB(x) - MC(x))\,dx, \text{ if } x_2 < x^*$$

6. By normal return, we simply mean the risk-adjusted market price or rate of return that each unit of a resource commands under perfect competition.

7. Thus, because we are presently assuming the existence of perfect competition and well-functioning markets, social opportunity costs, as we have defined them, correspond to private economic costs. In the absence of perfect competition (or, if externalities exist), private economic costs may differ from the costs that using resources imposes on society. These latter costs, *social opportunity costs*, are the relevant cost measure for purposes of CBA. The use of shadow pricing to obtain appropriate measures of social opportunity costs when markets are distorted is discussed in Chapters 5 and 6.

8. For an accessible discussion of the topics covered in this section and elsewhere in this chapter, and a history of the development of the concept of consumer surplus, see James R. Hines Jr., "Three Sides of Harberger Triangles." *Journal of Economic Perspectives*, 13(2), 1999, 167–88.

9. Of course, total costs equal total variable costs plus fixed costs. Here, for simplicity, we assume fixed costs are zero.

10. By definition, $NSB(x) = B(x) - C(x)$. To obtain the value of X that maximizes NSB we differentiate with respect to X and set the result equal to zero:

$$\frac{dNSB}{dX} = \frac{dB}{dX} - \frac{dC}{dX} = 0$$

Which implies

$$\frac{dB}{dX} = \frac{dC}{dX}$$

Thus, net social benefits are maximized when marginal benefit equals marginal cost.

11. In this discussion, we are assuming that marginal (private) costs equal marginal social costs. In Chapter 5, we consider situations where marginal (private) costs do not equal marginal social costs – for example, when externalities exist.

12. For a clear discussion of the distinction between producer surplus, rents, and profits see Margaret F. Sanderson and Ralph A. Winter, "Profits Versus Rents in Antitrust Analysis: An Application to the Canadian Waste Services Merger." *Antitrust Law Journal*, 70(2), 2002, 485–511.

13. Thomas W. Ross and Ralph A. Winter, "The Efficiency Defense in Merger Law: Economic Foundations and Recent Canadian Developments." *Antitrust Law Journal*, 72(2), 2004, 471–503.

14. Given no externalities, the deadweight loss can also be computed as the area between the marginal cost curve and the marginal benefit curve between the optimal output level, X^*, and the output level under target pricing, X^T.

15. For an explanation about how to evaluate public–private partnerships in terms of providing either value to society (social surplus) or value for money to government, see Anthony E. Boardman and Mark Hellowell, "A

Comparative Analysis and Evaluation of Specialist PPP Units' Methodologies for Conducting Value for Money Appraisals." *Journal of Comparative Policy Analysis*, 19, 2016, 197–206.

16. A somewhat similar table in concept and design has been coined "the Kaldor–Hicks tableau" by Kerry Krutilla, "Using the Kaldor–Hicks Tableau Format for Cost–Benefit Analysis and Policy Evaluation." *Journal of Policy and Management*, 24(4), 2005, 864–75. Krutilla argues that by illuminating the distributional implications of a policy intervention, the Kaldor–Hicks tableau provides "greater clarity and transparency" and is "useful for understanding the political ramifications of a particular project or policy."

17. In some cases, as we discuss in Chapter 5, taxes may increase social surplus. For example, if prior to being taxed a good was overconsumed due to a negative externality, then the introduction of a tax could increase allocative efficiency by reducing the overconsumption. In this case the METB would be negative. More generally, the efficiency implications of interventions depend on the distortions already in the market. For example, Charles Ballard demonstrates that when labor markets for low-income groups are distorted by high effective marginal tax rates, redistributing through wage subsidies can actually result in efficiency gains. Charles L. Ballard, "The Marginal Efficiency Cost of Redistribution." *American Economic Review*, 78(5), 1988, 1019–33.

18. Some discussions refer to the "social marginal cost of public funds," which differs from the marginal cost of public funds because the cost of raising an additional dollar of tax revenue is distributionally weighted. See K. W. Kevin Hsu and C. C. Yang, "Political Economy and the Social Marginal Cost of Public Funds: The Case of the Melzer–Richard Economy." *Economic Inquiry*, 46(3), 2008, 401–10. Distributional weighting is discussed in Chapter 19.

19. Such an argument is made, for example, by Daniel Fujiwara, *The Department for Work and Pensions Social Cost–Benefit Analysis Framework: Methodologies for Estimating and Incorporating the Wider Social and Economic Impacts of Work in Cost–benefit analysis of Employment Programmes*, Working Paper No. 86 (London: Department for Work and Pensions, 2010).

20. See Bev Dahlby, *The Marginal Cost of Public Funds: Theory and Application* (Cambridge, MA: The MIT Press, 2008, especially chapter 2); and Per-Olov Johansson and Bengt Kristrom, A Note on Cost–Benefit Analysis, The Marginal Cost of Public Funds, and the Marginal Excess Burden of Taxes," CERE Working Paper 2010:5 (Umea, Sweden, 2010).

21. The original sources of these estimates are as follows: B. Dahlby, "The Distortionary Effect of Rising Taxes," in W. Robson and W. Scarth, editors, *Deficit Reduction: What Pain, What Gain* (Toronto: C. D. Howe Institute, 1994); Charles E. Stuart, "Welfare Costs per Dollar of Additional Tax Revenue in the United States." *American Economic Review*, 74(3), 1984, 452–62; D. Fullerton and Y.K. Henderson, "The Marginal Excess Burden of Different Capital Tax Instruments." *Review of Economics and Statistics*, 71, 1989, 435–42; Charles L. Ballard, John B. Shoven, and John Whalley, "General Equilibrium Computations of the Marginal Welfare Costs of Taxes in the United States." *American Economic Review*, 75(1), 1985, 128–38; Charles L. Ballard, John B. Shoven, and John Whalley, "The Total Welfare Cost of the United States Tax System: A General Equilibrium Approach." *National Tax Journal*, 38(2), 1985, 125–40; Harry F. Campbell and K. Bond, "The Costs of Public Funds in Australia." *Economic Record*, 73, 1997, 28–40.

22. The original sources of these estimates are as follows: S. Ahmad and D. Croushore, "The Marginal Cost of Funds with Nonseparable Public Spending." *Public Finance Quarterly*, 24, 1996, 216–36; J. Gruber and E. Saez, "The Elasticity of Taxable Income: Evidence and Implications." *Journal of Public Economics*, 84, 2002, 1–32; H. Kleven and C. Kreiner, "The Marginal Cost of Public Funds: Hours of Work versus Labor Force Participation." *Journal of Public Economics*, 90, 2006, 1955–73; and G. Ruggeri, "The Marginal Cost of Public Funds in Closed and Small Open Economies." *Fiscal Studies*, 20, 1999, 41–60.

23. Charles L. Ballard, John B. Shoven, and John Whalley, "General Equilibrium Computations of the Marginal Welfare Costs of Taxes in the United States."

24. The derivation of the estimates in Table 3.2 are, of course, considerably more complicated, as they are based on sophisticated statistical procedures and most rely on general equilibrium models.

25. One can argue that these parameters are not unity on distributional (equity) grounds as well as efficiency grounds. For this argument applied to γ_g see, for example, Joel Slemrod and Shlomo Yitzhaki, "Integrating Expenditure and Tax Decisions: The Marginal Cost of Funds and the Marginal Benefits of Projects." *National Tax Journal*, 54(2), 2001, 189–201.

Appendix Notes

1. The slope of an indifference curve is called the marginal rate of substitution, where the marginal rate of substitution $\frac{dX}{dP}\Big|_{\bar{U}} < 0$ and $\bar{U}$ indicate that utility is being held constant.

2. At equilibrium, the marginal rate of substitution equals the ratio of the price of good X to the price of good Y.

3. Thus, in Figure 3A.1(a), $0I = (1/2)0H$ or $I = H/2$.

4. Depending on the slopes of the indifference curves, the consumption of good Y could either increase or decrease. As shown in Figure 3A.1(a), it slightly decreases in this particular example.

5. In calculus notation, this decomposition can be represented as follows:

$$\frac{dX}{dP} = \frac{dX}{dP}\Big|_{\bar{U}} - X \frac{dX}{dP}\Big|_{\bar{P}}$$

This equation is known as the *Slutsky equation*. The first term to the right of the equal sign is the substitution effect, where utility is held constant. The second term is the income effect, where prices are held constant, and X is the amount of the good consumed prior to the price change.

6. One way of doing this first requires obtaining estimates of the relation between quantity purchased and prices and the relation between quantity purchased and income and then (as implied by the preceding note) using the Slutsky equation to derive the income-compensated (rather than the utility-compensated) relation between prices and quantity purchased. In practice, however, it is not always feasible to estimate the relation between quantity purchased and income and, hence, to use the Slutsky equation.

7. For analyses of the size of the bias, see Ian J. Irvine and William A. Sims, "Measuring Consumer Surplus with Unknown Hicksian Demands." *American Economic Review*, 88(1), 1998, 314–22; Robin W. Boadway and Neil Bruce, *Welfare Economics* (Oxford: Basil Blackwell, 1984), 216–19; Julian M. Alston and Douglas M. Larson, "Hicksian vs. Marshallian Welfare Measures: Why Do We Do What We Do?" *American Journal of Agricultural Economics*, 75(3), 1993, 764–69; Jerry A. Hausman, "Exact Consumer's Surplus and Deadweight Loss." *American Economic Review*, 71(4), 1981, 662–76; and Robert D. Willig, "Consumer's Surplus Without Apology." *American Economic Review*, 66(4), 1979, 589–97.

8. Specifically, using compensating variation is only theoretically correct if consumers have homothetic preferences (i.e., the slopes of all indifferent curves are constant along any ray from the origin), which implies that each good in a consumer's utility function has an income elasticity of one. Equivalent variation does not require a similarly restrictive assumption. See George W. McKenzie, *Measuring Economic Welfare: New Methods* (New York, NY: Cambridge University Press, 1983). Also see Marco Becht, "The Theory and Estimation of Individual and Social Welfare Measures." *Journal of Economic Surveys*, 9(1), 1995, 53–87; and the references therein.

   Although equivalent variation is an appropriate measure of the welfare change resulting from a price increase or decrease, it has been argued that either compensating surplus or equivalent surplus is more appropriately used when the quantity of a good, rather than its price, increases or decreases. In this appendix, we focus on price rather than quantity changes. For a discussion of when each of the welfare change measures is most appropriately used, as well as a useful graphical presentation of each, see V. Kerry Smith and William H. Desvousges, *Measuring Water Quality Benefits* (Boston, MA: Kluwer-Nijhoff Publishing, 1986), chapter 2.

9. A fairly simple procedure for using the Slutsky equation to approximate the Hicksian measures of consumer surplus is described by Irvine and Sims ("Measuring Consumer Surplus …"). Also, see appendix note 6.

4 Valuing Impacts from Observed Behavior: Direct Estimation of Demand Schedules

A key concept for valuing policy impacts is change in social surplus. As discussed in Chapter 3, changes in social surplus are represented by areas, often as triangles or trapezoids, bounded by supply and demand schedules (curves). Measurement of changes in social surplus is relatively straightforward when we know the shapes (functional forms) and positions of the supply and demand curves in the relevant primary market, before and after the policy change. In practice, however, these curves are usually not known. Analysts have to estimate them from available data or find alternative ways to measure benefits and costs. In this chapter, we consider estimation of demand curves.

Although the empirical strategies we consider also apply to estimating supply curves, we focus on estimating demand curves for two reasons. First, whereas both short- and long-term demand curves tend to be upward-sloping, long-term supply curves tend to be perfectly elastic (flat) so that there is neither producer surplus in the pre-policy market nor a change in producer surplus resulting from policy-induced changes in the quantity demanded. In the absence of unique factors of production that create scarcity rents, positive producer surplus attracts new firms to the industry that simply replicate existing firms. Only if production factors are unique or there are barriers to entry to new firms does measurement of social surplus require estimation of supply curves to take account of changes in producer surplus. Second, for *ex post* CBA, changes in producer surplus can usually be computed more easily from changes in profits, which can often be obtained directly from affected firms.

For goods traded in well-functioning markets, we can usually observe the market-clearing price. We may also be able to observe the aggregate quantity bought and sold from government or trade association statistics so that we have the point of intersection of the demand and supply curves. The task in this chapter is to estimate changes in social surplus where there is limited additional information. We consider three situations. First, we suppose that we have only one observation on the demand curve but previous research provides knowledge of its shape (functional form), and either its elasticity or slope. Second, we suppose that we have a few observations (points) on the demand curve. Third, we suppose that we have many observations of prices and quantities from different regions or from different time periods. In the first two situations we can make simple extrapolations. In the third situation we can apply standard econometric techniques to estimate the demand curve. Appendix 4A contains an introduction to multiple regression analysis, the common starting point for demand curve estimation.

4.1   Knowing the Slope or Price Elasticity of Demand

Many municipalities charge annual fees for household refuse collection that do not depend on the quantity of refuse disposed of by households. In such communities, the marginal private cost (MPC) of an additional unit of garbage collected is effectively zero, whereas the marginal social cost (MSC) of collecting and disposing of it is shared equally among all households.[1] This divergence between MPC and MSC leads to free-riding and a socially excessive amount of refuse disposal. Raising the price of refuse disposal would reduce the quantity of refuse disposed of by households and thereby reduce the social surplus loss from excess refuse disposal.

Imagine that you have been asked to measure the social benefits that would result if a town, Wasteville, which currently does not charge households by volume for refuse collection, imposes a fee of $2.20 (2017 dollars) for each 30-gallon container. That is, households would be charged $2.20 for each container put at the curbside for emptying by the sanitation department. As a 30-gallon container holds about 20 pounds of waste, the new policy implies a price increase from zero to about $0.11/lb, assuming the containers were full.

From the sanitation department's records, you find that the current refuse disposal rate averages 2.60 pounds per person per day (lb/p/d), and the MSC of each ton of refuse collected is approximately $264 per ton, or $0.14/lb. (One ton equals 2,000 pounds in the United States.) This MSC is the sum of the marginal collection costs of $88 per ton and the tipping fee at the landfill of $176 per ton. Although the proposed fee still leaves the MPC, the actual price, below the MSC, the socially optimal price, you expect it will produce a gain in social surplus by reducing the amount of waste generated.

To measure the social surplus gain, however, you need to know the demand curve for refuse disposal. You know only one point on the demand curve: 2.60 lb/p/d of garbage at a price equal to zero. To progress any further, you must find a way of estimating the rest of the demand curve. Usually, demand curves are assumed to be linear or linear in logarithms. To begin, we assume the demand curve is linear.

4.1.1   *Linear Demand Curve*

A market demand curve for a good indicates how many units of the good consumers wish to purchase at each price. A linear functional form assumes a linear relationship between the quantity of the good demanded and its price; that is, the (ordinary) demand curve can be written as:

$$q = \alpha_0 + \alpha_1 p \tag{4.1}$$

where q is the quantity demanded at price p, α_0 is the quantity that would be demanded if the price were zero (the intercept on the q axis), and α_1 indicates the change in the quantity demanded as a result of a one-unit increase in price (the slope).

For Wasteville, q is measured in terms of *quantity demanded per person* per day. Therefore, we can assume $\alpha_0 = 2.60$ (the average amount of refuse disposed of daily by each person at a price of zero). Although we do not know the slope, α_1, we do know that other researchers have addressed this problem and have estimated either the slope or the price elasticity of demand.

Using a Slope Estimate. If you conducted some research, then you might turn up a study that gave you an estimate of the slope of the demand curve for refuse disposal. Indeed, Robin Jenkins conducted such a study.[2] She based her estimate on data from nine US communities that employed a variety of refuse fees, ranging from zero to $1.73 per 30- to 32-gallon container, over the period from 1980 to 1989. She estimated that each dollar increase in the price of a 30- to 32-gallon container reduced waste by 0.40 lb/p/d, that is, $\alpha_1 = -0.40$. Adjusting the $1 for inflation would correspond to a price increase today of $2.20.[3] In turn, adjusting the coefficient for inflation would result in an inflation adjusted slope, α_{1new}, equal to $(-0.40)/(2.20)$, or -0.18. Using this estimate leads to a prediction that if Wasteville imposed a fee of $2.20 per container ($0.11/lb), then residential waste disposal would fall by 0.40 lb/p/d from 2.60 lb/p/d to 2.20 lb/p/d.

Figure 4.1 shows the linear demand curve implied by Jenkins' slope estimate: $q = 2.60 - 0.18p$, drawn in the usual way with price on the vertical axis.[4] This line goes through the status quo point of 2.60 lb/p/d at zero dollars per pound (point c) and the predicted point of 2.20 lb/p/d at $0.11 per pound (point d). It also goes through the point 2.10 lb/p/d at the price of $0.14 per pound (point a).

This curve can be used to estimate the change in social surplus. Remembering that the MSC, which is the socially optimal price, is $0.14 per pound, the area of the triangle abc, $0.5(2.60 \text{ lb/p/d} - 2.10 \text{ lb/p/d})(\$0.14/\text{lb}-0.00) = \$0.035$ per pound per day (p/d), is the social surplus loss per person at a price of $0, and the area of the small triangle aed, $0.5(2.20 \text{ lb/p/d} - 2.10 \text{ lb/p/d})(\$0.14/\text{lb}-\$0.11/\text{lb})= \$0.0015/\text{p/d}$, is the social

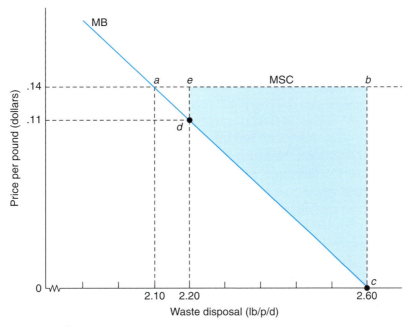

Figure 4.1 Social surplus gain from refuse fee.

surplus loss per person at the price of $0.11/lb. Thus, the area of the shaded trapezoid *debc*, $0.0335/p/d, is the gain in social surplus per person that would result from the price increase from zero to $0.11/lb. If the population of Wasteville is 100,000 people, then the annual gain in social surplus from imposing a container fee of $2.20 is ($0.0335/p/d)(365 days)(100,000 persons) = $1.2 million. To obtain the net social benefit of this policy, we would have to subtract the administrative cost of collecting the fee, any social losses that result if people dump illegally to avoid the fee, the revenue from the fee (a transfer from consumers to the municipality), and the avoided marginal excess burden resulting from the revenue allowing a reduction in the property tax.

Using a Price Elasticity Estimate. Suppose now that the analyst has a valid estimate of the price elasticity of demand for garbage disposal in Wasteville and, as above, the demand curve is linear. As discussed in Chapter 3, the price elasticity of demand, E_d, measures the responsiveness of the quantity demanded to changes in price. For a linear demand curve as in Equation (4.1), the price elasticity of demand equals:

$$E_d = \alpha_1 \frac{p}{q} \tag{4.2}$$

It is always negative because $\alpha_1 < 0$ (demand curves slope down), and p and $q > 0$, and it is always non-constant – it varies with both price and quantity. By rearranging Equation (4.2) we can estimate the slope of an ordinary demand curve, α_1, if we have an estimate of its price elasticity and also know the price and quantity at which the elasticity was estimated:

$$\alpha_1 = E_d \frac{q}{p} \tag{4.3}$$

Returning to our garbage fee example, suppose Jenkins had not provided an estimate of the slope, but instead had reported an estimate of the price elasticity of demand for residential refuse disposal of −0.12, which had been estimated at the average price charged by those communities in her sample that had non-zero fees, $0.81/container, or about $0.027 per pound, and at the average residential waste disposed by the communities in her sample of 2.62 lb/p/d.[5] Substituting this information into Equation (4.3) gives $\alpha_1 = (-0.12)$ (2.62 lb/p/d)/($0.027/lb) $\cong$ −11.6 p/d/$. As in the previous section, one would convert this estimate in 1985 dollars to 2017 dollars by dividing by 2.2, which would yield a slope of –5.3 p/d/$. A price change of $0.11/lb leads to a prediction of a reduction in quantity demanded of 0.58 lb/p/d. Note that this prediction differs from the prediction based on the reported slope. The difference arises because mean quantity in the sample is inconsistent with the current quantity at zero price in Wasteville. As the characteristics of the sample used to estimate elasticity almost never exactly match those of the application, such differences should be expected. Although there is no clear resolution, the simplest approach is generally to recover the actual estimate of the slope used to calculate the reported elasticity.

The general point is that construction of a linear demand curve to measure changes in social surplus requires either a direct estimate of the slope itself or an estimate of the price elasticity of demand and the price and quantity at which the elasticity was estimated.

Validity. When using a slope or elasticity estimate from previous research, it is important to consider issues of *internal validity* and *external validity*. Internal validity involves the sort of evaluation design issues discussed in Chapter 14, as well as issues related to the proper use of econometric techniques, which we discuss later in this chapter. External validity concerns the appropriateness of using estimates derived from data collected at other times, in other places, and with different populations. Applying estimates to circumstances similar to those under which they were obtained has high external validity. Specifically, the closer Wasteville is in economic, policy, demographic, and geographic characteristics to the communities in Jenkins' sample, the more confident we can be in the accuracy of our estimated change in waste disposal following the introduction of a volumetric user fee in Wasteville. The fact that her estimate comes from data collected in the 1980s is of some concern because there has been considerable time for other unmeasured variables, such as the level of environmental awareness or recycling infrastructure, to have changed.[6]

4.1.2   *Constant Elasticity Demand Curve*

The market demand curve may not be linear. Economists have found that many goods have a *constant elasticity demand curve* in which the elasticity of demand does not change as price and quantity change. That is

$$q = \beta_0 p^{\beta_1} \tag{4.4}$$

where q denotes quantity demanded at price p, as before, and β_0 and β_1 are parameters. In order to interpret β_1 it is useful to take the natural logarithm, denoted by ln, of both sides of Equation (4.4), which gives:

$$\ln q = \ln \beta_0 + \beta_1 \ln p \tag{4.5}$$

Exhibit 4.1

Researchers have used a variety of econometric methods to estimate the price elasticity of demand for various energy goods. Xavier Labandeira, José M. Labeaga, and Xiral López-Otero reviewed 428 of these studies and summarized their results in a meta-analysis that took account of the research design and empirical context of the studies. They treated estimates of elasticities from the studies as dependent variables in a regression model in which their independent variables included characteristics of the country in which the study was done, the time period covered by the study's data, and the type of statistical methods employed by the study's authors. They report average short-term and long-term price elasticities of demand for five energy goods: electricity (–0.126, –0.365), natural gas (–0.180, –0.684), gasoline (–0.293, –0.773), diesel fuel (–0.153, –0.443), and heating oil (–0.017, –0.185). Note that demand for these goods is inelastic with short-term demand more inelastic than long-term demand for each good.

Source: Adapted from Xavier Labandeira, José M. Labeaga, and Xiral López-Otero, "A Meta-Analysis on the Price Elasticity of Energy Demand," *Energy Policy*, 102(March), 2017, 549–68.

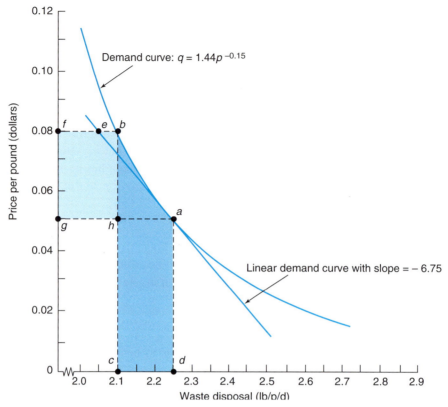

Figure 4.2 Constant elasticity demand curve.

We see immediately that the constant elasticity demand curve is linear in logarithms.[7] Furthermore, β_1, the slope of this demand curve, equals E_d, the price elasticity of demand.[8] As E_d does not depend on price or quantity it is said to come from a constant elasticity demand curve.

With quantity on the vertical axis and price on the horizontal axis, the slope of the constant elasticity demand curve is not constant; specifically, it equals $\beta_1 q/p$.[9] Similar to other demand curves, it slopes downward and $\beta_1 < 0$. It is also asymptotic to both the price and quantity axes, that is, as price becomes infinite, the quantity demanded approaches zero, and as price approaches zero, the quantity demanded approaches infinity. Because we are most often interested in the region of the demand curve where price is finite and greater than zero, and the estimates of elasticities are based on data in this range, these asymptotic extremes are usually not relevant to our analysis.

As an illustration of how to use a constant elasticity demand curve, consider the following situation. A community (not Wasteville) currently charges a refuse collection fee of $0.05/lb, and waste disposal is 2.25 lb/p/d. This status quo point is labeled point a in Figure 4.2. Imagine that you have been asked to estimate the change in consumer surplus that would result if the collection fee were raised to $0.08/lb, assuming that the demand for refuse collection and disposal has a constant elasticity functional form. This change in consumer surplus is represented by area *fbag* in Figure 4.2.

After some research we find an applicable study that reports an estimate of the price elasticity of demand of −0.15. Substituting this estimate of the price elasticity into Equation (3.4) and setting $P^* = \$.05/lb$ and $X^* = 2.25$ lb/p/d suggests that the loss in consumer surplus is approximately $\$0.0645/p/d$ for a linear demand curve, represented by area *feag* in Figure 4.2. For a town with a population of 100,000, the annual loss in consumer surplus would be calculated as (0.0645)(365)(100,000), or approximately $2.35 million.

A more accurate approach begins with the exact formula for the area under a constant elasticity demand curve from quantity q_0 to quantity q_1 which is given (exactly) by:[10]

$$\text{Area} = \left(\frac{1}{\beta_0}\right)^{1/\beta_1}\left(\frac{q_1^\rho - q_0^\rho}{\rho}\right) \tag{4.6}$$

where $\rho = 1 + (1/\beta_1)$. To estimate q_1 we first need to estimate β_0, which we can obtain from Equation (4.5): $\beta_0 = (2.25)/(0.05)^{-0.15} \approx 1.44$lb/p/d/\$, which gives $q = 1.44\, p^{-0.15}$ as the underlying demand curve for our application.[11] This equation implies that the area under the demand curve where q ranges from 2.10 lb/p/d to 2.25 lb/p/d, which is equivalent to the dark-shaded area *badc*, equals $\$0.0097/p/d$. If we now subtract area *hadc*, which measures the reduction in fee payments due to the reduction in quantity [(\$0.05/lb)(2.25 lb/p/d − 2.10 lb/p/d) =.0075/p/d], we obtain an estimate of area *bah* equal to $\$0.0022/p/d$. Finally we add the lightly shaded area *fbhg*, the increase in fee payments on the quantity remaining after the price increase [(\$0.08 − \$0.05)(2.10 lb/p/d) = 0.063/p/d], to provide an estimate of overall loss in consumer surplus equal to $\$0.0652/p/d$.[12] For a town with a population of 100,000, the consumer surplus lost annually would be $2.38 million, which is slightly larger than if one assumes a linear demand curve.

A complication arises when we wish to use an elasticity estimated from a constant elasticity functional form to predict the effect of raising a price from zero to some positive level. As the constant elasticity demand curve is inconsistent with an observation of zero price, there is no fully satisfactory way to make use of the elasticity estimate. We are forced to postulate some other functional form that goes through the status quo point where price equals zero and use the constant elasticity estimate as a rough guide for specifying its parameters. This expediency should be thought of as an informed guess that can serve as the starting point for sensitivity analysis.

4.2   Extrapolating from a Few Observations

Recent policy or other fortuitous changes (at least from the analyst's perspective) sometimes provide a basis for predicting the impacts of future policy changes. For example, imagine that the Metropolitan Transit Authority (MTA) for a small city faces a large budget deficit for the coming year. To reduce the deficit, the MTA is considering increasing the bus fare from the current $1.25 to $1.75 per ride. A few years ago, the

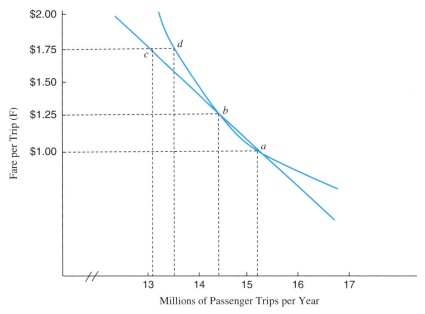

Figure 4.3 Imputing a demand curve from two points.

MTA increased the fare from $1.00 to the current fare. How could analysts use the impact of the last price increase as a guide for predicting the impact of the proposed increase?

Lacking any better information, the MTA analysts might treat the earlier fare increase as if it were a treatment in a simple "before and after" quasi-experimental design. (See Chapter 14.) If the increase in the fare from $1.00 to $1.25 per trip decreased the annual number of trips from 15.2 million to 14.5 million, then a reasonable starting point would be to assume a linear relationship between fare and the quantity of trips. Figure 4.3 shows the fare and annual number of trips before the price increase at point *a* and the fare and annual number of trips after the price increase at point *b*. A straight line through these two points has the following equation with quantity measured in millions:

$$q_{trips} = 18 - 2.8F \tag{4.7}$$

where *F* is the fare. For the proposed fare of $1.75, this equation predicts the number of annual trips would fall to 13.1 million, which is shown as point *c* in Figure 4.3.

The MTA analysts could have assumed some other functional form. For example, they could have fit a constant elasticity demand curve to the two observed points. A constant elasticity function through the two points would have the following equation with quantity measured in millions:[13]

$$q_{trips} = 15.2F^{-0.2} \tag{4.8}$$

For the proposed fare of $1.75, this equation predicts the number of annual trips would fall to 13.6 million, which is shown as point *d* in Figure 4.3. Thus, these alternative assumptions about functional form yield predictions that differ by a half-million trips per year.

Note that in this particular case, the linear and constant elasticity demand curves are close together over the observed range. Measuring a change in social surplus over this range, say to assess a rollback of the fare to $1.00, would be similar using either functional form. However, the equations are being used to make "out of sample" predictions beyond the previously observed values of ridership and fare. Figure 4.3 illustrates an important point: *the further analysts extrapolate from past experience, the more sensitive are their predictions to assumptions about functional form.* In the absence of theoretical guidance or other empirical evidence, analysts have no basis for choosing between the two widely different predictions. Analysts typically confront their uncertainty about functional form in sensitivity analysis as discussed in Chapter 11.

A second consideration concerns the validity of attributing the change in the outcome to the change in the policy variable. Analysts are implicitly assuming that no other variable of relevance to the outcome changed during the time period under consideration. It is possible, for example, that some of the decline in bus ridership after the observed price increase resulted from the opening of a new highway that made commuting by automobile more convenient. If this were the case, then it is unlikely that a similar further change in the fare would produce as large a reduction in ridership as predicted by either functional form.

4.3   Econometric Estimation with Many Observations

If many observations of quantities demanded at different prices are available, then it may be possible to use econometric techniques to estimate demand functions. The linear regression model typically serves as the starting point for such efforts. We assume here that the reader is familiar with the basic concepts of linear regression. Readers unfamiliar with these concepts, or desiring to review them, should read Appendix 4A. Readers requiring a fuller treatment should consult a basic econometrics text.[14]

4.3.1   *Model Specification*

The starting point for econometric estimation of demand functions is to specify the important explanatory (or independent) variables, such as price and income, that affect the quantity demanded and the functional form of the relationship.[15] For example, we may have theoretical reasons to believe that the demand for a particular good, q, is a function of the price of that good, p, income, I, and temperature, T:

$$q = f(p, I, T) \qquad (4.9)$$

The functional form, represented by f, may be linear, linear in logarithms, or have some other form.

Sometimes the set of explanatory variables varies slightly from one study to another. The model should include all variables that affect demand in theory. Even though we may not have a substantive interest in some of the explanatory variables, such as temperature, they should be included to "control" for their effects on the dependent variable and thereby allow us to isolate the *independent effects* of the variables of interest, such as price and income. For example, and returning to waste disposal, a study by James Strathman, Anthony Rufolo, and Gerard Mildner assumed that the demand for waste disposal depended on the tipping fee, manufacturing income, and construction employment.[16] In their study, construction employment was included as a control variable.

In practice, the set of included explanatory variables is usually limited for four reasons. First, measures of variables may not be available at reasonable cost. For example, the demand for waste disposal may depend on attitudes toward recycling that we cannot measure without a costly specialized survey. Second, some variables may have relatively small expected effects. For example, temperature may be anticipated to have only a small effect on the demand for a good. Third, a variable may be excluded because it is too highly correlated with other explanatory variables – the problem of *multicollinearity*, which we discuss in Appendix 4A. Fourth, the number of observations may be small so that additional variables noticeably reduce the "degrees of freedom" that help determine the precision of estimates.

The seriousness of excluding a theoretically important variable depends on two factors. First, it depends on the degree to which the excluded variable is correlated with an included variable of interest – one whose coefficient we require for predicting policy effects.[17] The higher the correlation, the greater is the bias in the estimated coefficient of the included variable.[18] Bias results because the estimated coefficient would incorporate part of the effect of the excluded variable with which it is correlated. Second, it depends on the true coefficient of the excluded variable if it were included. If this coefficient is very small, then the bias from excluding it is likely to be small.

After identifying the theoretically important and practically available variables, the next task is to specify the functional form of the model. As previously discussed, linear and constant elasticity forms are the most commonly used. Sometimes we have theoretical reasons for choosing between them; other times we simply see which fits the observed data better.

Assuming the model represented by Equation (4.9) has a linear functional form gives the following model:

$$q = \alpha_0 + \alpha_p p + \alpha_I I + \alpha_T T + \varepsilon \qquad (4.10)$$

where ε denotes an error term that captures the effect of unmeasured variables on q. This model can be estimated by *ordinary least squares* (OLS), assuming no simultaneity (i.e., identification) problem, which we discuss later.

A linear model may still contain non-linear functions of the explanatory variables. For example, by adding the square of temperature as an explanatory variable along with temperature itself, we allow for a non-linear relationship between the quantity demanded and temperature. We can also allow for the possibility of different demand curves for different subgroups in our sample by introducing interaction terms. For example, if we have individual-level data and we suspect that men have a steeper demand curve than women, we could include a new variable that is the product of price and the dummy variable (or indicator variable) for gender (e.g., "0" for men and "1" for women) along with the variables used to construct the interaction. We would then interpret the coefficient of price as the slope of the demand curve for men, and the sum of the coefficient of the price variable and the coefficient of the price–gender interaction variable as the slope of the demand curve for women. The general point is that we can have quite complicated functional forms within the basic linear specification that can be estimated by OLS.

Assuming a constant elasticity functional form gives the following model:

$$q = \beta_0 p^{\beta_p} I^{\beta_I} T^{\beta_T} e^{\varepsilon} \tag{4.11}$$

where the βs are parameters to be estimated, e is the base of the natural logarithm, and ε is the unobserved random error. Taking the natural logarithm of both sides of this equation gives:

$$\ln q = \ln \beta_0 + \beta_p \ln p + \beta_I \ln I + \beta_T \ln T + \varepsilon \tag{4.12}$$

This "linearized" model can be estimated by OLS with $\ln q$ as the dependent variable and $\ln p$, $\ln I$, and $\ln T$ as explanatory variables. The parameters, the βs, can be interpreted in the standard way, noting that the intercept is an estimate of $\ln \beta_0$ rather than β_0. The coefficient of the variable $\ln p$ is the price elasticity of demand, and the coefficient of the variable $\ln I$ is the income elasticity of demand.

<table>
<tr><td>4.3.2</td><td>*Types of Data*</td></tr>
</table>

Data availability is usually the limiting factor in estimating demand curves. Analysts sometimes have sufficient resources to assemble their own data. More often, however, resource limitations force them to rely on *convenience samples*, that is, data that happen to be available at acceptable cost. These include previously published data, data collected by researchers for other purposes, and samples of administrative records for program clients. Nevertheless, it is worthwhile briefly reviewing the major considerations in the choice of data and their implications for demand function estimation.

Level of Aggregation. The first major consideration is the level of aggregation. Individual-level data measure the behavior of persons, families, households, or other consuming units. Aggregate-level data measure the combined (aggregate) behavior of groups of consumers, usually organized by geographic jurisdictions or demographic characteristics.

Consumer theory is based on models of individual utility maximization. Individual-level data are generally preferable because they provide a close congruence between theory and data. Furthermore, theoretically important variables, such as income, can often be measured directly with individual-level data. In contrast, when using aggregate-level data, a mean or median typically serves as the measure of income.

In using aggregate data, there is a risk of making serious errors about the effects of policy-relevant variables on demand. For example, suppose that we use individual-level data from different states to estimate the price elasticity of demand for each state. Further suppose, as expected, each of these price elasticity estimates is negative. Now suppose that another less-fortunate analyst has only aggregate-level data that consist of one observation for each state (such as the average price and average quantity demanded in each state). She might hope that her estimated price elasticity is approximately a weighted average of the price elasticities of demand for each state and that her estimates of the effects of price changes are reasonably accurate. It is possible, however, that her estimated price elasticity is very different from the price elasticities that we estimate for each state. In fact, depending on the aggregate-level price and quantity observations, it could have the wrong sign.[19]

In practice, however, individual-level data are often not available. For example, in estimating the "demand" for criminal acts, an important theoretical variable is the "price," which depends on the perceived probability of arrest. We cannot directly observe the probability of arrest perceived by an individual, but we can assume that it is related to the objective (group) probability, which can be estimated as the fraction of crimes that result in arrest within a region or among a group of individuals. Perceived probabilities of arrest, however, almost certainly deviate somewhat from the objective probability, introducing measurement error that likely biases the estimated effect of the probability of arrest toward zero.

Cross-sectional Data versus Time Series Data. The second major consideration in selecting data concerns the choice between cross-sectional data and time series data. A cross-section involves observations on a number of comparable units at the same point in time, whereas a time series involves making repeated observations on the same unit at several points in time. For example, if we wished to determine the price elasticity of demand for wine, we might take advantage of different excise tax rates across different states. Using observations for each of the 50 states for a particular year, we would regress per-capita consumption of wine on after-tax retail prices and other explanatory variables, such as average state levels of income and education. Alternatively, if the real price of wine has varied over time, we might estimate a price elasticity by regressing national per-capita consumption in each year on the real price of wine in each year and other variables, such as real per-capita income in each year. Cross-sectional and time series data are prone to different types of econometric problems and yield coefficient estimates that have somewhat different interpretations.

Cross-sectional data generally provide estimates of long-run elasticities, whereas time series data usually provide estimates of short-run elasticities. In estimating elasticities from cross-sections, we usually assume that the variations in demands across units reflect long-run adjustments to previous price changes. Thus, we obtain estimates of long-run elasticities. In estimating elasticities from time series data, we observe responses to price changes occurring as frequently as the time unit of the observations. Thus, annual data provide estimates of annual elasticities, and monthly data provide estimates of monthly elasticities. For most goods, monthly elasticities would be interpreted as short-run. Annual elasticities, however, may be either short-run or long-run, depending on the extent to which full adjustment to price changes requires changes in capital goods, location, and other factors that consumers alter gradually.

We would expect short-run price elasticities to be smaller in absolute value than long-run price elasticities because, by definition, there is less time for consumers to adjust to price changes. Indeed, based on a review of 120 empirical studies, Molly Espy found an average short-run price elasticity of demand for gasoline of −0.26 and an average long-run price elasticity of −0.58, and an average short-run income elasticity of 0.47 and an average long-run income elasticity of 0.88.[20] P. B. Goodwin reviewed 120 empirical studies and reported average elasticities of the demand for automobile "traffic" with respect to motor fuel prices that were −0.16 in the short run and −0.33 in the long run.[21]

Cross-section and time series data tend to suffer from different econometric problems. Cross-sections, especially when they consist of units of different sizes, often have error terms with different variances – the *heteroscedasticity* problem. For example, the variance in the number of accidental deaths from fire is likely to be larger among larger cities, such as New York City, than among smaller cities, such as Utica, New York. If the variances of the error terms are unequal, then the OLS estimates of the coefficients are unbiased, but their calculated standard errors are smaller than the true standard errors. That is, the reported precision of OLS estimates would be overly optimistic. If the relative sizes of the variances of the error terms were known, then estimating the model by *generalized least squares* (GLS) would give more precise estimates of the coefficients. Discussions of tests for detecting heteroscedasticity and for appropriate estimation procedures can be found in most econometrics texts.

Time series data also suffer from a common problem with the error term. Remember that the effects of excluded explanatory variables are incorporated into the error term. If an excluded variable tends to change gradually over time, then it may produce correlation between successive error terms. This is one example of the more general problem of *autocorrelation*, which often exists in one form or another in time series data. It has similar effects to heteroscedasticity: OLS coefficient estimates, although unbiased, are not as precise as reported. More precise estimates can be obtained by using GLS if the pattern of the autocorrelation is known. The most widely used test for autocorrelation is the Durbin–Watson statistic, which should always be a component of time series analysis. Again, discussions of methods for detecting autocorrelation and correcting for it can be found in econometrics texts.

It is also possible to pool cross-sectional and time series data into a panel, for example, by using data from each state for each of a number of years. Although modeling with panel data can be quite complex and cannot be discussed here, three points are worth noting. First, panel data provide a rich source of information. Second, panel data are vulnerable to the econometric problems encountered with both cross-sectional and time series data. Third, panel data may help identify causal effects by allowing researchers to control for unmeasured variables that affect all the units in the cross-section.

4.3.3   *Identification*

In a perfectly competitive market, price and quantity result from the simultaneous interaction of supply and demand. Changes in price and quantity can result from shifts in the supply curve, shifts in the demand curve, or both. In the absence of variables that affect only one side of the market, it may not be possible to estimate separately the supply and demand curves. Indeed, if quantity supplied and quantity demanded depended only on price, then the equations for estimating both the demand curve and the supply curve would look identical. Determining whether we are estimating a demand curve or a supply curve is one example of the problem of *identification*. It occurs in multiple equation models in which some variables, such as price and quantity, are determined simultaneously. Such variables are called *endogenous variables*. In contrast, variables that are fixed or are determined outside of the model are called *exogenous variables*.

In order to identify a demand curve we need to have a variable that affects supply but not demand. Consider a competitive and unregulated market for wheat. If rainfall affects the supply of wheat but not the demand for wheat, then including rainfall in the supply equation but not in the demand equation identifies the demand equation. The reason is that changes in rainfall result in systematic shifts in supply but not demand, which will trace out the demand curve. Similarly, if income affects demand but not supply, then including income in the demand equation but not in the supply equation allows us to examine systematic shifts in the demand curve, which will trace out the supply curve. In general, a two-equation model will be identified if there is one exogenous variable that belongs in the first equation but not in the second, and another exogenous variable that belongs in the second equation but not in the first. By "belong," we mean that it has a non-zero coefficient; by "not belong," we mean that it theoretically has a zero coefficient. The zero coefficient conditions are most important. One cannot identify a model by excluding an exogenous variable from an equation that theoretically belongs in that equation.

Identification of demand curves tends to be less of a problem in the markets typically of interest in cost–benefit analysis than in markets generally. One reason is that CBA often deals with markets that are subject to exogenous government interventions. For example, the demand for cigarettes is probably easily identified in cross-sectional analysis because differences in state excise taxes shift the supply curve by a different amount in each state.

Another reason is that the identification problem does not arise in markets where the price is set exogenously. In some markets of interest to cost–benefit analysts, the government either provides the product or service, as is often the case with municipal waste disposal, or regulates the prices charged, as is the case with electricity. When government supplies a good or effectively sets price, price is exogenous, and we avoid the identification problem.

Although generally not applicable to the estimation of market demand curves, researches can sometimes identify policy effects through *natural experiments*, in which fortuitous random, or nearly random, events mimic true experiments that provide causal estimates of policy impacts.[22] Nearly random assignment may occur because of administrative rules that result in nearly identical units being above or below some arbitrary threshold. Such *regression discontinuities* may result in similar units around the threshold either receiving or not receiving the policy "treatment" in a nearly random way. For example, the federal government provided technical assistance to the 300 poorest counties in the United States to help them apply for participation in the newly created Head Start Program. As a result, counties slightly richer than the cut-off were much less likely to participate in the program than counties slightly poorer. Treating these counties as effectively equivalent allowed researchers to treat them as if they had been randomly assigned to the program and infer that an increase in funding for Head Start by from 50 to 100 percent reduced mortality from relevant causes by 33 to 50 percent.[23]

4.3.4   *Confidence Intervals*

The standard errors of the estimated coefficients of a model can be used to construct confidence intervals for the coefficients. A 95 percent confidence interval is commonly interpreted as there being a 95 percent chance that the true value of the coefficient lies within the interval. Strictly speaking, this is an incorrect interpretation. The correct interpretation is that if we were to repeat our estimation procedure many times, with a new data sample for each repetition, the estimated confidence intervals would contain the true value of the coefficient in about 95 percent of the repetitions. Nevertheless, confidence intervals provide some guidance for sensitivity analysis. Most analysts would consider it reasonable to treat the ends of a 95 percent confidence interval as best and worst cases. However, as discussed in Chapter 11, the standard errors of slopes, elasticities, or other parameters can be used directly to guide the selection of probability distributions in sensitivity analyses based on Monte Carlo simulations.

4.3.5   *Prediction versus Hypothesis Testing*

As a final topic on estimating demand functions, it is important to keep in mind the distinction between hypothesis testing and estimation. Social scientists are typically interested in testing hypotheses about one or more coefficients in a regression model. If the estimated coefficients are not statistically significantly different from zero, then social scientists do not reject the null hypothesis that the variables have no effect on the dependent variable. In other words, there is not a statistically convincing case that the variables have any effect.

As cost–benefit analysts, however, we have to make predictions. For such purposes we should use the estimated value of the coefficient, even if it is not statistically significant from zero at conventional levels. Although we may not be very confident that the true value of the coefficient is not zero, the estimated coefficient may be our best estimate of the true value. If so, it will give the best predictions. Sensitivity analysis should reflect the imprecision of our estimate. If we were to use only the statistically significant coefficients from an estimated model, we would bias our prediction and potentially underestimate the variance of our estimate of net benefits. Rather than treating statistically insignificant estimated parameters as if they and their standard errors are zero, using them directly or after statistical adjustment is generally more appropriate to predict net benefits.[24]

4.4   Conclusion

Estimating the net social benefits of policies often requires predictions of change in social surplus. Predicting changes in social surplus in turn requires knowledge of the appropriate market demand and supply curves. This chapter concerns estimation of these curves, focusing on demand curves.

Direct estimation of demand curves is possible if we know at least one point on the demand curve, its functional form, and either its slope or the price elasticity of demand. In many practical situations we do not know the slope or the price elasticity of demand. We may be able to infer such information from a few observations. Preferably, there may be many observations, and the analyst can use econometric techniques to estimate the demand curve. It is important to consider the advantages and potential limitations of these different estimation methods.

APPENDIX 4A

Introduction to Multiple Regression Analysis

Linear regression provides a manageable way to examine statistically the effects of one or more explanatory variables on a variable of interest – the dependent variable.[1] Its use requires us to assume that the effects of the various explanatory variables on the dependent variable are additive; that is, the model has the following functional form:

$$y = \beta_0 + \beta_1 x_1 + \beta_2 x_2 + \ldots + \beta_k x_k + \varepsilon \qquad (4A.1)$$

where y is the dependent variable, $x_1, x_2, \ldots, x_k$ are k explanatory (or independent) variables, $\beta_0, \beta_1, \beta_2, \ldots, \beta_k$ are parameters (coefficients) to be estimated, and ε is an error term that incorporates the cumulative effect on y of all the factors not explicitly included in the model. The basic model assumes that the explanatory variables are non-random and are measured without error.

The intercept parameter, β_0, also called the *constant*, is the expected value of y if all of the explanatory variables equal zero. The other parameters, 1,2, ..., k, which are called slope parameters, measure the marginal impacts of explanatory variables on the dependent variable. If, for instance, we were to increase x_1 by one unit while holding the values of the other explanatory variables constant, then y would change by an amount β_1.

Imagine that we set the values of all the explanatory variables except x_1 equal to zero. We could then plot y against x_1 in a two-dimensional graph. The equation $y = \beta_0 + \beta_1 x_1$ would represent the true regression line. The slope of this line is β_1; it measures the magnitude of the change in y that will result from a one-unit change in x_1. The actual observations will usually not lie exactly on the line. The vertical deviation between an observed point and the line will equal the random error, represented in our model by ε. If the values of ε are small in absolute value, then the true regression line fits the data well in the sense that the actual observations are close to it.

Estimating the Parameters of the Model

The most commonly used procedure for fitting a line to the data is the method of ordinary least squares (OLS). When we have only one explanatory variable so we can plot our data on a two-dimensional graph, the OLS procedure picks the line for which the sum of squared vertical deviations from the estimated line to the observed data is smallest.

Suppose we denote the OLS estimates of the $k + 1$ parameters by "hats": $\hat{\beta}_0, \hat{\beta}_1, \ldots, \hat{\beta}_k$. The $\hat{\beta}_j$ provides an estimate of the change in y due to a small (one unit) change in x_j holding *all other variables constant*. For the ith observation $(y_i, x_{i1}, x_{i2}, \ldots, x_{ik})$, the predicted value of the dependent variable is

$$\hat{y}_i = \hat{\beta}_0 + \hat{\beta}_1 x_{i1} + \hat{\beta}_2 x_{i2} + \ldots + \hat{\beta}_k x_{ik} \quad i = 1, 2, \ldots, n \tag{4A.2}$$

and the ith *prediction error*, or *residual*, is

$$\hat{\varepsilon} = y_i - \hat{y}_i \quad i = 1, 2, \ldots, n \tag{4A.3}$$

Thus, the residual is the observed value of the dependent variable minus the value we would predict for the dependent variable based on our estimated parameters and the values of our explanatory variables. OLS selects the parameter estimates so as to minimize the sum of squares of these residuals.[2]

The square of the correlation between the actual and predicted values of the dependent variable, R^2, is commonly used as a measure of the goodness-of-fit of a regression. Assuming the model includes a constant, the R^2, which ranges between 0 and 1, measures the percentage of variation in the dependent variable that is explained by the estimated model. It can be used to help select between alternative model specifications when theory is ambiguous, or to test alternative theories.

Multicollinearity

As long as the number of observations in our sample exceeds the number of coefficients that we want to estimate, regression software packages will usually enable us to obtain the OLS estimates. However, when one explanatory variable can be written as a linear combination of the others, we have a case of *perfect multicollinearity*, which prevents estimation of the model. A less severe but much more common form of the problem occurs when the explanatory variables in the sample are highly correlated. This condition is called *multicollinearity*. If two or more variables are highly correlated, OLS has difficulty identifying the independent effect of each explanatory variable on the dependent variable. As a result, these parameter estimates are not very reliable or, in the extreme case, they cannot be estimated. When two explanatory variables are highly correlated, the sum of their estimated coefficients will be closer to the sum of their true coefficients than will either individual coefficient estimate be to its true value. Often, researchers respond to a multicollinearity problem by excluding one or more explanatory variables, although this may lead to biased estimates of some parameters. Two alternative ways to deal with multicollinearity problems include using ridge regression or combining collinear variables into indices using principal components analysis.[3]

Properties of OLS Estimators

The OLS estimator will generally have a number of very desirable properties. (*Note*: An *estimator* is the formula we use to calculate a particular parameter from the data. The resultant specific value is an *estimate*.) If all of the explanatory variables are uncorrelated with the error term, ε, and if the expected value of the error term is zero, then the OLS estimators will be *unbiased*. To understand what it means for an estimator to be unbiased, we must keep in mind that a particular estimate depends on the errors in the actual sample of data. If we were to select a new sample, then we would realize different errors and, hence, different coefficient estimates. When an estimator is unbiased, the average of our estimates across different samples will be very close to the true coefficient value. For example, if the price of gasoline had no true effect on the quantity of gasoline demanded, then we would almost certainly estimate its coefficient to be positive or negative rather than exactly zero. Repeating OLS on a large number of samples and averaging our estimates of the coefficient of gasoline price, however, would generally yield a result very close to zero. Indeed, by adding more and more samples, we could get the average as close to zero as we wanted.

The OLS estimator is also consistent because it is unbiased and its variance approaches zero as the sample size is increased.[4] Consequently, as the sample size increases, we become more confident about the accuracy of our estimates – the distribution of the estimator gets tighter around the true value of the parameter being estimated. In the limit, the distribution of the estimator collapses around the true value of the parameter.

A problem arises, however, if an important variable is excluded from the estimation and that variable is correlated with an included variable. Suppose, for example, that the weather (temperature) affects the quantity of gasoline demanded, and that temperature is also correlated with gasoline price, but that temperature is excluded from the model. Now, the coefficient of gasoline price will reflect both the effect of gasoline price on quantity demanded and the indirect effect of temperature for which it serves as a proxy. Other things being equal, the stronger the true effect of temperature on quantity demanded, and the higher the absolute value of the correlation between gasoline price and temperature, the greater will be the bias in the coefficient of gasoline price. This problem cannot be solved by increasing the sample size.

If each error is drawn from a distribution with the same variance, then the OLS estimators will also be efficient in the sense that among the class of unbiased estimators that are linear functions of the dependent variable, the OLS estimators will have the smallest possible variance of any estimators.

Statistical Significance and Hypothesis Testing

It is often important to determine whether an estimate deviates enough from zero for us to conclude that the true value of the parameter is not zero. If we make the reasonable assumption that the error term for each observation can be treated as a draw from a normal distribution with constant variance, σ^2, then we can show that the OLS estimators will be distributed according to the normal distribution.[5] Specifically, we can interpret the particular numerical estimate of a coefficient, $\hat{\beta}$, as a draw from a random variable having a normal distribution centered around the true value of the coefficient, β, with variance, $\sigma_{\hat{\beta}}^2$, which depends on σ^2. (The OLS estimator is the random variable; the actual estimate based on the data is a particular realization of that random variable.) Because we want to know how likely it is that we would observe a coefficient estimate as large as we did if the true value of the coefficient were zero, we now suppose that the true value of the coefficient is zero (the null hypothesis) so that the distribution of our estimator is centered around zero. We then standardize our distribution to have a variance of one by dividing our coefficient estimate by its *estimated standard deviation*. The resultant statistic, called a *t* statistic or *t* ratio, has a *Student's* t *distribution*, or *t* distribution.[6] The *statistical significance* of our coefficient estimate can be determined by comparing the *t* statistic to the critical values in a table of the *t* distribution, which can be found in the appendix of almost any statistics text. For example, we might decide that we will reject the null hypothesis that the true value of the coefficient is zero if there is less than a 5 percent probability of observing a *t* ratio (in absolute value) as large as we did if the null hypothesis is true.[7]

The *t* distribution is tabulated by degrees of freedom. The OLS estimators have degrees of freedom equal to the total number of observations, denoted by n, minus the number of coefficients being estimated, $k + 1$. As the degrees of freedom increase, the Student's *t* distribution looks more like a standardized normal distribution. Regression software packages typically report both the *t* ratio and *p* value, that is, the probability of obtaining a value so large in absolute value if the true value of the parameter is zero.

Returning to our gasoline example, suppose that the analyst wants to test whether gasoline price has a statistically significant effect on gasoline demand at the 5 percent level of significance. She may specify a one-tailed alternative hypothesis test or a two-tailed alternative hypothesis test. For example, she may test the null hypothesis against the alternative that the true coefficient is less than zero (the one-tailed alternative), which means that the *critical region* consists of the entire 5 percent in the negative tail. Alternatively, she may test the null hypothesis against the alternative that the true coefficient value is not equal to zero (the two-tailed alternative), which means that the critical region consists of the 2.5 percent in the negative tail and the 2.5 percent in the positive tail.

Now suppose that the t statistic for the coefficient of gasoline price equals -1.84. Further, suppose that the sample size was 122, and there was only one explanatory variable, so that only two parameters were estimated (the intercept and slope) and there were 120 degrees of freedom. The absolute values of the critical values of the t distribution with 120 degrees of freedom are 1.658 for the one-sided alternative and 1.98 for the two-sided alternative. Thus, at the 5 percent level of significance, the analyst would reject the null hypothesis if she had specified a one-sided alternative, but she would accept the null hypothesis if she had specified a two-sided alternative.

Most regression software saves us the trouble of looking up critical values in tables by directly calculating the probability under the null hypothesis of observing a t statistic as large as that estimated, assuming we want to test the null hypothesis that the true parameter equals zero against a two-sided alternative. To do this classical hypothesis test, we simply see if the reported probability is less than the maximum probability of falsely rejecting the null hypothesis that we are willing to accept – for example, 5 percent. If it is smaller, then we reject the null hypothesis.

Exercises for Chapter 4

1. Consider the example presented in Figure 4.3. Compute the annual loss in consumer surplus for the price increase from $1.25 to $1.75.

    a. Assume a linear demand curve as per equation (4.7)

    b. Assume a constant elasticity demand curve as per equation (4.8)

2. (Regression software required; instructor-provided spreadsheet recommended.) An analyst was asked to predict the gross social benefits of building a public swimming pool in Dryville, which has a population of 70,230 people and a median household income of $31,500. The analyst identified 24 towns in the region that already had public swimming pools. He conducted a telephone interview with the recreation department in each town to find out what fee it charged per visit (Fee) and how many visits it had during the most recent summer season (Visits). In addition, he was able to find each town's population (Pop) and median household income (Income) in the most recent census. His data are as follows:

	Visits	Fee	Income	Pop
1	168,590	0	20,600	36,879
2	179,599	0	33,400	64,520

(continued)

(cont.)

	Visits	Fee	Income	Pop
3	198,595	0	39,700	104,123
4	206,662	0	32,600	103,073
5	170,259	0	24,900	58,386
6	209,995	0.25	38,000	116,592
7	172,018	0.25	26,700	49,945
8	190,802	0.25	20,800	79,789
9	197,019	0.25	26,300	98,234
10	186,515	0.50	35,600	71,762
11	152,679	0.50	38,900	40,178
12	137,423	0.50	21,700	22,928
13	158,056	0.50	37,900	39,031
14	157,424	0.50	35,100	44,685
15	179,490	0.50	35,700	67,882
16	164,657	0.75	22,900	69,625
17	184,428	0.75	38,600	98,408
18	183,822	0.75	20,500	93,429
19	174,510	1.00	39,300	98,077
20	187,820	1.00	25,800	104,068
21	196,318	1.25	23,800	117,940
22	166,694	1.50	34,000	59,757
23	161,716	1.50	29,600	88,305
24	167,505	2.00	33,800	84,102

a. Show how the analyst could use these data to predict the gross benefits of opening a public swimming pool in Dryville and allowing free admission.

b. Predict gross benefits if admission is set at $1.00 and Dryville has marginal excess tax burden of 0.25. In answering this question, assume that the fees are used to reduce taxes that would otherwise have to be collected from the citizens of Dryville to pay for expenses incurred in operating the pool.

Notes

1. More accurately, each household incurs a marginal private cost of refuse disposal that is only $1/n$ of the marginal social costs; that is, $\text{MPC} = \text{MSC}/n$, where n is the number of households. The MPC approaches zero for large n. Such sharing of marginal social cost characterizes common property resources.

2. Robin R. Jenkins, *The Economics of Solid Waste Reduction: The Impact of User Tees* (Brookfield, VT: Edward Elgar Publishing Company, 1993).

3. The Bureau of Labor Statistics provides an on-line calculator to adjust for general price inflation: www.bls.gov/data/inflation_calculator.htm.

4. Rearranging Equation (4.1) gives the following inverse market demand curve:

$$p = -\alpha_0/\alpha_1 + (1/\alpha_1)q$$

The slope of this curve equals $1/\alpha_1$. The intercept, $-\alpha_0/\alpha_1$, indicates the lowest price at which the quantity demanded equals zero; it is sometimes called the *choke price*. For the demand curve shown in Figure 4.1, the inverse demand curve is $p = 14.4 - 5.6q$, and the choke price is \$14.40.

5. Jenkins, *The Economics of Solid Waste Reduction: The Impact of User Tees*, pp. 88–90, 101.

6. A meta-analysis of 25 studies did not find an effect of the availability of curbside recycling on elasticity. However, elasticity does appear to depend on whether fees are based on weight or number of bags as well as by the pricing of compostable waste. Germà Bel and Raymond Gradus, "Effects of Unit-Based Pricing on Household Waste Collection Demand: A Meta-Regression Analysis." *Resource and Energy Economics*, 44(May), 2016, 69–182.

7. Some economists call this functional form a *log-linear demand curve*; others call it a *log-log demand curve* or a *double-log demand curve*. In order to minimize potential confusion, we will not use any of these terms, but will refer to the curve as linear in logarithms.

8. Because β_1 is the slope of the linear in logarithms demand curve, $\beta_1 = \partial \ln q / \partial \ln p$. By definition, the price elasticity of demand $\epsilon_d = \partial \ln q / \partial \ln p$. Consequently, $\epsilon_d = \beta_1$.

9. The slope is given by:

$$\partial q / \partial p = \beta_1 \beta_0 p^{\beta_1-1} = \beta_1 \beta_0 p^{\beta_1} / p = \beta_1 q / p.$$

10. The area is calculated by integrating the inverse demand curve from q_0 and q_1 that is, as $\int p \, dq = \int (q / \beta_0)^{1/\beta_1} dq$ with q_0 and q_1 as the limits of integration.

11. Note that our estimate of $\beta_0 = 1.44$ will generally differ from the original estimate of β_0 obtained by the researchers from whom we took our price elasticity estimate. This difference arises because we force the demand curve to pass through point a, our known data point, whereas the original, estimated equation probably will not pass through point a.

12. The change in consumer surplus is the area under the demand curve between p_0 and p_1 that is, $\int q \, dp = \int \beta_0 p^{\beta_1} dp$ with p_0 and p_1 as the limits of integration.

13. Solve for β_0 and β_1 as follows: $\beta_1 = \ln(q_0/q_1)/\ln(p_0/p_1) = -0.2$ and $\beta_0 = q_0 / p_0^{\beta_1} = 15.2$

14. For an excellent treatment of the econometric issues raised in this section, see William H. Greene, *Econometric Analysis*, 7th edn (Upper Saddle River, NJ: Prentice Hall, 2011).

15. Thus far, this chapter has focused on demand curves that relate quantity demanded to price. Other variables also affect demand. A demand function relates the quantity demanded to price and other variables. Because a demand function is more general than a demand curve, this section focuses on demand functions.

16. They estimated an elasticity of disposal demand with respect to tipping fees of -0.11 for communities in the region around Portland, Oregon, over a seven-year period; see James G. Strathman, Anthony M. Rufolo, and Gerard C. S. Mildner, "The Demand for Solid Waste Disposal." *Land Economics*, 71(1), 1995, 57–64.

17. If the estimated regression equation contains more than one explanatory variable, then the bias in the coefficient of a particular variable depends on the *partial correlation* between that variable and the omitted variable, controlling for all other variables in the regression.

18. If an excluded variable is not correlated with an included variable, then excluding it will not bias the estimated coefficient of the included variable. However, the overall fit of the model, measured by its R^2, will be poorer, and the precision of the estimated coefficients will be lower.

19. See, for example, Henri Theil, *Principles of Econometrics* (New York, NY: Wiley, 1971), 556–57.

20. Molly Espey, "Gasoline Demand Revisited: An International Meta-Analysis of Elasticities." *Energy Economics*, 20(3), 1998, 273–95.

21. P. B. Goodwin, "A Review of New Demand Elasticities with Special Reference to Short and Long Run Effects of Price Changes." *Journal of Transport Economics and Policy*, 26(2), 1992, 155–70 at pp. 158–59. See also Tae Moon Oum, W. G. Waters II, and Jong-Say Yong, "Concepts of Price Elasticities of Transport Demand and Recent Empirical Estimates." *Journal of Transport Economics and Policy*, 26(2), 1992, 139–54.

22. In a true experiments the researcher randomly assigns subjects or other experimental units into treatment and

control groups and controls the treatment (see Chapter 14). Natural experiments involve fortuitously occurring random, or as "good as random," assignment into treatment and control groups, but not direct control of the treatment. See Thad Dunning, *Natural Experiments in the Social Sciences: A Design-Based Approach* (New York, NY: Cambridge University Press, 2012).

23. Jens Ludwig and Douglas L. Miller, "Does Head Start Improve Children's Life Chances? Evidence from a Regression Discontinuity Design." *Quarterly Journal of Economics*, 122(1), 2007, 159–208. For a discussion of the use of Head Start evidence on CBA see Jens Ludwig and Deborah A. Phillips, "Long-Term Effects of Head Start on Low-Income Children." *Annals of the New York Academy of Sciences*, 1136(1), 2008, 257–68.

24. David L. Weimer, "The Thin Reed: Accommodating Weak Evidence for Critical Parameters in Cost–Benefit Analysis." *Risk Analysis*, 35(6), 2015, 1101–13.

Appendix Notes

1. For a clear introduction to regression analysis, see Jeffrey M. Wooldridge, *Introductory Econometrics: A Modern Approach* (Boston, MA: South-Western Publishing, 2000).

2. Formally, OLS minimizes $\sum_{i=1}^{n} \hat{\varepsilon}_b^2$.

3. See Greene, *Econometric Analysis.* For an application that presents both OLS and ridge regression estimates, see A. E. Boardman, S. Miller, and A. P. Schinnar, "Efficient Employment of Cohorts of Labor in the U.S. Economy: An Illustration of a Method." *Socio-Economic Planning Sciences*, 13(6), 1979, 297–302.

4. The OLS estimators are also *efficient.* Here, efficiency means that among all estimators whose formulas are linear in the dependent variable, the OLS estimator has the smallest variance. It therefore has the greatest "power" for rejecting the null hypothesis that a coefficient is zero.

5. *The central limit theorem* tells us that the distribution of the sum of independent random variables approaches the normal distribution as the number in the sum becomes large. The theorem applies for almost any starting distributions with finite variances. If we think of the error term as the sum of all the many factors excluded from our model and, furthermore, we believe that these excluded factors are not systematically related to one another or to the included variables, then the central limit theorem suggests that the distribution of the error terms will be approximately normal.

6. Student is the pseudonym of William Gosset, a quality control engineer at the Guinness Brewery in Dublin, who originally derived the *t* distribution.

7. The probability we choose puts an upward bound on the probability of falsely rejecting the null hypothesis. Falsely rejecting the null hypothesis is referred to as Type I error. Failing to reject the null hypothesis when in fact the alternative hypothesis is true is referred to as Type II error. We usually set the probability of Type I error at some low level, such as 5 percent. Holding the sample size constant, the lower we set the probability of a Type I error, the greater the probability of a Type II error.

Case 4

Use of Demand Schedules in Regulatory Impact Analyses

Although many countries require that proposed regulations be subjected to CBA, the United States does so most extensively in its regulatory process.[1] In 1981 President Ronald Reagan issued an executive order that established the framework for the mandatory use of CBA in the rule-making process by federal agencies.[2] His Executive Order 12291 introduced the Regulatory Impact Analysis (RIA) as a requirement for major rules – those that would have an annual effect on the economy of $100 million or more in terms of costs, benefits, or transfers. Agencies were directed to conduct RIAs to guide selection of rules that offered the largest net benefits. Executive Order 12866 issued by President Bill Clinton extended the definition of major rules. President Barack Obama reaffirmed the RIA process (Executive Order 13563), and required agencies to submit plans to OMB for retrospective RIAs that would review existing rules (Executive Order 13610). He also asked independent agencies with commissioners serving fixed terms, like the Federal Communications Commission or the Nuclear Regulatory Commission, to comply voluntarily with the RIA requirements imposed on cabinet departments (Executive Order 13579).

The number of major federal rules subjected to RIAs each year is large. Over the 10-year period from fiscal year 2005 through fiscal year 2014, the Office of Management and Budget (OMB) reviewed about 3000 RIAs, including 549 required for major rules.[3] The 120 RIAs that monetized costs and benefits for major rules predicted aggregate annual benefits of between $260.9 billion and $981.0 billion and annual costs of between $68.4 billion and $102.9 billion (2010 dollars). These large amounts show both the extensive role of regulation in the US economy and the substantial analytical resources marshalled in the efforts to make them more efficient.

Most RIAs do not directly measure changes in consumer and producer surplus. Rather, they do so indirectly by applying "shadow prices," imputed marginal valuations, to predicted impacts. Measurement of costs and benefits involves predicting impacts, such as reduced mortality from exposure to a carcinogenic chemical, and then monetizing these predictions with estimates of how people value reductions in mortality risk derived from observing their behavior when they face other trade-offs between risk and things they value, such as wages or time. However, in some RIAs, analysts do value costs and benefits directly in terms of changes in social surplus. We present here cases drawn from two substantial RIAs that do estimate consumer surplus. In the first example, analysts predicted net changes in consumer surplus resulting from tightening requirements for organic labeling that would induce some current sellers in the organic egg market to shift supply to the related cage-free egg market. In the second example, analysts used information from a variety of sources to "construct" a market for public swimming pool use by the wheelchair-bound in order to predict the value of rules that make the pools more accessible to the disabled.

Spillovers between Markets: 2017 Organic Food Production Rulemakings

The Organic Foods Production Act of 1990 (P.L. 101–624) authorizes the United States Department of Agriculture's Agricultural Marketing Service (AMS) to create and establish standards for a national organic certification program. Producers who meet these standards are allowed to advertise their goods as USDA organic products. In 2016, the AMS published a notice of proposed rulemaking to clarify rules and to add new provisions pertaining to livestock handling and avian living conditions.[4] The AMS noted the wide disparities in how producers comply with the outdoor access requirement for organic poultry certification. The AMS argued that these disparities undermine consumer confidence in the USDA organic designation. A final rule was adopted in 2017 with some regulations going into effect on March 20, 2017.[5] The final RIA was published concurrently with the final rule.[6] The discussion that follows focuses on the predicted effect of the more stringent requirement for outdoor space for layers (chickens kept to produce eggs in contrast to broilers raised for meat) on egg consumers.

The analysts faced the task of predicting what fraction of the current organic egg producers would find the outdoor space requirements too costly to meet and as a consequence leave the market. At one extreme, the analysts assumed that all current organic egg producers would meet the new requirements and stay in the market. Under this scenario, they estimated the cost of the rule as the additional real costs borne by the existing producers. At the other extreme, they assumed that 50 percent of the current organic egg producers would leave the market. In particular, as they already meet the requirements for cage-free eggs, the analysts assumed that these producers would simply switch their sales to that market. We discuss how the analysts valued this "spillover" scenario.

The starting point for the analysts was baseline predictions of prices and quantities of eggs in the organic and cage-free egg markets in future years in the absence of the new regulations. The analysts estimated compound growth rates for quantity and price in each of these markets for the 10-year period from 2007 to 2016. Both markets showed similar growth rates in quantity and nominal prices. Of particular relevance, the analysts predicted that in the absence of the regulation the quantity of eggs offered in the cage-free market would grow from 460.4 million dozen in 2016 to 1005.2 million dozen in 2022 and the quantity of eggs offered in the organic market would grow from 325.8 million dozen in 2016 to 667.6 million dozen in 2022. Over the same period, the analysts predicted that the average price per dozen would grow from $3.16 to $3.78 per dozen in the cage-free market and from $3.93 to $4.50 per dozen in the organic market. These projections along with those for other years from 2017 through 2029, the 13-year period over which layer houses are fully depreciated, provided the base case against which the incremental impacts of the outdoor space requirements were assessed.

In order to predict the impact of production moving from the organic market to the cage-free market, analysts needed to estimate the price elasticity of demand in each market. They were able to find several estimates for the organic market. They relied most heavily on a study that estimated demand elasticities for eggs with different attributes, such as brand name, egg size, package quantity, and labeled attributes such as organic.[7] The study offered several advantages. It was based on national data collected between April 2008 and March 2010 from supermarket scanners for over 2000 individual products with different combinations of attributes. The purchase data were augmented with monthly prices for inputs to production that could serve as instrumental variables to address the inherent endogeneity of price and quantity in a demand equation.[8] The study reported a price elasticity of demand for organic eggs of approximate –1.1. That is, a 1 percent increase (decrease) in price appears to reduce (increase) the quantity demand by 1.1 percent. The analysts ultimately considered elasticities from –1.25 to –0.50 in their estimates of consumer surplus changes.

The study did not, however, report a price elasticity of demand for cage-free eggs. Although another study based on data from two markets (San Francisco and Dallas) did report price elasticities for cage-free eggs that were twice the magnitude of elasticities for organic eggs,[9] the analysts decided to assume that the elasticities are the same. As using a less-elastic demand (larger absolute value of elasticity) for cage-free eggs than for organic eggs would substantially increase the estimated gain in consumer surplus from spillover, the decision to treat the two elasticities as equal is a conservative assumption in terms of estimating net benefits.

The rule provides a five-year phase-in. Consequently, 2022 would be the first year in which current organic producers who choose not to meet the higher standards would leave that market and by assumption switch to the less lucrative cage-free market. The analysts presented sample calculations, summarized in Table 4A.1, showing the impact of switching 50 percent of the 2017 organic production to the cage-free market in 2022.

Table 4A.1 *Egg Prices and Consumer Surplus Change in 2022*

Elasticity	Organic price ($/dozen)	Change in surplus ($million)	Cage-free price ($/dozen)	Change in surplus ($million)	Aggregate change ($million)
Baseline	$4.50	$0.00	$3.78	$0.00	$0.00
−1.25	$6.05	−$891.19	$2.92	$946.26	$55.07
−1.00	$5.74	−$712.95	$3.09	$757.01	$44.06
−0.75	$5.43	−$534.71	$3.26	$567.75	$33.04
−.50	$5.12	−$356.47	$3.43	$378.50	$22.03

Source: Department of Agriculture: Agricultural Marketing Service, *Regulatory Impact Analysis and Final Regulatory Flexibility Analysis, Final Report*, January 2017, table 4, p. 48.

The steps in the calculation are as follows:

First, the scenario assumes that 50 percent of the 2017 organic production will be switched to supply in the cage-free market in 2022. Thus, relative to the base case of 667.6 million dozen, the supply in the organic market in 2022 would be 484.0 million dozen, the base case projection of 667.6 million dozen minus the lost spillover of 183.6 million dozen (one-half of the 2017 production by "legacy producers," those in the organic market when the regulation would take effect). Relative to the base case supply of 1,005.2 million dozen in the cage-free market in 2022, supply in the cage-free market would be 1,188.8 million dozen, the base case projection of 1,005.2 million dozen plus the gained spillover of 183.6 million.

Second, the scenario predicts prices in these markets in 2022 using an assumed elasticity. The organic price is predicted to increase as a result of decreased supply from legacy producers. Assuming a price elasticity of demand of −1.0, prices are predicted to increase in the organic egg market by $1.24 per dozen, from a base price of $4.50 per dozen to a price with spillovers of $5.74 per dozen. In the cage-free market, prices are predicted to decrease as a result of the increased supply from producers who switch over to the cage-free market. Relative to the base case price of $3.78 per dozen, prices in the cage-free market would decrease by $0.69 per dozen to $3.09 per dozen.

Third, the analysts assumed a linear demand function in each market to predict consumer surplus changes.[10] The loss in consumer surplus in the organic market is the sum of the greater expenditure on infra-marginal consumption (the quantity that consumers continue to buy) and the loss of surplus from reduced consumption equal to 1/2 the product of the increase in price times the reduction in quantity – the sum of the shaded rectangle and shaded triangle in shown in Figure 3.2(b). The gain in consumer surplus in the cage-free market is the sum of the smaller expenditure on infra-marginal consumption (the quantity that consumers bought previously and continue to buy) and the value of increased consumption equal to 1/2 the product of the decrease in price times the increase in quantity – the sum of the shaded rectangle and shaded triangle shown in Figure 3.2(a). The magnitudes of consumer surplus changes depend on the assumed price elasticity of demand. Assuming an elasticity of −1, the change in consumer surplus in the organic market is −$713 million. In the cage-free market, the change in consumer surplus is $757 million. The change in aggregate consumer surplus, the sum of the change in consumer surplus in both the organic and cage-free market, is a gain of $44 million. The larger magnitude of consumer surplus change in the cage-free market results from the much larger size of its infra-marginal consumption compared to the organic market.

The analysts estimated the net cost of the rule under this scenario to be the increased real resource costs for the 50 percent of the legacy producers who stay in the organic market plus the change in consumer surplus resulting from the spillover of production of the other 50 percent of legacy producers to the cage-free market. Similar calculations were done for successive years and were discounted back to 2016 using the rates of 3 and 7 percent recommended by OMB.

The cost estimates resulting from the spillover analysis are incomplete, however, because they ignore changes in producer surplus. It is most reasonable to assume that the loss in consumer surplus on infra-marginal consumption in the organic market would be offset by increased producer surplus. Again, assuming an elasticity of –1.0 in each market, the social surplus loss from reduced consumption in the organic market would be (.5) ($1.24 per dozen)(183.6 million dozen) = $114 million.

To estimate the gain in social surplus in the cage-free market the price elasticity of supply must be taken into account – the lower price resulting from the influx of supply is likely to drive some of the firms that supplied cage-free eggs before the rule out of the market. For purposes of illustration, assume that the supply elasticity is 0.5. Using the predicted pre-rule price of $3.78 and quantity of 1005.2 million dozen in Equation (4.3) implies a slope of the supply schedule equal to 133 million dozen/dollar. (A similar calculation yields a slope of –266 million dozen/dollar as the slope of the demand schedule when the price elasticity of demand is assumed to be –1.0.)

Figure C4.1 shows the demand schedule in the cage-free market as D_0 and the pre-rule supply schedule as S_0, which intersect at point a. The spillover in supply from the organic market induced by the rule shifts the supply schedule horizontally by 183.6 million dozen to S_1. The post-rule equilibrium price and quantity, $3.32 and 1127.6 million dozen, occur at the intersection of D_0 and S_1, which is labeled b. Note that taking account of the upward-sloping supply schedule results in a smaller price decrease and a smaller quantity increase than assumed in the RIA. The change in social surplus in the market is represented by the area of triangle abc, which equals (0.5)($3.78 – $3.32)(1127.6 million dozen – 1005.2 million dozen), or $28 million. (Note that the rectangle bounded by the prices and points a and c represents a gain in consumer surplus exactly offset by a loss in producer surplus.) Thus, rather than the spillover resulting in a net gain of $44 million, it actually results in a net loss of $86 million ($114 million – $28 million).

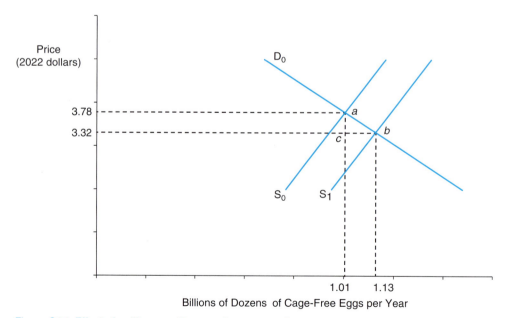

Figure C4.1 Effect of spillover on the cage-free egg market.

It should not be surprising that taking account of social surplus rather than just consumer surplus indicates a loss from induced spillover: both the organic and cage-free markets are themselves assumed to be efficient, so it should not be possible to increase social surplus by shifting supply from one of the markets to the other. It is surprising that the critics of the rule did not challenge this aspect of the RIA! Nonetheless, despite the analysts' omission of producer surplus, the case shows the process of interpreting policy impacts in terms of markets, drawing on empirical evidence to position demand curves within the markets, and valuing the impacts in terms of changes in consumer surplus.

"Constructing" Demand Schedules to Measure Benefits: 2010 ADA Rules

The Americans with Disability Act of 1990 (PL 101–336) was adopted to eliminate discrimination against people with disabilities and major implementing regulations followed in 1991. The Department of Justice published a notice of proposed rule-making to begin the process of updating and strengthening the regulations in 2004.[11] It also set out how it would conduct an RIA to assess the costs and benefits of proposed rules to comply with relevant executive orders. After obtaining feedback, the Department published a notice of a final proposed rule in 2008.[12] Simultaneously, the Department posted on its website an initial RIA conducted for it by HDR/HLB Decision Economics, Inc. for review by interested parties. The final rules, which have the effect of law, were published in 2010,[13] together with the final version of the RIA.[14]

The RIA estimated costs and benefits of the rules for 68 different types of facilities. A major monetized benefit estimated for each type of facility was the estimated

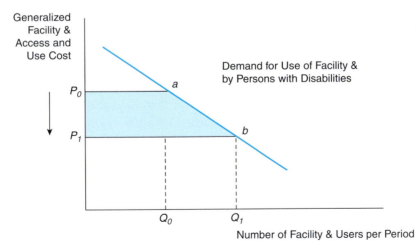

Figure ES-1 Economic framework for estimating benefits from changes in access time.
Source: Department of Justice: Disability Rights Section of the Civil Rights Division, *Final Regulatory Impact Analysis of the Final Revised Regulations Implementing Titles II and III of the ADA, Including Revised ADA Standards for Accessible Design, Final Report*, July 23, 2010, p. xvii.

increase in consumer surplus that would result from reductions in the "generalized facility access and use cost." That benefit category represents an estimate of the reduced cost (a benefit) disabled consumers would incur to use of these facilities because of a lower expenditure of time. The RIA illustrated this approach for some facility k in Figure ES-1.

The analysts drew on a variety of sources to specify plausible values of Q_0, and Q_1 and the difference in the values of P_0 and P_1, in order to predict the changes in consumer surplus that would result from the new regulations. In addition to economic activity data and published estimates of the price elasticity of demand, they used information about the impacts of particular regulations supplied by panels made up of disability experts and disabled persons.

The starting point for estimating Q_0 is typically the number of units of the good consumed annually. The next step is to apply both an income adjustment (IA) and an "ease of access" adjustment (EOA) to the initial number. The IA is a percentage adjustment that takes account of the generally lower income of the disabled. The EOA is a percentage reduction to take account of the difficulty of accessing the facility for the disabled prior to implementation of the rule. The final step is to multiply the adjusted total quantity by the fraction of the population with the disability.

As an example, consider Requirement 79, which sought to ensure more accessible means of entry to privately owned swimming pools to facilitate use by those with ambulatory disabilities. Based on average price of entry for commercial facilities and the total annual revenue of such facilities, the analysts estimated the total number of swimming pool visits in the United States to be about 401 million annually. Applying an IA adjustment of 60 percent and an EOA adjustment of 60 percent resulted in an adjusted total of 144.4 million. Assuming a rate of 11.9 percent of ambulatory disability, leads to an estimated total number of 17.18 million uses of pools by those with the relevant disabilities. This 17.18 million consists of 15.16 million uses by the non-wheelchair ambulatory disabled and 2.02 million uses by the disabled in wheelchairs. Although benefits were calculated for each of these types of use, in this case example we focus on use by disabled in wheelchairs, so that $Q_0 = 2.02$ million uses.

The first step in predicting Q_1 is to calculate the time savings from Requirement 79, and other requirements at pools that would reduce time costs for the ambulatory disabled. An expert panel estimated the direct time-savings from Requirement 79 to be 0.27 hours. This number was further adjusted for estimates of the fraction of users who would likely benefit from the requirement, the likelihood that the requirement would be in place, and the number of uses per visit. These adjustments resulted in an estimate of 14.1 minutes of time saved per visit. Following a similar procedure for 18 other requirements relevant to visits to pools resulted in a total time savings of about 43 minutes for all the ambulatory disabled (that is, the wheelchair and the non-wheelchair ambulatory disabled). Assuming a value of time of $10 per hour implies that the new requirements result in a reduction of the total "price" of pool use seen by the ambulatory disabled of $7.10 dollars.

The next step requires the price elasticity of demand. As no useful estimates of pool-use elasticity could be found in the research literature, the analysts used an estimate of the elasticity for recreation in general, 0.813.[15] This elasticity implies a slope of 0.164 million visits per dollar change in price for wheelchair disabled if one ignores changes in EOA. To take account of the assumption that the requirement would raise the EOA from 60 percent to 100 percent, the analysts multiplied this slope by the ratio of the new-to-original EOA to obtain a slope of 0.274 million uses per dollar for the wheelchair disabled. (A similar procedure resulted in a slope of 2.05 million uses per dollar for non-wheelchair ambulatory disabled.)

Finally, the increase in quantities demanded can be obtained by multiplying the price decrease by the slope of the demand schedule. This resulted in increases in use of 1.95 million and 14.56 million uses for the wheelchair and non-wheelchair disabled, respectively. Adding these amounts to the initial quantities of uses yields $Q_1 = 3.97$ million for the wheelchair disabled and $Q_1 = 29.72$ million for the non-wheelchair ambulatory disabled.

The annual gain in consumer surplus for the wheelchair disabled would equal the area of rectangle in the figure representing the lower cost for existing use ($7.10 × 2.02 million = $14.3 million) plus the area of the triangle representing the increased surplus from new use (.5 × $7.10 × 1.95 = $6.9 million) for a total of $21.2 million.

Exercises for Chapter 4 Case Study

1. (Instructor-provided spreadsheet recommended.) Figure C4.1 shows the effect of adding 183.6 million dozen eggs to the cage free market assuming a price elasticity of supply of 0.5. Recalculate the equilibrium price and quantity and the change in social surplus assuming a price elasticity of supply 0.75.

2. An overlook in the state's Scenic Park offers a spectacular view of Angel's Lake and the surrounding countryside. The overlook is accessible to people in wheelchairs by a special park bus that takes about 60 minutes to reach the overlook. The overlook is accessible to people not in wheelchairs by a tram that takes 15 minutes to reach the overlook. During the most recent park season, 600 people in wheelchairs visited the park. A local economist has estimated that the demand schedule for overlook visits by people in wheelchairs is linear and has a price elasticity of demand equal to −.8. Assume that people in wheelchairs value their recreational time at $10 per hour. What is the annual benefit of making the tram accessible to people in wheelchairs?

Notes

1. Rex Deighton-Smith, Angelo Erbacci, Céline Kauffmann, *Promoting Inclusive Growth through Better Regulation: The Role of Regulatory Impact Assessment*. OECD Regulatory Policy Working Papers, No. 3 (Paris: OECD Publishing, 2016).

2. For an overview of RIAs and other analytical requirements in rulemaking, see Curtis W. Copeland, *Cost–Benefit and Other Analysis Requirements in the Rulemaking Process*. (Washington, DC: Congressional Research Service, 2011).

3. Office of Management and Budget, *2015 Report to Congress on the Benefits and Costs of Federal Regulations and Unfunded Mandates on State, Local, and Tribal Entities* (Washington, DC: Office of Information and Regulatory Affairs, 2015).

4. Agricultural Marketing Service, "National Organic Program; Organic Livestock and Poultry Practices." *Federal Register*, 81(71), 2016, 21955–2209.

5. Agricultural Marketing Service, "National Organic Program (NOP); Organic Livestock and Poultry Practices." *Federal Register*, 82(12), 2017, 7042–92.

6. Department of Agriculture: Agricultural Marketing Service, *Regulatory Impact Analysis and Final Regulatory Flexibility Analysis, Final Report*, January 2017.

7. Yan Heng and Hikaru Peterson, "Estimating Demand for Differentiated Eggs Using Scanner Data." Presented to the Agricultural and Applied Economics Association Annual Meeting, Minneapolis, Minnesota, July 2014.

8. In a market, both price and quantity are jointly determined. That is, price does not vary independently of quantity. To identify a demand relationship, the effect of price on quantity, one generally requires variables that affect supply but not demand for use in instrumental variable methods. In the case of eggs, input prices are reasonable instruments because they almost certainly affect the supply price of eggs but do not directly affect consumer demand for eggs. For a clear introduction to the topic of identification, see Joshua D. Angrist and Jön-Steffen Pischke, *Mostly Harmless Econometrics: An Empiricist's Companion* (Princeton, NJ: Princeton University Press, 2009), chapter 4.

9. Jayson Lusk, "The Effect of Proposition 2 on the Demand for Eggs in California." *Journal of Agricultural & Food Industrial Organization*, 8(3), 2010, 1–18.

10. If the analysts had decided to rely on a specific estimate from the Heng and Peterson study, then a constant elasticity demand schedule would have been more appropriate. However, in view of all the other assumptions required to estimate changes in consumer surplus for this scenario, the simplifying assumption of linear demand has relatively little impact on the prediction of changes in consumer surplus.

11. Department of Justice, "Nondiscrimination on the Basis of Disability by Public Accommodations and in Commercial Facilities." *Federal Register*, 69(189), 2004, 58768–86.

12. Department of Justice, "Nondiscrimination on the Basis of Disability by Public Accommodations and in Commercial Facilities." *Federal Register*, 73(117), 2008, 34508–57.

13. Department of Justice, "Nondiscrimination on the Basis of Disability in State and Local Government Services." *Federal Register*, 75(178), 2010, 56164–236 and "Nondiscrimination on the Basis of Disability by Public Accommodations and in Commercial Facilities." *Federal Register*, 75(178), 2010, 56236–358.

14. Department of Justice, Disability Rights Section of the Civil Rights Division, *Final Regulatory Impact Analysis of the Final Revised Regulations Implementing Titles II and III of the ADA, Including Revised ADA Standards for Accessible Design, Final Report*, July 23, 2010.

15. Jon P. Nelson, "Hard at Play! The Growth of Recreation in Consumer Budgets." *Eastern Economic Journal*, 27(1), 2001, 35–53.

5 Valuing Impacts in Output Markets

Chapter 3 presents the basic microeconomic foundations of cost–benefit analysis. As discussed there, the change in allocative efficiency (i.e., the change in social surplus) due to a new project or a change in government policy depends on changes in consumer surplus, producer surplus, and net government revenues. This chapter and the next two illustrate how changes in these variables could be estimated if the pertinent market demand and supply curves were known.

One can think about a government project as using inputs, such as materials and labor, and transforming them into outputs, such as better-educated people or a new subway. Thus, a new project has output market impacts and input market impacts. If a city builds a new subway system, the main output markets are the markets for subway trips. In addition, we consider the effects of pollution and other externalities associated with the policy or project as outputs even though there are no markets for these "goods." Building the subway requires inputs, such as the land the stations occupy, the materials used to build the subway stations and, of course, labor. These goods or services are called factor inputs. Markets for these inputs are "upstream" of the output markets. The effects of a new government project or policy on these input markets should be taken into account. A policy may also have "knock-on" or indirect effects that occur "downstream." For example, a new subway or a new subway station may affect the market for housing near to the station or may affect the market for gasoline if some commuters switch from driving to riding the new subway. Such markets are called "secondary markets." In sum, analysts need to consider the impacts of a government policy on output markets, input markets, and secondary markets.

The change in allocative efficiency due to a new project or a change in government policy, ΔSS, equals the sum of the changes in social surpluses that arise in the three markets discussed above:

$$\Delta SS = \Delta SS_O + \Delta SS_I + \Delta SS_S \tag{5.1}$$

where ΔSS_O, ΔSS_I and ΔSS_S denote changes in the social surplus occurring in the output, input, and secondary markets, respectively.

Equation (3.12b) includes the net change in government surplus (government cash flow) as a single term equal to change in government revenues from the policy, ΔR, minus change in government expenditures on the policy, ΔE.[1] It is useful to think about government revenues as occurring in the output markets because that is where they are collected and government expenditures as occurring in the input markets because that is where the money is spent. Thus, the change in social surplus in the output market equals:

$$\Delta SS_O = \gamma_g \Delta R + \Delta CS_o + \Delta PS_o \tag{5.2}$$

where ΔCS_o and ΔPS_o denote the changes in consumer surplus and producer surplus in the output markets, respectively, and γ_g equals one plus the marginal excess tax burden. It is natural to interpret the change in social surplus in the output market as measuring the primary (gross) benefits of a policy. Analogously, the change in social surplus in the input market equals:

$$\Delta SS_I = -\gamma_g \Delta E + \Delta CS_I + \Delta PS_I \tag{5.3}$$

where ΔCS_I and ΔPS_I denote the changes in consumer surplus and producer surplus in the input markets. It is natural to interpret the change in social surplus in the input market as measuring the opportunity costs of a policy. Finally, the change in social surplus in the secondary markets equals:

$$\Delta SS_S = \Delta CS_S + \Delta PS_S \tag{5.4}$$

where ΔCS_S and ΔPS_S denote the changes in consumer surplus and producer surplus in the secondary markets. It is natural to interpret the change in social surplus in the secondary market as measuring the secondary or indirect benefits or costs of a policy. This chapter focuses on valuing impacts in output markets, given by Equation (5.2). Chapter 6 focuses on valuing impacts in input markets, given by Equation (5.3), and Chapter 7 focuses on valuing impacts in secondary markets, given by Equation (5.4). In these chapters we assume for convenience that the marginal excess tax burden equals zero so that $\gamma_g = 1$.

This chapter begins with a brief discussion of shadow pricing. Next, it discusses valuing impacts in efficient markets, followed by a discussion about how to value impacts in distorted markets where market failures are found. We provide brief explanations of common types of market failures including monopoly, externalities, information asymmetries, public goods, and addictive goods. The reason for discussing market failures is that their presence provides the *prima facie* rationale for most, although not all, proposed government interventions that are assessed through CBA. If markets worked perfectly, then Pareto efficiency would be obtained without government intervention: a set of prices would arise that distributes resources to firms and goods to individuals in such a way that it would not be possible to find a reallocation that would make at least one person better off without also making at least one other person worse off. Furthermore, as shown in Chapter 3, such an outcome would be allocatively efficient and would maximize net social benefits. It is only when markets fail that allocative efficiency grounds exist for government interventions. However, no more than a *prima facie* case exists. It is up to CBA to demonstrate that a specific intervention is worthwhile from society's perspective. If a particular intervention is already in place, the analyst can perform a CBA to determine whether or not the current policy is inefficient and, therefore, exhibits "government failure."[2]

5.1   Shadow Pricing

For the most part, this chapter and the following two chapters explain how to value impacts if the necessary market demand and supply curves were known. Often we use market prices as a measure of value. However, a market price may be distorted. For example, persons entering a US National Park pay a fee, but this fee is set by the National Park Service, not by the market. Consequently, it is unlikely that this fee bears a strong relation to the value of the benefits visitors actually receive from visiting the park. Also, prices charged by paper factories may understate the true social cost of paper if the production process generates pollution. In some situations the market price may not even exist. For example, no market provides a direct estimate of the value of human life. Thus, a continuum exists. At one end of this continuum are values that can be measured in terms of prices that are set in well-functioning, competitive markets. At the other end is the complete absence of markets that can be used to value benefits and costs resulting from a government policy.

When observed prices fail to reflect the social value of a good accurately or observed prices do not exist, analysts adjust observed prices or assign values that are as close as possible to the theoretically correct social values. The resultant prices are called *shadow prices* because they are not directly observable in any market. Economists have put much work into trying to determine the shadow price of many "goods" that are needed in CBA, including estimates of the shadow price of the value of a statistical life saved or of the social cost of various pollutants. Chapters 14, 15, and 16 describe several techniques to obtain shadow prices, while Chapter 17 provides estimates of important shadow prices. Shadow prices may be necessary in valuing impacts in any market.

5.2   Valuing Impacts in Efficient Markets

We examine two common situations. First, we consider policies that directly affect the quantity of a good available to consumers. For example, a publicly operated childcare center shifts the supply curve to the right, as it results in more child care being offered to consumers at each price. This often (but not always) reduces prices, resulting in benefits to consumers. Second, we consider policies that shift the supply curve down by altering the price or availability of some input used to produce the good. An example is deepening a harbor so that it accommodates larger ships, thus reducing the cost of transporting bulk commodities to and from the port for shipping companies. This results in direct reductions in costs to producers.

5.2.1   *Direct Increase in Supply Available to Consumers*

Suppose the government directly increases the supply of a good in a well-functioning market, but the increase is so small that the price of the good is unaffected. For example, a government may have surplus office equipment that it sells in sufficiently small quantities that the market price of office equipment does not change. The assumption of a negligible effect on price is more reasonable for goods traded in large, national markets than for goods traded in small, local markets. It is also more reasonable for homogeneous goods, such as surplus equipment, than for heterogeneous goods, such as land, which may differ in desirability from one parcel to another.

Figure 5.1 shows the impacts when a project directly increases the available supply of a good in a well-functioning market, but the increase is so small that the price of the good is unaffected. If the government sells the additional units of the good at the market price, then it may be treated like other competitors in an efficient market. Hence, as shown in the figure, it faces a horizontal demand curve, D, for the good at the market price, P_0. If the project directly adds a quantity, q', to the market, then the supply curve as seen by consumers shifts from S to $S + q'$.[3] Because the demand curve is horizontal, the price of the good and, hence, consumer surplus and producer surplus are unaffected by the shift in the supply curve. Assuming consumers purchase the additional units of the good, the government receives revenue equal to P_0 times q', the area of rectangle $q_0 abq_1$. This rectangle also, of course, represents a cost to those consumers who purchase the good. Because the demand curve represents willingness to pay, this "cost" is exactly offset by gains that these persons enjoy in consuming the good and, consequently, can be ignored in our analysis: there is no change in consumer surplus. Therefore, the revenues received by the government are the only benefits that accrue from the project selling q' units in the market.

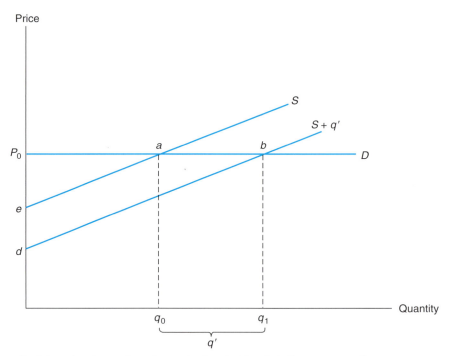

Social surplus change (ignoring costs of project inputs to the government):
Project (a): Direct increase in supply of q'—gain of project revenue equal to area of rectangle $q_0 abq_1$
Project (b): Supply schedule shift through cost reduction for producers—gain of trapezoid *abde*

Figure 5.1 Measuring impacts in an efficient market with no price effects.

If the government adds a sufficiently large quantity of a good to a market so that the price of the good is reduced, however, then consumers will enjoy an increase in consumer surplus. Figure 5.2 illustrates this possibility by showing a downward-sloping demand curve, D. The intersection of the demand curve and the supply curve, S, indicates the equilibrium price, P_0, prior to the project. The equilibrium price of the good falls to P_1 after the government provides the q' units of the good. This time, because of the reduction in the price facing consumers, there is a gain in consumer surplus corresponding to the area of trapezoid P_0abP_1. Because private-sector suppliers continue to operate on the original supply curve, S, the output they sell falls from q_0 to q_2, and they suffer a loss of producer surplus equal to the area of trapezoid P_0acP_1. Thus, the net gain in surplus among private actors (consumers and producers) equals the area of the lightly shaded triangle abc. In addition, the government receives revenues from the project equal to the area of rectangle q_2cbq_1. The sum of project revenues and the gain in social surplus in the market equals area q_2cabq_1, which is the incremental benefit from the government selling q' units in the market.

What benefits would accrue if the additional q' units of the good were instead distributed free to selected consumers? If the price of the good does not change, as in the situation depicted in Figure 5.1, then the answer is straightforward: as a result of receiving q' units of the good free, consumers gain surplus equal to the area of rectangle q_0abq_1, an area that exactly corresponds to the revenues that would have accrued had the project's output been sold. Therefore, as before, the incremental benefit would equal q_0abq_1.

The answer is more complex if the q' units of the good are distributed free, but the increase in supply causes its price to fall. This situation is shown in Figure 5.2. Under

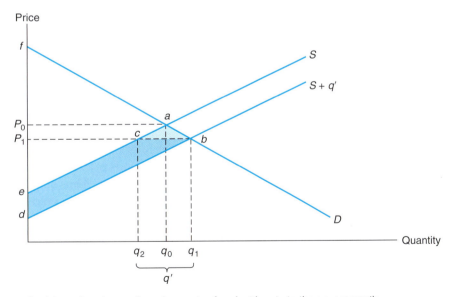

Social surplus change (ignoring costs of project inputs to the government):
Project (a): Direct increase in supply of q'—gain of triangle abc plus project revenue equal to area of rectangle q_2cbq_1
Project (b): Supply schedule shift through cost reductions for producers—gain of trapezoid $abde$

Figure 5.2 Measuring impacts in an efficient market with price effects.

these circumstances, if the q' units are given only to those consumers who would have valued these units at P_1 or higher, then the project's benefit measure is again exactly the same as it would have been had the output been sold. As before, the reduction in price from P_0 to P_1 results in an increase in social surplus equal to area abc. With free distribution, however, no revenue accrues to the project. Instead, as a result of receiving q' units of the good free, consumers enjoy an additional surplus equal to the area of rectangle q_2cbq_1. Thus, gains from the project once again equal the area of trapezoid q_2cabq_1.

It is more likely, however, that if q' units of the good are distributed for free, some would go to consumers who are located below point b on the market demand curve shown in Figure 5.2. In other words, some units would be distributed to some consumers in greater quantities than they would have purchased at price P_1. If these consumers keep the excess units, then area q_2cabq_1 overestimates the project's benefit because these persons value their marginal consumption of these units at less than P_1. Area q_2cabq_1 approximates project benefits, however, if recipients of the excess units sell them to others who would have been willing to buy them at a price of P_1 (provided the transaction costs associated with the sale of the excess units are zero).

Suppose, for example, that a project provides previously stockpiled gasoline free to low-income consumers during an oil supply disruption (an in-kind subsidy). Some low-income households will find themselves with more gasoline than they would have purchased on their own at price P_1; therefore, they will try to sell the excess. Doing so will be relatively easy if access to the stockpiled gasoline is provided through legally transferable coupons; it would obviously be more difficult if the gasoline had to be physically taken away by the low-income households. If the gasoline coupons could be costlessly traded among consumers, then we would expect the outcome to be identical to one in which the gasoline is sold in the market and the revenue given directly to low-income consumers.

5.2.2   *Direct Reduction in Costs to Producers*

We now turn to a different type of public-sector project, such as harbor deepening, which lowers the private sector's cost of supplying a market. Figure 5.2 can again be used to analyze this situation. In this case, however, the supply curve shifts to $S + q'$, not because the project directly supplies q' to the market, but rather because reductions in marginal costs allow private-sector firms to offer q' additional units profitably at each price.[4] As in the case of direct supply of q', the new equilibrium price is P_1. Thus, the gain in consumer surplus corresponds to the area of trapezoid P_0abP_1. The change in producer surplus corresponds to the difference in the areas of triangle P_0ae (the producer surplus with supply curve S) and triangle P_1bd (the producer surplus with supply curve $S + q'$). Area P_1ce is common to the two triangles and therefore cancels. Hence, producers enjoy a net gain in surplus equal to area $ecbd$ minus area P_0acP_1. Adding this gain to the gain in consumer surplus, area P_0abP_1, means that the net gain to consumers and producers resulting from the project equals the area of trapezoid $abde$. (That is, area $ecbd$ + area P_0abP_1 − area P_0acP_1 = area $ecbd$ + area abc = area $abde$.[5]) Because no project revenue is generated, area $abde$ alone is the gain from the project.

5.3   Valuing Impacts in Distorted Markets

If market or government failures distort the relevant output market, complications arise in determining the correct surplus changes. We illustrate these complications by examining five different types of market failures: monopoly, information asymmetry, externalities, public goods, and addictive goods. We do not attempt to provide a comprehensive discussion of market failures in this chapter, just an overview. For a comprehensive discussion, we recommend a book by David Weimer and Aidan Vining, which is cited in the second endnote.[6]

5.3.1   *Monopoly*

It is useful to examine monopoly first because it is an excellent example of a topic introduced in Chapter 3: a deviation from the competitive equilibrium that results in a deadweight loss and, hence, reduces social surplus.[7] One key to understanding monopoly is to recognize that because, by definition, a monopolist is the only firm in its market, it views the market demand curve as the demand curve for its output.

Because market demand curves slope downward, if the monopolist sells all its output at the same price, then it can sell an additional unit of output only by reducing the price on every unit it sells. Consequently, the monopolist's marginal revenue – the additional revenue it receives for each additional unit of output it sells – is less than the selling price of that unit. For example, if a monopolist could sell four units of output at a price of $10 but must reduce its price to $9 in order to sell five units, its revenue would increase from $40 to $45 as a result of selling the fifth unit. Therefore, the $5 in marginal revenue it receives from the fifth unit is less than the $9 selling price of the unit. Thus, as shown in Figure 5.3, the monopolist's marginal revenue curve, denoted MR, is located below its demand curve, denoted AR.

Given this situation, the monopolist would maximize profit by producing at Q_m, where its marginal cost equals its marginal revenue. The price it can charge is determined by what people are willing to pay for those units, which is given by the demand curve it faces. At the output level Q_m it would set its price equal to P_m.

As before, the social surplus generated by the output produced and sold by the monopolist is represented graphically by the area between the demand curve, which reflects the marginal benefit to society, and the marginal cost curve that is to the left of the intersection of the marginal revenue and marginal cost curves. This is the sum of consumer surplus plus producer surplus. The consumer surplus, which is captured by buyers, is the lightest shaded area above the price line. The producer surplus, which is captured by the monopolist, is the medium dark shaded area below the price line.

Although the term *monopolist* is sometimes used pejoratively, in a CBA any increase in producer surplus received by a monopolist that results from a government policy is counted as a benefit of the policy. The rationale is that owners of monopolies, like consumers and the owners of competitive firms, are part of society; therefore, benefits accruing to them "count."[8]

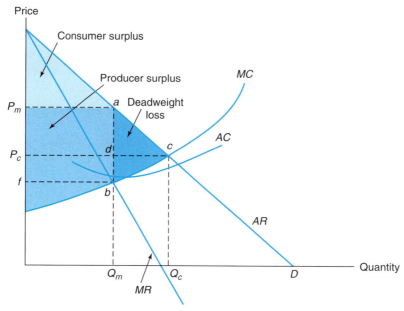

Figure 5.3 Monopoly.

Notice that, unlike the perfectly competitive case, social surplus is not maximized if the monopolist is left to its own devices. This is because the monopolist maximizes profits, not net social benefits. Net social benefits are maximized at point c on Figure 5.3, where the marginal cost curve intersects the marginal benefit curve (demand curve). The "lost" social surplus, which is the deadweight loss resulting from monopoly, is represented in Figure 5.3 by the darkly shaded triangular area abc. Were it possible for the government to break up the monopoly into a large number of competing firms, each firm would produce where price equals MC.[9] In Figure 5.3 this occurs where industry output and price are Q_c and P_c, which are sometimes referred to as the "competitive" output and price. If this competitive outcome was reached, two things would happen: first, the deadweight loss would disappear and social surplus would increase by the area abc. In CBA, this would count as a benefit of the government's actions. Second, because the competitive price, P_c, is less than the monopolistic price, P_m, consumers would capture that part of the monopolist's producer surplus that is represented by the rectangular area $P_m adP_c$. In CBA, this is viewed as a transfer.

5.3.2   *Natural Monopoly*

So far, we have been focusing on a general form of monopoly. We now turn to a specific type of monopoly: *natural monopoly*. The essential characteristic of a natural monopoly is that it enjoys *economies of scale* over a wide range of output. Usually, its fixed costs are very large relative to its variable costs; public utilities, roads, and bridges all provide good examples. As shown in Figure 5.4, these large fixed costs cause average costs to fall over a large range of output. Put another way, and as shown in Figure 5.4, (long-run)

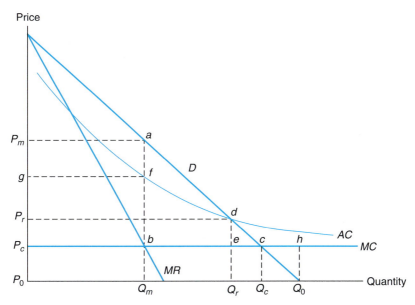

Figure 5.4 Natural monopoly.

average costs exceed (long-run) marginal costs over what we term the *relevant range of output*, which is the range between the first unit of output and the amount consumers would demand at a zero price, Q_0.

In principle, marginal costs could be rising or falling over the relevant output range, but for the sake of simplicity, we have drawn the marginal cost curve as horizontal. The important point is that (long-run) marginal costs are less than (long-run) average costs over the relevant range, so that average costs fall over the relevant range of output as output increases. As a result, one firm, a natural monopolist, can provide a given amount of output at a lower average cost than could two or more firms.

In these circumstances, it is reasonable for the government to permit a monopoly to exist. If it does, however, it must decide whether to regulate the monopoly, and if it regulates it, what type of policies to invoke. To make our discussion of these policies as concrete as possible, we will assume that the natural monopoly represented in Figure 5.4 is a road and that output is the number of cars that travel the road. Although most roads are built under government contract and operated by the government, they could instead be built and operated by private-sector firms under various regulatory frameworks. In fact, some roads have been built by private companies or public–private partnerships over the past 200 years.[10]

The government could follow one of four policies. The first is simply to allow the road-operating authority, whether a private-sector firm or a government agency, to maximize profits. As discussed previously, profits are maximized at output Q_m, where marginal cost equals marginal revenue. The road-operating authority could obtain this output level by charging a toll (i.e., a price) set at P_m. However, under this policy, output is restricted below the competitive level of Q_c, and willingness to pay, P_m, exceeds marginal costs, P_c. This results in a deadweight loss equal to area *abc*. The policy is also unattractive politically because it typically permits substantial monopoly profits, corresponding to area $P_m afg$.

An alternative policy that is often used in regulating natural monopolies is to require the road-operating authority to set its price at P_r, where the average cost curve crosses the demand curve. This policy eliminates monopoly profits by transferring social surplus from the road-operating authority to persons using the road. It also expands output, increasing social surplus and reducing deadweight loss from area *abc* to area *dec*. Thus, as compared to allowing the road-operating authority to maximize profits, society receives a benefit from the policy that corresponds to area *adeb*. However, deadweight loss is not completely eliminated. In other words, society could benefit still further if output could be expanded.

The third policy alternative does this by requiring the road construction and operating authority to set its price at P_c, where the marginal cost curve intersects the demand curve – in other words, by requiring competitive market pricing. This completely eliminates the deadweight loss, thereby maximizing net social benefits. However, a problem exists with this policy: price is below average costs; hence, revenues no longer cover costs. As a result, tax money must be used to subsidize the road construction and operating authority.

The fourth policy alternative is the one most often used in the case of roads: to allow free access, or in other words, to charge a zero price. In this case, output would expand to Q_0, the point at which the demand curve intersects the horizontal axis. The problem with this policy is that output expands to a level at which marginal costs exceed marginal benefit (i.e., WTP). This results in a deadweight loss equal to the triangular area chQ_0. Moreover, because no tolls are collected directly from road users, the entire construction and operating costs of the road must be paid through government subsidies obtained from taxes.

5.3.3   *Information Asymmetry*

The term *information asymmetry* implies that information about a product or a job may not be equal on both sides of a market. For example, sellers may have more information concerning how well made or safe a product is than buyers, doctors may know more about needed care than patients, or employers may know more about job-related health risks than their workers.

The implications of information asymmetry are easy to show in a diagram. To do this, we focus on the case in which sellers of a product have more information than buyers. Such a situation is represented in Figure 5.5, which shows two demand curves. One of these curves, D_i, represents how many units of the product buyers would desire if they had full information concerning it, while the other demand curve, D_u, indicates how many units they actually desire, given their lack of full information.[11] In other words, the two demand curves represent, respectively, consumers' WTP with and without full information concerning the product. They indicate that if buyers had full information, their WTP would be lower.[12]

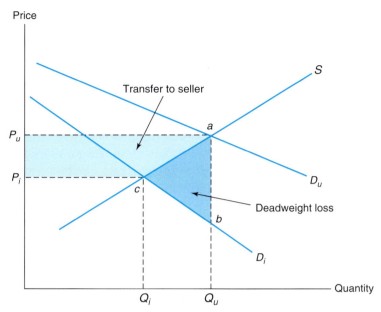

Figure 5.5 Information asymmetry.

Figure 5.5 shows that there are two effects of information asymmetry. First, by raising the price and the amount of the good purchased, information asymmetry increases producer surplus and reduces consumer surplus, resulting in a transfer from consumers to sellers. This transfer is shown by the lighter-shaded trapezoidal $P_u a c P_i$. Second, by increasing the amount of the good sold relative to the full information case, information asymmetry results in a deadweight loss, which is shown as the darker-shaded triangle area abc.

These two effects, especially the second one, suggest a rationale for the government to intervene by providing the missing information. If the government does this effectively, society will benefit because deadweight loss is reduced. In addition, there will be a transfer of surplus (back) from sellers to buyers. However, there are also costs associated with the government obtaining and disseminating information. These costs, which do not explicitly appear in the diagram, may be sizable.[13] Hence, for a government information program to have positive net benefits, and not just positive (gross) benefits, the deadweight loss associated with the lack of information in the absence of government intervention must usually be substantial.

It is useful to discuss the circumstances under which information asymmetry is sufficiently important that the benefits from government intervention are likely to exceed the costs. This largely depends upon two factors: first, the ease with which consumers can obtain the information for themselves; and second, whether third parties that could provide the missing information are likely to arise through market forces. To discuss these factors, it is helpful to distinguish among three types of products: (1) search goods, (2) experience goods, and (3) post-experience goods.[14]

Search goods are products with characteristics that consumers can learn about by examining them prior to purchasing them. For example, a student who needs a notebook for a class can go to the bookstore and easily learn pretty much everything he or she wants to know about the characteristics of alternative notebooks. Under such circumstances, information asymmetry is unlikely to be serious.

Experience goods are products about which consumers can obtain full knowledge, but only after purchasing and experiencing them. Examples are tickets to a movie, a meal at a new restaurant, a new television set, and a house. At least to a degree, information asymmetry concerning many such products takes care of itself. For example, once consumers have been to a restaurant, they acquire some information concerning the expected quality of the meal should they eat there again. Warranties, which are typically provided for televisions and many other major consumer durables, serve a similar purpose. In addition, market demand for information about experience goods often prompts third parties to provide information for a fee. This reduces information asymmetry. For example, newspaper reviews provide information about movies and restaurants; in the United States, *Consumer Reports* provides information about many goods; and inspection services examine houses for perspective buyers.

In the case of *post-experience goods*, consumption does not necessarily reveal information to consumers. Government intervention to reduce information asymmetry associated with post-experience goods is most likely to be efficiency-enhancing because learning through individual action does not always occur. Examples of this situation include adverse health effects associated with a prescription drug and a new automobile with a defective part. Employee exposure to an unhealthy chemical at work is similar. In these cases, information asymmetry may persist for long periods of time, even after the health of some people has been ruined. Moreover, because the needed information is often expensive to gather and individuals may be unwilling to pay for it, third parties may not provide the necessary information. Under these circumstances, there may be a strong rationale for government intervention.

5.3.4   *Externalities*

An *externality* is an effect that production or consumption has on third parties – people not involved in the production or consumption of the good. It is a byproduct of production or consumption for which there is no market. Indeed, externalities are sometimes referred to as the problem of "missing markets." Examples include pollution caused by a factory and the pleasure derived from a neighbor's beautiful garden. Externalities may occur for a wide variety of reasons. For example, some result because a particular type of manufacturing technology is used (e.g., air pollution caused by smokestack industry). Others arise because of interdependencies (or synergies) between producers and consumers or different groups of producers (e.g., beekeepers who unintentionally provide pollination services for nearby fruit growers). Still other externalities occur because of networks (e.g., the larger the number of persons who purchase a particular type of automobile, the greater the number of qualified service garages available to each owner). Because the number of externalities is enormous, a careful CBA should first be conducted before the government intervenes to correct any specific externality.[15]

We first examine a negative externality (i.e., one that imposes social costs) and then a positive externality (i.e., one that produces benefits). Figure 5.6 illustrates a market in which the production process results in a negative externality, such as air or water pollution. The supply curve, S^*, reflects only the private marginal costs incurred by the suppliers of the good, while the second supply curve, $S^\#$, incorporates the costs that the negative externality imposes on third parties, as well as the private marginal costs incurred by suppliers. The vertical distance between these two curves, measured over the quantity of the good purchased, can be viewed as the amount those subjected to the negative externality would be willing to pay to avoid it. In other words, it represents the costs imposed by the externality on third parties. The extent of this distance depends in part upon whether the market somehow compensates third parties for the negative externality. For example, it would be smaller if homeowners were able to purchase their houses at lower prices because of pollution in their neighborhood than if they were not.

Figure 5.6 indicates that, if left to its own devices, the market sets too low a price for the good ($P^* < P^\#$) because it fails to take account of the cost to third parties of producing the good. As a result, too much output is produced ($Q^* > Q^\#$). This causes deadweight loss, which is represented by the shaded triangular area labeled C. This deadweight loss reflects the fact that for each unit of additional output produced in excess of $Q^\#$, marginal social costs (shown by the supply curve $S^\#$) increasingly exceed marginal social benefits (shown by the demand curve D).

The standard technique for reducing deadweight loss resulting from negative externalities is to impose taxes.[16] For example, the suppliers of the good represented in Figure 5.6 could be required to pay a tax, t, on each unit they sell, with the tax set equal to the difference between marginal social costs and marginal social benefits (shown in

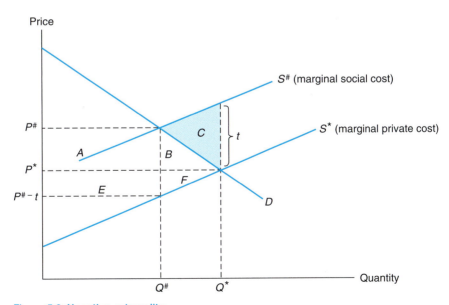

Figure 5.6 Negative externality.

the figure as the vertical distance at Q^* between the two supply curves). As production costs would now include the tax, the supply curve of sellers, S^*, would shift upward to $S^\#$. Consequently, the price paid by consumers would increase from P^* to $P^\#$, the net price received by producers would fall from P^* to $P^\# - t$, and output produced and sold would fall from Q^* to $Q^\#$. Note that pollution associated with the good would be reduced, but not completely eliminated, because the good would continue to be produced, although in smaller amounts.[17]

Figure 5.6 implies that the benefits and costs of the government's tax policy are distributed unequally among different groups in the economy. These are displayed in the following social accounting ledger.

	Gains	Losses	Change
Consumers of good		A + B	–(A + B)
Producers of good		E + F	–(E + F)
Third-party consumers	B + C + F		B + C + F
Government revenue	A + E		A + E
Society			C

Because the tax causes consumers to pay a higher price for less of the good, they lose surplus equal to areas A and B. Similarly, because the tax causes producers to sell less of the good but increases their production costs (they have to pay the tax), they lose producer surplus equal to areas E and F. On the other hand, because of the reduction in the number of units produced and, hence, in pollution, third parties receive benefits from the policy equal to areas B, C, and F. Finally, the government receives tax revenues equal to areas A and E. The areas A, B, E, and F represent transfers from one group to another. Therefore, the benefit of the tax policy, given by the change in revenue plus the changes in consumer surplus and producer surplus, equals area C, as shown in the social accounting ledger above. This area corresponds to the deadweight loss eliminated by the tax policy. To compute the *net* social surplus from the tax, the cost of administering it would have to be subtracted from the benefit represented by C.

Now let us look at an example of a positive externality, a program that subsidizes the purchase of rodent extermination services in a poor neighborhood. One mechanism for doing this is to provide residents with vouchers that are worth a certain number of dollars, v, for each unit of extermination services they purchase. After subtracting the face value of these vouchers from what they charge neighborhood residents for their services, exterminators would then be reimbursed the face value of the voucher by the government.

By increasing the use of extermination services, such a program may result in a positive externality: the fewer the rodents in the neighborhood, the easier it is for residents in adjoining neighborhoods to control their own rodent populations. This situation is illustrated in Figure 5.7, where the market demand curve, D_M, is shown as understating the social demand curve, D_S. The area between these two demand curves represents the WTP for the extermination voucher program by residents of adjoining neighborhoods,

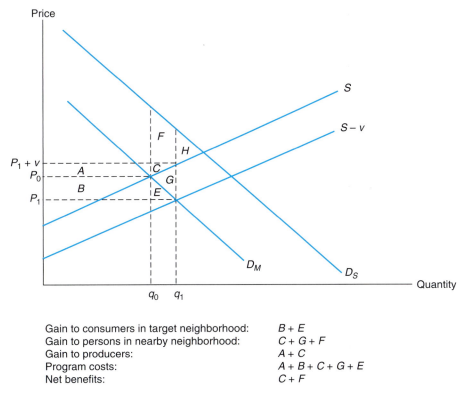

Gain to consumers in target neighborhood: $B + E$
Gain to persons in nearby neighborhood: $C + G + F$
Gain to producers: $A + C$
Program costs: $A + B + C + G + E$
Net benefits: $C + F$

Figure 5.7 Social benefits for direct supply of a good with a positive externality.

assuming they had knowledge of the potential benefits from the program to them. Thus, the market equilibrium price, P_0, and quantity, q_0, are both too low from the social perspective, resulting in deadweight loss equal to $C + F + H$.

What are the social benefits of a program that distributes vouchers worth \$$v$ per unit of extermination service to the residents of the poor neighborhood? As implied by Figure 5.7, when the vouchers become available, residents of the poor neighborhood face a supply curve that is below the original market supply curve, S, by \$$v$. As a consequence of a voucher-induced shift in the supply curve, neighborhood residents increase their purchases of extermination services from q_0 to q_1, paying an effective price of P_1. Consumers in the targeted neighborhood enjoy a surplus gain equal to the area of trapezoid $B + E$; producers, who now receive a higher supply price of $P_1 + v$, enjoy a surplus gain equal to the area of trapezoid $A + C$; and people in the surrounding neighborhoods, who enjoy the positive externality, gain surplus equal to the area of parallelogram $C + G + F$, the area between the market and social demand curves over the increase in consumption. The program must pay out \$$v$ times q_1 in subsidies, which equals the area of rectangle $A + B + C + G + E$. Subtracting this program cost from the gains in social surplus in the market yields program benefits: the area of trapezoid $C + F$. This benefit results because the program succeeds in eliminating part (although not all) of the deadweight loss in the market for extermination services.

Public Goods

Once produced, public goods – for example, flood control projects or national defense – are available for everyone. No one can or, indeed, should be excluded from enjoying their benefits. In this sense, public goods may be regarded as a special type of positive externality. Similar to other positive externalities, private markets, if left to their own devices, tend to produce fewer public goods than is socially optimal. Pure public goods have two key characteristics: they are non-excludable, and they are non-rivalrous.

A good is non-excludable if it is impossible, or at least highly impractical, for one person to prevent others from consuming it. If it is supplied to one consumer, it is available for all consumers, a phenomenon sometimes called *jointness in supply*. For example, it would be very difficult for a user of the light emitted from a particular streetlight to prevent others from using that light. In contrast, most private goods are excludable. For instance, a purchaser of a hamburger can exclude others from taking a bite unless overcome by physical force.

The reason non-excludability causes market failure is easy to see. Once a non-excludable good such as street lighting or national defense exists, it is available for everyone to use. Because people cannot be excluded from using it, a *free-rider problem* results. As a consequence, there is not sufficient incentive for the private sector to provide it. Usually it must be publicly provided, if it is going to be provided at all.

Non-rivalry implies that one person's consumption of a good does not prevent someone else from also consuming it; consequently, more than one person can obtain benefits from a given level of supply at the same time. For example, one person's use of a streetlight to help him see at night does not diminish the ability of another person to use the same light. However, if one person eats a hamburger, another cannot consume the same hamburger. The hamburger is rivalrous; a streetlight is non-rivalrous. Thus, unlike the hamburger, even if it were feasible to exclude a second person from using street lighting, it would be inefficient to do so because the marginal cost of supplying lighting to the second person is zero.

The reason non-rivalry causes market failure can be examined by contrasting how a *total marginal benefit curve*, a curve that reflects the incremental benefits to consumers from each additional unit of a good that is available for their consumption, is derived for a rivalrous good with how such a curve is derived for a non-rivalrous good. To do this graphically as simply as possible, we assume that there are only two potential consumers of each of the two goods. Thus, Figure 5.8 displays two graphs: one for the rivalrous good (hamburger) and one for the non-rivalrous good (streetlight). Each graph contains three curves: a demand curve representing consumer A's WTP (d_A), a demand curve representing consumer B's WTP (d_B), and a total marginal benefit (MB) curve, which is derived from the demand curves for the two consumers.

The total marginal benefit curve for the rivalrous good is equivalent to a market demand curve. To derive this curve, the two demand curves for individual consumers are summed horizontally. For example, at a price of P^*, consumer A would want to consume q_1 and consumer B would want q_2 of the good. Total market demand for the good at a price of P^* is equal to $q_1 + q_2$, a total of Q^*. Thus, WTP for (or equivalently, marginal benefits from) the last unit of the total of Q^* units consumed is P^*. Notice that until the price falls below $P^\#$, the marginal benefit curve would correspond to B's demand curve because A would not demand any of the good.

In contrast, the total marginal benefit curve for the non-rivalrous good is derived by adding the demand curves for individual consumers vertically rather than horizontally.

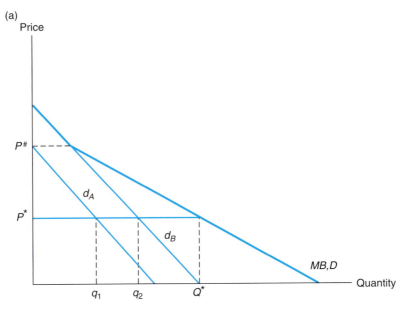

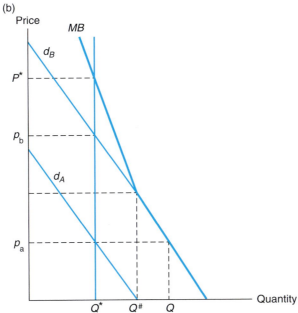

Figure 5.8a Rivalrous good (e.g., hamburger).
Figure 5.8b Non-rivalrous good (e.g., streetlight).

At an output level of Q^*, for example, total WTP (i.e., the total marginal benefits from the last unit of the good that is made available) is equal to $p_a + p_b$ or P^*. Notice that at output levels above $Q^\#$, consumer A's WTP falls to zero and, consequently, the marginal benefit curve corresponds to consumer B's demand curve.

The reason the demand curves for individual consumers must be summed horizontally in the presence of rivalry and vertically in its absence can be clarified through use of a numerical example. If at a price of $2 consumer B wanted to buy two hamburgers and consumer A one hamburger, then total demand would equal three hamburgers – the horizontal sum of demand at a particular price. However, if at a price of $1,000 B wanted two streetlights on the block on which he and A both lived, but A wanted only one, then two streetlights would completely satisfy the demands of both. Thus, the total demand for a non-rivalrous good cannot be determined by summing the quantity of the good each consumer desires at a given price. It must be determined instead by summing each consumer's WTP for a given quantity of the good. Hence, although A and B have a different WTP for the two streetlights, their total WTP for the two streetlights can be determined by adding A's WTP for two lights to B's.

The distinction between how the total demand for rivalrous and non-rivalrous goods is determined has an important implication. In the case of the rivalrous good, consumers will reveal to the market how much they want. For example, if the price of hamburgers is set at P^*, consumer A will actually purchase q_1 of the good and consumer B will actually purchase q_2, but in the case of a non-rivalrous good, no market mechanism exists that causes consumers to reveal how many units they would purchase at different prices. For example, if the price of streetlight is at p_b, consumer B would be willing to purchase Q^* of the good, but if B did that, A would not purchase any because, as a result of B's purchase, he could consume all he wanted. In other words, A would free-ride on B. Because of this free-rider problem, B might refuse to make any purchase until A agreed to make some sort of contribution.[18]

When only a small group of people is involved, they may be able to work out the free-rider problems caused by the non-excludability and non-rivalry of public goods through negotiations. For example, a neighborhood association might make arrangements for installing and paying for streetlights, but too much or too little of the good may be produced. For example, if consumers A and B are to be charged for streetlights on the basis of their WTP, each will probably try to convince the other that they place a low value on streetlights regardless of how they actually value them. It is therefore difficult to determine where the total marginal benefit curve for a public good is located, even if only a small group of people is involved. When a large group of people shares a good that is non-excludable and non-rivalrous, such as national defense, negotiations become impractical. Consequently, if the good is going to be produced at all, the government must almost certainly intervene by either producing the good itself or subsidizing its production.

Because streetlighting is both non-rivalrous in consumption and non-excludable, it is close to being a pure public good. Examples of other goods that are close to being pure public goods are flood control, national defense, and crime deterrence resulting from police patrolling the streets. Other goods may be either non-rivalrous or non-excludable, but not both. For example, an uncrowded road is essentially non-rivalrous in nature. One person's use of it does not keep another from using it. Yet, it is excludable. Individuals could be required to pay a toll to use it. Thus, it is sometimes called a *toll good*. Fish in international waters provide an example of a good that is rivalrous but non-excludable. Fish and fishers move around so it is difficult to preclude fishers from catching a particular species of fish, for example, tuna. However, if a fisher catches a tuna, then that tuna is no longer available to other fishers. This type of good is called an *open-access resource*. Goods that are either non-rivalrous or non-excludable, but not both, exhibit some but not all of the characteristics of public goods. However, for the sake of brevity, we have focused on pure public goods, which are both non-rivalrous and non-excludable.

As suggested by the preceding analysis, because of both non-rivalry and non-excludability, actual markets for pure public goods are unlikely to exist. However, marginal benefit and marginal cost curves, which are analogous to market demand and supply curves, do exist. We have already shown how to derive a marginal benefit curve for a public good. And, as in the case of a private good, the marginal cost curve for a public good simply reflects the costs of producing each incremental unit of the good. Social welfare is maximized when marginal benefits equal marginal costs, while deadweight loss results at either smaller or larger output amounts. However, because of the absence of a true market, little or none of a pure public good would be produced without government intervention, or at least some sort of negotiation process. Thus, in the absence of government intervention or negotiations, society would forgo social surplus resulting from consumption of the good. Even if the government does intervene or negotiations do take place, there is nonetheless no guarantee that output of the good will be at the point where marginal benefits equal marginal costs because the marginal benefit curve for a pure public good is inherently unknowable. As a consequence, too much or too little of it may be produced. However, as described in Chapter 16, techniques exist that can be used to obtain information about WTP for public goods.

5.3.6   *Addictive Goods: Intrapersonal Externalities*

For some people, the consumption of a particular good today increases their demand for its consumption in the future. For example, exposure to classical music during childhood may contribute to a demand for such music in adulthood. Economic models of addictive goods assume that the amount demanded at any time depends on the amount of previous consumption. *Rational addiction* occurs when consumers fully take account of the future effects of their current consumption.[19] If current consumption is myopic or fails to take account of future risks, then addiction is not rational. For example, some children may fail to anticipate the consequences of tobacco addiction during their adulthood or some adults may fail to anticipate the risk that their casual gambling may become a disruptive compulsion. Such cases involve *negative intrapersonal externalities* – harm imposed by current consumers on their future selves.

The presence of negative intrapersonal externalities brings into question the appropriateness of using changes in consumer surplus measured under market demand curves as the basis for assessing the benefits of alternative policies. On the one hand, the demand curve reveals the marginal willingness of the market to pay for additional units of the good. On the other hand, the satisfaction from addictive consumption may not actually make consumers better off – it avoids the pain of abstinence but does not provide as much happiness as would alternative consumption in a non-addicted state. The stated desire and costly efforts made by many adult smokers to quit smoking suggests that they perceive benefits from ending their addiction. In other words, they wish they had not been addicted by their younger selves.

A plausible approach to measuring consumer surplus in the presence of undesirable addiction involves assessing consumer surplus using unaddicted demand curves.[20] Figure 5.9 illustrates the approach taking as an example addicted, or so-called problem, gamblers. It shows two demand curves: D_A, the demand curve for gambling in the presence of the addiction, and D_R, the demand curve for the same group of addicted gamblers if they were instead like the majority of recreational gamblers who enjoy gambling but do not have a strong compulsion to gamble that leads them to regret their gambling behaviors. The quantity of gambling demanded by these addicted gamblers at price P is Q_A. If they were not addicted, however, then they would consume only Q_R at that price. Q_A minus Q_R is the excess consumption due to the addiction. Consumption up to level Q_R involves a positive consumer surplus of PaP_C. The consumption from Q_R to Q_A involves expenditures of Q_RabQ_A but consumer value equal to only Q_RacQ_A as measured under their recreational demand curve, resulting in a deadweight loss equal to area abc. Overall, participation in this market by these addicted gamblers yields consumer surplus equal to

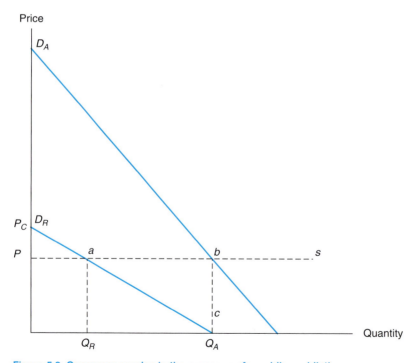

Figure 5.9 Consumer surplus in the presence of gambling addiction.

$PaP_C - abc$. If a policy resulted in these addicted gamblers becoming unaddicted recreational gamblers, then a surplus gain of *abc* would result.

The Australian Productivity Commission applied this approach to estimate consumer surplus losses and gains from the Australian gambling industry. It estimated a consumer surplus gain for recreational gamblers (97.9% of all gamblers) to be between AU$2.7 billion and AU$4.5 billion annually but a consumer surplus loss of almost AU$2.7 billion annually for problem gamblers (2.1% of all gamblers).[21]

5.4   Conclusions

This chapter has shown that the gains and losses associated with government programs and projects are appropriately determined by valuing the resulting changes in net government revenue flows, producer surplus, and consumer surplus. Even when the relevant demand and supply curves are known, great care must be exercised in order to measure the changes appropriately, especially when the relevant markets are distorted. The chapter demonstrates how policies to correct five prominent types of market failures – monopoly, information asymmetries, externalities, public goods, and addictive goods – can be analyzed within a CBA framework.

The chapter focused on output markets, the markets in which policy interventions take place. The following chapter considers factor markets in which the government purchases the inputs required by the program or project. These markets, primary markets, are the ones that are directly affected by a particular policy. Markets that are indirectly affected – secondary markets – are the focus of Chapter 7.

Exercises for Chapter 5

1. Suppose the government is considering an increase in the toll on a certain stretch of highway from $.40 to $.50. At present, 50,000 cars per week use that highway stretch; after the toll is imposed, it is projected that only 45,000 cars per week will use the highway stretch.

   Assuming that the marginal cost of highway use is constant (i.e., the supply curve is horizontal) and equal to $.40 per car, what is the social change in surplus attributable to the increase in the toll? (Hint: the toll increase will cause the supply curve, not the demand curve, to shift.)

2. A country imports 3 billion barrels of crude oil per year and domestically produces another 3 billion barrels of crude oil per year. The world price of crude oil is $90 per barrel. Assuming linear curves, economists estimate the price elasticity of domestic supply to be 0.25 and the price elasticity of domestic demand to be 0.1 at the current equilibrium.

a. Consider the changes in social surplus that would result from imposition of a $30 per barrel import fee on crude oil that would involve annual administrative costs of $250 million. Assume that the world price will not change as a result of the country imposing the import fee, but that the domestic price will increase by $30 per barrel. Also assume that only producers, consumers, and taxpayers within the country have standing. Determine the quantity consumed, the quantity produced domestically, and the quantity imported after the imposition of the import fee. Then estimate the annual social benefits of the import fee.

b. Economists have estimated that the marginal excess burden of taxation in the country is 0.25 (see Chapter 3). Reestimate the net social benefits assuming that 20 percent of the increase in producer surplus is realized as tax revenue under the existing tax system. In answering this question, assume that increases in tax revenues less the cost of administrating the import fee are used to reduce domestic taxes.

c. The reduction in the country's demand for imports may affect the world price of crude oil. Assuming that the import fee reduces the world price from $90 to $80 per barrel, and thus, the after-tax domestic price is $80 + $30 = $110 per barrel, a net increase in domestic price of $20 per barrel, repeat the analysis done in parts a and b.

Notes

1. Usually, ΔR takes into account the cost of collecting the revenues.

2. For a detailed examination of government failures, see David L. Weimer and Aidan R. Vining, *Policy Analysis: Concepts and Practice*, 6th edn (New York, NY: Taylor & Francis, 2017).

3. A change in price only causes a movement along the supply curve, a change in quantity supplied. However, a project that provides more of a good increases the supply of the good, resulting in a shift of the supply curve.

4. This assumes, of course, that the market is sufficiently competitive and the firms in it are sufficiently efficient that all of the cost savings are passed on to consumers in the form of a price decrease.

5. An alternative method of measuring the gain in social surplus is simply to compare total social surplus with and without the project. In the absence of the project, total social surplus would be represented by the triangular area *fae*, while in the presence of the project, total social surplus would be represented by the triangular area *fbd*. Subtracting the smaller triangle from the larger triangle, we again find that the net gain in social surplus equals the trapezoidal area *abde*.

6. For a theoretical treatment of externalities, public goods, and club goods, see Richard Corres and Todd Sandler, *The Theory of Externalities, Public Goods and Club Goods*, 2nd edn (New York, NY: Cambridge University Press, 1996).

7. There are, of course, other types of markets in which individual firms have market power – for example, those characterized by oligopoly or monopolistic competition. We focus on markets characterized by monopoly, and especially natural monopoly, because government intervention is most likely to occur in these markets.

8. Of course, foreign-owned firms, regardless of whether they are competitive or monopolistic, usually would not be given standing. Therefore, their benefits would not be counted in a CBA.

9. There are, of course, alternative policies that the government might adopt in response to the monopoly. For example, it might tax the monopolist's profits, regulate the prices the monopolist charges, or operate it as a state-owned enterprise.

10. For comprehensive analyses of public–private partnerships, see Anthony E. Boardman, Matti Siemiatycki and Aidan R. Vining, "The theory and evidence concerning public-private partnerships in Canada and elsewhere". SPP Briefing Paper 9.12, 2016; and Graeme A. Hodge, Carsten Greve and Anthony E. Boardman, *International Handbook on Public-Private Partnerships* (Cheltenham, UK: Edward Elgar, 2010).

11. In principle, it is possible that D_u could be to the left of D_i, rather than to the right of it as shown in Figure 5.5. This would occur if instead of desiring more of the product in the absence of information concerning it than they would with the information, consumers desire less of it. In practice, however, such situations are unlikely to continue for long because strong incentives would exist for sellers to eliminate such information asymmetry by providing buyers with the needed information, thereby increasing their demand for the product. When the actual demand curve is to the right of the fully informed demand curve, the incentive, in contrast, is for sellers to withhold the information.

12. The two demand curves are drawn closer together at high prices rather than at low prices to imply that at higher prices buyers would go to more trouble to obtain additional information about the product than they would at lower prices. Whether or not this is actually the case, however, is not essential to the analysis.

13. This is discussed more fully in Aidan R. Vining and David L. Weimer, "Information Asymmetry Favoring Sellers: A Policy Framework." *Policy Sciences*, 21(4), 1988, 281–303.

14. For a more extensive discussion of these three types of products, see Vining and Weimer, "Information Asymmetry Favoring Sellers: A Policy Framework."

15. For an entertaining discussion of possible misuses of the term "externality" and when intervention may or may not be appropriate for correcting externalities, see Virginia Postrel, "External Cost: The Dangers of Calling Everything Pollution." *Reason*, 1999.

16. This tax can be levied either in the traditional manner – that is, on the good itself – or, alternatively, by the government issuing transferable permits that, in effect, tax effluents emitted by firms, rather than the goods they produce. Under the latter approach, which is currently being used in the United States to control sulphur dioxide emissions, firms that have found ways to control their pollution relatively inexpensively can sell their permits to pollute to firms for which pollution control would be relatively more costly.

17. Indeed, when, as in the case illustrated in Figure 5.6, the tax is levied on the good, there is no special incentive for firms to reduce the amount of pollution resulting from their production process. However, when the effluent itself is taxed – for example, through use of the transferable pollution permits discussed in the previous endnote – such incentives do exist.

18. The free-rider problem is also closely linked to difficulties in remedying problems resulting from externalities. For example, because clean air is both non-rivalrous and non-excludable, in the absence of government

intervention, limited incentives exist for the private sector to produce clean air by reducing air pollution.

19. Gary S. Becker and Kevin M. Murphy, "A Theory of Rational Addiction." *Journal of Political Economy*, 96(4), 1988, 675–700.

20. Independent developments of this approach can be found in Fritz L. Laux, "Addiction as a Market Failure: Using Rational Addiction Results to Justify Tobacco Regulation." *Journal of Health Economics*, 19(4), 2000, 421–37; and Australian Productivity Commission, *Australia's Gambling Industries*, Inquiry Report No. 10, 26 1999, Appendix C, 11–13. Available at www.pc.gov.au/inquiry/gambling/finalreport/index.html.27.

21. Australian Productivity Commission, *Australia Gambling Industries*, chapter 5, p. 24.

6 Valuing Impacts in Input Markets

Public policies usually require resources (i.e., inputs) that could be used to produce other goods or services instead. Public works projects such as dams, bridges, highways, and subway systems, for example, require labor, materials, land, and equipment. Similarly, social service programs typically require professional employees, computers, telephones, and office space; wilderness preserves, recreation areas, and parks require at least land. Once resources are devoted to these purposes, they obviously are no longer available to produce other goods and services. As a result, almost all public policies incur opportunity costs. Conceptually, these costs equal the value of the goods and services that would have been produced had the resources used in carrying them out been used instead in the best alternative way.

The opportunity cost of the resources used by a program or policy equals the change in social surplus in the input markets. Furthermore, this change equals the expenditure on the inputs adjusted, when necessary, by the changes in consumer surplus and producer surplus in the input markets. Analogous to the previous chapter, this chapter first shows how to compute opportunity costs when the market for a resource is efficient and then it shows how to compute the opportunity cost when the market for the resource is inefficient (i.e., there is a market failure). As will be seen, in the first of these situations, budgetary expenditures usually accurately measure project opportunity costs if there are no price effects and will slightly overstate project opportunity costs if there are price effects. In the second situation, expenditures may substantially overstate or understate project opportunity costs. In this situation, analysts often use shadow prices in order to obtain the best estimates of social costs.

Before beginning, it may be helpful to make a general point concerning opportunity costs: the relevant determination is what must be given up today and in the future, *not* what has already been given up. The latter costs are *sunk* and should be ignored. In CBA, the extent to which costs are sunk depends importantly on whether an *ex ante, ex post*, or *in medias res* analysis is being conducted. For instance, suppose you are asked to evaluate a decision to complete a bridge after construction has already begun. The opportunity cost of the steel and concrete that is already in place is the value of these materials in their current best alternative use, which is most likely measured by the maximum amount for which they could be sold as scrap, less the costs of scrapping them. The latter costs may exceed the scrap value of the materials and, therefore, the opportunity cost will be negative when calculating the incremental gain of continuing construction.

6.1   Valuing Costs in Efficient Markets

6.1.1   *Perfectly Elastic Supply Curves*

An example of this situation is when a government agency that runs a training program for unemployed workers purchases pencils for trainees. Assuming an absence of failures in the market for pencils, and that the agency buys only a small proportion of the total pencils sold in the market, the agency is realistically viewed as facing a horizontal supply curve for pencils. Thus, the agency's purchases will have a negligible effect on the price of pencils; it can purchase additional pencils at the price they would have cost in the absence of the training program.

This situation is depicted in Figure 6.1. If a project purchases q' units of the input factor represented in the diagram (e.g., pencils), the demand curve, D, would shift horizontally to the right by q'. As implied by the horizontal supply curve, marginal costs remain unchanged and, hence, the price remains at P_0. The area under the supply curve represents the opportunity cost of the factor and P_0 is the opportunity cost of one additional unit of the factor. Consequently, the opportunity cost to society of the q' additional units of the factor needed by the project is simply the original price of the factor times the number of units purchased (i.e., P_0 times q'). In Figure 6.1, this is represented by the shaded rectangle abq_1q_0. There is no change in consumer surplus or producer surplus in the factor market. Thus, the opportunity cost of the additional pencils used by the agency equals the expenditure it must incur to buy them.

Because most input factors have neither steeply rising nor declining marginal cost curves, *it is often reasonable to presume that expenditures required for project inputs equal their social costs.* This is the case when the quantity of the resource purchased

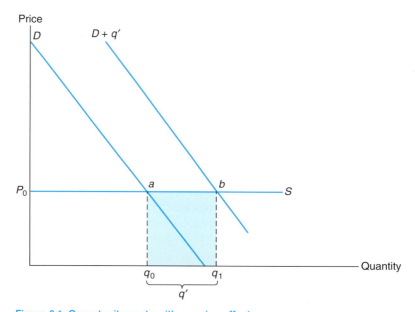

Figure 6.1 Opportunity costs with no price effects.

makes only a small addition to the total demand for the resource, and where, in addition, there is no reason to suspect the existence of significant market failures.

6.1.2   *Perfectly Inelastic Supply Curves*

In contrast to pencils, let us now examine a government purchase of a parcel of land for a park. We assume that, unlike the pencils, the quantity of land in a specified area is fixed at A acres. Thus, the government faces a vertical rather than horizontal supply curve. In addition, we assume that if the government does not purchase the land, it will be sold in one-acre parcels to private buyers who will build houses on it.

This situation is represented in Figure 6.2, where S is the supply curve and D the private-sector demand curve. If the owners of the land sell it in the private market, they receive the amount represented by the rectangle $PbA0$. Now let us assume that the government secures all A units of the land at the market price through its eminent domain powers, paying owners the market price of P. Thus, the government's budgetary cost is represented in Figure 6.2 by area $PbA0$.

Here, however, the government's budgetary outlay understates the opportunity cost of removing the land from the private sector. The reason is that the potential private buyers of the land lose consumer surplus (triangle aPb in Figure 6.2) as a result of the government taking away their opportunity to purchase land, a real loss that is not included in the government's purchase price. The full cost of the land if it is purchased by the government is represented in Figure 6.2 by all of the area under the demand curve to the left of the vertical supply curve, area $abA0$, not only the rectangular area below the price line.[1]

6.1.3   *Efficient Markets with Noticeable Price Effects*

It is possible that even when a resource is purchased in an essentially efficient market its price is bid up. This could occur, for example, if the construction of a very large dam requires massive amounts of concrete. In such a situation, the project should be

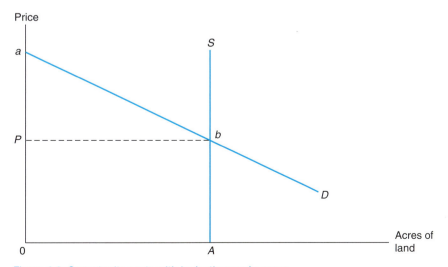

Figure 6.2 Opportunity costs with inelastic supply curve.

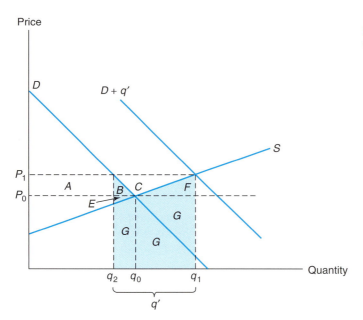

Figure 6.3 Opportunity costs with price effects.

viewed as facing an upward-sloping supply curve for the resource input. Such a supply curve is illustrated in Figure 6.3. In this example, project purchases of q' units of the resource would shift the demand curve, D, to the right. Because the supply curve, S, is upward-sloping, the equilibrium price rises from P_0 to P_1, indicating that the large purchase causes the marginal cost of the resource to rise. The price increase causes the original buyers in the market to decrease their purchases from q_0 to q_2. However, total purchases, including those made by the project, expand from q_0 to q_1. Thus, the q' units of the resource purchased by the project come from two distinct sources: (1) units bid away from their previous buyers, and (2) additional units sold in the market.

Total project expenditures on the resource are equal to P_1 times q'. In Figure 6.3, these expenditures are represented by areas $B + C + G + E + F$, which together form a rectangle. To calculate the opportunity cost we need to add changes in consumer and producer surplus. Area labeled A plus area labeled B in Figure 6.3 represent a decrease in the consumer surplus of the original buyers because of the price increase. However, sellers gain producer surplus as a result of the price represented by areas $A + B + C$. Therefore, the net *increase* in consumer plus producer surplus equals area C. This amount should be *subtracted* from government expenditures to obtain the cost equal to areas $B + G + E + F$. The effects of the purchase are summarized in the following social accounting ledger.

	Gains	Losses	Net gains
Consumers		$A + B$	$-\{A + B\}$
Producers	$A + B + C$		$A + B + C$
Government		$B + C + G + E + F$	$-\{B + C + G + E + F\}$
Society			$-\{B + G + E + F\}$

When prices change, the opportunity cost equals budgetary outlay less an adjustment, which is given by area C. If the demand and supply curves are linear, this adjustment can be readily calculated. It equals the amount of the factor purchased for the project, q', multiplied by $1/2(P_1 - P_0)$, half the difference between the new and the old prices.[2] The social cost of purchasing the resource for the project, areas $B + G + E + F$, equals the amount purchased multiplied by the average of the new and old prices, $1/2(P_1 + P_0)(q')$.[3] The average of the new and old prices reflects the social opportunity cost of purchasing the resource more accurately than either the old price or the new price. It is an example of a shadow price. As an examination of Figure 6.3 suggests, area C will be small relative to the budgetary cost unless the rise in prices is quite substantial. In many instances, therefore, the budgetary outlay will provide a good approximation of the social cost even when there is an effect on prices.

The social cost of using a resource for a project or program does not necessarily depend upon the mechanism that a government uses to obtain it. Suppose, for example, that instead of paying the market price for q' units of the resource represented in Figure 6.3, the government instead first orders supplying firms to increase their prices to the original customers in the market from P_0, to P_1, thereby causing sales to these buyers to fall from q_0 to q_2. Next, suppose that the government orders these firms to supply q' units to the government at the additional cost required to produce them. The social surplus loss resulting from the price increase to the original buyers is area $B + E$, which is the deadweight loss attributable to the increase in price. The social opportunity cost of producing the additional q' units of the resource for the government, which in this case corresponds to the government's budgetary expenditure, is the trapezoidal area $G + F$. Thus, the social cost that results from the government's directive is $B + G + E + F$. This cost is exactly the same as the social cost that results when the government purchases the resource in the same manner as any other buyer in the market. Notice, however, that this time the government's budgetary outlay, $G + F$, is smaller, rather than larger, than the social opportunity cost of using the resource.

6.2　　Valuing Costs in Distorted Markets

As indicated in Chapter 3, in an efficient market, price equals marginal social cost. When price does not equal marginal social cost, allocative inefficiency results. A variety of circumstances can lead to inefficiency: absence of a working market, market failures, and distortions due to government interventions (such as taxes, subsidies, regulations, price ceilings, and price floors). Any of these distortions can arise in factor markets, complicating the estimation of opportunity cost.

Because of space limitations, it is possible to examine only five distortions here. First, we consider the situation in which the government purchases an input at a price below the factor's opportunity cost. Second, we look at the situation when the government makes purchases of an input that is in fixed supply. Third, we examine the case in which the government hires from a market in which there is unemployed labor. Fourth, we consider a project in which government hiring for a project induces labor to migrate from rural to urban areas, as often occurs in a developing country. Fifth, we explore the situation in which the government purchases inputs for a project from a monopolist. In each of these situations, shadow pricing is needed to measure more accurately the opportunity cost of the input.

6.2.1   *Purchases at Below Opportunity Costs*

Consider a proposal to establish more courts so that more criminal trials can be held. Budgetary costs include the salaries of judges and court attendants, rent for courtrooms and offices, and perhaps expenditures for additional correctional facilities (because the greater availability of trial capacity leads to more imprisonment). For these factors, budgetary costs may correspond well to social opportunity costs. However, the budget may also include payments to jurors, payments that typically just cover commuting expenses. If any compensation is paid to jurors for their time, then it is usually set at a nominal *per diem* not related to the value of their time as reflected, perhaps, by their wage rates. Thus, the budgetary outlay to jurors almost certainly understates the opportunity cost of jurors' time. Consequently, a shadow price is necessary. A better estimate of jurors' opportunity cost is, for example, their commuting expenses plus the number of juror-hours times either the average or the median pre-tax hourly wage rate for the locality. The commuting expenses estimate should include the actual resource costs of transporting jurors to the court, not just out-of-pocket expenses. The hourly pre-tax wage rate times the hours spent on jury duty provides a measure of the value of goods forgone because of lost labor, although several criticisms of it are discussed in Chapter 15.

6.2.2   *Purchases When Inputs Are in Fixed Supply*

Sometimes the government needs to make a purchase of an input that is in fixed supply. A situation in which supply is fixed is illustrated in Figure 6.4, which pertains to the electricity that would be required for a project. The production of electricity is often characterized as having constant marginal costs up to a capacity constraint. Consistent with this, the supply curve in the figure is perfectly elastic prior to Q_1 and then becomes completely inelastic when the nation's generating capacity is exhausted. Let D_a represent the demand curve for electricity without the project for which the government requires electricity and D'_a represent the demand curve with the project. Under these circumstances, the electricity capacity constraint is not binding. As a result, the project would not affect the current consumers of electricity. However, it would require that additional inputs be used to produce the additional electricity needed by the project. Consequently, the cost of the electricity used on the project would simply be the government's purchase expenditure.

Now assume that without the project the demand curve for electricity is D_b and with the project it is D'_b. Thus, the project would increase the market price of electricity from P_1 to P_2 and reduce the consumption of electricity by current consumers from Q_1 to Q_2. Because of the price increase, current consumers lose surplus, while the producers of electricity gain surplus. As explained earlier in the chapter, these changes in surplus can be appropriately taken into account in determining the cost of electricity to the project by simply using the average of the old and new market prices, $(P_1 + P_2)/2$, as a shadow

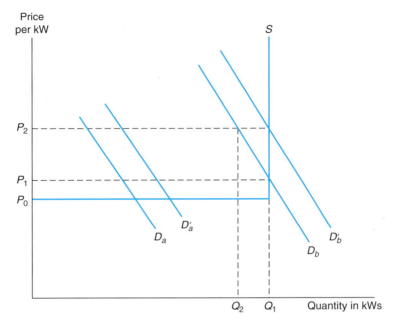

Figure 6.4 Electricity market supply is either completely elastic or completely inelastic.

price. Thus, measured in market prices, the cost of electricity for the project would equal $[(P_1 + P_2)/2](Q_1 - Q_2)$.

6.2.3   *Hiring Unemployed Labor*

We have stressed that assessing opportunity costs in the presence of market failures or government interventions requires a careful accounting of social surplus changes. Analysis of the opportunity cost of workers hired for a government project who would otherwise be unemployed illustrates the kind of effort that is required.

Let us examine the opportunity costs of labor in a market in which minimum wage laws, union bargaining power, or some other factor creates a wage floor that keeps the wage rate above the market-clearing level and, consequently, there is unemployed labor. Notice that we are focusing here on a very specific form of unemployment: that which occurs when the number of workers who desire jobs at the wage paid in a particular labor market exceeds the number of workers employers are willing to hire at that wage.[4] Workers who are unemployed for this reason are sometimes said to be *in surplus*. We focus on surplus workers so that we can examine their opportunity costs when they are hired for a government project. This issue is of particular importance because there are government projects that are specifically designed to put surplus workers to work and numerous other projects that are likely to hire such workers. Of course, there are other forms of unemployment than the type considered here. For example, some persons are briefly unemployed while they move from one job to another.

Before discussing how the opportunity cost of surplus labor might be measured, it may be useful to consider more explicitly the extent to which the labor hired to work on a government project reduces the number of unemployed workers. Consider, for example, a project that hires 100 workers. How many fewer workers will be unemployed as a result? In considering this question, it is important to recognize that the project does not have to hire directly from the ranks of the unemployed. Even if the project hires 100 previously employed persons, this will result in 100 job vacancies, some of which may be filled by the unemployed. If the unemployment rate for the type of workers hired for the project (as determined by their occupation and geographic location) is very high (say, over 10 percent), the number of unemployed workers may approach 100. However, if the unemployment rate for the workers is low (say, below 4 percent or so), most of the measured unemployed are probably between jobs rather than in surplus. As a consequence, the project is likely to cause little reduction in the number of persons who are unemployed. Instead, the project will draw its workforce from those employed elsewhere or out of the labor force. To illustrate, a recent study by Donald Vitaliano found that in July 2009, when the national unemployment rate was 9.5 percent, over half of the workers hired for a government project (55 percent) would have been drawn from among persons who were either unemployed or who had withdrawn from the labor force but stated that they wanted a job. Based on Vitaliano's estimated relationship, the percentage drawn from the ranks of the unemployed would have only been 16 percent in November 2016, when the unemployment rate was 5.0 percent.[5]

Figure 6.5 depicts a situation in which a government project reduces unemployment. In this figure, the pre-project demand curve for labor, D, and the supply curve for labor, S, intersect at P_e, the equilibrium price in the absence of the wage floor, P_m. At the wage floor, L_s, workers desire employment, but only L_d workers are demanded so that $L_s - L_d$ workers are in surplus and thus unemployed. Now imagine that L' workers are

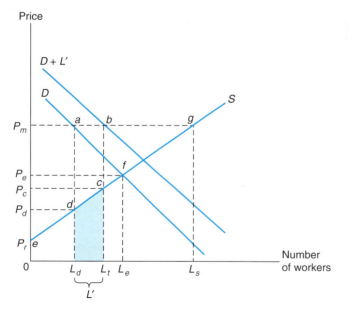

Figure 6.5 Opportunity costs with a price floor.

hired for a government project at a wage of P_m. This shifts the demand curve to the right by L'. As long as L' is less than the number of unemployed laborers, the price remains at the floor.

We now consider five alternative measures of the social cost of hiring the L' unemployed workers. All five of these measures are subject to criticism. Indeed, it is not obvious that, as a practical matter, it is possible to obtain an accurate value of the social cost of hiring the unemployed. However, some of the alternative measures described here are far better approximations of the true social cost than others.

1. **Measure A.** It is sometimes suggested that because the unemployed are not working, there are zero opportunity costs in putting them to work. However, this treats the unemployed as if their time is valueless. This is clearly inappropriate on two grounds. First, many unemployed persons are in fact engaged in productive enterprises such as job search, child care, and home improvements. Second, even if they were completely at leisure, leisure itself has value to those who are enjoying it. Consequently, few, if any, unemployed persons are willing to work at a zero wage. Indeed, the supply curve in Figure 6.5 represents the value that various individuals, both those who are employed and those who are unemployed, place on their time when they are not employed. For example, an individual located at point f would only be willing to accept employment at a price of P_e or greater. Thus, P_e provides a measure of the value that this person places on his or her time. In other words, his or her opportunity cost of giving up leisure time to work is P_e. Similarly, individuals located on the supply curve at points c and d value their time at P_c and P_d, respectively. No individual is willing to work at a price below P_r, and, as P_r has a positive value, Figure 6.5 implies that the opportunity cost of hiring the unemployed must be above zero.

2. **Measure B.** Figure 6.5 indicates that total budgetary expenditure on labor for this project is P_m times L', which equals the area of rectangle abL_tL_d. This budgetary outlay for labor, however, is likely to overstate substantially the true social cost of hiring workers for the project. As implied by the supply curve in Figure 6.5, although employed workers are paid a price of P_m, most would be willing to work for less. This difference between the value they place on their time, as indicated by the supply curve, and P_m, the price they are actually paid while employed, is producer (i.e., worker) surplus, which may be viewed as a transfer to the workers from the government agency hiring them. To obtain a measure of the social cost of hiring workers for the project, this producer surplus must be subtracted from the budgetary expenditure on labor.[6] Measure B fails to do this.

3. **Measure C.** As the project expands employment in the market represented by Figure 6.5 from L_d to L_t, one might assume that the trapezoid $abcd$ represents producer surplus enjoyed by the newly hired. Given this assumption, one would subtract area $abcd$ from area abL_tL_d to obtain a measure of the social

cost of hiring workers for the project. Thus, the social cost would be measured as the shaded trapezoid cdL_dL_t, the area under the supply curve between L_d and L_t. This shaded area would equal the opportunity cost of the newly hired workers – that is, the value of the time they give up when they go to work.

4. **Measure D.** One shortcoming of measure C is that it is implicitly based on an assumption that all the unemployed persons hired for the project value their time at less than P_c and at greater than P_d. In other words, this approach assumes that these workers are all located between points c and d on the supply curve. However, there is no basis for such an assumption. Indeed, it is quite likely that some of the hired unemployed persons value their time at well above P_c and that others value their time at well under P_d. In fact, the figure implies that unemployed persons who value their time as low as P_r and as high as P_m would be willing to work on the project because the project would pay them a price of P_m. Thus, perhaps, a better assumption is that the unemployed persons who would actually get hired for the project are distributed more or less equally along the supply curve between points e and g, rather than being confined between points d and c. This assumption implies that the unemployed persons who are hired for the project value their time by no more than P_m, by no less than P_r, and, on average, by $1/2(P_m + P_r)$. Thus, the social cost of hiring L' workers for the project would be computed as equal to $1/2(P_m + P_r)(L')$.

5. **Measure E.** One practical problem with using measure D in an actual CBA is that the value of P_r, the lowest price at which any worker represented in Figure 6.5 would be willing to accept employment, is unlikely to be known. Given this, some assumption about the value of P_r must be made. One possible, and perhaps not unreasonable, assumption is that the supply curve passes through the origin and, hence, the value of P_r equals zero. The fact that the probabilities of illness, divorce, and suicide all increase with unemployment, while job skills deteriorate, suggest that P_r could, in practice, be very low for at least some unemployed persons. If we once again assume that the unemployed persons who are hired for the project are distributed more or less equally along the supply curve between the point at which it intersects the vertical axis and point g, then this implies that the unemployed persons who are hired for the project value their time by no more than P_m, by no less than zero, and, on average, by $1/2(P_m + 0) = 1/2\,P_m$. Hence, the social cost of hiring workers for the project would be computed as $1/2\,P_m(L')$. Note that the estimate provided by this computation is equal to half the government's budgetary outlay. While this cost estimate would be smaller and almost certainly less accurate than that computed using measure D, it is usually easier to obtain.

Given our preceding argument that non-work time has a positive value, measure E is probably best viewed as providing an easily obtainable lower-bound estimate of the true project social costs for labor, while the project budgetary cost for labor, measure B, provides an upper-bound estimate.

6.2.4   *Hiring Labor when Rural to Urban Migration within a Developing Country is Important*

A substantial fraction of the unskilled workers for a project in a developing country are ultimately likely to be drawn from the countryside. This will be true not only of projects in rural areas, but also of projects in cities, even if the workers who are directly hired by the project currently reside in urban areas. The reason is that as employment increases in urban areas in developing countries, workers in rural areas are induced to migrate to the areas where employment has increased.

Why this migration occurs is suggested by a well-known model developed by John Harris and Michael Todaro.[7] Their model is based on two observations about developing countries: unemployment is often very high in urban areas, and earnings are typically considerably higher in urban than in rural areas. Although Harris and Todaro do not explain the reasons for the higher urban wages, they could be due to minimum wage laws that are enforced in urban areas but not rural areas, the role of unions, decisions by foreign corporations that are under pressure in their home countries to pay wages that exceed subsistence levels, or a belief on the part of employers that higher wages result in higher productivity because higher paid workers are healthier, less likely to leave the firm, and more motivated.[8] The key point for purposes of the Harris–Todaro model is that urban wages are above their equilibrium level and, consequently, result in urban unemployment.[9] Rural wages, in contrast, are at their equilibrium level and, consequently, lower than urban wages.

Harris and Todaro suggest that because of the higher urban wages, workers will migrate from the countryside to the cities, even though some of them will not be able to find jobs. More specifically, they postulate that the probability that a rural worker will obtain employment upon migrating to a city equals $(L - U)/L$, where L is the size of the workforce in the city, U is the number of unemployed persons, and $E = (L - U)$ is the number of employed workers. Therefore, the model implies that workers will have an incentive to migrate from the countryside to the city as long as:

$$RW < UW(E/L) \tag{6.1}$$

where RW is the rural wage, UW is the urban wage, and $UW(E/L)$ is the wage that migrating workers will receive on average (in other words, $UW(E/L)$ is their expected wage). Thus, according to the model, rural–urban migration will cease when:

$$RW = UW(E/L) \tag{6.2}$$

Two important implications of this model are that even when there is no incentive for further migration, urban unemployment may continue to be high, and urban wages may continue to exceed rural wages.

We now use the Harris–Todaro model to examine the effects of locating a new project in a city. Assume that prior to initiating the project the equilibrium condition specified in Equation (6.2) is being met. Now assume that ΔE unskilled workers are hired to work on the project. If ΔE is fairly small relative to the size of the workforce, then wage rates are unlikely to be affected. Moreover, urban wage rates may also be unaffected because they are already above their equilibrium level. However, because of the increase in the number of available urban jobs, the expected urban wage facing rural workers will increase to $UW[(E + \Delta E)/L]$, inducing some rural workers to migrate. Consequently, the equilibrium can only be re-established if:

$$E/L = (E + \Delta E)/(L+\Delta L) \tag{6.3}$$

where ΔL is the number of workers added to the urban labor force.

There are two things to notice here. First, if there are no changes in urban wage rates, then current residents of the city who are presently outside the labor force (that is, not already employed or seeking employment) will not be induced to join it, except perhaps by the increase in the number of available jobs. Therefore, many, if not most, of the workers added to the urban labor force will be migrants from rural areas. Second, according to the model, the number of migrants is likely to exceed the number of jobs created by the project. This can be seen by first rearranging the terms in Equation (6.3) to obtain:

$$L + \Delta L = L(E+\Delta E)/E \tag{6.4}$$

and then by subtracting $L = L(E)/E$ from Equation (6.4) and rearranging the terms to obtain:

$$L+\Delta L-L = L(E + \Delta E)/E - L(E)/E \text{ or } \Delta L/\Delta E = L/E \tag{6.5}$$

Because the urban labor force consists of both workers and the unemployed (that is, $L = E + U$), the ratio L/E must exceed 1 and, thus, as Equation (6.5) implies, so will the ratio $\Delta L/\Delta E$.

The implications of this simple model can be illustrated with an example. If the urban wage is 50 percent higher than the rural wage (that is, if $1.5RW = UW$), then Equation (6.2) implies that E/L equals 0.67. Hence, one-third of the urban workforce will be unemployed. Moreover, Equation (6.5) implies that for each job created by a project, 1.5 persons will enter the urban labor force (that is, $\Delta L = \Delta E(L/E) = 1(3/2) = 1.5$). For reasons already stressed, many, if not most, of these persons are likely to be rural migrants.

Because most of the unskilled workers added to the workforce as a result of a government project would probably be drawn from the countryside, the output that is forgone is production in rural areas. If the project is located in a rural area, then rural–urban migration is not a consideration, and the shadow wage used in estimating the value of the foregone output would simply be the rural wage. In other words, to determine the cost of labor for the project, the number of workers hired would be multiplied by the rural wage. However, if the project is located in an urban area, then account must be taken of the number of workers who would leave the countryside for each job created. According to the Harris–Todaro model, if *all* the workers added to the workforce as a result of the project are rural migrants, then this can be accomplished by multiplying the rural wage by the ratio, L/E. Alternatively, the urban wage can be used instead, given that Equation (6.2) implies that $RW(L/E) = UW$.[10]

However, the urban wage rate should be viewed as an *upper bound* because fewer than L/E rural workers may actually migrate in response to each job created by an urban project. First, as previously mentioned, some urban residents may be induced into the labor force as jobs are created by the project. Second, the actual number of migrants could be less if workers are risk-averse or there are monetary or psychic costs associated with migrating. Third, if the project is sufficiently large, then the migration of rural workers could cause rural wages to rise, thereby reducing the ultimate number of migrants. If fewer than L/E workers migrate, then the appropriate market wage to use in determining the shadow wage rate would be less than the urban wage. Thus, Caroline Dinwiddy and Francis Teal demonstrate that, under a wide variety of assumptions, the appropriate shadow wage is likely to fall somewhere between the rural and the urban market wage.[11] Consequently, *if large numbers of unskilled workers will be employed on an urban project in a developing country, and there are wide differences between rural and urban wages, a sensitivity test should be conducted in determining the shadow wage rate by first using the rural market wage and then using the urban wage.*

While urban wage rates for unskilled workers can be obtained from survey data – for example, the average manufacturing wage can be used[12] – many rural workers produce crops for their own consumption. Hence, the effective wage rate of these workers is more difficult to ascertain. One way to construct an estimate of the rural market wage is to first determine how a typical rural worker who is likely to be affected by the project being evaluated allocates his or her productive time and then estimate the value of the worker's output. For instance, suppose that the typical worker is employed on a cacao plantation for half the year and receives a daily wage of 40 pesos and food and transportation valued at 10 pesos a day, for a total of 50 pesos. Because the worker is only needed at the plantation for six months, he or she works at home during the remainder of the year, growing corn for three months and bananas for the remaining three months. Although the corn and bananas are mostly grown for home consumption, if they were brought to the local market they could be sold for 910 pesos and 1,365 pesos, respectively. Dividing the market value of corn and bananas by the 91 days during which the work to grow each was performed suggests that the worker earned a daily market wage of 10 pesos from growing corn and a daily market wage of 15 pesos from growing bananas. Given this information, the worker's daily wage can be computed as a weighted average of his or her daily return from each endeavor, where the weights are the fraction of time he or she devoted to each activity. That is:

$$RW = .5(50) + .25(10) + .25(15) = 31.25 \text{pesos} \tag{6.6}$$

In principle, at least two additional factors should be taken into account in determining the shadow wage rate of rural, unskilled workers, although in practice they rarely are because of the lack of adequate information. First, it is possible that moving to the city requires the worker to work longer hours, places the worker under greater stress, and results in a less-satisfactory lifestyle. If so, then the shadow wage rate should, in principle, be adjusted upward to account for the resulting loss of utility.

Second, many rural workers in developing countries live in large, extended families. If a project induces a rural worker to migrate to the city, then the effects on the remaining family members should, in principle, be taken into account. The remaining family members lose the migrating worker's output, of course, but they gain because the worker no longer consumes the income available to the family. These two amounts are not necessarily entirely offsetting; it is possible that the gain exceeds the loss. This would occur, for example, if the family shares its income (the total value of the output produced by all family members) equally among its members. Under these circumstances, each family member's consumption level would be equal to the average value of the output produced by the family. The family member's contribution to family output, however, would correspond to his or her marginal product. Because rural families typically produce much of their output at home on a fixed amount of land, it is likely that the family would be producing on the declining segment of its marginal product curve. If so, the value of a family member's marginal product will be smaller than the value of the output that he or she consumes. Thus, if a family member is induced by a project to migrate in such circumstances, the consumption levels of the remaining family members will increase.

Exhibit 6.1

In 1974, the World Bank led an international effort to eradicate onchocerciasis (river blindness) in West Africa. The project, which extended over more than two decades and covered 11 countries, used insecticides to kill the blackfly, the carrier of the parasite that causes onchocerciasis. The benefits of the program stem from the reduction in the number of cases of river blindness. A CBA of a similar program in a developed country would likely have measured benefits by monetizing the morbidity and mortality effects with shadow prices. (See Chapter 17 for estimates of these prices.) However, estimating the necessary shadow prices in these very poor countries was impractical. Instead, the CBA of the project conducted by the World Bank in 1995 measured benefits in terms of the value of increased agricultural output resulting from increased labor and land. As the average person who develops blindness lives with it for 8 years and dies 12 years prematurely, each avoided case adds about 20 years of productive life. Assuming that these years are employed in agriculture, the percentage increase in the rural labor supply resulting from the project was projected and multiplied by an estimated output elasticity of labor of 0.66 to obtain the predicted percentage increase in agricultural output. The value of the increase in agricultural output was in turn estimated by the World Bank. A similar procedure was used to value the additional agricultural land made available through eradication. Overall, the project offered net positive benefits, even when assuming labor force participation rates and land utilization rates of only 70 percent.

Source: Adapted from Aehyung Kim and Bruce Benton, "Cost–Benefit Analysis of the Onchocerciasis Control Program," World Bank Technical Paper Number 282, May 1995.

6.2.5   *Purchases from a Monopoly*

We now turn to a final example of measuring the social cost of project or program purchases in an inefficient market – the purchase of an input supplied by a monopoly. In this circumstance, a government agency's budgetary outlay overstates the true social costs

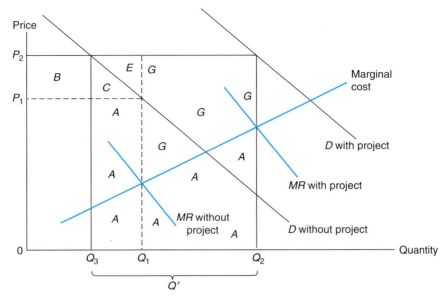

Figure 6.6 Opportunity costs when buying from a monopoly.

resulting from the purchase. This overstatement occurs because the price of the input exceeds the social cost of producing it. As a consequence, a substantial share of the revenues a monopolist receives are transfers or *monopoly rents*. Thus, in principle, a CBA should not use the budgetary outlay as a measure of social cost.

Figure 6.6 illustrates a government agency's purchase of an input from a monopoly. Prior to the purchase, the input is produced at level Q_1, where the monopolist's marginal cost and marginal revenue curves intersect. The price at Q_1, as determined by the demand curve, is P_1. Now, as a result of the agency's purchase of Q' units, the monopolist's demand curve and marginal revenue curve shift to the right. The price of the input increases to P_2 and the quantity sold increases to Q_2. At the new higher price, the agency purchases a quantity equal to the distance between Q_3 and Q_2, while the original buyers in the market reduce the quantity they purchase from Q_1 to Q_3.

As in our previous examples, the direct budgetary cost of the agency's purchase equals the price times the quantity purchased: $P_2(Q_2 - Q_3)$. In Figure 6.6, this is represented by the rectangle between Q_3 and Q_2 and bounded by P_2 (i.e., areas $A + C + G + E$). However, these budgetary costs overstate the true social cost. To find the true social cost of the agency's purchase, one must examine the effects of the purchase on the monopolist and the original buyers of the input, as well as on the agency's revenues.

Because the monopolist sells more of the input at higher prices as a result of the government's purchase, its producer surplus increases. This increase has two parts: (1) that resulting from the higher price the monopolist now receives for the units that it previously sold (which is represented in Figure 6.6 by areas $B + C + E$), and (2) that resulting from the additional units that the monopolist now sells (area G). Thus, as can be seen from the figure, part of the cost to the agency, areas $C + G + E$, is a transfer to the monopolist.

Original buyers in the market are clearly worse off as a result of the agency's purchase because they now have to pay a higher price for the input. In measuring their loss of consumer surplus, it is the original demand curve that is pertinent because this is the curve that reflects the original buyers' WTP for the input. Thus, the original buyers' total loss in consumer surplus, all of which is a transfer to the monopolist, is equal to areas $B + C$.

The following distributional social accounting ledger summarizes the effects of the purchase:

	Gains	Losses	Net gains
Consumers		$B + C$	$-\{B + C\}$
Monopolistic producer	$B + C + G + E$		$B + C + G + E$
Government		$A + C + G + E$	$-\{A + C + G + E\}$
Society			$-\{A + C\}$

The major conclusion from this analysis is that in the case of input purchases from a monopolist, budgetary expenditures are larger than the social costs. The reason is that the price the monopoly charges exceeds the marginal cost of producing the input. Consequently, in conducting a CBA, the government's budgetary cost should be adjusted downward through shadow pricing. In practice, however, the error that would result from using the unadjusted budgetary expenditures would often not be very large. As an examination of Figure 6.6 suggests, the size of the bias, areas $G + E$, depends on the extent to which the price the monopoly charges exceeds its marginal costs – in other words, on how much monopoly power it actually has. This, in turn, depends on how steeply sloped the demand curve is. Thus, before an analyst develops shadow prices, a sometimes difficult undertaking, he or she should ask whether it is really necessary to do so.

6.2.6   *The General Rule*

Other market distortions in input markets also affect opportunity costs in predictable ways. It is useful to summarize the direction of the bias created by some of these distortions. In input markets in which supply is taxed, direct expenditure outlays overestimate opportunity cost; in input markets in which supply is subsidized, expenditures underestimate opportunity cost. In input markets exhibiting positive externalities of supply, expenditures overestimate opportunity cost; in input markets exhibiting negative externalities of supply, expenditures underestimate opportunity costs. To determine opportunity costs in such cases, apply the rule: *opportunity cost equals direct expenditures on the input minus (plus) gains (losses) in producer surplus or consumer surplus occurring in the input market*.

6.3   Conclusions

This chapter has focused on input markets where the government purchases the inputs required by the program or project. It has shown that the government's budgetary expenditure on an input will differ from the social value of the purchase, its opportunity cost, if prices are affected or if, for a variety of reasons, the market in which the purchase is made is distorted. Because data on budgetary expenditures are often readily obtained and estimates of conceptually appropriate measures (which should take account of resulting changes in net government revenue flows, producer surplus, and consumer surplus) are sometimes difficult to make, those conducting CBAs need to consider how great an error results if they rely on budgetary expenditures and if correcting it is worth the cost of the effort. Sometimes upper- and lower-bound estimates are quite possible (for example, in hiring from the ranks of the unemployed). In any event, it is essential to be as transparent as possible about possible errors and their direction in reporting cost estimates of purchases in input markets.

Exercises for Chapter 6

1. Consider a low-wage labor market. Workers in this market are not presently covered by the minimum wage, but the government is considering implementing such legislation. If implemented, this law would require employers in the market to pay workers a $5 hourly wage. Suppose all workers in the market are equally productive, the current market-clearing wage rate is $4 per hour, and that at this market-clearing wage there are 600 employed workers. Further suppose that under the minimum wage legislation, only 500 workers would be employed and 300 workers would be unemployed. Finally, assume that the market demand and supply curves are linear and that the market reservation wage, the lowest wage at which any worker in the market would be willing to work, is $2.

    Compute the dollar value of the impact of the policy on employers, workers, and society as a whole.

2   Assume that a typical unskilled rural worker in a developing country would be paid 2 dubyas a week if he migrates to the city and finds a job. However, the unemployment rate for unskilled workers is 40 percent in the city.

    a.   What does the Harris–Todaro model predict the worker's rural wage is?

    b.   Assume now that the government is considering funding a project in the city that would use substantial numbers of unskilled workers. Using your answer to part (a), suggest a reasonable upper-bound and lower-bound estimate of the market wage rate for unskilled workers that the government might use in conducting a CBA of the proposed project.

3. (Instructor-provided spreadsheet recommended.) A proposed government project in a rural area with 100 unemployed persons would require the hiring of 20 workers. The project would offer wages of $12 per hour. Imagine that the reservation wages of the 100 unemployed fall between $2 and $20.

a. Estimate the opportunity cost of the labor required for the project assuming that the government makes random offers to the 100 unemployed until 20 of them accept jobs. (First, generate a list of the reservation prices of 100 persons according to the formula $2 + 18u$ where u is a random variable distributed uniformly [0, 1]. Second, work down the list to identify the first 20 workers with reservation wages less than $12. Third, sum the reservation wages of these 20 workers to get the opportunity cost of the labor used for the project.)

b. Estimate the opportunity cost of the labor required for the project assuming that the government can identify and hire the 20 unemployed with the lowest reservation wages.

c. Repeat part (a) 15 times to get a distribution for the opportunity cost and compute its standard deviation.

Notes

1. If the government were to purchase only a small part of the fixed supply of land on the open market, its budgetary outlay would very closely approximate the opportunity cost of removing the land from the private sector. In this case, the government's entry into the market would bid up the price of the land slightly, crowding potential private-sector land buyers who are just to the left of point b on the demand curve out of the market. These buyers would lose a negligible amount of surplus. In addition, those private-sector buyers who remain in the market would pay a slightly higher price. Hence, surplus would be transferred between these buyers and the sellers of the land.

2. This formula is based on a bit of geometry. The triangular area C equals one-half the rectangular area from which it is formed, $B + C + F$. Thus, area C is equivalent to $1/2(P_1 - P_0)$ (q').

3. This amount is derived as follows:

$$P_1 q' - \tfrac{1}{2}(P_1 - P_0)q' = \tfrac{1}{2}(P_0 + P_1)q'.$$

4. For a discussion of various forms of wage rigidity that result in unemployment, see Ronald G. Ehrenberg and Robert S. Smith, *Modern Labor Economics: Theory and Public Policy*, 12th edn (New York, NY: Taylor & Francis, 2015), chapter 13.

5. Donald F. Vitaliano, "An Empirical Estimate of the Labor Response Function for Benefit–Cost Analysis." *Journal of Benefit–Cost Analysis*, 3(3), 2012, Article 1. The relationship that Vitaliano estimated appears below: percentage of hired workers drawn from unemployed = 0.67 – 14.11(vacancy rate). This estimate is based on a time series covering the period from January 2001 to November 2011. "Unemployed" is defined broadly to include those officially unemployed in US government statistics plus those out of the labor force who state that they want a job. The vacancy rate (job openings divided by the size of the labor force) is strongly inversely related to the unemployment rate. The vacancy rate in July 2009 at the height of the Great Recession was .009. In November 2016, it was .037 (www.bls.gov/news.release/pdf/jolts.pdf). The pioneering study of the relationship between government spending and reducing unemployment is Robert H. Haveman and John V. Krutilla, *Unemployment, Idle*

Capacity and the Evaluation of Public Expenditure: National and Regional Analysis (Baltimore, MD: Johns Hopkins University Press, 1968).

6. A similar conclusion is reached by Robert H. Haveman and Scott Farrow, "Labor Expenditures and Benefit–Cost Accounting in Times of Unemployment." *Journal of Benefit–Cost Analysis*, 2(2), 2011, Article 7; and Robert H. Haveman and David L. Weimer, "Public Policy Induced Changes in Employment Valuation Issues for Benefit–Cost Analysis." *Journal of Benefit–Cost Analysis*, 6(1), 2015, 112–53.

7. John. R. Harris and Michael. P. Todaro, "Migration, Unemployment, and Development." *American Economic Review*, 60(1), 1970, 126–42. This model is quite simple, making no attempt to capture all important labor market phenomena in developing countries, yet it provides some very useful insights.

8. See Caroline Dinwiddy and Francis Teal, *Principles of Cost–Benefit Analysis for Developing Countries* (Cambridge: Cambridge University Press, 1996), 145–47 and 151. Higher living costs could also contribute to higher urban wages but, unlike the factors listed in the text, would not induce workers to migrate from rural to urban areas.

9. The urban wage is still equal to the marginal product of labor because urban employers hire workers until the point where the marginal product of labor equals the marginal cost of hiring an additional worker.

10. The conclusion that the urban wage should be used was also reached by Christopher J. Heady ("Shadow Wages and Induced Migration." *Oxford Economic Papers*, 33(1), 1981, 108–21) on the basis of a model that incorporated more general and complex assumptions than the Harris–Todaro model. However, Heady also discussed certain circumstances under which a lower wage, but one that is probably higher than the rural wage, should be used.

11. Dinwiddy and Teal, *Principles of Cost–Benefit Analysis for Developing Countries*, chapter 9.

12. This particular measure is suggested by Christopher J. Heady ("Shadow Wages and Induced Migration").

7 Valuing Impacts in Secondary Markets

In conducting CBAs of government policies, there is a natural tendency to list as many effects of the policies as one's imagination permits. For example, an improvement in public transportation in a particular city may increase bus usage and reduce car usage. It may also reduce downtown pollution and congestion. Further, it may subsequently reduce the demand for automobile repairs, parking places, and gasoline.

To assess these effects, one must first determine which of them occur in primary markets and which of them occur in secondary markets. Primary markets refer to markets that are directly affected by a policy (that is, the output and input markets discussed in Chapters 5 and 6), while secondary markets are markets that are indirectly affected. Changes in bus usage clearly occur in the primary market for public transportation. The reductions in pollution and congestion also can be thought of as occurring in that primary market, though these particular impacts are in the external, or missing, part of that market. Any effect that occurs in a primary market should be accounted for in a CBA. On the other hand, effects on the demand for auto repairs, parking places, and gasoline occur in secondary markets and, as will be seen, often can (and indeed should) be ignored in conducting CBA. This last group of effects is often referred to as *secondary, second-round, spillover, side, pecuniary*, or *indirect effects*.

While Chapters 5 and 6 examined the benefits and costs of government policies that occur in primary markets, this chapter focuses on policy impacts in secondary markets. As in those chapters, we distinguish between efficient and distorted markets. In addition, the chapter takes a brief look at the special implications of secondary market effects for local communities, as the benefits of such effects are often touted by advocates of local infrastructure projects such as sports stadiums and convention centers.

7.1 Valuing Benefits and Costs in Efficient Secondary Markets

7.1.1 *Complements and Substitutes*

Secondary market effects result because government policies affect the prices of goods in primary markets, and this, in turn, noticeably affects the demand for other goods. These latter goods are referred to as *complements to* and *substitutes for the good traded in the primary market*.

Consider the following example. Stocking a lake near a city with fish lowers the effective price of access to fishing grounds for the city's residents. They not only fish more often, but they also demand more bait and fishing equipment. We say that access to fishing grounds and fishing equipment are complements because a decrease (increase) in the price of one will result in an increase (decrease) in the demand for the other. In contrast, fishing is a substitute for golfing because as the price of fishing goes down (up), the demand for golfing goes down (up).

If government policies affect the demand for goods in secondary markets, then prices in these secondary markets may or may not change as a result. We first discuss the simpler situation in which prices do not change. We then analyze the more complex situation in which prices do change in secondary markets.

7.1.2   *Efficient Secondary Market Effects without Price Changes*

Because most goods have substantial numbers of complements and substitutes, many government projects cause effects in large numbers of secondary markets. Accounting for all these effects would impose an enormous burden on analysts. Fortunately, however, such effects can often be ignored in CBA without substantially biasing the estimates of net benefits. When can we ignore secondary market effects? *We can, and indeed should, ignore impacts in undistorted secondary markets as long as the change in social surplus in the primary market resulting from a government project is measured and prices in the secondary markets do not change.* The reason for this is that in the absence of price adjustments in secondary markets in response to price changes in primary markets, impacts are typically fully measured as surplus changes in primary markets. Measuring the same effects in both markets will, therefore, result in double counting. Thus, for example, if prices of fishing equipment do not change, then the increased consumption of fishing equipment is not relevant to the CBA of a project that increases access to fishing grounds.

A closer look at the fishing example should make the rule for the treatment of secondary markets clearer. For simplicity, we assume that the price of fishing equals the marginal social cost of fishing and that this marginal social cost is constant. This, in turn, implies that no producer surplus or externalities exist in the primary market (e.g., highway congestion does not result because of increased travel to the newly stocked lake).

Figure 7.1(a) shows the market for "fishing days." Prior to the stocking of the nearby lake, the effective price of a day of fishing (largely the time costs of travel) was P_{F_0}, the travel cost to a lake that contains plentiful fish but is much further away. Once fishing is available at the nearby lake, the effective price falls to P_{F_1} and, as a consequence, the number of days spent fishing by local residents rises from q_{F_0} to q_{F_1}. The resulting increase in social surplus equals the area of trapezoid $P_{F_0} abP_{F_1}$, the gain in consumer surplus. We measure this gain in consumer surplus using the demand schedule for fishing, D_F. As is customary in textbooks, this demand schedule should be viewed as the relation between price and quantity that would exist in the primary market if the prices of all secondary goods were held constant. Later we discuss the importance of this assumption.

Now consider the market for fishing equipment. The decline in the effective price of fishing days shifts the demand schedule for fishing equipment from D_{E_0} to D_{E_1} as shown in Figure 7.1(b). If the supply schedule is perfectly elastic – likely when the local market accounts for only a small fraction of regional or national demand – then the shift in demand will not increase the price of fishing equipment.

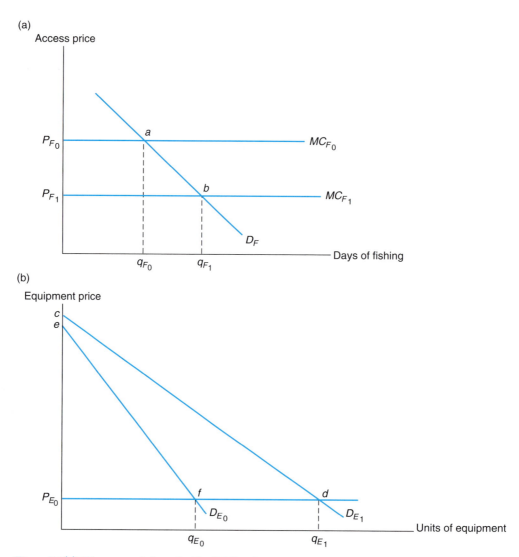

Figure 7.1(a) Primary market: market for fishing days.
Figure 7.1(b) Secondary market: market for fishing equipment (no price effect).

Does this shift in demand for fishing equipment represent a change in consumer welfare that should be counted in a CBA of the fish-stocking project? In other
words, should the gap between the old and new demand schedules that is above the
price line be counted as an additional increase in consumer surplus? It is tempting to
treat the increase in consumer surplus from efP_{E_0} to cdP_{E_0} in panel (b) as an additional
increase in social benefits that should be added to $P_{F_0}abP_{F_1}$ in panel (a), but this should
not be done. As discussed next, doing so would result in double counting. As long as
price does not change in the equipment market as a result of stocking the lake, the
social surplus change in the fishing market measures the entire benefit from the stocking project.

To see this, first consider fishers who already own all the fishing equipment they need at the time the lake is stocked and, hence, presently contribute no demand to the market for fishing equipment. The value that these persons place on their existing fishing equipment will tend to increase as a result of stocking the nearby lake. However, because they are not in the market for new fishing equipment, the gap between the old and new demand schedules for new fishing equipment does not reflect this increase. Of course, these fishers' willingness to pay for fishing days will presumably be higher than it otherwise would have been because they will not have to make further expenditures for fishing equipment. However, any additional increase in consumer surplus that these fishers enjoy as a result of already owning fishing equipment at the time the nearby lake is stocked will already be reflected by the primary market demand schedule for fishing days, which will be further to the right than it otherwise would be. It cannot show up in the secondary market for fishing equipment.

Now consider individuals who do not own fishing equipment at the time the lake is stocked but are now induced to make such purchases. The gap between the two demand schedules in Figure 7.1(b) accurately reveals the increased value that these persons place on fishing equipment. That is, these people are now willing to pay more for fishing equipment, and indeed they will buy more fishing equipment. It is the only way they can fully realize surplus gains from the stocking project, but having to make this expenditure is not an additional benefit from the stocking project. Just like the fishers who already own fishing equipment, the increase in consumer surplus that these persons receive from the stocking project is fully captured by the consumer surplus measured using the primary market demand schedule for fishing days. This includes any consumer surplus that they receive from their purchases of fishing equipment. Thus, counting the gap between the two demand schedules in panel (b) as benefits and also counting the increase in consumer surplus shown in panel (a) as benefits would result in counting the same benefits twice.

Persons who do not own fishing equipment at the time the lake is stocked would have been even better off if, like the current owners of fishing equipment, they did not have to buy new equipment in order to take advantage of the newly stocked lake. Thus, everything else being equal, WTP for fishing days is presumably greater among those who already own fishing equipment than among those who must purchase it. The increase in consumer surplus that results from the stocking project for both groups, even if different from one another, will be fully reflected in the primary market demand schedule for fishing days.

It is important to stress that secondary market effects can be ignored only if social surplus in the primary market is measured directly. As discussed in greater detail in Chapter 15, in situations in which cost–benefit analysts are unable to measure social surplus changes in primary markets, they may infer them instead from the demand shifts in secondary markets. For example, imagine that analysts have no information about the demand schedule for fishing days, but they do know how the demand schedule for fishing equipment will change. With no direct measure of the benefits from stocking the lake, they might measure the difference between the social surplus in the fishing equipment market after the project (based on demand schedule D_{E_1}) and the social surplus in the equipment market prior to the project (based on demand schedule D_{E_0}). They would then apply some sort of scaling factor to correct for the underestimation that would result because not all the consumer surplus from fishing will be reflected in the equipment market. (As already indicated, because some fishers will use old equipment and collect their own bait, their surplus will not appear in the equipment market. Moreover, equipment and bait comprise only some of the inputs to fishing.)

7.1.3   *Efficient Secondary Market Effects with Price Changes*[1]

The situation is more complex when the supply schedule in the secondary market is upward-sloping. To see this, we examine the effect of stocking the lake on the demand for golfing. In Figure 7.2, panel (a) once again shows the demand for fishing days, while panel (b) now shows the demand for golfing days. As before, the reduction in the price of fishing days from P_{F_0} to P_{F_1} as a result of stocking the lake causes an increase in social surplus equal to the area $P_{F_0}abP_{F_1}$ (for the moment ignore demand schedules D_{F_1} and D^*).

As fishing and golf are presumed to be substitutes, a reduction in the price of fishing days from P_{F_0} to P_{F_1} would cause the demand for golfing to fall. Thus, the demand schedule for golfing in panel (b) would shift to the left from D_{G_0} to D_{G_1}. As previously emphasized, by itself this shift does not represent a change in consumer surplus that is not already fully accounted for in measuring the change in consumer surplus in the primary market. Golfers are obviously not made worse off by stocking the lake, although some may now place a lower valuation on golf. Instead, by itself, the shift in demand merely indicates that in the absence of golf, the consumer surplus gains from stocking the lake would have been even larger. The existence of golf is reflected in the location of D_{F_0}, the demand schedule for fishing days, which is farther to the left than it would have been if golf were not available as a substitute for fishing.

The shift of demand from D_{G_0} to D_{G_1}, however, causes the fees for golf course use to fall from P_{G_0} to P_{G_1}. This, in turn, results in an increase in consumer surplus, one represented by the area $P_{G_0}efP_{G_1}$, which has not previously been taken into account. Note that the consumer surplus resulting from a reduction in price is measured relative to the new demand schedule, which gives marginal valuations of golf after the decline in the price of fishing. In addition, the fall in golfing fees also causes a reduction in producer surplus equal to area $P_{G_0}gfP_{G_1}$. As the reduction in producer surplus exceeds the increase in consumer surplus, a net loss in social surplus equal to the area of triangle *efg* results.[2]

Should this loss in social surplus in the golfing market be subtracted from the social surplus gain in the fishing market in measuring net gains from the project? It is frequently unnecessary to do so. The reason is that the increase in consumer surplus gain in the fishing market is often, in practice, likely to be measured as the area $P_{F_0}acP_{F_1}$ rather than as the area $P_{F_0}abP_{F_1}$. If measured in this way, the increase in consumer surplus in the fishing market would be understated by the triangular area *abc*, but this triangle closely approximates triangle *efg*, the net loss in social surplus in the golfing market.

To see why the consumer surplus gain in the fishing market is often, in practice, measured as the area $P_{F_0}acP_{F_1}$ rather than as the area $P_{F_0}abP_{F_1}$, one must recognize that our fishing story does not end with the shift in the demand schedule in the secondary

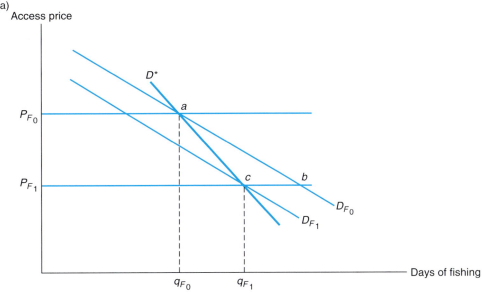

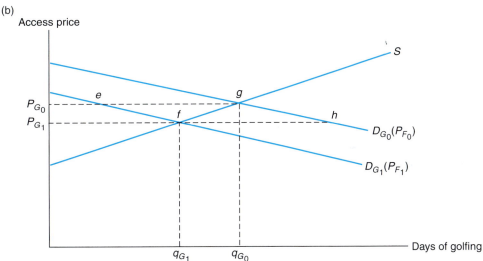

Figure 7.2(a) Primary market: market for fishing days.
Figure 7.2(b) Secondary market: market for golfing days (price effects).

market. If golf and fishing are substitutes, the reduction in golf course fees will cause some people to switch from fishing to golf, and the demand for fishing days will fall. This is shown in panel (a) as a leftward shift in the demand schedule for fishing days from D_{F_0} to D_{F_1}. Because prices in the market for fishing days are unaffected given that the supply of fishing days is perfectly elastic, by itself, this shift does not cause any further changes in social surplus. Note, however, that by drawing a line between the original and the final equilibrium points in Figure 7.2(a) – that is, between points a and c – one can derive a special type of demand schedule, D^*.

This demand schedule, which is sometimes called an *observed* or *equilibrium demand schedule*,[3] indicates what the demand for fishing days will be once prices in other markets, including the market for golfing days, have fully adjusted to the change in prices in the market for fishing days. Thus, D^* differs from the demand schedules D_{F_0} and D_{F_1}, which indicate the number of fishing days demanded at each price for fishing days, *holding the prices of all other goods constant*. As it is frequently difficult statistically to hold the prices of secondary goods constant while estimating the relation between price and quantity demanded in a primary market, empirically estimated demand schedules – the ones actually observed and available for use in a CBA – often more closely resemble equilibrium demand schedules such as D^* than "textbook-style" demand schedules such as D_{F_0} and D_{F_1}.[4]

Thus, the equilibrium demand schedule, D^*, is the one that is often used in practice to obtain a measure of the increase in social surplus resulting from the reduction in the price of fishing days. If so, however, the resulting measure, $P_{F_0} ac P_{F_1}$, understates the true measure of the gain in social surplus in the primary market, $P_{F_0} ab P_{F_1}$, by the triangular area *abc*. However, as previously suggested, area *abc* provides a good approximation of area *efg* in panel (b),[5] the area that should be subtracted from the social surplus gain in the primary market, area $P_{F_0} ab P_{F_1}$, to obtain an accurate measure of the overall net gains from stocking the lake. In other words, area *abc* represents part of the benefits from the fish-stocking project and area *efg* an approximately offsetting cost of the project. Hence, by using the equilibrium demand schedule to measure the change in social surplus in the primary market for fishing, we incorporate social surplus changes that occur in the secondary market for golfing days, as well as those that occur in the market for fishing days. We do not have to obtain separate measures of the surplus changes that occur in secondary markets.[6]

This is important because it illustrates an important general point: by using an equilibrium demand schedule for the primary market – the type of demand schedule that is often empirically estimated, and thus available – one can capture the effects of policy interventions in both the primary market in which they were initiated *and* in all secondary markets. Thus, we can restate our earlier rule concerning project impacts in secondary markets: *we should ignore effects in undistorted secondary markets, regardless of whether there are price changes, if we are measuring benefits in the primary market using empirically measured demand schedules that were estimated without holding prices in secondary markets constant.*

7.2 Valuing Benefits and Costs in Distorted Secondary Markets

Unfortunately, the use of equilibrium demand schedules in primary markets misses some of the relevant effects that occur in distorted secondary markets – that is, in secondary markets in which prices do not equal social marginal costs. To see why, examine Figure 7.3, a slightly altered version of Figure 7.1(b). This new figure is based on the assumption that because of negative externalities, the market price of fishing equipment,

P_{F_0}, underestimates the marginal social cost by x cents. (Think of the equipment as lead sinkers, some of which eventually end up in the lake, where they poison ducks and other wildlife. The x cents would then represent the value of the expected loss of wildlife from the sale of another sinker.) In this case, the expansion of consumption involves a social surplus loss equal to x times $q_{E_1} - q_{E_0}$, which is represented in Figure 7.3 by the shaded rectangle. This loss, which is not reflected at all by market demand or supply schedules in the fishing market, should be subtracted from the benefits occurring in that market in order to obtain an accurate measure of net gains from the program.

Although the marginal social cost curve is drawn horizontal in Figure 7.3 for simplicity, actual schedules in distorted markets could be more complex. For example, congestion on roads may increase at an increasing rate, causing the marginal social cost curve to slope upward non-linearly. Indeed, immediately prior to traffic gridlock (sometimes called "breakdown"), the marginal social cost approaches infinity. In such situations, changes in the primary market that result in demand increases (decreases) in the secondary market can lead to substantial increases (decreases) in social costs in the secondary market, which should be counted in a CBA.

Another type of distortion in secondary markets is imposed by the presence of taxes. For example, Figure 7.4 illustrates local produce markets for beef and chicken, which are substitutes for one another. For simplicity, the supply schedules in both markets are assumed to be perfectly elastic. In the absence of any taxes on these products, the price of beef (the primary good) would be P_B and the price of chicken (the secondary good) would be P_C.

For the purposes of our illustration, let us assume that chicken is currently subject to a tax of t_C cents per pound, but beef is not presently taxed. In this situation, the existing demand schedules for beef and chicken are represented by D_{B_0} and D_{C_0}, respectively. As panel (b) of Figure 7.4 indicates, the tax on chicken provides the government

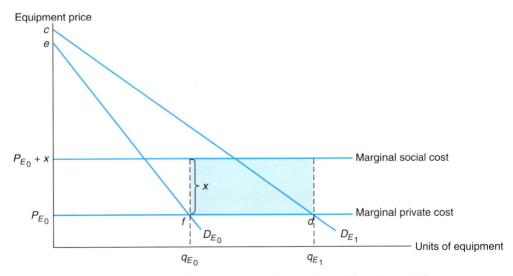

Figure 7.3 Distorted secondary market: market for fishing equipment (no price effect).

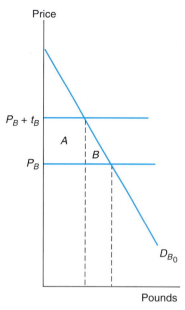

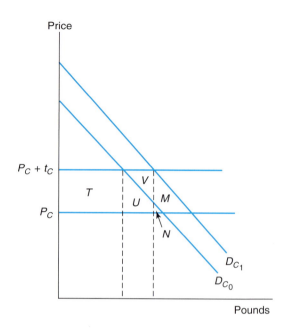

Figure 7.4(a) Market for beef.
Figure 7.4(b) Market for chicken.

with revenue equal to area T but reduces consumer surplus by areas $T + U$. Thus, the tax on chicken results in deadweight loss equal to the triangular area U.

Now assume that the government is considering imposing a tax of t_B cents per pound on beef. As indicated in panel (a), if the new tax is adopted, the government will collect revenue represented by area A, but consumers of beef will lose surplus equal to the areas $A + B$. Consequently, imposition of the new tax will result in deadweight loss in the beef market equal to area B.

The increase in the market price of beef shifts the demand schedule for chicken, a substitute, from D_{C_0} to D_{C_1}. For reasons discussed previously, this shift does not represent a change in consumer surplus. Indeed, the deadweight loss in the market for chicken remains the same, although it does shift from area U to areas $M + N$. However, the shift causes an increase in the sale of chicken, as consumers substitute chicken for beef, resulting in an increase in tax revenues collected by the government. This increase, which is represented in panel (b) by area $U + V$, is a benefit from the tax imposed on beef that could conceivably more than offset the deadweight loss occurring in the beef market. The various effects of the tax on beef are summarized in the following social accounting ledger:

	Benefits	Costs
Consumers	–	$A + B$
Government revenue	$A + U + V$	–
Social benefit and costs	$U + V$	B

Notice that while *all* of the change in consumer surplus takes place in the primary market, increases in tax revenues occur in both markets.

The important lesson from this illustration is that, unlike situations in which there are no distortions in secondary markets, benefits and costs of a policy intervention cannot be fully measured by observing only the effects that occur in primary markets. Effects that occur in distorted secondary markets should, in principle, be valued separately. A method for doing this is described in Exhibit 7.1. Yet, in practice and as indicated in the exhibit, it is usually very difficult to do so. Estimation problems usually preclude accurate measurement of welfare changes that occur in secondary markets. Estimating the own-price effect (how quantity demanded changes as the price of the good changes) is often difficult; estimating cross-price effects (how the quantity demanded of good Y changes as the price of good Z changes) is even more difficult. Consequently, we are rarely very confident of predictions of demand shifts in secondary markets. Moreover, when secondary markets are distorted, it is also difficult to measure the size of the distortions. (Recall the x-cent loss of wildlife from the sale of another sinker. How is the value of x to be estimated?) Nonetheless, such measures are usually needed if program effects in distorted secondary markets are to be taken into account.

Fortunately, price changes in most secondary markets are likely to be small. Most pairs of goods are neither strong complements nor strong substitutes. Hence, large price changes in the primary markets are usually necessary to produce noticeable demand shifts in the secondary markets. Thus, even when secondary markets are distorted, ignoring these markets may result in relatively little bias to CBA.

Exhibit 7.1

It is sometimes both desirable and feasible to build models of closely linked markets to estimate changes in social surplus. They are commonly referred to as *computable general equilibrium* (CGE) models, but this is a misnomer – they take account of a small set of the many markets that make up an economy and thus might be more accurately called computable multimarket equilibrium models. Considering multiple markets rather than limiting analysis to the equilibrium demand schedule in the primary market is appropriate when markets are not neatly separable because of externalities in consumption or production.

One application of CGE models is to assess policy changes in markets for heterogeneous goods with production externalities. For example, what is commonly referred to as the oil market involves the extraction of crude oils of various qualities in various locations, their transportation to refineries employing different technologies to produce petroleum products, and the sale of these petroleum products in various regional markets. George Horwich, Hank Jenkins-Smith, and David Weimer use such a model to assess the efficiency of various public policy responses to oil supply disruptions.

Constructing, calibrating, and using industry-level CGE models are demanding tasks that require substantial resources and thus often are not worth developing for purposes of a single CBA. For example, a proper CBA of changes in the capacity of O'Hare International Airport would require a model that takes account of the network externality inherent in the airline system – delays originating at O'Hare propagate to flights into and out of other US airports. Creating a CGE model of the US airline industry would likely be too costly a task for analysts doing a one-time study of a proposed O'Hare expansion, but might be an appropriate investment for the Federal Aviation Administration to provide as a tool for assessing the net benefits of any proposed airport expansions.

Despite the difficulty of creating useful CGE models, they are being increasingly used in policy analysis. For example, Thomas Nechyba has developed models of public education to take into account the effect of school outcomes on residential choice and the consequences of residential choice on student body composition and tax revenues, important factors in schooling outcomes.

Sources: George Horwich, Hank Jenkins-Smith, and David L. Weimer, "The International Energy Agency's Mandatory Oil-Sharing Agreement: Tests of Efficiency, Equity, and Practicality." In George Horwich and David L. Weimer, editors, *Responding to International Oil Crises* (Washington, DC: American Enterprise Institute for Public Policy Research, 1988), 104–33; Thomas J. Nechyba, "What Can Be (and What Has Been) Learned from General Equilibrium Simulation Models of School Finance?" *National Tax Journal*, 54(2), 2003, 387–414. See also Allen H. Klaiber and V. Kerry Smith, "Developing General Equilibrium Benefit Analyses for Social Programs: An Introduction and Example." *Journal of Benefit–Cost Analysis*, 3(2), 2012, 1–52.

7.3   Indirect Effects of Infrastructure Projects

Public infrastructure projects that improve transportation or communications, such as road building or harbor deepening, may substantially reduce the cost of production in some industries. These reductions in costs may have indirect effects in markets for consumption goods by reducing the prices at which the goods are sold. These indirect effects are similar but not quite the same as the secondary market effects that are the main topic of this chapter. In the case of secondary markets, a government policy influences prices in a primary market, which in turn influences demand in secondary markets in which goods that are complements of or substitutes for the primary market good are sold. In the case of an indirect effect, a government infrastructure project reduces the production costs of firms by reducing their expenditures on various inputs, and this direct effect of the project causes indirect effects by reducing prices in markets in which the goods produced by the firms are sold.

Although the two situations differ, both raise a similar question: can the change in social surplus that results from the government's policy be adequately measured by focusing on the market in which the intervention takes place? In both cases the answer is similar: it can if the markets that are indirectly affected are not seriously distorted.[7]

We have already demonstrated this point when secondary market effects occur. To illustrate this in the case of indirect effects that result from public expenditures on infrastructure improvement, consider the harbor-deepening project that was discussed in Chapter 5. The direct effect of the project on shippers that use the harbor is a gain in surplus that is represented by area $P_0 ab P_1$ in Figure 5.3. However, the shippers do not necessarily keep this entire gain. Competitive pressures will likely result in firms paying lower prices for productive inputs that are shipped through the harbor. This, in turn, will cause cost curves in the markets in which these firms sell their goods to shift downward and to the right. If prices in these markets fall as a result, then consumer surplus will increase.

In competitive markets for these goods, this indirect gain in consumer surplus is already captured by the direct surplus gain represented by area $P_0 ab P_1$ in Figure 5.3.[8] The reason is that some of the surplus gains initially enjoyed by shippers are ultimately passed on to the buyers of consumption goods through the reductions in the prices of these goods. If markets where the indirect effects occur are distorted, however, then some of the changes in surplus in these markets may not be captured by surplus changes in the market where the direct effects take place. For example, the price reductions may engender increases in sales in markets with either positive or negative externalities. If so, third parties will enjoy an increase in surplus when positive externalities are present and will suffer a decrease in surplus when negative externalities exist. These changes are not reflected by the direct changes in surplus.

7.4   Secondary Market Effects from the Perspective of Local Communities

Advocates of localized recreational facilities – for example, advocates of new sports stadiums, museums, and parks – frequently contend that major benefits will occur in secondary markets. For example, they predict that the demand for the services of local restaurants, hotels, and other businesses will increase. In addition, they often claim that such projects result in *multiplier effects*; that is, as purchases from nearby businesses increase, these businesses will, in turn, also spend their newly gained revenues nearby, and this, in turn, will generate still more revenues that will be spent locally, and so forth.

As long as secondary markets in a community are not distorted, one should be very cautious in counting revenues from local projects that are generated by secondary market effects and multiplier effects as project benefits. There are several reasons for exercising this caution.

First, absent market distortions, these revenues are relevant only when standing is restricted to some group smaller than society as a whole, such as to residents of a specific geographic area. As discussed in this chapter, when society is broadly defined, such claims cannot be justified unless the secondary market is distorted. For example, in evaluating the fish-stocking project from the narrow perspective of the local county, one might count as a benefit increases in revenues received by local businesses resulting from non-residents buying fishing equipment in the county or frequenting local hotels and restaurants. From the broader social or national perspective, however, these expenditures simply represent a transfer from non-residents to residents because they occur only as a result of consumers shifting their spending from one geographic area to another. Similarly, tax payments by non-residents may count as a local benefit, but would likely be offset by lower tax payments elsewhere with national standing.

Second, when standing is restricted to residents of a local community, any social surplus gains that accrue to non-residents as a result of a local project can no longer be counted as project benefits. For example, surplus gains enjoyed by sports team fans or owners who reside outside the community no longer count. Thus, the case for a local project could actually be stronger if standing is not restricted to the local community than if it is.

Third, as indicated earlier in this chapter, even if the demand for local products and services increases as a result of a local project, suppliers do not receive increases in surplus unless prices increase. Even when prices do increase, the resulting increase in producer surplus is at least partially offset because consumers who are residents of the local community must now pay more for goods and services and, as a result, lose consumer surplus. However, some residents may value the growth that occurs in the local economy in and of itself. Moreover, expansions in local businesses may provide some opportunities for taking advantage of economies of scale and, therefore, could produce benefits in the form of lower production costs.

Fourth, localized multiplier effects generally tend to be relatively small because local businesses are often owned by non-residents. Moreover, many of the purchases by local businesses are made outside the local area. Thus, expenditures made within a local area readily dissipate elsewhere, and this becomes increasingly true as standing is restricted to smaller geographic areas.

It is only when secondary markets are distorted that effects in these markets can potentially generate important benefits for the community. However, negative impacts can also occur, such as increases in pollution and congestion that result when non-residents use local roads to reach a recreational facility. Local projects are most likely to generate significant positive benefits in secondary markets when local rates of unemployment are high or other local resources are idle and substantial barriers to resource mobility exist. Under such circumstances, increases in demand in secondary markets and the multiplier effects that accompany these demand increases could significantly reduce levels of unemployment and increase the utilization of other idle resources such as empty buildings. The utilization of idle resources such as empty buildings has very low opportunity costs, and as discussed in Chapter 6, large increases in surplus accrue to many unemployed workers when they are hired. However, as also pointed out in Chapter 6, it is only when the rate of unemployment is fairly high that a substantial fraction of those hired are likely to be drawn from the ranks of the unemployed.

7.5   Conclusion

Most of the key concepts from Chapters 5, 6, and 7 are summarized in Table 7.1. As the table indicates, changes in social surplus serve as the basis for measuring the costs and benefits of policies. The concept of opportunity cost helps us value the inputs that policies divert from other uses; the concept of WTP helps us value policy outputs. The key to valuing outputs is to identify the primary markets in which they occur. When the outputs are not traded in organized markets, ingenuity is often needed to infer supply and demand schedules (remember the market for "fishing days"). For this purpose, various shadow pricing techniques, such as those discussed in Chapters 14–17 of this book, are often needed. Costs and benefits that occur in undistorted secondary markets are typically very difficult to value, but generally need not and, indeed, should not be added to costs and benefits that are measured in primary markets. Doing so will usually result in double counting.

The rules that appear in Table 7.1 cannot be used without first determining the type of market in which the various potential impacts of a project or program occur – input, output, or secondary market – and then determining whether the market is efficient or inefficient. In practice, this is sometimes difficult. To illustrate the sorts of judgments that must be made in practice, we conclude by listing selected impacts of a

Table 7.1 *Rules for Measuring Social Benefits and Costs of Government Interventions*

Type of intervention	Efficient markets	Inefficient markets
Change in input markets (Concept: value costs as the opportunity cost of the purchased resources.)	If supply schedule is flat, value cost as direct budgetary expenditure. (Example: purchase of materials from a competitive national market.) If supply schedule is not flat, value cost as direct budgetary expenditure less (plus) any increase (decrease) in social surplus in market. (Example: purchases of materials from a competitive local market.)	Value costs as direct budgetary expenditure less (plus) any increase (decrease) in social surplus in market. (Examples: hiring unemployed labor; purchases of materials from a monopoly.)
Changes in output markets (Concept: value benefits as WTP for the change and costs as WTP to avoid the change.)	Value change as net change in social (i.e., consumer and producer) surplus plus (less) any increase (decrease) in government revenues. (Example: government provision of goods and services to consumers or producers.)	Value change as net change in social (i.e., consumer, producer, and third party) surplus plus (less) any increase (decrease) in government revenues. (Example: tax or subsidy in market with externality.)

(continued)

Table 7.1 (cont.)

Type of intervention	Efficient markets	Inefficient markets
Changes in quantities exchanged in secondary markets as a result of government intervention in input or output markets (Concept: commodities exchanged in secondary markets are typically complements of or substitutes for commodities exchanged in primary markets; most impacts in secondary markets can be valued in primary markets.)	If prices do not change in secondary market, ignore secondary market impacts. If prices do change, but benefits in primary market are measured using a demand schedule with other market prices held constant, then social surplus changes in the secondary market will always represent reductions in social surplus that should be subtracted from changes in the primary market. However, if benefits in the primary market are measured using a demand schedule that does not hold other prices constant, ignore secondary market impacts. (Example: price changes in primary market cause demand schedule shifts in competitive secondary market.)	Costs or benefits resulting directly from increases in the size of the distortion should, in principle, be measured. Other impacts in secondary market should be ignored if prices do not change. (Example: price change in primary market causes the demand schedule to shift in a secondary market with an externality.)

These rules pertain only to measuring impacts of government interventions on society as a whole. Issues concerning standing are ignored in the rules.

hypothetical street-widening project that would substantially increase traffic along the route and ask the reader to consider what type of market each occurs in and, hence, whether each should be included in a cost–benefit analysis of the project. Our own judgment concerning each, which is based on the assumption that surplus gains by those who drive on the street are measured by using an equilibrium demand schedule for trips, appears in Exhibit 7.2.

Exhibit 7.2

1. The increased traffic would cause vibrations that crack the walls of adjacent houses. The cracked walls in houses that would result from the increased traffic are a negative externality. Although the externality would occur in the secondary market for housing, it should be taken into account in the study.

2. Profits of gasoline at filling stations that are located along the route would increase. The increased purchases of gasoline would occur in a secondary market. If this market is not seriously distorted (e.g., by externalities or monopoly power), then the increase in gasoline purchases should be ignored because any effects on surplus will be captured by measuring surplus in the output market. (Notice, however, that doing this neglects the fact that it is the owners of the filling stations, rather than automobile drivers, who receive the increase in surplus from increased purchases of gasoline; it also ignores the possibility that filling station owners who are located on other streets may face reductions in surplus.)

3. The property values of these stations would also increase. The property market is also a secondary market. Hence, these effects should be ignored.

4. Traffic on adjacent streets would decline. Therefore, the remaining motorists would experience quicker and cheaper journeys. The decrease in traffic on adjacent streets can be viewed as a reduction in a negative externality – congestion – that distorts a secondary market (the adjacent streets are presumably substitutes for the street that would be widened). This is a real benefit that should be taken into account.

5. Air pollution along the route would increase. Air pollution is a negative externality that distorts the output market. Hence, it should be taken into account.

6. The increased auto traffic would require the city to hire three more police officers to enforce traffic regulations. The hiring of three additional police officers would take place in an input market for labor and can be viewed as a direct cost of the project.

7. The greater number of motorists would lead to an increased number of traffic violations, and the resulting fines would mean that the city receives increased revenue. The increase in traffic fines would simply be a transfer between motorists and the city and, except for their distributional implications, can be ignored.

8. Fewer people would ride buses; as a consequence the bus company would lay off 10 bus drivers. The 10 laid off bus drivers would lose their

jobs because the demand schedule in the secondary market for public transportation would shift to the left. Unless this market or the factor markets that serve this market are distorted, the shift in demand can be ignored. Examples of such distortions are the loss of monopoly profits by the bus company or the inability of the bus drivers to find new jobs because of high rates of unemployment. Otherwise, the bus drivers would simply find new jobs at a similar level of compensation, implying that widening the road would have no effect on the social value of the output they produce.

9. Widening the road would necessitate cutting down a number of trees. These trees would then be sold to a nearby sawmill. The benefits and costs of cutting down the trees and selling them to a sawmill can be assessed independently of the street-widening project. If the benefits from cutting down the trees exceed the costs, then the trees should be cut regardless of whether the street-widening project is undertaken. However, if the costs exceed the benefits, then the costs and benefits of cutting the trees should be included in the CBA of the street-widening project.

Exercises for Chapter 7

1. Recall exercise 1 from Chapter 5 in which an increase in the toll on a highway from $.40 to $.50 would reduce use of the highway by 5,000 cars per week.

    a. Because of the reduced use of the highway, demand in the secondary market for subway rides increases. Assuming that the price of subway rides is set equal to the marginal cost of operating the subway and marginal costs are constant (i.e., the supply schedule is horizontal), and no externalities result from the reduced use of the highway and the increased use of the subway, are there additional costs or benefits due to the increased demand for subway rides? Why or why not?

    b. Because of the reduced use of the highway, demand in the secondary market for gasoline falls by 20,000 gallons per year. There is a stiff tax on gasoline, one that existed prior to the new toll. Assuming that the marginal cost of producing gasoline is $1 per gallon, that these marginal costs are constant (i.e., the supply schedule is horizontal), that no externalities result from the consumption of gasoline, and that the gasoline tax adds 30 percent to the supply price, are there any additional costs or benefits due to this shift? If so, how large are they?

2. Recall exercise 2 from Chapter 5 in which a country imposes an import fee on the crude oil it imports. Assume that prior to the imposition of the import fee, the country annually consumed 900 million short tons of coal,

all domestically mined, at a price of $66 per short ton. How would the CBA of the import fee change if, after imposition of the import fee, the following circumstances are assumed to result from energy consumers switching from crude oil to coal?

   a.   Annual consumption of coal rises by 40 million short tons, but the price of coal remains unchanged.

   b.   Annual consumption of coal rises by 40 million short tons and the price of coal rises to $69 per short ton. In answering this question, assume that the prices of other goods, including coal, were not held constant in estimating the demand schedule for crude oil.

   c.   Annual consumption of coal rises by 40 million short tons and the price of coal rises to $69 per short ton. In answering this question, assume that the prices of other goods, including coal, were held constant in estimating the demand schedule for crude oil. Also assume that the demand schedule for coal is completely inelastic.

   d.   The market price of coal underestimates its marginal social cost by $7 per short ton because the coal mined in the country has a high sulphur content that produces smog when burned. In answering this question, assume that the annual consumption of coal rises by 40 million short tons, but the price of coal remains unchanged.

3.   Recall exercise 2 from Chapter 5 in which a country imposes an import fee on the crude oil it imports. Imagine that all the crude oil imports to the country are made by ships owned by its nationals. The Association of Petroleum Shippers argues that the reduction in imports resulting from the import fee will drive down the price of shipping services and thereby inflict a loss on them. The Committee for Energy Independence, which favors the import fee, argues that the reduction in shipping prices will benefit consumers of shipping services. Which argument is correct? In preparing an answer, make the following assumptions: the import fee will reduce the quantity of imported crude oil from 3 billion to 2.5 billion barrels per year; the reduction in barrels shipped will drive per-barrel shipping costs down from $4 per barrel to $3 per barrel; and the elasticity of demand in the shipping market at the new equilibrium ($3, 2.5 billion barrels) is −0.3. Also assume that the shipping market is undistorted and that the prices of other goods, including shipping services, were held constant in estimating the demand schedule for crude oil.

4.   (Instructor-provided spreadsheet recommended.) Consider an individual's utility function over two goods, q_m and q_s, where m indicates the primary market in which a policy will have its effect and s is a related secondary market:

$$U = q_m + \alpha q_s - (\beta_m q_m^2 + \gamma q_m q_s + \beta_s q_s^2)$$

where α, β_m, β_s, and γ are parameters such that $\beta_m > 0$, and $\beta_s > 0$, $\beta_m < (1 - \gamma q_s)/2q_m$, $\beta_s < (1 - \gamma q_m)/2q_s$, and $\gamma < p_m \beta_s/p_s + p_s \beta_m/p_m$. For purposes of this exercise, assume that $\alpha = 1$, $\beta_m = 0.01$, $\beta_s = 0.01$, and $\gamma = -0.015$. Also assume that the person has a budget of \$30,000 and the price of q_m, p_m, is \$100 and the price of q_s, p_s, is \$100. Imagine that the policy under consideration would reduce p_m to \$90.

The provided spreadsheet has two models. Model 1 assumes that the price in the secondary market does not change in response to a price change in the primary market. That is, p_s equals \$100 both before and after the reduction in p_m. Step 1 solves for the quantities that maximize utility under the initial p_m. Step 2 solves for the quantities that maximize utility under the new p_m. Step 3 requires you to make guesses of the new budget level that would return the person to her original level of utility prior to the price reduction – keep guessing until you find the correct budget. (You may wish to use the Tools|Goal Seek function on the spreadsheet instead of engaging in iterative guessing.) Step 4 calculates the compensating variation as the difference between the original budget and the new budget. Step 5 calculates the change in the consumer surplus in the primary market.

Model 2 assumes that $p_s = a + bq_s$. Assume that $b = 0.25$ and a is set so that at the quantity demanded in step 2 of model 1, $p_s = 100$. As no analytical solution for the quantities before the price change exists, step 1 requires you to make guesses of the marginal utility of money until you find the one that satisfies the budget constraint for the initial p_m. Step 2 repeats this process for the new value of p_m. Step 3 requires you to guess both a new budget to return the person to the initial level of utility and a marginal utility of money that satisfies the new budget constraint. A block explains how to use the Tools|Goal Seek function to find the marginal utility consistent with your guess of the new budget needed to return utility to its original level. Step 4 calculates the compensating variation. Step 5 calculates the change in the consumer surplus in the primary market and bounds on the change in consumer surplus in the secondary market.

Use these models to investigate how well the change in social surplus in the primary market approximates compensating variation. Note that as utility depends on consumption of only these two goods, there are substantial income effects. That is, a price reduction in either of the goods substantially increases the individual's real income. Getting started: the values in the spreadsheet are set up for a reduction in p_m from \$100 to \$95. Begin by changing the new primary market price to \$90 and resolving the models.

Notes

1. For a helpful analysis that uses a somewhat different approach than the one presented in this section but reaches very similar conclusions, see Herbert Mohring, "Maximizing, Measuring, and Not Double Counting Transportation-Improvement Benefits: A Primer on Closed- and Open-Economy Cost–Benefit Analysis." *Transportation Research*, 27(6), 1993, 413–24.

2. As advocates of a policy often claim benefits in secondary markets, it is ironic that demand shifts in undistorted secondary markets that cause price changes always involve losses in social surplus. This can be seen by using panel (b) in Figure 7.2 to illustrate the case of an outward shift in demand in a secondary market, as well as the case of an inward shift in demand. Simply take D_{G_1} as the original demand schedule and D_{G_0} as the post-project demand schedule. Using the post-project demand schedule for measuring social surplus changes, we see that the price increase from P_{G_1} to P_{G_0} results in a producer surplus increase equal to the area of trapezoid $P_{G_1}fgP_{G_0}$ and a consumer surplus loss equal to the area of $P_{G_1}hgP_{G_0}$ so that social surplus falls by the area of triangle *fgh*.

3. See Richard E. Just, Darrell L. Hueth, and Andrew Schmitz, *Applied Welfare Economics and Public Policy* (Englewood Cliffs, NJ: Prentice Hall, 1982), chapter 9.

4. For greater detail concerning this point, see Just, Hueth, and Schmitz, *Applied Welfare Economics and Public Policy*, 200–13.

5. Indeed, under certain assumptions, areas *abc* and *efg* will almost exactly equal one another. The most important of these assumptions is that the price changes in the two markets represented in Figure 7.2 are small and that no income effects result from these price changes. If there are no income effects, there will be symmetry in substitution between the two goods. In other words, their cross-substitution effects will be equal. That is, $\partial q_F/\partial P_G = \partial qG/\partial P_F$. Therefore, $\Delta P_F \Delta q_F \approx \Delta P_G \Delta q_G$. Hence, area *abc* approximately equals area *efg*. Typically, income effects do occur as a result of price changes, but as discussed in Appendix 3A, these effects tend to be small for most goods. Consequently, one would anticipate that area *abc* would generally closely approximate area *efg*.

6. Separate measures would have to be obtained, however, to examine how benefits and costs were distributed among various groups. For example, area *abc* is a gain to consumers, while area *efg* is a loss to producers. To the extent these two areas are equal, they represent a transfer of surplus from producers to consumers. In addition, surplus corresponding to area $P_{G_0}efP_{G_1}$ is also transferred from producers to consumers.

7. For a detailed analysis of the secondary market effects of transportation and land use projects, see David M. Newberry, "Spatial General Equilibrium and Cost–Benefit Analysis," in K. Puttaswamaiah, editor, *Cost–Benefit Analysis: Environmental and Ecological Perspectives* (New Brunswick, NJ: Transaction Publishers, 2002), 1–18.

8. For a formal demonstration of this assertion, see Jan Rouwendal, "Indirect Welfare Effects of Price Changes and Cost–Benefit Analysis," unpublished paper (Amsterdam: Tinbergen Institute Discussion Paper No. 02–011/3, 2002).

8 Predicting and Monetizing Impacts

Imagine that you completed the first three steps in CBA set out in Chapter 1. You have identified the alternative policies, determined standing, and catalogued the relevant impacts with appropriate units of measure. Next you must predict the impacts of each alternative and monetize them. As mentioned in Chapter 1, sometimes prediction and monetization can be done together (for example, when a demand curve is available), but often they must be done separately (for example, when a policy potentially affects health or crime rates). Because so much of the effort in a typical CBA goes into these two steps, whether done together or separately, this chapter provides a brief overview of approaches you can use to do them. One of these approaches, estimating demand curves, was discussed earlier in Chapter 4, but sometimes such estimation is infeasible. Therefore, other approaches are also briefly described in the chapter. Greater detail on these approaches appears later in the book.

In this chapter, we presume you are conducting an *ex ante* analysis (that is, you are making predictions of impacts of a policy that is under consideration). However, much of what we say is also applicable to *in media res* analysis. Moreover, we presume that you are conducting a "pure" cost–benefit analysis. That is, that you are predicting *all* impacts as best you can, even in the absence of strong supporting evidence. To do this, you should use policy research, relevant theory, and, when all else fails, learn about the subject and make informed guesses. Many actual CBAs take this approach, especially if the analysts face severe budgetary and time constraints. As we indicated in Chapter 2, however, there are other alternatives, such as qualitative CBA and cost–effectiveness analysis. Moreover, as in all CBAs, there will be many uncertainties associated with many or even all of the predicted monetized impacts, but we are focusing in this chapter on only two of the 10 CBA steps listed in Chapter 1. An elaboration of the sorts of uncertainties that can occur and how they can be treated in CBA appear in Chapters 11 and 12. Of course, you need to be self-conscious about the uncertainties and be forthright in presenting them. And ultimately, you need to complete all 10 steps.

8.1 Predicting Impacts

Prediction concerns impacts occurring in the future. Yet, the primary basis for prediction is usually what has happened in the past. Sometimes policy analysts, but more often policy researchers working in universities and research institutes, use observed data to assess the consequences of past policy changes. Their inferences about the effects of these prior policy changes drawn from evaluations can inform predictions about what is likely to happen if the policy were continued, terminated, expanded, or replicated. Obviously, analysts must move beyond this evaluation-as-the-basis-for-prediction approach when predicting the consequences of either novel policies or policies in place that have not been evaluated. Perhaps a similar policy intervention that has been evaluated can be found to provide at least some guidance for prediction. Or perhaps estimates of elasticities made in other contexts can be used to predict impacts.

Three major sources of error arise during the application of CBA.[1] First, *omission errors*, the exclusion of impacts with associated costs or benefits, prevent CBAs from being comprehensive. Sometimes impacts are not anticipated. Other times they are anticipated but not included in the analysis for lack of quantitative predictions of their magnitudes or plausible shadow prices for their monetization. As discussed in Chapter 2, the inability or unwillingness to predict or monetize forces a retreat to qualitative CBA. In cases in which only one major impact cannot be predicted or monetized, the analyst may first calculate net benefits without it and then ask the question: how large would the monetized value of the excluded impact have to be to change the sign of net benefits?

Second, *forecasting errors* arise simply because we cannot predict the future with certainty. The past, which is the empirical focus of the social sciences, is an imperfect guide to the future. The larger and more novel the policy being assessed, the greater the danger that the future will differ from the past. Much of the discussion that follows considers the ways that the past can be used as a basis for making predictions. As noted below, psychological biases of individuals tend to make some types of forecasts overly optimistic. There may also be unanticipated difficulties and adaptations that make actual experience deviate from forecasts. Forecasts of the real resources required for large and complex infrastructure projects are often too low because of the need for redesign as implementation reveals information about the site and the actual performance of the capital equipment employed. Forecasts of regulatory impacts are often too large because they fail to anticipate offsetting behaviors that reduce either risk reductions[2] or compliance costs.[3]

Third, *valuation errors* occur because we often do not have confident estimates of appropriate shadow prices for converting each predicted impact into an opportunity cost or a WTP. As with forecasting, the more novel is the impact being monetized, the greater is the challenge of finding an appropriate shadow price. Plausible shadow prices can often be gleaned from available research, but sometimes they must be developed and defended by the analyst.

Analysts must often be innovative and bold to complete comprehensive CBAs. They should also anticipate the errors inherent in their efforts and consciously assess them to the greatest extent possible.

8.1.1   *Simplify by Predicting Incremental Impacts Relative to the Status Quo*

Good policy analysis always keeps the status quo as a potential option in case none of the alternatives under consideration are superior to it. CBA also keeps the status quo as an alternative, albeit usually implicitly. It does so by *predicting the incremental impacts of policy alternatives relative to those that would occur under the status quo policy.* As discussed in Chapter 1, the most efficient alternative project has both the largest net benefits among the alternatives to the status quo and has positive net benefits to ensure that it offers larger net benefits than the status quo.

For example, imagine that the alternatives being assessed will have four types of impacts, Z_1, Z_2, Z_3, and Z_4. If an alternative policy and the status quo have logically identical impacts Z_1 and Z_2, then assessing the alternative relative to the status quo obviates the need to predict these impacts quantitatively because they net out when the predicted impacts of the status quo are subtracted from the predicted impacts of the alternative. The analyst would have to predict the difference in impacts Z_3 and Z_4 between the alternative and the status quo. For example, suppose an alternative criminal justice policy would use the same real resources as the status quo policy: the incremental resources required would be zero. However, if the alternative would reduce crime relative to the status quo, then it would be necessary to predict this difference quantitatively.

8.1.2   *Predict Using Data from an Ongoing Policy*

Policies often take the form of programs for specific populations, such as those in a particular geographic area or those with a particular condition. These existing policies may provide data useful for predicting the impacts of similar policies applied for other populations. As discussed in Chapter 14, true experiments with random assignment of subjects into treatment and control groups, with the latter continuing under the status quo, generally provide the most confident inferences of the impacts that a policy has actually produced. Quasi-experiments with non-random assignment into treatment and comparison groups generally provide less-confident assessment of impacts and often require statistical adjustments to account for non-random assignment. In any event, an analysis of an existing program provides at least some basis for predicting the impacts of a similar policy.

Even in the absence of an experimental or quasi-experimental evaluation, investigation of the policy in place may prove useful in identifying the resources needed to implement it. Also, in the case of social programs, data may be available on relevant outcomes for at least program participants. To make use of these program measures, the analyst must find a relevant "comparison" group to answer the question, "Compared to what?"

Consider, for example, an intervention aimed at supporting schizophrenics in community living situations that keeps track of the contacts of participants with the criminal justice system, their hospitalizations, their employment records, and their suicides. Absent an explicit control or comparison group as part of an experimental or quasi-experimental design, analysts may take population averages or reports from specific studies as a basis for comparison. With respect to hospitalizations, for instance, a study of California Medicaid recipients with schizophrenia found annual rates of psychiatric hospitalizations of 27 percent and medical hospitalizations of 11 percent.[4] A first cut at an estimate of the impact of the intervention on rates of hospitalizations would be to subtract the observed rates for those in the intervention from these reported rates for

California. A more sophisticated approach might use the statistical model presented in the article to estimate what the hospitalization rates would have been for a group with the demographic characteristics of those in the intervention. It would also be important to consider if there are likely to be any systematic differences between California schizophrenics participating in the Medicaid program from 1998 to 2000 and the schizophrenics in the intervention. The estimate that results after taking account of these sorts of considerations would be the basis for predicting the effect of the intervention on hospitalizations if it were to be continued or replicated.

8.1.3   *Predict Based on Single Evaluation of a Similar Policy*

An evaluation of a policy similar to the one being analyzed may be available. Its value as a basis for prediction depends on how closely it matches the policy being considered and how well the evaluation was executed.

Policies can be similar in the sense of having the same underlying model, but differ in the intensity and type of inputs used and their target populations. Consider, for example, two visiting nurse programs aimed at reducing child abuse in at-risk families. One might involve one-hour visits every two weeks by public health nurses to families with adults who are suspected of having abused their children. The other might involve one-hour visits every month by nurse's aids to families with adults who were formally found to have abused their children. Which of these differences are relevant in using the evaluation of one program to predict the consequences of the other? These two programs may have too many differences to allow confident prediction. Perhaps if they differed only in terms of the frequency of visits, the analyst could make various assumptions about the relationship between frequency of visits and impacts to get a range of plausible predictions. So, if a linear relationship were assumed, a program with half the frequency would be predicted to produce half the impact. Assumptions of non-linear relationships would yield different predictions. Analysts must fall back on their substantive knowledge and theory to decide how to take account of such differences.

The quality of the evaluation design is especially important to consider when using a single study as the basis for prediction. In general, true experimental designs with random assignment of subjects to treatment and control groups are most desirable. However, randomization can fail to provide comparable treatment and control groups if the number of subjects is small or the mechanism for randomization is flawed. Quasi-experimental designs in which comparisons are made without random assignment to the treatment and control groups can produce poor inferences for a variety of reasons discussed in Chapter 14.

Even when its evaluation design is sound, basing prediction on a single study risks making incorrect predictions for several reasons. First, there is the bias of academic journals to publish studies with statistically significant results, while, in fact, there may be other unpublished studies that did not find statistically significant effects.[5] Consequently, the one published study may show an unrepresentative effect.

Second, people tend to bring cognitive biases to their decision-making, including forecasting decisions that tend to lead to overoptimistic predictions.[6] These cognitive biases, as well as more careful implementation when the evaluator is closely associated with the policy than is likely in replication, tend to make findings of positive effects somewhat overly optimistic.[7] Analysts should guard against this *optimism bias* when they are predicting the consequences of policies they favor. For the same reason, some analysts routinely discount the size of effects from studies in which the evaluator was closely associated with the design or implementation of the program.[8]

Third, although rarely taken into account in practice, the most appropriate statistical inference about what has happened may not correspond to the best prediction of what will happen. As discussed in Chapter 4, the common approach for analysts seeking to predict an impact from evaluations is to interpret the estimated effect, perhaps a mean difference in an experiment or a coefficient in a regression analysis, as the predicted impact. However, when the sample size is small or the fit of the model to the data is poor, the estimated effect may give a prediction that is too large (in absolute value sense) from the perspective of being likely to be close to the impact that will actually result from a repetition of the experiment.[9] Consequently, a more reliable prediction may result if the estimated impact is "shrunk" in proportion to the poorness of the fit of the model to the data. In a regression context, for example, a recommended heuristic is to shrink the coefficient by $(F - 1)/F$, where F is the F-statistic for the fit of the model to the data.[10]

Simply relying on standard statistical approaches can also lead to an underestimation of effects. It is common for social scientists to treat estimated impacts as zero if the probability of observing them if they were truly zero is more than 5 percent. In other words, impacts that are not statistically significant at conventional levels are treated as zero. This may be an appropriate approach in the social sciences where researchers wish to have overwhelming evidence before rejecting a null effect in favor of some alternative theory. However, it is generally not the right approach in CBA where the estimated effect, perhaps shrunk, is likely to be a better prediction than zero. The standard error of the estimated effect conveys the degree of uncertainty in its value and should be used in Monte Carlo simulations of net benefits.[11] Indeed, the distribution of net benefits resulting from Monte Carlo simulations provides the basis for investigating the hypothesis of interest: predicted net benefits are positive.

Briefly, Monte Carlo simulations involve first determining the range of uncertainty around the estimates of benefits and costs – for example, by using the confidence intervals implied by the standard errors of the impacts. The estimates of each of the benefits and costs about which there is uncertainty are then replaced by a random draw within the range of uncertainty. This is repeated many times, thereby in effect conducting multiple CBAs. The fraction of the resulting multiple estimates of net benefits that is positive is a measure of the probability that the net benefits of the policy being studied is actually positive. Greater detail about Monte Carlo simulations is found in Chapter 11.

8.1.4   *Predictions Based on Meta-Analyses of Similar Policies*

Some policy interventions are replicated in many locations and evaluated with experimental or quasi-experimental research designs. In some policy areas a sufficient number of these evaluations are made public to permit a statistical assessment of their combined results. This process, called *meta-analysis*, seeks to use the information in the studies to find the magnitude of an impact (usually called its "effect size") and the variances of the impact.[12] Drawing information from multiple evaluations reduces the chances that the overall result will suffer from the limitations of any one of the evaluations.

Meta-analysis begins with an identification of the relevant evaluations that are the sources of its data. Social science researchers often limit the evaluations they consider to those found in articles published in refereed journals. Policy analysts seeking to apply CBA may choose to include unpublished evaluations of relatively new or unusual interventions if there are few published evaluations. The quality of the source of the evaluation can itself be a variable in the meta-analysis, along with direct classifications of the quality of the research design. In general, published studies, which have undergone peer review, are more credible. However, the reviewing process tends to bias publication decisions toward articles showing statistically significant effects, which potentially makes the pool of available published articles overly optimistic.[13] In addition, the delay in the publishing process from initial submission of manuscripts to publication of articles may be several years, so that relying solely on published studies may miss the most recent, and perhaps most relevant, findings.

In meta-analysis, a standardized measure of *effect size* is determined and extracted from each study so that findings based on somewhat different measures can be combined. For example, different achievement tests, which are not directly comparable without standardization, may be used in evaluations of a classroom intervention. The results from these different tests can be standardized in terms of their underlying distribution so that the units of measure become standard deviations. For example, an evaluation of the effect of tutoring on student performance measured the effect size as the difference between the test scores for the treatment and control groups divided by the standard deviation of scores for the control group.[14] Measures of the variation of effect size in each study are also extracted from the studies. In the simplest approach, the standardized effect sizes and their variances are combined to find an average effect size and its variance. More sophisticated approaches may use multivariate regression to estimate an average effect size and variance controlling for the qualities of the studies, variations in composition of subject populations in the studies, and differences in the details of the implementation of the intervention.

The Washington State Institute for Public Policy (WSIPP), which does analysis at the request of the state legislature, makes exemplary use of meta-analysis to support its application of CBA to prospective policies.[15] An example is the efforts of a team of its analysts to assess the costs and benefits of interventions in K–12 schooling policies. The team conducted a meta-analysis of 38 evaluations of class size reductions and a meta-analysis of 23 evaluations of moving from half-day to full-day kindergarten.[16] Measuring effect size in standard deviations of test scores, the meta-analysis of class reduction evaluations found an effect size of reducing classes from 20 to 19 students of 0.019 standard deviations for kindergarten through grade 2, 0.007 standard deviations for grades 3 through 6, and no statistically significant effect for higher grades. The team used these effects as a starting point for their analysis, allowing for annual decay of effects in later grades. They then related improved test scores to lifetime earnings and other social effects. The case study following this chapter provides a more detailed description of another study done by WSIPP that made exemplary use of meta-analysis.

When multiple evaluations relevant to predicting impacts for a CBA are available, it is worth considering whether to invest substantial resources to complete a competent meta-analysis. Even when only a few evaluations are available, it is worthwhile using meta-analysis methods to combine their effects. Indeed, with only a small number of available studies the costs of implementing the meta-analysis are likely to be low. Of course, analysts can take advantage of meta-analyses performed by others, whether they are directly related to CBA as are many of those done by the Washington State Institute for Public Policy, or they summarize the research relevant to predicting a specific impact.

8.1.5   *Predict Using Generic Elasticities*

Evaluations of policies similar to the alternative being analyzed often provide evidence relevant to prediction of all or many of the impacts. In their absence, analysts must seek out a variety of evidence to support their predictions. One common approach is to search for relevant elasticities. Often policies or programs change the effective prices of goods, either directly through changes in their price or indirectly through changes in the convenience of consumption. In these cases the impact is the change in the quantity of the good consumed. If an estimate of the price elasticity of demand is available, then the methods set out in Chapter 4 can be used to translate the change in effective price to a change in consumption.

Consider, for example, a program that would lower the price seen by its participants for access to health care. Absent any available evaluation of this or similar policies, an analyst might predict a change in medical care utilization caused by the reduction in price based on a price elasticity of demand of −0.2 as estimated using data from the RAND Health Insurance Experiment.[17] Although finding a relevant elasticity or other empirical basis for prediction from experiments may seem somewhat fortuitous, it is often worth searching for them among the numerous social policy experiments that have been completed in the United States.[18]

Much empirical work in the social sciences, medicine, and many other fields makes use of observational data. In economics, for instance, price and quantity variation can be observed over time or across jurisdictions with different taxes. Researchers often take advantage of such natural (unplanned) variation to estimate elasticities and other parameters useful in prediction. Analysts can find these studies by searching in both general (e.g., ECONLIT, Google Scholar, JSTOR, and Proquest Digital Dissertations) and substantively specific (e.g., ERIC for education and PubMed for health) electronic databases of articles. The World Wide Web not only makes it easier to access these databases, but also provides a way of potentially finding unpublished studies that, although not vetted by referees or editors, might provide estimates of elasticities not available elsewhere.

Some of the common elasticities that have been estimated many times have been assessed in meta-analyses. For example, meta-analyses of the price elasticity of demand for gasoline,[19] electricity,[20] residential water,[21] and cigarettes[22] are available. Other meta-analyses review tax elasticities for corporate behavior and tax elasticities for economic development,[23] and price, service quality, income, gasoline price, and car ownership elasticities for the demand for public transportation.[24]

It may be possible to identify a chain of elasticities that link an immediate policy impact to other impacts, including some future impacts, that should also be valued. For example, high school completion has a variety of potentially relevant effects ranging from greater success in the labor market to reduced crime to better-informed fertility choices.[25] Or consider an early childhood intervention that increases readiness for school. Although the increased readiness may have some direct value to children and parents, it may also have effects on the course of education, which in turn have other valued impacts – one can imagine the increased achievement in early grades contributing to a higher likelihood of high school completion and its relevant effects. Of course, the longer the chain of causality that links the initial estimated impact to the predictions of future impacts, the less-certain the predictions.

8.1.6 *Guesstimate*

Sometimes it is not possible to find any existing quantitative evidence to predict an impact. As a prediction must be made – excluding the impact is equivalent to predicting it is zero with certainty – one can turn to logic or theory to specify its plausible range. For example, if a policy will increase the price of some good, then it is almost certainly reasonable to assume that the amount consumed will not go up. You may be able to put an upper bound on reduction in consumption with an estimate of the price elasticity of demand of some other good that you can argue is likely to be more price elastic. The assumed range can be used in a Monte Carlo simulation to take account of your uncertainty of the magnitude of the impact. When your guesstimate has a very large range, you may also want to do sensitivity analysis in which, taking account of all other impacts first, you determine how large or small its value would have to be to change the sign of net benefits.

If none of the above approaches is acceptable, you may obtain advice from experts who have developed tacit knowledge that allows you make guesstimates. An expert, such as a highway engineer, may be able to provide fairly confident ranges of predictions for project costs based on her experience in using the prevalent rules-of-thumb, without conducting a major and perhaps quite expensive study. In some circumstances, there may be value in consulting multiple experts in a systematic way. The best-known approach for doing this is the Delphi Method, which was originally developed by the RAND Corporation to aid in the analysis of national defense issues. It requires participation by a number of experts. Each expert is consulted by the group coordinator in several rounds. In each round following the first, the coordinator provides feedback to the experts in the form of unattributed summaries of the answers provided by the fellow experts in the previous round. The final product is a statistical summary of the answers. The Delphi Method is sometimes used to generate input for economic analyses.[26]

8.2   Monetizing Impacts

CBA requires that the quantitatively predicted policy impacts be valued in terms of a common money metric based on the relevant national or regional currency, such as the dollar or Euro. The fundamental principles of WTP and opportunity cost introduced in Chapter 2 provide the conceptual bases for monetizing. Depending on the impact being valued, monetization can be relatively straightforward and certain or, like much of prediction, indirect and uncertain.

8.2.1   *Monetizing when Impacts Change Quantities Consumed in Markets*

Policies that change consumption of market goods are relatively straightforward to monetize. As discussed in Chapters 3, 5, 6, and 7, these changes should be monetized as the algebraic sum of the corresponding changes in social surplus, changes in government revenue, and the marginal excess tax burden of the changes in government revenue. In the simplest case, the policy involves purchasing an input in an undistorted market with a perfectly elastic supply schedule – the change in quantity of the input consumed in the market is monetized with the market price. Markets with less than perfectly elastic supply, distortion, or markets that exhibit both conditions require careful accounting of changes in social surplus, including those external to the market, and changes in government revenue. In general, impacts occurring in such markets are not monetized by directly observed market prices but rather by *shadow prices* taking account of all the relevant effects in the market. (One example of shadow prices is the marginal excess tax burden discussed in Chapter 3. A further example appears in Exhibit 8.1.) As long as the market supply and demand schedules and, if relevant, the social marginal benefit and social marginal cost schedules have been predicted, the monetization is still relatively straightforward. Further, the monetization itself in such cases does not add uncertainty beyond that inherent in the predictions of the relevant schedules.

Exhibit 8.1

Markets in some developing countries are much more distorted than in most developed countries. For example, it is often the case that: labor markets are segmented and labor mobility is limited by systems of land tenure; official exchange rates do not accurately reflect the value of the national currency; the prices of goods exchanged in international markets are distorted by trade taxes, import controls, and high tariffs; and credit markets are divided between formal and informal sectors. Consequently, experts have advocated that shadow prices, which are often and rather confusingly called *accounting prices*, be used instead of market prices in conducting CBAs in developing countries. Methods for using shadow prices were developed in the early 1970s by the United Nations Industrial Development Organization and by

Ian Little and James Mirrlees. These ideas were then synthesized by Lyn Squire and Herman G. van der Tak, two employees of the World Bank. Using the first surname initial of the economists who were prominent in promoting the approach, it is sometimes called the *LMST accounting price method*.

The LMST methodology makes a basic distinction between tradeable goods and non-tradeable goods. *Tradeable goods* include consumption goods and productive factors that are exported or imported, as well as products for which there might potentially be an international market – for example, close substitutes of the goods that are traded internationally. Thus, traded goods affect, or potentially can affect, a nation's balance of payments. *Non-tradeable goods* include all other consumption goods and productive factors such as local transportation, electricity, services, and (most importantly) local labor. The key to the LMST method is in using *world prices*, the prices at which goods are actually bought and sold internationally, to shadow price all project inputs and outputs that are classified as tradeable. Non-tradeable goods are often produced with inputs that are tradeable so that world prices can also be used to value them. Even the labor for a project may be drawn from other sectors of the economy where it was previously producing tradeable goods so that world prices can once more be used.

The rationale for using world prices is not that free trade prevails or that world prices are undistorted – although they are less distorted than the domestic market prices in many developing countries and are probably less distorted today than they were when the LMST methodology was initially developed – but that they more accurately reflect the opportunities that are available to a country, and these opportunities should be recognized in evaluating projects. For example, if a project input has to be imported, it is reasonable to value it at its import price. Similarly, if project output is to be exported, it is reasonable to value it on the basis of its export price because this indicates what it would contribute to the nation's foreign exchange. Thus, the methodology is based on the principle of *trade opportunity costs*.

To see the rationale for using world prices to value project outputs and inputs more clearly, consider a developing country that is conducting a CBA of a proposal to build a steel plant with government funds. Although the country currently has a high tariff on imported steel, it is nonetheless dependent on steel produced in other countries. Because the tariff is incorporated into the domestic market price of steel, it can be viewed as a transfer between domestic steel buyers and the government. However, world prices do not incorporate tariffs. Thus, the world price for importing steel is often considerably lower than its market price in a developing country. Consequently, a CBA that is based on domestic market prices could indicate that the steel plant project should proceed, when, in fact, the real resource cost of importing steel (that is, the cost net of the tariff) is smaller than the resource cost of producing it domestically. Similarly, if a project uses a locally produced (but potentially importable) input that has an artificially inflated price because of high tariffs or import quotas, the possibility of purchasing the input more cheaply on the world market than locally should be recognized in determining the project's cost. As a third example, consider a project to increase the production and foreign sales of an agricultural crop. In some developing countries, national policies keep the domestic market prices of some agricultural crops artificially low. When this occurs, a crop production project might not pass the cost–benefit test if domestic market prices are used, but could pass it if the analysis is based instead on world prices. Thus, the LMST method argues that the values of imports and exports on the world market should be the basis for decisions about domestic projects.

Sources: *United Nations Industrial Development Organization, Guidelines for Project Evaluation* (New York, NY: United Nations, 1972); I. M. D. Little and J. A. Mirrlees, *Project Appraisal and Planning for Developing Countries* (London: Heinemann Educational, 1974); and Lyn Squire and Herman van der Tak, *Economic Analysis of Projects* (Baltimore, MD: Johns Hopkins University Press, 1975). An excellent concise summary of the LMST approach can be found in Terry A. Powers, "An Overview of the Little-Mirrlees/Squire-van der Tak Accounting Price System," in Terry A. Powers, editor, *Estimating Accounting Prices for Project Appraisal* (Washington, DC: Inter-American Development Bank, 1981), 1–59. Book-length treatments include Caroline Dinwiddy and Francis Teal, *Principles of Cost–Benefit Analysis for Developing Countries* (Cambridge: Cambridge University Press, 1996); Robert J. Brent, *Cost–Benefit Analysis for Developing Countries* (Cheltenham: Edward Elgar Publishing, 1998); and Steve Curry and John Weiss, *Project Analysis in Developing Countries* (London: Macmillan, 1993).

8.2.2   *Monetizing Impacts in Missing Markets*

Most public policies, but especially those addressing social and environmental problems, have impacts that do not correspond to changes in consumption in well-functioning markets. Monetizing these impacts requires shadow prices. Researchers have to be clever in finding ways to estimate these shadow prices. As discussed in Chapter 15, hedonic pricing and asset valuation methods can often be used to make inferences about the social value of impacts from the indirect effects they have on observable behaviors. However, sometimes the impacts, such as changes in the availability of goods with an existence value, cannot be derived from observable behavior and therefore, as explained in Chapter 16, can only be estimated through contingent valuation surveys or other stated preference methods.[27]

Fortunately, as reviewed in Chapter 17, researchers have estimated a number of shadow prices for commonly encountered impacts. Some shadow prices, such as the willingness to pay for reductions in mortality risk (a basis for estimating the value of a statistical life), the social cost of noise, or the opportunity cost of commuting time, have been estimated in a sufficiently large number of studies to make meta-analyses possible. Other shadow prices must be gleaned from smaller numbers of studies and often differ in terms of their comprehensiveness. For example, an important impact of many social policies is reduction in crime. A comprehensive shadow price would include not only the direct costs to victims and the use of resources in the criminal justice system, but also the costs that fear of crime imposes on potential victims. Improving these key shadow prices is an important project for social scientists wishing to promote the application of CBA.[28]

As with prediction, even a single relevant study can provide an empirical basis for determining a needed shadow price. For example, imagine that you faced the task of monetizing an impact that pertains to children. Perhaps you have a plausible shadow price for adults. If so, then you might use the findings from a study by Mark Dickie and Victoria L. Messman that parents appear willing to pay twice as much for reductions of flu symptoms for their young children as for themselves.[29] (Interestingly, the ratio falls to one by the time children reach the age of 18 – a result probably very plausible for parents of teenagers!) Of course, the more the impact you are trying to monetize differs from flu symptoms, the less confident you should be about using ratios from this particular study.

More generally, empirically derived shadow prices should be treated as uncertain predictions. In calculating net benefits, analysts must usually multiply an uncertain prediction of effect by an uncertain shadow price. Again, the importance of Monte Carlo simulations to assess uncertainty in net benefits should be clear.

8.3   Conclusion

The range of quality of available evidence to support the prediction and monetization of policy impacts is very wide. Sometimes, but relatively rarely, multiple evaluations employing rigorous experimental designs provide the basis for making fairly confident predictions of the magnitudes of the impacts that would result from continuation or replication of policies. Even more rarely can these impacts be monetized with readily available and widely accepted shadow prices. More often, analysts must piece together evidence to support predictions from a variety of sources and use shadow prices with varying degrees of provenance. Doing so well requires both a sound conceptual grounding in CBA and the courage to predict and monetize even when the supporting evidence is weak. It also demands that analysts make their assumptions and uncertainties transparent, both in presentation and through Monte Carlo and other methods to take account of uncertainties.

Exercises for Chapter 8

1. Review the following CBA: David L. Weimer and Mark A. Sager, "Early Identification and Treatment of Alzheimer's Disease: Social and Fiscal Outcomes." *Alzheimer's & Dementia*, 5(3), 2009, 215–26. Evaluate the empirical basis for prediction and monetization.

2. Imagine that a project involves putting a high-voltage power transmission line near residential property. Discuss how you might predict and monetize its impact on residents.

Notes

1. For more detail see Anthony E. Boardman, Wendy L. Mallery, and Aidan R. Vining, "Learning from *Ex Ante/Ex Post* Cost–Benefit Analysis Comparisons: The Coquihalla Highway Example." *Socio-Economic Planning Sciences*, 28(2), 1994, 69–84.

2. For example, see Darren Grant and Stephen M. Rutner, "The Effect of Bicycle Helmet Legislation on Bicycling Fatalities." *Journal of Policy Analysis and Management*, 23(3), 2004, 595–611 at 606.

3. Winston Harrington, Richard D. Morgenstern, and Peter Nelson, "On the Accuracy of Regulatory Cost Estimates." *Journal of Policy Analysis and Management*, 19(2), 2000, 297–322.

4. Todd P. Gilmer, Christian R. Dolder, Jonathan P. Lacro, David P. Folsom, Laurie Lindamer, Piedad Garcia, and Dilip V. Jeste, "Adherence to Treatment with Antipsychotic Medication and Health Care Costs among Medicaid Beneficiaries with Schizophrenia." *American Journal of Psychiatry*, 162(4), 2004, 692–99. Rates reported in Chapter 8 are calculated using data in the article on hospitalization rates for drug compliance categories and the fraction of subjects in the categories.

5. David L. Weimer, "Collective Delusion in the Social Sciences." *Policy Studies Review*, 5(4), 1986, 705–08.

6. Charles R. Schwenk, "The Cognitive Perspective on Strategic Decision Making." *Journal of Management Studies*, 25(1), 1988, 41–55.

7. Anthony Petrosino and Haluk Soydan, "The Impact of Program Developers as Evaluators on Criminal Recidivism: Results from Meta-Analysis of Experimental and Quasi-Experimental Research." *Journal of Experimental Criminology*, 1(4), 2005, 435–50.

8. For example, analysts at the Washington State Institute for Public Policy routinely halve the intervention effects reported for programs in which the evaluator was closely involved in the design or implementation of the program. See, for instance, Steve Aos, Jim Mayfield, Marna Miller, and Wei Yen, *Evidence-Based Treatment of Alcohol, Drug, and Mental Health Disorders: Potential Benefits, Costs, and Fiscal Impacts for Washington State* (Olympia, WA: Washington State Institute for Public Policy, 2006), appendix A3.c.

9. For an intuitive introduction to this issue, see Bradley Efron and Carl Morris, "Stein's Paradox in Statistics." *Scientific American*, 236, 1977, 119–27.

10. J. B. Copas, "Using Multiple Regression Models for Prediction: Shrinkage and Regression to the Mean." *Statistical Methods in Medical Research*, 6(2), 1997, 167–83.

11. As an example, see David Greenberg, "A Cost–Benefit Analysis of Tulsa's IDA Program." *Journal of Benefit–Cost Analysis*, 4(3), 2013, 263–300.

12. For an introduction to doing meta-analysis, see Mark W. Lipsey and David B. Wilson, *Practical Meta-Analysis* (Thousand Oaks, CA: Sage Publications, 2001) or M. Borenstein, L. V. Hedges, J. T. P. Higgins, and H. R. Rothstein, *Introduction to Meta-Analysis* (Chichester: Wiley, 2009).

13. Weimer, "Collective Delusion in the Social Sciences."

14. Peter A. Cohen, James A. Kulik, and Chen-Lin C. Kulik, "Educational Outcomes of Tutoring: A Meta-Analysis of Findings." *American Educational Research Journal*, 19(2), 1982, 237–48.

15. For an overview of the WSIPP approach, see Elizabeth K. Drake, Steve Aos, and Marna G. Miller, "Evidence-Based Public Policy Options to Reduce Crime and Criminal Justice Costs: Implications in Washington State." *Victims and Offenders*, 4(2), 2009, 179–96. Analysts may find useful information for their own CBAs from those available on the WSIPP web page, www.wsipp.wa.gov.

16. Steve Aos, Marna Miller, and Jim Mayfield, *Benefits and Costs of K–12 Educational Policies: Evidence-Based Effects of Class Size Reductions and Full-Day Kindergarten* (Olympia, WA: Washington State Institute for Public Policy, Document No. 07–03-2201, 2007).

17. Willard G. Manning, Joseph P. Newhouse, Naihua Duan, Emmitt B. Keeler, and Arleen Leibowitz, "Health Insurance and the Demand for Medical Care: Evidence from a Randomized Experiment." *American Economic Review*, 77(3), 1987, 251–77.

18. David H. Greenberg and Mark Shroder, *Digest of Social Experiments*, 3rd edn (Washington, DC: Urban Institute Press, 2004) provides brief summaries of social experiments initiated by 2003. Abstracts of later experiments can be found in David H. Greenberg and Mark D. Shroder, editors, *The Randomized Social Experiments eJournal*, which is distributed on-line by the Economics Research Network (ERN), a division of Social Science Electronic Publishing (SSEP) and Social Science Research Network (SSRN).

19. Molly Espey, "Gasoline Demand Revisited: An International Meta-Analysis of Elasticities." *Energy Economics*, 20(3), 1998, 273–95; Martijn Brons, Peter Nijkamp, Eric Pels, and Piet Rietveld, "A Meta-Analysis of the Price Elasticity of Gasoline Demand: An SUR Approach." *Energy Economics*, 30(5), 2008, 2105–22.

20. James A. Espey and Molly Espey, "Turning on the Lights: A Meta-Analysis of Residential Electricity Demand

Elasticities." *Journal of Agricultural and Applied Economics*, 36(1), 2004, 65–81.

21. Jasper M. Dalhuisen, Raymond J. G. M. Florax, Henri L.T. de Groot, and Peter Nijkamp, "Price and Income Elasticities of Residential Water Demand: A Meta-Analysis." *Land Economics*, 79(2), 2003, 292–308.

22. Craig A. Gallet and John A. List, "Cigarette Demand: A Meta-Analysis of Elasticities." *Health Economics*, 12(10), 2003, 821–35.

23. Ruud A. de Mooij and Sjef Ederveen, "Corporate Tax Elasticities: A Reader's Guide to Empirical Findings." *Oxford Review of Economic Policy*, 24(4), 2008, 680–97; Joseph M. Philips and Ernest P. Goss, "The Effects of State and Local Taxes on Economic Development: A Meta-Analysis." *Southern Economic Journal*, 62(2), 1995, 320–33.

24. Johan Holmgren, "Meta-Analysis of Public Transport Demand." *Transportation Research: Part A, Policy and Practice*, 41(10), 2007, 1021–35.

25. For demonstrations of this approach, see Robert Haveman and Barbara Wolfe, "Schooling and Economic Well-Being: The Role of Nonmarket Effects." *Journal of Human Resources*, 19(3), 1984, 377–107 and Barbara Wolfe and Robert Haveman, "Accounting for the Social and Non-Market Benefits of Education," in John F. Helliwell, editor, *The Contribution of Human and Social Capital to Sustained Economic Growth and Well Being* (Vancouver, BC: University of British Columbia Press 2001), 221–50.

26. Jon Landeta, "Current Validity of the Delphi Method in the Social Sciences." *Technological Forecasting and Social Change*, 73(5), 2006, 467–82.

27. For British ideas on monetizing various benefits in missing markets, see the United Kingdom *Green Book*, Annex 2, "Valuing Non-Market Impacts," 57–67 (2003, updated 2011) and Daniel Fujiwara, *The Department for Work and Pensions Social Cost–benefit analysis Framework: Methodologies for Estimating and Incorporating the Wider Social and Economic Impacts of Work in Cost–Benefit Analysis of Employment Programmes*, Working Paper No. 86 (London: Department for Work and Pensions, 2010).

28. For a discussion of a number of shadow prices that would be useful in applying CBA to social programs, see David L. Weimer and Aidan R. Vining, *Investing in the Disadvantaged: Assessing the Benefits and Costs of Social Policies* (Washington, DC: Georgetown University Press, 2009).

29. Mark Dickie and Victoria L. Messman, "Parental Altruism and the Value of Avoiding Acute Illness: Are Kids Worth More than Parents?" *Journal of Environmental Economics and Management*, 48(3), 2004, 1146–74. For a general discussion of the issues, see Sandra Hoffmann, "Since Children Are Not Little Adults – Socially – What's an Environmental Economist to Do?" *Duke Environmental Law & Policy Forum*, 17(2), 2006, 209–32.

Case 8

WSIPP CBA of the Nurse–Family Partnership Program

The Washington State legislature asked the Washington State Institute for Public Policy (WSIPP) to identify programs that could be implemented in Washington to reduce the number of children entering and remaining in the child welfare system. We briefly review the approaches to prediction and monetization used by the analysts in conducting a CBA of a particular intervention, the Nurse–Family Partnership for Low-Income Families (NFP).

Aside from providing a rich illustration of approaches to predicting and monetizing, familiarity with the work of WSIPP is valuable for CBA analysts for several reasons. First, WSIPP demonstrates how CBA can actually be conducted and presented to influence public policy.[1] Second, its CBAs are exemplary in their systematic use of empirical evidence through careful meta-analyses. Third, although the complicated methods WSIPP uses are sometimes difficult to follow as presented, it does strive to make them as transparent as possible. Fourth, its meta-analyses are excellent resources for analysts assessing social policies. Fifth, the Pew-MacArthur Results First Initiative is assisting other states and local jurisdictions in adapting the WSIPP CBA model to their local conditions, thus increasing the chances that analysts in many US jurisdictions will have an opportunity to use it.[2]

The NFP is intended to promote child development and parenting skills through intensive visitation by nurses to low-income women during pregnancy and the two years following the birth of first children.[3] The following prediction strategy, summarized in the table at the end of the case, was employed by the analysts: First, a meta-analysis of the available evaluations of the implementation of the NFP in two sites was done to estimate the mean effect size for child abuse and neglect. That is, taking account of all the available studies, how much on average do NFP programs reduce abuse and neglect? This mean effect size was used by the WSIPP analysts as the predicted effect.

Second, the analysts conducted meta-analyses of studies linking child abuse and neglect to other impacts of interest. These meta-analyses provided estimates of the mean effect sizes of child abuse and neglect on the secondary impacts of crime, high school graduation, K–12 grade repetition, births, and pregnancies for mothers under 18 years, test scores, illicit drug use, and alcohol abuse.

Third, the predicted effects of an NFP program on each of the secondary impacts was obtained by multiplying the predicted effect size of an NFP on child abuse and neglect by the secondary impact mean effect size. So, following an example provided in the report, consider a target population with a lifetime child abuse and neglect rate of 13.7 percent and a high school graduation rate of 70 percent. Participation in an NFP program would reduce the lifetime child abuse and neglect rate by 2.7 percentage points.[4] Eliminating (that is, reducing the rate by 100 percentage points) child abuse and neglect would increase the rate of high school graduation by 7.9 percentage points. Multiplying these two percentage-point rate changes together yields a predicted increase in the probability of high school graduation of about 0.2 percentage points.

The analysts used a variety of approaches to monetize the predicted impacts. For example, as indicated in the table that appears below, the social cost of a case of child abuse and neglect has two major components, each of which was estimated. The first component is an estimate of the average cost to the Washington State child welfare system of a substantiated child abuse or neglect case. Estimation of its monetary value was based on a model of the welfare system that took into account the real resource costs and probabilities of the steps in processing child abuse complaints and the possible services provided to victims. The second component is an estimate of the medical and mental health treatment costs and quality of life costs resulting from a case of child abuse. These costs were estimated from a study of adult on juvenile crime conducted by researchers using Pennsylvania data from 1993.[5] As usually is the case when analysts gather data from published studies, the results must be translated into current dollars using the Consumer Price Index.

As the entries in the table indicate, the analysts used a variety of sources for estimating shadow prices for the other predicted impacts: models of processes within Washington State, national economic data, and empirical findings reported in research articles. Along the way, they had to make many assumptions to move from available evidence to the needed shadow prices. Their efforts are commendable both in terms of their creativity and transparency.

Predictions and Monetization for the NFP Program

Impact per participant	Prediction (meta-analyses)	Monetization
Child Abuse and Neglect (CAN)	Experimental evaluations of two NFP programs in Colorado and New York; lifetime prevalence of CAN in general population estimated from 10 studies (10.6 percent)	Welfare system costs: model of case processing and service use in Washington State
		Medical and mental health care costs and quality of life costs: based on estimates from study of juvenile violence in Pennsylvania[1]
Crime	10 studies of impact of CAN on crime	Criminal justice system costs: case processing model for Washington State

(continued)

(cont.)

Impact per participant	Prediction (meta-analyses)	Monetization
High school graduation	Three studies of impact of CAN on high school graduation	Victim costs: personal expenses, property losses, mortality[2] Discounted lifetime money earnings gain from high school graduation based on data from Census Bureau's Current Population Survey
Test scores	Seven studies of impact of CAN on test scores	Rate of return per standard deviation of test score gain based on review article[3] multiplied by earnings of those with a high school degree but no college degree based on Current Population Survey
K–12 grade repetition	Two studies of impact of CAN on grade repetition	Cost of a year of schooling multiplied by the probability of high school completion to take account of elimination of year at end of schooling
Alcohol abuse	Four studies of impact of CAN on alcohol abuse	After-tax lifetime earnings loss due to mortality and morbidity Treatment, medical, motor vehicle crashes, fire destruction, welfare administrative costs[4]
Illicit drug abuse	Four studies of impact of CAN on illicit drug abuse	After-tax lifetime earnings loss due to mortality and morbidity Treatment, medical, motor vehicle crashes, fire destruction, welfare administrative costs[5]
Program costs	Based on program descriptions	Washington State wage and benefit rates

[1] Ted R. Miller, Deborah A. Fisher, and Mark A. Cohen, "Costs of Juvenile Violence: Policy Implications." *Pediatrics*, 107(1), 2001, e3 (7 pages).

[2] Miller, Ted R., Mark A. Cohen, and Brian Wiersema, *Victim Costs and Consequences: A New Look* (Washington, DC: National Institute of Justice, 1996).

[3] Eric A. Hanushek, "The Simple Analytics of School Quality." National Bureau of Economic Research Working Paper W10229, January 2004.

[4] Based on: Henrick J. Harwood, "Updating Estimates of the Economic Costs of Alcohol Abuse in the United States." Report prepared by Lewin Group for the National Institute on Alcohol Abuse and Alcoholism, 2000.

[5] Based on: Office of National Drug Control Policy, *The Economic Costs of Drug Abuse in the United States 1992–1998* (Washington, DC: Executive Office of the President, 2001).

Exercise for Chapter 8 Case Study

1. Imagine Washington State is considering implementing a program that pays monetary awards to families when their high school age children meet certain goals (for example, school attendance, achievement on standardized tests, receiving regular dental checkups, and receiving flu shots). WSIPP has been asked by the state legislature to assess whether the state should adopt this policy.

   a. Name three potential *secondary* impacts that WSIPP might consider in evaluating the policy.

   b. Indicate how WSIPP might go about making predictions of *one* of these impacts and then monetize them. (You need not go beyond the level of detail provided in the table to the case, but write in complete sentences.)

Notes

1. For a discussion of WSIPP, see David L. Weimer and Aidan R. Vining, "An Agenda for Promoting and Improving the Use of CBA in Social Policy," in *Investing in the Disadvantaged*, 249–71.

2. By mid-2017, 23 states and eight counties were participating in the initiative. www.pewtrusts.org/en/projects/pew-macarthur-results-first-initiative.

3. Stephanie Lee, Steve Aos, and Marna Miller, *Evidence-Based Programs to Prevent Children from Entering and Remaining in the Child Welfare System: Benefits and Costs for Washington* (Olympia, WA: Washington State Institute for Public Policy, Document No. 08-07-3901, 2008).

4. Effect size for a dichotomous variable (e.g., abuse/no abuse) is approximated by

$$ES = \ln\left\{\left[p_e\left(1-p_c\right)\right]/\left[p_c\left(1-p_e\right)\right]\right\}/1.65$$

where ES is the effect size, p_c is the frequency in the control group, and p_e is the frequency in the treated population. With an estimate of ES and p_c it is possible to solve for p_e, the predicted frequency for program participants. A similar procedure can be used for continuous variables (e.g., test scores) to predict effects using the following formula

$$ES = \left(M_e - M_c\right)/\left[\left(V_e + V_c\right)/2\right]^5$$

where M_c is the mean effect in the control group, M_e is the mean effect in the treatment group, V_e is the square of the standard deviation in the treatment group, and V_c is the square of the standard deviation in the control group. See Lipsey and Wilson, *Practical Meta-Analysis*.

5. Ted R. Miller, Mark A. Cohen, and Brian Wiersema, *Victim Costs and Consequences: A New Look* (Washington, DC: National Institute of Justice, 1996).

9 Discounting Future Impacts and Handling Inflation

Both private and public investment decisions can have important consequences that extend over time. When consumers purchase houses, automobiles, or education, they generally expect to derive benefits and incur costs that extend over a number of years. When the government builds a dam, subsidizes job training, regulates carbon dioxide emissions, or leases the outer continental shelf for oil exploration, it also sets in motion impacts that extend over many years. In order to evaluate such projects, analysts discount future costs and benefits so that all costs and benefits are in a common metric – the present value. By aggregating the present values of the costs and benefits of each policy alternative that occur in each time period, analysts compute the net present value of each alternative. Typically, analysts recommend the alternative with the largest net present value.

This chapter covers practical techniques needed to compute the net present value of a project (or policy). It assumes that the social discount rate, the rate at which analysts should discount the future benefits and costs of a project, is known. As we discuss in the following chapter, some controversy remains over the appropriate value of the social discount rate. In practice, though, oversight agencies, such as the Office of Management and Budget in the United States, Her Majesty's Treasury in the United Kingdom, or the Treasury Board in Canada, almost always specify the discount rate that analysts should use. (We also provide such rates in the following chapter.) This chapter also ignores the topics of uncertainty and risk, that is, it treats expected costs and benefits as if they were actual costs and benefits.

The sections of this chapter cover the following important topics: the basics of discounting, compounding, and discounting over multiple years, the timing of benefits and costs, the problem of comparing projects with different time frames, using real versus nominal dollars, accounting for relative price changes, the particular issues associated with long-lived projects and calculating horizon values (also called terminal values), the appropriateness of time-declining discounting, and sensitivity analysis in discounting.

The appendix to the chapter presents useful short-cut formulas for calculating the present value of constant annuities and perpetuities, and for calculating the present value of annuities and perpetuities that grow or decline at a constant rate.

9.1 The Basics of Discounting

9.1.1 Projects with Lives of One Year

Technically speaking, discounting takes place over *periods* rather than years. However, because the discounting period is a year in almost all public-sector applications, and it is easier to think of years rather than periods, we generally use the term years.

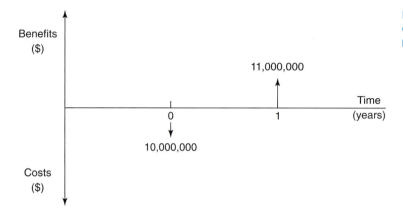

Figure 9.1 A timeline diagram for city land purchase example.

In this section, we consider projects that last for exactly one year. In the following section we consider projects that last for longer than one year. Suppose, for example, a city government has the opportunity to buy a parcel of land for $10 million. Also suppose that if it buys the land, then the land will be sold for $11 million one year from now. If it does not buy the land, then the city will invest the money in Treasury Bills (T-bills) at an interest rate of 5 percent.[1] Should the city buy the land? There are three ways to make this decision, each of which gives the same answer.

Whichever method the analyst uses, as an initial step, it is often useful to lay out the benefits and costs of a project on a *timeline*, as shown in Figure 9.1. The horizontal axis represents time measured in years. (Year 0 means now.) Benefits appear above the timeline and costs are below it. Although a timeline might seem unnecessary for this simple example, this tool clarifies the timing of the benefits and costs of a project and is particularly useful when the number of impacts and the timing of impacts is more complex.

9.1.2   *Future Value Analysis*

This method compares the amount the city will receive in the future if it engages in the project with the amount it will receive in the future if it invests the money. If the city invests the money in T-bills, then it will have $10.5 million in one year – the principal amount of $10 million plus interest of $500,000. This amount, $10.5 million, is called the *future value* (*FV*) of the T-bills because it is the amount the city will have in a future period if it buys them. The city can compare this future value with the future value it will receive if it buys the land, $11 million, and choose the alternative that has the highest future value. Thus, the city should buy the land because it would be better off in a year, in this case by $500,000.

The future value in one year of some amount *X* available today (called the principal amount) is given by the following formula:

$$FV = X(1 + i) \tag{9.1}$$

where *i* is the annual rate of interest. The concept of future value is intuitively understandable to anyone who has ever had a savings account. For example, if you invest $1,000 in a savings account at 4 percent, you will have $1,000(1 + 0.04) = $1,040 in a year. As is evident from Equation (9.1), the future value increases as the interest rate increases.

Note that interest rates are often stated as percentages, such as 5 percent. If so, the *interest rate, i,* in Equation (9.1) would equal 0.05. In order to use Excel to obtain the FV in one year of $1,000 invested at 5 percent one enters "=–FV(.05,1,,1000)" or "=FV(.05,1,,–1000)". Note that one enters the interest *rate* (usually $0 < i < 1$) and one needs to include a minus sign in front of the principal amount, which is a bit odd, but one gets used to it. The first argument (i.e., term in the parenthesis) is the interest rate; the second term is the number of periods; the third term pertains to annuities, which we discuss later (for now it is left blank); and the fourth term is the principal amount.

9.1.3   *Present Value Analysis*

We now switch from future values to present values. Present value analysis compares the current equivalent value of the project, which is called its *present value (PV)*, with the current equivalent value of the best alternative project. The present value of buying the land that will be worth $11 million in one year's time, given that the city could invest its money at 5 percent, is found by setting $X = PV$, $FV = \$11,000,000$ and $i = 0.05$ in Equation (9.1):

$$\$11,000,000 = PV(1 + 0.05)$$

Solving this equation for *PV* gives:

$$PV = \frac{\$11,000,000}{1.05} = \$10,476,190$$

In contrast, the present value of the best available alternative, buying the T-bills now, is $10 million ($10,500,000/1.05). Comparing these two present values shows that the city would be $476,190 better off in present value terms if it bought the land. Note that $500,000/(1.05) = $476,190. That is, receiving $476,190 now is equivalent to $500,000 (of interest) in one year.

In general, if the prevailing annual interest rate is *i*, then the present value (*PV*) of an amount received in one year, *Y*, is given by:

$$PV = \frac{Y}{1+i} \tag{9.2}$$

As is evident from Equation (9.2), the present value of some future amount decreases as the interest rate increases. In order to use Excel to obtain the *PV* of $1,000 received in one year when the interest rate is 5 percent one enters "=–PV(.05,1,,1000)" or "=PV(.05,1,,–1000)". Again, note that one needs to include a minus sign.

9.1.4   *Net Present Value Analysis*

This method calculates the present values of all the benefits and costs of a project, including the initial investment, and sums them to obtain the *net present value (NPV)* of that

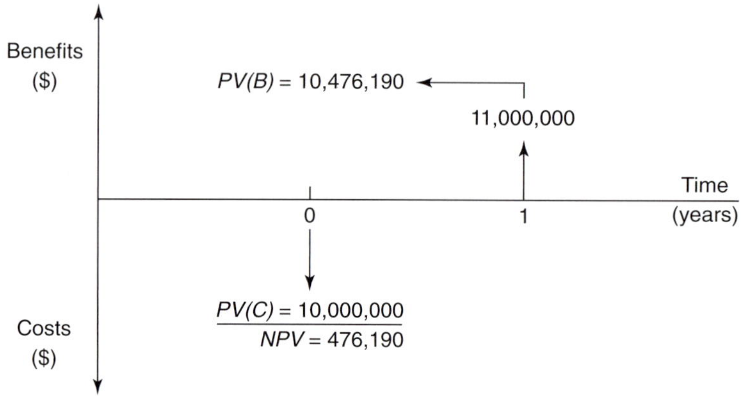

Figure 9.2 *NPV* of buying the land.

project. For the land purchase example, the *NPV* equals the present value of the land if the city buys it less the current cost of the land:

$$NPV = \$10{,}476{,}190 - \$10{,}000{,}000 = \$476{,}190$$

These amounts are represented graphically on a timeline in Figure 9.2. Because the *NPV* of buying the land is positive, the city should buy the land. It will be $476,190 better off in present value terms.

By definition, the *NPV* of a project equals the difference between the present value of the benefits, *PV(B)*, and the present value of the costs, *PV(C)*:

$$NPV = PV(B) - PV(C) \tag{9.3}$$

As discussed in Chapter 1, the *NPV* method provides a simple criterion for deciding whether to undertake a project. If the *NPV* of a project is positive, then one should proceed with it; if the *NPV* is negative, then one should not. The positive *NPV* decision rule assumes implicitly that no other alternative with a higher *NPV* exists. *If there are multiple, mutually exclusive alternatives, then one should select the alternative with the highest* NPV.

The foregoing example assumes that the city has $10 million available that could be used either to buy the land or to invest at interest rate *i*. Sometimes analysts calculate *NPV*s of projects for which the government does not have all the cash immediately available and may have to borrow some funds. *Implicitly, analysts assume that the government can borrow or lend funds at the same interest rate* i. *Under this assumption it does not matter whether the government currently has the money or not: the* NPV *rule still holds.* In Chapter 10 we discuss how the source of funding for a project may affect the choice of the discount rate. However, even in these situations, analysts should select the project with the largest *NPV*.

9.2   Compounding and Discounting over Multiple Years

We now generalize these results to apply to projects with impacts that occur over many years. Again, we first discuss future values, then present values, and finally net present values.

Future Value over Multiple Years

Suppose that the city could invest the $10 million for five years with interest at 5 percent per annum. Using Equation (9.1), at the end of the first year the city would have $10 million × 1.05 = $10.5 million. In order to calculate the interest in future years, we need to know if there is simple interest or compound interest.

If there is *simple interest*, then each year interest is received only on the original principal amount, that is, $500,000 per year. Thus, the future value of the investment in five years would be $12.5 million (the initial $10 million plus five years of interest of $0.5 million per year). No interest is paid on the interest received each year. However, if interest is *compounded annually*, then the investment would grow as shown in Table 9.1. At the end of the first year, the future value of the investment would be $10.5 million. Investing this amount at the beginning of the second year would result in a FV of $10.5 million × 1.05 = $11.025 million at the end of the second year. Notice that the interest in the second year, $0.525 million, is more than the interest in the first year, $0.5 million. With *compound interest*, interest is earned on the principal amount *and* on the interest that has been reinvested (*interest on the interest*). This process is called *compounding interest*. Henceforth, we shall always assume that interest is compounded annually, unless explicitly stated otherwise.

Table 9.1 illustrates that when interest is compounded annually, the future value will grow more quickly than under simple interest. Over longer periods (10 years or more), the divergence between compound interest and simple interest becomes quite large. This gap increases with time, thereby lending credence to the adage of many pension fund sales agents who exhort young adults "to invest early and leave it alone." Furthermore, the divergence between compound interest and simple interest increases with the interest rate.

In general, if an amount, denoted by X, is invested for n years and interest is compounded annually at rate i, then the future value, denoted FV, is:[2]

$$FV = X(1 + i)^n \qquad (9.4)$$

For example, if $10 million is invested for four years with interest compounded annually at 5 percent, then the future value is: $FV = 10(1 + .05)^4 = \$12.155$ million.

Table 9.1 *Investment of $10 Million with Interest Compounded Annually at 5 Percent Per Annum*

Year	Beginning of year balance ($ millions)	Annual interest ($ millions)	End of year balance ($ millions)
1	10.000	0.500	10.500
2	10.500	0.525	11.025
3	11.025	0.551	11.576
4	11.576	0.575	12.155
5	12.155	0.608	12.763

The term $(1 + i)^n$, which gives the future value of $1 in n years at annual interest rate i, compounded annually, is called the *compound interest factor*.[3] In this example, the compound interest factor is 1.216. In order to use Excel to obtain the compound interest factor for the *FV* in four years of $1 invested at 5 percent one enters "=–FV(.05,4,,1)" or "=FV(.05,4,,–1)". To obtain the FV of $10 invested at 5 percent for four years, one enters "=–FV(.05,4,,10)" or "=FV(.05,4,,–10)". The *FV* increases as the interest rate increases and as the number of periods increases.

9.2.2   *Present Value over Multiple Years*

Suppose that a government agency wants to undertake an organizational restructuring in three years that is expected to cost $100,000 at that time. If the interest rate is 6 percent, then the amount needed now to obtain $100,000 in three years, denoted *PV*, can be found by substituting into Equation (9.4):

$$PV(1 + 0.06)^3 = \$100,000.$$

Solving this equation for *PV* gives:

$$PV = \frac{\$100,000}{(1+0.06)^3} = \frac{\$100,000}{1.19102} = \$83,962$$

Consequently, the government agency would need $83,962 now to have $100,000 in three years.

In general, the present value of $Y received in n years with interest compounded annually at rate i is:

$$PV = \frac{Y}{(1+i)^n} \tag{9.5}$$

The term $1/(1 + i)^n$ is called the *present value factor*, or the *discount factor*. It equals the present value of $1 received in n years when the interest rate is i, compounded annually. For example, the present value factor in the foregoing example equals $1/(1 +.06)^3 = 0.8396$. In order to use Excel to obtain the present value factor for the *PV* of $1 received in three years with interest at 6 percent one enters "=–PV(.06,3,,1)" or "=PV(.06,3,,–1)". To obtain the FV of $10 invested at 6 percent for four years one enters "=–FV(.06,3,,10)" or "=FV(.06,3,,–10)".

The process of calculating the present value of a future amount is called *discounting*. As is evident from Equation (9.5), the present value of a future amount is less than the future amount itself – it is discounted. The amount of the discount increases as the interest rate increases and as the number of years increases. Furthermore, the effect of interest rates on the *PV* increases with time. Comparing Equations (9.4) and (9.5) shows that discounting is the reverse of compounding. The following formulas summarize the relationship between discounting and compounding:

$$PV = \frac{FV}{(1+i)^n} \tag{9.6A}$$

$$FV = PV(1 + i)^n \tag{9.6B}$$

If a project yields benefits in more than one period, then we can compute the present value of the whole stream by adding the present values of the benefits received in each period. Specifically, if B_t denotes the benefits received in period t for $t = 0, 1, ..., n$, then the present value of the stream of benefits, denoted $PV(B)$, is:

$$PV(B) = \frac{B_0}{(1+i)^0} + \frac{B_1}{(1+i)^1} + \cdots + \frac{B_{n-1}}{(1+i)^{n-1}} + \frac{B_n}{(1+i)^n}$$

$$PV(B) = \sum_{t=0}^{n} \frac{B_t}{(1+i)^t} \tag{9.7}$$

Similarly, if C_t denotes the costs incurred in period t for $t = 0, 1, ..., n$, then the present value of the stream of costs, denoted $PV(C)$, is:

$$PV(C) = \sum_{t=0}^{n} \frac{C_t}{(1+i)^t} \tag{9.8}$$

To illustrate the use of Equation (9.7), consider a government agency that has to choose between two alternative projects. Project I yields a benefit of $10,500 four years from now, whereas project II yields $5,500 four years from now and an additional $5,400 five years from now. Assume the interest rate is 8 percent. Which is the better project? The present values of the two projects follow:

$$PV(\text{I}) = \frac{\$10,500}{(1+0.08)^4} = \$7,718$$

$$PV(\text{II}) = \frac{\$5,500}{(1+0.08)^4} + \frac{\$5,400}{(1+0.08)^5} = \$4,043 + \$3,675 = \$7,718$$

In this example, the present values of the two projects happen to be identical. Thus, one would be indifferent between them. Timelines for these two projects are shown in Figure 9.3.

9.2.3   *Net Present Value of a Project*

We have now introduced all of the basics of discounting necessary for CBA. As discussed earlier, the NPV of a project is the difference between the present value of the benefits and the present value of the costs, as represented in Equation (9.3). Substituting Equations (9.7) and (9.8) into Equation (9.3) gives the following useful expression:

$$NPV = \sum_{t=0}^{n} \frac{B_t}{(1+i)^t} - \sum_{t=0}^{n} \frac{C_t}{(1+i)^t} \tag{9.9}$$

To illustrate the mechanics of computing the NPV of a project using this formula, suppose a district library is considering purchasing a new information system that would give users access to a number of online databases for five years. The benefits of this system are estimated to be $150,000 per annum, a figure that reflects both cost savings to the library and user benefits. The information system costs $500,000 to purchase and set up initially,

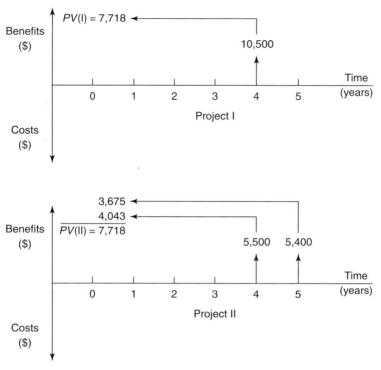

Figure 9.3 Timelines for Project I and Project II.

and $25,000 to operate and maintain annually. After five years, the system would be disman-tled and sold. In this example we assume that the costs of dismantling and selling it would equal the amount that it would be sold for. Thus, the terminal value equals zero. Suppose that the appropriate discount rate is 4 percent and there are no other costs or benefits.

A timeline for this project is shown in Figure 9.4. It shows the timing of each benefit and cost, their present values, the present value of all the benefits, the present value of all the costs, and the *NPV* of the project. The present value of the benefits is $667,773; the present value of the costs is $611,296; and the *NPV* of the project is $56,478. As the *NPV* is positive, the library should purchase the new information system.

It is often useful to present the results in a table of the kind shown in Table 9.2. In this case one must be careful about the timing of events. Unless stated otherwise, the amounts are implicitly assumed to occur at the end of each year. Thus, "Year 1" means one year from now and "Year 2" means two years from now, and so on. Similar to the timeline, Table 9.2 shows the annual benefits and the annual costs, and, in the last row, the PVs of these amounts.

An alternative way to compute the *NPV* of a project is to compute the present value of the annual *net social benefits*. Let $NSB_t = B_t - C_t$ denote the annual net social benefits that arise in year t ($t = 0, 1, 2, ..., n$). It follows from Equation (9.9) that the NPV *of a project equals the present value of the net social benefits:*[4]

$$NPV = \sum_{t=0}^{n} \frac{NSB_t}{(1+i)^t}$$

(9.10)

Table 9.2 *Analysis of the Library Information System*

Year	Event	Annual benefits	Annual costs	Annual net social benefits
0	Purchase and install	0	500,000	−500,000
1	Annual benefits and costs	150,000	25,000	125,000
2	Annual benefits and costs	150,000	25,000	125,000
3	Annual benefits and costs	150,000	25,000	125,000
4	Annual benefits and costs	150,000	25,000	125,000
5	Annual benefits and costs	150,000	25,000	125,000
	PV	667,773	611,296	56,478

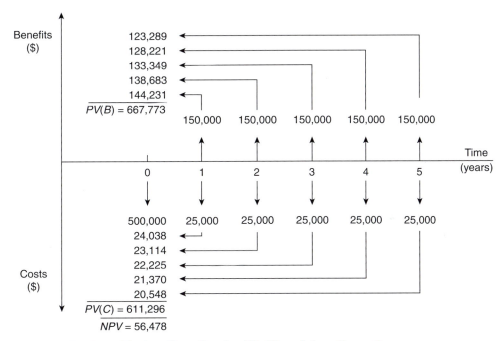

Figure 9.4 Timeline of the benefits and costs of the library information system.

Table 9.2 illustrates that Equations (9.9) and (9.10) produce the same *NPV*. The last column contains the annual net social benefits which have a NPV of exactly the same amount as before, $56,478.

In many respects, tables and timelines are substitutable. They both present key information succinctly, and they facilitate computation of project *PV*s and *NPV*s. Neither is necessary. Analysts can experiment with them and use them when helpful. For complicated projects it is often useful to start with a timeline to indicate precisely when impacts occur and then enter the data into a spreadsheet to compute the *PV*s and the *NPV*s.

One particular situation is worth mentioning. In some projects, all of the costs occur at the beginning ($t = 0$) and benefits only occur in the ensuing years ($t = 1, 2, ..., n$). In this situation, Equation (9.9) simplifies to:

$$NPV = \sum_{t=1}^{n} \frac{B_t}{(1+i)^t} - C_0$$

9.2.4   *Annuities and Perpetuities*

An *annuity* is an equal, fixed amount received (or paid) each year for a number of years. A *perpetuity* is an annuity that continues indefinitely. Suppose, for example, that in order to finance a new state highway, a state government issues $100 million worth of 30-year bonds with an annual interest rate of 4 percent. The annual interest payments of $40,000 are an annuity. If at the end of *each* 30-year period the state government refinances the debt by issuing another 30-year bond that also has an interest rate of 4 percent, then the annual interest payments of $40,000 would continue indefinitely, which is a perpetuity.

The library information system problem contains two annuities: the annual benefits of $150,000 per year for five years, which we refer to as annuity A1, and the annual costs of $25,000 per year for five years, which we refer to as annuity A2. From Figure 9.4 we see that the present value of A1 is $667,773. The present value of A2 is $111,296, easily computed by subtracting $500,000 from the PV of the costs. Sometimes it is useful to use equations to compute the present value of an annuity. From Equation (9.7) or (9.8), the present value of an annuity, A, for n years at interest rate i is given by:

$$PV = \sum_{t=1}^{n} \frac{A}{(1+i)^t}$$

Therefore,

$$PV = A \sum_{t=1}^{n} \frac{1}{(1+i)^t} = A a_i^n \qquad (9.11)$$

The term a_i^n, which equals the present value of an annuity of $1 per year for n years when the interest rate is i, is called an *annuity factor* and is given by Equation (9A.2) in Appendix 9A. Tables of annuity factors are built into most calculators and computer spreadsheets. Using Excel, the annuity factor for an annuity of $1 for 5 years at an interest rate of 4 percent is obtained by entering "=PV(.04,5,–1)", which equals 4.452. The third argument is the negative of the annuity amount, in this case $1. In previous PV examples this argument was left blank (or one could have entered zero) because there was no annuity.

Sometimes a benefit or a cost is like an annuity that grows or declines at a constant rate. Suppose, for example, that the benefits of the library information system are $150,000 the first year but then, due to more use of the system, they grow at 3 percent per annum, as shown in Table 9.3. Column 3 shows the benefits as growing annually at 3 percent and column 4 contains the present values of these amounts, resulting in a PV of the total benefits of $707,418. In this example, a 3 percent growth rate increases the PV by $39,645 or almost 6 percent. Clearly, assumptions about the growth of annuities can

Table 9.3 *Analysis of an Annuity that Grows at a Constant Rate*

Year	Event	Annual benefits	PV (annual benefits)
1	Annual benefits and costs	150,000	144,231
2	Annual benefits and costs	154,500	142,844
3	Annual benefits and costs	159,135	141,470
4	Annual benefits and costs	163,909	140,110
5	Annual benefits and costs	168,826	138,763
	PV		707,418

have a large impact on the NPV. Sometimes it is easier to use formulas to compute the PV of an annuity that grows or declines at a constant rate. These formulas are discussed in Appendix 9A; see, in particular, Equations (9A.4) and (9A.5).

A *perpetuity* is simply an annuity that continues indefinitely. Fortunately, it is easy to compute the present value of an amount, denoted by A, received at the end of each year in perpetuity by using the following formula:

$$PV = \frac{A}{i} \quad \text{if } i > 0 \tag{9.12}$$

To provide some intuition for this formula, suppose that a municipality has an endowment of $10 million. If interest rates are 6 percent, then this endowment will provide annual interest amounts of $600,000 indefinitely. More generally, if the municipality has an endowment of X and if the interest rate is i, then the perpetual annual income from the endowment, denoted by A, is given by $A = iX$. Rearranging this equation shows the present value of the perpetual annuity is given by $X = A/i$, which is Equation (9.12).

Equation (9.12) is straightforward to apply. For example, the present value of a perpetuity of $150,000 per year when interest rates are 8 percent is:

$$PV = \frac{\$150,000}{0.08} = \$1,875,000$$

When interest rates are 10 percent, the present value of a perpetuity simply equals the perpetuity multiplied by 10. For example, the present value of a perpetuity of $150,000 per year is $1,500,000 when interest rates are 10 percent.

9.2.5   *Continuous Compounding*

Throughout this chapter we assume that interest is compounded once per period, with the period being a year. In practice, interest on mortgages, savings accounts, and other investments is often compounded more than once per period. It may be compounded semi-annually, monthly, or even daily; sometimes, interest is compounded continuously. Assuming the interest rate is constant, the future value of a principal amount increases as the frequency of discounting increases and, analogously, the present value of a future amount declines as the frequency of discounting increases. However, the difference between compounding interest once per period and compounded it continuously is not great. For example, under continuous compounding, the *PV* of the benefits of the library information system would be $666,255, only $1,518 less than if interest was compounded only once per year.[5]

9.3   Timing of Benefits and Costs

The compounding and discounting formulas presented above assume that all benefits and costs occur at the end of each period (year), except for the initial costs, which occur immediately. This assumption is reasonable for many projects. Furthermore, when most of the costs of the project occur early and most of the benefits of the project occur late, this assumption is conservative in the sense that the *NPV* is lower than it would be if it were computed under alternative assumptions.

To illustrate this point, return to the library information system example, but now assume that the annual benefits of $150,000 all occur at the beginning of each year rather than at the end, while the timing of all of the costs remain unchanged. The present value of the benefits and the *NPV* of the project increase by $26,711. Clearly, the *NPV* of a project can vary considerably depending on the assumptions made about the timing of benefits and costs.

There are a variety of ways to compute the PV of the benefits under this new assumption. In order to understand them it useful to distinguish between an *ordinary annuity*, also called a *regular annuity*, where the payments are received (or paid) at the end of each year, as in Figure 9.4, and a *deferred annuity*, also called an *annuity due*, where the payments are received (or paid) at the beginning of each year.[6] One way to compute the PV of the benefits that are assumed to occur at the beginning of each year is to recognize that they can be thought of as consisting of two components: $150,000 received now plus an ordinary annuity of *four* payments of $150,000 per year. The latter amounts to $544,484 which, when added to $150,000, yields a PV of $694,484.[7] A second way is to compute the PV of an annuity due directly, either using the formula or a spreadsheet. In Excel the PV of an annuity due of $150,000 per period, received at the beginning of each year, is "=PV(.04,5,–150000,0,1)". The last argument indicates the type of annuity; it equals zero or is left blank for an ordinary annuity and it equals one for an annuity due.

When costs or benefits occur over the course of a year, they can be treated as if they occur in the middle of that year, rather than at the beginning or the end. Thus, for a project similar to the library information system project with some up-front costs (incurred at time 0) and with annual net social benefits that arise throughout the year, one could set $t = 0.5, 1.5, 2.5$, etc., in Equations (9.9) or (9.10) and use the formula:

$$NPV = -C_0 + \sum_{t=1}^{n} \frac{NSB_t}{(1+i)^{t-.5}}\tag{9.13}$$

Alternatively, one could compute the NPV in two ways: one assumes the impacts occur at the beginning of the year, while the other assumes they occur at the end of the year, and take the average.

9.4   Comparing Projects with Different Time Frames

Projects should always be compared over the same discounting period so that they have the same opportunity to accumulate costs and benefits, that is, they should be like-for-like. Projects with different time frames are not like-for-like and not directly comparable. The analyst must make adjustments.

Suppose that a government-owned electric utility company is considering two new alternative sources of power. The first alternative is a large hydroelectric dam (*HED*) which would last 75 years and the second is a cogeneration plant (*CGP*) which would last 15 years. After considering all relevant social benefits and costs, and assuming a discount rate of 6 percent, the *NPV* of the 75-year hydroelectric project is $40 million and the *NPV* of the 15-year cogeneration project is $25 million. Is the hydroelectric project preferable simply because it has the larger *NPV*? The answer is no. These projects are not like-for-like because they have different time spans. However, there are two methods for evaluating projects with different time frames: the *rollover method* and the *equivalent annual net benefit method*. As we show, they always lead to the same conclusion.

9.4.1   *Roll-Over Method*

If the utility initially built a CGP, it could be replaced by another CGP in 15 years. Further, the utility could build a third CGP in 30 years, a fourth in 45 years and a sixth in 60 years. If so, the length of these five sequential CGPs would be the same as the length of the single 75-year hydroelectric project. The HED project and five back-to-back CGP projects are directly comparable.

The *NPV* of five back-to-back CGPs equals $42.4 million as Table 9.4 shows. Because this *NPV* is higher than the *NPV* of the alternative hydroelectric project, the

Table 9.4 *The NPV of Five Back-to-Back Cogeneration Plants*

Year (*t*)	Event	PV in year *t*	PV in year 0
0	First CGP	25	25.0
15	Second CGP	25	10.4
30	Third CGP	25	4.4
45	Fourth CGP	25	1.8
60	Fifth CGP	25	0.8
	PV		42.4

utility should select this alternative. This method can be used to compare any two projects that only differ in terms of length. For example, if project A were two-thirds the length of project B, then the analyst can directly compare three back-to-back project A's with two back-to-back project B's.

9.4.2   *Equivalent Annual Net Benefit Method*

It is often easier to compare projects of unequal lengths using the *equivalent annual net social benefit method*, which, for convenience, we refer to as the equivalent annual net benefit (EANB) method. The *EANB* of a project equals its *NPV* divided by the *annuity factor* that has the same term and discount rate as the project itself (i.e., the present value of an annuity of $1 per year for the life of the project, discounted at the rate used to calculate the *NPV*):

$$EANB = \frac{NPV}{a_i^n} \tag{9.14}$$

where a_i^n is the annuity factor. The *EANB* is the amount which, if received each year for the life of the project, would have the same *NPV* as the project itself. This process is called *amortization* and is often applied to costs; here it is applied to the NPV of the two alternatives. The *EANBs* for the HED and the CGP projects equal:

$EANB(HED) = \$40/16.46 = \$2.43$ million

$EANB(CGP) = \$25/9.71 = \$2.57$ million

The *EANB* of the CGP project is $2.57 million, which implies that this project is equivalent to receiving an annuity of $2.57 million per year for 15 years. In contrast, the PV of the net social benefit of the HED alternative is equivalent to receiving an annuity of $2.43 million per year for 75 years. If one could continuously replace either alternative project at the end of its life with a similar project, then the CGP project would yield net annual social benefits equivalent to a perpetuity of $2.57 million per year, and the HED project would yield annual net social benefits equivalent to a perpetuity of $2.43 million per year. Consequently, the constant replacement CGP alternative is preferable, assuming replacement of both types of plant is possible at the end of their useful lives.

9.4.3   *An Additional Advantage of the Cogeneration Project*

In fact, if the utility chooses the CGP project at the beginning, then it may not be desirable to replace it with an identical CGP in 15 years. At that time a more efficient CGP is likely to be available. In contrast, if the utility builds the HED project, then it is probably locked in for 75 years. Thus, the CGP project has an additional benefit because of its flexibility in allowing the introduction of more efficient technology at a number of time points over the 75-year period. Chapter 11 discusses such benefits, called quasi-option value, in more depth. Here it is sufficient to recognize that the shorter project has an additional benefit which is not incorporated in the analysis above.

9.5   Inflation and Real versus Nominal Dollars

Conventional private-sector financial analysis measures revenues, expenditures, net income, assets, liabilities, and cash flows in terms of historical monetary units. Such units are referred to as *nominal dollars* (sometimes called *current dollars*). However, if you have ever listened to the reminiscences of an older person, then you probably know that a dollar purchased more goods and services in the past than it does now – "a dollar's not worth a dollar anymore!" For example, nominal per-capita disposable personal income in the United States was approximately 33 percent higher in 2014 than in 2004 ($40,690 versus $30,709), but the average person could not buy 33 percent more goods and services.[8] Purchasing power declines with price inflation. In order to control for the declining purchasing power of a dollar due to inflation, we convert nominal dollars to *real dollars* (sometimes called *constant dollars*).

To obtain real dollar measures, analysts *deflate* nominal dollars. There are a number of possible deflators. Usually, the *deflator* is based on the market price of a basket of goods and services purchased by consumers, that is, it is based on consumer prices. In the United States, the most commonly used deflator is the *all-items CPI* for all urban consumers, denoted CPI-U, which is published by the Bureau of Labor Statistics from January 1913 until the last month.[9] Sometimes analysts use the gross domestic product (GDP), which is broader and reflects the price of all goods and services in the economy, including the public sector. The choice of whether to use a consumer price deflator or the GDP deflator depends on whether the impacts of a project are concentrated on consumers or are much broader. In practice, most CBA studies use a consumer price deflator, especially when calculating consumer surplus. Some studies use a GDP deflator when calculating producer surplus.

Currently, the base year for CPI-U (that is, the period when the CPI-U = 100) is the period 1982–1984. CPI-U is expressed as the ratio of the cost of purchasing a standard basket of market goods in a particular year to the cost of purchasing the same (or very similar) basket of goods in the base year, multiplied by 100. For example, the CPI-U for 1980 was 82.4, which implies that the cost of a basket of goods in 1980 was 82.4 percent of the cost of a similar basket of goods in 1982–1984. In contrast, CPI-U for 2016 was 240.0, which implies that the cost of a basket of goods in 2016 was 240 percent of the cost of a similar basket in 1982–1984.

In order to convert amounts measured in nominal dollars for any year into amounts measured in real dollars for the base year (1982–1984), we simply divide the amount by the CPI for that year (divided by 100). For example, the average real income of people in 2004 measured in 1982–1984 dollars was $16,257 ($30,709/1.889), and the average real income of people in 2014 measured in 1982–1984 dollars was $17,188 ($40,690/2.36736). Therefore, after adjusting for inflation, people were able to purchase 5.7 percent more goods in 2014 than in 2004. Although their nominal incomes were 33 percent higher in 2014 than in 2004, their real incomes were only 5.7 percent higher.

To convert amounts expressed in base year dollars to, say, 2016 dollars, they are simply multiplied by the CPI for 2016 (divided by 100). Thus, the average real disposable incomes of people in 2004 and 2014, expressed in 2016 dollars, were $39,018 ($16,257 × 2.40007) and $41,252 ($17,188 × 2.40007), respectively.

More generally, to convert amounts expressed in year a nominal dollars into amounts expressed in year b real dollars, the year a dollar amounts are divided by the CPI for year a and multiplied by the CPI for year b. Fortunately for analysts in the US, the following government website contains an inflation calculator that does this automatically: www.bls.gov/data/inflation_calculator.htm.

9.5.1   *Problems with Indices Based on Consumer Prices*

The value of the CPI matters to cost–benefit analysts and the many people who receive payments affected by it. Many pensions, for example, are adjusted each year based on the CPI. The return to holders of index-linked bonds also depends on the value of the CPI. Although the CPI (or the CPI-U) is the most widely used price index in the US, it has been subject to a number of criticisms.

Most academic economists believe that the CPI somewhat overstates the rate of increase in market prices. In the mid-1990s, a commission set up by the Senate Finance Committee and chaired by Michael Boskin estimated that in the United States the CPI overestimated the increase in the cost of living by about 1 percentage point per annum, with a range between 0.8 percentage points and 1.6 percentage points.[10] As a result, people receiving entitlements linked to the CPI were, in effect, receiving a higher amount than was necessary to keep their purchasing power constant.

The main reason why the CPI might be biased upward is because it does not accurately reflect consumers' *current* purchases of goods.[11] This is sometimes called the *commodity substitution effect*. When the price of a good rises, consumers alter their spending patterns and buy similar, but less-expensive, products. The CPI does not immediately pick up this switch to less-expensive goods and so overestimates the cost of living.[12] Also, while government statisticians are visiting the same older, relatively expensive stores, consumers are switching to newer, cheaper discount stores and online stores; this is the so-called *discount stores effect*. A similar problem occurs when pharmaceutical patents expire. When a patent expires, some consumers switch to a new generic drug, which is often as effective as the patented drug, but is considerably less expensive. Such new generic drugs are not included in the sample basket. This *"new goods" problem* applies also to new "high-tech" goods, such as iPads or customized mail-order genetic testing kits, which both improve our quality of life and are also often cheaper than older substitutes. A second type of problem concerns incremental quality improvements to existing products. The CPI does not immediately reflect changes in product quality, such as safer and more reliable cars. The US government has corrected the CPI for some of these problems on an ongoing basis. In 1998, it undertook some major revisions that reduced the estimated bias to about 0.65 percent per annum.

The downward bias in consumer price indices is probably not as large in some other countries as it is in the US. For example, Allan Crawford estimates that the bias was about one-half a percentage point per annum in 1998 in Canada.[13] One reason why it was lower in Canada than the United States is that the base basket of goods has been updated every 4 years in Canada versus approximately every 10 years in the United States. Also, the Canadian index attaches a lower weight to medical services.

The United Kingdom has two main consumer-focused indices: the UK Consumer Price Index (also abbreviated by CPI) and the Retail Prices Index (RPI).[14] The UK's CPI is the main measure of inflation for macroeconomic policy purposes, currently targeted at 2 percent. It is constructed in a way that is consistent across the European Union and thereby allows inflation to be compared across the EU. The RPI is the more familiar index, going back to 1947, and is used for indexation of pensions, state benefits, and index-linked gilts (short-term government bonds). The weights in the UK's CPI and the RPI are updated annually. In general, the RPI index is considerably more variable over time than is the CPI index.

9.5.2   *Discounting Using Real or Nominal Dollars*

Analysts may work with project benefits and costs in either real dollars or in nominal dollars. Also, they may discount using either a real interest rate or a nominal interest rate. Care must be taken to ensure that the units of measurement of benefits and costs are consistent with the units of measurement of the discount rate. *If benefits and costs are measured in nominal dollars, then the analyst should discount using a nominal discount rate; if benefits and costs are measured in real dollars, then the analyst should discount using a real discount rate*. Both methods result in the same numerical answer.[15]

In the private sector, it is more natural to work in nominal dollars. Interest rates and other market data are expressed in nominal dollars; pro forma income and cash-flow projections are usually made in nominal dollars; and the tax system is based on nominal amounts. However, for the analysis of public policy projects, *it is usually easier and more intuitively appealing to express all benefits and costs in real dollars and to discount using a real discount rate*. Returning to our library information system example, it makes more sense to think about the current and future annual cost savings to the library at today's prices than in future inflated prices. Similarly, it is easier to think about user benefits in terms of the number of hours of use at today's value per hour than to think about them in terms of future valuations. If one expects that user benefits will increase over time, for example, due to more people using the system or because each person uses it more often, then the projected real annual benefits will increase. This would be immediately clear if annual benefits were measured in real dollars. If, alternatively, annual benefits were expressed in nominal dollars, then it would not be immediately obvious whether increases were due to real increases in benefits or due to inflation.

If the analyst prefers to work in real dollars, but benefits, costs, or the interest rate are expressed in nominal dollars, then nominal dollar amounts must be converted to real dollars. This process requires an estimate of *expected inflation throughout the life of the project*, denoted m. To convert future impacts (benefits or costs) measured in nominal dollars to real dollars *we use the formula for computing present values, Equations (9.7) or (9.8), but discount at rate* m.[16]

$$Real\ cost\ or\ benefit_t = \frac{Nominal\ cost\ or\ benefit_t}{(1+m)^t} \qquad (9.15)$$

For example, if a city could invest $10 million for five years at a nominal discount rate of 5 percent, then the nominal future value in 5 years would be $12.763 million; see Table 9.1. However, with an expected inflation rate of 2 percent throughout the period, the real value of this amount in year 0 dollars would be $11.56 million ($14.026/(1.02)^5), using Equation 9.15.

To derive the formula for the real interest rate, r, in terms of nominal interest rate, i, suppose we begin with $1 today. With a nominal interest rate, i, we would receive $\$(1 + i)$ one year from now. However, if the inflation rate is m, then $\$(1 + i)$ received one year from now would buy only as much as $\$(1 + i)/(1 + m)$ does today, using the formula immediately above or Equation (9.2). The real interest rate, r, is therefore defined by $(1 + r) = (1 + i)/(1 + m)$. Rearranging this expression gives the following equation, which we use to *convert a nominal interest rate, i, to a real interest rate, r, with an inflation rate, m.*[17]

$$r = \frac{i - m}{1 + m} \tag{9.16}$$

For example, if the nominal interest rate is 5 percent and inflation is 2 percent, then the real interest rate is $(.05 - .02)/1.02 = 0.0294$, or 2.94 percent. Therefore, if the city could invest $10 million for 5 years at a real interest rate of 2.94 percent then it would have $10(1.0294)^5 = $11.56 million in real terms, the same amount we computed above. If inflation is quite low (m is small), then the real interest rate *approximately* equals the nominal interest rate minus the rate of inflation: $r \approx i - m$. For example, if the nominal interest rate is 5 percent and inflation is 2 percent, then the real interest rate is approximately 3 percent.

In order to convert benefits or costs from real dollars to nominal dollars, analysts can use the formula for computing future values, Equation (9.4), but compound at the rate of inflation, m. To convert a real interest rate to a nominal interest rate, solve Equation (9.16) for i.

9.5.3   *An Example of Handling Inflation: New Garbage Trucks*

A practical example illustrates the basic technique of handling inflation and moving from market interest rates, which are nominal rates, to real interest rates. Consider a city that uses a rural landfill to dispose of solid refuse and is considering adding new, large trucks to the refuse fleet. By adding these trucks, the city would reduce the annual disposal costs. Specifically, the city would save $100,000 during the first year and the same amount in each successive year in real dollars. This assumption is based on several implicit assumptions, for example, that the amount of time that operators drive the trucks remains constant and vehicle operating costs and operator wages increase with inflation. The trucks would be purchased today for $500,000 and would be sold after four years when the city will open a resource recovery plant that will obviate the need for landfill disposal. The *current* market value of four-year-old trucks of the same type and quality as the city might buy is $200,000. This is the liquidation value of the trucks expressed in *real* dollars in 4 years.

Suppose the city can borrow money at a market interest rate of 5 percent and analysts expect that inflation will be 2 percent during the next four years. Should the city buy the trucks? As usual, the answer should be yes if the *NPV* is positive. Is it?

9.5.4   *Using Real Dollars*

The annual benefits and costs in real dollars are given in column 3 of Table 9.5. Because benefits and costs are expressed in real dollars, we need to discount them using the real discount rate, which equals 2.94 percent using Equation (9.16). Generally analysts assume that benefits and costs arise at the end of a year. Suppose, however, *we assume that the savings arise throughout the year*. The discounted amounts are shown in column 4, which, when summed, yield an *NPV* equal to $55,772. Thus, as long as no alternative equipment configuration offers a greater *NPV*, the city should purchase the larger trucks.

9.5.5   *Using Nominal Dollars*

If an analyst takes the market interest rate facing the city as the appropriate discount rate, which is a nominal rate, then she must predict future costs and benefits in nominal dollars. To convert amounts in real dollars to nominal dollars, one simply inflates them using Equation (9.4) by the expected rate of inflation, m. For the annual savings one might be tempted to use $n = 1, 2, 3, 4$. However, because these savings are assumed to arise during the year, one must use $n = 0.5, 1.5, 2.5$, and 3.5, respectively. Because the trucks are sold at the end of period 4, then one would set $n = 4$ when applying Equation (9.4). Column 5 of Table 9.5 shows the estimated benefits and costs of this project in nominal dollars, assuming a 2 percent annual inflation rate. Notice that the city expects to receive $216,486 in nominal dollars when it sells the trucks at the end of the fourth year. This is called the *nominal liquidation value* of the trucks. Discounting the nominal

Table 9.5 *The Net Present Value of Buying New Garbage Trucks*

Year	Event	Annual benefits and costs (in real dollars)	PV (real annual benefits and costs) [a]	Annual benefits and costs (in nominal dollars)	PV (nominal annual benefits and costs) [b]
0	Truck purchase	−500,000	−500,000	−500,000	−500,000
1	Annual savings	100,000	98,561	100,995	98,561
2	Annual savings	100,000	95,745	103,015	95,745
3	Annual savings	100,000	93,009	105,075	93,009
4	Annual savings	100,000	90,352	107,177	90,352
4	Truck liquidation	200,000	178,104	216,486	178,104
	NPV		55,772		55,772

[a] Discounted using a real discount rate of 2.94 percent.
[b] Discounted using a nominal discount rate of 5 percent.

benefits using a nominal interest rate of 5 percent gives the amounts in column 6, which sum to $55,772, as before. Thus, the two methods give exactly the same answer.

9.5.6   *Estimates of Future Inflation*

As the above example illustrates, performing ex ante CBA does not necessarily require an estimate of the expected rate of inflation over the life of a proposed project. However, it is necessary if some impacts (generally benefits) are measured in real dollars and some impacts (generally costs) are measures in nominal dollars. It is tempting for analysts to use the current annual inflation rate, but this could be extremely inaccurate, especially for longer projects.

Short-term inflation forecasts are available from federal governments or the Organisation for Economic Co-operation and Development (OECD). Each month *The Economist* presents forecasts of the change in consumer prices for the current year and the following year for some countries, and there are more data on its website. In the United States, there are three potentially useful surveys: the Livingston Survey of professional economists, the University of Michigan Survey of Consumers, and the Survey of Professional Forecasters (SPF).[18]

Longer-term estimates are harder to find. However, SPF respondents have provided 10-year-ahead inflation forecasts of the CPI since 1991. Another option is to use the inflationary expectations implied by the price of *inflation-indexed government bonds*.[19] Although it is possible to use this approach to infer inflationary expectations over fairly long time periods (up to 30 years), these bonds are sometimes thinly traded and, therefore, the estimates may be unreliable.[20]

9.6   Relative Price Changes

The preceding section discusses how to handle general price increases due to inflation. It assumes relative prices do not change, that is, the price of each good or service is assumed to increase at the same rate. In practice, however, some prices increase (or decrease) faster than others. That is, relative prices may change. Analysts should always consider this possibility, especially for long-lived projects. Fortunately, there is no conceptual difficulty in handling relative price changes. As before, all prices should be converted to real dollars and discounted at the real SDR (social discount rate) or all prices should be converted to nominal dollars and discounted at the nominal SDR. The importance of relative price changes is illustrated by the end of chapter case study of a CBA of a development project in British Columbia to supply coal to Japanese customers.

9.7   Terminal Values and Fixed-Length Projects

The costs and benefits of many CBA projects have the same structure as the new garbage truck project, that is, up-front costs are incurred at time zero, project benefits and operating costs arise in years 1 through n, and the assets are liquidated at the end of year n. For such projects, the NPV can be computed using the following formula:

$$NPV = -C_0 + \sum_{t=1}^{n} \frac{RNSB_t}{(1+i)^{t-.5}} + \frac{T_n}{(1+i)^n} \tag{9.17}$$

where C_0 is the initial cost, $RNSB_t$ are the "regular" annual net social benefits (i.e., excluding the terminal value, $t = 1,2, ..., n$), T_n is the terminal value at the end of year n, and i is the appropriate discount rate. In the garbage truck example, using real dollars, $C_0 = \$500,000$, $RNSB_t = \$100,000$ each year, $T_n = \$200,000$, and $i = 2.94$ percent.

In this example, the terminal value is the liquidation value of the assets. Assuming that there are no externalities and there is a well-functioning market in which to value garbage trucks, then the second-hand market price would reflect the asset's social value at that time. Some projects have negative terminal values. For example, there may be costs associated with decommissioning the site used for a World Exposition, the Olympic Games, or a nuclear power plant, which exceed the value of the assets sold. For some projects the terminal value equals zero. Indeed, the library information system example made this assumption.

9.8   Terminal (or Horizon) Values, and Long-Lived Projects

In all projects discussed thus far, the social benefits and costs arise during a limited number of years, typically the period when the project was being implemented. At the end of the project, the remaining assets are immediately sold or used in some other way and it is assumed there are no subsequent costs or benefits. That is, application of Equations (9.9), (9.10), or (9.17) assumes that there is no benefit or cost after the nth year. This assumption is often reasonable in private-sector decision-making because project evaluation requires only the consideration of private benefits and costs that are usually zero after the project ends. However, the impacts of a government project might arise many years in the future, perhaps indefinitely, even though it is finished from an engineering or administrative perspective. In England, for example, cars travel on roads that were laid out by the Romans more than 18 centuries ago. The Great Wall of China continues to generate tourism benefits even though it was built to discourage particularly unwelcome "visitors" many centuries ago. The same issue also arises in human capital investment programs, especially training and health programs. For example, pre-school training programs may benefit participants throughout their entire lives, years after they completed the program; some benefits may even accrue to their children. All of these impacts should be included in a CBA. However, in practice, it is often not clear how to handle costs and benefits that arise after the program has finished.

If benefits or costs occur indefinitely, then the NPV can be calculated using Equations (9.9) or (9.10) with n replaced with infinity, ∞:

$$NPV = \sum_{t=0}^{\infty} \frac{NSB_t}{(1+i)^t} \tag{9.18}$$

The difficulty of applying this formula lies in predicting the NSBs far into the future. Usually, analysts break the infinite time period into two parts: *the discounting horizon* and all time periods thereafter. Annual net social benefits are discounted over the discounting horizon of, say, k years. The present value of all subsequent net social benefits *at the end of the discounting horizon* is called the *horizon value* and is denoted H_k. Thus, the NPV can be written:

$$NPV = \sum_{t=0}^{k} \frac{NSB_t}{(1+i)^t} + \frac{H_k}{(1+i)^k} \tag{9.19}$$

where

$$H_k = \sum_{t=k+1}^{\infty} \frac{NSB_t}{(1+i)^t} \tag{9.20}$$

In practice, the terms horizon value and terminal value are used interchangeably.

The length of the discounting period, k, is arbitrary in theory. In practice, it is usually determined by the nature of each project and the confidence of the analyst to predict costs and benefits during the "near future" (the first k periods) rather than the "far future," thereafter. The first k years might be the *useful life* of the project. For example, as illustrated in the Coquihalla Highway example introduced in Chapter 1, analysts often use a 20-year discounting period for highways because they tend to last about 20 years before they require major repairs. Once the discount period has been selected there are two ways to estimate the horizon value.

9.8.1   *Horizon Value Estimated Directly*

For many long-lived projects it is probably most appropriate to assume that, after some point in time, the *NSBs* grow or decline at a constant rate. If so, the equations in Appendix 9A are useful to compute PVs.

9.8.2   *Horizon Value Based on Depreciated Value of the Asset(s)*

For projects with a high percentage of capital assets one could try to estimate the *economic value* of the assets at the end of the discounting period, assuming that this value equals the present value of its future net social benefits. One way to estimate this value is to subtract *economic depreciation* from the initial capital cost. The economic value of most assets declines at a geometric rate; that is, the value in one year is a constant proportion of the value in the previous year. The depreciation rate is high for assets with short lives, such as tires, motor vehicles, and medical equipment, and is low for assets with long lives, such as steam turbines, warehouses, railroad structures, and water systems. Barbara Fraumeni describes the methodology used by the US Bureau of Economic Analysis (BEA) for calculating economic depreciation and presents a comprehensive summary of the depreciation rates and service lives of many assets.[21] It is important to emphasize that this method is based on economic depreciation, not accounting depreciation. The latter often has little relationship to economic value. *Accounting depreciation should never be included as a cost in CBA.*

A somewhat similar approach is to assume that the economic value of an asset equals some fraction of the initial project cost. For example, the Coquihalla highway illustration in Chapter 1 assumed that the real horizon value of the highway was equal to 75 percent of the initial construction cost: 0.75 × $661.8 million = $496.35 million.[22] Obviously, though, the 75 percent figure is somewhat arbitrary.

Of course, one should make adjustments where appropriate. For example, if the asset will be used more heavily or maintained more poorly than normal, then one should raise the depreciation rate. Also, the horizon value should depend on future net social benefits which, in turn, depend on its future use. Although an aircraft may have a fairly high depreciated value, its social value is low if it will be mothballed and nobody will fly it. Similarly, if the government is considering building a "white elephant," for example, a so-called "bridge to nowhere," then simple application of economic depreciation would overestimate the horizon value.

9.8.3   *Reprise of Horizon Values*

The analyst must decide on both the discounting period and the method for calculating the horizon value. These may be interdependent. If, for example, the analyst is going to assume the horizon value is zero, then she should use a relatively long discounting period. If the analyst is going to estimate the horizon value separately, then it makes sense to discount over the project's useful life. Because of uncertainty concerning the actual magnitude of the horizon value, *sensitivity analysis* is often conducted by selecting alternative horizon values and seeing how this affects the findings. A further consideration is that for some very long-lived projects analysts should use time-declining discount rates. We now turn to that issue.

9.9   Time-Declining Discounting

Thus far this chapter has assumed that the discount rate is constant; that is, it does not vary over time. This assumption is reasonable for projects with relatively short-term impacts. However, it is not reasonable for projects with some impacts that occur in the far future, such as those that affect climate change. In Chapter 10 we discuss the use of time-declining discount rates and suggest that for developed countries, benefits and costs should be discounted at 3.5 percent for the first 50 years, at 2.5 percent for years 50–100, 1.5 percent for years 100–200, 0.5 percent for years 200–300, and 0.0 percent for years more than 300 years in the future.

In order to understand how to perform time-declining discounting, suppose that a project has a cost of $1 million today and a benefit of $1 billion in 400 years' time. Assuming continuous discounting, the *PV* of the benefit would be $1 billion × [(e^{-0.035*50})

$\times$ ($e^{-0.025(100-50)}$) $\times$ ($e^{-0.015(200-100)}$) $\times$ ($e^{-0.005(300-200)}$)], which is approximately $6,737,945, yielding a project *NPV* of $5,737,945. To obtain the PV of the benefits, we first compute the value in year 300 using a discount rate of 0 percent, which is $1 billion. We then discount this value at 0.5 percent for 100 years from years 300 to 200, then take the resulting value in year 200 and discount for 100 years to year 100 at 1.5 percent, then take the resulting value in year 100 and discount it back to year 50 at 2.5 percent, and finally discount the resulting amount to year 0 at 3.5 percent. This is equivalent to applying a single, constant rate of 1.26 percent over 400 years.

9.10   Sensitivity Analysis in Discounting

This chapter assumes that the rate (or rates with time declining discounting) that should be used to discount future benefits and costs is known. However, for reasons discussed in Chapter 10, there are significant differences of opinion about the correct value of the social discount rate. Therefore, one should determine the sensitivity of the NPV with respect to the discount rate. The terminal value is also a candidate for sensitivity analysis.

As we discuss more fully in Chapter 11, the most straightforward way to perform sensitivity analysis is to vary each parameter about which there is uncertainty and recalculate the *NPV*. This is easy to do on a spreadsheet. If the policy recommendations are robust (i.e., the *NPV* remains either positive or negative) under all plausible values of the parameters, we can have greater confidence that the recommendations are valid.

Figure 9.5 plots the *NPV* of buying new garbage trucks against the real discount rate for two different real terminal values, one of $200,000 (the top curve) and the other $150,000 (the bottom curve). Holding the terminal value constant, the *NPV* of the project decreases as the discount rate increases. This common pattern arises for investment projects whose costs occur early and whose benefits occur late. A higher discount rate results in a lower *NPV* because the future benefits are discounted more than the more immediate costs.

By definition, the *internal rate of return* (*IRR*) of the project (sometimes referred to as the *breakeven discount rate*) equals the discount rate that yields an *NPV* = 0. This amount can be read off the graph on the horizontal axis where the *NPV* = 0, found by trial and error on a spreadsheet or found analytically.[23] If the real horizon value equals $200,000 then the real IRR equals 7.25 percent. If the appropriate real discount rate were less than 7.25 percent, then the project would have a positive *NPV* and should be adopted. Conversely, if the appropriate real discount rate were more than 7.25 percent, then the project would have a negative NPV and it should not be adopted.

If the horizon value equals $150,000 in real dollars, then the NPV curve shifts down by the discounted value of $50,000. As the NPV decreases as the discount rate increases, the curve shifts down less for high interest rates than for low interest rates. Although the *NPV* is smaller than before at every discount rate, it is still positive as long as the real discount rate is less than 3.86 percent.

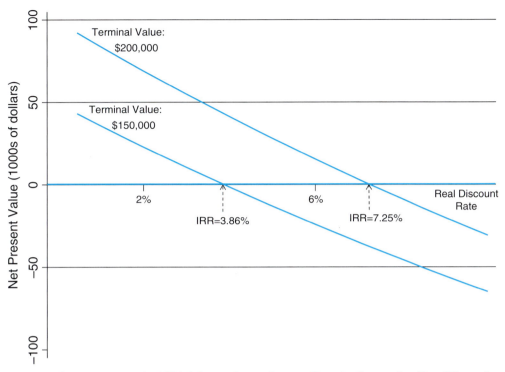

Figure 9.5 Sensitivity analysis: *NPV* of the purchase of new garbage trucks as a function of the real discount rate and the real horizon value.

9.10.1 *The Internal Rate of Return as a Decision Rule*

The real *IRR* of the new garbage trucks project is 7.25 percent, which implies that this project is equivalent to a project of similar size that provides annual benefits equal to 7.25 percent of the original amount for 5 years (the length of the project) and returns all of the initial invested capital at the end of the fifth year. The *IRR* may be used for selecting projects *when there is only one alternative to the status quo* as in this example. The basic idea, which we discuss in depth in Chapter 10, is that society (or a government acting in the interests of society) should only invest in projects that earn a higher return than could be earned by investing the resources elsewhere. In other words, the appropriate discount rate should reflect the opportunity cost of the funds.

There are, however, a number of potential problems with using the *IRR* for decision-making. First, the *IRR* may not be unique; that is, there may be more than one discount rate at which the *NPV* is zero. This problem may arise when annual net benefits change more than once from positive to negative (or vice versa) during the discounting period. Second, *IRR*s are percentages (i.e., ratios), not dollar values. Therefore, they should not be used to select one project from a group of projects that differ in size. This scale problem always arises with the use of ratios, including benefit–cost ratios, cost–effectiveness ratios, and *IRR*s. Nonetheless, if it is unique, the *IRR* conveys useful information to decision-makers or other analysts who want to know how sensitive the results are to the choice of discount rate.[24]

9.11   Conclusion

This chapter presents the main issues concerning the mechanics of discounting. It assumes that the appropriate discount rate is known. In fact, determination of the appropriate discount rate to use in CBA is a somewhat contentious issue, which we discuss in Chapter 10.

APPENDIX 9A

Formulas for Calculating the Present Value of Annuities and Perpetuities

Present Value of an Annuity

The present value of an annuity of A per annum (with payments received at the end of each year) for n years with interest at i percent is given by:

$$PV = \sum_{t=1}^{n} \frac{A}{(1+i)^t}$$

This amount is the sum of n terms of a geometric series with the common ratio equal to $1/(1 + i)$. Consequently,

$$PV = Aa_i^n \tag{9A.1}$$

where,

$$a_i^n = \frac{1-(1+i)^{-n}}{i} \tag{9A.2}$$

Note that the *present value of an annuity decreases as the interest rate increases, and vice versa*. This is a partial explanation for why bond prices rise as interest rates fall. Another important observation is that *annuity payments received after about the twentieth year add little to the present value when interest rates are 10 percent or higher*. Thus, private companies are often reluctant to make very long-term investments such as reforestation.

The Present Value of an Annuity that Grows or Declines at a Constant Rate

Sometimes a project's benefits (or costs) grow at a constant rate. Let B_t denote the annual benefits in year t. Thus, the annual benefits that arise in year 1 are denoted B_1. Suppose these benefits grow each year at a constant rate, g. Then the benefits in year t will be:

$$B_t = B_{t-1}(1 + g) = B_1(1 + g)^{t-1} \quad t = 2, \ldots, n \tag{9A.3}$$

The present value of the total benefits – the stream over n years – can (if $i > g$) be shown to be:[1]

$$PV(B) = \frac{B_1}{(1+g)} a_{i_0}^n \tag{9A.4}$$

where $a_{i_0}^n$ is defined by Equation (9A.2) and:

$$i_0 = \frac{i-g}{1+g}, \quad i > g \tag{9A.5}$$

Comparing Equation (9A.1) with (9A.4) shows that the PV of a benefit stream that starts at B_1 in year 1 and grows at a constant rate g for $n - 1$ additional years, when the interest rate is i, equals the PV of an annuity of $B_1/(1 + g)$ for n years when the interest rate, i_0, is given by Equation (9A.5). *Note that when using Equation (9A.5), the annuity equals $B_1/(1 + g)$, not B_1.*

To illustrate how to calculate the present value of a stream of benefits that grows at a constant rate using these formulas, return to the library information system example and assume that benefits grow at 3 percent per annum *after the first year*. From above, the present value of this stream of benefits equals the present value of an annuity of $150,000/1.03 = 145,631$ per annum for 5 years, discounted at the following rate:

$$i_0 = \frac{i-g}{1+g} = \frac{.04 - .03}{1.03} = 0.0097087$$

which amounts to $707,418, as before.

If the growth rate is small, then $B_1/(1 + g) \cong B_1$ and $i_0 \cong i - g$. Therefore, from Equation (9A.5), the present value of a benefits stream that starts at B_1 and grows at rate g for $n - 1$ additional years approximately equals the present value of an annuity of B_1 for n years discounted at rate $i - g$, as long as $i > g$. This approximation makes it clear that when benefits grow at a positive rate, the annuity is discounted at a lower rate, which will yield a higher PV. On the other hand, if the benefits are declining at a constant rate, then the annuity is discounted at a higher rate, which will yield a lower PV.

Equation (9A.5) only holds if the interest rate exceeds the growth rate: $i > g$. If $i \leq g$, then it should not be used. Importantly, though, it can always be used if g is negative, that is, if benefits decline at a constant rate.

The Present Value of a Perpetuity that Grows or Declines at a Constant Rate

If the first year's net social benefits, NSB_1, grow indefinitely at a constant rate g and if the interest rate equals i, then the PV of the net social benefits is found by taking the limit of Equation (9A.4) as n goes to infinity. That is,

$$NPV = \frac{NSB_1}{(i-g)} \quad if \; i > g \tag{9A.6}$$

Some finance students may recognize this formula as the Gordon growth model, which is also called the dividend growth model. It is often used to value a stock that yields a constant flow of dividends that grow at a constant rate. As before, this formula holds only if $i > g$.

Exercises for Chapter 9

1. A highway department is considering building a temporary bridge to cut travel time during the three years it will take to build a permanent bridge. The temporary bridge can be put up in a few weeks at a cost of $730,000. At the end of three years, it would be removed and the steel would be sold for scrap. The real net *costs* of this would be $81,000. Based on estimated time savings and wage rates, fuel savings, and reductions in risks of accidents, department analysts predict that the benefits in real dollars would be $275,000 during the first year, $295,000 during the second year, and $315,000 during the third year. Departmental regulations require use of a real discount rate of 4 percent.

   a. Calculate the present value of net benefits assuming that the benefits are realized at the end of each of the 3 years.

   b. Calculate the present value of net benefits assuming that the benefits are realized at the beginning of each of the 3 years.

   c. Calculate the present value of net benefits assuming that the benefits are realized in the middle of each of the 3 years.

   d. Calculate the present value of net benefits assuming that half of each year's benefits are realized at the beginning of the year and the other half at the end of the year.

   e. Does the temporary bridge pass the net benefits test?

2. A government data-processing center has been plagued in recent years by complaints from employees of back pain. Consultants have estimated that upgrading office furniture at a net cost of $430,000 would reduce the incidence and severity of back injuries, allowing the center to avoid medical care that currently cost $68,000 each year. They estimate that the new furniture would also provide yearly benefits of avoided losses in work time and employee comfort worth $18,000. The furniture would have a useful life of 5 years, after which it would have a real scrap value equal to 10 percent of its initial net cost. The consultants made their estimates of avoided costs assuming that they would be treated as occurring at the beginning of each year.

In its investment decisions, the center uses a nominal discount rate of 9 percent and an assumed general inflation rate of 3 percent. It expects the inflation rate for medical care will be either 3 percent, the same as other goods, or 6 percent. Should the center purchase the new furniture?

3. A town's recreation department is trying to decide how to use a piece of land. One option is to put up basketball courts with an expected life of 8 years. Another is to install a swimming pool with an expected life of 24 years. The basketball courts would cost $180,000 to construct and yield net benefits of $40,000 at the end of each of the 8 years. The swimming pool would cost $2.25 million to construct and yield net benefits of $170,000 at the end of each of the 24 years. Each project is assumed to have zero salvage value at the end of its life. Using a real discount rate of 5 percent, which project offers larger net benefits?

4. The environmental protection agency of a county would like to preserve a piece of land as a wilderness area. The current owner has offered to lease the land to the county for 20 years in return for a lump sum payment of $1.1 million, which would be paid at the beginning of the 20-year period. The agency has estimated that the land would generate $110,000 per year in benefits to hunters, bird watchers, and hikers. Assume that the lease price represents the social opportunity cost of the land and that the appropriate real discount rate is 4 percent.

    a. Assuming that the yearly benefits, which are measured in real dollars, accrue at the end of each of the 20 years, calculate the net benefits of leasing the land.

    b. Some analysts in the agency argue that the annual real benefits are likely to grow at a rate of 2 percent per year due to increasing population and county income. Recalculate the net benefits assuming that they are correct.

5. Imagine that the current owner of the land in the previous exercise was willing to sell the land for $2 million. Assuming this amount equaled the social opportunity cost of the land, calculate the net benefits if the county were to purchase the land as a permanent wildlife refuge. In making these calculations, first assume a zero annual growth rate in the $110,000 of annual real benefits; then assume that these benefits grow at a rate of 2 percent per year.

6. (Instructor-provided spreadsheet recommended.) New City is considering building a recreation center. The estimated construction cost is $12 million with annual staffing and maintenance costs of $750,000 over the 20-year life of the project. At the end of the life of the project, New City expects to be

able to sell the land for $4 million, although the amount could be as low as $2 million and as high as $5 million. Analysts estimate the first-year benefits (accruing at the end of the year of the first year) to be $1.2 million. They expect the annual benefit to grow in real terms due to increases in population and income. Their prediction is a growth rate of 4 percent, but it could be as low as 1 percent and as high as 6 percent. Analysts estimate the real discount rate for New City to be 6 percent, although they acknowledge that it could be a percentage point higher or lower.

a.   Calculate the present value of net benefits for the project using the analysts' predictions.

b.   Investigate the sensitivity of the present value of net benefits to alternative predictions within the ranges given by the analysts.

Notes

1. T-bill is an abbreviation of Treasury bill. A T-bill is a short-term bond issued by the Treasury Department of the U.S. government.

2. At the end of the first year, one would have $FV = X(1 + i)$. At the end of the second year, one would have $FV = [X(1 + i)](1 + i) = X(1 + i)^2$, and so on.

3. There is a useful rule for computing approximate future values called the "rule of 72." Capital roughly doubles when the interest rate (expressed in percentage points) times the number of years equals 72: $100 \times i \times n = 72$. For example, if the interest rate is 8 percent, then your capital doubles in $72/8 = 9$ years. Similarly, in order to double your capital in 10 years, you need an interest rate of at least $72/10 = 7.2$ percent.

4. $NPV = \sum_{t=0}^{n} \dfrac{B_t}{(1+i)^t} - \sum_{t=0}^{n} \dfrac{C_t}{(1+i)^t} = \sum_{t=0}^{n} \dfrac{B_t - C_t}{(1+i)^t}$

$= \sum_{t=0}^{n} \dfrac{NSB_t}{(1+i)^t}$

5. If interest is compounded continuously, then the present value of \$$Y$ received in n years with interest rate i is given by:

$$PV = \frac{Y}{e^{in}}$$

where $e = \lim_{n \to \infty}\left(1 + \dfrac{1}{n}\right)^n$ is the base of the natural logarithm, which equals 2.71828 to five decimal places. For example, the present value of \$150,000 received in five years with interest at 4 percent compounded continuously is:

$$PV = \frac{\$150,000}{e^{.04 \times 5}} = \frac{\$150,000}{1.221} = \$122,810$$

6. The semantics are counterintuitive because one might expect that a deferred annuity starts later than an ordinary annuity, not sooner. The confusion arises because one often saves first and then receives annuity payments at some future date and these payments occur at the beginning of a period. For CBA purposes one should simply consider an ordinary annuity as one where the impacts (inputs or outputs) arise at the end of a period while for an annuity due they arise at the beginning of a period.

7. If a spreadsheet (or calculator) computes only the PV of ordinary annuities, then one could calculate the PV of an annuity due for n years by computing the PV of an ordinary annuity for $n - 1$ years and adding the value of the initial payment or receipt made today.

8. Source: www.bls.gov/emp/ep_table_410.htm (accessed May 3, 2017).

9. Source: www.usinflationcalculator.com/inflation/consumer-price-index-and-annual-percent-changes-from-1913-to-2008/

(accessed May 3, 2017). The most recent CPI figures for Canada are available from Statistics Canada in table 326–0020; see www5.statcan.gc.ca/cansim/a26?id=3260020 (accessed May 3, 2017). For the latest statistics for the United Kingdom see the Office for National Statistics' website at www.ons.gov.uk/.

10. See Michael J. Boskin, Ellen R. Dulberger, Robert J. Gordon, Zvi Griliches, and Dale W. Jorgenson, *Toward a More Accurate Measure of the Cost of Living*, Final Report to the Senate Finance Committee from the Advisory Committee to Study the Consumer Price Index (Washington, DC: Senate Finance Committee, 1996).

11. For more detail see Brent R. Moulton, "Bias in the Consumer Price Index: What Is the Evidence?" *Journal of Economic Perspectives*, 10(4), 1996, 159–77 and Allan Crawford, "Measurement Biases in the Canadian CPI: An Update." *Bank of Canada Review*, Spring 1998, 39–56.

12. For practical reasons the CPI is a Laspeyres index, which uses the quantities of each good consumed in a previous period to compute expenditures in the current period.

13. See Allan Crawford, "Measurement Biases in the Canadian CPI: An Update."

14. There are three main differences between the CPI and the RPI. The first concerns the goods. The CPI covers the full range of consumer purchases made by households, excluding council tax and most owner-occupier housing costs, such as mortgage interest payments, which are included in the RPI. Other items included in the RPI but not in the CPI include vehicle excise duty and trade union subscriptions. Items included in the CPI but not in the RPI include unit trust and stockbroker charges, overseas students' university fees and accommodation costs. The second key difference is that the CPI has a broader population base: the RPI (unlike the CPI) excludes households in the top 4 percent of income and some pensioners. The third key difference is the weights: the CPI weights are based on household expenditure from the National Accounts, while the RPI uses the Expenditure and Food Survey. Fourth, the aggregation formulas are different.

15. Recall that the NPV for a project is given by Equation (9.9), and suppose that the benefits, B_t, and costs, C_t, are in nominal dollars and i is the nominal interest rate. Let b_t denote real benefits, c_t denote real costs, and suppose the rate of inflation is m, then, using Equation (9.4), $B_t = b_t(1 + m)^t$ and $C = c_t(1 + m)^t$. Consequently,

$$NPV = \sum_{t=0}^{n} \frac{B_t - C_t}{(1+i)^t} = \sum_{t=0}^{n} \frac{(b_t - c_t)(1+m)^t}{(1+i)^t}$$

Now, to simplify, set $1/(1 + r) = (1 + m)/(1 + i)$, which gives:

$$NPV = \sum_{t=0}^{n} \frac{b_t - c_t}{(1+r)^t}$$

As we discuss later, we can interpret r as the real interest rate.

16. The expected CPI in t periods in the future equals $(1 + m)^t$ times the current CPI. Therefore, dividing the future impacts measured in nominal dollars by $(1 + m)^t$, in accordance with Equation (9.5), is exactly the same as the method implied above for converting amounts expressed in year b dollars into amounts expressed in year a dollars, namely: dividing by the expected CPI in t periods in the future and multiplying by the CPI for the current year.

17. This relationship is known as the Fisher effect. An alternative derivation follows. Suppose that we invest \$1 for a year, the real rate of return is r and the rate of inflation during the year is m, then we would have \$$(1 + r)(1 + m)$ in a year. Thus, the nominal rate of return i is:

$$i = (1 + r)(1 + m) - 1, \text{ or } (1 + i) = (1 + r)(1 + m)$$

Rearranging this expression also gives Equation (9.16).

18. For the Livingston survey data and more information about this survey see www.phil.frb.org/research-and-data/real-time-center/livingston-survey/ (accessed May 5, 2017). For more information about the SPF see www.phil.frb.org/research-and-data/real-time-center/survey-of-professional-forecasters/ (accessed May 5, 2017), and for more information about the University of Michigan's Survey of Consumers see http://research.stlouisfed.org/fred2/series/MICH/ (accessed May 5, 2017). See also Lloyd B. Thomas Jr., "Survey Measures of Expected U.S. Inflation." *Journal of Economic Perspectives*, 13(4), 1999, 125–44, who found the median Michigan consumer survey forecast performing best.

19. This type of bond is called a Treasury Inflation Protected Security (TIPS) in the United States, an index-linked gilt in the United Kingdom, or a real return bond in Canada. The semi-annual coupon payments and the final principal payment are linked to the inflation rate in the issuing country. An estimate of expected inflation during the life of a project is provided by taking the difference between the nominal yield on a conventional bond that has the same term as the project and the real yield on real-return bonds with the same term.

20. A final approach is to infer inflationary expectations from *inflation swaps*. However, we will not discuss this more complicated method as it should, in theory, provide the same estimates as using inflation-indexed bonds. Matthew Hurd and Jon Rellen explain this method in detail and discuss discrepancies between the results obtained from this method and using inflation-indexed bonds; see www.bankofengland.co.uk/publications/quarterlybulletin/qb060101.pdf (accessed May 5, 2017).

21. Barbara M. Fraumeni, "The Measurement of Depreciation in the U.S. National Income and Product Accounts." *Survey of Current Business*, 77(7), 1997, 7–23.

22. This figure is an estimate of the future value of the highway 20 years after construction is completed, which is 21.5 years from when the decision was made. Discounting this horizon value at 7.5 percent for 21.5 years yields a PV equal to \$104.8 million.

23. By definition, the internal rate of return can be found by setting the left-hand side of Equations (9.9) or (9.10) equal to zero and solving for i. In practice, this can be quite difficult. It is usually easier to enter the data into a spreadsheet and use trial and error.

24. If expenditures equal social costs and if the total amount of expenditures is constrained, then ranking projects on the basis of the IRR criterion may maximize the total NPVs. For example, if three projects cost a *total* of \$1 billion and, in addition, each has a higher IRR than a fourth project that costs \$1 billion by itself, then the first three projects will also have a larger *combined NPV* than the NPV of the fourth project. In effect, the IRR provides an estimate of the average annual net benefit per unit of (constrained) expenditure. Problems with ranking project in terms of their IRRs only arise when the total expenditure on the projects with the highest IRRs does not exactly equal the total amount available. Even if the first, second, and third projects have higher IRRs than the fourth project, the fourth project *may* still have a higher NPV than the three smaller projects combined if its total cost is larger (but still no more than \$1 billion). In any constrained project choice setting, the optimal set of projects can be found by using linear programming.

Appendix Note

1. Assuming all benefits arise at the end of each year,

$$PV(B) = \sum_{t=1}^{n} \frac{B_1(1+g)^{t-1}}{(1+i)^t} = \sum_{t=1}^{n} \frac{B_1}{(1+g)} \left(\frac{1+g}{1+i}\right)^t. \text{ Setting } i_0 =$$

$(i - g)/(1 + g)$ implies $1/(1 + i_0) = (1 + g)/(1 + i)$. Therefore,

$$PV(B) = \sum_{t=1}^{n} \frac{B_t}{(1+g)} \left(\frac{1}{(1+i_0)^t}\right) = \frac{B_1}{(1+g)} a_{i_0}^n$$

Case 9

A CBA of the North-East Mine Development Project

The prices of most goods and services tend to rise over time, that is, we experience inflation. However, in practice, not all prices (or values) increase at the same rate. Some prices, such as house prices and fuel prices, are often much more volatile than others. For this reason, some countries exclude such volatile items from their basket of goods when computing the CPI. And the prices of some goods and services sometimes go in a different direction to other prices. For example, from December 2010 to December 2016 in the US, the all-items CPI rose about 10 percent; however, the price of houses rose about 21 percent, while the price of gold fell about 15 percent.[1]

The importance of relative price changes is illustrated by a CBA of a mine development project in British Columbia (BC) to supply a mineral for export. The mine was located in the north-east quadrant of the province and was projected to supply exclusively offshore (primarily Japanese) customers in the 1980s. The estimates shown in Case Table 9.1 are converted to 2016 dollars to facilitate a realistic understanding of the relevant numbers.[2] The second, third, and fourth columns summarize the proposed project's expected benefits, costs, and net social benefits. These columns show the "base case" estimated numbers. Overall, the analysis estimated the PV of the net social benefits to be $960 million (column 4). The main categories of beneficiaries were expected to be the Canadian National Railway (CNR) and the Canadian federal government. At the time, CNR was the national, state-owned railway company that would transport the mine output. The Canadian federal government would receive corporate taxes. The mine owner was also expected to benefit in terms of increased profits (producer surplus). The BC government would pay for a rail branch line to the mine as well as other required infrastructure, but would benefit from royalties and higher corporate taxes. Unemployed workers in BC and the rest of Canada at that time were expected to enjoy employment benefits.

The fifth column contains the expected net social benefits if the mineral price were to fall to 90 percent of the base price. All other prices were assumed to stay the same. Under these assumptions, the aggregate net social benefits would fall by $770 million, but would still be positive. Thus, this demonstrates that a relative price change can have a substantial impact on the estimated NPV.

Moving further from the base case, the sixth column shows the expected net social benefits if the mineral price were to fall to 90 percent of the expected base price and offshore customers were to cut back their mineral purchases to 90 percent of their previously expected orders.[3] Under these assumptions, the overall expected net social benefits would turn negative.

Case Table 9.1 *CBA of North-East Mine Development Project (2016 $ Millions)*

Sector	Benefits	Costs	Net social benefits	90% base price	90% base price and quantity
Mining sector	9,677	9,513	163	−426	−700
Transport sector					
Trucking	96	96	0	0	0
Canadian National Railway	1,471	1,045	426	426	353
BC Rail	630	589	41	41	18
Port terminal	394	438	−44	−44	−67
Analysis and survey	32	32	0	0	0
British Columbia					
Royalties and taxes	674	0	674	566	493
Producer surplus (labor)	73	0	73	73	73
Environment	29	15	15	15	15
Infrastructure*	0	257	−257	−257	−257
Rail branch line	266	779	−514	−514	−540
Canada					
Corporate taxes	385	0	385	312	268
Highways, port navigation	0	76	−76	−76	−76
Producer surplus (labor)	73	0	73	73	73
Totals	13,800	12,840	959	189	−347

* Highways, electric power, townsite.
Source: Based on W. G. Waters II, "A Reanalysis of the North East Coal Development" (undated), tables 2 and 3. All figures are present values in millions of 2016 Canadian dollars, assuming a real discount rate of 10 percent with the discounting period ending in 2003 and no terminal value.

Case Table 9.1 also shows that, under the base case assumptions, the main anticipated "winners" would be CNR, the federal government of Canada and, to a lesser extent, the mining sector. If the mineral price fell by 10 percent, then the mining sector would switch to being a net loser. Also, the residents of British Columbia would switch from being marginal "winners" to marginal "losers," largely because royalties and corporate taxes would decrease while the costs of highways and the branch line extension would have already been incurred. If the price and quantity levels were to fall to 90 percent of the anticipated levels, then the mining sector would lose badly.

In fact, the branch line extension opened in 1983, operated by BC Rail. Unlike most lines of this kind, it was powered by electricity because of its proximity to a major dam producing hydroelectric power and because it went through two long tunnels. Although the line was profitable initially, the freight volumes never achieved the forecasted levels, partially due to overestimation of the size of the mineral deposit. After approximately 12 years of operation the line was de-electrified and leased to CNR under a long-term contract. The line is currently mothballed. However, CNR (now privatized) claims that it will put the line back into service before the end of 2017.

Exercises for Discounting Case Study

1. Would you describe this study as a distributional CBA?

2. Why is there no consumer surplus included as a benefit?

3. What weaknesses do you see in this CBA? If corrected, would they increase or decrease the expected NPV?

Notes

1. Sources: for the US CPI see www.usinflationcalculator. com/inflation/consumer-price-index-and-annual-percent-changes-from-1913-to-2008/; for the all-transactions house price index for the US see https://fred.stlouisfed.org/series/USSTHPI; for the price of gold, see www.jmbullion.com/charts/gold-price/# (all accessed June 18, 2017).

2. An initial study was prepared by the government of British Columbia, "A Benefit–Cost Analysis of the North East Coal Development" (Victoria, BC: Ministry of Industry and Small Business, 1982). Subsequent analysis was conducted by W. W. Waters, II, "A Reanalysis of the North East Coal Development" (Working paper, University of British Columbia, undated). Case Table 9.1 is based on Waters' later study.

3. This scenario of declining prices and declining quantities sold was quite plausible for this project. The major Japanese customers were simultaneously encouraging development of Australian and other sources. If these alternative sources came on line at the same time, there would be a worldwide excess supply, internationally determined prices would fall, and demand for the BC mineral would fall.

10 The Social Discount Rate

When evaluating government policies or projects, analysts must decide on the weights to apply to policy impacts that occur in different periods, which are normally measured in years.[1] Using weights, denoted by w_t, and estimates of the real annual net social benefits, NSB_t, the estimated net present value (NPV) of a project is given by:[2]

$$NPV = \sum_{t=0}^{\infty} w_t \, NSB_t$$

(10.1)

The weights in Equation (10.1) are called *social discount factors*. The use of weights makes costs, benefits, or net benefits that occur in the future commensurable with (i.e., comparable to) costs, benefits, or net benefits realized today. By doing this, we can aggregate social costs and benefits that occur over different time periods to obtain a single measure of the value of a project, the NPV.

Usually in CBA, the social discount factors are given by:

$$w_t = \frac{1}{(1 + SDR)^t} \quad t = 0, 1, 2, \ldots$$

(10.2)

where SDR is the real *social discount rate*, a constant.[3] If Equation (10.2) holds, then Equation (10.1) is equivalent to the formulas for calculating the NPV of a project that were introduced in Chapter 9, with discounting at the SDR. Equation (10.2) implies that selecting the SDR is equivalent to selecting a set of social discount factors to use in Equation (10.1).

Discounting reflects the idea that resources available at some future date are worth less today than the same amount available right now. There are two basic reasons. First, through investing, resources today can produce a greater amount of resources for use in the future. This defines the opportunity cost of consuming the resources today – future resources forgone from not investing. Second, people prefer to consume now rather than in the future (they are impatient). For these reasons, it is generally accepted that the weights decline over time: $0 \leq w_t \leq w_{t-1} \leq \ldots \leq w_1 \leq w_0 = 1$.

If Equation (10.2) holds, then $w_t = \frac{w_{t-1}}{(1 + SDR)}$, where $t > 0$ and $w_0 = 1$. In this case, the social discount factors decline geometrically: the weight in one period is proportional to the weight in the previous period and this relationship remains constant over time. The rate of decline in the weights equals the SDR.[4] The assumption that the SDR is constant is appropriate for intra-generational projects. However, Equation (10.1) is more general than the formulas for calculating the NPV of projects that were introduced in Chapter 9. Later in this chapter we discuss situations where it is more reasonable to assume that the social discount factors do not decline at a constant rate; rather, there are *time-declining social discount rates*. This important issue arises in the analysis of climate change policies and other policies that have very long-term (intergenerational) impacts.

In practice, as we discuss later in this chapter, governments or government agencies usually prescribe the discount rate that they want analysts to use. However, there is disagreement about what that rate *should* be, even for relatively short-lived projects.[5] This chapter deals with theoretical issues *pertaining to the selection of the appropriate set of social discount factors* to use in Equation (10.1) or, in short, the selection of the appropriate SDR given that the objective is to maximize social welfare. It is possible to do a CBA without fully comprehending the theoretical issues pertaining to the choice of the social discount rate. However, while someone might therefore be able to easily compute the *NPV*, that person would not be able to give advice or answer questions about the choice of the value of the discount rate without reading this chapter.

Scholars have proposed two primary methods to determine the SDR: the social opportunity cost of capital (SOC) method and the social time preference (STP) method; this chapter describes both methods and explains the differences between them. The SOC method relies on market-based estimates and consequently is sometimes referred to as the descriptive approach. The STP method derives shadow prices for the parameters of an optimal growth model and consequently is sometimes referred to as the prescriptive approach.

One issue that invariably arises in the discussion of the appropriate social discount rate is the treatment of risk and uncertainty. One approach is to add a risk premium to the discount rate to reflect that risk. In our view, it is preferable to treat risk and discounting separately. The most appropriate way to handle risk is to convert net benefits to certainty equivalents and then discount the certainty equivalents at a risk-free social discount rate, as discussed in Chapter 12. However, computing certainty equivalents is onerous in most circumstances. Fortunately, however, as we also discuss in Chapter 12, social risk premiums would typically be small and, therefore, *analysts can reasonably discount expected net benefits at a risk-free SDR*.[6]

10.1   Does the Choice of Discount Rate Matter?

Yes! The choice of the SDR is one of the most important topics in CBA. For many, its importance was driven home in the debate around the *Stern Review* on the economics of climate change.[7] The authors of that review argued for an immediate current sacrifice of 1 percent of global GDP to slow climate change. However, in response, William Nordhaus argued that this call was based on "an extreme assumption about discounting" and that if "we substitute more conventional discount rates used in other global-warming analyses … the *Review*'s dramatic results disappear."[8] Although the level of the SDR would not have as dramatic an impact on most policy questions as it does for global warming, it nearly always plays an important role in determining the present value of the net benefits of public investments and, therefore, on the recommended policy alternative.

Table 10.1 *Annual Net Benefits and Net Present Values for Three Alternative Projects (dollars)*

Year	Project A	Project B	Project C
0	−80,000	−80,000	−80,000
1	25,000	80,000	0
2	25,000	10,000	0
3	25,000	10,000	0
4	25,000	10,000	0
5	25,000	10,000	140,000
NPV (SDR = 2%)	37,836	35,762	**46,802**
NPV (SDR = 10%)	14,770	**21,544**	6,929

To see why the value of the SDR matters, consider $100 of costs that arise 100 years from now. With a SDR of 3.5 percent, one would be willing to pay $3.2 now to avoid these costs. However, with a SDR of 7 percent, one would be willing to pay only 11.5 cents now to avoid these costs. Clearly, the choice of the SDR affects how we currently value costs and benefits occurring far in the future.

To see how the value of the SDR can change the ranking of projects, even for short-duration projects, consider a government agency with a budget of $100,000 that can be spent on only one of three potential projects. The annual net benefits of each of these projects are shown in Table 10.1. Choosing the lower SDR of 2 percent would favor project *C*, while using the higher SDR of 10 percent would favor project *B*. Thus, the ranking of projects depends importantly on the choice of discount rate.

Generally, for projects with similar costs, a low discount rate favors projects with the highest total benefits, irrespective of when they occur, because all of the social discount factors (weights) are quite close to 1 (i.e., high). Increasing the discount rate applies smaller weights to benefits or costs that occur further in the future and therefore weakens the case for projects such as project *C* with benefits that are back-end loaded. In contrast, it strengthens the case for projects with benefits that are front-end loaded, such as project *B*.

10.2   When There's No Doubt about the Value of the Social Discount Rate

Welfare economics frames policy choices as an attempt to maximize social welfare – an aggregation of the well-being or utility of the individuals that make up the society. Social welfare analysis generally assumes that well-being depends on consumption (of both privately consumed goods and services, such as food, as well as public goods, such as environmental quality). Individuals tend to prefer present consumption benefits to the same level of consumption benefits occurring in the future. Economists refer to this preference to consume sooner rather than later as *time preference.* The rate at which an individual is willing to make trade-offs between consuming a bit more in one year and less in the next is called an individual's *marginal rate of time preference* (MRTP). Also, individuals face an opportunity cost of forgone interest when they spend dollars today rather than invest them for future use, assuming the *marginal rate of return on investment* (ROI) is positive. These considerations provide a basis for deciding how costs and benefits realized by society in different years should be discounted.

10.2.1   *The Individual Marginal Rate of Time Preference*

The concept of time preference can be most easily understood in the context of borrowing and lending. Suppose that a graduate student will receive stipends of $15,000 this year and $20,000 next year. Suppose you are that student and a rich uncle offers you a sum of money and asks if you would prefer $1,000 this year or $1,200 next year. Suppose that you are indifferent between these gifts; that is, you are just willing to sacrifice $200 additional consumption next year in order to consume the extra $1,000 this year rather than next year.[9] In this case, you would have a marginal rate of time preference, MRTP, of 20 percent. Put another way, the MRTP tells us that you require more than 20 percent more next year in order to decrease your current consumption by a small amount.

Absent a rich uncle, you might be able to consume more today through borrowing. Although many banks may not be interested in lending to you because you are an impecunious graduate student who may not repay them, let us assume that the local credit union is willing to lend to you at an annual interest rate of 10 percent. That is, you can borrow $1,000 if you contract to repay this amount plus $100 in interest next year. If you were willing to give up $200 to get an additional $1,000 immediately from your uncle, then you would surely take advantage of a loan that requires you to give up only $100 in consumption next year in order to consume $1,000 more this year.

Once you take out the loan of $1,000, you will have $16,000 to spend this year and $18,900 to spend next year. Now that you have reduced the gap between what you have to spend this year relative to next year, you probably have an MRTP of less than 20 percent. After taking out the loan you might now, if given the choice, prefer a gift of $1,200 next year over a gift of $1,000 this year. If so, this indicates your MRTP is now less than 20 percent. This example illustrates how the MRTP changes as one shifts consumption from one year to another.

10.2.2   *Equality of MRTPs and Market Rates in Perfect Markets*

As long as individuals can borrow as much as they wish, they can incrementally shift consumption from the future to the present until their MRTPs fall to the rate of interest that they must pay. If banks offer a rate of interest in excess of your MRTP, then you will happily save now and defer some consumption to the future. For example, if you are indifferent between an additional $1,000 today and an additional $1,050 next year, but can deposit $1,000 for one year to obtain an additional $1,060 next year, then you would want to make the deposit. Only when the rate of interest you earn just equals your MRTP will you be indifferent between spending or depositing an additional dollar.

In an idealized perfectly competitive market, with no market failure and no taxes or transaction costs, each individual's MRTP equals the market interest rate. To see this, suppose that a consumer's utility is a function of consumption over two years: C_1 denotes consumption this year (year 1) and C_2 denotes consumption next year (year 2). The consumer maximizes her utility, denoted by $U(C_1, C_2)$, subject to a budget constraint in which T denotes the present value of total income available to be spent over the two years and i denotes the market interest rate:

$$Max \ U(C_1, C_2) \tag{10.3}$$

$$\text{s.t.} \ C_1 + \frac{C_2}{1+i} = T \tag{10.4}$$

This problem is represented graphically in Figure 10.1.

The curves labeled U^1 and U^2 are *indifference curves*. Each indifference curve represents combinations of current and future consumption that provide the individual with the same level of utility. Thus, the individual is indifferent between any two points on an indifference curve. All points on curve U^2 are preferred to all points on curve U^1; that is, the preference directions are north and east.

The slope of each indifference curve is negative, reflecting the fact that a consumer requires more consumption in the next period in order to give up some consumption in this period. If a person is indifferent between an additional $1,000 today and an additional $1,050 next year, for example, then the slope of her indifference curve equals $-1,050/1,000 = -1.05$. The absolute value of the slope of the indifference curve measures

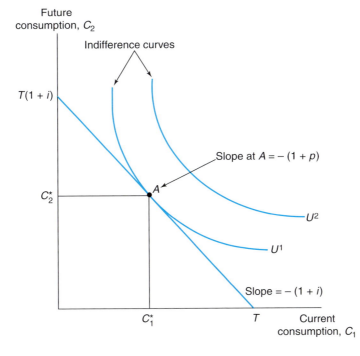

Figure 10.1 Equality of MRTP and the market interest rate.

the rate at which an individual is indifferent between substituting current consumption for future consumption and is called the consumer's *marginal rate of substitution* (MRS) between consumption this year and consumption next year.

In this example, the individual requires 5 percent more next year in order to defer consumption; therefore that person's MRTP equals 0.05. *In general, if an individual requires* 1 + p *more units in the future in order to give up one unit of current consumption, then the slope of that individual's indifference curve is* −(1 + p); *the marginal rate of substitution is* 1 + p; *and the marginal rate of time preference is* p. In the relevant range, $p > 0$ and the slope of the indifference curve is greater than 1 in absolute value.

As consumption in the current period increases, the indifference curves become flatter, indicating that the person requires relatively smaller additional amounts of future consumption in order to forgo a given amount of current consumption. That is, as current consumption increases, the marginal rate of substitution and the marginal rate of time preference decrease.

An individual who receives all of her income in the first period can choose to invest all or part of it at interest rate i.[10] Thus, she could spend all of her income in year 1, which means $C_1 = T$ and $C_2 = 0$; she could spend all of it in year 2, in which case $C_1 = 0$ and $C_2 = (1 + i)T$, or she could consume at any other point on the budget constraint represented by the straight line between $(1 + i)T$ and T. The slope of this line is $−(1 + i)$.[11] Thus, each additional unit of consumption in period 1 costs $(1 + i)$ units of consumption in period 2 and each additional unit of consumption in period 2 costs $1/(1 + i)$ units of consumption in period 1.

To determine an individual's optimal consumption levels, we find where her indifference curve is tangent to the budget constraint. This tangency occurs at point A in Figure 10.1 where the optimal consumption levels are denoted C_1^* and C_2^*. At this point the slope of indifference curve U^1, $−(1 + p)$, equals the slope of the budget constraint, $−(1 + i)$. Therefore, at her optimum consumption level, $p = i$; that is, the market interest rate equals the individual's MRTP.

This result holds generally in a perfectly efficient market in which individuals can borrow or lend as much as they want at the same interest rate and have "well-behaved" preference functions.[12] *Every* individual would have an MRTP equal to the market interest rate in such a world. Because all consumers face the same market interest rate, they would have the same MRTP. Consequently, everyone would be willing to trade current and future consumption at the same rate. Because this rate equals the market interest rate, it would be natural to use the market interest rate as the social discount rate.

10.2.3   *Equality of the Social Rate of Time Preference and the Return on Investment in Perfect Markets*

We now extend the analysis to a two-period model that incorporates production. It applies to some hypothetical country that does not trade with any other country, that is, it is a closed economy. Moreover, as before, the analysis simplifies things by assuming there are no market failures or taxes, and that there are no transaction costs associated with borrowing and lending.

The economy of this hypothetical country is depicted in Figure 10.2. The horizontal axis indicates consumption during the current period and the vertical axis indicates consumption during the future period. The curve labeled *CPF* is a consumption possibility frontier which represents all the combinations of current and future consumption that are feasible if the country utilizes its resources efficiently. Suppose that at the beginning of the first period, the country has T units of resources, which can be allocated between current consumption and investment. At one extreme, which is represented by point T on the horizontal axis, "society" (i.e., the country's citizens) consumes all T units in the current period, invest none, and therefore has no future consumption. At the other extreme, which is represented by point S on the vertical axis, society consumes no unit in the current period, invests all T units, and consumes S units in the future period. Note that $S > T$; this implies there is a positive rate of return on all resources invested in the current period.

Point X represents a more realistic intermediate position where current consumption equals C_t^* and future consumption equals C_{t+1}^*. At this point, society would relinquish for investment $I_t = T - C_t^*$ units of potential consumption in the current period. In the future period, society would consume $C_{t+1}^* = I_t + R$ units, where I_t represents the amount invested in the first period and R represents the return on this investment. Future consumption can be partitioned into two components by drawing a 45° line from point T to the line between X and C_t^* on Figure 10.2. The lower segment corresponds to I_t and the upper segment corresponds to R.

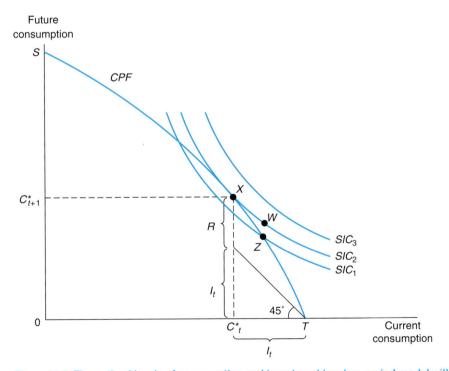

Figure 10.2 The optimal levels of consumption and investment in a two-period model with production.

The investment, I_t, can be thought of as the sum of a number of small investments. The *average* rate of return on these investments equals R/I_t. Let ROI denote the *marginal rate of return on a small investment* and let ROI_X denote the marginal rate of return on investment at X.[13] The slope of the CPF at X equals $-(1 + ROI_X)$. As it is shown in Figure 10.2, the CPF curve is concave, that is, ROI decreases as society moves from T towards S. Implicitly, the shape of the CPF assumes society makes the best investments first. Consequently, the marginal rate of return at any point is less than the average rate of return on investments at this point.

The set of three curves labeled *SIC* in Figure 10.2 are *social indifference curves*. Each curve represents combinations of current and future consumption that provides society with an equal level of utility. For example, society is indifferent between points X and W on SIC_2. The negative slope of the *SIC*s implies that this hypothetical society is only willing to give up some units of current consumption if future consumption is increased. The *marginal social rate of time preference* (STP) is the *extra* amount of future consumption that society requires as compensation for giving up one unit of current consumption. At X, this society requires at least $1 + STP_X$ units in the future to give up one unit of current consumption.

Society, of course, desires to reach the highest possible indifference curve. As Figure 10.2 shows, this curve is SIC_2 given the *CPF* and an initial endowment of T units. Although SIC_3 is preferable to SIC_2, the country's resources are insufficient to reach SIC_3. Indeed, the country's economy can only reach SIC_2 at a single point, X. At X, SIC_2 and the *CPF* curve are tangential and their slopes are equal. Consequently, $1 + STP_X = 1 + ROI_X$ at point X, and therefore *the marginal social rate of time preference equals the marginal rate of return on investment*. Furthermore, these rates would equal the market rate of interest, i. In addition, if the rates of interest for borrowing and lending were equal and available to all individuals, then every member of society would have the same marginal rate of time preference, equal to i. The choice of the SDR would be obvious and unambiguous.

To see why everybody would have the same MRTP, suppose that an individual initially had an MRTP in excess of i; that is, the person wanted to consume more now. This person could borrow at i, a lower rate than she is willing to pay, and thereby increase her current consumption at the expense of her future consumption. This increase in current consumption would increase the relative value of future consumption, causing her MRTP to decline until it eventually equaled i. Analogously, another individual with an MRTP below i would willingly postpone some current consumption in exchange for increased future consumption. By doing so her MRTP would rise until it equaled i. Thus, at X every individual would have the same MRTP, equal to i.

10.2.4   *Complications in Real Economies*

The example considered above showed that in perfectly competitive markets in a closed economy there is no ambiguity about the choice of the value of the SDR. Every individual's marginal rate of time preference, society's marginal rate of time preference, the marginal rate of return on investment, and the market interest rate would all equal each other. Unfortunately, real economies are not perfectly competitive and these rates do diverge!

An actual economy with taxes and transaction costs would be more likely to function at point Z in Figure 10.2 rather than at point X. Here, society would underinvest (actual investment $< I_t$); it would only be able to reach SIC_1, rather than SIC_2; and the marginal rate of return on investment (ROI) would exceed the marginal social rate of time preference (STP).[14] To illustrate the wedge between the ROI and STP, consider a firm that earns a one-year rate of return of 6 percent on a shareholder investment of $100. If the firm faced a corporate tax rate of 40 percent, then it would pay $2.40 to the government and return only $3.60 to the shareholder. A shareholder who faces a personal income tax rate of 30 percent would pay $1.08 of the $3.60 to the government, leaving the shareholder with only $2.52. Further, it is inevitable that a shareholder would face transaction costs (searching for the investment opportunity, gathering information about its risks, taking steps to reduce the risk, etc.). If those costs amounted to $0.52, the actual return realized by the shareholder would be only $2. For future purposes, we note that the rate at which individuals can, *in practice*, trade-off consumption today for consumption in the future is called the *consumption rate of interest*, denoted CRI. It is usually assumed to equal the *after-tax* return on savings, 2 percent in this example, versus the 6 percent ROI on the $100 investment.

Typically, as in this example, an investment opportunity with a particular rate of return would only elicit investments from individuals with a much lower MRTP than the ROI. Because different individuals and different firms have different preferences, face different tax rates, and face varying transactions costs associated with investments that vary across investment projects and across individuals, numerous individual values exist for both the MRTP and the ROI. Thus, there is no obvious choice of value of the SDR. As mentioned above, there are two proposed methods for determining the value of the SDR. We first discuss the SOC method and then follow with the STP method.

10.3   The Social Opportunity Cost of Capital (SOC) Method

The social opportunity cost of capital (SOC) method builds on influential work by Arnold Harberger.[15] Harberger analyzed a closed domestic market for investment and savings, such as the one shown in Figure 10.3. In the absence of taxes and government borrowing, the demand curve for investment funds by private-sector borrowers is represented by D_0, and the supply curve of funds from lenders (savers) is represented by S_0. The demand curve reflects the CPF in Figure 10.2 and points on the demand curve show the ROI for different levels of investment. The supply curve reflects the SICs in Figure 10.2. More specifically, the points on the supply curve show the *CRI* measured by the after-tax returns to savings associated with different levels of savings, reflecting the opportunity cost of forgone consumption.

Now consider the introduction of a corporate income tax and a personal income tax. The tax on corporate profits would shift the demand curve down to D_t because part of the returns from investments must now be paid to the government, whereas the tax on interest income would shift the supply curve up to S_t because part of the interest on savings must now be paid to the government. Thus, both taxes would reduce investment. Given the initial demand and supply curves and these taxes, the market-clearing interest

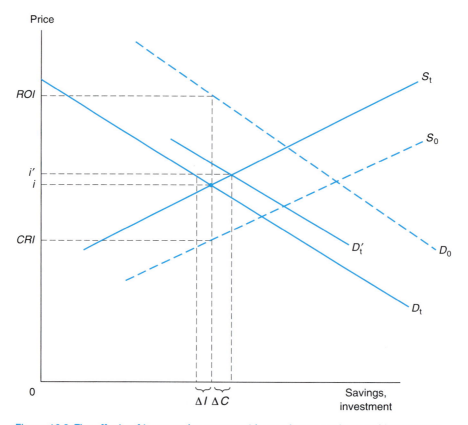

Figure 10.3 The effects of taxes and government borrowing on savings and investment.

rate would be i. That is, investors would pay an interest rate of i to borrow funds, and savers would receive an interest rate of i prior to paying taxes. However, the marginal rate of return on investment before taxes (i.e., the opportunity cost of forgone private-sector investment), ROI, would exceed i with the gap between them representing taxes paid by firms and investors. The CRI, which equals the opportunity cost of forgone consumption, would be less than i with the gap between them representing taxes paid by savers.

Now consider the effects of a government project that is financed entirely by borrowing in this closed, domestic financial market. Suppose the demand for funds for the new project shifts the market demand curve up from D_T to D_t'. The market rate of interest would rise from i to i'. Private-sector investment would fall by ΔI, and savings would increase by ΔC.

Harberger argues that the social discount rate should reflect the social opportunity cost of capital, which can be obtained by weighting ROI and CRI by the size of the relative contributions that investment and consumption would make toward funding the project. That is, he suggests that the SDR should be computed using the social opportunity cost of capital, denoted SOC:

$$SOC = a*CRI + b*ROI \tag{10.5}$$

where a = ΔC/(ΔI +ΔC), b = ΔI/(ΔI +ΔC), and a + b = 1.[16]

Lind and others argue that foreign borrowing is another potential source of funding in most economies.[17] If so, a government project need not necessarily crowd out domestic private consumption or investment on a dollar-for-dollar basis. If a is the proportion of the project's resources that displace private domestic consumption, b is the proportion of the resources that are financed by private domestic investment, and c =1 – a – b is the proportion of the resources obtained by borrowing from foreign sources, then the SOC is given by:

$$SOC = a*CRI + b*ROI + c*CFF \tag{10.6}$$

where CFF is the *marginal cost of foreign funds*. If the country faces a completely elastic supply of foreign funds at the government's long-term borrowing rate, i, then the CFF = i.[18]

10.3.1 *Special Cases of the SOC*

Some economists and policy makers have argued that the social opportunity cost of capital equals ROI, which is equivalent to setting b = 1 in Equations (10.6) and (10.7). This approach would be appropriate if all government funding came at the expense of private-sector investment, not through taxes (which affect consumption) or borrowing from foreigners. Because this condition is unlikely to hold, we do not recommend discounting at the ROI. However, as we discuss later, many countries have, in fact, adopted this method. Unfortunately, it can also create some semantic confusion. This confusion arises because it is often not clear whether the term social opportunity cost of capital refers to Equation (10.5), (10.6), or to the ROI. Some economists label Equations (10.5) or (10.6) as either the Harberger method or as the weighted social cost of capital method, and refer to the ROI as the social opportunity cost of capital. To minimize confusion, we refer to Equations (10.5) and (10.6) as the social opportunity cost of capital and will refer to the ROI as the ROI.

Other economists have suggested setting a = 1 in equations (10.5) or (10.6), that is, using the CRI as the social discount rate. Usually, authors justify this approach by arguing that the CRI is a proxy for the social rate of time preference, which we discuss in the following section.

Some economists have proposed using the government's (or Treasury's) risk-free borrowing rate, TBR, as the SDR. This rate equals the CFF and this method is, therefore, equivalent to setting a = b = 0 in Equation (10.6). However, proponents of this method do not justify it on the grounds that all financing comes from borrowing overseas. Instead, they argue that the government's borrowing rate is appropriate because it is what a government pays to finance a project. Anthony Boardman and Mark Hellowell point out that this rate might be appropriate if the goal were to maximize the present value of net revenue (cash flow) to the government (or its Treasury), but not to maximize allocative efficiency.[19]

Finally, some authors argue that the risk-free rate should be adjusted for the systematic risk of a particular project.[20] The ROI is the marginal return on a "bundle" of assets, some low-risk and others high-risk. It does not vary from project to project. A variant of the ROI method, which we refer to as the ROI (SRP) method, adds a project-specific risk premium (SRP) to the risk-free rate. Usually, the SRP depends on the systematic risk born by investors in private-sector projects in the same sector as the project being evaluated.[21] Again, this method might be appropriate if the goal were to maximize the present value of net revenue (cash flow) to the government (or its Treasury), but not to maximize allocative efficiency. Interestingly, though, Boardman and Hellowell point out that if this rule were applied correctly, it would often imply discounting at a *lower* rate than the risk-free rate because the project-specific systematic risk to the government itself (or its Treasury) is often negative.

10.3.2   Estimation of, and Numerical Values for, the SOC

Estimation of the SOC requires estimates of the parameters in Equation (10.6). There are many ways to estimate the ROI. To begin, recall that it should be the marginal ROI. One relatively straightforward method assumes that profit maximizing firms will not make an investment unless the expected net present value of the investment is positive. Thus, a firm will invest in a new project only if the after-tax ROI on that investment is greater than the firm's weighted average cost of capital.[22] Using this approach, evidence suggests that, the real marginal ROI for the United States has averaged about 6.8 percent from 1947 to 2010.[23]

A direct estimate of the marginal CRI is provided by the real, expected after-tax return to holding government bonds or equivalent savings vehicles, such as savings deposits. To estimate this return, one needs an estimate of the nominal yield available to savers, the marginal income tax rate for savers, and expected inflation. This is difficult because savers face a myriad of saving rates and different individuals face different tax rates. Using the average real, expected return to 10-year US Treasury bonds from 1953 to 2011 and an individual tax rate on savings of 30 percent implies that the real CRI is about 1.2 percent.

One way to estimate the real marginal cost of foreign borrowing is to use the real, expected pre-tax return on 10-year US Treasury bonds. This return averaged 2.6 percent from 1953 to 2011.

David Burgess and Richard Zerbe propose that $a = .10$, $b = .54$ and $c = .36$.[24] Using these weights and the above estimates of *CRI*, *ROI*, and *CFF* equal to 1.2, 6.8, and 2.6 percent, respectively, leads to an estimate of the *SOC* for the United States equal to 4.7 percent, or approximately 5 percent in round numbers.[25] Burgess and Zerbe propose estimates of the *CRI*, *ROI*, and *CFF* of 3.5, 8.5, and 5.5 percent, respectively. Using their own weights leads to a SOC of 7 percent. Thus, we suggest a "best" estimate of the SOC for the United States equal to 5 percent, with sensitivity analysis at 3 percent and 7 percent.

10.3.3   Criticisms of the SOC Method and the Resultant SDR Estimate

The SOC method and the estimates of the SOC parameters are subject to a number of criticisms. First, the weights may be incorrect. Specifically, the weight on ROI, which has the largest value among the three components, may be too high. The above estimate of b is consistent with Harberger's argument that funding comes primarily at the expense of private-sector investment. However, prior to the 2008–2009 financial crisis, governments and the public in most developed countries usually viewed new federal expenditures as necessitating additional taxes, and they viewed reductions in debt levels as enabling tax reductions. In the United States, almost all state governments are subject to requirements that they balance their budgets. Thus, in most circumstances one can assume that government projects are tax-financed, not debt-financed. Furthermore, the majority of taxes are obtained from consumers.[26] In addition, there is fairly strong evidence that in "normal times," changes in consumers' disposable incomes lead to changes in consumption rather than changes in savings.[27]

A second criticism is that different projects might be funded in different ways, that is, the weights may differ among projects and, therefore, the SOC should differ from project to project. For example, some specific projects are largely or completely deficit financed in which case c would be large, and a and b would be small. Third, analysts often estimate the average ROI, not the smaller marginal ROI. Fourth, market estimates of the ROI include a risk premium that should not be included in the SDR. Fifth, ROI estimates might be biased upward because they reflect actual returns, which are higher than social returns, because of market failures, such as barriers to entry, or negative externalities. Each of the above criticisms suggests that the SOC method leads to overestimates of the SDR.

There are further concerns about using the SOC. One pertains to the value of the CRI, a proxy for the social rate of time preference. Individuals differ in their preferences and opportunities: while some are saving, others are borrowing. At the margin some save, in effect, by reducing their debt. Because consumer borrowing rates exceed savings rates and because reducing debt is not taxed, consumers who save by reducing their debt earn a much higher real, after-tax return than savers do. It is not obvious how to aggregate these different rates of interest into a single CRI. A second concern is that people sometimes fail to make rational, consistent choices in intertemporal contexts.[28] Individuals display time-inconsistency; specifically, individual rates of time preference and implied discount rates decline over the time horizon to which they are applied.[29] Choices made at one time may be overturned later, even if no new information becomes available. A decision *not* to engage in a project may later appear to have been a mistake, even though nothing has changed except the passage of time. Further, there is evidence that the way intertemporal choices are framed affects individuals' implicit rates of time preference. Individuals use different rates to discount losses versus gains (loss aversion), large losses versus small ones, choices involving the near future as against choices further out in time, and choices between speeding up consumption versus delaying it.[30] Also, many individuals simultaneously borrow and lend: they pay down mortgages, buy bonds and stocks for retirement, and even borrow on their credit cards.[31] While such behavior may not be irrational per se, it is unreasonable to assume that individuals are equating marginal rates of time preference with a single market rate.

Finally, the use of market rates of interest reflects the preference only of individuals currently alive and not the preferences of future generations. This is especially problematic when a project's impacts span generations. Those yet unborn do not have a direct voice in current markets, yet we may believe that they should have standing in our current CBAs.[32] All of these considerations seriously weaken the case for using the SOC method to derive an estimate of the SDR.

10.4   The Social Time Preference (STP) Method

The STP method focuses on society's willingness to trade off present consumption for future consumption. It builds on the work of Frank Ramsey, who proposed a model with infinite periods in which society (or a single representative individual) attempts to maximize a social welfare function that reflects the values society places on per-capita consumption over time.[33] This model reflects the preferences of future generations as well as those currently alive. Through investment, consumption increases over time. Policy makers choose the amount of public investment in order to maximize the well-being of society now and in the future. Even if individuals do not make consistent, well-behaved intertemporal consumption choices over public and private goods, as discussed above, society should make its public investments as though they do.

A number of economists have demonstrated that maximization of such a social welfare function implies that, on the optimal growth path, society's *marginal rate of time preference*, STP, would equal the sum of two components: one that reflects the reality of impatience and the other that reflects society's preference for smoothing consumption over time.[34] They argue that the STP should be used to discount future benefits and costs.

This method presumes that funds for government projects ultimately come from the reduced consumption of individuals. However, it is possible that a project might be funded from borrowing that crowds out some higher-yielding private investment(s). To take this possibility into account, funds from (or into) investment should be converted to consumption equivalents by multiplying them by the shadow price of capital (SPC) prior to discounting at the STP. Sometimes, therefore, this method is known as the *STP–SPC method*. Later we argue that most funds for government projects actually come from consumption and shadow pricing is unnecessary in most circumstances.

10.4.1   *The Ramsey Formula*

Assuming society's well-being is a function of consumption, the SDR should reflect the weights that society puts on present and future consumption flows, where consumption includes privately consumed goods and services, such as food, as well as public goods, such as national defense or environmental quality. To derive these weights, Ramsey argued that policy makers should act as though they are maximizing a social welfare function, W, that equals the present value of current and future utilities from per-capita consumption:

$$W = \int_0^\infty e^{-\rho t} U(c_t) dt$$

(10.7)

Here, $U(c_t)$ is the utility that society (or a representative individual) derives from per-capita consumption during period t, $e^{-\rho t}$ is the discount factor (or weight) that applies to the incremental utility from more consumption in period t, e is the exponential function, and ρ is the rate at which future utility is discounted. The parameter ρ is the rate of decrease in the utility of incremental consumption just because it is in the future. It reflects impatience and is sometimes called the *pure rate of time preference*.

To determine the STP, we first compute the discount factor that society should apply to incremental consumption in period t to maximize social welfare as set out in Equation (10.7).[35] The STP equals the proportionate rate of decrease in this discount factor over time, which can be shown to equal:[36]

$$STP = \rho + g\varepsilon \tag{10.8}$$

where g is the percentage change in per-capita consumption (i.e., consumption growth), and ε is the absolute value of the elasticity of the marginal utility of consumption with respect to changes in consumption; and $\rho, g, \varepsilon \geq 0$. This equation is known as the Ramsey formula (for computing the SDR). In principle, ρ, g, or ε could vary over time periods. However, we will assume that they are constant and, therefore, the STP is constant, at least within a generation.

The STP given by Equation (10.8) is the rate at which consumption should be discounted in order for society to maximize the present value of utility from its current and future per-capita consumption. If government invested in projects until the real return on investment were equal to this rate, then society would achieve the optimal growth rate of consumption. For this reason, this method of deriving the SDR is sometimes referred to as the "optimal growth rate model."

The Ramsey formula implies that society discounts future consumption for two reasons. First, from the first term in Equation (10.8), society (or a representative individual) is impatient and prefers to consume now rather than in the future, other things being equal. Second, from the second term in Equation (10.8), society prefers more equality in per-capita consumption over time than would otherwise occur (i.e., consumption smoothing) assuming economic growth that will increase future consumption.

This model supposes that individuals have declining marginal utility of consumption. Assuming growth, the future has a lower weight than the present as incrementally higher levels of consumption are valued less. The parameter e measures how fast the marginal utility of consumption falls as per-capita consumption rises. Setting e equal to zero (with $\rho = 0$) implies no discounting of future consumption: society treats each unit of consumption received in the future as identical to a unit of consumption in the present. It signifies a complete lack of concern for our current lower wealth and, therefore, for intergenerational inequality. In contrast, as e approaches infinity, society completely discounts each unit of consumption received in the (richer) future, signifying an overwhelming desire to equalize per-capita consumption over time. When e equals one, the relative weight on society's consumption in each time period equals the inverse of its relative per-capita consumption. Thus, a 10 percent reduction in consumption today, for example, from \$40,000 to \$36,000, is an acceptable trade-off for a 10 percent increase in consumption at a richer, future time, for example, from \$80,000 to \$88,000. Society weighs the loss of \$1 of consumption today as twice as important as a gain of \$1 to its future self, because the future society is twice as rich.

10.4.2   *Estimation of, and Numerical Values for, the STP*

The value of the STP depends on the value of three parameters: ρ, g, and ε. There has been considerable debate about the value of ρ since Ramsey's original article. It may seem reasonable for society to discount consumption next year relative to consumption this year because of pure time preference, or impatience. Also, current members of society will not live forever and would, therefore, rather consume sooner than risk not consuming at all. However, when applied to long-term projects with intergenerational impacts, positive values of ρ would be equivalent to treating the utility of future generations as less valuable than the utility of the current generation. Ramsey himself thought that it is ethically indefensible to use a positive value. However, Kenneth Arrow shows that weighting all generations' welfare equally results in unreasonably high rates of savings being required of the current (or even of every) generation.[37] To avoid this result, a positive pure rate of time preference should be employed. Arrow suggests a figure of around 1.0 percent for ρ.

The future growth rate of per-capita consumption, g, can be derived by estimating past growth rates and making assumptions about whether the future growth rate will be similar. Although the annual US growth rate averaged approximately 2.2 percent over 1947–2009, it has been trending down.[38] During the most recent decade for which data are available (1999–2009), it averaged only 1.63 percent per annum. Recent US growth rates have been even lower. Based on the above, we think g will equal about 1.9 percent in the future.

There are a variety of ways to estimate or prescribe a value for ε, the absolute value of the elasticity of the marginal utility of consumption. Proposed values range between 1 and 4, but with most of them in the range of 1–2.[39] One way to infer ε is from the progressivity built into the federal income tax schedule.[40] This estimate is about 1.35 for developed countries, which seems reasonable to us.

With $g = 1.9$ *percent,* $\varepsilon = 1.35$, *and* $\rho = 1.0$ *percent, our best estimate of the STP (for developed countries) is 3.5 percent. Other scholars have proposed different estimates.*[41] *It would be reasonable to conduct sensitivity analysis at 2.0 and 5.5 percent.*

10.4.3   *Special Case of the STP: The Shadow Price of Capital (SPC)*

A potential problem with using the STP as the social discount rate is that resources invested in the private sector generally earn a higher return than the STP.[42] If a government used a lower discount rate than the private sector, then it would undertake projects that the private sector would not undertake and it would grow undesirably large. Also, whether or not a project was undertaken would depend on whether the assets were state-owned or privately owned and not exclusively on the merits of the project. A public-sector project should be undertaken if its benefits would exceed the opportunity cost of the resources; otherwise, it should not. To ensure that society would be better off through government projects, changes in private-sector investment flows associated with a particular project should be converted into *consumption equivalents* by weighting them by a parameter, which is greater than 1, called *the shadow price of capital, SPC*, prior to discounting.[43]

Consumption and private-sector investment are treated differently because consumption provides an immediate benefit while investment generates a stream of benefits that occur in future periods. To see this, suppose a dollar is invested in the private sector for an indefinite period. Suppose also that it earns a return of ROI each period and this return is consumed each period, while the original dollar is reinvested. Thus, ROI is consumed each period in perpetuity. The present value of this perpetual consumption flow, using the formula for a perpetuity introduced in Chapter 9, is:

$$SPC = \frac{ROI}{STP}$$

(10.9)

Because ROI is greater than STP, the value of the SPC is greater than 1, reflecting the situation that, at the margin, *displaced private-sector investment is more costly to society than displaced consumption and that increments to private-sector investment are more beneficial than increments to consumption.*

To explore the shadow price approach a bit further, suppose that a project yields real annual net benefits of *NB* indefinitely. If these net benefits are consumed as they arise, then the present value of this perpetual consumption flow, discounted at the STP, is *NB/STP*. Now consider two extreme cases. If the project's capital costs arise in year 0, C_0, and all these funds are raised from consumption, then the *NPV* rule implies the project should be undertaken if *NB/STP* > C_0. Thus, in this extreme situation, the STP–SPC method is equivalent to discounting benefits and costs at the STP. Now suppose instead that all the capital costs, which occur in year 0, displace private investment. Under this assumption, the STP–SPC method implies the project should be undertaken if *NB/STP* > SPC*C_0 = (ROI/STP)C_0 or, equivalently, if *NB/ROI* > C_0. This condition is equivalent to discounting the benefits and costs at the ROI.

The expression for the SPC in Equation (10.9) is based on the simplifying assumption that the entire return from the investment would be consumed during the period in which it occurs. It seems more likely that some of it would be consumed and some of it would be reinvested. Consideration of this possibility leads to a more general expression for the SPC:

$$SPC = \frac{(1-f)ROI}{STP - fROI}$$

(10.10)

where *f* is the fraction of the return that is reinvested each period.[44] Note that in the absence of reinvestment, *f* = 0, and this formula reduces to Equation (10.9).

Although this method has strong theoretical appeal, it is somewhat difficult to use in practice and there are few examples of it actually being used to evaluate public-sector projects. The following subsection explains how to apply it and, in the process, illustrates the difficulties when projects are, in fact, debt-financed.

10.4.4   *Numerical Values of the SPC*

Computation of the SPC requires values for STP, ROI and *f*. We have already suggested that STP equals 3.5 percent and ROI equals 6.8 percent. The gross investment rate (the ratio of real gross fixed investment to real GDP) provides a rough estimate of f, the fraction of the gross return that is reinvested. Using data from the Federal Reserve Bank of St. Louis Economic Research database (FRED), we calculate that the average ratio of real gross private domestic investment to real GDP for 1947–2011 is 12.8 percent. Plugging these estimates into Equation (10.10) yields a value of SPC equal to about 2.2.[45] This implies that one dollar of private-sector investment would produce a stream of consumption benefits with an NPV equal to $2.2. If the STP was very low (2.3 percent) and the ROI was very high (8 percent) and the fraction reinvested was high (15 percent), then the SPC would equal approximately 6. *Thus, our best estimate of the SPC is 2.2 with sensitivity analysis at 1 and 6.*

10.4.5   *Illustration of the SPC Method*

Consider a project to improve the physical plant of a city's schools that will cost $3 million funded out of taxes. Further suppose that the annual benefits will be $700,000 for five years and there will be no other impact. Ignoring the SPC and discounting the annual benefits at 3.5 percent yields a PV of the benefits equal to $3,160,537. Thus, the NPV of the project equals $160,537 and one would recommend it should proceed.

Now suppose that the project is to be funded by a bond issue that will yield a return of 4 percent (real) and will be repaid over five years. Suppose that the bonds would be purchased solely by city citizens and would be paid for through five equal annual installments of $673,854. The bond issue would displace private investment and, therefore, it would be appropriate to use the SPC method.[46] This method requires that discounting be done in three steps. First, the costs and benefits in each period are divided into those that directly affect consumption and those that directly affect investment. Second, flows into and out of investment are multiplied by the SPC to convert them into consumption equivalents. Third, the resultant consumption equivalents and the original consumption flows are discounted at the STP.

The government's annual bond payments are likely to come from taxes and, therefore, from consumption. However, what do the bond-holder recipients do with the money they receive? Each annual payment consists of a combination of interest and reduction of principal. We will assume that the bond-holders consume the interest they receive and invest the amount equal to the reduction in principal.[47] These amounts are shown in Table 10.2. Time in years appears in column 1, the annual bond payments are shown in column 2, the amount of interest in these payments is shown in column 3, and the amount of principal reduction is shown in column 4.[48]

Step 1 is to separate the flows into changes in investment and changes in consumption. The changes in investment are shown in column 5. They consist of the original amount of the bond and the annual reductions in the principal. The changes in consumption are shown in column 6. They consist of the annual benefits of $700,000 less the annual repayments of the principal of $673,991 (column 1) plus the interest payments (in column 3). Step 2 requires the change in investment to be multiplied by the shadow price of capital, which we assume equals 2.2, to convert them to their consumption equivalents. The result is shown in column 7. Step 3 discounts these amounts at the STP, to obtain their PV, which is equal to –$633,997. Finally, this amount is added to

Table 10.2 *An Illustration of the SPC Method*

Year	Bond payments	Interest	Principal reduction	Change in investment	Change in consumption	Change in investment x SPC
0				−3,000,000		−6,600,000
1	673,881	120,000	553,881	553,881	146,119	1,218,539
2	673,881	97,845	576,037	576,037	123,963	1,267,281
3	673,881	74,803	599,078	599,078	100,922	1,317,972
4	673,881	50,840	623,041	623,041	76,959	1,370,691
5	673,881	25,919	647,963	647,963	52,037	1,425,518
PV					458,803	−633,997

the PV of the changes in consumption, which equals $458,803. Thus, the resultant NPV equals −$175,194.

This example illustrates that the SPC can matter. With the above assumptions, the project has a negative NPV and should not proceed. If the SPC were ignored (i.e., set equal to unity), then the estimated NPV would be positive and the project would receive a positive recommendation.

10.4.6   *When Shadow Pricing is Unnecessary*

For many policy evaluations shadow pricing is not necessary because the project does not displace private investment. For example, many regulations primarily affect private consumption (e.g., through higher prices), not investment. More generally, if the government sets an overall target for the government deficit and debt, then at the margin, any new project must be tax-financed. Income taxes (and other taxes) primarily reduce consumption rather than investment because most income is spent on consumption.[49] Thus, the main effect of engaging in a government project will be to reduce consumption, not investment, making shadow pricing largely unnecessary. The case for using the SPC is strongest for deficit-financed projects in a closed economy where the supply of savings and foreign funds are very unresponsive to the interest rate.

10.4.7   *Criticisms of the STP and SPC Methods and the Resultant SDR Estimate*

The SPC method accounts for increases and displacement of private investment and consumption in a theoretically appropriate fashion, which is an important advantage over other methods. Nonetheless, there are several potential objections. First, as opposed to just choosing a discount rate and using it in the *NPV* formula, when the SPC is used, it is difficult to explain to policy makers how the *NPV* calculations are made, let alone why. Second, as the above illustration makes clear, the informational requirements of the SPC are more substantial than for the other discounting approaches. Judgment plays an important role in deciding how to allocate benefits and costs between investment and consumption. These decisions are somewhat subjective and open to manipulation. However, as we have argued, if projects are funded out of consumption rather than investment then there is no need to use the SPC method.

Critics of the STP argue that, in fact, government funds come from borrowing, which reduces private-sector investment. If the SPC is ignored inappropriately, then society may overinvest in public-sector projects and underinvest in private-sector projects. A second criticism is that there is uncertainty associated with the estimates of the STP (and the SPC). Past estimates of growth may not be good predictors of the future long-run growth rate in consumption. Also, the parameters ε and ρ are based on value judgments about intergenerational equality. Other scholars propose different parameter values.[50]

10.5   Discounting Intergenerational Projects

So far we have considered only a constant (time-invariant) SDR. We have assumed, for example, the same SDR is used to discount costs and benefits between years 401 and 400 as between years 1 and 0. As discussed below, however, there are at least four reasons to consider using time-declining SDRs (i.e., to use lower rates to discount costs and benefits that occur farther in the future). Most of these considerations become relevant when project impacts cross generational lines. However, there is no obvious way to decide when a project is intergenerational. In many circumstances, those as yet unborn when a project is initiated will live to be affected by it, whether as beneficiaries, taxpayers, or both. Those alive bear some of the startup costs, but may not live to reap the benefits. Nonetheless, both the serious ethical dilemmas and the practical differences that occur when considering long-term projects do not begin before a span of about 50 years. Thus, for discounting purposes, it is reasonable to define intra-generational projects as those whose effects occur within a 50-year horizon.[51] We consider projects with significant effects beyond 50 years as intergenerational.

The first reason for using time-declining discount rates, which we briefly discussed earlier, is that individuals appear to be "time-inconsistent."[52] Empirical behavioral evidence suggests that individuals apply lower rates to discount events that occur farther into the future, that is, they have decreasing time aversion. Exhibit 10.1 presents evidence that an individual's MRTP for saving lives now versus saving lives in the future declines as the time horizon extends farther into the future. David Laibson cites evidence that individuals' discount functions are approximately hyperbolic, implying that they engage in *hyperbolic discounting*.[53] He explains that individuals recognize that, if they do not commit to saving, then on a day-to-day basis (using a high short-term discount rate) they will never save as much for the future as they know they should (using a low long-term discount rate). Recognizing their lack of self-control, individuals may commit to savings plans with large penalties for early withdrawals, while using their available credit to otherwise maximize their current consumption. They may simultaneously save by purchasing an illiquid asset with a relatively low, after-tax real return (such as a government savings bond), make predetermined monthly mortgage payments, and borrow short-term on a credit card at a high real interest rate. These observed patterns of saving and borrowing simply reflect individuals' recognition of their lack of self-control and the time-declining discount rates that result from this.

Exhibit 10.1

Maureen Cropper and colleagues have conducted surveys to measure how participants are willing to trade off lives saved today with lives saved in the future. In round numbers, this research suggests that people are indifferent between one life saved today and two lives saved in 5 years' time, three lives saved in 10 years' time, six lives saved in 25 years' time, 11 lives saved in 50 years' time, and 44 lives saved in 100 years' time. More precisely, and expressing the results in terms of marginal rate of time preference (MRTP), the research found an implicit marginal rate of time preference of 16.8 percent over a 5-year horizon, 11.2 percent over a 10-year horizon, 7.4 percent over a 25-year horizon, 4.8 percent over a 50-year horizon, and 3.8 percent over a 100-year horizon. These results suggest that individual MRTPs are significantly greater than zero, but they decline as the time horizon extends farther into the future.

Source: Adapted from Maureen L. Cropper, Selma K. Aydede, and Paul R. Portney, "Rates of Time Preference for Saving Lives." *American Economic Review: Papers and Proceedings*, 82(2), 1992, 469–72.

The second reason pertains to evaluating decisions with impacts that occur far in the future, such as environmental effects, including reforestation, efforts to mitigate global climate change by greenhouse gas abatement, preserving biodiversity through the protection of unique ecosystems, and the storage of radioactive waste. Discounting at a time-constant discount rate can pose ethical dilemmas. With a constant SDR the social discount factors decline geometrically. Even using a modest SDR, costs and benefits that occur sufficiently far in the future have a negligible value. The use of a constant discount rate much in excess of 1.0 or 2.0 percent implies that it is not allocatively efficient for society to spend even a small amount today in order to avert a very costly environmental disaster, provided that the disaster occurs sufficiently far in the future. For example, if greenhouse gas buildup imposes a huge cost of, say, $1 trillion in 400 years' time, this has an *NPV* of less than $336 million today at a constant discount rate of 2 percent and an *NPV* of less than $113,000 at a discount rate of 4 percent. Thus, if CBA used a discount rate of more than 4 percent, we would conclude that it is not worth spending $113,000 today to avert a major disaster with a cost of $1 trillion in 400 years.

A third reason for using a time-declining SDR is because members of the current generation may fail to account appropriately for the effects of long-term projects on the welfare of future generations. Primarily for this reason, Nicholas Stern concluded that for projects addressing climate change it is "entirely inappropriate" to use market rates of return as a basis for the SDR.[54] In contrast, the STP method considers the welfare of future generations.[55] However, the social welfare function in Equation (10.7) treats society as a single, representative individual whose well-being is equal to the discounted sum of the utility derived from present and future per-capita consumption. This may make sense for evaluating 50-year investments, but may be less relevant for evaluating 400-year or 10,000-year investments involving multiple generations, such as for climate change or storage of nuclear waste.

The fourth reason for using a time-declining SDR is that the farther we look into the future, the greater the inherent uncertainty as to the future growth rate of the economy and, therefore, the future STP. Allowing for this uncertainty means that lower discount rates should be used to discount impacts that occur farther in the future.[56] Suppose that a project delivers a single benefit of $1 billion in 400 years. Suppose further that there is a 50 percent chance that the appropriate (constant) discount rate over this period will be 7 percent and a 50 percent chance that it will be 1 percent. One might imagine that we should average these two rates to obtain the expected discount rate, 4 percent, and then use this rate to compute the expected PV of the future benefit as $1 billion $\times e^{-(0.04) \times 400}$, which is approximately $110. However, this is incorrect. The expected PV equals $9,157,800, that is, $1 billion $\times (e^{-(0.07)400} + e^{-(0.01)400})/2$. This amount is equivalent to using a single, certain discount rate of approximately 1.2 percent. We average the discount factors of $e^{-(0.07)400}$, which equals a very small number (6.9×10^{-13}), and $e^{-(0.01)400}$, which equals 0.0183. The discount factors associated with the larger discount rate approach zero as the time horizon becomes longer. They have less influence as the horizon increases, resulting in time-declining discount rates.

10.5.1   *Numerical Values of Time-Declining Discount Rates*

Based on the Ramsey formula and research by Richard Newell and William Pizer, we suggest the following schedule of time-declining discount rates: *3.5 percent from year 0 to year 50, 2.5 percent from year 50 to year 100, 1.5 percent from year 100 to year 200, 0.5 percent from year 200 to year 300, and 0 percent thereafter.*[57] For a single benefit in year 300, this schedule is equivalent to applying a single, constant rate of 1.67 percent to all periods. This schedule allows the effects on far future generations to be given more weight than time-invariant discount rates. After a given period of time, all future generations are essentially treated alike.

10.6   The Social Discount Rate in Practice

Current discounting practices in governments vary considerably. There is some evidence that local government agencies do not discount at all. At the federal level, most governments do discount impacts, but there is considerable variation across countries. One important trend is that the prescribed rates in many governments and federal agencies have been trending lower. For example, in the 1970s and 1980s, both the Office of Management and Budget (OMB) in the United States and the Federal Treasury Board Secretariat (TBS) in Canada required most agencies to use a SDR of 10 percent. More recently, the OMB has revised this rate downward to 3 percent and 7 percent, and the TBS has revised its rate downward to 8 percent. The European Commission (EC) and most other European countries have also reduced their recommended rates, as have governments in New Zealand, Mexico, Peru, and the Philippines. These lower rates have been motivated by increased acceptance of the STP method, led by the UK government in 2003.

Table 10.3 presents the prescribed (real) SDR in several countries and the social discount rate method upon which the rate is based. These countries were selected because their government agencies provide, at a minimum, reasonably clear and consistent information and explanations; many other agencies do not.[58] Table 10.3 illustrates a number of points. First, agencies appeal to a variety of discounting methods to support their prescribed SDR, including the SOC, ROI, ROI (SRP), TBR, STP, and SPC (i.e., STP–SPC) methods. Second, even though the STP method is increasing in influence, descriptive (market-based) discount rate methods, like the ROI and the SOC, are more prevalent

Table 10.3 *The Discount Rate Method and Prescribed Social Discount Rates in Selected Countries*

Country and agency	Method	SDR (%)	Declining SDR
North America			
Canada (Base)[59]	SOC	8	No
Canada (sometimes)[60]	SPC	3	No
Mexico[61]	SOC	10	No
US (OMB)[62,63]	SPC theoretically preferred, but use CRI and ROI	3 and 7	Sensitivity analysis if intergenerational
US (OMB: CEA)[64]	TBR	–0.5 to 0.7	No
US (CBO)[65]	STP	2	No
US (GAO)[66]	TBR	–0.5 to 0.7	Sensitivity analysis
US (EPA)[67]	SPC theoretically preferred, but use CRI and ROI	3 and 7	After 50 years
Europe			
European Union (EC)[68]	STP	4	Consider alternative lower rate
France[69]	ROI (SRP)	4.5 + SRP	Effectively no
Netherlands[70]	ROI	5.5	No
Norway[71]	ROI	4	After 40 years
Sweden[72]	STP	3.5	No
United Kingdom[73]	STP	3.5	After 30 years
Other countries			
Australia (Base)[74,75]	ROI	7	Include "supplementary discussion"
Chile[76]	SOC	6	No
New Zealand (Default)[77]	ROI (SRP)	6	No
New Zealand (Telecoms, Media, Technology)	ROI (SRP)	7	No
Philippines[78]	ROI	10	No

than prescriptive methods. The SOC method is preferred only in Canada and Mexico. Third, agencies may draw on different methods to make recommendations pertaining to different types of projects. Even though Canada, Australia, the OMB in the United States, and other countries favor the ROI or SOC methods for most CBAs (the base case), they recommend lower (STP-based rates) for health or environmental projects (including climate change). Fourth, the prescribed rates vary considerably from potentially negative for short-term cost-effectiveness (CEA) projects considered by the OMB to 10 percent for most projects in Mexico and the Philippines. Fifth, the discount rates are generally lower in European countries than in other countries. While the SDRs are generally lower in developed countries than in developing countries, the base SDRs in Canada, the United States (OMB), Australia, and New Zealand are high at 7 percent or more. Sixth, few countries advocate time-declining discount rates. Finally, although not shown in the table, recommendations for sensitivity analysis vary considerably. Some guides discuss sensitivity analysis without specifying particular values, some agencies recommend ±2 percent, others encourage Monte Carlo analysis. Overall, there is little consistency.

Most multilateral development banks, such as the World Bank or the Inter-American Development Bank (IDB), use relatively high discount rates in the region of 10–12 percent.[76] Recently, however, the Asian Development Bank switched to using the STP method and reduced its recommended rate to 9 percent and even 6 percent for some projects.[80]

10.7   Conclusion

There has been considerable debate as to the appropriate method of discounting, as well as the specific value of the SDR. There is now widespread agreement that the correct conceptual method of discounting is to shadow price investment flows and to discount the resulting consumption equivalents and the consumption flows using a consumption-based discount rate. We believe that the most appropriate practical method for determining the value of the SDR is the optimal growth rate method. We advocate the use of time-declining discount rates in projects with significant intergenerational impacts. Our discussion should have made it clear that analysts are unlikely to have complete confidence in whatever discount rate they use. It is almost always desirable, therefore, to test the sensitivity of one's results to changes in the parameters used in discounting.

Exercises for Chapter 10

1. (Instructor-provided spreadsheet recommended.) The following table gives cost and benefit estimates in real dollars for dredging a navigable channel from an inland port to the open sea.

Year	Dredging and patrol costs ($)	Saving to shippers ($)	Value of pleasure boating($)
0	2,548,000	0	0
1	60,000	400,000	60,000
2	60,000	440,000	175,000
3	70,000	440,000	175,000
4	70,000	440,000	175,000
5	80,000	440,000	175,000
6	80,000	440,000	175,000
7	90,000	440,000	175,000

The channel would be navigable for seven years, after which silting would render it unnavigable. Local economists estimate that 75 percent of the savings to shippers would be directly invested by the firms or their shareholders, and the remaining 25 percent would be used by shareholders for consumption. They also determine that all government expenditures come at the expense of private investment. The marginal social rate of time preference is assumed to be 3.5 percent, the marginal rate of return on private investment is assumed to be 6.8 percent, and the shadow price of capital is assumed to be 2.2.

Assuming that the costs and benefits accrue at the end of the year they straddle and using the market-based interest rate approach, calculate the present value of net benefits of the project using each of the following methods.

a. Discount at the rates suggested by the US Office of Management and Budget.

b. Discount using the shadow price of capital method.

c. Discount using the shadow price of capital method. However, now assume that the social marginal rate of time preference is 2.0 percent, rather than 3.5 percent.

d. Discount using the shadow price of capital method. However, now assume that the shadow price of capital is given by Equation (10.9). Again, assume that the social marginal rate of time preference is 3.5 percent.

e. Discount using the shadow price of capital method. However, now assume that only 50 percent of the savings to shippers would be directly invested by the firms or their shareholders, rather than 75 percent. Again, assume that the social marginal rate of time preference is 3.5 percent, and that the shadow price of capital is 2.23.

2. An analyst for a municipal public housing agency explained the choice of a discount rate as follows: "Our agency funds its capital investments through nationally issued bonds. The effective interest rate that we pay on the bonds is the cost that the agency faces in shifting revenue from the future to the present. It is, therefore, the appropriate discount rate for the agency to use in evaluating alternative investments." Comment on the appropriateness of this discount rate.

3. Assume the following: Society faces a marginal excess tax burden of raising public revenue denoted METB; the shadow price of capital equals θ; public borrowing displaces private investment dollar for dollar; and public revenues raised through taxes displace consumption (but not investment). Consider a public project involving a large initial capital expenditure, C, followed by a stream of benefits that are entirely consumed, B.

    a. Discuss how you would apply the shadow price of capital method to the project if it is financed fully out of current taxes.

    b. Discuss how you would apply the shadow price of capital method to the project if it is financed fully by public borrowing, which is later repaid by taxes.

4. Assume a project will result in benefits of $1.2 trillion in 500 years by avoiding an environmental disaster that otherwise would occur at that time.

    a. Compute the present value of these benefits using a time-constant discount rate of 3.5.

    b. Compute the present value of these benefits using the time-declining discount rate schedule suggested in this chapter.

Notes

1. This chapter draws on Mark A. Moore, Anthony E. Boardman, Aidan R. Vining, David L. Weimer, and David H. Greenberg, "'Just Give Me a Number!' Practical Values for the Social Discount Rate." *Journal of Policy Analysis and Management*, 23(4), 2004, 789–812; Anthony E. Boardman, Mark A. Moore, and Aidan R. Vining, "The Social Discount Rate for Canada Based on Future Growth in Consumption." *Canadian Public Policy*, 36(3), 2010, 323–41; and Mark A. Moore, Anthony E. Boardman, and Aidan R. Vining, "More Appropriate Discounting: The Rate of Social Time Preference and the Value of the Social Discount Rate." *Journal of Benefit–Cost Analysis*, 4(1), 2013, 1–16. We thank Mark Moore for his many contributions to this chapter.

2. Throughout this chapter we assume that impacts (costs and benefits) and discount rates are all measured in real dollars.

3. Equation (10.2) can also be recognized as exponential discounting. It is the only functional form that guarantees time consistency in choice: that is, the ranking of A today over B tomorrow is the same as the ranking of A one year from now and B one year and one day from now. See R. H. Strotz, "Myopia and Inconsistency in Dynamic Utility Maximization." *Review of Economic Studies*, 23(3), 1955–56, 165–80.

4. That is, $\Delta w / w_t = -i$.

5. Moore, Boardman, and Vining, "More Appropriate Discounting: The Rate of Social Time Preference and the Value of the Social Discount Rate." David F. Burgess and Richard O. Zerbe, "The Most Appropriate Discount Rate." *Journal of Benefit–Cost Analysis*, 4(3), 2013, 391–400.

6. In practice, analysts usually do not convert net benefits to certainty equivalents or option prices. Specifically, they use expected values rather than option prices because the former can be estimated from observable behavior, while the latter requires contingent valuation surveys. Unless strong assumptions are made about individuals' utility functions, even the sign, let alone the magnitude, of the difference between expected values and option prices is usually theoretically uncertain, except in the case of uncertainty about income (see Chapter 12, and the references therein). It is important, however, both conceptually and in practice, to treat risk and discounting separately. Nonetheless, in order to compensate for risk, analysts sometimes discount expected net benefits using a higher rate than they would in the absence of risk. Unfortunately, this procedure generally results in an incorrect estimate of the *NPV*. For example, suppose that a project has a relatively large expected terminal cost that is subject to risk. Using a higher rate to account for this risk will reduce, rather than magnify, the present value of this cost, making a positive *NPV* more, rather than less, likely. In contrast, the certainty equivalent for a negative net benefit is a more negative net benefit. As this example illustrates,

it is inappropriate to attempt to take account of risk by adjusting the discount rate. For other reasons why doing this is problematic, see Coleman Bazelon and Kent Smetters, "Discounting Inside the Washington D.C. Beltway." *Journal of Economic Perspectives*, 13(4), 1999, 213–28.

7. Nicholas Stern, *The Economics of Climate Change: The Stern Review* (New York, NY: Cambridge University Press, 2007).

8. William D. Nordhaus, "A Review of the *Stern Review on the Economics of Climate Change*." *Journal of Economic Literature*, 45(3), 2007, 682–702. See also Partha Dasgupta, "Commentary: The Stern Review's Economics of Climate Change." *National Institute Economic Review*, 199(1), 2007, 4–7 and Martin L. Weitzman, "A Review of the *Stern Review on the Economics of Climate Change*," *Journal of Economic Literature*, 45(3), 2007, 703–24.

9. Assume here that, in order to reveal your true preferences, there is no arbitrage opportunity; that is, you could not borrow or lend money. Arbitrage means that you can simultaneously buy something in one market and sell it in another market and thereby make a guaranteed profit. If interest rates were less than 20 percent and arbitrage were allowed, you could say that you would rather have the $1,200 next year and then immediately borrow between $1,000 and $1,200 from the bank. Thus, you would say that you would prefer to have the $1,200 next year even though you would actually prefer to have $1,000 now.

10. It would make no conceptual difference if the consumer received income in both periods.

11. The budget constraint, Equation (10.4), can be rewritten as $C_2 = T(1 + i) - (1 + i)C_1$, which implies that its slope equals $-(1 + i)$. The absolute value of the slope of the budget constraint exceeds 1, indicating that the consumer earns positive interest (at rate i) on the part of income saved the first year.

12. Formally, the result holds as long as the problem has an interior solution. A very impatient person would have an MRTP $> i$, which leads to a corner solution on the C_1 axis. For simplicity, we ignore this possibility.

13. This example assumes that the marginal return on investment to the private sector equals the marginal social return on this investment. In other words, there are no market failures or externalities.

14. At point Z, in Figure 10.2, the absolute value of the slope of the *CPF*, $(1 + r)$, exceeds the absolute value of the slope of the *SIC*, $(1 + p)$.

15. Arnold C. Harberger, "The Discount Rate in Public Investment Evaluation." *Conference Proceedings of the Committee on the Economics of Water Resource Development*

(Denver, CO: Western Agricultural Economics Research Council, Report No. 17, 1969).

16. In fact, Harberger (op. cit.) asserts that savings are not very responsive to changes in interest rates. Some empirical evidence supports this assertion, implying that the SS curve is close to vertical, and as a consequence, ΔC is close to zero. This, in turn, suggests that the value of the parameter a is close to 0 and the value of b is close to 1. In other words, almost all of the resources for public-sector investment would be obtained by crowding out private-sector investment. Harberger, therefore, argues that the marginal rate of return on investment is a good approximation of the SDR. However, there is currently little support for this view, although proponents of the SOC method attach larger weight to b. For evidence about the responsiveness of savings to changes in interest rates, see, for example, John Muellbauer and Ralph Lattimore, "The Consumption Function: A Theoretical and Empirical Overview," in M. H. Pesaran and M. R. Wickens, editors, *The Handbook of Applied Econometrics: Macroeconomics* (Cambridge, MA: Blackwell, 1995), 221–311.

17. Robert C. Lind, "Reassessing the Government's Discount Rate Policy in Light of New Theory and Data in a World Economy with a High Degree of Capital Mobility." *Journal of Environmental Economics and Management*, 18(2), 1990, S8–S28.

18. David Burgess and Richard Zerbe present a more general version of this equation which allows for multiple sectors of the economy with different effective tax rates on capital in each sector and with different groups of savers with different rates of personal income taxes; see David F. Burgess and Richard O. Zerbe, "Appropriate Discounting for Benefit–Cost Analysis." *Journal of Benefit–Cost Analysis*, 2(2), 2011, article 2.

19. Anthony E. Boardman and Mark Hellowell, "A Comparative Analysis and Evaluation of Specialist PPP Units' Methodologies for Conducting Value for Money Appraisals." *Journal of Comparative Policy Analysis*, 19(3), 2017, 191–206.

20. Systematic risk depends on the correlation between the returns to a project and the growth in consumption. It is important to clarify whether one is referring to financial systematic risk which concerns the correlation between the financial returns to a project and growth in consumption or social systematic risk which concerns the correlation between the net social benefit returns and consumption. See Boardman and Hellowell ("A Comparative Analysis and Evaluation of Specialist PPP Units' Methodologies for Conducting Value for Money Appraisals").

21. The risk premiums are usually based on the capital asset pricing model (CAPM).

22. The weighted average cost of capital, WACC, is given by: $WACC = w_e\, k^e + w_d\, (1 - t)\, k^d$, where k^e is the cost of equity, k^d is the cost of debt, w_e is the proportion of equity, w_d is the proportion of debt, and t is the corporate tax rate.

23. See Mark A. Moore, Anthony E. Boardman, and Aidan R. Vining, "More Appropriate Discounting: The Rate of Social Time Preference and the Value of the Social Discount Rate" for derivation of the estimated values in the United States of this and other parameters discussed in this section.

24. David F. Burgess and Richard O. Zerbe, "Appropriate Discounting for Benefit–Cost Analysis," *Journal of Benefit–Cost Analysis*. For Canada, Jenkins and Kuo suggests $a = .15$, $b = .46$ and $c = .39$. Glenn P. Jenkins and C.-Y. Kuo, "The Economic Opportunity Cost of Capital for Canada – An Empirical Update," Queen's Economics Department, February 2008.

25. For Canada, Anthony Boardman, Mark Moore and Aidan Vining obtain a similar estimate of the SOC. See Anthony Boardman, Mark Moore and Aidan Vining, "The Social Discount Rate for Canada Based on Future Growth in Consumption," *Canadian Public Policy* 36(3), 2010, 323–41.

26. In the United States, for example, since 1980 individual income tax provides about 46 percent of revenues while corporate income taxes provide about 10 percent of revenues; see www. gpoaccess.gov/usbudget/fy10/sheets/hist02z1.xls (accessed February 13, 2010).

27. Dynan and colleagues find that marginal propensities to save out of disposable income vary between 2.4 and 11 percent in the United States (K. E. Dynan, J. Skinner, and S. P. Zeldes, "Do the Rich Save More?" Federal Reserve Board, Financial and Economic Discussion Series, 2000). Souleles (2002) finds that the Reagan tax cuts of the 1980s had very strong effects on current consumption when enacted (rather than when announced), inducing marginal propensities to consume of non-durables of between 0.6 and 0.9 (N. S. Souleles, "Consumer Response to the Reagan Tax Cuts." *Journal of Public Economics*, 85(1), 2002, 99–120). Even predictable tax refunds are largely spent when received, indicating that consumption is very responsive to the actual, rather than the predictable, permanent level of income, contrary to standard economic theory. See N. S. Souleles, "The Response of Household Consumption to Income Tax Refunds." *American Economic Review*, 89(4), 1999, 947–58.

28. S. Frederick, G. Loewenstein, and T. O'Donoghue, "Time Discounting and Time Preference: A Critical Review." *Journal of Economic Literature*, 40(2), 2002, 351–401.

29. If you think you have only a short time to live, then you will value the present very highly because, quite literally, there may be no tomorrow for you. Thus, it is reasonable to expect that older people have a higher MRTP rate than younger people. See Maureen L. Cropper, Sema K. Aydede, and Paul R. Portney, "Rates of Time Preference for Saving Lives." *American Economic Review*, 82(2), 1992, 469–72, who found a positive relationship between age and the MRTP, but found no significant relationship between respondents' MRTP

and their sex, education, marital status, or income. Laibson explains that individuals may have precommitted themselves to saving a certain amount of their income in an illiquid asset, while borrowing for current consumption from ready sources of credit. However, they are still not equating their marginal rates of time preference to a single market rate. See David Laibson, "Golden Eggs and Hyperbolic Discounting." *Quarterly Journal of Economics*, 112(2), 1997, 443–77.

30. George Loewenstein and Drazen Prelec, "Anomalies in Intertemporal Choice: Evidence and an Interpretation." *Quarterly Journal of Economics*, 107(2), 1992, 573–97.

31. Individuals who recognize that they are likely to make time-inconsistent choices may choose to use various commitment devices, e.g., to ensure that they save enough for retirement. This may explain the observation that individuals simultaneously borrow and lend. See, among others, Robert C. Lind, "Reassessing the Government's Discount Rate Policy in Light of New Theory and Data in a World Economy with a High Degree of Capital Mobility." *Journal of Environmental Economics and Management*, 18(2), 1990, S8–S28.

32. For a discussion of this issue, see Daniel W. Bromley, "Entitlements, Missing Markets, and Environmental Uncertainty." *Journal of Environmental Economics and Management*, 17(2), 1989, 181–94. Note, however, that the willingness of people to pass inheritances to their children and to pay to preserve certain natural resources indicates they give standing to future generations.

33. Frank P. Ramsey, "A Mathematical Theory of Saving." *Economic Journal*, 38(152), 1928, 543–59.

34. See Stephen A. Marglin, "The Social Rate of Discount and the Optimal Rate of Investment." *Quarterly Journal of Economics*, 77(1), 1963, 95–111; James A. Mirrlees and Nicholas Stern, "Fairly Good Plans." *Journal of Economic Theory*, 4(2), 1972, 268–88; W. R. Cline, *The Economics of Global Warming* (Washington, DC: Institute for International Economics, 1992); Kenneth J. Arrow, "Intergenerational Equity and the Rate of Discount in Long-Term Social Investment." Paper presented at the IEA World Congress, 1995. Available at www-siepr.stanford.edu/workp/swp97005.pdf [accessed August 27, 2017]; Nicholas Stern, *The Economics of Climate Change: The Stern Review* (New York, NY: Cambridge University Press, 2007).

35. This discount factor is obtained by taking the derivative of W with respect to consumption in period t: $\frac{dW}{dc_t} = U'(c_t)e^{-\rho t}$. It equals the product of $U'(c_t)$, the derivative of $U(c_t)$ with respect to c_t, which is the marginal utility of consumption, and the discount factor for utility of consumption, $e^{-\rho t}$.

36. Given that $\dfrac{d\left(\dfrac{dW}{dc}\right)}{dt} = U''\dfrac{dC}{dt}e^{-\rho t} + U'e^{-\rho t}\left(-\rho\right) < 0$, then the rate of change of the absolute value of the discount

factor, which equals $-\dfrac{d\left(\dfrac{dW}{dc}\right)}{dt}$ divided by $\dfrac{dW}{dc}$, is $\rho + g\varepsilon$, where $g = \dfrac{dC/dt}{c}$ is the rate of change in per-capita consumption, and $\varepsilon = -\dfrac{dU'}{dc}\dfrac{c}{U'}$ is the absolute value of the elasticity of the marginal utility of consumption with respect to consumption. We drop the time subscript for simplicity.

37. Kenneth J. Arrow, "Intergenerational Equity and the Rate of Discount in Long-Term Social Investment."

38. This value was obtained by regressing the natural logarithm of real per-capita consumption on time using data from Robert Shiller's website.

39. See Martin L. Weitzman, "A Review of the *Stern Review on the Economics of Climate Change*." Arrow et al. suggest that ε is between 1 and 2. K. J. Arrow, W. R. Cline, K. G. Maler, M. Munasinghe, R. Squitieri, and J. E. Stiglitz, "Intertemporal Equity, Discounting and Economic Efficiency." In J. P. Bruce et al., editors, *Climate Change 1995* (Cambridge: Cambridge University Press, 1995), 128–44.

40. David J. Evans and Haluk Sezer, "Social Discount Rates for Six Major Countries." *Applied Economic Letters*, 11(9), 2004, 557–560, and David J. Evans, "The Elasticity of Marginal Utility of Consumption: Estimates for 20 OECD Countries." *Fiscal Studies*, 26(2), 2005, 197–224.

41. For example, Kula estimates or argues $g = 2.3$ percent, $\varepsilon = 1.89$, and $\rho = 0.9$, and therefore he suggests STP = 5.2 percent. See E. Kula, "Derivation of the Social Time Preference Rates for the United States and Canada." *Quarterly Journal of Economics*, 99(4), 1984, 873–82. Cline, assuming the likely future world growth rate is 1 percent, $\rho = 0$, and $\varepsilon = 1.5$, estimates STP = 1.5 percent. See W. R. Cline, *The Economics of Global Warming* (Washington, DC: Institute for International Economics, 1992).

42. For example, in Figure 10.3, ROI > CRI.

43. This approach was first suggested by Otto Eckstein and systematically developed by David Bradford. See Otto Eckstein, *Water Resource Development: The Economics of Project Evaluation* (Cambridge, MA: Harvard University Press, 1958) and David F. Bradford, "Constraints on Government Investment Opportunities and the Choice of Discount Rate." *American Economic Review*, 65(5), 1975, 887–99.

44. Suppose a dollar invested yields a return of ROI, and of that return a constant fraction f is reinvested each period, while the fraction $1 - f$ is consumed. In the first period $(1 - f)$ ROI is consumed and f ROI is reinvested (as is the original $1). In the second period, $(1 + f$ ROI) is invested which yields a return of ROI $(1 + f$ ROI). Again, suppose that fraction f of this return is reinvested and $1 - f$ is consumed.

If this process is repeated it yields a consumption stream of: $(1 - f)$ ROI, $(1 - f)$ ROI $(1 + f$ ROI$)$, $(1 - f)$ ROI $(1 + f$ ROI$)^2$, ... This consumption stream is a perpetuity with initial (year one) annual benefits of $(1 - f)$ ROI that grow at a constant rate, f ROI. Application of the formulas in the appendix to Chapter 6 yields Equation (10.10). For more information see Randolph M. Lyon, "Federal Discount Policy, the Shadow Price of Capital, and Challenges for Reforms." *Journal of Environmental Economics and Management*, 18(2), 1990, S29–50, appendix I.

45. See also Evans and Sezer, who provide theoretically grounded estimates of the SDR for a variety of countries. D. J. Evans and H. Sezer, "Social Discount Rates for Six Major Countries," and D. J. Evans and H. Sezer, "Social Discount Rates for Member Countries of the European Union." *Journal of Economic Studies*, 32(1), 2005, 47–60.

46. For a more detailed illustration see Mark A. Moore, Anthony E. Boardman, and David H. Greenberg, "The Social Discount Rate in Canada." In A. R. Vining and J. Richards, editors, *Building the Future: Issues in Public Infrastructure in Canada* (Toronto, ON: C. D. Howe Institute, 2001), 73–130.

47. If the loans for the project were obtained from persons residing outside the community instead of local citizens, one might believe that benefits and costs accruing to these persons are irrelevant to its investment decisions and, therefore, ignore them in computing the project's net present value. Also, if there was the possibility of borrowing from abroad, then there will be less than complete crowding out of domestic private investment. Private investment may also be less than completely crowded out if there were unemployed resources in the local economy.

48. For example, of the installment of $673,854 paid at the end of the first year, the interest on the loan is $120,000 $(0.04 \times 3,000,000)$, and the remainder, $553,854 $(673,854 - 120,000)$, is repayment of principal.

49. Arrow, "Intergenerational Equity and the Rate of Discount in Long-Term Social Investment." Paper presented at the IEA World Congress, 1995.

50. Cline proposes using a value of θ equal to 1.56 and then discounting using p_x measured at 1.5 percent for all CBAs, including greenhouse gas abatement projects. His estimate of θ uses r_z 8.0 percent, assumes that all investments have 15-year lives, and that $f = 0.2$. See W. R. Cline, *The Economics of Global Warming.*

51. One rationale for this 50-year cut-off is that most equipment, structures, and buildings will not last much longer than 50 years. Depreciation rates appear to range between 3.4 and 13.3 percent per year, implying that between 80 and 100 percent has depreciated after 50 years. Thus, there are likely to be few public investments that are intergenerational in our sense. Another argument is that 50 years corresponds

approximately to two generations – our generation and our children's – and that events beyond this time period truly belong to future generations. See C. R. Hulten and F. C. Wykoff, "The Measurement of Economic Depreciation"; and M. Nadir and I. Prucha, "Estimation of the Depreciation Rate of Physical and R&D Capital." *Economic Inquiry*, 34(1), 1996, 43–56. A third rationale is provided by Newell and Pizer, which we discuss later. R. G. Newell and W. A. Pizer, "Discounting the Distant Future: How Much do Uncertain Rates Increase Valuations?" *Journal of Environmental Economics and Management*, 46(1), 2003, 52–71.

52. After reviewing the literature on counterexamples to constant discounting, George Loewenstein and Drazen Prelec conclude that "unlike the EU [expected utility] violations, which in many cases can only be demonstrated with a clever arrangement of multiple choice problems (e.g., the Allais paradox), the counterexamples to *DU* [constant discounting] are simple, robust, and bear directly on central aspects of economic behavior." See George Loewenstein and Drazen Prelec, "Anomalies in Intertemporal Choice: Evidence and an Interpretation," at p. 574.

53. David Laibson, "Golden Eggs and Hyperbolic Discounting."

54. Nicholas Stern, "The Economics of Climate Change." *American Economic Review: Papers and Proceedings*, 98(2), 2008, 1–37.

55. Otto Eckstein, *Water Resource Development: The Economics of Project Evaluation*; Edmund Phelps, "The Golden Rule of Accumulation: A Fable for Growthmen." *American Economic Review*, 51(4), 1961, 638–43; Stephen Marglin, "The Social Rate of Discount and the Optimal Rate of Investment"; Kenneth J. Arrow, "Intergenerational Equity and the Rate of Discount in Long-Term Social Investment"; P. Dasgupta, K. Maler, and S. Barrett, "Intergenerational Equity, Social Discount Rates, and Global Warming."

56. See M. Weitzman, "Gamma Discounting." *American Economic Review*, 91(1), 2001, 260–71; R. G. Newell and W. A. Pizer, "Discounting the Distant Future: How Much do Uncertain Rates Increase Valuations?"; B. Groom, C.J. Hepburn, P. Koundouri and D. Pearce, "Discounting the Future: The Long and the Short of It." *Environmental and Resource Economics*, 32(4), 2005, 445–93; C. Gollier, P. Koundouri and T. Pantelidis, "Declining Discount Rates: Economic Justifications and Implications for Long-Run Policy." *Economic Policy*, 23, 2008, 759–95; C. Hepburn, P. Koundouri, E. Panopoulous, and T. Pantelidis, "Social Discounting under Uncertainty: A Cross-Country Comparison." *Journal of Environmental Economics and Management*, 57(2), 2009, 140–50; K. J. Arrow et al., "How Should Benefits and Costs be Discounted in an Intergenerational Context? The Views of an Expert Panel." *Resources for the Future Discussion Paper*, 12–53, October.

Available online at www.rff.org/files/sharepoint/WorkImages/Download/RFF-DP-12–53.pdf.

57. Newell and Pizer ("Discounting the Distant Future: How Much do Uncertain Rates Increase Valuations?") adopt an approach based on the historical behavior of interest rates. Their model captures the uncertainty in forecasting the rates that will prevail in the far future. They examine the US government's real, long-term bond rate over the past 200 years and find the data do not clearly distinguish between a random-walk and a mean-reversion model. They prefer the random-walk version and use it to simulate the future path of the bond rate, from both a 4 percent and a 2 percent initial value. They generate thousands of different time paths and use these to construct expected discount factors. This results in a time-declining scale of effective discount rates. Hepburn, Koundouri, Panopoulou, and Pantelidis ("Social Discounting Under Uncertainty: A Cross-Country Comparison") apply this method to four other countries. In an alternative approach, Weitzman ("Gamma Discounting") surveyed almost 2200 economists, asked each to provide a single, real rate to use in discounting the costs and benefits of global climate change, and found that the frequency distribution of the respondents' rates approximated a gamma distribution. His main finding is that even if every respondent believes in a constant discount rate, the widespread of opinion results in the SDR declining significantly over time. Based on the distribution of his respondents' preferred discount rates, Weitzman suggests a scale for SDRs that approaches zero after 200 years. Newell and Pizer derive rates that are generally higher than Weitzman's rates and fall more slowly, with the declining rate kicking in after about 50 years.

58. See Organisation for Economic Cooperation and Development (OECD), *Explanatory Note for a Survey of RIA Systems in OECD Countries*. Paris, France: 29th Session of the Committee. 2004, April 15–16.

59. Treasury Board of Canada Secretariat (TBS), *Canadian Cost–Benefit Analysis Guide: Regulatory Proposals*, 2007.

60. The SPC method may *also* be used where consumption is involved, such as for health and environmental goods, and there are minimal resources involving opportunity costs

61. Coppola, Fernholz and Glenday proposed enhancing the (top-down) SOC method with a supply price (bottom-up) approach; see Andrea Coppola, Fernando Fernholz, and Graham Glenday, "Estimating the Economic Opportunity Cost of Capital for Public Investment Projects: An Empirical Analysis of the Mexican Case." *World Bank Policy Research Working Paper 6816*, 2016. Their recommendations led the government to reduce the SDR from 12 percent to 10 percent.

62. Office of Management and Budget (OMB), *Circular No. A-4*, September 17, 2003. These guidelines discuss declining discount rates and suggest performing sensitivity analysis at lower rates.

63. See also Office of Management and Budget (OMB), *Circular No. A-94 Revised*, October 29, 1992, and Office of Management and Budget (OMB), *Economic Analysis of Federal Regulations Under Executive Order 12866*, January 11, 1996. The base case excludes water resource policy and cost–effectiveness analysis.

64. Office of Management and Budget (OMB), *Memorandum for the Heads of Department and Agencies M-17–10*, December 12, 2016. The rates vary according to the duration of the project from 3-year to 30-year.

65. Coleman Bazelon and Kent Smetters, "Discounting Inside the Washington D.C. Beltway." *Journal of Economic Perspectives*, 13(4), 1999, 213–28. Costs and benefits should be converted to consumption equivalents "ideally." The CBO sets the STP equal to the CRI, which it estimates based on real government T-bill rates.

66. General Accounting Office (GAO), *Discount Rate Policy*, May 1991. The SDR should equal the interest rate on T-bills with the same maturity as the project being evaluated. Private-sector discount rates should be used for asset divestiture decisions. The ROI method or the STP-SPC method may be used for some types of evaluations.

67. Environmental Protection Agency (EPA), *Guidelines for Preparing Economic Analyses*, 2010.

68. European Commission (EC), *Better Regulation 'Toolbox'*, 2017. However, the current EC guide for Cohesion policy recommends an SDR equal to 5% in cohesion countries and 3% in other member states; see, European Commission (EC), *Guide to Cost–Benefit Analysis of Investment Projects: Economic Appraisal Tool for Cohesion Policy 2014–2020*, 2014.

69. France Strategie, "Discount Rate in Project Analysis," March 2017.

70. MKBA, "Why Do Discount Rates Differ? Analyzing the Differences Between Discounting Policies for Transport Cost–Benefit Analysis in Five Practices" (undated). Similar to Canada, climate change projects may be discounted at a lower rate.

71. Kare Hagen et al., *Cost–Benefit Analysis*, Official Norwegian Reports NOU 2012:16, 2012.

72. Swedish Transport Administration, *Method of Analysis and Socio-Economic Calculation Values for the Transport Sector: ASEK 6.0*, 2016. However, Hansson, Lilieqvist, Björnberg, and Johansson find that Swedish authorities differ widely in the discount rates used in their policy evaluations; see Sven Ove Hansson, Kristin Lilieqvist, Karin Edvardsson Björnberg, and Maria Vredin Johansson, "Time Horizons and Discount Rates in Swedish Environmental Policy: Who Decides and on What Grounds?" *Futures*, 2015.

73. HM Treasury, *The Green Book: Appraisal and Evaluation in Central Government* (London: Treasury Stationary Office), 2008.

74. Office of Best Practice Regulation (OBPR), *Cost–Benefit Analysis Guidance Note*, February 1, 2016. Most states have their own guidelines, some of which are similar to the Commonwealth while others are not; see Georgre Argyrous, "A Review of Government Cost–Benefit Analysis Guidelines." The Australian and New Zealand School of Government, March 2013. See also appendix 4 in Leo Dobes, Joanne Leung, George Argyrous, *Social Cost–Benefit Analysis in Australia and New Zealand* (Acton, Australia: Australian National University Press, 2016).

75. However, the CRI (3 percent) may be used for some environmental projects; see Commonwealth of Australia, *Handbook of Cost–Benefit Analysis*, Financial Management Reference Material No. 6, 2006 (archived).

76. Ehtisham Ahmed and Hernan Viscarra, *Public Investment for Sustainable Development in Chile.*

Inter-American Development Bank Discussion Paper No: IDB-DO-469, 2016.

77. New Zealand Treasury, *Guide to Social Cost Benefit Analysis*, 2015. The Treasury recommends using a rate equal to the long-run return on similar investments made by shareholders. This return varies by sector. See also New Zealand Treasury, *Public Sector Discount Rates for Cost Benefit Analysis*, 2008.

78. Investment Coordination Committee, *Revisions on ICC Guidelines and Procedures (Updated Social Discount Rate for the Philippines)*. National Economic and Development Authority, September 30, 2016.

79. Javier Campos, Tomás Serebrinsky, and Ancor Suárez-Alemán, "Time Goes By: Recent Developments on the Theory and Practice of the Discount Rate." *Inter-American Development Bank, Technical Note IDB-TN-861*, September 2015.

80. Asian Development Bank, *Guidelines for the Economic Analysis of Projects* (Manila, Philippines: Asian Development Bank, 2007).

11 Dealing with Uncertainty: Expected Values, Sensitivity Analysis, and the Value of Information

Cost–benefit analysis almost always requires the analyst to predict the future. Whether it is efficient to begin a project depends on what one expects will happen after the project has begun. Yet, analysts can rarely make precise predictions about the future. Indeed, in some cases, analysts can reasonably assume that uncontrollable factors, such as epidemics, floods, bumper crops, or fluctuations in international oil prices, will affect the benefits and costs that would be realized from proposed policies. How can analysts reasonably take account of these uncertainties in CBA?

We focus on three topics relevant to uncertainty: *expected value* as a measure to take account of risks, *sensitivity analysis* as a way of investigating the robustness of net benefit estimates to different resolutions of uncertainty, and the *value of information* as a benefit category for CBA and as a guide for allocating analytical effort. Expected values take account of the dependence of benefits and costs on the occurrence of specific contingencies, or "states of the world," to which analysts are able to assign probabilities of occurrence. Sensitivity analysis is a way of acknowledging uncertainty about the values of important parameters in prediction; therefore, it should be a component of almost any CBA. When analysts have opportunities for gaining additional information about costs or benefits, they may be able to value the information by explicitly modeling the uncertainty inherent in their decisions. A particular type of information value, called *quasi-option value*, is relevant when assessing currently available alternatives that have different implications for learning about the future.

11.1 Expected Value Analysis

One can imagine several types of uncertainty about the future. At the most profound level, an analyst might not be able to specify the full range of relevant circumstances that may occur. Indeed, the human and natural worlds are so complex that one cannot hope to anticipate every possible future circumstance. Yet, in many situations of relevance to daily life and public policy, it is reasonable to characterize the future in terms of two or more distinct contingencies. For example, in deciding whether to take an umbrella to work, it is reasonable to divide the future into two contingencies: Either it will or it will not rain sufficiently to make the umbrella useful. Of course, other relevant contingencies can be imagined as well – it will be a dry day, but one may or may not be the victim of an attempted mugging in which the umbrella would prove valuable in self-defense! If these additional contingencies are highly unlikely, then it is usually reasonable to ignore them.

Modeling the future as a set of relevant contingencies involves yet another narrowing of uncertainty: How likely are each of the contingencies? If it is feasible to assign probabilities of occurrence to each of the contingencies, then uncertainty about the future becomes a problem of dealing with *risk*. In relatively simple situations, risk can be incorporated into CBA through expected value analysis.

11.1.1   *Contingencies and their Probabilities*

Modeling uncertainty as risk begins with the specification of a set of *contingencies* that, within a simplified model of the world, are *exhaustive* and *mutually exclusive*. A contingency can be thought of as a possible event, outcome, or state of the world such that one and only one out of the relevant set of possibilities will actually occur. What makes a set of contingencies the basis of an appropriate model for conducting a CBA of a policy?

The set of contingencies ideally should capture the full range of plausible variations in net benefits of the policy. For example, in evaluating the construction and filling of an oil stockpile for use in the event of an oil price shock sometime in the future, the analyst would want to consider at least two contingencies: There will never be another future oil price shock (a situation in which the policy is likely to result in net losses), or there will be some specified major oil price shock (a situation in which the policy is likely to result in net gains).

The analyst should also assess how comprehensively the set of contingencies represents the possible outcomes between the extremes. In some circumstances, the possible contingencies can be listed exhaustively, so that they can be treated as fully representative. More often, however, the selected contingencies sample from an infinite number of possibilities. In these circumstances, each contingency can be thought of as a *scenario*, which is just a description of a possible future. The practical question is: Do the specified contingencies provide a sufficient variety of scenarios to convey the possible futures adequately? If so, then the contingencies are representative.

Figure 11.1 illustrates the representation of a continuous scale with discrete contingencies. The horizontal axis gives the number of inches of summer rainfall in an agricultural region. The vertical axis gives the net benefits of a water storage system, which increase as the amount of rainfall decreases. Imagine that an analyst represents uncertainty about rainfall with only two contingencies: "excessive" rain, and "deficient" rain. The excessive rain contingency assumes 22 inches of rainfall, which would yield zero net benefits from the storage system. The deficient rain contingency assumes zero inches of rainfall, which would yield $4.4 million in net benefits. If the relationship between rainfall and net benefits follows the straight line labeled *A*, and all the rainfall amounts between 0 and 22 are equally likely, then the average of net benefits over the full continuous range would be $2.2 million. If the analyst assumed that each of the contingencies were equally likely, then the average over the two contingencies would also be $2.2 million, so that using two scenarios would be adequately representative.[1]

Now assume that net benefits follow the curved line labeled *B*. Again, assuming that all rainfall amounts between 0 and 22 inches are equally likely, the average of net benefits over the full continuous range would only be about $1.1 million, so that using only these two contingencies would grossly overestimate the average net benefits from the

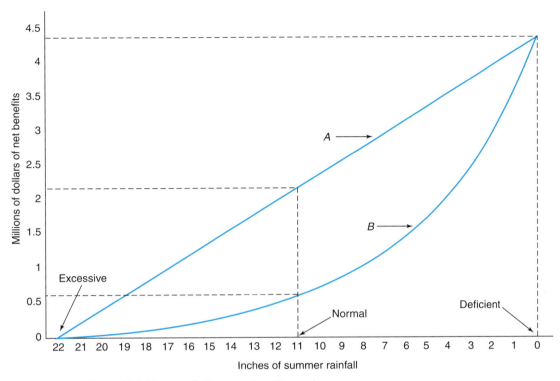

Figure 11.1 Representativeness of contingencies.

storage system.[2] Adding "normal" rainfall as a contingency that assumes 11 inches of rainfall and averaging net benefits over all three contingencies yields net benefits of $1.6 million, which is more representative than the average calculated with two contingencies, but still considerably larger than the $1.1 million predicted over the full continuous range. The inclusion of even more contingencies would be desirable. For example, moving to five equally spaced contingencies gives an average benefit of $1.3 million, which is much closer to the average over the continuous range.[3]

Once we have specified a tractable but representative set of contingencies, the next task is to assign probabilities of occurrence to each of them. To be consistent with the logical requirement that the contingencies taken together are exhaustive and mutually exclusive, the probabilities that an analyst assigns must each be non-negative and sum to exactly 1. Thus, if there are three contingencies, C_1, C_2, and C_3, the corresponding probabilities are $p_1 \geq 0$, $p_2 \geq 0$, and $p_3 \geq 0$ such that $p_1 + p_2 + p_3 = 1$.

The probabilities may be based solely on historically observed frequencies or on subjective assessments by clients, analysts, or other experts based on a variety of information and theory or on both history and expertise. For example, return to the contingencies in Figure 11.1: agriculturally "excessive" rain, "normal" rain, and "deficient" rain in a river valley for which a water storage system has been proposed. The national weather service may be able to provide data on average annual rainfall over the last century that allows an analyst to estimate the probabilities of the three specified levels of precipitation from their historical frequencies. If such data were not available, then the analyst would have to base the probabilities on expert opinion, comparison with similar valleys in the region for which data are available, or other subjective assessment. As such subjective assessments are rarely made with great confidence, it is especially important to investigate the sensitivity of the results to the particular probabilities chosen.

11.1.2   *Calculating the Expected Value of Net Benefits*

The specification of contingencies and their respective probabilities allows an analyst to calculate the *expected net benefits* of a policy. She does so by first predicting the net benefits of the policy under each contingency and then taking the weighted average of these net benefits over all the contingencies, where the weights are the respective probabilities that the contingencies occur. Specifically, for I contingencies, let B_i be the benefits under contingency i, C_i be the costs under contingency i, and p_i be the probability of contingency i occurring. Then the expected net benefits, $E[NB]$, is given by the formula:

$$E[NB] = p_1(B_1 - C_1) + p_2(B_2 - C_2) + \ldots + p_I(B_I - C_I) \qquad (11.1)$$

which is just the expected value of net benefits over the I possible outcomes.[4]

Exhibit 11.1

Being explicit about contingencies, their probabilities, and their consequences helps structure complex decision problems. Consider the following letter that President Abraham Lincoln wrote to Major General George B. McClellan on February 3, 1862:

My dear Sir:

You and I have distinct, and different plans for a movement of the Army of the Potomac – yours to be down the Chesapeake, up the Rappahannock to Urbana, and across land to the terminus of the Railroad on the York River – mine to move directly to a point on the Railroad South West of Manassas.

If you will give me satisfactory answers to the following questions, I shall gladly yield my plan to yours.

First. Does not your plan involve a greatly larger expenditure of time and money than mine?

Second. Wherein is a victory more certain by your plan than mine?

Third. Wherein is a victory more valuable by your plan than mine?

Fourth. In fact, would it not be less valuable, in this, that it would break no great line of the enemy's communications, while mine would?

Fifth. In case of disaster, would not a safe retreat be more difficult by your plan than by mine?

Yours truly, Abraham Lincoln

Source: John G. Nicolay and John Hay, editors, *Abraham Lincoln: Complete Works, Volume Two* (New York, NY: The Century Company, 1894), 120.

When facing complicated risk problems, analysts often find it useful to model them as *games against nature*. A game against nature assumes that nature will randomly, and non-strategically, select a particular state of the world. The random selection of a state of the world is according to assumed probabilities. The selection is non-strategic in the sense that nature does not alter the probabilities of the states of the world in response to the action selected by the analysts. A game against nature in *normal form* has the following elements: *states of nature* and their *probabilities of occurrence*, *actions* available to the decision-maker facing nature, and *pay-offs* to the decision maker under each combination of state of nature and action.

Exhibit 11.2

In their evaluation of alternative government oil stockpiling programs in the early 1980s, Glen Sweetnam and colleagues at the US Department of Energy modeled the uncertainty surrounding oil market conditions with five contingencies: *slack market* – oil purchases for the US stockpile of up to 1.5 million barrels per day (mmb/d) could be made without affecting the world oil price; *tight market* – oil purchases increase the world price at the rate of $3.60 per mmb/d; *minor disruption* – loss of 1.5 mmb/d to the world market (e.g., caused by a revolution in an oil-exporting country); *moderate disruption* – loss of 6.0 mmb/d to the world market (e.g., caused by a limited war in the Persian Gulf); *major disruption* – loss of 12.0 mmb/d to the world market (e.g., caused by a major war in the Persian Gulf). For each of the 24 years of their planning horizon, they assumed that the probabilities of each of the contingencies occurring depended only on the contingency that occurred in the previous year. For each year, they calculated the social surplus in the US oil market conditional on each of the five market contingencies and changes in the size of the stockpile.

The model they constructed allowed them to answer the following questions. For any current market condition and stockpile size, what change in stockpile size maximizes the present value of expected net benefits? How much storage capacity should be constructed? How fast should it be added? The model and the answers it provided were influential in policy debates concerning expansion of the US stockpile, the Strategic Petroleum Reserve.

Sources: Adapted from Glen Sweetnam, "Stockpile Policies for Coping with Oil-Supply Disruptions," in George Horwich and Edward J. Mitchell, editors, *Policies for Coping with Oil-Supply Disruptions* (Washington, DC: American Enterprise Institute for Public Policy Research, 1982), 82–96. On the role of the model in the policy-making process, see Hank C. Jenkins-Smith and David L. Weimer, "Analysis as Retrograde Action: The Case of Strategic Petroleum Reserves." *Public Administration Review*, 45(4), 1985, 485–94.

Table 11.1 shows the analysis of alternatives for planetary defense against aster-oid collisions as a game against nature in normal form. It considers three possible states of nature over the next 100 years: exposure of Earth to collision with an asteroid larger than 1 km in diameter, which would have enough kinetic energy to impose severe regional or even global effects on society (10 on the Torino Scale); exposure of Earth to collision with an asteroid smaller than 1 km but larger than 20 m in diameter, which would have severe local or regional effects on society (8 or 9 on the Torino Scale); and no exposure of Earth to an asteroid larger than 20 m in diameter. The game shows three alternative actions: Build a forward-based asteroid defense, which would station nuclear devices sufficiently deep in space to attain a good possibility of their timely use in diverting asteroids from col-lision courses with Earth; build a near-Earth asteroid defense, which would be less expen-sive but not as effective as the forward-based defense; or do not build any asteroid defense.

Although actually estimating the pay-offs for this game would be both a monu-mental and a controversial analytical task, Table 11.1 displays some hypothetical figures. The pay-offs, shown as the present value of net costs over the next century, range from $30 trillion (Earth is exposed to a collision with an asteroid larger than 1 km in diameter in the absence of any asteroid defense) to $0 (Earth is not exposed to collision with an asteroid larger than 20 m and no defense system is built). Note that estimating the costs of a collision between Earth and an asteroid would itself involve expected value calcula-tions that take account of size, composition, and point of impact of the asteroid. The $30 trillion figure is about one-third of the world's annual gross domestic product.

The last column of Table 11.1 shows expected values for each of the three alter-natives. The expected value for each alternative is calculated by summing the products

Table 11.1 *A Game against Nature: Expected Values of Asteroid Defense Alternatives*

State of nature	Exposure to a collision with an asteroid larger than 1 km in diameter	Exposure to a collision with an asteroid between 20 m and 1 km in diameter	No exposure to collision with an asteroid larger than 20 m in diameter	
Probabilities of states of nature (over next century)	.001	.004	.995	
Actions (alternatives)	**Pay-offs (net costs in billions of 2000 dollars)**			**Expected value**
Forward-based asteroid defense	5,060	1,060	60	69
Near-Earth asteroid defense	10,020	2,020	20	**38**
No asteroid defense	30,000	6,000	0	54

Choose near-Earth asteroid defense: Expected net cost = $38 billion.

of its pay-off conditional on states of nature with the probabilities of those states. For example, the expected value of pay-offs (present value of net costs) for no asteroid defense is:

$$(0.001)(\$30{,}000 \text{ billion}) + (0.004)(\$6{,}000 \text{ billion}) + (0.995)(\$0) = \$54 \text{ billion}$$

Similar calculations yield $69 billion for the forward-based asteroid defense alternative and $38 billion for the near-Earth asteroid defense alternative. As the maximization of expected net benefits is equivalent to minimizing expected net costs, the most efficient alternative is near-Earth asteroid defense. Alternatively, one could think of near-Earth asteroid defense as offering expected net benefits of $16 billion relative to no defense ($54 billion in expected net costs minus $38 billion in expected net costs equals $16 billion in expected net benefits), while forward-based asteroid defense offers negative $15 billion in expected net benefits relative to no defense ($54 billion in expected net costs minus $69 billion in expected net costs equals negative $15 billion in expected net benefits).

In CBA, it is common practice to treat expected values as if they were certain amounts. For example, imagine that a perfect asteroid defense system would have a present value cost of $100 billion under each of the states of nature. In this case, assuming accurate prediction of costs, the $100 billion *would be certain* because it does not depend on which state of nature actually results. CBA generally treats a certain amount such as this as fully commensurate with expected values, even though the latter will not actually result in its expected value. In other words, although the expected net cost of no asteroid defense is $54 billion, assuming an accurate prediction of pay-offs, the actually realized net cost will be $30 trillion, $6 trillion, or $0. If the perfect defense system cost $54 billion, then CBA would rank it and no defense as equally efficient.

Treating expected values as if they were certain amounts implies that the person making the comparison has preferences that are *risk-neutral*. A person has risk-neutral preferences when he or she is indifferent between certain amounts and lotteries with the same expected pay-offs. A person is *risk-averse* if he or she prefers the certain amount and is *risk-seeking* if he or she prefers the lottery. Buying insurance, which offers a lower expected pay-off than the certain premium charged, indicates risk-aversion; buying a lottery ticket, which offers a lower expected value than its price, indicates risk-seeking.

Chapter 12 considers the appropriateness of treating expected values and certain equivalents as commensurate (e.g., risk neutrality). Doing so is not conceptually correct in measuring willingness to pay in circumstances in which individuals face uncertainty. Nevertheless, in practice, *treating expected values and certain amounts as commensurate is generally reasonable when either the pooling of risk over the collection of policies, or the pooling of risk over the collection of persons affected by a policy, will make the actually realized values of costs and benefits close to their expected values.* For example, a policy that affects the probability of highway accidents involves reasonable pooling of risk across many drivers (some will have accidents, others will not) so that realized values will be close to expected values. In contrast, a policy that affects the risk of asteroid collision does not involve pooling across individuals (either everyone suffers from the global harm if there is a collision or no one does if there is no collision), so that the realized value of costs may be very far from their expected value. As discussed in Chapter 12, such unpooled risk may require an adjustment, called *option value*, to expected benefits.

11.1.3   *Decision Trees and Expected Net Benefits*

The basic procedure for expected value analysis, taking weighted averages over contingencies, can be directly extended to situations in which costs and benefits accrue over multiple years, as long as the risks in each year are independent of the realizations of risks in previous years. Consider, for example, a CBA of a dam with a 20-year life and assuming that the costs and benefits of the dam depend only on the contingencies of below-average rainfall and above-average rainfall in the current year. Additionally, provided the analyst is willing to make the plausible assumption that the amount of rainfall in any year does not depend on the rainfall in previous years, then the analyst can simply calculate the present value of expected net benefits for each year and then calculate the present value of this stream of net benefits in the usual way.

The basic expected value procedure cannot be so directly applied when either the net benefits accruing under contingencies or the probabilities of the contingencies depend on the contingencies that have previously occurred (in other words, they are not independent). For example, above-average rainfall in one year may make the irrigation benefits of a dam less in the next year because of accumulated ground water. In the case of a policy to reduce the costs of earthquakes, the probability of a major earthquake may change each year depending on the mix of earthquakes that occurred in the previous year.

Such situations require a more flexible framework for handling risk than basic expected value analysis. *Decision analysis* provides such a framework.[5] Though it takes us too far afield to present decision analysis in any depth here, we sketch its general approach and present simple illustrations that demonstrate its usefulness in CBA. A number of book-length treatments of decision analysis are available for those who wish to pursue this topic in more depth.[6]

Decision analysis can be thought of as a *sequential, or extended form, game against nature*. It proceeds in two basic stages. First, one specifies the logical structure of the decision problem in terms of sequences of decisions and realizations of contingencies using a diagram, called a *decision tree*, that links an initial decision (the trunk) to final outcomes (branches). Second, using *backward induction* thinking, one works from final outcomes back to the initial decision, calculating expected values of net benefits across contingencies and pruning dominated branches (i.e., eliminating branches with lower expected values of net benefits).

Consider a vaccination program against a particular type of influenza that involves various kinds of costs.[7] The costs of the program result from immunization expenditures and possible adverse side effects; the benefits consist of the adverse health effects that are avoided if an epidemic occurs. This flu may infect a population over the next two years before sufficient immunity develops worldwide to stop its spread. Figure 11.2 presents a simple decision tree for a CBA of this vaccination program. The tree should be read from left to right to follow the sequence of decisions, denoted by an open

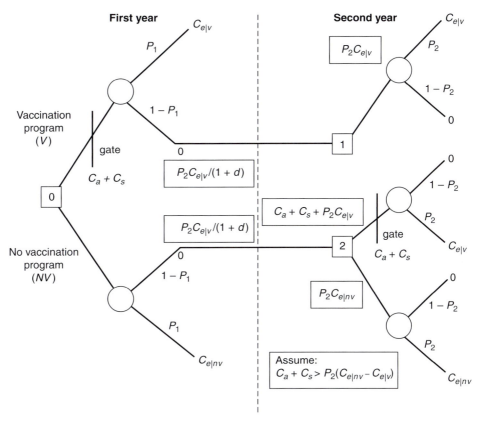

Figure 11.2 Decision tree for vaccination program analysis.

box, and random selections of contingencies, denoted by an open circle. The tree begins with a decision node, the square labeled 0 at the extreme left. The upper bough represents the decision to implement the vaccination program this year; the lower bough represents the decision not to implement the program this year.

Upper Bough: The Vaccination Program. First, follow the upper bough. If the program were implemented, then it would involve direct administrative costs, C_a, and the costs of adverse side effects, such as contracting the influenza from the vaccine itself, suffered by those who are vaccinated, C_s. Note that C_s, like most of the other costs in this example, is itself an expected cost based on the probability of the side effect, the cost to persons suffering the side effect, and the number of persons vaccinated. The solid vertical line on the bough can be thought of as a toll gate at which point the program costs, $C_a + C_s$, are incurred. A chance node, represented by a circle, appears next. Either the influenza infects the population (the upper branch, which occurs with probability P_1 and results in costs $C_{e|v}$, where the subscript should be read as "the epidemic occurs given that the vaccination program has been implemented"), or the influenza does not infect the population (the lower branch, which occurs with probability $1 - P_1$ and results in zero costs at that time). If the influenza does occur, then the population will be immune in the next year. Thus, the upper branch does not continue. If the influenza does not occur, then there is still a possibility that it might occur in the next year. Therefore, the lower branch continues to the second year, where the square labeled 1 notes the beginning of the second year. It leads directly to another chance node that specifies the two contingencies in the second year: The influenza infects the population (the upper subbranch, which occurs with probability P_2 and results in costs $C_{e|v}$), or the influenza does not infect the population (the lower subbranch, which occurs with probability $1 - P_2$ and results in zero costs).[8] We assume that P_2 is known at the time of the initial decision.[9]

Lower Bough: No Vaccination Program. We now return to the initial decision node and follow the lower bough that represents no vaccination program in the first year. Initially there is no cost associated with this decision. A chance node follows with two branches: Either the influenza infects the population (the lower branch, which occurs with probability P_1 and results in costs $C_{e|nv}$), or the influenza does not infect the population (the upper branch, which occurs with probability $1 - P_1$ and results in zero costs).[10] If the influenza does occur, then there is no need to consider the next year. If it does not occur, then the tree continues to decision node 2: Either implement the vaccination program in the second year (the upper subbranch crossing the gate where program costs $C_a + C_s$ are incurred) or do not implement it (the lower subbranch).

If the program is implemented, then a chance node occurs: The influenza infects the population (the lower twig, which occurs with probability P_2 and results in costs $C_{e|v}$), or the influenza does not infect the population (the upper twig, which occurs with probability $1 - P_2$ and results in zero costs). One completes the tree by considering the parallel chance node following the decision not to implement the program in the second year: The influenza infects the population (the lower twig, which occurs with probability P_2 and results in costs $C_{e|nv}$), or the influenza does not infect the population (the upper twig, which occurs with probability $1 - P_2$ and results in zero costs).

Solving the Decision Tree. To solve the decision problem, work from right to left, replacing chance nodes with their expected costs and pruning off parallel nodes that are dominated. Consider the chance node following decision node 1. Its expected cost, calculated by the expression $P_2 C_{e|v} + (1 - P_2)0$, equals $P_2 C_{e|v}$.

Now consider the chance nodes following decision node 2. The lower chance node, following a decision not to implement the vaccination program, has an expected cost of $P_2 C_{e|nv}$. The upper chance node has an expected cost of $P_2 C_{e|v}$, to which must be added the certain program costs so that the full expected cost of implementing the vaccination program in the second year is $C_a + C_s + P_2 C_{e|v}$. The analyst can now compare the expected cost of the two possible decisions at node 2: $P_2 C_{e|nv}$ versus $C_a + C_s + P_2 C_{e|v}$. To illustrate, assume that program costs are greater than the expected cost reduction from the vaccine, that is, $C_a + C_s > P_2(C_{e|nv} - C_{e|v})$, then $P_2 C_{e|nv}$ is smaller than $C_a + C_s + P_2 C_{e|v}$ so that not implementing the program dominates implementing it. (If this were not the case, then the lower branch would be unequivocally dominated by the upper branch.[11]) The analyst can now prune off the upper subbranch. If we reach decision node 2, then we know that we can obtain expected second-year costs of $P_2 C_{e|nv}$.

At decision node 0 the expected costs of implementing the vaccination program (i.e., following the upper bough) consist of direct costs plus the expected costs of following the chance node, which now has the pay-offs $C_{e|v}$ if there is an epidemic and the discounted expected value of node 1, $P_2C_{e|v}/(1 + d)$ if there is not an epidemic. Note that because this latter cost occurs in the second year, it is discounted using rate d. Thus, the present value of expected costs from implementing the vaccination program is given by:

$$E[C_v] = C_a + C_s + P_1C_{e|v} + (1 - P_1)P_2C_{e|v}/(1 + d) \qquad (11.2)$$

where the last term incorporates the expected costs from the second year.

The expected costs of not implementing the vaccination program are calculated in the same way: The pay-off if there is not an epidemic becomes the discounted expected costs from decision node 2, $P_2C_{e|nv}/(1 + d)$; the pay-off if there is an epidemic is still $C_{e|nv}$. Therefore, the expression:

$$E[C_{nv}] = P_1C_{e|nv} + (1 - P_1)P_2C_{e|nv}/(1 + d_1) \qquad (11.3)$$

gives the present value of expected costs of not implementing the program.

The final step is to compare the present values of expected costs for the two possible decisions at node 0. We prune the bough with the larger present value of expected costs. The remaining bough is the optimal decision.

As an illustration, suppose that we have gathered data suggesting the following values for parameters in the decision tree: $P_1 = .4$, $P_2 = .2$, $d = .05$, $C_{e|v} = .5C_{e|nv}$ (the vaccination program cuts the costs of influenza by half), $C_a = .1C_{e|nv}$ (the vaccination costs 10 percent of the costs of the influenza), and $C_s = .01C_{e|nv}$ (the side-effect costs are 1 percent of the costs of the influenza). For these values, $E[C_v] = .367C_{e|nv}$ and $E[C_{nv}] = .514C_{e|nv}$. Therefore, the vaccination program should be implemented in the first year because $E[C_v] < E[C_{nv}]$.

Calculating Expected Net Benefits of the Vaccination Program. Returning explicitly to CBA, the benefits of the vaccination program are the costs it avoids or simply $E[C_{nv}] - E[C_v]$, which in the numerical example shown in the preceding paragraph equals $0.147C_{e|nv}$. In Chapter 12, we return to the question of the appropriateness of expected net benefits as a generalization of net benefits in CBA.

Extending Decision Analysis. Decision analysis can be used for both public- and private-sector issues, and to structure much more complicated analyses than the CBA of the vaccination program. Straightforward extensions include more than two alternatives at decision nodes, more than two contingencies at chance nodes, more than two periods of time, and different probabilities of events in different periods. Analyses of the US oil stockpiling program typically involve trees so large that they can only be fully represented and solved by computers.[12] *For all problems, whether complex or not, decision analysis can be very helpful in showing how risk should be incorporated into the calculation of expected net benefits.*

11.2   Sensitivity Analysis

Whether or not one structures a CBA explicitly in terms of contingencies and their probabilities, analysts always face some uncertainty about the magnitude of the predicted impacts and the assigned values. Initial analyses usually suppress uncertainty by using the most likely estimates of unknown quantities. These estimates comprise what is called the *base case*. The purpose of sensitivity analysis is to acknowledge and clarify the underlying uncertainty. In particular, it should convey how sensitive predicted net benefits are to changes in assumptions. If the sign of net benefits does not change when the analyst considers the range of reasonable assumptions, then the results can be considered robust.

The presence of large numbers of unknown quantities is the usual situation in CBA. It makes a brute-force approach of looking at all combinations of assumptions unfeasible. For example, the vaccination program analysis, which is further developed in the next section, requires 17 different uncertain numerical assumptions. If an analyst considered just three different values for each assumption, there would still be over 129 million different combinations of assumptions to assess.[13] Even if it is feasible to compute net benefits for all these combinations, an analyst would still face the daunting task of sorting through the results and communicating them in an effective way.

Instead, we consider three more manageable approaches to doing sensitivity analysis. First, we demonstrate *partial sensitivity analysis*: How do net benefits change as a single assumption is varied while holding all others constant? Partial sensitivity is most appropriately applied to what the analyst believes to be the most important and uncertain assumptions. It can be used to find the values of numerical assumptions at which net benefits equal zero, or just break even. Second, we consider *worst- and best-case analysis*: Does any combination of reasonable assumptions reverse the sign of net benefits? Analysts are generally most concerned about situations in which their most plausible estimates yield positive net benefits, but they want to know what would happen in a worst case involving the least favorable, or most conservative, assumptions. Third, we consider the use of *Monte Carlo simulation*: What distribution of net benefits results from treating the numerical values of key assumptions as draws from probability distributions? The distribution of net benefits conveys information about the riskiness of the project: its mean (or median) provides a measure of the center of the distribution; its variance, spread around the mean, and the probability of positive net benefits provide information about the riskiness of a policy.

A Closer Look at the Vaccination Program Analysis

We illustrate these techniques by considering a more detailed specification of the costs relevant to the decision analysis of the hypothetical vaccination program presented in Figure 11.2. This program would vaccinate some residents of a county against a possible influenza epidemic.[14]

Consider the following general description of the program. Through an advertising and outreach effort by its Department of Health, the county expects to be able to recruit a large fraction of older residents in poor health who are at high mortality risk from influenza, and a much smaller fraction of the general population, for vaccination. As the vaccine is based on a live virus, some fraction of those vaccinated will suffer an adverse reaction that, in effect, converts them to high-risk status and gives them influenza, a cost included in the side effects of the vaccine, C_s. As the vaccine does not always confer immunity, often because it is not given sufficiently in advance of exposure to the influenza virus, its effectiveness rate is less than 100 percent. Everyone who contracts influenza must be confined to bed rest for a number of days. Analysts can value this loss as the average number of hours of work lost times the average wage rate for the county, although this procedure might overestimate the opportunity costs of time for older persons and underestimate the cost of the unpleasantness of the influenza symptoms for both younger and older persons. They can place a dollar value on the deaths caused by the influenza by multiplying the number of expected deaths times an estimate of the dollar value of life. The various numerical assumptions for the analysis appear in Table 11.2. Notice, for example, that the base case value used for each saved life is $10 million. That is, it is assumed that people make decisions about how much value they place on small changes in risks of death as if they valued their lives at $10 million.

Table 11.2 *Base-Case Values for Vaccination Program CBA*

Parameter	Value [range]	Comments
County population (N)	380,000	Total population in the county
Fraction high risk (r)	.06 [.04, .08]	One-half population over age 64
Low-risk vaccination rate (v_l)	.05 [.03, .07]	Fraction of low-risk persons vaccinated
High-risk vaccination rate (v_h)	.60 [.40, .80]	Fraction of high-risk persons vaccinated
Adverse reaction rate (α)	.03 [.01, .05]	Fraction vaccinated who become high-risk
Low-risk mortality rate (m_l) [.000025, .000075]	.00005	Mortality rate for low-risk infected
High-risk mortality rate (m_h) [.0005, .00015]	.001	Mortality rate for high-risk infected
Herd immunity effect (θ)	1.0 [.5, 1.0]	Fraction of effectively vaccinated who contribute to herd immunity effect
Vaccine effectiveness rate (e)	.75 [.65, .85]	Fraction of vaccinated who develop
Hours lost (t)	24 [18, 30]	Average number of work hours lost to illness
Infection rate (i)	.25 [.20, .30]	Infection rate without vaccine
First-year epidemic probability (p_1)	.40	Chance of epidemic in current year
Second-year epidemic probability (p_2)	.20	Chance of epidemic next year
Vaccine dose price (q)	$9/dose	Price per dose of vaccine
Overhead cost (o)	$120,000	Costs not dependent on number vaccinated
Opportunity cost of time (w)	$20/hour	Average wage rate (including benefits) in the county
Value of life (L)	$10,000,000	Assumed value of life
Discount rate (d)	.035	Real discount rate
Number high-risk vaccinations (V_h)	13,680	High-risk persons vaccinated: $v_h r N$
Number low-risk vaccinations (V_l)	17,860	Low-risk persons vaccinated: $v_l(1-r)N$
Fraction vaccinated (v)	.083	Fraction of total population vaccinated: $rv_h + v_l(1-r)$

The benefits of vaccination arise through two impacts. First, those effectively vaccinated are immune to the influenza. Thus, the program targets persons with high mortality risk because they benefit most from immunity. Second, through what is known as the *herd immunity* effect, a positive externality, vaccinated persons reduce the risks of infection to those not vaccinated – this is the reason why some low-risk persons are recruited for vaccination to increase the total fraction of the population that is vaccinated.[15] These two effects cause the expected costs of the epidemic with vaccination, $C_{e|v}$, to be less than the expected costs of the epidemic without the vaccination program, $C_{e|nv}$.

Table 11.3 relates the specific numerical assumptions in Table 11.2 to the parameters in Figure 11.2. From Table 11.3, we see that the direct program costs, C_a, depend on the overhead (i.e., fixed) costs, o, and cost per vaccination, q, times the number of vaccinations given ($V_h + V_l$). The costs of side effects, C_s, depend on the adverse reaction rate, α, the number vaccinated, and the cost per high-risk infection, $wt + m_h L$, where wt is the opportunity cost of lost labor and $m_h L$ is the cost of loss of life. The epidemic's costs without the vaccination program, $C_{e|nv}$, depend on the infection rate, i, the number of high-risk susceptibles, rN, the number of low-risk susceptibles, $(1 - r)N$, and the costs per high- and low-risk infections. Finally, the cost of the epidemic with the vaccination program, $C_{e|v}$, depends on the post-vaccination infection rate, $i - \theta ve$, the number of high-risk individuals remaining susceptible, $rN - eV_h$, the number of low-risk individuals remaining susceptible, $(1 - r)N - eV_l$, and the costs per low- and high-risk infections. Working through these formulas in Table 11.3 yields expected net benefits equal to $20.3 million for the base-case assumptions presented in Table 11.2.

Partial Sensitivity Analysis. An important assumption in the analysis is the probability that the epidemic occurs. In the base case, we assume that the probability of the epidemic in the next year, given no epidemic in the current year, p_2, is one-half the probability of the epidemic in the current year, p_1. To investigate the relationship between net benefits and the probability of epidemic, we vary p_1 (and, hence, p_2) holding all other base-case values constant. Specifically, we vary p_1 from 0 to 0.5 by increments

Table 11.3 *Formulas for Calculating the Net Benefits of Vaccination Program*

Variable	Value (millions of dollars)	Formula
C_a	0.404	$o + (V_h + V_l)q$
C_s	9.916	$\alpha(V_h + V_l)(wt + m_h L)$
$C_{e|nv}$	147.3	$i[rN(wt + m_h L) + (1 - r)N(wt + m_l L]$
$C_{e|v}$	87.9	$(i - \theta ve)\{(rN - eV_h)(wt + m_h L) + [(1 - r)N - eV_l](wt + m_l L)\}$
ECv	55.7	$C_a + C_s + p_1 C_{e|v} + (1 - p_1)p_2 C_{e|v}/(1 + d)$
EC_{nv}	76.0	$p_1 C_{e|v} + (1 - p_1)p_2 C_{e|v}/(1 + d)$
$E[NB]$	20.3	$EC_{nv} - EC_v$

of 0.05. We thereby isolate the marginal partial effect of changes in probability on net benefits.

The results of this procedure are displayed as the line labeled $L = \$10$ million in Figure 11.3. This label reminds us of another base-case assumption: the value of life equals $10 million, which we vary next. Because the equations underlying the calculation of net benefits were embedded in a spreadsheet on a personal computer, it was easy to generate the points needed to draw this line by simply changing the values of p_1 and recording the corresponding net benefits.

As expected, this line is upward-sloping: the higher the probability of the epidemic, the larger the net benefits of the vaccination program. For values of p_1 less than about 0.12, net benefits become negative (i.e., the upward-sloping line lies below the solid horizontal line). In other words, if we think that the probability of the epidemic in the current year is less than 0.12, and we are willing to accept the other base-case assumptions, then we should not implement the program. The probability at which net benefits switch sign is called the *breakeven value*. Finding and reporting breakeven values for various parameters is often a useful way to convey their importance.

The line labeled $L = \$5$ million repeats the procedure changing the base-case assumption of the value of life from $10 million per life to $5 million per life.[16] The graph thus conveys information about the impact of changes in two assumptions: Each line individually gives the marginal impact of epidemic probability; looking across lines

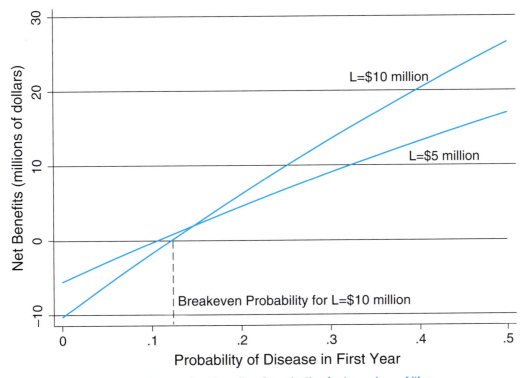

Figure 11.3 Expected net benefits of vaccination for two values of life.

conveys information about the impact of changes in the assumed value of life. As this illustration suggests, we can easily consider the sensitivity of net benefits to changing two assumptions at the same time by constructing families of curves in a two-dimensional graph. Although computers make it feasible to produce graphs that appear three-dimensional, the added information that these graphs convey is often difficult to process visually and therefore should be avoided.

Figure 11.4 considers one more example of partial sensitivity analysis. It repeats the investigation of the marginal impact of epidemic probability on net benefits for two different assumptions about the size of the herd immunity effect, θ. The upper curve is for the base case that assumes a full herd immunity effect ($\theta = 1$). The lower curve assumes that only one half of the effect occurs ($\theta = .5$), perhaps because the population does not mix sufficiently uniformly for the simple model of herd immunity assumed in the base case to apply. (Both cases return to the base-case assumption of $10 million per life saved.) Now the breakeven probability rises to over 0.16 for the weaker herd immunity effect. Of course, we could instead give primary focus to the herd immunity effect by graphing net benefits against the size of the herd immunity effect, holding epidemic probability constant.

A thorough investigation of sensitivity ideally considers the partial marginal impacts of changes in each of the important assumptions. However, there is a "chicken and egg" problem: Identifying the important assumptions often cannot be done before

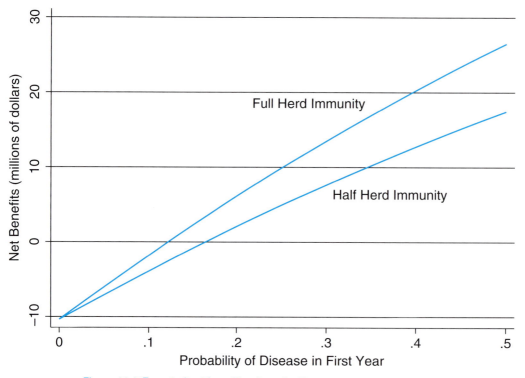

Figure 11.4 Expected net benefits of vaccination.

actually doing the sensitivity analysis because importance depends on the marginal response of net benefits to changes in assumptions, as well as the plausible range of the assumptions. In the analysis of the vaccination program, for example, partial sensitivity analysis might well be warranted for most of the assumptions presented in Table 11.2.

Worst- and Best-Case Analysis. The base-case assumptions, which generally assign the most plausible numerical values to unknown parameters, produce an estimate of net benefits that we think is most likely. In the vaccination program example, these assumptions yield fairly large positive net benefits. We can put a plausible lower bound on net benefits by considering the least favorable of the *plausible range* of values for each of the assumptions. In this way, we can calculate a pessimistic prediction of net benefits. Also, we can calculate an optimistic prediction of net benefits by using the most favorable assumptions. As we discuss later in the chapter, information usually has value in decision-making to the extent it can potentially lead us to make a different choice. Therefore, worst-case analysis is generally most valuable when the base-case expected net benefits are positive; best-case analysis is generally most valuable when the base-case expected net benefits are negative. It should be kept in mind, however, that even if the ranges are plausible, the probability of actually realizing net benefits as extreme as either the worst or the best case gets very small as the number of parameters gets large.

Worst-case analysis acknowledges that society, or specific decision-makers, may be risk-averse. That is, they often care not just about expected net benefits, the appropriate consideration in most cases, but also about the possible "downside." Furthermore, as we point out in Chapters 1 and 8, there are often cognitive limitations and bureaucratic incentives to generate optimistic forecasts. Worst-case analysis may provide a useful check against these biases.

As a demonstration of worst-case analysis, we take the lower end of each of the ranges presented in Table 11.2 for r, v_h, v_l, m_l, m_h, θ, e, t, and i, and the higher end of the range for α. For example, we assume that r, the fraction of the population at high mortality risk, equals 0.04 rather than the base-case value of 0.06. (For the time being, we keep p_1, p_2, q, o, w, L, and d at their base-case values.) With worst-case assumptions, net benefits fall to $0.11 million. Although still positive, this more conservative estimate is more than two orders of magnitude (10^2) less than under the base-case assumptions.

Return to the question of the sensitivity of net benefits to the probability of epidemic. The breakeven probability rises from about 12 percent under the base-case assumptions to almost 42 percent under the more conservative worst-case assumptions. In other words, expected net benefits would no longer be positive if we assessed the probability of an epidemic to be only 0.4, the assumed value under the base case.

Care must be taken in determining the most conservative assumptions. Under the base-case assumptions, for example, net benefits increase as our assumed value of life increases. Under the conservative assumptions, however, net benefits decrease as the value of life increases. This reversal in the direction of the marginal impact of the value of life occurs because the higher rate of adverse reactions, α, under the conservative case is sufficiently large so that the expected number of deaths is greater with the vaccination program (1.8 deaths) than without it (1.7 deaths).

More generally, caution is warranted when net benefits are a non-linear function of a parameter. In such cases, the value of the parameter that either minimizes or maximizes net benefits may not be at the extreme of its plausible range. Close inspection of partial sensitivity graphs generally gives a good indication of the general nature of the relationship, although these graphs can sometimes be misleading because they depend on the particular assumed values of all other parameters. A more systematic approach is to inspect the functional form of the model used to calculate net benefits. When a non-linear relationship is present, extreme values of assumptions may not necessarily result in extreme values of net benefits. Indeed, inspection of Table 11.3 indicates that net benefits are a quadratic function of vaccination rates v_l and v_h because they depend on $C_{e|v}$, which involves the product of direct effects and the herd effect. Under the base-case assumptions, for instance, net benefits would be maximized if all high-risk persons were vaccinated and 46 percent of low-risk persons were vaccinated. As these rates are well above those that could realistically be obtained by the program, we can reasonably treat the upper and lower bounds of vaccination rates as corresponding to extreme values of net benefits.

If the base-case assumptions generate negative net benefits, then it would have been reasonable to see if more optimistic, or best-case, assumptions produce positive net benefits. If the best-case prediction of net benefits is still negative, then we can be very certain that the policy should not be adopted. If it is positive, then we may want to see if combinations of somewhat less-optimistic assumptions can also sustain positive net benefits.

Monte Carlo Simulations. Partial- and extreme-case sensitivity analyses have two major limitations. First, they may not take account of all the available information about assumed values of parameters. In particular, if we believe that values near the base-case assumptions are more likely to occur than values near the extremes of their plausible ranges, then the worst and best cases are highly unlikely to occur because they require the joint occurrence of a large number of independent low-probability events. Second, these techniques do not directly provide information about the variance, or spread, of the statistical distribution of realized net benefits, which conveys the riskiness of the point estimates. Further, if we cannot distinguish between two policies in terms of expected values of net benefits, then we may be more confident in recommending the one with the smaller variance because it has a higher probability of producing realized net benefits near the expected value.

Monte Carlo simulation provides a way of overcoming these problems. The name derives from the casinos of that famous gambling resort. It is apt because the essence of the approach is playing games of chance many times to elicit a distribution of outcomes. Monte Carlo simulation plays an important role in the investigation of statistical estimators whose properties cannot be adequately determined through mathematical techniques alone. The low opportunity cost of computing makes Monte Carlo simulation feasible for most practicing policy analysts. Because it effectively accounts for uncertainty in complex analyses, it should be in every analyst's tool kit. *Indeed, it should be routinely used in CBA.*

There are three basic steps in performing Monte Carlo simulations. First, the analyst should specify probability distributions for all the important uncertain quantitative assumptions. For the Monte Carlo simulation of the vaccine program, the analysis focuses on the 10 parameters with expressed ranges in Table 11.2. If one does not have theory or empirical evidence that suggests a particular distribution, then it is reasonable to specify a uniform distribution over the range. That is, the most reasonable assumption is that any value between the upper and lower bound of plausible values is equally likely. For example, the analysis assumes that the distribution of the fraction of the population at risk, r, is uniformly distributed between 0.04 and 0.08. Often, though, a more reasonable assumption is that some values near the most plausible estimate should be given more weight. For example, analysts may believe that hours lost due to influenza follow a normal distribution. They could then center it at the best estimate of 24 hours and set the standard deviation at 3.06 so that there is only a 5 percent chance of values falling outside the most plausible range of 18 to 30 hours. (See Appendix 11A for a brief discussion of working with probability distributions.) As discussed in Chapter 4, analysts can sometimes estimate unknown parameters statistically using regression analysis or other techniques. Commonly used regression models allow analysts to approximate the distribution of an unknown parameter as normal with mean and standard deviation given by their empirical estimates.

The second step is to execute a trial by taking a random draw from the distribution for each parameter to arrive at a set of specific values for computing realized net benefits. For example, in the case of the vaccination program analysis, analysts have to determine which contingencies are likely to occur in each of the two periods. To determine if an epidemic occurs in the current year, they take a draw from a Bernoulli distribution with probability p_1 of yielding "epidemic" and $(1 - p_1)$ of yielding "no epidemic." That is, it is as if one were to flip a coin that has a probability of p_1 of landing with "epidemic" face up. Almost all spreadsheets allow users to take draws from random variables uniformly distributed between 0 and 1 – a draw from the uniform distribution produces an outcome within this range that is as likely to occur as any other outcome in the range. Thus there is a p_1 probability of a value between zero and p_1 occurring. To implement a draw from a Bernoulli distribution that has a probability of p_1 of yielding "epidemic," one simply compares the draw from the uniform distribution to p_1: If the random draw from the uniform distribution is smaller (larger) than p_1, then assume that an epidemic does (not) occur in the current year; if an epidemic does not occur in the current year, then follow a similar procedure to determine if an epidemic occurs in the second year. Three mutually exclusive realizations of net benefits are possible:

Epidemic in neither year: $NB = -(C_a + C_s)$

Epidemic in current year: $NB = -(C_a + C_s) + (C_{e|nv} - C_{e|v})$

Epidemic in next year: $NB = -(C_a + C_s) + (C_{e|nv} - C_{e|v})/(1 + d)$

where the value of NB depends on the particular values of the parameters drawn for this trial.[17]

Exhibit 11.3

Influenza vaccination programs are usually targeted to those in high-risk groups, such as infants, the elderly, and people with compromised immune systems. Is vaccination of healthy workers cost-beneficial? Kristin L. Nichols attempts to answer this question with a cost–benefit analysis. Benefits of vaccination include avoided lost work days, hospitalizations, and deaths. Costs include the costs of the vaccination and lost work days, hospitalizations, and deaths from side effects. She employed Monte Carlo analysis to estimate net benefits. Noting that previous studies reported that managers generally took fewer sick days than other personnel, she built a negative correlation between sick days and wage rate, two of the important parameters, into the Monte Carlo trials. She estimated the mean value of net benefits to be $18.27 (2010 dollars) with a 95 percent confidence interval ranging from $44.10 in positive net benefits to $2.92 in negative net benefits. In order to assess the relative importance of various assumed parameters to net benefits, she regressed the net benefits from each trial on the randomly drawn values of the parameters. Net benefits were most sensitive to the illness rate, the work absenteeism rate due to influenza, and the hourly wages. In addition, a poor match between the vaccine and the circulating virus strain gave negative net benefits. Not surprisingly, the 95 percent confidence interval from the Monte Carlo analysis was much tighter than the best/worst-case range of positive net benefits of $233.15 to negative net benefits of $28.45.

Source: Adapted from Kristin L. Nichol, "Cost–Benefit Analysis of a Strategy to Vaccinate Healthy Working Adults Against Influenza." *Archives of Internal Medicine*, 161(5), 2001, 749–59.

Note that these estimates of *NB* no longer involve expectations with respect to the contingencies of epidemics, though the cost estimates themselves are expected values.

In the third step, one repeats the trial described in the second step many times – typically a thousand times or more – to produce a large number of realizations of net benefits. The average of these trials provides an estimate of the expected value of net benefits. An approximation of the probability distribution of net benefits can be obtained by breaking the range of realized net benefits into a number of equal increments and counting the frequency with which trials fall into each one. The resulting *histogram* of these counts provides a picture of the distribution. The more trials that go into the histogram, the more likely it is that the resulting picture gives a good representation of the distribution of net benefits. Underlying this procedure is the law of large numbers: as the number of trials approaches infinity, the frequencies will converge to the true underlying probabilities.

Figure 11.5 presents a histogram of 10,000 replications of random draws from the bracketed assumptions in Table 11.2. The assumed distributions are all uniform except that for hours lost, *t*, which follows a normal distribution, and whether or not the epidemic occurs, which, although a Bernoulli distribution, is implemented with the readily available uniform distribution. The height of each bar is proportional to the number of trials that had net benefits falling in the corresponding increment.

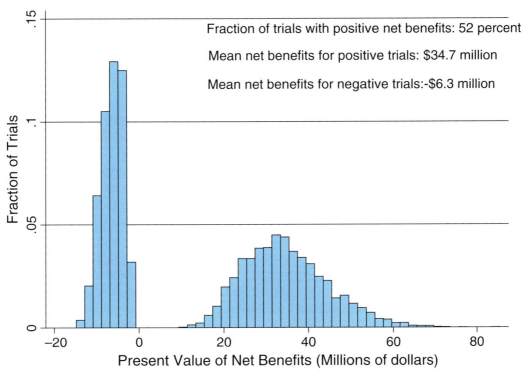

Figure 11.5 Histogram of realized net benefits.

The average of net benefits over the 10,000 trials is $15.0 million. This differs from our base-case calculation of $20.3 million because the base-case value of the herd immunity factor, θ, was set at 1 rather than at the middle point of the plausible range. Repeating the Monte Carlo procedure with the herd immunity factor set to 1 yields an average of realized net benefits of $18.7 million, which is close to the base-case calculation of expected net benefits.[18]

The histogram provides a visual display of the entire distribution of net benefits so that its spread and symmetry can be easily discerned. The trials themselves can be used to calculate directly the sample variance, standard deviation, fraction of positive trials, and other summary statistics describing net benefits.

The most striking feature of the histogram is that it reveals a bimodal distribution. If an epidemic occurs in either year, then the vaccination program has positive net benefits and it is as if we are drawing only from the right-most hump of the distribution. If an epidemic occurs in neither year, then the vaccination program has negative net benefits and it is as if we are drawing from the left-most hump of the distribution. The assumed probabilities of epidemic in the two years leads one to expect positive net benefits 52 percent of the time $[p_1 + (1 - p_1) p_2]$, which is close to the 52.8 percent of trials with positive net benefits in the Monte Carlo simulation.

The Monte Carlo results presented in Figure 11.5 treat several parameters as if they are certain. Most importantly, they treat the values of time, the value of a statistical life, and the discount rate as certain. As we explain in Chapter 17, however, these values are uncertain. Distributions for the values of these parameters could be specified and included in an expanded simulation. Doing so would be most appropriate for the values of time and the value of a statistical life. Another approach, more appropriate for uncertainty about the discount rate, would be to repeat the Monte Carlo simulation for specific values of the parameters rather than including them within a single simulation. For example, as noted in the discussion of the regulatory cases following Chapter 4, the Office of Management and Budget recommends discounting at real rates of 3 and 7 percent. This recommendation could be followed by conducting a separate Monte Carlo simulation at each of these discount rates.

The illustration also assumes that the parameters are independent of one another. In practice, they may be correlated. However, in order to take these correlations into account, one would need to know the variance–covariance matrix of the parameters. Such more sophisticated approaches are beyond the scope of this book.

Sensitivity Analysis Strategy. We recommend the following strategy for conducting sensitivity analysis: First, when there are more than a few uncertain parameters, the most common situation in doing real-world CBA, the analyst should use Monte Carlo simulation as the framework for the analysis. Rather than reporting net benefits based on beliefs about the most likely values of parameters, report the mean value of net benefits from the Monte Carlo trials. To convey the degree of uncertainty about prediction of net benefits, show the histogram of net benefits across trials and report the fraction of trials with positive net benefits.[19] Second, use partial sensitivity analysis to focus attention on how the values of particularly important parameters affect net benefits. The parameters may be important because they have large effects on net benefits, their values are highly uncertain, or because of expectations that specific values of certain parameters, such as the discount rate, be used. Finally, only use worst- and best-case analyses as a fallback expediency when Monte Carlo simulation is impractical.

11.3   Information and Quasi-Option Value

The various analytical techniques developed in the previous sections provide a basis for assessing uncertainty in information about assumed or estimated parameters used in CBA. In this section we demonstrate the use of games against nature to place value on information itself. Use of the normal form illustrates the basic concepts. One then uses decision trees to explicate a particular information value, the quasi-option value, which arises in the context of delaying irreversible decisions, which allows time for the gathering or revelation of information about the future.

11.3.1   *Introduction to the Value of Information*

The value of information in the context of a game against nature answers the following question: by how much would the information increase the expected value of playing the game? As an example of how to answer this question, return to the asteroid defense game presented in Table 11.1. Imagine that scientists have proposed developing a detection device that would allow them to determine with certainty whether the Earth would be exposed to a collision with a large asteroid (diameter greater than one kilometer) in the next 100 years. What is the maximum investment that should be made to develop this device?

If the device were to be built, then it would reveal which of two possible futures were true: First, with a probability of 0.001, it would show that there would be a collision with a large asteroid. Second, with a probability of 0.999, it would show that there would be no collision with a large asteroid. Each of these two futures implies a different game against nature, as shown in Table 11.4.

Game One, shown on the left side of Table 11.4, results if the detection device indicates that the Earth will be exposed to collision with a large asteroid. Not surprisingly, in this game the best action is to choose forward-based asteroid defense, which has the smallest net costs of the three actions ($5,060 billion). Game Two, shown on the right side of Table 11.4, results if the detection device indicates that the Earth will not be exposed to collision with a large asteroid. As exposure to collision with a large asteroid is ruled out, the probabilities of the other two possible states of nature are adjusted upward so that they sum to 1 (0.004004 and 0.995996). In this game, the best action is

Table 11.4 *Reformulated Games against Nature: Value of Device for Detecting Large Asteroids*

State of nature	Game One $p = 0.001$	Game Two $p = 0.9999$	
	Exposure to a collision with an asteroid larger than 1 km in diameter	Exposure to a collision with an asteroid between 20 m and 1 km in diameter	No exposure to collision with an asteroid larger than 20 m in diameter
Probabilities of states of nature (over next century)	1	0.004004	0.995996

Actions (alternatives)	Pay-offs (net costs in billions of 2000 dollars)	Expected value	Pay-offs (net costs in billions of 2000 dollars)		Expected value
Forward-based asteroid defense	5,060	**5,060**	1,060	60	64.01
Near-Earth asteroid defense	10,020	10,020	2,020	20	28.01
No asteroid defense	30,000	30,000	6,000	0	**24.02**

Game One: Choose forward-based asteroid defense: Expected net cost = $5,060 billion.
Game Two: Choose no asteroid defense: Expected net cost = $24.02 billion.
Expected net cost of decision with detection device:
(0.001)($5,060 billion) + (0.999)($24.02 billion) = $29.06 billion.
Value of information provided by detection device: $38 billion − $29.06 billion = $8.94 billion.

to choose no asteroid defense, which has the smallest net costs of the three alternative actions ($24.02 billion).

Prior to developing the detection device, we do not know which of these two games nature will give us to play. We do know, however, that it will indicate Game One with probability 0.001 and Game Two with probability 0.999. Thus it is possible to compute an expected net cost over the two games as (0.001)($5,060 billion) + (0.999)($24.02 billion) = $29.06 billion. In order to place a value on the information provided by the device, the analyst compares the expected net cost of the optimal choice in the game without it (the $38 billion shown in Table 11.1) with the expected net cost resulting from optimal choices in the games with it ($29.06 billion). The difference between these net costs ($38 billion −$29.06 billion) equals $8.94 billion, which is the value of the information provided by the device. Consequently, as long as the detection device costs less than $8.94 billion, it would be efficient to develop it.

Note that the value of the information derives from the fact that it leads to different optimal decisions. The optimal choice without the device is near-Earth asteroid defense. The optimal choice with the device is either forward-based asteroid defense if collision exposure is confirmed or no asteroid defense if the absence of collision exposure is confirmed.

In practice, analysts rarely face choices requiring them to value perfect information of the sort provided by the asteroid detection device. They do, however, routinely face choices involving the allocation of resources – time, energy, budgets – toward reducing uncertainty in the values of the many parameters used to calculate net benefits. For example, a statistical estimate based on a random sample size of 600 will be much more precise than one based on a sample of 300. How can the analyst determine if the investment in the larger sample size is worthwhile?

In a CBA involving many assumed parameters, Monte Carlo simulation can provide especially useful information. For example, suppose an agency is deciding whether it is worthwhile to invest analytical resources in conducting a study that would reduce the estimate of the variance of hours lost from the influenza described in the previous section. One could replicate the analysis presented in Figure 11.5 with a smaller assumed variance of hours lost and compare the resulting distribution of net benefits to that resulting with the larger variance. A necessary condition for the investment of analytical resources to be worthwhile is a meaningful change in the distribution of realized net benefits.

Exhibit 11.4

Research and development projects typically have very uncertain costs and benefits when they are initiated. Based on an assessment of detailed case studies of six research and development projects (Supersonic Transport, Applications Technology Satellite Program, Space Shuttle, Clinch River Breeder Reactor, Synthetics Fuels from Coal, and Photovoltaics Commercialization), Cohen and Noll concluded: "The final success of a program usually hinges on a few key technical objectives and baseline economic assumptions about demand or the cost of alternative technologies, or both. The results of the research that addressed the key technical issues, and realizations a few years after that program was started of the key unknown economic parameters, typically made the likely success of a project very clear" (p. 82).

For example, Susan Edelman prepared CBAs of the supersonic transport project with the information that would have been available to conscientious analysts in each of a number of years. She reports that the plausible range of benefit–cost ratios fell from 1.97 to 4.97 in 1963 to 1.32 to 1.84 in 1971. They declined as it became clear that either higher operating costs or reduced loads would result from failures to achieve technical objectives and that operations over land would likely be restricted to reduce the impacts of sonic booms on people (pp. 112–21).

Source: Adapted from Linda R. Cohen and Roger G. Noll, editors, *The Technology Pork Barrel* (Washington, DC: The Brookings Institution, 1991).

11.3.2   *Quasi-Option Value*

It may be wise to delay a decision if better information relevant to the decision will become available in the future. This is especially the case when the costs of returning to the status quo once a project has begun are so large that the decision is effectively irreversible. For example, consider the decision of whether to develop a virgin wilderness area. Analysts may be fairly certain about the costs and benefits of development to the current generation, but be very uncertain of the opportunity cost to future generations of losing the virgin wilderness. If information revealed over time would reduce uncertainty about how future generations will value the wilderness area, then it may be desirable to delay a decision about irreversible development to incorporate the new information into the decision process. The expected value of information gained by delaying an irreversible decision is called *quasi-option value*.[20]

Quasi-option value can be quantified by explicitly formulating a multiperiod decision problem that allows for the revelation of information about the value of options in later periods.[21] Although some environmental analysts see quasi-option value as a distinct benefit category for policies that preserve unique assets such as wilderness areas, scenic views, and animal species, it is more appropriately thought of as a correction to the calculation of expected net benefits through an inappropriate one-period decision problem. As the calculation of quasi-option value itself requires specification of the proper decision problem, *whenever quasi-option value can be quantified, the correct expected net benefits can and should be calculated directly.*

As background for an illustration of quasi-option value, Table 11.5 sets out the parameters for a CBA of alternatives for use of a wilderness area. The value of net benefits from full development (*FD*) and limited development (*LD*) are measured relative to no development (*ND*) for two contingencies. Under the contingency labeled "Low Value," which will occur with a probability *p*, future generations place the

Table 11.5 *Benefits and Costs of Alternative Development Policies Assuming No Learning*

	Preservation contingencies	
	Low value	High value
Full development (*FD*)	B_F	$-C_F$
Limited development (*LD*)	B_L	$-C_L$
No development (*LD*)	0	0
Probability of contingency	p	$1 - p$
Expected value of full development:	$E[FD] = pB_F - (1-p)C_F$	
Expected value of limited development:	$E[LD] = pB_L - (1-p)C_L$	
Expected value of no development:	$E[ND] = 0$	
Adopt full development if:	$pB_F - (1-p)C_F > pB_L - (1-p)C_L$ and $pB_F - (1-p)C_F > 0$	

same value as current generations on preservation of the wilderness area. Under the contingency labeled "High Value," which will occur with a probability $1 - p$, future generations place a much higher value than current generations on preservation of the wilderness area. If the Low Value contingency occurs, then *FD* yields a positive present value of net benefits equal to B_F and *LD* yields a positive present value of net benefits equal to B_L. That is, after taking account of all costs and benefits, the present value of net benefits for *FD* and *LD* are the positive amounts B_F and B_L, respectively. If, instead, the High Value contingency occurs, then *FD* yields a negative present value of net benefits equal to $-C_F$ and *LD* yields a negative present value of net benefits equal to $-C_L$, where C_F and C_L are net costs and therefore signed negative to be the present value of net benefits. Assume that $B_F > B_L > 0$ and $C_F > C_L > 0$ so that *FD* yields greater net benefits under the Low Value contingency and greater net costs under the High Value contingency than *LD*.

Imagine that the analyst conducts a CBA assuming that no learning will occur over time. That is, assuming that no useful information will be revealed in future periods. The expected net benefits of *FD* equal $pB_F - (1-p)C_F$; the expected net benefits of *LD* equal $pB_L - (1-p)C_L$; and the expected net benefit of *ND* equals 0. One would simply choose the alternative with the largest expected net benefits.

Now consider the case of *exogenous learning*. That is, one assumes that after the first period one discovers with certainty which of the two contingencies will occur. Learning is exogenous in the sense that the information is revealed irrespective of what action is undertaken.

Figure 11.6 presents a decision tree for the exogenous learning situation. The square box at the extreme left-hand side of the figure represents the initial decision. If one selects *FD*, then the result is the same expected value as in the case of no learning – the decision is irreversible and, hence, learning has no value because there is no decision left to make in period 2. If one selects either *LD* or *ND* in the first period, then there is a decision left to make in period 2 once one knows which contingency has occurred. The

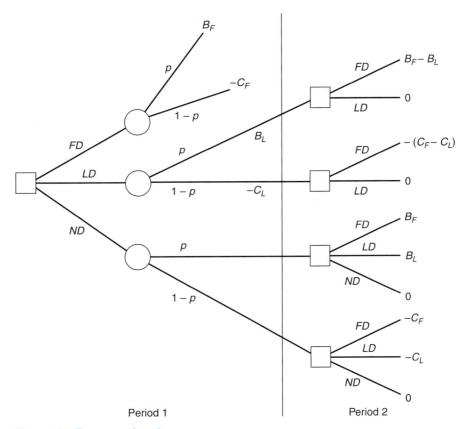

Figure 11.6 Exogenous learning.

expected values of the LD and ND decisions in period 1 can be found using the backward induction method introduced in the vaccine example developed earlier in the chapter.

First, consider LD. If the Low Value contingency is revealed at the beginning of period 2, then the optimal decision will be to complete the development to obtain net benefits $B_F - B_L$. The present value of this amount is obtained by discounting at rate d. It is then added to B_L, the period 1 net benefits, to obtain the net benefits of LD conditional on the Low Value contingency occurring. If the High Value contingency is revealed at the beginning of period 2, then the optimal decision is to forgo further development so that the net benefits conditional on the High Value contingency occurring consist only of the $-C_L$ realized in period 1. Multiplying these conditional net benefits by their respective probabilities yields the expected net benefits for limited development in period 1 of $p[B_L + (B_F - B_L)/(1 + d)] - (1 - p)C_L$. Note that it differs from the expected value in the no-learning case by the expected net benefits of the period 2 option, $p(B_F - B_L)/(1 + d)$, which is the quasi-option value of LD.

Next consider the decision ND in period 1. If the Low Value contingency is revealed at the beginning of period 2, then the optimal decision is FD, which has a present value of $B_F/(1 + d)$. If the High Value contingency is revealed at the beginning of period 2, then the optimal decision is ND, which has a present value of 0. Consequently, the expected net benefits from choosing ND in period 1 are $pB_F/(1+d)$, which equal the quasi-option value of ND.

The middle column of Table 11.6 summarizes the expected values of the period 1 alternatives for the case of exogenous learning.

Figure 11.7 presents a decision tree for the endogenous learning situation. Unlike the situation with exogenous learning, information is generated only from development itself. For example, the value placed on preservation by future generations may depend on the risk that development poses to a species of bird that feeds in the wilderness area during its migration. The effect of limited development on the species may provide

Table 11.6 *Expected Values for Decision Problems: Quasi-Option Values (QOV) Measured Relative to No Learning Case*

	No learning	Exogenous learning	Endogenous learning
$E[FD]$	$pB_F - (1-p)C_F$	$pB_F - (1-p)C_F$	$pB_F - (1-p)C_F$
QOV		0	0
$E[LD]$	$pB_L - (1-p)C_L$	$p[B_L + (B_F + B_L)/(1+d)] - (1-p)C_L$	$p[B_L + (B_F - B_L)/(1+d)] - (1-p)C_L$
QOV		$p(B_F - B_L)/(1+d)$	$p(B_F - B_L)/(1+d)$
$E[ND]$	0	$pB_F(1+d)$	0
QOV		$pB_F/(1+d)$	$= 0$

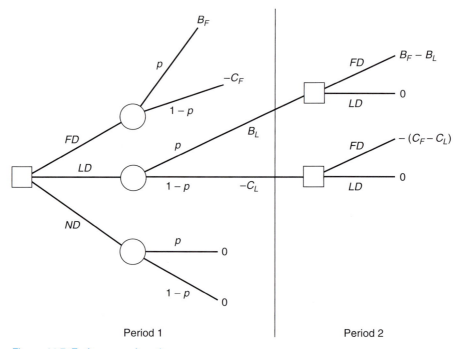

Period 1   Period 2

Figure 11.7 Endogenous learning.

enough information to permit a reliable prediction of the effect of full development. If no development is undertaken, then no new information will be available at the beginning of the second period. If full development is undertaken, then new information will be generated, but there will be no decision for it to affect.

As shown in the last column of Table 11.6, the expected net benefits for the *FD* and *LD* alternatives with endogenous learning are identical to those with exogenous learning. The expected net benefits of *ND* are zero, however, because there will be no new information to alter the decision not to develop in the future.

Table 11.7 compares the different learning cases for a specific set of parameter values. If the analyst specifies the decision problem as one of no learning, then *FD* has the largest expected net benefits. Imagine that instead one specifies the decision problem as one of exogenous learning. Now *ND* has the largest expected net benefits. Furthermore, relative to the case of no learning, the quasi-option value of *ND* is $46.3 million ($46.3 million − 0) and the quasi-option value of *LD* is $23.15 million ($28.15 million − $5 million). Now instead specify the decision problem as one with endogenous learning. *LD* now has the largest expected net benefits. Relative to the case of no learning, the quasi-option value of *LD* is $23.15 million ($28.15 million − $5 million), and the quasi-option value of *ND* is 0 (0 − 0).

This simple numerical illustration conforms to the common intuition about quasi-option value: *It tends to be large for no development in cases of exogenous learning and large for limited development in cases of endogenous learning.* It is important to keep in mind, however, that the illustration is based on very stylized models of learning. Differently specified models could yield different rankings and different quasi-option values for the alternatives. Even with this simple model, different numerical assumptions could lead to different rankings of alternatives.

Note that the numerical estimates of quasi-option values in the illustration depend on expected values calculated by comparing what was assumed to be the correct two-period decision problem to a one-period decision problem that fails to consider the potential for learning. Of course, if one knows the correct decision problem, then there would be no need to concern ourselves with quasi-option value as a separate benefit

Table 11.7 *Numerical Illustration of Quasi-Option Value (millions of dollars)*

Expected value	No learning	Exogenous learning	Endogenous learning
$E[FD]$	10.00	10.00	10.00
$E[LD]$	5.00	28.15	28.15
$E[ND]$	0.00	46.30	0.00

Assumptions:

$B_F = 100$ $C_F = 80$
$B_L = 50$ $C_L = 40$
$p = .5$ $d = .08$

category because solving the decision problem would lead to the appropriate calculations of expected net benefits.

Quasi-Option Value in Practice

How should analysts treat quasi-option value in practice? Two heuristics seem warranted. First, *quantitative quasi-option values should be based on an explicit decision problem that structures the calculation of the expected net benefits.* An explicit decision problem focuses attention on the key assumptions that determine the magnitude of quasi-option value. It also makes it unnecessary to consider quasi-option value as a distinct benefit category. Second, *when insufficient knowledge is available to formulate a decision problem for explicitly calculating the magnitude of quasi-option value, it should be discussed as a possible source of bias rather than added as an arbitrary quantitative adjustment to expected net benefits.* As with other biases, one can ask the question: How big would quasi-option value have to be to affect the ranking of policies?

11.4   Conclusion

Uncertainty is inherent to some degree in every CBA. Through expected value analysis, the analyst attempts to average over the possible contingencies to arrive at expected net benefits as a plausible prediction of net benefits. In situations not explicitly involving risk, one often assumes parameter values that are more appropriately thought of as draws from probability distributions rather than as certainties. The purpose of sensitivity analysis is to determine how net benefits change if these parameters deviate from their assumed values. Partial sensitivity analysis, the most commonly used approach, focuses attention on the consequences of alternative assumptions about key parameters. Extreme-case analysis examines whether combinations of plausible assumptions exist that reverse the sign of net benefits. Monte Carlo simulation attempts to estimate the distribution of net benefits by explicitly treating assumed parameter values as random variables. It is especially useful when the risk of the policy is of particular concern and the formula for the calculation of net benefits involves the uncertain parameters in other than simple sums; that is, when uncertain parameters are multiplied or divided. While the nature of the policy under consideration and the resources available to the analysts attempting to estimate its benefits and costs determine the appropriate form of sensitivity analysis, every CBA should be subjected to tests of its sensitivity to the assumptions it employs.

Explicit decision analysis frameworks, including games against nature in both normal and extensive form, provide a basis for assessing the value of information in risky circumstances. It allows an explicit calculation of quasi-option value, which is sometimes treated as a separate benefit category in CBAs. Quasi-option values take account of the value of being able to act upon future information. As solving a correctly specified decision problem naturally incorporates quasi-option values, they need not be treated as distinct benefits. Quantitative claims about quasi-option values should be based on an explicit decision problem.

APPENDIX 11A

Monte Carlo Sensitivity Analysis using Commonly Available Software

Two types of generally available software allow analysts to do Monte Carlo simulations easily. Spreadsheets allow it to be done by making rows correspond to trials; statistical packages allow it to be done by making observations correspond to trials. Spreadsheets greatly reduce the labor needed to conduct all the types of sensitivity analysis. Although specialized software is available for doing Monte Carlo analysis, such as Crystal Ball (Decisioneering, Inc.) for use with Excel and DATA (TreeAge, Inc.) for decision analysis, with a bit of effort Monte Carlo simulation can be done with any simple spreadsheet that provides random number generators. Similarly, any statistical package that provides a random number generator can be used. For very complicated simulations, statistical packages that allow structured programming, such as the creation of macros and subprograms, offer greater transparency that helps avoid errors.

Specifying Distributions for Uncertain Parameters

In many situations, analysts are willing to put bounds on the value of uncertain parameters, but unwilling to assume that any values within these bounds are more or less likely than any others. In such cases, uniform distributions are appropriate. Most spreadsheets and statistical packages provide a function for generating random variables that are distributed uniformly from 0 to 1. For example, in Excel, the function RAND() returns a draw from this distribution; in the statistical package Stata, runiform() does so. To generate uniform random variables with other ranges, one simply multiplies the draw from the random variable uniformly distributed from 0 to 1 by the desired range and then adds the minimum value. So, for example, to get the appropriate random variable for the fraction of high-risk persons in the population, r in Table 11.2, use the following formula: $0.04 + (0.08 - 0.04)z$, where z is the uniform random variable with range 0 to 1.

Some other useful distributions can be generated directly from the uniform distribution for parameters whose values analysts believe fall within bounds, but are more likely to fall closer to the center of the bounds. For example, to obtain a draw from a symmetric triangular distribution between zero and one, simply take one-half of the sum of two independent draws from a uniform distribution over 0 to 1. Generating asymmetric triangular distributions from uniform distributions is a bit more complicated. First, create a variable $t = (\text{mode-minimum})/(\text{maximum-minimum})$, where minimum is the smallest value, maximum is the largest value, and mode is the location of the peak, which falls between the minimum and the maximum.

Second, draw a value, u, from the uniform distribution. Third, if $u < t$, then the value equals

$$\text{minimum} + \sqrt{u(\text{mode} - \text{minimum})(\text{maximum} - \text{minimum})}$$

Fourth, if $u \geq t$, then the value equals

$$\text{maximum} - \sqrt{(1-u)(\text{maximum} - \text{mode})(\text{maximum} - \text{minimum})}$$

Simply adding together three uniformly distributed random variables produces a distribution bounded between 0 and 3 with much of its density around its center, producing a distribution that looks somewhat like a normal distribution over the range of the bounds.

Assuming actual normal distributions for uncertain parameters is quite common for two reasons. First, the Central Limit Theorem suggests that if the value of the parameter is determined by the sum of many independent random events, then its distribution will be approximately normal. Consistent with the Central Limit Theorem, adding together increasing numbers of independent uniform distributions results in a distribution approximating the normal distribution. Indeed, when spreadsheets and statistical packages only provided uniform random number generators, it was common to approximate normal distributions by summing large numbers of uniform distributions.

Second, analysts often rely on statistical analyses of data for estimates of needed parameters. For example, regression coefficients often serve as point estimates of parameters. Under conventional assumptions for continuous dependent variables, the estimator of the coefficient has approximately a normal distribution. Assuming a normal distribution with a mean equal to the point estimate and a standard deviation equal to the standard error of the estimator naturally follows.

Today spreadsheets and statistical packages provide functions for drawing from normal distributions. For example, in Excel, NORM.INV(RAND(),μ,σ) returns a draw from a standard normal distribution (mean equal to μ, and variance equal to σ^2). In Stata, normal() provides a standard normal (mean equal to zero; variance equal to 1) that can be converted to a normal distribution with any mean and variance through simple transformations: add a constant equal to the desired expected value and multiply by the square root of the desired variance. A range of 3.92 standard deviations includes 95 percent of the area of the normal distribution. To get the random variable we used in the Monte Carlo simulation for hours lost, t in Table 11.2, we added 24 to the standardized normal and multiplied it by $(30 - 18)/3.92$ so that there was only a 5 percent chance that a value of t would be generated outside the range 18–30.

Table A11.1 summarizes the common applications of the uniform and normal distributions in Monte Carlo simulations for Excel, Stata, and R, an open-source computer language used widely in statistical analysis. Other distributions may also be useful. Most books on mathematical statistics indicate how random variables distributed as chi-square, Student's t, F, and multivariate normal can be generated using combinations of functions of normally distributed random variables. Increasingly, these and other potentially useful distributions, such as the gamma, Poisson, and exponential, are built-in functions in common software packages.

Table A11.1 *Common Distributions for Use in Monte Carlo Simulations*

Distribution	Excel	Stata	R*
Uniform Minimum = a Maximum = b	+a+ (b − a)*RAND()	gen x =a+(b − a)*runiform()	x < −runif(n,a,b)
Normal Mean = μ Variance = σ²	+NORM. INV(RAND(),μ,σ)	gen x = μ+σ*rnormal()	x < −rnorm(n,μ,σ)
Symmetric *triangular* Minimum = a Maximum = b	+a +(b-a)* (RAND()+RAND())/2	gen c = runiform() + runiform() gen x = a+(b − a)*c/2	x < −(runif(n,a,b) + runif(n,a,b))/2
Asymmetric *triangular* Minimum = a Maximum = b Mode = c	+RAND() in cell Z + IF(Z < (c − a)/(b −a), a + SQRT(Z*(c − a)*(b − a)), b − SQRT((1 − Z)*(b − c)*(b − a)))	gen t = (c − a)/(b − a) gen u = runiform() gen x = a + sqrt(u*(c − a)*(b − a)) if u < t replace x = b − sqrt((1 − u)* (b − c)*(b − a) if u >= t	t < −(c − a)/(b − a) u < − runif(n,0,1) x < −ifelse(u < t, a + sqrt(u*(c − a)* (b −a)), b − sqrt((1 − u)*(b − c)* (b − a)))
Bounded *Normal-like* Minimum = a Maximum = b	+a + (b − a)* (+RAND() + RAND() +(RAND())/3	gen c = runiform() + runiform() + runiform() gen x = a + (b − a)*c/3	x < −(runif(n,a,b) + runif(n,a,b) + runif(n,a,b))/3

* R uses arrays so their length, n, the number of trials, must be specified in creating random variables.

Basic Steps Using a Spreadsheet

Once procedures have been developed for generating appropriately distributed random variables, Monte Carlo simulation can be implemented in the following steps.

First, construct a row of appropriate random variables and the formulas that use them to compute net benefits. The last cell in the row should contain net benefits.

Second, copy the entire row a number of times so that the last column of the resulting block contains different realizations of net benefits. Most spreadsheet should be able to handle blocks of more than 1000 rows without memory or speed problems.

Third, analyze the accumulated realizations in the last column along the lines of Figure 11.5, calculating the mean and standard deviation, and plotting them as a histogram.

Basic Steps Using a Statistical Package

In using statistical packages for Monte Carlo simulation, trials are represented as observations. First, create a data set with the number of observations corresponding to the number of trials sought, say 1000, and open a file of the commands that you will employ to create the necessary variables.

Second, give each of the uncertain parameters a variable name and draw values for each observation from its distribution.

Third, combine the parameters in appropriate formulas for costs, benefits, and net benefits. Employing intermediate variables can reduce the chances of errors and facilitate interpretation and modification of the simulation by yourself or others. Indeed, the record of commands provides a transparent record of your calculations. For CBAs that involve complicated calculations, this record is likely to be much easier to interpret than the comparable spreadsheet would be.

Fourth, use available statistical and graphical commands to analyze the variable containing net benefits and display its distribution.

Exercises for Chapter 11

1. The initial cost of constructing a permanent dam (i.e., a dam that is expected to last forever) is $830 million. The annual net benefits will depend on the amount of rainfall: $36 million in a "dry" year, $58 million in a "wet" year, and $104 million in a "flood" year. Meteorological records indicate that over the last 100 years there have been 86 "dry" years, 12 "wet" years, and 2 "flood" years. Assume the annual benefits, measured in real dollars, begin to accrue at the end of the first year. Using the meteorological records as a basis for prediction, what are the net benefits of the dam if the real discount rate is 5 percent?

2. Use several alternative discount rate values to investigate the sensitivity of the present value of net benefits of the dam in exercise 1 to the assumed value of the real discount rate.

3. The prevalence of a disease among a certain population is 0.40. That is, there is a 40 percent chance that a person randomly selected from the population will have the disease. An imperfect test that costs $250 is available to help identify those who have the disease before actual symptoms appear. Those who have the disease have a 90 percent chance of a positive test result; those who do not have the disease have a 5 percent chance of a positive test. Treatment of the disease before the appearance of symptoms costs $2000

and inflicts additional costs of $200 on those who do not actually have the disease. Treatment of the disease after symptoms have appeared costs $10,000.

The government is considering the following possible strategies with respect to the disease:

S1. Do not test and do not treat early.

S2. Do not test but treat early.

S3. Test and treat early if positive and do not treat early if negative.

Find the treatment/testing strategy that has the lowest expected costs for a member of the population.

In doing this exercise, the following notation may be helpful: Let D indicate presence of the disease, ND absence of the disease, T a positive test result, and NT a negative test result. Thus, we have the following information:

$$P(D) = .40, \text{ which implies } P(ND) = .60$$
$$P(T|D) = .90, \text{ which implies } P(NT|D) = .10$$
$$P(T|ND) = .05, \text{ which implies } P(NT|ND) = .95$$

This information allows calculation of some other useful probabilities:

$$P(T) = P(T|D)P(D) + P(T|ND)P(ND) = .39 \text{ and } P(NT) = .61$$
$$P(D|T) = P(T|D)P(D)/P(T) = .92 \text{ and } P(ND|T) = .08$$
$$P(D|NT) = P(NT|D)P(D)/P(NT) = .07 \text{ and } P(ND|NT) = .93$$

4. In exercise 3, the optimal strategy involved testing. Does testing remain optimal if the prevalence of the disease in the population is only 0.05? Does your answer suggest any general principle?

5. (Use of a spreadsheet recommended for parts a through e and necessary for part f.) A town with a population of 164,250 persons who live in 39,050 households is considering introducing a recycling program that would require residents to separate paper from their household waste so that it can be sold rather than buried in a landfill like the rest of the town's waste. Two major benefits are anticipated: revenue from the sale of waste paper and avoided tipping fees (the fee that the town pays the owners of landfills to bury its waste). Aside from the capital costs of specialized collection equipment, household containers, and a sorting facility, the program would involve higher collection costs, inconvenience costs for households, and disposal costs for paper that is collected but not sold. The planning period for the project has been set at eight years, the expected life of the specialized equipment.

The following information has been collected by the town's sanitation department.

Waste Quantities: Residents currently generate 3.6 pounds of waste per person per day. Over the last 20 years, the daily per capita amount has grown by about 0.02 pounds per year. Small or no increases in the last few years, however, raise the possibility that levels realized in the future will fall short of the trend.

Capital Costs: The program would require an initial capital investment of $1,688,000. Based on current resale values, the scrap value of the capital at the end of eight years is expected to be 20 percent of its initial cost.

Annual Costs: The department estimates that the separate collection of paper will add an average of $6/ton to the cost of collecting household waste. Each ton of paper collected and not sold would cost $4 to return to the landfill.

Savings and Revenues: Under a long-term contract, tipping fees are currently $45 per ton with annual increases equal to the rate of inflation. The current local market price for recycled paper is $22 per ton, but has fluctuated in recent years between a low of $12 per ton and a high of $32 per ton.

Paper Recovery: The fraction of household waste made up of paper has remained fairly steady in recent years at 32 percent. Based on the experience of similar programs in other towns, it is estimated that between 60 and 80 percent of paper included in the program will be separated from other waste and 80 percent of the paper that is separated will be suitable for sale, with the remaining 20 percent of the collected paper returned to the waste stream for landfilling.

Household Separation Costs: The sanitation department recognized the possibility that the necessity of separating paper from the waste stream and storing it might impose costs on households. An average of 10 minutes per week per household of additional disposal time would probably be needed. A recent survey by the local newspaper, however, found that 80 percent of respondents considered the inconvenience of the program negligible. Therefore, the department decided to assume that household separation costs would be zero.

Discount Rate: The sanitation department has been instructed by the budget office to discount at the town's real borrowing rate of 6 percent. It has also been instructed to assume that annual net benefits accrue at the end of each of the eight years of the program.

a.   Calculate an estimate of the present value of net benefits for the program.

b. How large would annual household separation costs have to be per household to make the present value of net benefits fall to zero?

c. Assuming that household separation costs are zero, conduct a worst-case analysis with respect to the growth in the quantity of waste, the price of scrap paper, and the percentage of paper diverted from the waste stream.

d. Under the worst-case assumptions of part c, how large would the average yearly household separation costs have to be to make the present value of net benefits fall to zero?

e. Investigate the sensitivity of the present value of net benefits to the price of scrap paper.

f. Implement a Monte Carlo analysis of the present value of net benefits of the program.

6. Imagine that, with a discount rate of 5 percent, the net present value of a hydroelectric plant with a life of 70 years is $25.73 million and that the net present value of a thermal electric plant with a life of 35 years is $18.77 million. Rolling the thermal plant over twice to match the life of the hydroelectric plant thus has a net present value of ($18.77 million) + ($18.77 million)/$(1 + 0.05)^{35}$ = $22.17 million.

Now assume that at the end of the first 35 years, there will be an improved second 35-year plant. Specifically, there is a 25 percent chance that an advanced solar or nuclear alternative will be available that will increase the net benefits by a factor of three, a 60 percent chance that a major improvement in thermal technology will increase net benefits by 50 percent, and a 15 percent chance that more modest improvements in thermal technology will increase net benefits by 10 percent.

a. Should the hydroelectric or thermal plant be built today?

b. What is the quasi-option value of the thermal plant?

Notes

1. A more realistic assumption (e.g., rainfall amounts closer to the center of the range are more likely) would not change this equality as long as the probability density function of rainfall is symmetric around 11 inches.

2. Assuming that rainfall is distributed uniformly over the range, the expected value of net benefits is simply the area under curve B from 22 inches to 0 inches. See note 4 on how to calculate this area for any distribution of rainfall.

3. The representativeness is very sensitive to the particular shape of the probability density function of rainfall. The use of two contingencies would be even less representative if amounts of rainfall near 11 inches were more likely than more extreme amounts.

4. In the case of a continuous underlying dimension, such as price, the expected value of net benefits is calculated using integration, the continuous analog of addition. Let $NB(x)$ be the net benefits given some particular value of x, the underlying dimension. Let $f(x)$ be the probability density function over x. Then,

$$E[NB] = \int NB(x)f(x)dx$$

where the integration is over the range of x.

5. The term *decision analysis* was originally used to include both choice under risk (statistical decision analysis) and games against strategic opponents (game theory). Now it is commonly used to refer only to the former.

6. We recommend Howard Raiffa, *Decision Analysis: Introductory Lectures on Choices under Uncertainty* (Reading, MA: Addison-Wesley, 1969); Morris H. DeGroot, *Optimal Statistical Decisions* (New York, NY: Wiley Interscience, 2004); Robert L. Winkler, *Introduction to Bayesian Inference and Decision*, 2nd edn (Gainesville, FL: Probabilistic Press, 2003); and Robert D. Behn and James W. Vaupel, *Quick Analysis for Busy Decision Makers* (New York, NY: Basic Books, 1982) as general introductions. For more direct application to CBA, see Miley W. Merkhofer, *Decision Science and Social Risk Management: A Comparative Evaluation of Cost–Benefit Analysis, Decision Analysis, and Other Formal Decision-Aiding Approaches* (Boston, MA: D. Reidel Publishing Company, 1987).

7. Although this example is hypothetical, it captures the essence of the problem that faced public health officials in confronting the N1H1 virus in 2009 and 2010. For an analysis of the issues that arose in the Swine Flu episode in the 1970s, see Richard E. Neustadt and Harvey V. Fineberg, *The Swine Flu Affair: Decision-Making on a Slippery Disease* (Washington, DC: US Government Printing Office, 1978).

8. Note that in this example the probability of an epidemic in the second year is conditional on whether an epidemic occurred in the first year. If an epidemic has occurred in the first year, then the population gains immunity and there is zero probability of an epidemic in the second year. If an epidemic has not occurred, then there is some probability, p_2, that one will occur in the second year.

9. Instead, we might have allowed the estimate of P_2 to be adjusted after information was revealed, or gathered, during the first year. If this were the case, then we might use *Bayes' theorem* to update the initial beliefs about P_2 in the face of the new information. Bayes' theorem provides a rule for updating subjective probability estimates on the basis of new information. Let A and B be events. A basic axiom of probability theory is that: $P(A \text{ and } B) = P(A|B)P(B) = P(B|A)P(A)$ where $P(A \text{ and } B)$ is the probability of both A and B occurring, $P(A)$ is the probability of A occurring, $P(B)$ is the probability of B occurring, $P(A|B)$ is the conditional probability that A occurs given that B has occurred, and $P(B|A)$ is the conditional probability of B occurring given that A has occurred. It follows directly from the axioms that: $P(A|B)=P(B|A)P(A)/P(B)$ which is the simplest statement of Bayes' rule. Its application is quite common in diagnostic tests. For example, we may know the frequency of a disease in the population, $P(A)$, the probability that a test will yield a positive result if randomly given to a member of the population, $P(B)$, and the conditional probability that, given the disease, the test will be positive, $P(B|A)$. We would thus be able to calculate $P(A|B)$, the conditional probability that someone with a positive test has the disease.

10. Note the assumption that the probability of the influenza reaching the population, p_1, is independent of whether or not this particular population is vaccinated. This would not be a reasonable assumption if the vaccination were to be part of a national program that reduced the chances that the influenza would reach this population from some other vaccinated population.

11. In this particular problem, it will never make sense to wait until the second year to implement the program if it is going to be implemented at all. If, however, the risk of side effects were expected to fall in the second year, say, because a better vaccine would be available, then delay could be optimal. In terms of the decision tree, we could easily model this alternative scenario by using different values of C_s in the current and next years.

12. For a discussion of the application of decision analysis to the stockpiling problem, see David L. Weimer and Aidan R. Vining, *Policy Analysis: Concepts and Practice*, 6th edn (New York, NY: Routledge, 2017), chapter 17.

13. Calculating the number of combinations: $3^{17} = 129{,}140{,}163$.

14. For examples of CBA applied to hepatitis vaccine programs, see Josephine A. Mauskopf, Cathy J. Bradley,

and Michael T. French, "Benefit–Cost Analysis of Hepatitis B Vaccine Programs for Occupationally Exposed Workers." *Journal of Occupational Medicine*, 33(6), 1991, 691–98; Gary M. Ginsberg and Daniel Shouval, "Cost–Benefit Analysis of a Nationwide Neonatal Inoculation Programme against Hepatitis B in an Area of Intermediate Endemicity." *Journal of Epidemiology and Community Health*, 46(6), 1992, 587–94; and Murray Krahn and Allan S. Detsky, "Should Canada and the United States Universally Vaccinate Infants against Hepatitis B?" *Medical Decision Making*, 13(1), 1993, 4–20.

15. Call the basic reproductive rate of the infection R_0. That is, each primary infection exposes R_0 individuals to infection. If i is the fraction of the population no longer susceptible to infection because of previous infection, then the actual reproductive rate is $R = R_0(1 - i - v)$, where v is the fraction of the population effectively vaccinated. If R falls below 1, then the infection dies out because, on average, each infection generates less than one new infection. Assuming that the population is homogeneous with respect to susceptibility to infection and that infected and non-infected individuals uniformly mix in the population, a rough estimate of the ultimate i for the population is given by the formula $i = 1 - (1/R_0) - v$, where $1 - 1/R_0$ is the estimate of the infection rate in the absence of the vaccine. For an overview, see Roy M. Anderson and Robert M. May, "Modern Vaccines: Immunisation and Herd Immunity." *The Lancet*, 8690(March), 1990, 641–45; and Joseph W. G. Smith, "Vaccination Strategy," in Philip Selby, editor, *Influenza, Virus, Vaccines, and Strategy* (New York, NY: Academic Press, 1976), 271–94.

16. The $L = \$10$ million and $L = \$5$ million lines cross because lives are at risk both from the vaccination side effects and from the epidemic. At low probabilities of epidemic, the expected number of lives saved from vaccination is negative so that net benefits are higher for lower values of life. At higher probabilities of epidemic, the expected number of lives saved is positive so that net benefits are higher for higher values of life.

17. Note that these estimates of NB no longer involve expectations with respect to the contingencies of epidemics, although the cost estimates themselves are expected values. For each random draw, only one combination of contingencies can actually occur. (The epidemic poses a collective risk to the population, while the costs result from the realizations of independent risks to individuals in the population.)

18. In general, if the calculation of net benefits involves sums of random variables, using their expected values yields the expected value of net benefits. If the calculation involves sums and products of random variables, then using their expected values yields the expected value of net benefits only if the random variables are uncorrelated. In the Monte Carlo approach, correlations among variables can be taken into account by drawing parameter values from either multivariate or conditional distributions rather than from independent univariate distributions as in this example. Finally, if the calculation involves ratios of random variables, then even independence (i.e., an absence of correlations) does not guarantee that using their expected values will yield the correct expected value of net benefits. In this latter situation, the Monte Carlo approach is especially valuable because it provides a way of estimating the correct expected net benefits.

19. Aidan R. Vining and David L. Weimer, "An Assessment of Important Issues Concerning the Application of Benefit–Cost Analysis to Social Policy." *Journal of Benefit–Cost Analysis*, 1(1), 2010, 1–38.

20. The concept of quasi-option value was introduced by Kenneth J. Arrow and Anthony C. Fisher, "Environmental Preservation, Uncertainty, and Irreversibility." *Quarterly Journal of Economics*, 88(2), 1974, 312–19.

21. Jon M. Conrad, "Quasi-Option Value and the Expected Value of Information." *Quarterly Journal of Economics*, 44(4), 1980, 813–20; and Anthony C. Fisher and W. Michael Hanemann, "Quasi-Option Value: Some Misconceptions Dispelled." *Journal of Environmental Economics and Management*, 14(2), 1987, 183–90. The concept of quasi-option value also applies to private-sector investments involving large initial costs that cannot be recovered if abandoned. For overviews, see Robert S. Pindyck, "Irreversibility, Uncertainty, and Investment." *Journal of Economic Literature*, 29(3), 1991, 1110–48; Avinash Dixit and Robert Pindyck, *Investment Under Uncertainty* (Princeton, NJ: Princeton University Press, 1994); Gilbert E. Metcalf and Donald Rosenthal, "The 'New' View of Investment Decisions and Public Policy Analysis: An Application to Green Lights and Cold Refrigerators." *Journal of Policy Analysis and Management*, 14(4), 1995, 517–31; and Anthony Edward Boardman and David H. Greenberg, "Discounting and the Social Discount Rate," in Fred Thompson and Mark T. Green, editors, *Handbook of Public Finance* (New York, NY: Marcel Dekker, 1998), 269–318.

Case 11

Using Monte Carlo Simulation: Assessing the Net Benefits of Early Detection of Alzheimer's Disease

Alzheimer's disease (AD), the most common form of dementia, currently affects at least 5 percent of the US population aged 65 years and older. This chronic progressive neurodegenerative disorder increases in prevalence with age, affecting almost half of those persons aged 85 and older. Aging of the US population will likely increase the prevalence of AD from a total of about 5 million people today to 14 million people by 2050.[1] The expected rapid increase in the number of persons with AD will translate into higher public and private long-term care costs paid by households, the Medicaid program, and long-term care insurers. Although studies have estimated a wide range of total annual costs to the US economy resulting from AD, the most plausible estimates now have surpassed two-hundred billion dollars.[2] Primary care physicians often fail to detect the mild cognitive impairment that is usually apparent in the early stages of AD; they enter diagnoses of AD into medical records even less frequently.[3] Nonetheless, fairly inexpensive but effective protocols exist for diagnosing AD[4] – one well-designed study found that screening those over 70 years old would cost less than $4,000 per positive diagnosis.[5] Assuming that 70 percent of those diagnosed participate in treatment or counseling interventions, the cost per treated diagnosis would be about $5,700. Do the benefits of early detection of AD justify the diagnosis cost?

Early detection of AD could be beneficial in three ways. First, although available drugs can neither reverse nor stop the progression of AD, they can slow it. Use of the drugs during the early stages of the disease can potentially delay the entry of those with AD into expensive long-term care. Second, there is strong evidence that providing support to the caregivers of AD patients can enable them to keep their loved ones in the home longer and with fewer adverse psychological costs for themselves. Third, despite common perceptions to the contrary, most people want to know if they are in the early stages of AD.[6] This knowledge enables them to participate in planning for their own long-term care as well as to engage in desirable activities, such as travel, while they can still do so.

Early treatment and caregiver support provides large potential benefits by reducing the total time AD patients spend in nursing homes. The median annual nursing home cost in the United States is over $90,000. Not surprisingly, most AD patients admitted to nursing homes fairly quickly exhaust their financial resources and must rely on public subsidy through the Medicaid program, which now pays for just over half of all nursing home costs in the United States. Avoiding a year of nursing home care thus saves resources for society as well as reduces state and federal Medicaid expenditures. Studies also suggest that at each stage of the disease, AD patients experience a higher quality of life if living in the community rather than in nursing homes. This is offset somewhat by a lower quality of life for caregivers when AD patients they are caring for live in the community rather than in nursing homes. Treatment and caregiver support have costs that must be taken into account. Further, the time costs of caregivers are substantially larger for AD patients living in the community rather than in nursing homes.

The net benefits of early detection equal the costs without intervention minus the costs with it. In other words, the net benefits of early detection are the avoided costs that it facilitates. Table C11.1 summarizes the cost categories included in a cost–benefit analysis of early detection, which was implanted through the Monte Carlo simulation described below.

Totting up these costs poses a number of analytical challenges. First, as with many public policies, costs precede beneficial impacts. Expenditures on early detection and treatment occur now, but the delayed entry into nursing homes will likely occur years in the future when the disease progresses to a stage that overwhelms caregivers. Second, life-course uncertainties affect whether benefits will actually be realized by any particular patient. People in the relevant age group die from many causes. Consequently, some will die before any benefits from delayed nursing home care can be realized. Third, as is common in analyses of social policies, predicting impacts involves assumptions about uncertain parameters. Most importantly, assumptions about the progression of AD with and without drug treatment and the impacts of caregiver support come from studies with estimation error.

To address these challenges, David Weimer and Mark Sager (henceforth W&S) built a Monte Carlo simulation that tracks patients over their remaining life courses with and without the interventions made possible by early identification of AD.[7] Each trial of the simulation provides an estimate of net benefits from intervention, sometimes positive as when the patient lives long enough to show a reduced stay in a nursing home, but sometimes negative as when the patient dies before a reduced stay in a nursing home can be realized. The simulation also allowed for the uncertainty about costs displayed in Table C11.1 as well as important uncertainties in the impacts of drug treatment and caregiver

Table C11.1 *Costs Borne by AD Patients, Caregivers, and the Rest of Society*

Cost category	Monetization strategy	Values used (2009 dollars)
Time in nursing home	Annual nursing home cost	66,795/year
Patient utility	Statistical value of life year	93,500 to 187,000 (uniform distribution)
Caregiver utility		
Caregiver time	Median wage and benefit rate	14.69/hour
Drug treatment	Market price	1,825/year
Caregiver support	Wage and benefit rate	35.05/hour
In-home services	Expenditures	0 to $2,968/year (uniform distribution)

Source: Information extracted from David L. Weimer and Mark A. Sager, "Early Identification and Treatment of Alzheimer's Disease: Social and Fiscal Outcomes." *Alzheimer's & Dementia*, 5(3), 2009, 215–26.

support based on the available estimates in the research literature. For example, the statistical value of a life-year and in-home services were allowed to vary over uniform ranges, although other costs, such as the annual cost of a nursing home, were treated as point estimates. In addition, the impact of caregiver counseling on institutionalization risk was based on the reported confidence interval for the odds ratio for participation in the counseling. In aggregate, the trials provide a distribution of possible outcomes. The average of the trials provides an estimate of the likely net benefit conditional on intervention. If the conditional net benefit is larger than costs per diagnosis, then early detection is efficient.

Modeling the Life Course of AD Patients

A commonly used cognitive metric, the Mini-Mental State Examination (MMSE), plays a central role in W&S modeling the life course of those with AD. The MMSE is a scale ranging from a high of 30 corresponding to normal cognitive ability to 1 for loss of all cognitive ability. Scores of 28–21, 20–11, and 10–1 represent mild, moderate, and severe AD, respectively. Research provides estimates of the rates of decline in MMSE for AD patients both with and without drug treatment. Research also provides estimates of the probability of AD patients being institutionalized as a function of MMSE, age, sex, and marital status (married patients are more likely to have a caregiver).

The general approach adopted by W&S involved separate Monte Carlo simulations for different types of AD patients defined by combinations of initial MMSE, age, sex, marital status, and either an intervention (drug treatment, caregiver counseling, and drug treatment combined with caregiver counseling) or no intervention. Each patient progresses year by year until death. During each year of life, costs of various sorts were incurred: time costs based on estimates from the literature of the time spent by caregivers contingent on whether the patient was in the community or institutionalized and whether the AD was mild, moderate, or severe (monetized at median wage rates); utility costs for both caregivers and patients for mild, moderate, and severe AD (monetized at the value of a life year); nursing home costs for those institutionalized (monetized at average annual cost); and the costs of interventions (monetized at drug prices, counselor wages, and incremental expenditures on in-home services).

After the first year of the simulation, the AD patient has some probability of living to the next year based on survival probabilities for men and women in the general population adjusted for their higher mortality rate. If the AD patient begins with a spouse, then unadjusted survival probabilities are used to determine if the spouse survives to the next year. At the beginning of each subsequent year in which the patient resides in the community, the probability of being institutionalized, based on the updated MMSE, age, and marital status as well as sex and whether caregiver counseling is provided, determines if the patient remains in the community or enters a nursing home. Once the patient enters a nursing home, he or she remains there until death.

W&S modeled the disease progression in two different ways. The first approach was based on estimates that MMSE declines with and without drug treatment. The second approach was based on research suggesting that patients could be divided into slow and fast decliners and that drug treatment increased the probability of a patient being a slow decliner. Each of these approaches drew parameters from specified distributions. For example, the mean decline model drew declines from a normal distribution with mean 3.5 MMSE points and standard deviation of 1.5 MMSE points for patients not receiving drug treatment.

Simply comparing incurred costs with and without intervention would overestimate the benefits of intervention because some AD patients not identified early would eventually be identified when their symptoms became more obvious. Consequently, the counterfactual to early detection took account of subsequent diagnosis and intervention. In particular, based on available research, it gave each patient not identified initially a 25 percent chance of being diagnosed when MMSE fell to 19 points.

Net benefits for each of the interventions were computed in the following steps: First, the net benefits of intervention in each year were computed as the difference between the costs without the initial intervention (but potentially with it later as specified in the counterfactual) and the costs with it. Second, these differences were discounted back to the present to obtain a present value of net benefits. Third, the first two steps were repeated in 10,000 trials to produce a distribution of the present value of net benefits. Fourth, the mean present value of net benefits was computed by averaging over the trials. The intervention would be assessed as efficient if the average present value of net benefits it produced were larger than the costs of diagnosing an AD patient through screening. A similar method was used to estimate the fiscal impacts of early detection for Wisconsin and the federal government to assess the budgetary implications of early detection.

Table C11.2 shows representative results from the analysis for a married male using the more conservative model of AD progression and drug response. Several general patterns are apparent. First, other things being equal, interventions offer larger net benefits for younger AD patients – younger patients are likely to survive longer and are therefore at greater risk of long stays in nursing homes. Second, drug treatment provides larger net benefits for patients earlier in the AD progression. Slowing disease progression early keeps patients in the mild phase of AD longer, which reduces both caregiver costs and the probability of an early institutionalization. Third, the net benefit from caregiver counseling does not change very much across this range of AD progression. Note that the present values reported in Table C11.2 would be larger for a female patient, but smaller for an unmarried patient.

Policy Implications

The scenarios presented in Table C11.2 all show the net benefits of intervention following early diagnosis of AD to be larger than the $5,700 cost per treated diagnosis that could be obtained from screening those over 70 years of age. Some caution is warranted in basing policy on the estimates of benefits from drug treatment because the available research from which the estimates were taken typically followed patients for only a few years. Consequently, the drug treatment model in the simulations involves extrapolation

Table C11.2 *Present Value of Net Benefits from Interventions Following Early AD Detection in Married Males (1,000s dollars)*

Age	Intervention	MMSE		
		26	**24**	**22**
	Drug treatment only	94.5	71.4	48.7
65	Counseling only	12.0	11.6	11.9
	Drug treatment and counseling	119.3	96.6	72.9
	Drug treatment only	80.9	62.3	41.5
70	Counseling only	9.2	10.5	11.5
	Drug treatment and counseling	103.0	82.2	66.1
	Drug treatment only	66.5	51.6	34.9
75	Counseling only	7.4	11.7	10.7
	Drug treatment and counseling	82.7	69.3	56.8

Source: Calculated using the W&S model.

beyond observed data and may be overly optimistic in assuming that drugs can slow progression over more than a few years. The costs and impacts of caregiver counseling are based on a long-term study with random assignment of caregivers to counseling and a control group, and therefore have a much stronger empirical basis.[8] As the net benefits from counseling alone are larger than the diagnostic costs, the analysis strongly supports screening combined with caregiver support. W&S also estimated that about half of the net benefits from caregiver counseling would accrue as fiscal savings to the state of Wisconsin, suggesting that screening and caregiver counseling would be fiscally as well as socially beneficial. The W&S analysis was influential in promoting state support for AD screening in Wisconsin and Minnesota.[9]

Accommodating the Different Types of Uncertainty

The W&S analysis shows how Monte Carlo simulation can be used to model three types of uncertainty. First, Monte Carlo simulation can be used to take account of parameter uncertainty, its most common use in CBA. The key is to represent the uncertainty as a probability distribution over possible values of the parameter and then draw values of the parameter from the distribution in the multiple trials. For example, rather than using the point estimate of the reduction in risk of institutionalization reported in the study of caregiver counseling, W&S randomly drew values from the reported confidence interval around the point estimate in their Monte Carlo trials. Second, Monte Carlo simulation can be used to model processes that involve random events by assigning probabilities to them. This capability was especially important in the W&S analysis because of the importance of random events, such as nursing home institutionalization and patient death, to the accruing of costs and benefits. Third, multiple Monte Carlo simulations can be conducted to take account of model uncertainty. For example, in the W&S analysis, separate Monte Carlo simulations employed two different models of AD progression. Although not done in the W&S analysis, results can be reported as weighted averages across the models.

Exercises for Chapter 11 Case

1. What information would be needed to estimate the net benefits of a state-wide Alzheimer's disease screening program for 65-year-olds?

2. Imagine that you wanted to use a life-course model similar to the Alzheimer's disease model to estimate the net benefits of helping someone quit smoking. What would be the most important similarities and differences?

Notes

1. Centers for Disease Control and Prevention, *Alzheimer's Disease* (www.cdc.gov/aging/aginginfo/alzheimers.htm).

2. Michale D. Hurd, Paco Martorell, Adeline Delavande, Kathleen J. Mullen, and Kenneth M. Langa, "Monetary Costs of Dementia in the United States." *New England Journal of Medicine*, 368, 2013, 1326–34.

3. Alex J. Mitchell, Nicholas Meader, and Michael Pentzek, "Clinical Recognition of Dementia and Cognitive Impairment in Primary Care: A Meta-analysis of Physician Accuracy." *Acta Psychiatrica Scandinavica*, 124(3), 2011, 165–83.

4. Common protocols have three stages: first, a simple screen, such as whether or not the person can name 14 animals in 1 minute; second, for those who screen positive on the animal naming test, the Neurobehavioral Cognitive Status Examination, which requires about 20 minutes to administer; and third, for those who screen positive on the Neurobehavioral Cognitive Status Examination, diagnosis by a physician to rule out other causes of dementia.

5. Malaz Boustani, Christopher M. Callahan, Frederick W. Unverzagt, Mary G. Austrom, Anthony J. Perkins, Bridget A. Fultz, Siu L. Hui, and Hugh C. Hendrie, "Implementing a Screening and Diagnosis Program for Dementia in Primary Care." *Journal of General Internal Medicine*, 20(7), 2005, 572–77.

6. Louise Robinson, Alan Gemski, Clare Abley, John Bond, John Keady, Sarah Campbell, Kritika Samsi, and Jill Manthorpe, "The Transition to Dementia – Individual and Family Experiences of Receiving a Diagnosis: A Review." *International Psychogeriatrics*, 23(7), 2011, 1026–43.

7. David L. Weimer and Mark A. Sager, "Early Identification and Treatment of Alzheimer's Disease: Social and Fiscal Outcomes." *Alzheimer's & Dementia*, 5(3), 2009, 215–26.

8. Mary S. Mittleman, William E. Haley, Olivio J. Clay, and David L. Roth, "Improving Caregiver Well-Being Delays Nursing Home Placement of Patients with Alzheimer Disease." *Neurology*, 67(9), 2006, 1592–99.

9. Alzeimer's Disease Working Group, *Preparing Minnesota for Alzheimer's: Budgetary, Social and Personal Impacts*, Summary of Report to the Legislature, 2010.

12 Risk, Option Price, and Option Value

In the actual practice of *ex ante* CBA in circumstances involving significant risks, analysts almost always apply the Kaldor–Hicks criterion to expected net benefits. They typically estimate changes in social surplus conditional on particular contingencies occurring, and then they compute the expected value over the contingencies as explained in Chapter 11. Economists, however, now generally consider *option price*, the amount that individuals are willing to pay for policies prior to the realization of contingencies, to be the theoretically correct measure of willingness to pay in circumstances of uncertainty or risk. Whereas social surplus can be thought of as an *ex post* measure of welfare change in the sense that individuals value policies as if contingencies have already occurred, option price is an *ex ante* welfare measure in the sense that consumers value policies without knowing which contingency will actually occur. These measures generally differ from one another. In this chapter, we consider the implications of the common use of expected social surplus, rather than option price, as the method for measuring net benefits.

The central concern of this chapter is the conceptually correct measure of willingness to pay in circumstances in which individuals face uncertainty. Individuals may face uncertainties about their demand for a good, the supply of a good, or both. With respect to demand, one may be uncertain about one's future income, utility function (tastes), and the prices of other goods. For example, one's utility from skiing may depend on the sturdiness of one's knees, a physical condition that cannot be predicted with certainty. With respect to supply, one may be uncertain about the future quantity, quality, or price of a good. For example, the increase in the quality of fishing that will result from restocking a lake with game fish depends on such circumstances as weather and spills of toxic chemicals, and thus is uncertain to some degree.

In contrast to Chapter 11, we limit our attention to uncertainties of direct relevance to individuals. We ignore uncertainties that are not of direct individual relevance, but instead arise because analysts must make predictions about the future to estimate WTP. In the context of the CBA of the vaccination program discussed in Chapter 11, for example, the probability of an epidemic, the probability an unvaccinated individual will be infected, the probability a vaccinated individual will be infected, and the probability a vaccinated individual will suffer a side effect are exactly the types of uncertainties considered in this chapter. The analyst's uncertainties about the magnitude of these probabilities, the appropriate shadow price of time, or the number of people who will choose to be vaccinated were adequately addressed in the discussion of sensitivity analysis presented in Chapter 11. Although these analytical uncertainties are usually of greatest practical concern in CBA, we seek here to provide the conceptual foundation required for understanding the appropriate measure of costs and benefits when individuals face significant uncertainties. We are especially interested in how to assess government policies that increase or reduce the uncertainties that individuals face.

Frequently in this chapter we use the word "uncertainty." However, as we have just stated, this chapter assumes that we know the magnitude of the probabilities. Thus, this chapter really concerns *risk*. In practice, risk means different things to different people. It often refers to downside risk, for example, the risk of overestimating benefits or underestimating costs. In contrast, we define risk as the variance in net benefits.[1] A risk-reducing policy reduces the variance in net benefits relative to current policy, while a risk-increasing policy increases the variance in net benefits relative to the status quo.

This chapter has three major sections. The first introduces option price and clarifies its relationship to expected surplus. The second section introduces the concept of *option value*, the difference between option price and expected surplus, and reviews the theoretical literature that attempts to determine its sign. Although sometimes thought of as a conceptually distinct category of benefits, option value is actually an adjustment to measured net benefits to account for the fact that they are usually based on expected surplus rather than option price. The third section provides a general assessment of the appropriateness of the use of expected surplus as a proxy for option price.

12.1   *Ex Ante* WTP: Option Price and Certainty Equivalents[2]

Viewing benefits (or costs) in terms of the willingness of individuals to pay to obtain desirable (or avoid undesirable) policy impacts provides a clear perspective on the appropriateness of treating expected net benefits as if they were certain amounts. By identifying the conceptually correct method for valuing uncertain costs and benefits, we can better understand the circumstances under which the use of expected net benefits is more or less appropriate.

There is now a near-consensus among economists that the conceptually correct way to value the benefits of a policy in circumstances involving risk is to sum the *ex ante* amounts that the individuals affected by the policy would be willing to pay to obtain it.[3] To see this, imagine that each person, knowing the probabilities of each of the contingencies that would occur under the policy, would give a truthful answer to the following question: *Prior to knowing which contingency will actually occur, what is the maximum amount that you would be willing to pay to obtain the policy?* Each individual's answer to this question is what economists call the person's *option price* for the policy. If we think of the policy as a lottery having probabilities of various pay-offs to the person, then the individual's option price is the *certainty equivalent* of the lottery – that is, an amount the person would pay for a ticket without knowing the pay-off (or contingency) that is actually realized. (It is called a certainty equivalent because the amount paid for a lottery ticket is certain even if the pay-off is not.)

By summing the option prices of all persons, we obtain the aggregate benefits of the policy, which can then be compared to its opportunity cost in the usual way. If the opportunity cost is not dependent on which contingency actually occurs, then we have fully taken account of risk by comparing the aggregate WTP, which is independent of the contingency that actually occurs, with the certain opportunity cost.

12.1.1   *Illustrations of Option Price*

To illustrate the concept of option price, return to the asteroid defense policies set out in Table 11.1 in the previous chapter. Assume that the United Nations wishes to evaluate forward-based asteroid defense from the perspective of humankind. Analysts might employ a contingent valuation survey of the sort described in Chapter 16. It would require surveyors to explain to each person the possible contingencies (exposure to collision with an asteroid larger than 1 km diameter, exposure to collision with an asteroid between 20 m and 1 km in diameter, and no exposure to collision with an asteroid larger than 20 m in diameter), the probabilities of each contingency, and the consequences to the Earth under each contingency with and without forward-based asteroid defense. Each person would then be asked questions to elicit the maximum amount that he or she would be willing to pay to have forward-based asteroid defense. These amounts would be summed over all earthlings to arrive at the social benefits of forward-based asteroid defense. As this sum represents aggregate WTP before people know which contingency occurs, and therefore is the WTP irrespective of which one actually occurs, it can be thought of as a certainty equivalent. Let us assume that the net benefits, the sum of individual option prices, equaled $100 billion. The net benefits of forward-based asteroid defense would then be calculated as this amount minus the certain program costs of $60 billion, or $40 billion.

Recall that in actual CBA, analysts more commonly measure benefits by first estimating the social surplus under each contingency and then taking the expected value of these amounts using the probabilities of the contingencies. For example, the information in Table 11.1 indicates that the expected net benefits of forward-based asteroid defense relative to no program to be −$15 billion (the expected value of the net costs of no program, $54 billion, minus the expected value of the net costs of forward-based asteroid defense, $69 billion). Thus, in this example, the expected surplus would underestimate net benefits by $55 billion ($40 billion less −$15 billion). This difference between option price and expected surplus is the option value of forward-based asteroid defense. In this case, the option value can be thought of as an additional "insurance benefit" of the program. It is the maximum amount beyond expected net benefits that individuals are willing to pay to have the defense program available to reduce the risk of the catastrophic consequences that would result from an undefended collision with a large asteroid.

In general, how does this expected surplus measure compare to the option price? Assuming that individuals are risk-averse, *expected surplus can either underestimate or overestimate option price depending on the sources of risk. For an individual who is risk-averse and whose utility function depends only on income, expected surplus will underestimate option price for policies that reduce income risk and overestimate option price for policies that increase income risk.* In order to understand how these possibilities can arise, it is necessary to look more carefully at the relationship between option price and expected surplus from the perspective of an individual consumer. The following diagrammatic expositions illustrate cases where option price exceeds expected surplus (a temporary dam) and expected surplus exceeds option price (a bridge).

Table 12.1 shows the contingent pay-offs for building a temporary dam that provides water for irrigation. With or without the dam, the farmer can be viewed as facing two contingencies: it rains a lot (wet contingency), or it does not rain very much (dry contingency). If it is wet, then he will always produce more crops than if it is dry. Without the dam, the farmer would receive an income of $100 if it rains a lot and only $50 if it does not rain very much. As a result of the dam, his income will increase by $50 if it is dry but by only $10 if it is wet. These $50 and $10 figures are the surpluses that the farmer receives from the dam under each contingency. In expected value terms, assuming that the dry and wet contingencies are equally likely, this surplus equals $30. This $30 expected surplus figure corresponds to the measure of benefits that is used in CBA when option price is not estimated.[4]

Notice that this example assumes that the dam will store water that can be used for irrigation purposes if it is dry. Consequently, the dam will do more for the farmer if it turns out to be dry than if it turns out to be wet. As a result, his income depends much less on which contingency actually occurs once the dam is built than it did without the dam. In other words, the dam reduces the income risk faced by the farmer by reducing the variation in his income. Without the dam, the variance of the farmer's income is $625, but with the dam it is only $25.[5]

To determine the farmer's option price we need to know the farmer's utility function. Normally, we would not have this information, which is why, in practice, expected surplus rather than option price is normally used to determine net benefits. For purposes

Table 12.1 *Example of a Risk-reducing Project*

Contingency	Policy		Probability of contingency
	Dam	No dam	
Wet	110	100	.5
Dry	100	50	.5
Expected value	105	75	
Variance	25	625	

Surplus point:	$U(110 - S_w) = U(100)$ implies $S_w = 10$
	$U(100 - S_d) = U(50)$ implies $S_d = 50$
Expected surplus:	$E(S) = 0.5S_w + 0.5S_d = 30$
Expected utility of no dam:	$EU = 0.5U(100) + 0.5U(50)$
Willingness-to-pay locus:	(s_w, s_d) such that
	$0.5U(110 - s_w) + 0.5U(100 - s_d) = EU$
Option price:	$0.5U(110 - OP) + 0.5U(100 - OP) = EU$
	$EU = 4.26$ and $OP = 34.2$
	for $U(c) = \ln(c)$, where c is net income
Comparison:	$OP > E(S)$

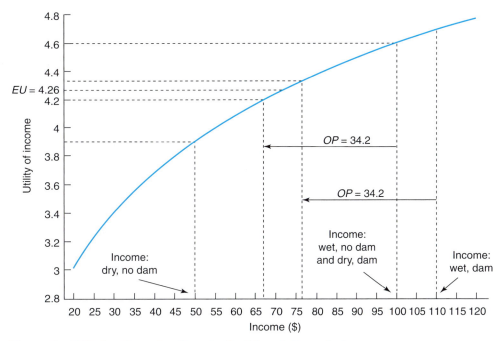

Figure 12.1 Utility function and option price for risk-reducing project.

of our illustration, however, we assume that the farmer's utility is given by the natural log of his income as shown by the curved line in Figure 12.1.

To determine the farmer's option price from the dam, we first calculate his expected utility without the dam, denoted *EU*. In the absence of the dam, the farmer realizes an income of $50 dollars if it is dry, which has utility equal to 3.912, and $100 if it is wet, which has utility equal to 4.605. Because the probabilities of wet and dry are each one-half, the farmer's expected utility if the dam is not built equals 4.26. The option price for the dam, denoted *OP*, is the amount of income the farmer would be willing to give up to have the dam that gives him the same expected utility as he would have without the dam. In this example, *OP* = 34.2. To see this, note that if we subtract 34.2 from each of the contingent incomes with the dam ($100 if it dry, $110 if it is wet), then the net contingent incomes are now $65.80 and $75.80. The corresponding utilities are 4.187 and 4.328, resulting in an expected utility equal to 4.26, which is the expected utility of no dam. Thus, either no dam or a dam with a certain payment of $34.20 gives the farmer the same expected utility.[6]

The farmer's option price for the dam of $34.20 exceeds his expected surplus of $30. Thus, if the opportunity cost of the project were $32 and the farmer were the only beneficiary, then the common practice of using expected surplus would result in rejecting building the dam when, in fact, the option price indicates that building the dam would increase the farmer's utility.

Figure 12.2 provides an alternative graphical representation of the relationship between expected surplus and option price for the farmer. The vertical axis indicates the farmer's willingness-to-pay amounts if it is dry; the horizontal axis represents his

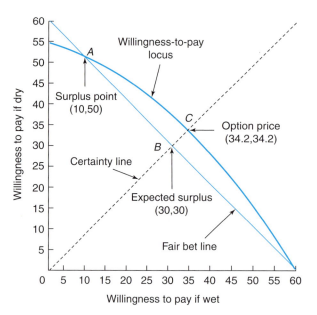

Figure 12.2 Risk-reducing project: expected surplus and option price.

willingness-to-pay amounts if it is wet. Thus, point A represents his surplus under each contingency.

There is a slightly different way to view point A. Imagine that before the government will build the dam the farmer would be required to sign a contract, Contract A, that stipulates that he will pay the government an amount equal to $\$X_w$ if it turns out to be wet and an amount equal to $\$X_d$ if it turns out to be dry. This is called a *contingent contract* because its terms depend on events that will not be known until sometime in the future. Although the government is unlikely to require a contingent contract in practice, it is a useful device for thinking about how much the farmer values the dam or, in other words, his benefit from the dam. This benefit corresponds to the maximum value that the government could assign to $\$X_w$ and $\$X_d$ and still get the farmer to sign Contract A, $\$10$ and $\$50$, respectively. The farmer would be just willing to sign at these amounts because he would be exactly back to the situation he faced without the dam, when his income equaled $\$100$ if it rained and $\$50$ if it was dry. In other words, $\$10$ and $\$50$ are his maximum WTP under Contract A.

Notice that because the $\$10$ payment if it is wet and the $\$50$ payment if it is dry put the farmer back to where he would be without the dam, they measure the surplus he receives but not the utility he receives because the dam reduces the income risk he faces. If the farmer makes these payments, then his income variability would be exactly what it was without the dam. To examine the change in income risk resulting from the dam, imagine now that the government is also willing to let the farmer choose an alternative contract, Contract B, that allows him to pay the same amount, $\$30$, regardless of which contingency actually occurs. If the government does this, then the expected value of the payment it will receive would be equal under the two contracts. However, Contract B would place the farmer on a line that bisects the origin of Figure 12.2. This line is called the *certainty line* because payment amounts along it are the same regardless of which contingency actually occurs. Thus, any point along this line, including *B*, represents a certainty equivalent.

The certainty line intersects another line. This one passes through the surplus point, but every point along it has the same expected value. For example, in the case of our illustration, the expected value would always be equal to $30 along this line. This line is called the *fair bet line*. To see why, imagine flipping a coin. A pay-off of $10 if you get heads and $50 if you get tails would have exactly the same expected value as $20 if you get heads and $40 if you get tails. Thus, the slope of the fair bet line, −1, is equal to the negative of the ratio of the probabilities of the contingencies. Moving along the fair bet line toward the certainty line, the expected value always remains the same, but the variation in income decreases. Finally, at point *B* on the certainty line, the pay-off is equal regardless of which contingency, heads or tails, actually occurs.[7] In our example, this pay-off is $30.

We now return to our farmer and the dam and ask whether he would be indifferent between signing Contract A, under which he must pay $10 if it is wet and $50 if it is dry, and Contract B, under which he must pay $30 regardless of whether it is wet or dry, noting that the expected value of his income would be equal under the two contracts. To answer this, we look at what his income would be under the two contracts.

Although the expected value of income under the two contracts would be identical, the variation in income between the two contingencies is obviously much less under Contract B. Thus, by comparing Contracts A and B, as we do in Table 12.2, we can examine the effect of the dam on the risk facing the farmer, while holding the expected value of his income constant. If the farmer is risk-averse and, hence, would prefer a more stable to a less stable income from year to year, then he will not be indifferent between the two contracts but will prefer B to A because he will face less risk with B than with A.

Now, recall that at point *A* in Figure 12.2 the farmer was willing to sign a contract that would require him to pay $10 if it is wet and $50 if it is dry and that the expected value of these payments was $30. Because the farmer prefers point *B* to point *A*, this suggests that in order to reach the certainty line, the farmer would be willing to sign a contract requiring him to pay a certainty equivalent greater than $30. The maximum such amount that he would pay is represented by point *C* in Figure 12.2, a point that is farther north-east along the certainty line than point *B*. Point *C* represents the farmer's option price, the maximum amount that he would be willing to pay for *both* the increase in expected income and the reduction in income risk resulting from the dam.

Table 12.2 *Comparison of Contingent Contracts for the Dam*

Contingency	Probability	Income under Contract A	Income under Contract B
Wet	.5	$100	$80
Dry	.5	$50	$70
EV		$75	$75

In other words, it incorporates the full value of the dam to the farmer. Conceptually, it is the correct measure of benefits that the farmer would receive from the dam. Instead, however, CBAs typically predict point *B*, the expected value of the surpluses resulting from the dam. While point *B* captures the effect of the dam on expected income, it does not incorporate the effect of the dam on income variability or risk.

Although the farmer would prefer point *B* to point *A*, he would be indifferent between points *A* and *C*. Indeed, a curve drawn between these points is very similar to an indifference curve. This curve, the *willingness-to-pay locus*,[8] shows all of the combinations of contingent payments for the dam that give the farmer the same expected utility with the dam as without it.[9] It is based on knowledge of the probabilities of the contingencies prior to knowing which one will actually occur. If the option price lies farther to the north-east along the certainty line than does the certain project cost, then the project would increase the farmer's welfare.

Table 12.3 describes a policy involving constructing a bridge in an area where the probability of an earthquake is 20 percent. The bridge would increase the expected value of income that the individual described in the table receives, but at the same time, it would make her income more dependent on whether a quake actually occurs. In other words, the bridge increases the income risk facing the individual. Consequently, as shown in the table, the expected surplus of $84 exceeds the option price of $71.10. Thus, if the opportunity cost of the bridge were a certain $75 and the person were the only beneficiary, then the option price indicates that building it would reduce her expected utility if she actually had to pay the opportunity cost of its construction. Hence, the bridge should not be built, even though the expected surplus from building it is positive.

Table 12.3 *Example of a Risk-increasing Project*

	Policy		
Contingency	Bridge	No bridge	Probability of contingency
No earthquake	200	100	.8
Earthquake	100	80	.2
Expected value	180	96	
Variance	1,600	64	

Surplus point:	$U(200 - S_n) = U(100)$ so $S_n = 100$
	$U(100 - S_e) = U(80)$ so $S_e = 20$
Expected surplus:	$E(S) = .8S_n + .2S_e = 84$
Expected utility of no bridge:	$EU = .8U(100) + .2U(80)$
Willingness-to-pay locus:	(s_n, s_e) such that
	$.8U(200 - s_n) + .2U(100 - s_e) = EU$
Option price:	$.8U(200 - OP) + .2U(100 - OP) = EU$
	$EU = 4.56$ and $OP = 71.1$
	for $U(c) = \ln(c)$, where c is net income
Comparison:	$OP < E(S)$

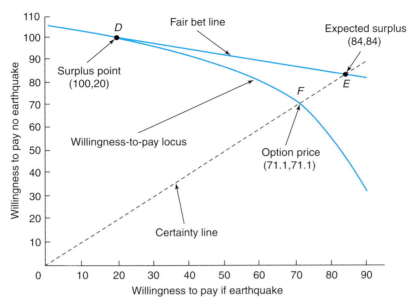

Figure 12.3 Risk-increasing project: expected surplus and option price.

Figure 12.3 illustrates this situation. The bridge can be viewed as initially placing the individual at point *D*. Once again, we can imagine the government requiring the individual to sign a contingent contract, Contract D. In this case, the individual would be willing to pay up to $100 in the event that there is not a quake but only $20 if there is a quake. By signing such a contract, she would be no worse off than she was without the bridge.

We have taken account of the fact that the bridge would increase expected surplus but not the fact that it would also affect income risk. Thus, as before, we imagine that the government is also willing to sign a different contract, Contract E, as long as the expected value of the payments continues to equal $84, their expected value under Contract D.

Which contract would she prefer? If she is risk-averse, she would prefer Contract D to Contract E because, in Table 12.4, even though the expected value of her income is identical under the two contracts, her income would be subject to less risk.

Table 12.4 *Contingent Contracts for the Bridge*

Contingency	Probability	Income under Contract D	Income under Contract E
No quake	.8	$100	$116
Quake	.2	$80	$16
EV		$96	$96

Because a risk-averse individual would prefer Contract D to Contract E, her willingness-to-pay locus for the bridge would be below her fair bet line. Consequently, her option price, which is represented by point *F*, is less than $84. As in the previous illustration, the individual would be indifferent between points *D* and *F*, but not between points *D* and *E*.

12.1.2   *Is Option Price the Best Measure of Benefits?*

The dam and bridge illustrations demonstrate that, in general, option price does not equal expected surplus in circumstances of uncertainty. In the first illustration, option price was larger than the expected value; in the second illustration, it was smaller. We have implicitly taken option price to be the correct benefit measure. Is this generally the case? The answer to this question requires a clearer specification of the institutional environment of policy choice.

The key consideration concerns the availability of insurance against the risks in question. *If complete and actuarially fair insurance is unavailable against the relevant risks, then option price is the conceptually correct measure of benefits.* Insurance is complete if individuals can purchase sufficient coverage to eliminate their risks entirely. It is actuarially fair if its price depends only on the true probabilities of the relevant contingencies. In the case of two contingencies, with the probability of contingency 1 equal to p and the probability of contingency 2 equal to $1 - p$, actuarially fair insurance would allow the individual to trade contingent income in contingency 1 for contingent income in contingency 2 at a price of $p/(1 - p)$. For example, if p equals .2, then the price of insurance equals .25 (.2/.8), so that to increase income in contingency 1 by $100, the individual would have to give up $25 in contingency 2. Graphically, the availability of actuarially fair insurance means that individuals could move along the fair bet lines toward the certainty lines shown in Figures 12.2 and 12.3 through purchases of insurance.

Complete and actuarially fair insurance is rarely if ever available in the real world.[10] The problem of *moral hazard*, the changes in risk-related behavior of insurees induced by insurance coverage, encourages profit-maximizing insurers to limit coverage through copayments.[11] Insurers may be unwilling to provide full insurance against losses to unique assets that cannot be easily valued in markets.[12] *Adverse selection* occurs when insurees have better information about their true risks than do insurers. Adverse selection may result in either the combining of low- and high-risk persons in the same price pool or in limiting the extent of coverage in order to induce high-risk persons to reveal themselves.[13] The pooling of high- and low-risk persons implies that at least one of the groups receives an actuarially unfair price; limiting available coverage to high-risk persons means that complete insurance is unavailable. Routine administrative costs, as well as efforts to control moral hazard and adverse selection, inflate prices above the actuarially fair levels. Limited pools of insurees or uncertainty about the magnitudes of risks may require a further increment in prices to reduce the risk of bankruptcy for insurers.[14] Finally, some risks are so highly correlated across individuals that risk pooling does not sufficiently reduce aggregate risk to allow actuarially fair prices.[15] In order to manage the risk of going bankrupt, insurers facing correlated risks must charge an amount above the actuarially fair price to build a financial cushion or buy reinsurance to guard against the possibility of having to pay off on many losses at the same time.

Imagine that, despite these practical limitations, complete and actuarially fair insurance were available for the risk in question. It would then be possible for the sponsor of the project to trade the contingent surplus amounts for a certain payment by purchasing sufficient insurance to move along the fair bet line, which represents actuarially fair insurance, to the certainty line. In this way, a certain payment corresponding to the expected surplus could be achieved. For example, returning to Figure 12.3, the project sponsor could guarantee a certain payment of $84, which is larger than the option price of $71.10. Notice, however, that if the option price exceeds the expected surplus (the situation illustrated in Figure 12.2), then the latter will understate the conceptually correct measure of project benefits, even if complete and actuarially fair insurance can be purchased. In general, therefore, *if complete and actuarially fair insurance is available, then the larger of option price or expected surplus is the appropriate measure of benefits.*

This generalization ignores one additional institutional constraint: it is not practical to specify contingency-specific payments that would move an individual from his or her contingent surplus point to other points on his or her willingness-to-pay locus. The impracticality may arise from a lack of either information about the shape of the entire willingness-to-pay locus or the administrative capacity to write and execute contingent contracts through taxes and subsidies whose magnitudes depend on the occurrence of events. Yet, if such contracts were administratively feasible *and* the analyst knew the entire willingness-to-pay locus, then the policy could be designed with optimal contingent payments so that the person's post-payment contingent surpluses would have the greatest expected value, which could then be realized with certainty through insurance purchases.

Figure 12.4 illustrates this possibility. In the absence of payments, the person realizes either S_1 or S_2 depending on which contingency occurs. If, in addition to the direct effects of the policy, the person were given a payment equal to $FB_1 - S_1$ if contingency 1 occurred or paid a fee of $S_2 - FB_2$ if contingency 2 occurred, then the person's post-payment contingent surpluses would be given by point FB^*. Because FB^* is the point of tangency between the willingness-to-pay locus and a fair bet line, it has the largest expected value of any point on the willingness-to-pay locus. Starting at this point, complete and actuarially fair insurance would allow the policy sponsors to move along the fair bet line to the certainty line. The resulting certain payment, $E(FB^*)$, would be the maximum certain amount of benefit produced by the payment-adjusted policy.[16]

Thus, *in the exceedingly unlikely circumstance that optimal contingent payments are feasible and complete and actuarially fair insurance is available, the expected value of the point on the willingness-to-pay locus that is just tangent to the fair bet line is the appropriate measure of benefits.*

In summary, if the policy under consideration involves costs that are certain and complete and actuarially fair insurance is unavailable, then option price is the appropriate measure of benefits because it allows us to compare certain willingness-to-pay amounts with certain costs. In practice, however, option prices are difficult to measure. Indeed, as will be evident from the discussion of option values in the next section, very

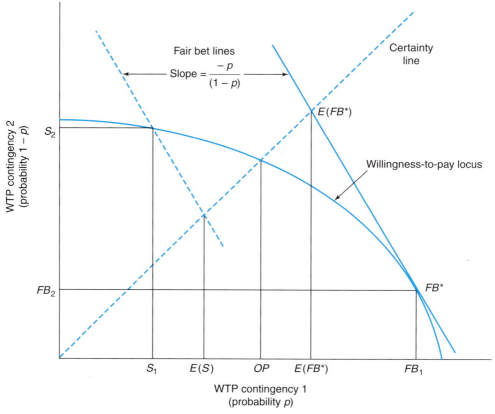

Figure 12.4 Option price and the maximum expected value of willingness to pay.

specific assumptions about the nature of risks must be made to be able to determine whether option price is larger or smaller than the commonly measured expected surplus.

12.2   Determining the Bias in Expected Surplus: Signing Option Value

Early attempts to apply CBA to recreational resources such as national parks raised uneasiness about the appropriateness of expected surplus as a net benefit measure. In a seminal article dealing with the issue, Burton Weisbrod pointed out that estimates of the benefits of preserving a national park based solely on the benefits accruing to actual visitors do not capture its value to those who anticipate the possibility of visiting it sometime in the future but actually never do.[17] He argued that these non-visitors would be willing to pay something to preserve the option of visiting. He called this amount *option value*, which has been interpreted by many as a separate benefit category of relevance to valuing assets, such as natural resources, that offer opportunities for future consumption.

CBA requires a more precise definition of option value, however.[18] The key to formulating it lies in the recognition that option price fully measures a person's *ex ante* willingness to pay for a policy in the presence of uncertainty about the benefits that will accrue *ex post*. The uncertainty may arise from a variety of sources, including not only uncertainty about the demand the person will actually have for the goods produced by the policy if it is implemented (Weisbrod's point), but also uncertainty about the quantities, qualities, and prices of the goods, as well as the prices of other goods. Because, even with such uncertainties, it is a full measure of willingness to pay, option price includes option value.

It is now standard to define *option value* as the difference between option price and expected surplus:

$$OV \equiv OP - E[S] \tag{12.1}$$

where OV is option value, OP is the option price, and $E[S]$ is expected surplus. For example, the option value for the dam presented in Table 12.1 is $4.20, the option price of $34.20 minus the expected surplus of $30. The option value of the bridge presented in Table 12.3 is −$12.90, the option price of $71.10 minus the expected surplus of $84.

Rearranging the equation defining option value gives the practical interpretation of option value as an adjustment to expected surplus required to make it equal to option price:

$$OP = E[S] + OV \tag{12.2}$$

where the left-hand side is the certain amount a person is willing to pay, the conceptually correct measure of benefits, and the right-hand side consists of expected surplus, which is what is typically measurable, and option value, which is the amount that would have to be added to expected surplus to make it equal to option price. Although it may seem natural to interpret option value as a distinct benefit category, it is better to interpret it as the bias in estimated benefits resulting from measurement by expected surplus rather than option price. Unfortunately, either interpretation requires caution because the sign, let alone the magnitude, of option value are often difficult to determine.

In a related literature, the difference between option price (certainty equivalent) and expected surplus is referred to as the risk premium, RP, that is:

$$RP = E(S) - OP \tag{12.3}$$

Thus, somewhat confusingly, $RP = -OV$. The RP is the minimum extra amount above the risk-free net benefit (OP) that the individual requires as compensation for exposure to a risky investment. Alternatively, one can think of it as the maximum amount that the individual would pay to insure the net benefit against risk.

12.2.1   *Determining the Sign of Option Value*

The sign of option value may be positive or negative, depending on a variety of assumptions concerning the source and nature of risk, the characteristics of the policy being analyzed, and the underlying structure of individual utility. With only a few exceptions, the sign of option value has proven to be theoretically ambiguous. This raises the issue of the usefulness of the concept of option value for even determining the direction of bias when expected surplus is used as an approximation of option price.

The earliest studies (see Appendix 12A) attempted to determine the sign of option price when the change in the price or quantity of the good being valued is certain but the demand for the good is uncertain. For example, in the earliest effort to sign option value, Charles J. Cicchetti and A. Myrick Freeman III assumed that there is some probability that a person will have positive demand for the good.[19] Their conclusion that option price is always positive when demand is uncertain was later contradicted by Richard Schmalensee, who showed that the sign was ambiguous under general assumptions.[20]

Subsequent efforts to sign option value without making specific assumptions about individuals' utility functions have produced an unequivocal result only with respect to uncertainty in income. Specifically, in valuing a certain change in the price or quantity of a normal good (quantity demanded increases with increases in income), option value will be negative for a risk-averse person with uncertain income because the change in price or quantity of the good accentuates the income uncertainty. Conversely, in valuing a certain change in the price or quantity of an inferior good (quantity demanded decreases with increases in income), option value will be positive for a risk-averse person. As CBA typically involves valuing changes in normal goods, this general result suggests caution against the tendency of thinking of option value as a positive adjustment to expected surplus.

Exhibit 12.1

In 1980 Richard G. Walsh, John B. Loomis, and Richard A. Gillman combined survey and recreational use data in an effort to estimate the willingness of Colorado households to pay for increments of land designated for wilderness. They estimated that residents of the state were willing to pay a total of $41.6 million annually for 2.6 million acres. Approximately $6.0 million, or almost 15 percent, of this total was option value.

Source: Adapted from Richard G. Walsh, John B. Loomis, and Richard A. Gillman, "Valuing Option, Existence, and Bequest Demands for Wilderness." *Land Economics*, 60(1), 1984, 14–29.

On the other hand, with the imposition of a variety of different restrictive assumptions, it appears that for risk-averse persons, uncertainty about the quantity, quality, or price of a normal good (supply-side uncertainty) will usually result in a positive option value. For example, Douglas M. Larson and Paul R. Flacco show that if the demand for a normal (inferior) good is linear, semilog, or loglinear in price, then option price is positive (negative) for uncertainty in the price or quality of the good being valued.[21] They also show that uncertainty about the prices of other goods and tastes – demand-side uncertainty – similarly yields positive (negative) option values for normal (inferior) goods for these demand functions.[22]

It should not be surprising that in view of the difficulty in establishing the sign of option value, even less progress has been made in putting bounds on its size relative to expected surplus. Calculations by V. Kerry Smith suggest that the size of option value relative to expected surplus is likely to be greater for assets that have less perfect substitutes.[23] Larson and Flacco derived expressions for option value for the specific demand functions that they investigated, but the implementation of these expressions is computationally very difficult.[24] Consequently, it is generally not possible to quantify option value using the information from which estimates of expected surplus are typically made. However, as shown in the next section, we may be able to identify situations in which it is reasonable to assume that option value associated with changes in income risk will be sufficiently small so that option values will be sufficiently small, and therefore, expected surplus will be a close approximation for option price.

12.3   Rationales for Expected Surplus as a Practical Net Benefit Measure

Although option price is generally the conceptually correct measure of net benefits in circumstances of uncertainty and risk, because of data limitations analysts most often estimate net benefits in terms of expected surpluses. As indicated in the preceding discussion of option value, determining even the sign of the bias that results from the use of expected surplus rather than option price is not always possible. In this section we consider the reasonableness of expected surplus as a practical measure.

If society were risk-neutral, then choosing policies that individually maximized expected net benefits would be efficient in the sense of maximizing the expected value of society's entire portfolio of policies.[25] It is generally assumed, however, that individuals are risk-averse. Nonetheless, we present three arguments often made in defense of the use of expected surplus. One argument applies at the level of the individual when people face small changes in risks so that realized net benefits are likely to be close to expected net benefits. Another argument is based on the consideration of the impact of a new project on aggregate social risk. A third argument is based on pooling risks across individuals. We consider each of these arguments in turn.

12.3.1   *Small Changes in Individual Risks*

A new project affects the risk experienced by individuals. Suppose that if there were no project an individual would consume a risky amount of consumption (or income) denoted c. If the project proceeds she would also receive a fraction λ of the net benefits of the new project ($\lambda \geq 0$). The extra risk that she experiences due to the project is given by the change in the variance of her consumption:

$$Var(c + \lambda NB) - Var(c) = \lambda^2 Var(NB) + 2\lambda Cov(c, NB) \qquad (12.4)$$

where $Cov(c, NB)$ represents the covariance between the two risky amounts c and NB. For example, the "no dam" option in Table 12.1 gives her consumption if the dam were not built, and the "dam" option gives her consumption if the dam were built. $Var(c + \lambda NB)$ = 25, $Var(c) = 625$, and the *reduction* in her risk equals 600.

The first term on the right-hand side of Equation (12.4) is a measure of project-specific risk or *non-systematic risk*. The second term on the right-hand side of Equation (12.4) is a measure of *systematic risk*.[26] We consider them in turn.

The parameter λ is small if the project's net benefits are spread broadly over a large population and each individual consumes only a small portion of the net benefits. In this case, the direct effect of project risk is a second-order phenomenon (its effect is multiplied by λ^2), and can be ignored. The change in risk depends only on the second term, $Cov(c, NB)$. If the project's net benefits are independent of non-project consumption, the covariance will be zero and the expected net benefit equals the option price. For a normal good, such as an airport or a highway infrastructure project, the demand for and net benefits from the infrastructure services would be positively correlated with income and consumption. Therefore, the project would be risk-increasing. For a risk-averse individual, the option price would be less than expected net benefits and the option value would be negative. Using expected values would overestimate the net benefits. Conversely, for an inferior good, the correlation would be negative, the option price would be more than expected net benefits, and the option value would be positive for a risk-averse individual.

Even when a project has systematic risk, there are many circumstances in which the option value is relatively small. John Quiggin assumes a power function for individual utility, and shows that for small projects the option value as a proportion of expected surplus depends on four parameters.[27] For reasonable values of these parameters, option value is less than 1 percent of expected net benefits. *Thus, for projects with broadly spread impacts, analysts can reasonably use expected net benefits.*

12.3.2   *Risk Reduction through Policy Portfolios*

The above argument is based on the assumption that each individual receives only a small fraction of the net benefits. However, the benefits and costs of some projects may be unevenly distributed. Policies that are targeted at specific groups, such as the unemployed, or at geographical regions often impose substantial costs on and produce substantial benefits for specific individuals. In these situations, it may not be appropriate to act as if society were risk-averse.

But, in fact, society holds a large portfolio of projects. Therefore, the non-systematic risk associated with a project can be virtually eliminated through portfolio diversification. That is, society can self-insure against the risk of any particular project: it is able to pool risk across projects so that it effectively has complete and actuarially fair insurance. In this case analysts can act as if λ is small.[28] *If, in addition, the systematic risk is small, then analysis of a new government project can proceed by discounting its expected net benefits at the risk-free social discount rate.*[29]

12.3.4   *Pooling Risks across Individuals: Collective and Individual Risk*

We next consider the possibility of risk pooling at the level of the individual policy. It is important to make a distinction between collective risk and individual risk.

By *collective risk*, we simply mean that the same contingency will result for all individuals in society. For example, in the context of doing a CBA for a nuclear power plant, the contingencies might be "no accident" and "nuclear accident" – everyone in the geographic area experiences the same realized contingency. The actual realized net benefits can differ substantially from the expected net benefits because all individuals share the same outcome, whether favorable or unfavorable, rather than the weighted average of the two. In such circumstances, the world does not offer us a "middle" outcome corresponding to the expected value. Realized net benefits will, therefore, differ substantially from expected net benefits.

In contrast, consider the case of a large number of individuals who have identical preferences and who face the same probabilities of realizing each of the contingencies, but the contingency that each individual realizes is independent of the contingency realized by any other individual. This is a case of *individual risk*. This might occur, for instance, in the context of evaluating an automobile safety device using a model of traffic accidents in which there is some probability that a driver will have a potentially fatal accident for each mile driven. Multiplying the expected net benefits for one individual by the number of individuals yields a measure of total expected net benefits for the policy that can appropriately be treated as approximately certain. The reason is that in circumstances of individual risk with large numbers of individuals exposed to the risk, the proportion of individuals realizing each contingency approximates the probability associated with that contingency. In other words, the averaging process tends to produce realizations of total net benefits close to those calculated by the expected value procedure.

This averaging is analytically equivalent to the availability of actuarially fair insurance – it effectively translates, through a movement along a fair bet line, any contingent surplus point to a point on the certainty line. Thus, *in cases of individual risk, the larger of option price and expected surplus is the appropriate benefit measure*.

12.3.5   *Reprise: Expected Surplus as a Practical Measure*

How reasonable is the use of expected surplus as a practical net benefit measure? Although social risk-neutrality argues for expected surplus as the correct benefit measure, its underlying assumptions are not plausible. Somewhat more plausibly, if each individual receives only a small fraction of the net benefits of a project and if the systematic risk is small, then diversification across policies argues for expected surplus as an approximate measure of benefits. Overall, these arguments suggest that when neither option prices nor option values can be estimated, and risks are individual rather than collective, analysts can reasonably use expected surplus as an approximate measure of benefits. When dealing with cases involving collective risk, they should take special care to consider the potential bias in this approach.

12.4   Conclusion

We rarely have much opportunity to infer option prices directly from observable behavior, although insurance premiums and self-protection investments may convey some useful information about people's WTP for reductions in risk. Contingent valuation surveys provide an alternative approach for directly eliciting option prices through structured conversations with respondents, but they are prone to the problems we discuss in Chapter 16. Consequently, we often have no alternative but to predict policy effects under the specified contingencies, value them with shadow price estimates from observed market behavior, and calculate expected net benefits. In cases of individual risk, it is unlikely that this procedure will result in an overestimation of net benefits. In cases of collective risk, however, these expected net benefits may either understate or overstate the conceptually correct benefits based on option price by an amount called the option value. Unfortunately, confidently signing, let alone quantifying, option price is often not possible.

APPENDIX 12A

Signing Option Value

The following table shows the progression of theoretical investigations of the sign of option value.

Study	Assumptions and conclusions	Comments
Douglas M. Larson and Paul R. Flacco, "Measuring Option Prices from Market Behavior." *Journal of Environmental Economics and Management*, 22(2), 1992, 178–98.	(1) Linear, semilog, or loglinear demand functions; uncertainty in own-price, other prices, quality, or tastes: Option value positive for normal goods; option price negative for inferior goods. (2) Linear demand, uncertainty about income, normal or inferior goods: Option value is zero. (3) Semilog or loglinear demand; uncertainty about income; normal or inferior goods: Option value is negative.	Assumption of specific functional forms for demand allow signing of option value for nonincome uncertainty. Linear demand implies risk-neutrality; semilog and loglinear demands imply risk-aversion for normal goods and risk-seeking for inferior goods.
Richard C. Hartman and Mark L. Plummer, "Option Value under Income and Price Uncertainty." *Journal of Environmental Economics and Management*, 14(3), 1987, 212–25.	(1) Uncertainty in income: Option value is negative for normal goods. (2) Uncertainty in own-price and other prices: Sign of option value is ambiguous.	General in the sense that preferences may depend on contingencies.

(continued)

(cont.)

Study	Assumptions and conclusions	Comments
Mark L. Plummer and Richard C. Hartman, "Option Value: A General Approach." *Economic Inquiry*, 24(3), 1986, 455–71.	(1) Uncertainty in income and risk-aversion: Option value is negative for normal goods. (2) Uncertainty in quality and risk-aversion: Option value is positive for normal goods. (3) Uncertainty in tastes and risk aversion: Option value ambiguous for more than two contingencies.	Sign of option value for uncertain parameter depends on signs of the changes in surplus and marginal utility with respect to the parameter.
A. Myrick Freeman III, "The Sign and Size of Option Value." *Land Economics*, 60(1), 1984, 1–13.	(1) Uncertainty in demand due to exogenous factors and risk-aversion: Option value is positive. (2) If probability of demand is low, expected consumer surplus is large, and person is highly risk-averse, then option value may be large.	Depends on assumption that marginal utilities and attitudes toward risk independent of exogenous factors; demonstrated for only two contingencies.
Richard C. Bishop, "Option Value: An Exposition and Extension." *Land Economics*, 58(1), 1982, 1–15.	(1) Uncertainty in demand: Sign of option value is ambiguous. (2) Uncertainty in supply (price uncertainty): Option value is positive.	Supply-side case demonstrated for only two contingencies.
Richard Schmalensee, "Option Demand and Consumer's Surplus: Valuing Price Changes under Uncertainty." *American Economic Review*, 62(5), 1972, 813–24.	Uncertainty in demand: Sign of option value is ambiguous.	Sign depends on risk-aversion and whether surplus is measured by equivalent or compensating variation.
Charles J. Cicchetti and A. Myrick Freeman III, "Option Demand and Consumer Surplus: Further Comment." *Quarterly Journal of Economics*, 85(3), 1971, 528–39.	Uncertainty in demand: Option value is positive.	Overly strong assumptions imply the same utility results under each contingency.

Exercises for Chapter 12

1. A large rural county is considering establishing a medical transport unit that would use helicopters to fly emergency medical cases to hospitals. Analysts have attempted to estimate the benefits from establishing the unit in two ways. First, they surveyed a random sample of residents to find out how much they would be willing to pay each year for the unit. Based on responses from the sample, the analysts estimated a total willingness to pay of $8.5 million per year. Second, the analysts estimated the dollar value of the improvements in health outcomes and avoided medical costs of users of the unit to be $6.2 million per year. Taking the analysts' estimates at face value, specify the following:

    a. The aggregate of individuals' annual option prices for the unit.

    b. The annual total expected gain in social surplus from use of the unit.

    c. The annual aggregate option value for the unit.

2. Imagine that we want to value a cultural festival from the point of view of a risk-averse person. The person's utility is given by $U(I)$ where $I is her income. She has a 50 percent chance of being able to get vacation time to attend the festival. If she gets the vacation time, then she would be willing to pay up to $S to attend the festival. If she does not get the vacation time, then she is unwilling to pay anything for the festival.

    a. What is her expected surplus from the cultural festival?

    b. Write an expression for her expected utility if the festival does not take place.

    c. Write an expression incorporating her option price, OP, for the festival if the festival takes place. (To do this, equate her expected utility if the festival takes place to her expected utility if the festival does not take place. Also, assume that if the festival does take place, then she makes a payment of OP whether or not she is able to attend the festival.)

    d. Manipulate the expression for option price to show that the option price must be smaller than her expected surplus. (In doing this, begin by substituting $0.5S - e$ for OP in the equation derived in part c. Also keep in mind that because the person is risk averse, her marginal utility declines with income.)

    e. Does this exercise suggest any generalizations about the benefits of recreational programs when individuals are uncertain as to whether they will be able to participate in them?

3. (Spreadsheet required.) Imagine that a rancher would have an income of $80,000 if his county remains free from a cattle parasite but only $50,000 if the county is exposed to the parasite. Further imagine that a county program to limit the impact of exposure to the parasite would reduce his income to $76,000 if the county remains free of the parasite but increase it to $70,000 if the county is exposed to the parasite. Assume that there is a 60 percent chance of exposure to the parasite and that the rancher's utility is the natural logarithm of his income. What is the rancher's option price for the county program? (Set up the appropriate equation and solve through iterative guessing.)

Notes

1. The variance in net benefits is defined as: $Var[NB] = E\{(NB - E[NB])^2\}$. For a discrete random variable with possible outcomes NB_i, $i = 1, 2, \ldots n$,

$$E(NB) = \sum_{i=1}^{n} p_i \, NB_i \text{ and}$$

$$VAR(NB) = \sum_{i=1}^{n} p_i (NB_i - E(\text{NB}))^2$$

where, p_i is the probability of the ith outcome.

2. Our discussion in this section is based on Daniel A. Graham, "Cost–Benefit Analysis Under Uncertainty." *American Economic Review*, 71(4), 1981, 715–25; V. Kerry Smith, "Uncertainty, Benefit–Cost Analysis, and the Treatment of Option Value." *Journal of Environmental Economics and Management*, 14(3): 1987, 283–92; and Charles E. Meier and Alan Randall, "Use Value Under Uncertainty: Is There a 'Correct' Measure?" *Land Economics*, 67(4), 1991, 379–89. The latter is the best overview of this topic despite a pedagogically relevant typographical error (the slope of the fair bet line is misstated in several diagrams).

3. Measuring benefits by persons' *ex ante* willingness to pay assumes that they correctly assess and process risks. Lack of information about risks, or biases in processing the information, muddies the comparison between this approach and the expectational approach if the latter involves more accurate risk assessments. For overviews, see Colin F. Camerer and Howard Kunreuther, "Decision Processes for Low Probability Risks: Policy Implications." *Journal of Policy Analysis and Management*, 8(4), 1989, 565–92, and W. Kip Viscusi, *Fatal Trade-offs: Public and Private Responsibilities for Risk* (New York, NY: Oxford University Press, 1992).

4. Formally, let m_i be the person's wealth under contingency i and let Z be an indicator of whether the policy under consideration is adopted ($Z = 0$ if not adopted; $Z = 1$ if adopted). The person's utility under contingency i can be written as $U(m_i, Z)$. The person's surplus (willingness to pay) for the project given that contingency i occurs, S_i, satisfies the equation:

$$U(m_i - S_i, 1) = U(m_i, 0)$$

The expected value of the person's contingent surpluses is $E(S) = p_1 S_1 = p_2 S_2$ in the case of two contingencies with probabilities p_1 and p_2, respectively.

5. In the case of the pay-offs from the dam given in Table 12.1:

$$E[X] = (.5)(110) + (.5)(100) = 105$$
$$\text{and Var}[X] = (.5)(110 - 105)^2$$
$$+ (.5)(100 - 105)^2$$
$$= 25$$

6. The option price in this example is found by solving $0.5U(110 - OP) + 0.5U(100 - OP) = 4.26$.

7. The intersection of the fair bet line and the certainty line corresponds to the solution of the following equations:

$$E(S) = p_1 x_1 + p_2 x_2 \text{ (expected value line)}$$
$$x_1 = x_2 \text{ (certainty line)}$$
$$p_1 = 1 - p_2$$

where x_1 defines the location of points on the vertical axis and x_2 defines the location of points on the horizontal axis. Solving these equations gives $E(S) = x$, where x is the point of intersection.

8. Two aspects of the relation among the fair bet line, the certainty line, and the willingness-to-pay locus are worth noting. First, if insurance were available in unlimited quantity at an actuarially fair price, then the person could actually move from any point on the willingness-to-pay locus along the fair bet line to the certainty line by buying insurance. The near consensus that option price is the appropriate benefit measure is based on the reasonable assumption that complete and actuarially fair insurance markets generally do not exist in the real world. Second, a fair bet line can be drawn through any point. Thus, for example, if we wanted to know which point on the willingness-to-pay locus has the largest expected value, then we would find the point that is just tangent to a fair bet line.

9. Continuing with the notation from note 4, points on the willingness-to-pay locus, $(w_1 \, w_2)$, satisfy the following equation:

$$p_1 U_1 (m_1 - w_1, 1) + p_2 U_2 (m_2 - w_2, 1) = EU$$

where $EU = p_1 U_1(m_1, 0) + p_2 U_2(m_2, 0)$ is the person's expected utility without the project.

10. For a general introduction to the theory of insurance, see Isaac Ehrlich and Gary S. Becker, "Market Insurance, Self-Insurance, and Self-Protection." *Journal of Political Economy*, 80(4), 1972, 663–48.

11. Mark V. Pauly, "The Economics of Moral Hazard: Comment." *American Economic Review*, 58(3), 1968, 531–37.

12. Philip J. Cook and Daniel A. Graham, "The Demand for Insurance and Protection: The Case of Irreplaceable Commodities." *Quarterly Journal of Economics*, 91(1), 1977, 141–56.

13. One way to get high-risk persons to reveal themselves is to offer two insurance options: one that gives full coverage at a premium that is actuarially fair for high risks and another that gives only limited coverage at a premium that

is actually fair for low risks. If the level of coverage under the latter option is sufficiently low, then high risks will be better off revealing themselves to get the full coverage. The result is a so-called *separating equilibrium* in which both risk groups honestly reveal themselves. However, the information is gained at the cost of limiting coverage to low-risk persons. See Michael Rothschild and Joseph Stiglitz, "Equilibrium in Competitive Insurance Markets: An Essay on the Economics of Imperfect Information." *Quarterly Journal of Economics*, 90(4), 1976, 629–50. An extension of the Rothschild–Stiglitz model, which incorporates contracting costs, allows for the possibility that low-risk persons receive more favorable coverage. See Joseph P. Newhouse, "Reimbursing Health Plans and Health Providers: Efficiency in Production versus Selection." *Journal of Economic Literature*, 34(3), 1996, 1236–63.

14. J. David Cummins, "Statistical and Financial Models of Insurance Pricing and the Insurance Firm." *Journal of Risk and Insurance*, 58(2), 1991, 261–301.

15. Jack Hirshleifer and John G. Riley, *The Analytics of Uncertainty and Information* (New York, NY: Cambridge University Press, 1992).

16. The difference between $E(FB^*)$ and $E(S)$ is called the *option premium*. Unlike option value, it is always nonnegative. See Dennis C. Cory and Bonnie Colby Saliba, "Requiem for Option Value." *Land Economics*, 63(1), 1987, 1–10. Unfortunately, the extreme assumptions of complete and actuarially fair insurance, knowledge of the entire willingness-to-pay locus, and the feasibility of contingent-specific payments give the notion of option premium little practical relevance to CBA.

17. Burton A. Weisbrod, "Collective Consumption Services of Individual Consumption Goods." *Quarterly Journal of Economics*, 78(3), 1964, 71–77.

18. The possibility of double-counting benefits with this formulation was soon pointed out by Millard F. Long, "Collective-Consumption Services of Individual-Consumption Goods." *Quarterly Journal of Economics*, 81(2), 1967, 351–52.

19. Charles J. Cicchetti and A. Myrick Freeman III, "Option Demand and Consumer Surplus: Further Comment." *Quarterly Journal of Economics*, 85(3), 1971, 528–39.

20. Richard Schmalensee, "Option Demand and Consumer's Surplus: Valuing Price Changes under Uncertainty." *American Economic Review*, 62(5), 1972, 813–24. Robert Anderson later showed that the contradictory results arose because of additional assumptions made by Cicchetti and Freeman that had the unattractive consequence of guaranteeing the option buyer a certain utility level no matter which contingency arose. Robert J. Anderson

Jr., "A Note on Option Value and the Expected Value of Consumer's Surplus." *Journal of Environmental Economics and Management*, 8(2), 1981, 187–91.

21. Douglas M. Larson and Paul R. Flacco, "Measuring Option Prices from Market Behavior." *Journal of Environmental Economics and Management*, 22(2), 1992, 178–98.

22. Larson and Flacco, "Measuring Option Prices from Market Behavior." As discussed in Chapter 13, empirical estimation of demand equations usually involves at least income and own-price as explanatory variables for quantity. If the sign of the estimated coefficient of income is positive (negative), then the good is normal (inferior).

23. V. Kerry Smith, "A Bound for Option Value." *Land Economics*, 60(3), 1984, 292–96.

24. Their expressions require not only estimates of the parameters of the demand equations, but also fairly complicated expectations over the parameters that are treated as uncertain.

25. To say that society is risk-neutral implies that there is a social welfare function that ranks alternative distributions of goods among individuals. That is, it gives a "score" to each possible distribution such that a distribution with a higher score is preferred by society to a distribution with a lower score. Aggregation of individual preferences, however, cannot guarantee a social welfare function that satisfies minimally desirable properties as noted in Chapter 2. Again, see Tibor Scitovsky, "The State of Welfare Economics." *American Economic Review*, 51(3), 1951, 301–15. More generally, see Kenneth J. Arrow, *Social Choice and Individual Values*, 2nd edn (New Haven, CT: Yale University Press, 1963).

26. Note, importantly, that in welfare economics and cost–benefit analysis, (social) systematic risk depends on the covariance (or correlation) between net (social) benefits of a new project and non-project aggregate consumption. It is completely different from (financial) private-sector systematic risk, which depends on the covariance (or correlation) between the financial returns to a new project and the returns to the market portfolio. Indeed, one may be positive while the other is negative, and vice versa; see Anthony E. Boardman and Mark Hellowell, "A Comparative Analysis and Evaluation of Specialist PPP Units' Methodologies for Conducting Value for Money Appraisals." *Journal of Comparative Policy Analysis*, 19(3), 2017, 191–206.

27. John C. Quiggin, "Risk and Discounting in Project Evaluation." In *Risk and Cost Benefit Analysis*, M. Harvey (Ed.) (Bureau of Transport and Regional Economics), Report 110. Australian Government Department of Transport and Regional Services, 2005, 67–116. The four parameters are: the (constant) elasticity of the marginal

utility of consumption; a term that is proportional to the systematic risk; the coefficient of variation (standard deviation divided by expected value) for the project's net benefits; and the coefficient of variation for consumption.

28. Kenneth J. Arrow and Robert C. Lind, "Uncertainty and the Evaluation of Public Investment Decisions." *American Economic Review*, 60(3), 1970, 364–78.

29. See Mark M. Moore, Anthony E. Boardman and Aidan R. Vining, "Risk in Public Sector Project Appraisal: It Mostly Does Not Matter!" *Public Works Management and Policy*, 22(4), 2017, 55–78.

13 Existence Value

Within the CBA framework, people's willingness to pay (WTP) for a policy change comprehensively measures its social benefits. Although analysts sometimes elicit willingness-to-pay amounts through contingent valuation surveys (see Chapter 16), they prefer to make inferences about them from observations of people's behaviors (see Chapters 4, 14, and 15). Observed changes in consumption of a good whose price or quantity is affected by the policy change allow WTP to be estimated. For many, perhaps most, applications of CBA, analysts can reasonably assume that such estimates capture the entire WTP. Yet in some applications of CBA, especially those involving changes to unique environmental resources, people may be willing to pay for the existence of "goods" that they themselves will never actually "consume." Correctly conceptualizing and measuring such *existence values* poses a challenge to the application of CBA.

In this chapter, we consider existence value as an additional category of benefit. It is often grouped with option value and quasi-option value under the heading of *non-use* or *passive use* benefits. As discussed in Chapters 11 and 12, however, option and quasi-option values are better thought of as adjustments to standard benefit measures to take account of various aspects of uncertainty rather than as distinct categories of benefits. In contrast, existence value is another meaningful benefit category, although one that poses problems of definition and measurement.[1] After framing existence value as a special benefit category, we discuss the theoretical and empirical problems analysts face in measuring it.

13.1 Active and Passive Use Value

The notion that people may place a value on the very existence of "unique phenomena of nature" that they neither visit, nor ever anticipate visiting, was introduced into the CBA literature around half a century ago by John V. Krutilla.[2] Consider, for example, a unique wilderness area. Hunters might be willing to pay to preserve the area because it either lowers the price or increases the quality of hunting. Naturalists might be willing to pay to preserve the area because it provides a desirable area for hiking or bird-watching. Nearby residents may be willing to pay to preserve the area because they enjoy its scenic beauty and it prevents commercial development that they find undesirable. People who enjoy nature films may be willing to pay to preserve the area because it provides a unique setting for filming rare species. All of these people value the area because they make use of it in some way. Yet one can imagine that some people might be willing to pay to preserve the area even though they do not use it in any of these ways. In commonly used terminology, these people are said to derive *non-use value* from the wilderness area. Note that while it might make sense to think about these people as additional people, they may not be: that is, some people may derive both use value and non-use value from an asset.

While most economists accept the general idea that people may derive value from mere knowledge of the existence of unique assets such as scenic wilderness, animal species, or works of art, clearly defining non-use value is a complicated issue, and there is not yet a clear consensus on its precise meaning.

One complication is the difficulty of drawing a sharp line between use and non-use. In terms of standard consumer theory, any good that a person values is an argument in his or her utility function. The good need not involve any observable activity by the person to secure its value. The quantity of a pure public good such as national defense, for instance, is "consumed" by individuals, however passively. Existence value can also be thought of as a pure public good.[3] It is non-rivalrous – the value one person derives from it does not diminish the values derived by others. It is non-excludable – no one can be excluded from deriving value from the quantity of the good, which is provided commonly to all. Viewed as a public good, it seems more appropriate to describe existence value as *passive use* rather than non-use.

Yet, how passive must the "consumption" be in order to distinguish use from non-use? It is probably safe to say that merely thinking about the good does not constitute use as the term is commonly understood. What about discussing the good with other people? Consumption now involves observable behavior, the consumption of a complementary good, time, but most economists would probably consider it non-use. Consuming films and photography books based on the good, however, probably crosses the line between use and non-use because it leaves a behavioral trace in the markets for these complementary goods. These distinctions hinge not just on the intrinsic attributes of the good, but also on our ability to observe and value behavior. Thus, in actual application, distinguishing between use and non-use is not just a purely conceptual issue.

A second complication, which we consider in more detail in Appendix 13A, arises because individuals derive both use and non-use value from a given asset. A person's WTP for preservation of a wilderness area may be motivated by the anticipation of hunting *and* the pleasure of knowing that future generations will be able to enjoy it as well. While the person's total WTP, or as it is often called in this context *total economic value*, is conceptually clear, the division between these two categories of value is ambiguous because the order of valuation is generally relevant. One ordering is to elicit first the person's WTP for use and then, taking this amount as actually paid, to elicit the person's WTP for non-use. The other possible ordering is to elicit first the person's WTP for non-use and then, taking this amount as actually paid, elicit the person's WTP for use. The orderings should yield the same total WTP, but they probably will yield different values for use and non-use. Obviously, the ordering problem blurs the boundary between use and non-use.

A third complication has to do with differences in the way quantity changes affect use and non-use benefits. In general, non-use benefits tend to be less quantity-sensitive than use benefits. For example, consider a species of mammal that will remain viable as long as its population exceeds 20,000. Someone may very well have a non-use value for the existence of this species that is the same for total populations of either 25,000 or 25 million because either level of population is large enough to avoid extinction. Hikers who wish to see this species in its natural habitat, however, may have a use value that is substantially higher for a larger population because it offers a greater likelihood of an encounter with the species.

Finally, the non-use category raises issues of motivation that are typically avoided by economists. If non-use does not leave a behavioral trace, then its value must usually be discovered empirically through stated rather than revealed preferences, in other words, by contingent valuation surveys, which are discussed in Chapter 16. Sometimes economists may be able to find behavioral traces outside of normal market transactions. For example, especially at the local level, binding referenda on the provision of public goods are sometimes held. By relating percentages of affirmative votes to district-level property values or incomes, it may be possible to make inferences about WTP. Nonetheless, most empirical estimates of non-use values rely on stated rather than revealed preferences.

A theory about the motivations behind non-use value can help guide the formulation and interpretation of questions for eliciting stated preferences. For example, a possible motivation for non-use value is altruism toward either current people or future generations. Yet, it makes a difference whether the altruism is either individualistic or paternalistic. A concern about the general utility levels of others can be described as *individualistic altruism*; a concern about the consumption of specific goods by others is *paternalistic altruism*. For example, giving money to homeless alcoholics is consistent with individualistic altruism, while contributing to a program that gives them only meals is consistent with paternalistic altruism. If the analyst believes that individualistic altruism is the motivation for existence value, then it is important that contingent valuation survey respondents be given sufficient context to understand the implications of provision of the good on the overall wealth of others. Because the targets of altruism usually bear some share of the costs of the provided goods, individualistic altruism generally results in lower existence values than paternalistic altruism.[4] For example, altruism might motivate someone to want to bequeath the current world climate to subsequent generations. If the altruism is paternalistic rather than altruistic, then, in determining WTP for current policies, the survey ignores the possibility that members of future generations might prefer some climate change and a higher endowment of capital to no climate change and a lower endowment of capital.

With these caveats in mind, we present Table 13.1 as a way of thinking about existence value as a benefit category within the broader framework of benefit categories.[5] The distinction between use benefit and non-use benefit partially reflects our ability to measure them.

Consider first benefits that arise from active use of a good. The most obvious benefit category is *rivalrous consumption* of goods, such as trees for wood products, water for irrigation, and grasslands for cattle grazing. As markets usually exist for rivalrous goods, they are the category most amenable to valuation through the estimation of demand schedules and consumer surplus.

Table 13.1 *Taxonomy of Benefits: Possible Partitioning of WTP*

Type of use	Benefit category	Example
Active use	Rivalrous consumption	Logging of old-growth forest
	Non-rivalrous consumption: direct	Hiking in wilderness
	Non-rivalrous consumption: indirect	Watching a film of wilderness area
	Option value	Possibility of visiting wilderness area in the future
Passive use (non-use)	Pure existence value: good has intrinsic value	Perceived value of natural order
	Altruistic existence value: gift to current generation	Others hiking in wilderness
	Altruistic existence value: bequest to future generation	Future others hiking in wilderness

The other use categories are for non-rivalrous goods. Those consumed onsite, such as hiking and bird-watching, which do not interfere with other users or uses, are labeled *direct non-rivalrous consumption*. Although rarely traded in markets, such goods often can be valued by observing the travel and time costs people are willing to bear to consume them (see Chapter 15). In alternative taxonomies of benefits, this category is sometimes labeled *non-destructive consumption*.

Indirect non-rivalrous consumption takes place offsite. For example, a person may derive value from watching a film about wildlife in a particular wilderness area. Expenditures of time and money on offsite non-rivalrous consumption provide some information for estimating its value, although much less reliably than for the other use categories.

Consider next passive use benefits. Four categories can be distinguished in terms of motivation. The first category, *option value*, was discussed in Chapter 12. It is the amount that someone is willing to pay to keep open the option of use, active or passive, in the future. It is only passive in the sense that it would not be fully captured by estimates of WTP based on observations of active use.

The other categories pertain to different types of existence value. The second category, *pure existence value*, arises because people believe the good has intrinsic value apart from its use. For example, some people might be willing to pay to preserve a wilderness area because they think that it is right that some natural habitats exist for rare animal species.

The remaining two categories are based on altruism. Some people may be willing to pay to preserve a wilderness area, for example, because they get pleasure from knowing that it is used by others. Generally, the motivation for such *altruistic existence value* is paternalistic in the sense that it is driven by the desire for others to consume this particular good, rather than by the desire to increase their consumption overall. It may be based on the belief that exposure to nature, art, or historical sites is intrinsically good or perhaps on the desire to share with others a type of experience one has found to be emotionally enriching. When the altruism is directed toward future generations, the good is said to have a *bequest value*. People get pleasure from knowing that those not yet born will be able to use (and not use!) the good. Just as people often wish to leave their children a share of the wealth they have accumulated, they may want to bequeath them access to unique goods as well.

The distribution of benefits across these categories obviously depends on the specific attributes of the project being evaluated. By their very nature, projects involving the conservation of wilderness areas are likely to derive a high fraction of their benefits from non-use values. For example, based on survey data, K. G. Willis estimated existence values for three nature "Sites of Special Scientific Interest" in Great Britain.[6] Consumer surplus associated with use of the sites appeared to account for only about 10–12 percent of people's total WTP. Option value accounted for a comparable percentage. The remaining portion of WTP consisted of existence (pure and bequest) value. Only if the non-use benefits were included did conservation of these areas appear to have positive net benefits.

13.2   The Measurement of Existence Value

Despite the difficulty economists have in clearly defining existence value as a benefit category, few economists would deny that sometimes people are willing to pay a total amount for the preservation of assets that exceeds their WTP for their use or anticipated possible future use. Yet, some economists believe that the method of measurement currently available, the contingent value survey, lacks sufficient reliability for existence values to be reasonably included in CBA. Because we consider contingent valuation in detail in Chapter 16, our discussion here raises only the general issues most relevant to the measurement of existence value.

13.2.1   *Directly Eliciting Total Economic Value*

One way to avoid some of the conceptual problems in defining existence value is to measure WTP for a policy change holistically rather than disaggregating it into component parts. In the context of contingent valuation, the analyst poses questions aimed at getting respondents to state their WTP amounts based on consideration of *all* their possible motivations for valuing policy changes. The total economic value revealed through this *structured conversation* is each respondent's benefit from the policy change.

The viability of this approach obviously depends on the analyst's ability to structure a meaningful conversation. The analyst must convey a full description of the policy effect being valued. Considerably more context must be provided in the valuation of effects on passive than active use. People typically know their own current levels of use as a starting point for valuing marginal changes. They are less likely to know the total stock of a good that has non-use value to them. Yet their valuation of marginal changes in the good is likely to depend on how much they think is currently available. For example, people who think that a particular species lives only in one particular wilderness area are likely to place a much higher value on the preservation of that area than if they knew that the species lived in several other already protected areas. Indeed, one can imagine that, given enough information and time for reflection, some people may place a zero or negative value on the existence of more of some good when its quantity is above some threshold. One may place a negative value on policies that increase the number of deer in an area if, for instance, their number is already so large as to threaten the survival of other species.

Exhibit 13.1

Public opinion and economic analysis frequently conflict in the evaluation of public subsidies for the construction and operation of stadiums for professional sports teams. Valid CBAs of sports stadiums based only on use benefits almost never find positive social net benefits, especially if conducted from the national perspective. In its early years, for example, the baseball stadium built for the Baltimore Orioles at Camden Yards appears to have increased average attendance from 30,000 to 45,000 per game, with approximately 70 percent of the increase in attendance consisting of residents from outside Maryland, suggesting that net benefits might be positive if a CBA were conducted from a state rather than a national perspective.

Bruce W. Hamilton and Peter Kahn did exactly that, but still did not obtain positive net benefits. Conducting a detailed CBA from the perspective of the residents of Maryland, they reported the following annual benefits and costs:

Annual benefits:		$3.36 million
Job creation	$0.48 million	
Out-of-stadium incremental taxes	$1.25 million	
Incremental admission tax	$1.20 million	
Sales tax on incremental stadium spending	$0.43 million	
Annual costs:		$14.00 million
Annual net benefit:		−$10.64 million

The net cost of the stadium to Maryland taxpayers is $10.64 million per year, which is equivalent to about $14.20 per Baltimore household per year. Hamilton and Kahn note, however, that building the stadium was probably necessary to keep the Orioles from eventually moving to another city, and that citizens of Maryland, even if they never attend Orioles games, may place a value on the stadium because they get pleasure from simply having the Orioles in Baltimore. Hamilton and Kahn call these values "public consumption benefits," which can be thought of as passive-use benefits, consisting of some combination of option value and existence value. Only if the annual value of public consumption benefits exceeds $10.64 million would Oriole Park at Camden Yards pass the net benefits test.

Source: Adapted from Bruce W. Hamilton and Peter Kahn, "Baltimore's Camden Yards Ballparks," in Roger G. Noll and Andrew Zimbalist, editors, *Sports, Jobs, and Taxes: The Economic Impact of Sports Teams and Stadiums* (Washington, DC: The Brookings Institution, 1997), 245–81. Corrections to original provided by Bruce W. Hamilton.

Existence value based on altruism poses special problems. When individuals are concerned only about their own consumption, it is reasonable to separate costs from benefits. Each can be estimated separately and combined to find net benefits. Altruistic values, however, may depend on the distribution of both costs and benefits. Respondents thus need to know who is likely to use the good being valued and who is likely to bear the costs of preserving it. Failure to include information on the latter may inflate existence values if it leads to respondents not taking into account all the effects on others.

Let us assume that these concerns, along with the more general problems of contingent valuation discussed in Chapter 16, are adequately addressed so that analysts can be confident that they have correctly elicited individuals' total economic value for the policy change under consideration. If their sample of respondents included all the people with standing, then these total valuations would suffice for completing the CBA. Often, however, analysts wish to combine benefits estimated from behavioral data with existence value estimates from a relatively small sample drawn from people with standing. As already mentioned, partitioning respondents' total WTP into use and non-use values is sensitive to the ordering of categories. If non-use values from the sample are to be added to use values estimated by other methods to get total economic benefits, then it is important that questions be asked so as to elicit non-use values after respondents have considered and reported their use values.

In contrast to use, non-use does not occur in easily defined geographic markets. Aggregate existence values are very sensitive to the geographic assumptions made in extrapolating from survey samples to the population with standing.[7] People appear to place a higher existence value on resources in closer proximity.[8] Therefore, using average existence values estimated from local samples to obtain aggregate existence values for a more geographically extensive population may be inappropriate. Indeed, the question of geographic extrapolation appears to be one of the most controversial aspects of the use of existence values in damage assessment cases.[9]

As a final point, note that as long as the structured conversation leads respondents to consider all the sources of uncertainty relevant to their valuation of the policy change, their total WTP amount is an option price. It is thus fully inclusive of option value so that no adjustments for uncertainty are required.

13.2.2   *Behavioral Traces of Existence Value?*

Many economists would be more comfortable measuring existence value through the observation of related behavior. As a pure public good, however, its behavioral trace is likely to be so weak that considerable ingenuity will be required to find ways of measuring it through readily accepted methods. Nevertheless, the history of the development of increasingly sophisticated methods for measuring benefits offers some hope that a way will be found.

Bruce Madariaga and Kenneth McConnell suggest one line of investigation.[10] They note that people are willing to pay to join such organizations as the Nature Conservancy and the Audubon Society. Some part of their membership fees can be thought of as voluntary contributions for a public good, the preservation of wilderness areas. Ways of making inferences about existence values from the patterns of contributions to such organizations have yet to be developed. Doing so is complicated by the problem of *free riding* – some who benefit from the public good will not voluntarily contribute to its provision. However, M. Shechter, B. Reiser, and N. Zaitsev used donation in response to fire damage to a national park in Israel to assess the passive value of the damage and then compared their results to contingent valuation survey findings, concluding that the evidence from donations (which they interpret as revealed behavior) is not strongly consistent with the contingent valuation findings.[11]

More sophisticated models of individual utility may also provide some leverage on the measurement of existence value. Douglas Larson notes that public goods are sometimes complements of, or substitutes for, private goods.[12] If investigators are willing to impose assumptions about the form of the demand for market goods and the nature of the complementarity between market goods and existence values, then they may be able to make inferences about the magnitudes of the existence values from observation of the consumption of the market goods. Larson also suggests that explicitly treating time as a constraint in utility maximization may open up possibilities for measurement based on people's allocations of time. For example, the time people spend watching films or reading books about habitats of endangered species might, with sufficient cleverness, provide a basis for estimating their existence values for the habitats.

13.2.3   *Should Existence Value Be Included in CBA?*

A growing number of efforts to estimate existence values through surveys can be found in the literature.[13] The particular estimates are often controversial.[14] Should existence values be used in CBA? The answer requires a balancing of conceptual and practical concerns. On the one hand, recognizing existence values as pure public goods argues for their inclusion. On the other hand, in view of the current state of practice, estimates of existence values are very uncertain. This trade-off suggests the following heuristic: *Although existence values for unique and long-lived assets should be estimated whenever possible, costs and benefits should be presented with and without their inclusion to make clear how they affect net benefits.* When existence values for such assets cannot be measured, analysts should supplement CBA with discussion of their possible significance for the sign of net benefits.

13.3   Conclusion

As CBA is increasingly applied to environmental policies, concern about existence values among analysts will almost certainly grow. Unless methods of measurement improve substantially, however, deciding when and how to include existence values in CBA will continue to be difficult. By being aware of the limitations of these methods, analysts can be better producers and consumers of CBA.

APPENDIX 13A

Expenditure Functions and the Partitioning of Benefits

Policies that have multiple effects – for example, they can affect both use and non-use values – pose conceptual problems for the aggregation of benefits. In most situations, we approximate willingness-to-pay by summing the changes in social surplus associated with each of the effects. In general, however, this procedure tends to overestimate total economic value (*TEV*). In this appendix, we introduce some notation for formally representing the measurement of utility changes from policies with multiple effects with expenditure functions, an analytical approach commonly used in more theoretical treatments of social welfare.[1] A stylized numerical example follows to show the ambiguity in the partitioning of benefits among the various effects.

Imagine that a person has a budget B and also has a utility function U that depends on the quantities of goods $X_1, X_2, ..., X_n$. Assume that the prices of these goods are $p_1, p_2, ..., p_n$, respectively. The problem facing the consumer is to choose the quantities of the goods that maximize U such that $p_1 X_1 + p_2 X_2 + ... + p_n X_n \leq B$. Let U^* be the maximum utility that the person can obtain given B and the prices of the goods. We can construct an expenditure function, $e(p_1, p_2, ..., p_n; U^*)$, which is defined as the minimum dollar amount of budget necessary to obtain utility U^* at the given prices. Obviously, for the original set of prices that we used to find U^*, $e(p_1, p_2, ..., p_n; U^*) = B$.

Assume that we instituted a policy that *increased* the price of the first good from p_1 to q_1. Associated with this new price is the expenditure function $e(q_1, p_2, ..., p_n; U^*) = B'$, where B' is greater than B because the person must be given more budget to keep the utility equal to U^* in the face of the higher price. A measure of the consumer surplus loss from the price increase is given by:

$$e(q_1, p_2, ..., p_n; U^*) - e(p_1, p_2, ..., p_n; U^*)$$

which equals $B' - B$. This amount equals the compensating variation for the price change as discussed in the appendix to Chapter 3.[2]

Imagine now that X_1 and X_2 are goods, perhaps existence value and hiking, provided to the person by a particular wilderness area. How would we use the expenditure function to value the wilderness area, using the original budget and set of prices?

We want to know how much compensation we would have to give to the person to restore his or her utility level to $U*$ after making X_1 and X_2 equal zero. In terms of the expenditure function, we do this by setting p_1 and p_2 sufficiently high so that the person's demand for X_1 and X_2 is "choked off" at zero quantities. Assume that p_{1c} and p_{2c} choke off demand. To get the TEV of the wilderness area to the individual, we calculate how much additional budget we would have to give the person to return him or her to the original utility level:

$$TEV = [e(p_{1c}, p_{2c}, p_3, \ldots p_n; U*) - e(p_1, p_2, p_3, \ldots p_n; U*)]$$

which is an unambiguous and correct measure of the person's WTP for the wilderness area.

Now consider how we might partition TEV into the two components associated with X_1 and X_2. One way would be to first value X_1 and then X_2. We can express this by adding and subtracting $e(p_1, p_{2c}, \ldots, p_n; U*)$ to the equation for TEV to get the following equation:

$$TEV = \left[e\left(p_{1c},\ p_{2c}, p_3,\ \ldots\ p_n; U^*\right) - e\left(p_1,\ p_{2c}, p_3,\ \ldots\ p_n; U^*\right) \right]$$
$$+ \left[e\left(p_1,\ p_{2c}, p_3,\ \ldots\ p_n; U^*\right) - e\left(p_1,\ p_2, p_3,\ \ldots\ p_n; U^*\right) \right]$$

where the part of the equation in the first set of brackets represents the WTP to obtain X_1 at price p_1 and the part of the equation in the second set of brackets represents the WTP to obtain subsequently X_2 at price p_2.

The other possible partition is to first restore X_2 at price p_2 and then restore X_1 at price p_1. It is expressed by the following equation:

$$TEV = \left[e\left(p_{1c},\ p_{2c}, p_3,\ \ldots\ p_n; U^*\right) - e\left(p_{1c},\ p_2, p_3,\ \ldots\ p_n; U^*\right) \right]$$
$$+ \left[e\left(p_{1c},\ p_2, p_3,\ \ldots\ p_n; U^*\right) - e\left(p_1,\ p_2, p_3,\ \ldots\ p_n; U^*\right) \right]$$

where the part of the equation in the first set of brackets represents the WTP to obtain X_2 at price p_2 and the part of the equation in the second set of brackets represents the WTP to subsequently obtain X_1 at price p_1.

These alternative ways of partitioning generally will not yield the same WTP amounts for X_1 and X_2. Typically, the WTP for a good will be greater if the good is introduced in the partitioning sequence earlier rather than later. The rough intuition behind this result is that a good will be relatively less valuable at the margin if it is added to an already full bundle of goods.

If one can measure TEV directly, then this ambiguity in partitioning is of little concern.[3] In most circumstances, however, analysts attempt to construct TEV from independent estimates of separate benefit categories. In terms of expenditure functions, what is commonly done can be expressed as follows:

$$TB = \left[e\left(p_{1c},\ p_{2c}, p_3,\ \ldots\ p_n; U^*\right) - e\left(p_1,\ p_{2c}, p_3,\ \ldots\ p_n; U^*\right) \right]$$
$$+ \left[e\left(p_{1c},\ p_{2c}, p_3,\ \ldots\ p_n; U^*\right) - e\left(p_{1c},\ p_2, p_3,\ \ldots\ p_n; U^*\right) \right]$$

where the part of the equation in the first set of brackets is the compensating variation for making only X_1 available, the part of the equation in the second set of brackets is the compensating variation for making only X_2 available, and *TB* is the total estimated benefits. In general, *TB* does not equal *TEV*. *TB* systematically overestimates *TEV*. The overestimation tends to increase as the number of benefit components increases.[4]

We next illustrate these concepts with the stylized numerical example presented in Table 13A.1. The model assumes that the person's utility, U, depends on three goods: E, the size of the wilderness area (existence value); X, a particular use of the wilderness area such as hiking; and Z, a composite good that represents all goods other than E and X. It also depends on the parameter Q, an index of the quality of the wilderness area. The person has a budget of $B = 100$ and faces prices for E, X, and Z of $p_e = \$0.50$, $p_x = \$1$, and $p_z = \$2$, respectively.[5] The quantities of E, X, and Z that maximize utility for the parameter

Table 13A.1 *An Illustration of the Benefits Partitioning Problem*

Utility function	$U(E, X, Z; Q) = QE^\gamma + QX^\beta + Z^\theta$ where E is the quantity of wilderness that exists, X is the use level of the wilderness, Z is a market good, and Q is an index of quality of the wilderness
Budget constraint	$B = p_e E + p_x X + p_z Z$ where B is the available budget, and p_e, p_x, and p_z are the respective prices of E, X, and Z
Optimization problem	Maximize $L = U + \lambda [B - p_e E - p_x X - p_z Z]$ where λ is the marginal utility of money
Numerical assumptions	$Q = 1$; $\gamma = 0.5$; $\beta = 0.75$; $q = 0.9$; $p_e = 0.5$; $p_x = 1$; $p_z = 2$; $B = 100$ $E = 9.89$; $X = 30.90$; $Z = 32.08$; $\lambda = .318$
Solution values	$U(9.89, 30.90, 32.08; 1) = 38.93 = U^*$ $e(p_e, p_x, p_z; Q; U^*) = e(0.5, 1, 2; 1; 38.93) = 100$
Expenditure functions	Wilderness area not available: $e(\infty, \infty, 2; 1; 38.93) = 116.95$ Wilderness existence, no use: $e(0.5, \infty, 2; 1; 38.93) = 111.42$ Wilderness use only: $e(\infty, 1, 2; 1; 38.93) = 105.04$
Existence-use partition $TEV = 16.95$	Existence value $= e(\infty, \infty, 2; 1; 38.93) - e(0.5, \infty, 2; 1; 38.93)$ $\qquad\qquad = 116.95 - 111.42 = 5.53$ Use value $= e(0.5, \infty, 2; 1; 38.93) - e(0.5, \infty, 2; 1; 38.93)$ $\qquad\qquad = 111.42 - 100 = 11.42$
Use-existence partition $TEV = 16.95$	Existence value $= e(\infty, 1, 2; 1; 38.93) - e(0.5, \infty, 2; 1; 38.93)$ $\qquad\qquad = 116.95 - 105.04 = 11.91$ $\qquad\qquad = 105.04 - 100 = 5.04$
Independent summation $TB = 17.44$	Existence value $= e(\infty, \infty, 2; 1; 38.93) - e(0.5, \infty, 2; 1; 38.93)$ $\qquad\qquad = 116.95 - 111.42 = 5.53$ Use value $= e(\infty, \infty, 2; 1; 38.93) - e(\infty, 1, 2; 1; 38.93)$ $\qquad\qquad = 116.95 - 105.04 = 11.91$

values listed in the table can be found through numerical methods to be $E = 9.89$, $X = 30.90$, and $Z = 32.08$.[6] The utility from this combination of goods, U^*, equals 38.93.

The expenditure function follows directly. Obviously, the budget that gives $U^* = 38.93$ is just the budget of $100 in the optimization. Therefore, we can write the expenditure function for the initial position as:

$$e(p_e = .05, p_x = 1, p_z = 2; Q = 1; U^* = 38.93) = 100$$

Before illustrating the partitioning problem, it may be helpful to consider how expenditure functions can be used to find compensating variations for independent policy effects. Consider, for instance, how one can find the compensating variation for a reduction in the price of X from $1 to $.50. The procedure involves finding the expenditure function:

$$e(p_e = .5, p_x = 0.5, p_z = 2; Q = 1; U^* = 38.93) = 63.25$$

by asking what budget amount would allow the person to obtain the original utility at the lower price. The compensating variation for the price reduction is just the difference between the values of the expenditure function with the lower price, $63.25, and the value of the original expenditure function, $100. That is, the person would be indifferent between facing the original price of $1 with a budget of $100 and facing the reduced price of $0.50 with a budget of $63.25. Therefore, the willingness-to-pay for the price reduction is the difference between $100 and $63.25, or $36.75.

Now consider how one could value a policy that would increase the quality index, Q, by 10 percent. The expenditure function for the quality improvement relative to the initial position is:

$$e(p_e = .05, p_x = 1, p_z = 2; Q = 1.1; U^* = 38.93) = 94.45$$

which indicates that the compensating variation for the quality improvement is $-$5.55 ($94.45 $-$ $100), indicating that the original utility could be obtained with a smaller budget.

Returning to the initial position, let us now consider the total value of wilderness, TEV, and the two ways of partitioning it between existence and use. We choke off consumption of E and X by setting their prices at infinity. This yields the expenditure function:

$$e(p_e = \infty, p_x = \infty, p_z = 2; Q = 1; U^* = 38.93) = 116.95$$

which implies that the wilderness area has a total value of $16.95 ($116.95 $-$ $100). If we partition first by existence value and then by use value, we calculate:

$$e(p_e = .05, p_x = \infty, p_z = 2; Q = 1; U^* = 38.93) = 111.42$$

which implies an existence value of $5.53 ($116.95 $-$ $111.42) and a use value of $11.42 ($111.42 $-$ $100).[7] If instead we partition first by use value and then by existence value, we calculate:

$$e(p_e = \infty, p_x = 1, p_z = 2; Q = 1; U^* = 38.93) = 105.04$$

which implies a use value of $11.91 ($116.95 − $105.04) and an existence value of $5.04 ($105.04 − $100).[8] Thus, we see that the sequence of valuation makes a difference: Existence value and use value are each larger when they are valued first rather than second.[9]

Finally, consider the independent summation of benefits. Existence is valued as in the existence–use sequence and use is valued as in the use–existence sequence. Thus, we would estimate the total economic value of the wilderness to be $17.44 ($5.53 + $11.91), which exceeds the correct compensating variation by $0.49 ($17.44 − $16.95).

In summary, the partitioning of benefits between existence and use is conceptually ambiguous when the same individuals derive both values from a policy change. More generally, policies that affect people's utilities in multiple ways are prone to overestimation of WTP when each effect is valued independently as a separate benefit category.

Exercises for Chapter 13

1. Imagine a wilderness area of 200 square miles in the Rocky Mountains. How would you expect each of the following factors to affect people's total WTP for its preservation?

   a. The size of the total wilderness area still remaining in the Rocky Mountains.

   b. The presence of rare species in this particular area.

   c. The level of national wealth.

2. An analyst wishing to estimate the benefits of preserving a wetland has combined information obtained from two methods. First, she surveyed those who visited the wetland – fishers, duck hunters, and bird-watchers – to determine their WTP for these uses. Second, she surveyed a sample of residents throughout the state about their WTP to preserve the wetland. This second survey focused exclusively on non-use values of the wetland. She then added her estimate of use benefits to her estimate of non-use benefits to get an estimate of the total economic value of preservation of the wetland. Is this a reasonable approach? (Note: In responding to this question assume that there was virtually no overlap in the persons contacted in the two surveys.)

Notes

1. Put another way, and in the context of the discussion in Chapter 12, existence value is part of option value. That is, option value includes use value and non-use value. We simply ignored existence value in Chapter 12.

2. John V. Krutilla, "Conservation Reconsidered." *American Economic Review*, 57(4), 1967, 777–86 at p. 784. For a discussion of the importance of this article, see V. Kerry Smith, "Krutilla's Legacy: Twenty-First Century Challenges for Environmental Economics." *American Journal of Agricultural Economics*, 86(5), 2004, 1167–78.

3. Charles Plourde, "Conservation of Extinguishable Species." *Natural Resources Journal*, 15(4), 1975, 791–97.

4. Bruce Madariaga and Kenneth E. McConnell, "Exploring Existence Value." *Water Resources Research*, 23(5), 1987, 936–42.

5. For an alternative framework, see R. Kerry Turner, Jouni Paavola, Philip Cooper, Stephen Farber, Valma Jessamy, and Stavros Georgiou, "Valuing Nature: Lessons Learned and Future Research Directions." *Ecological Economics*, 46(3), 2003, 493–510 at p. 495 (table 1).

6. K. G. Willis, "Valuing Non-Market Wildlife Commodities: An Evaluation and Comparison of Benefits and Costs." *Applied Economics*, 22(1), 1990, 12–30.

7. For an overview, see V. Kerry Smith, "Nonmarket Valuation of Environmental Resources." *Land Economics*, 69(1), 1993, 1–26.

8. Ronald J. Sutherland and Richard G. Walsh, "The Effect of Distance on the Preservation Value of Water Quality." *Land Economics*, 61(3), 1985, 281–91; and Ian J. Bateman and Ian H. Langford, "Non-Users' Willingness to Pay for a National Park: An Application and Critique of the Contingent Valuation Method." *Regional Studies*, 31(6), 1997, 571–82.

9. Raymond J. Kopp and V. Kerry Smith, "Benefit Estimation Goes to Court: The Case of Natural Resource Damage Assessment." *Journal of Policy Analysis and Management*, 8(4), 1989, 593–612.

10. Bruce Madariaga and Kenneth E. McConnell, "Exploring Existence Value." *Water Resources Research*, 23(5), 1987, 936–42.

11. M. Shechter, B. Reiser and N. Zaitsev, "Measuring Passive Use Value: Pledges, Donations and CV Responses in Connection with an Important Natural Resource." *Environmental and Resource Economics*, 12(4), 1998, 457–78.

12. Douglas M. Larson, "On Measuring Existence Value." *Land Economics*, 69(1), 1992, 116–22.

13. Richard G. Walsh, John B. Loomis, and Richard A. Gillman, "Valuing Option, Existence, and Bequest Demands for Wilderness." *Land Economics*, 60(1), 1984, 14–29; K. G. Willis, "Valuing Non-Market Wildlife Commodities: An Evaluation and Comparison of Benefits and Costs." *Applied Economics*, 22(1), 1990, 13–30; Thomas H. Stevens, Jaime Echeverria, Ronald J. Glass, Tim Hager, and Thomas A. More, "Measuring the Existence Value of Wildlife: What Do CVM Estimates Really Show?" *Land Economics*, 67(4), 1991, 390–400; John B. Loomis and Douglas S. White, "Economic Benefits of Rare and Endangered Species: Summary and Meta-Analysis." *Ecological Economics*, 18(3), 1996, 197–206; John Loomis, "Estimating Recreation and Existence Values of Sea Otter Expansion in California Using Benefit Transfer." *Coastal Management*, 34(4), 2006, 387–404; John Horowitz, "Existence Values for Maryland Forests" (Queenstown, MD: Queenstown, MD Harry R. Hughes Center for Agro-Ecology, University of Maryland Wye Research and Education Center, 2008); Pieter van Beukering, Wouter Botzen, and Esther Wolfs, "The Non-Use Value of Nature in the Netherlands and the Caribbean Netherlands: Applying and Comparing Contingent Valuation and Choice Modelling Approaches" (Amsterdam, The Netherlands: Institute for Environmental Studies, 2012); Xin Jin, Jianzhang Ma, Tijiu Cai, and Xiaoxin Sun, "Non-use Value Assessment for Wetland Ecosystem Service of Hongxing National Nature Reserve in Northeast China." *Journal of Forestry Research*, 27(6), 2016, 1435–42.

14. See, for example, Donald H. Rosenthal and Robert H. Nelson, "Why Existence Value Should Not Be Used in Cost–benefit analysis." *Journal of Policy Analysis and Management*, 11(1), 1992, 116–22; Raymond J. Kopp, "Why Existence Value Should Be Used in Cost–Benefit Analysis." *Journal of Policy Analysis and Management*, 11(1), 1992, 123–30; Hans-Peter Weikard, "Why Non-Use Value Should Not Be Used," Working Paper No. 22 (Netherlands: Mansholt Graduate School, 2005). One practical problem is that the estimates of values are quite sensitive to the empirical model used; see, for example, Aurelia Bengochea-Morancho, Ana M. Fuertes-Eugenio, and Salvador del Saz-Salazar, "A Comparison of Empirical Models to Infer the Willingness to Pay in Contingent Valuation." *Ecological Economics*, 30(1), 2005, 235–44.

Appendix Notes

1. A more formal treatment can be found in Alan Randall, "Total and Nonuse Values," in John B. Braden and Charles D. Kolstad (editors), *Measuring the Demand for Environmental Quality* (New York, NY: North-Holland, 1991), 303–21. The original analysis of the importance of the sequence of valuation can be found in J. R. Hicks, *A Revision of Demand Theory* (Oxford: Clarendon Press, 1956), 169–79.

2. Although we use compensating variation as a measure of the dollar value of utility here because we find it most intuitive (as discussed in the appendix to Chapter 3), equivalent variation, which measures welfare changes relative to the utility level after the price change, is generally considered a superior money metric for utility because it provides an unambiguous ordinal measure for ranking price changes. If $U\sim$ is the utility after the price change, then the equivalent variation is:

$$e(q_1, p_2, ..., pn; U\sim) - e(q_1, p_2, ..., pn; U\sim)$$

where $e(q_1, p_2, pn; U\sim) = B$. Compensating and equivalent variation typically differ by a small amount due to income effects. In the case of quantity changes of public goods, however, the size of their difference also depends on the availability of close substitutes for the public good. See W. Michael Hanemann, "Willingness-to-Pay and Willingness-to-Accept: How Much Can They Differ?" *American Economic Review*, 81(3), 1991, 635–47.

3. Of course, the value of *TEV* will depend on whether it is measured in terms of compensating variation or equivalent variation.

4. John P. Hoehn and Alan Randall, "Too Many Proposals Pass the Benefit Cost Test." *American Economic Review*, 79(3), 1989, 544–51.

5. If E is a public good, then we would interpret p_e as the tax per unit of E that the person pays. As everyone would have to consume the same quantity, the person would not be able to choose the value of E so that the optimization of utility would be over only X and Z.

6. The partial derivatives of L with respect to E, X, Z, and λ give four equations with four unknowns. Although these *first-order conditions* cannot be solved analytically, they can be rearranged so that E, X, and Z are each expressed as a function of λ and parameters. A solution can be found by guessing values of λ until a value is found that implies values of E, X, and Z that satisfy the budget constraint.

7. If we assume that E is fixed at its initial level, the more realistic case in evaluating an existing wilderness area, then the existence value equals only \$5.47. It is smaller than in the example because the person does not have the opportunity to purchase more E when X is not available. This assumption changes neither the *TEV* nor the existence value as estimated by the use-existence partition.

8. It may seem strange to partition in this way because one would normally think of existence as being a prerequisite for use. Some types of uses, however, could be provided without maintaining existence value. For example, through stocking it may be possible to provide game fishing without preserving a stream in its natural form.

9. Using equivalent variation rather than compensating variation as the consumer surplus measure leads to the following:

$e(pe = \infty, px = \infty, pz = 2; Q = 1; U\sim = 33.81) = 100.00$
$e(pe = 0.5, px = 1, pz = 2; Q = 1; U\sim = 33.81) = 84.10$
$e(pe = \infty, px = 1, pz = 2; Q = 1; U\sim = 33.81) = 89.00$
$e(pe = 0.5, px = -, pz = 2; Q = 1; U\sim = 33.81) = 94.68$
$TEVev = 100.00 - 84.10 = 15.90$

| Existence-use partition: | existence value = 100.00 − 94.68 = 5.32 |
| | use value = 94.68 − 84.10 = 10.58 |

| Use-existence partition: | use value = 100.00 − 89.00 = 11.00 |
| | existence value = 89.00 − 84.10 = 4.90 |

| Independent summation: | existence value = 100.00 − 94.68 = 5.32 |
| | use value = 100.00 − 89.00 = 11.00 |

$TBev = 16.32$

14 Valuing Impacts from Observed Behavior: Experiments and Quasi-Experiments

Sometimes the benefits and costs of program interventions can be estimated through experimental and quasi-experimental designs.[1] This chapter first describes experimental and quasi-experimental designs, indicating how they are used in estimating the impacts of social programs in policy areas such as health, education, training, employment, housing, and welfare. It then describes how these impacts are incorporated into CBAs of employment and training programs, illustrating how concepts developed in earlier chapters can be used in actual cost–benefit analyses. The case study that follows the chapter examines CBAs of a number of employment and training programs that were targeted at welfare recipients.

14.1 Alternative Evaluation Designs

CBAs of any intervention require comparisons between alternatives: the program or policy that is subject to the CBA is compared to the situation that would exist without the program (the so-called *counterfactual*), and impacts are measured as differences in outcomes (e.g., in health status or earnings) between the two situations. The term *internal validity* refers to whether this measured difference can be appropriately attributed to the program being evaluated. Internal validity, in turn, depends on the particular way in which the comparison between the program and the situation without the program is made. There are numerous ways in which this comparison can be made. Researchers usually refer to the specific scheme used for making comparisons in order to measure impacts as an *evaluation design*.

Diagrams that represent five commonly used evaluation designs,[2] as well as brief summaries of the advantages and disadvantages of each of these designs, appear in Table 14.1. In these diagrams, the symbol O represents an outcome measurement point, X represents a treatment point, and R indicates that subjects were assigned randomly to treatment and control groups.

The evaluation designs that are listed in Table 14.1 are not the only ones that exist. There are numerous others, but these designs provide a good sampling of the major alternatives. So that we can make our discussion of them as concrete as possible, we assume that they all pertain to alternative ways in which a program for training the unemployed might be evaluated. In this context, "being in the treatment group" means enrollment in the training program.

Table 14.1 *Five Commonly Used Evaluation Designs*

Type	Structure[1]	Major advantages	Major disadvantages
Design 1: Comparison of net changes between treatment and true control groups	$R: O_1 X O_2$ $R: O_3 O_4$	Random assignment guards against systematic differences between control and treatment groups so highest internal validity	Direct and ethical costs of random assignment; as with all evaluations external validity may be limited
Design 2: Comparison of post-treatment outcomes between true control and treatment groups	$R: X O_2$ $R: O_4$	Random assignment guards against systematic differences between control and treatment groups so high internal validity	Direct and ethical costs of random assignment; danger that a failure of randomization will not be detected
Design 3: Simple before/after comparison	$O_1 X O_2$	Often feasible and relatively inexpensive; reasonable when factors other than treatment are unlikely to affect outcome	Does not control for other factors that may cause change
Design 4: Comparison of post-treatment outcomes between quasi-control and treatment groups	$X O_1$ O_2	Allows for possibility of statistically controlling for factors other than treatment	Danger of sample selection bias caused by systematic differences between treatment and quasi-control groups
Design 5: Comparison of net changes between treatment and quasi-control group	$O_1 X O_2$ $O_3 O_4$	Allows for possibility of statistically controlling for factors other than treatment; permits detection of pre-treatment measurable differences between treatment and quasi-control groups	Danger of sample selection bias caused by systematic differences between treatment and quasi-control group in terms of nonmeasurable differences

O, observation; X, treatment; R, random assignment.

[1] Draws on notation introduced by Donald T. Campbell and Julian Stanley, *Experimental and Quasi-Experimental Designs for Research* (Chicago, IL: Rand McNally College Publishing Company, 1963).

14.1.1   *Design 1: Classical Experimental Design*

Design 1 is a classical experimental design. The symbols indicate that unemployed persons are randomly allocated between a treatment group and a control group. Members of the treatment group can receive services from the training program, while persons in the control group cannot. The way this might work in practice is that after the training program is put into place, unemployed persons are notified of its existence. Some of these persons apply to participate in it. A computer is used, in effect, to flip a fair coin: Heads the applicant is selected as a member of the treatment group and, consequently, becomes eligible to participate in the program; tails the applicant becomes a member of the control group. Control group members are not eligible to participate in the program, but can receive whatever other services are available for the unemployed.

The procedure just described for establishing treatment and control groups is called *random assignment*.[3] Random assignment evaluations of social programs – for instance, a training program – are often called *social experiments*.

To see how well the training program works, data on outcomes are collected for both the treatment group and the control group, both before the treatment is administered and after. Using the collected data, members of the experimental and control groups are then compared.[4] For example, the earnings of the two groups can be compared sometime after the training is completed to measure the size of the program's impact on earnings.[5]

Although it is sometimes impractical or infeasible to use,[6] design 1 is the best of the five design schemes summarized in Table 14.1 for many types of evaluations. Its major advantage is the use of random assignment. Because of random assignment, the characteristics of people in the treatment and control groups should be similar, varying only by chance alone. With a reasonably large number of participants, this randomization should result in similar treatment and control groups. As a result, random assignment helps ensure that the evaluation has internal validity; that is, members of the experimental groups can be directly compared in terms of such outcomes as earnings, and any differences that are found between them can be reasonably attributed to the treatment.

It is important to recognize, however, that although design 1 helps ensure internal validity, like the other evaluation designs discussed in this section, it may not provide *external validity*. That is, there is no assurance that findings from the evaluation, even though valid for the group of persons who participated in the evaluated program, can be generalized to any other group. The reason for this is that personal and community characteristics interact in complex ways with the services provided by a program.[7] As a result, the program may serve some persons more effectively than others. For example, findings for a training program for unemployed, male, blue-collar workers who live in a community with low unemployment may provide little information concerning how well the program would work for unemployed female welfare recipients who live in a community with high unemployment. In addition, the findings may also not hold for future time periods when relevant social or economic conditions have changed.

14.1.2   *Design 2: Classical Experimental Design without Baseline Data*

Design 2 is similar to design 1 in that random assignment is also used to allocate individuals between the treatment and control groups, and both are referred to as *experimental designs*. The difference between the two designs is that collection of pre-treatment, baseline information on members of the treatment and control groups is not part of design 2 but is part of design 1. The problem with not collecting pre-treatment information is that there is no way of checking whether the treatment and control groups are basically similar or dissimilar.

For the comparison between the two groups to measure program effects accurately, the groups should, of course, be as similar as possible. Yet, they could be dissimilar by chance alone. This is more likely if each group has only a few hundred members, as is sometimes the case in social experiments. It is also possible that those running an experiment fail to implement the random assignment process correctly. If information is available on pre-treatment status – for example, on pre-treatment earnings – then statistical adjustments can be made to make the comparison between the treatment and the control groups more valid. Hence, there is less certainty concerning internal validity with design 2 than design 1.

Nonetheless, design 2 may be more appropriate than design 1 when it is possible that the collection of pre-treatment information predisposes the participants to certain relevant behaviors. For example, pre-treatment questions about knowledge of health risks may make the treatment group in a study of health education more prone to learning than the general public would be.

Exhibit 14.1

Much of this chapter focuses on cost–benefit analyses of social programs, especially employment and training (E&T) programs that have been based on random assignment experiments. Random assignment, of course, has also been used extensively to assess medicine and medical procedures. Health experiments, in fact, have been conducted for considerably longer than social experiments. And like social experiments, they sometimes provide the basis for CBAs, although they are used far more frequently in cost–effectiveness and cost–utility analyses (see Chapter 18).

Health experiments, especially those involving new drugs, differ from social experiments in an important respect. In experimentally testing new drugs, subjects in the control group are usually given a placebo and members of the treatment and control groups do not know whether they are receiving the new drug or the placebo. For example, in a recent randomize trial of LMTX, a drug to treat Alzheimer's disease, which included 891 patients with mild or moderate Alzheimer's disease in 16 countries and took place over a 15-month period, researchers compared results in patients treated with LMTX with those treated with a placebo. Those administering the drug also did not know who was in the treatment and control groups, a procedure that is often used in drug treatment experiments in combination with placebos and referred to as a "double-blind trial." In social experiments, in contrast, it is rarely feasible to keep assignment to treatment and control groups hidden (placebo social programs are difficult to envision). Thus, there is the risk that the behavior of people in the control group may be affected by knowledge of the fact that they missed out in receiving the treatment. For example, in the case of a training program experiment, some members of the control group may be discouraged, while others may be goaded into finding alternative sources of the services offered by the experimental program. It is also possible that some control group members are inappropriately provided some program benefits by sympathetic administrators.

Source: Susan Scutti, "Testing of New Alzheimer Drug Disappoints, but it's Not All Bad News," CNN, July 27, 2016.

14.1.3   *Design 3: Before and After Comparison*

Design 3 is by far the worst of the five designs, relying as it does on a simple *before and after comparison* of the same group of individuals. For example, the earnings of a group of individuals that went through a training program are compared with their earnings before going through the program. The problem with this design is that there is no information on what would have happened without the program. Consequently, there is no way to ensure internal validity. For example, the average earnings of people going into a training program are likely to be very low if most of these people are unemployed at the time of entry. That, perhaps, is why they decided to go into the program in the first place. Even without the program, however, they might have found jobs eventually. If so, their average earnings would have gone up over time even if the program did not exist. With a before and after comparison, this increase in earnings would be incorrectly attributed to the program.

Before and after comparisons, however, do offer certain advantages. They provide a comparatively inexpensive way of conducting evaluations. Moreover, when valid information cannot be gathered for a comparison group, a comparison of pre- and post-treatment outcomes may be the only feasible way of conducting an evaluation. Such a comparison is obviously most valid when non-program factors are not expected to affect the outcomes of interest (for example, earnings) or can be taken into account through statistical adjustments.

14.1.4   *Design 4: Non-experimental Comparison without Baseline Data*

Design 4 is based on a comparison of two different groups: one that has gone through a program and the other that has not. Unlike design 2, however, membership in the two groups is not determined by random assignment. For example, the comparison group could be made up of people who originally applied for training but ultimately decided not to participate. Alternatively, the comparison group could be drawn from a geographical area where the program does not exist. Because such a comparison group is not selected through random assignment, it is sometimes called a *quasi-control group*, and design 4 is called a *quasi-experimental design*. Use of a quasi-control group may be necessary when obtaining a comparison group through random assignment is infeasible or impractical.

Unfortunately, with this design there is no means of controlling for those differences between the two groups that existed prior to the treatment and, hence, no way to ensure internal validity. Perhaps, for example, at the time of application for training, those who ultimately went through the program had been unemployed for a longer period of time than persons in the comparison group, suggesting that in the absence of training they would have fared worse in the job market than members of the comparison group. Yet if at the end of training it is observed that they actually did just as well as persons in the comparison group, this suggests the training had an effect: it pulled the trainees up even with the comparison group. However, with design 4, there is no way to know the difference in the length of unemployment prior to training. As a result, it would just be observed that, after training, members of the treatment group were doing no better than people in the comparison group. This finding is subject to a bias known as *sample selection bias* that results because systematic differences between the treatment and quasi-control group are not, and indeed cannot be, taken into account. In this instance, sample selection bias is important because it could lead to the incorrect conclusion that the training made no difference.

14.1.5   *Design 5: Non-experimental Comparison with Baseline Data*

Design 5 utilizes both a treatment group and a control group. In addition, both pre-treatment and post-treatment data are collected. This provides information on how the treatment group differed from the comparison group prior to the training (for example, in terms of length of unemployment). This information can be used in a statistical analysis to control for pre-treatment differences between the treatment and control groups. For this reason, design 5 offers greater opportunity to obtain internal validity than either design 3 or 4.

Even so, because this design, which like design 4 is a quasi-experimental design, does not randomly assign individuals to the treatment and control groups, a major problem occurs if people in the treatment and the comparison groups differ from one another in ways that cannot be measured readily. Then it becomes very difficult to adjust statistically for differences between the two groups. Perhaps, for example, unemployed persons who enter training are more motivated than unemployed persons who do not. If so, they might receive higher earnings over time even without the training. If analysts cannot somehow take account of this difference in motivation – in practice, sometimes they can, but often they cannot – then they may incorrectly conclude that higher post-training earnings received by the trainees are due to the training when, in fact, they are really due to greater motivation on the part of the trainees. In the evaluation literature, such a situation creates a threat to internal validity that is known as the *selection problem*.[8]

The occurrence of selection problems can be greatly reduced by using design 1 or 2. The reason is that when random assignment is done properly, people assigned to the treatment group should not differ from members of the control group in terms of characteristics, including those that cannot be readily observed such as motivation, except by chance alone. Because of this advantage, an increasing number of evaluations of social programs that embody experimental designs have been conducted since the early 1960s.[9] However, large numbers of evaluations that utilize non-experimental designs, such as designs 3, 4, and 5, also continue to be done either because costs or administrative factors prevent randomization or evaluations are initiated after the program has begun operating.

14.2   CBAs of Experiments and Quasi-Experiments

Although numerous evaluations that have utilized the designs outlined above have been conducted, formal CBAs have been carried out for only a minority of them. Often the evaluations focus instead on only one or two outcomes of interest. For example, in the housing or health areas, they might focus on whether the evaluated program could be administered effectively or whether housing or health status improved, and do not attempt to measure other benefits and costs.

Many of the evaluations of social programs that have been subjected to CBA have focused on programs that attempt to increase the employment or earnings of unemployed or low-skilled workers,[10] and to keep the discussion specific, the remainder of this chapter focuses on such programs. The services provided by these programs have varied considerably but have included job search assistance, remedial education, vocational training, subsidizing private-sector employers who hire program participants, financial incentives to work, and the direct provision of public-sector jobs to participants. Although the individual programs that provide such services often differ greatly from one another, such programs are commonly referred to as *employment and training (E&T) programs*.[11]

E&T programs are often viewed as investments in the *human capital* of participants (i.e., attempts to improve their skills and abilities). Thus, the major economic rationale for funding them revolves around assertions that E&T programs help correct market or institutional failures that cause underinvestments in human capital. For example, low-income people may not have the resources to invest in certain kinds of training, such as classroom vocational training. Their access to private financing may be limited by a lack of collateral and a high risk of default. Moreover, public training may be justified as compensating for inadequacies in the public education system or as providing a second chance to those who prematurely terminate formal schooling because of imperfect foresight or a high subjective rate of time preference. In addition, E&T programs may help correct imperfect information among participants about human capital investment opportunities by guiding them into activities that yield the highest pay-off for them.

A distinct rationale for E&T programs stems from a widely accepted value that, all else equal, it is better to receive income from employment than from transfer programs. To meet this goal, increasingly stringent requirements to participate in E&T programs have been imposed on welfare and unemployment insurance recipients since the early 1980s.

14.3   The CBA Framework in the E&T Context

The basic CBA accounting framework has been described in previous chapters. However, different policy areas have developed variations of the basic CBA framework that address issues specific to each area. The particular accounting framework that is used today in conducting most CBAs of E&T programs was originally developed during the late 1960s

Table 14.2 *Stylized Cost–Benefit Framework Showing the Impacts of E&T Programs*

	Society (A) (B + C)	Participant (B)	Non-participant (C)
Output produced by participant			
In-program output	+	0	+
Gross earnings	+	+	0
Fringe benefits	+	+	0
Participant work-related expenditures			
Tax payments	0	−	+
Expenditures on child care, transportation, etc.	−	−	0
Use of transfer programs by participants			
Welfare payments	0	−	+
Other transfer payments	0	−	+
Transfer program operating costs	+	0	+
Use of support programs by participants			
Support services received by participants	−	0	−
Allowances received by participants	0	+	−
E&T operating costs	−	0	−

and refined in the early 1980s. A stylized version of this framework appears in Table 14.2. Although details of the framework vary somewhat from one E&T CBA to another, depending upon the specific nature of the services provided, the table lists the typically measured benefits and costs.

This framework offers several advantages: It is readily understandable to policy makers; by displaying benefits and costs from the perspectives of both participants and non-participants, it suggests some of the distributional implications of the program being evaluated; and, possibly most important, because measures of each cost–benefit component listed can actually be obtained from data collected during the evaluation, it is operationally feasible. Indeed, despite shortcomings in the framework, it is difficult to find practical alternatives to it.

In Table 14.2, plus signs indicate anticipated sources of benefits and minus signs anticipated sources of costs from different perspectives. The first column (A) shows aggregate benefits and costs from the perspective of society as a whole. The remaining columns show the distribution of benefits and costs to the two groups that are typically relevant in assessing E&T programs: participants or clients served by the evaluated program (B); and non-participants, including taxpayers who pay for the program (C).

Benefits and costs to society are simply the algebraic sum of benefits and costs to participants and to non-participants because society is the sum of these two groups. Hence, the table implies that if a program causes transfer payments received by participants (e.g., unemployment compensation or welfare payment receipts) to decline, then this should be regarded as a savings or benefit to non-participant taxpayers, a cost to program participants (albeit one that may be offset by earnings), and neither a benefit nor a cost to society as a whole but simply income transferred from one segment of the population to another.

This approach is consistent with the standard one used in CBA. As we have seen, in standard CBA "a dollar is a dollar," no matter to whom it accrues. Thus, in Table 14.2, a dollar gained or lost by an E&T participant is treated identically to a dollar gained or lost by a non-participant. Consequently, if an E&T program caused the transfer dollars received by participants to fall, then this would be viewed as not affecting society as a whole because the loss to participants would be fully offset by benefits to non-participants in the form of reductions in government budgetary outlays. Typically, however, E&T participants have much lower incomes, on average, than non-participants. For reasons that will be discussed in detail in Chapter 19, a case can sometimes be made for treating the gains and losses of low-income persons differently from those of higher-income persons. This is almost never done in CBAs of E&T evaluations, however. Instead, as can be seen in Table 14.2, they simply lay out the results so that the distributional consequences of a particular program can be observed.

Table 14.2 divides the benefits and costs associated with E&T programs into four major categories. The first two categories pertain to effects that result if a program increases the work effort or productivity of participants – for example, by providing work in a public-sector job where they perform useful services, providing them skill training, or helping them find private-sector employment through job search assistance. On the one hand, the value of the output they produce will rise, which in the private sector should be reflected by increases in earnings and fringe benefits. On the other hand, if hours at work rise, expenditures on child care and transportation will also increase. And if earnings rise, tax payments will increase. The third major cost–benefit category in Table 14.2 pertains to decreases in dependency on transfer payments that may result from an E&T program. Such reductions in dependency should cause both the amount of payments distributed under transfer programs and the cost of administering these programs to fall. The fourth major category refers to expenditures on the services received by program participants. Obviously, such expenditures increase when an E&T program is implemented. However, this increase will be partially offset because participants do not need to obtain similar services from other programs.

Three of the subcategories listed in Table 14.2 pertain to job-related expenditures and require clarification: participant expenditures on child care, transportation, and so forth; support services received by participants; and allowances received by participants. The first of these subcategories refers to total job-required outlays by E&T participants on such items as child care, transportation, and uniforms. The subcategory of support services pertains to the direct provision of such goods by a government agency, and the allowances subcategory refers to government reimbursement of job-required expenditures by participants. Table 14.2 reflects the philosophy that *all* program-induced increases in job-required expenditures should be treated identically, as resource costs to society engendered in producing goods and services, one that hopefully is offset by higher participant earnings. Of course, to the extent the government directly provides support services to participants, client outlays for this purpose will be smaller. In a CBA, this would be reflected by a smaller dollar amount appearing under the participant expenditures on job-related outlays and a larger dollar amount appearing under the subcategory of support services received by participants. Job-required expenditures are further discussed later in the chapter.

As previously indicated, all of the cost and benefit items listed in Table 14.2 would be measured as the difference between outcomes with and without the E&T program. In practice, many of the services offered by an E&T program may also be offered under other programs. For example, training provided by the programs may also be available through community colleges. Consequently, estimates of program effects on participants do not measure impacts of the receipt of service against the non-receipt of services. Rather, such estimates attempt to determine the *incremental* effect of the program over the environment that would exist without the program. Similarly, the measure of program operating services is an estimate of the cost of running the program being evaluated less the cost of the services program participants would receive without the program.[12]

Benefits and costs that are sometimes referred to as *intangible effects* but are rarely, if ever, actually estimated in evaluations of E&T programs do not appear in Table 14.2. Examples of intangible effects include the values of leisure forgone during training and while working and self-esteem from working. Almost by definition, intangible effects are difficult to measure, but they may be important. In fact, the non-measurement of important intangible costs and benefits is a key problem in conducing CBAs of most social programs.[13] In the next section, we examine the implications of not measuring certain intangible effects in conducting CBAs of E&T programs.

14.4   Conceptual Issues in Conducting CBAs of E&T Programs[14]

We now turn to a number of limitations of the accounting framework illustrated in Table 14.2. As will be seen, these arise because the framework is not completely consistent with the theoretical concepts discussed in Chapters 3, 5, 6, and 7. Because these limitations can result in incorrect policy conclusions, comparing some of the operational measures of benefits and costs typically used in conducting CBAs of E&T programs with their conceptually correct counterparts appears useful. In doing this, it is helpful to examine measures of benefits and costs associated with E&T programs separately from the participant and the non-participant perspectives, keeping in mind that social benefits and costs are simply the algebraic sum of benefits received and costs incurred by these two groups.

14.4.1   *The Participant Perspective*

Two Alternative Measures. The standard E&T framework, as Table 14.2 suggests, estimates participant net benefits as net changes in the incomes of program clients – that is, as increases in earnings and fringe benefits minus increases in taxes, decreases in transfer payments, and increases in work-related expenditures that result from participation in the program. However, as Chapters 3 and 5 emphasize, the conceptually appropriate measure of participant net benefits is net changes in the surplus of program participants, not net changes in their incomes. As will be seen, the difference between these two measures can be substantial.

The extent to which the two measures diverge depends on the precise mechanism through which E&T programs influence earnings. For instance, E&T programs may either increase the hourly wage rates of participants (e.g., by imparting new skills) or increase the hours they work (e.g., by aiding in job search or increasing the obligations that must be met in exchange for transfer payments). Numerous E&T programs have been found to increase hours worked. Meaningful impacts on wage rates are rarer but have occurred. In the discussion that follows, we compare the two alternative measures of net benefits from the perspective of three different hypothetical E&T participants, each of whom is assumed to respond differently to the program.

The first participant is represented in Figure 14.1. Curve S is the labor supply schedule of this participant, an individual who is assumed to have successfully participated in an E&T program that increased her market wage from W_0 to W_1.[15] As a result, the individual increases her hours of work from h_0 to h_1. In the diagram, area A represents the increase in participant surplus (earnings) that would have resulted from the wage increase even if the participant had not increased her hours. Areas $B + C$ represents an additional increase in participant earnings that resulting from the increase in hours that actually takes place at the higher wage. However, area C is fully offset by the individual's loss of leisure.[16] Consequently, although areas A, B, and C are counted as benefits when using the net income change measure of E&T effects, only A and B are counted in the conceptually correct (producer) surplus change measure.

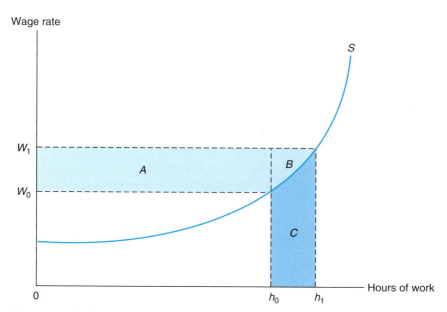

Figure 14.1 Social surplus change resulting from an induced wage increase.

In Figure 14.1, the first E&T participant was assumed to be in equilibrium both before entering the program and upon completing the program; that is, it was assumed that at both points she was able to work the number of hours she desired to work at her market wage. Many E&T participants, however, are not in equilibrium prior to entering a program. Indeed, many persons participate in E&T specifically because they are unemployed.

Such a situation is assumed to face the second participant, an individual who is represented in Figure 14.2. In this figure, the individual has a market wage of W_0 prior to entering E&T but is able to obtain only h_0 hours of work instead of the desired h_1 hours. Assume now that, although participating in E&T does not affect the participant's market wage, it does permit him to increase his hours of work from h_0 to h_1 As a result of this hours increase, the participant enjoys an earnings increase equal to areas $A + B$ but a (producer) surplus increase equal to only area A. Thus, once again, the net income change measure of E&T benefits is larger than the conceptually more appropriate (producer) surplus change measure.

The findings for the first two E&T participants imply that while any earnings increases that result from wage increases should be fully credited to the program, only part of earnings increases resulting from increases in hours should be credited. In Figure 14.3, we turn to a more complex situation facing a third E&T participant: a welfare recipient who, as a condition for receiving her welfare grant, is required to work at a public-sector job for h^* hours each month, where h^* is determined by dividing her grant amount by the minimum wage. Similar arrangements, which are often referred to as *workfare*, have sometimes been used to administer welfare programs. The welfare recipient's

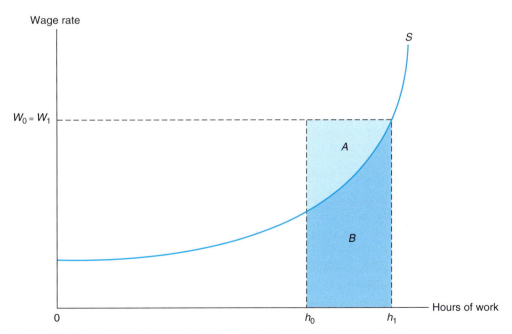

Figure 14.2 Social surplus change due to an induced increase in hours worked.

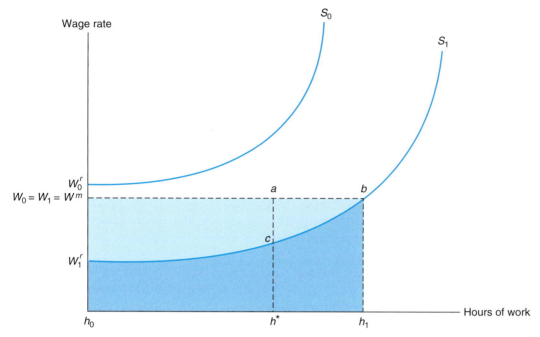

Figure 14.3 Social surplus change due to workfare.

market wage is assumed to equal W^m, the minimum wage, while curve S_0 represents her supply schedule in the absence of workfare. (Ignore curve S_1 for the moment.) Figure 14.3 implies that in the absence of workfare, W_0^r, the welfare recipient's reservation wage, i.e., the lowest wage at which she would be willing to work) would exceed her market wage. Thus, she would choose not to work.

Now imagine that the welfare recipient is enrolled in workfare in two distinct steps. In the first step, her welfare grant, which in the diagram corresponds to the rectangular area $W^m a h^* h_0$,[17] is withdrawn. This loss of income would cause her labor supply curve to shift to the right from S_0 to S_1. As a consequence, her reservation wage would fall from W_0^r to W_1^r, a value below the minimum wage. In the second step, she is offered the opportunity to work h^* hours at a public-sector workfare job at a wage of W^m. In other words, she is given the opportunity to earn back her welfare grant. Because W^m exceeds W_1^r, the participant represented in Figure 14.3 would prefer workfare to not working at all.

If the welfare recipient accepts the workfare offer, then the net income change and social surplus change measures of program impacts have quite different implications. Assuming she has no opportunities to work in addition to h^*, her net income would be unchanged from what it was prior to the program ($W^m a h^* h_0$); consequently, the measure based on changes in net income would imply that she is no worse off. However, the social surplus change measure does imply that she is worse off. Specifically, her social surplus would decline by an amount represented by the area $W_1^r c h^* h_0$, an amount equal to the value that the recipient places on her lost leisure.[18]

So far, the focus has been on benefits received by and costs incurred by welfare recipients while they are participating in workfare. Now let us consider a different situation: The benefits and costs associated with a participant's move from welfare to a regular private-sector job. This is, of course, one of the major objectives of programs such as workfare, and Figure 14.3 implies that the program would in fact have the desired effect on the participant. Although in the absence of the workfare she would prefer not to work at all, given a choice between participating in workfare (point *a*) or working at a regular minimum-wage job (point *b*), the participant would select the latter. By restricting her hours to h^*, workfare causes the participant to be "off her labor supply curve." Only by finding a regular job can she work h_1 hours, the number of hours she would desire to work at the minimum wage. In actual practice, the participant might move directly from welfare to the job upon being confronted with the workfare requirement, or alternatively, she might first participate in workfare while seeking private-sector employment.

A comparison of the net income change measure of workfare's impact on a participant who moves directly to private-sector employment with the corresponding conceptually correct measure of the change in social surplus yields an interesting finding. On the one hand, the net income change measure implies that the participant represented in Figure 14.3 enjoys a net gain. Her transfer payments fall from $W^m a h^* h_0$ to zero, but her earnings increase from zero to $W^m b h_1 h_0$, resulting in a net increase in income of $a b h_1 h^*$. On the other hand, the participant suffers a net social surplus loss because her gain in surplus from working, area $W^m b W_1^r$, is exceeded by the value of her lost transfer $W^m a h^* h_0$. Thus, under the circumstances represented in Figure 14.3, the net income change measure suggests a conclusion that is the diametrical opposite from that implied by the conceptually more correct social surplus change measure.

In measuring the impacts of E&T programs from the participant perspective, three rules can be drawn from the preceding analyses of the three illustrative E&T participants. First, *the full value of reductions in transfer payments should be counted as a cost to E&T participants*. Second, *the full value of increases in earnings that result from wage rate increases should be counted as a benefit to E&T participants*. Third, *only part of the value of earnings increases that result from hours increases should be counted as a benefit to E&T participants; namely, the part that represents an increase in participant surplus should be counted, while the part that is offset by reductions in leisure should not*.

In conducting CBAs of E&T programs, the first two of these rules are straightforward to implement. Implementing the third rule, however, requires an estimate of the percentage of earnings changes attributable to increases in hours that should be counted. The relatively few studies that have attempted to do this have found that the part of the earnings increase that should *not* be counted is potentially large and, if erroneously counted is likely to result in a substantial overstatement of estimated net benefits.[19]

Non-Pecuniary Benefits from Employment. It is sometimes suggested that there are benefits from being employed – for example, increased self-esteem, elimination of stigma that may result from not working, improved health and well-being,[20] greater status, and more social interaction. Although not really non-pecuniary, so-called "scarring effects," which result from the deterioration of human capital during periods of non-employment and employer reactions to gaps in employment, are avoided by maintaining employment. In addition, the income from employment may contribute to the welfare of workers' children and result in their achieving more education. If an E&T program helps individuals gain employment, they and their children may reap such benefits. If so, then these program benefits should, in principle, be included in CBAs of E&T programs, although it is difficult to do so directly.[21] However, to the extent an E&T participant recognizes the potential for achieving these non-pecuniary benefits through the program, her labor supply curve will be further to the right than otherwise, and program benefits measured as surplus would incorporate them. Program benefits that are measured as increases in participant earnings, instead of as increases in surplus, will also be larger the further her labor supply curve is to the right. However, her increase in earnings will not correspond very well to her increase in surplus. Moreover, at most, only part of the benefits from an improvement in self-esteem or a reduction in stigma is likely to be captured by the labor supply curve. Because of information asymmetry, potential non-pecuniary benefits from employment are unlikely to be fully recognized by E&T participants.

Job-Required Expenditures. The framework traditionally used in cost–benefit analyses of E&T programs counts increases in job-related expenditures such as child care and transportation that result from program participation as a social cost of the program, regardless of whether paid for by E&T participants or the government. As discussed next, however, this approach can sometimes result in double-counting.

For illustrative purposes, we focus on child care, although a similar analysis could be made for other work-related costs such as transportation. Figure 14.4(a) pertains to an individual who participated in an E&T program that increased her wage from W_0 to W_1. The supply curve, S, indicates the hours the individual would work if she must pay for child care. The diagram implies that, as a result of the program-engendered wage increase, she would go from not working to working h_1 hours. Thus the program would engender an increase in earnings equal to area $W_1 a h_1 0$ and a smaller surplus gain equal to area $W_1 a W_r$. Panel (b) illustrates the E&T participant's demand for child care. P_0 represents the market-set price for child care. As indicated in the figure, the demand curve for child care would shift out from D_0 to D_1 as a result of the wage increase and the increased hours worked resulting from the E&T.

As the reader may have noticed, Figure 14.4(b) is very similar to the diagrams of primary and secondary markets that appear in Chapter 7. This is hardly surprising. The direct effects of E&T programs typically occur in labor markets, while a complementary relationship exists between work effort and child care. Hence, the primary market is the labor market for E&T participants, while the market for child care is a secondary market.

As discussed in detail in Chapter 7, effects in undistorted secondary markets should usually be ignored if program benefits in primary markets are measured in terms of changes in surplus. Specifically, the individual represented in Figure 14.4 will presumably consider the child care expenses she will incur in determining the number of hours she would be willing to work at each wage rate. Thus, in using her labor supply curve to measure her surplus gain from participating in the E&T program, area $W_1 a W_r$, her child care expenditures are already fully taken into account. Consequently, her increase in expenditures in the secondary market represented in panel (b) – that is, area uvd_1d_0 – should be ignored, as should the area between the two demand curves in panel (b). Not doing so will result in double-counting.

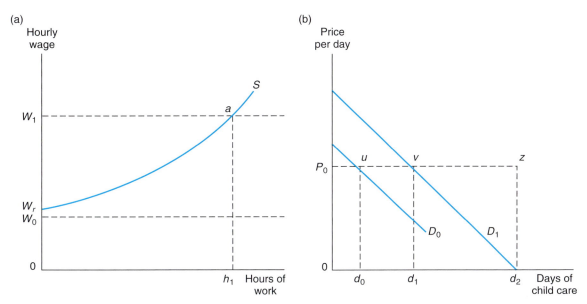

Figure 14.4(a) Labor market effects of an E&T program.
Figure 14.4(b) Child care market effects of an E&T program.

As emphasized earlier, benefits to E&T participants are traditionally measured as changes in net income, rather than as changes in surplus. To obtain this measure, increases in expenditures on child care would, of course, be subtracted from earnings increases. As indicated in Figure 14.4(a), the increase in earnings overstates the gain in surplus resulting from the E&T program by an amount represented by area $W_r a h_1 0$. Subtracting the increase in day care expenditures, area $u v d_1 d_0$, from the increase in earnings offsets this overstatement. However, area $u v d_1 d_0$ could be either larger or smaller than area $W_r a h_1 0$. Thus, the net income measure could be either larger or smaller than the more appropriate social surplus measure.

We next consider benefits and costs if the government directly provides child care or reimburses individuals for their expenditures on child care. To do this, we again use Figure 14.4. A seemingly natural way to examine such a policy is to compare the earnings increases that result from the government subsidizing child care with the government's cost. As will be seen, however, this approach is incorrect.

For illustrative purposes, we assume that child care is provided free to subsidized individuals, but the government pays the market price of P_0. As previously discussed, at a market wage of W_1 the demand curve for child care for the individual represented in Figure 14.4 would be D_1. Thus, if child care was provided to her free, she would consume d_2 units of child care.

As the direct effects of the government's subsidy occur in the market for child care, it should now be viewed as the primary market for purposes of analysis, while the labor market should be viewed as the secondary market. Thus, although the government's provision of subsidized child care would shift the labor supply curve to the right, and this, in turn, would affect earnings,[22] these effects should be ignored. Instead, the effects of the policy on individuals are best examined by measuring surplus changes in the primary market. For example, the individual represented in Figure 14.4 would enjoy a surplus gain corresponding to area d_1vd_2. However, the cost to the government, which is represented by area d_1vzd_2, would be considerably greater, resulting in dead-weight loss equal to area vd_2z.[23]

14.4.2   *The Non-participants' Perspective*[24]

Several categories of benefits and costs accrue to non-participants: intangible benefits, benefits from in-program output, reductions in crime, and costs resulting from the displacement of public-sector and private-sector workers.

Intangible Benefits Received by Non-participants. The preceding section emphasized that in measuring the benefits and costs of E&T programs to participants it is changes in their surplus that should be estimated rather than changes in their money income. Thus, the effects on participant surplus of E&T-induced reductions in participant leisure time should be taken into account.

The same concept applies in measuring benefits and costs of E&T programs to non-participants. For example, if non-participants positively value the substitution of earnings for welfare payments in and of itself, then the increase in surplus they received will exceed any reductions in their tax obligations that might result from E&T programs targeted at welfare recipients. Thus, in principle, it is changes in the surplus of non-participants that result from E&T programs, rather than changes in their incomes, that should be measured. In view of the practical difficulty of doing this, however, it has never been attempted. An approach that might be used for this purpose, contingent valuation, is taken up in Chapter 16.

Changes in Taxpayer Excess Burden. As discussed in Chapter 3, taxes result in losses of economic efficiency that economists refer to as deadweight loss or excess burden. If taxes increase, excess burden also rises; but if they fall, excess burden also diminishes. A particular E&T program could cause taxes to either increase or decrease, depending on whether the program results in positive or negative net expenditures by the government. This would be determined as part of a CBA of the program. Once determined, the program's effect on deadweight loss – that is, its marginal excess tax burden – must be estimated. Doing this requires an estimate of the efficiency cost of one dollar more of taxes or of one dollar less. Such estimates can be found in Chapter 3. The value of this variable can be multiplied by the government's net benefits or net costs to determine the change in deadweight loss resulting from the E&T program.

Benefits from In-Program Output. Some E&T programs involve the provision of public-sector jobs. Perhaps the best-known example of this is the Works Projects Administration (WPA), which operated in the United States during the Great Depression and was intended to absorb some of the massive number of workers who were unemployed during this period. More recently, the Comprehensive Employment and Training Act provided as many as 750,000 public-sector jobs for unemployed persons during the late 1970s. In still more recent years, as discussed earlier, welfare recipients in some states have been required to perform work at public-sector jobs in exchange for their payments.

How should the value to taxpayers of the in-program output produced by E&T participants be assigned to public-sector jobs? Ideally, this would be done by determining what taxpayers would be willing to pay for this output. This is usually infeasible, however, because the output is not purchased in market transactions. Consequently, an alternative approach is used that determines what the labor resources required to produce the output would have cost if purchased on the open market. Because agencies that "employ" E&T participants usually pay nothing for the services of these people, researchers use the wage rate that would have been paid to similar workers hired in the open market. Once an appropriate wage rate is determined, the basic calculation involves multiplying the number of hours E&T participants work by this wage and perhaps adjusting to account for differences between the average productivity of the E&T workers and workers hired in the open market.

This procedure can result in an estimate that either overstates or understates the true value of the in-program output produced by E&T participants. The reasons for this can be seen by examining a key assumption that underlies this valuation method: that the decisions of the public-sector agencies that employ E&T workers closely reflect the desires of taxpayers. More specifically, an analogy is drawn with the behavior of private-sector firms and consumers under perfect competition, and it is assumed that the amount that an agency would be willing to pay to employ an additional worker corresponds to the value that taxpayers would place on the additional output that the worker could potentially produce. Although this is not an appropriate place to assess the perfect competition analogy or discuss the extent to which bureaucratic behavior reflects taxpayer preferences, it should be obvious that a rather strong assumption is required to value output produced by E&T workers.[25]

The implications of this assumption can be explored by use of Figure 14.5, which depicts the demand curve for workers by a public-sector agency that might potentially be assigned E&T participants and the supply curve the agency faces in hiring workers in a competitive labor market. In using this diagram, we first examine a situation in which the assumption that bureaucratic behavior reflects taxpayer preferences is valid and then one where it is not.

In Figure 14.5, the horizontal line, S, represents the supply curve, which is set at the level of the market-determined wage, W, that must be paid to each regular worker hired by the agency; the downward-sloping line, D, represents the demand curve, which is assumed to slope downward as a result of diminishing returns and (as implied by the assumption about bureaucratic behavior) because the agency prioritizes its tasks so that, as its budget expands, successively less important services are performed. (Ignore curve D^* for the moment.) This demand curve reflects the WTP for workers by the agency and, in keeping with the assumption concerning bureaucratic behavior, the area under this curve is presumed to measure the value to taxpayers of output produced by workers hired by the agency.

Figure 14.5 indicates that in the absence of E&T workers the agency would hire R regular workers; however, if P E&T participants were assigned to the agency, a total

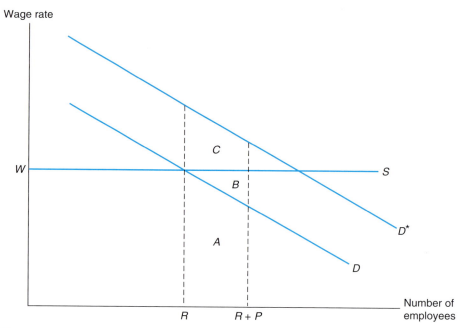

Figure 14.5 Demand for workers by a public-sector agency.

of $R + P$ workers would be employed. Thus, if the bureaucratic behavior assumption is valid, the value to taxpayers of the output added by the E&T workers would equal area A.

Unfortunately, however, area A typically cannot be directly measured. The reason for this is that the output produced by public-sector agencies is rarely sold in market transactions and, consequently, the agency's derived demand curve for labor, which is depicted in Figure 14.5, cannot actually be observed. However, even though government and non-profit agencies that "employ" E&T participants pay nothing for the services of these people, the area under the supply curve between R and $R + P$ can be valued by simply determining the wages that would have to be paid to similar workers hired on the open market to do the work performed by E&T participants. Consequently, it is the area under the supply curve – that is, area A plus area B – that is usually used in practice as the measure of the value of in-program participant output. As a glance at Figure 14.5 suggests, the size of the resulting overstatement of the value of the output produced by E&T participation, which is represented by area B, depends upon the slope of the agency demand curve.

So far, we have assumed that agency behavior simply reflects the value that taxpayers would place on the agency's output. Let us now look at one of the numerous possible situations where this is not the case. The specific example we examine is one in which the agency, perhaps because of budget constraints produces less output than taxpayers collectively desire. These circumstances are represented in Figure 14.5 by two demand curves. As before, curve D indicates *agency* WTP for workers, but the value that *taxpayers* place on the output produced by the agency is now represented by the area under demand curve D^*. Consequently, the value of the additional output produced by the P E&T participants now equals area A plus area B plus area C. Thus, under these circumstances, the measure based on the supply curve of the output produced by E&T workers, which as previously indicated equals area A plus area B, understates the true value by an area equal to C.

Possible Reduction in Crime. As implied by a number of studies, if an E&T program increases the employment and earnings among its participants, it might also decrease criminal activities among the participants.[26] For example, one study found that a 1 percent increase in income reduces the propensity to commit crime by 0.6 percent among male US youth who have permanently left school.[27]

A rough estimate of the benefits from reduced crime due to an E&T might be obtained by first multiplying an estimate of the reduced propensity to commit crime (e.g., the 0.6 percent) by an estimate of the percentage by which the program increased income and then multiplying the resulting figure by an estimate of dollar savings ensuing from a 1 percent reduction in the probability of committing a crime. Estimates of the latter can be derived from the costs of different types of crime, which are presented in Chapter 17.

Costs from Public-Sector Labor Displacement. So far, our discussion has been based on the assumption that the E&T workers made available to a public-sector agency would simply be added to the regular workforce that the agency would hire in the absence of the program. However, the agency might instead substitute E&T workers for regular workers. In terms of Figure 14.5, this behavior on the part of the agency, which is usually referred to as *displacement*, would mean that agency employment would increase by less than the P workers provided by E&T. Indeed, with 100 percent displacement, the agency's workforce would remain at R, rather than increase to $R + P$. Consequently, at first blush, it would appear that displacement leads to overstatement of the value of output produced by E&T participants.[28]

The issue is actually a bit more subtle and complex, however. If the displaced workers have a similar risk of joblessness as E&T participants, then increases in output produced by E&T participants assigned to public-sector agencies may be entirely offset by losses in the output formerly produced by those workers who are displaced. This need not be the case, however, if the E&T participants are exceptional in terms of lack of skills or if they face exceptional barriers to labor market access. Moving such persons directly into jobs under these circumstances will change the characteristics of the general pool of unemployed in ways that may allow a reduction in the net incidence of joblessness, especially if local labor market conditions are tight. Thus, to the extent that E&T participants are unskilled relative to those they replaced, the labor market consequences will differ from a simple one-for-one replacement.

Costs from Private-Sector Labor Displacement. A major objective of most E&T programs is to increase the unsubsidized private-sector employment of program participants. If programs are successful, some participants undoubtedly end up in jobs that would otherwise have been held by non-participants. If, as a result, these non-participants become unemployed or accept lower-wage jobs, their earnings obviously fall. This earnings reduction, which is another type of displacement effect, is potentially a cost of E&T

programs to non-participants. Because there is little agreement concerning the magnitude of private-sector labor displacement, it has rarely been taken into account in CBAs of E&T programs.[29]

The failure to take account of private-sector displacement may not be very serious, however. CBA usually assumes that full employment is maintained. If it is, then it should be relatively easy for displaced non-participants to find alternative job opportunities (although this may take some time), and E&T programs will raise the feasible employment level. Nonetheless, if E&T programs add workers with a particular set of skills to the workforce, they may still depress the wages of workers with similar skills. Private-sector displacement is a more serious issue if unemployment is high. Even then, however, it is possible that E&T programs may impart skills that allow trainees to leave slack occupational labor markets for tight ones. If they do, then they will decrease the competition for job vacancies in the slack labor markets, making it easier for unemployed workers who remain in these markets to find jobs. To the extent this occurs, E&T programs will again raise feasible employment levels.

14.5   Choosing Prediction Parameters

In using the cost–benefit framework illustrated in Table 14.2, it is necessary to take account of any benefits and costs of E&T programs that are likely to extend beyond the typically two- or three-year period for which postprogram data on outcomes are collected. For example, as a result of having participated in an E&T program, some individuals could potentially enjoy increased earnings but pay higher taxes, incur greater job-required expenses, and receive fewer transfer payments over the remainder of their working lives. These streams of future benefits and costs must be incorporated into the CBAs of the program. Doing this requires that three important parameters be specified: the social discount rate, the discounting time horizon, and the decay rate of program effects. Chapter 10 discussed the social discount rate in detail. Discussion of the other two parameters follows.

14.5.1   *The Discounting Time Horizon*

As described in Chapter 9, the time horizon is the total period over which benefit and cost streams are either observed or predicted. CBAs of E&T programs usually assume that benefits and costs beyond the specified time horizon equal to zero. One procedure for determining the length of the time horizon is to subtract the age of program participants at the time they entered the program from the age at which they are expected to retire from the workforce. Often, however, a shorter, somewhat arbitrarily selected time horizon – for example, five years – is used instead. Doing this is simply an acknowledgment on the part of analysts that because they do not possess crystal balls, uncertainty increases the further one attempts to extrapolate beyond the period for which evaluation data were collected. However, because most E&T operating costs are generally incurred shortly after program entry, basing a CBA of an E&T program on a short time horizon

Table 14.3 *The Sensitivity of a $1 Improvement in Annual Earnings to Alternative Time Horizons and Discount Rates (dollars)*

	Discount rate (percent)	
Time horizon	3.0	5.0
5 years	4.58	4.33
10 years	8.53	7.72
20 years	14.85	12.46
30 years	19.60	15.37

will understate E&T benefits if the key potential benefit, earnings improvements, persists well beyond the time horizon. Program operating costs, however, will not be similarly understated.

This understatement of benefits relative to costs could be substantial. Table 14.3 shows the present discounted value of an improvement of $1 in annual earnings under alternative assumptions about time horizons over which the improvement persists and for the value of the discount rate. The figures in the table have two important implications. First, it is evident that the magnitude of benefit and cost estimates are quite sensitive to the choice of the time horizon. For example, if a 5 percent discount rate and a five-year time horizon are used for extrapolation purposes, the present value of an improvement of $1 in earnings equals $4.33. However, if a 5 percent discount rate and a 20-year time horizon are used instead, the present value equals $12.46, almost a threefold increase. Second, the longer the time horizon that is used, the more sensitive are projections of benefits and costs to the choice of the discount rate.

How long are program effects on earnings likely to last for actual E&T programs? While evidence on this topic is sketchy, a study that pooled findings from a large number of E&T evaluations found that program effects on earnings continue to exist for about six years for adult men and about four years for youth after they complete an E&T program, while program effects continue indefinitely for adult women.[30] However, results that are based on random assignment evaluations alone suggest that program earnings effects may last somewhat longer for adult men. Findings from a separate study that is based solely on random assignment evaluations of E&T programs targeted at female welfare recipients suggest that the effects of these programs on earnings continue for five to six years.[31]

Taken together, this evidence seems to suggest that, except for adult women participating in E&T programs, using fairly short time horizons in CBAs of these programs is probably appropriate. It is important to recognize, however, that these findings are based on averages for a variety of evaluated programs. The effects of a particular program could last for either a longer or a shorter period of time depending on its particular features.

14.5.2   *The Decay Rate*

A decay rate is necessary in extrapolating E&T effects that persist beyond the period over which post-program data on outcomes are collected in order to take account of the possibility that the size of these effects may change over time. For example, it is usually argued that programs that provide training or job placement for low-wage workers initially may give them a competitive advantage in the labor market, but this advantage may decay over time. In the case of training, however, one could alternatively argue that doors are opened on the job that allow participants to obtain additional training after leaving an E&T program and, consequently, the program's effects on earnings will grow over time.

Unfortunately, only limited empirical evidence exists as to whether the earnings effects of E&T programs tend to grow or decay over time, let alone the magnitude of the actual rate of decay or growth. Because policy makers are often anxious for findings from evaluations of E&T programs, data on program outcomes are usually limited to three years or less, making predictions of decay rates highly subject to forecasting error, a common CBA problem discussed in Chapter 20.[32] However, one of the studies mentioned previously in discussing time horizons found that earnings effects for adult men, adult women, and youth who participated in E&T programs all initially grew after they completed training but only for a short period of time (perhaps a year or so). Earnings then declined for the men and youth but remained constant for the women.[33] The other previously mentioned study indicated that the earnings effects of programs targeted at welfare recipients increased for two or three years and then begin declining until they disappeared altogether after five or six years.[34] It is again important to recognize that these patterns pertain to a "typical" program and may not hold for a particular program that is being subjected to a CBA.

Once values for the discount rate, time horizon, and decay rate are chosen, Equation (9A.6) in Appendix 9A can be used to compute present values. In using these formulas, care must be taken to use a negative value for g if it is determined that the effects of the E&T program will decay over time and a positive value for g if it seems likely that these impacts will grow over time. For benefit and cost components that neither grow nor shrink over time, g should, of course, be set equal to zero.

14.6   Conclusion

The analysis presented in this chapter suggests that CBAs of E&T programs are more difficult both to conduct successfully and to interpret than they may first appear, even when the CBA is based on a classical experimental design. Nevertheless, as the case study that follows this chapter illustrates, they can provide useful insights. However, some uncertainty exists concerning the reported values, both because of uncertainty over how long the program impacts persisted and because of benefits and costs that were not estimated, such as the value of reductions in the leisure time of participants, changes in the self-esteem of program participants, possible labor displacement resulting from the programs, and society's preference for work over welfare.

Exercises for Chapter 14

1. Using the scheme shown in Table 14.1, diagram the evaluation design used in the CBA of each of the following programs.

   a. To evaluate a government training program that provides low-income, low-skilled, disadvantaged persons job-specific training, members of the target population are randomly assigned to either a treatment group that is eligible to receive services under the program or to a control group that is not. Data are collected on the earnings, welfare receipts, and so forth of both groups during the training period and for two years thereafter.

   b. To evaluate a government training program that provides low-income, low-skilled, disadvantaged persons job-specific training, members of the target population who live in the counties in the eastern half of a large industrial state are assigned to a treatment group that is eligible to receive services under the program, while members of the target population who live in the counties in the western half of the state are assigned to a comparison group that is not. Information is collected on the earnings, welfare receipts, and so forth of both groups for one year prior to the beginning of training, during the training period, and for two years thereafter.

   c. To evaluate a government training program that provides low-income, low-skilled, disadvantaged persons job-specific training, information is collected on the earnings, welfare receipts, and so forth of those persons who receive training. This information is collected for the year prior to the beginning of training, during the training period, and for two years thereafter.

2. Consider a government training program that provides low-skilled men job-specific training. To evaluate this program, members of the target population were randomly assigned to either a treatment group that was eligible to receive services under the program or to a control group that was not. Using this evaluation design, the following information was obtained:

   • Members of the treatment group were found to remain in the program an average of one year, during which time they received no earnings but were paid a tax-free stipend of $4,000 by the program to help them cover their living expenses. During the program year, the average annual earnings of members of the control group were $10,000, on which they paid taxes of $1,000. During the program year, the welfare and unemployment compensation benefits received by the two groups were virtually identical.

- Program operating costs (not counting the stipend) and the cost of services provided by the program were $3,000 per trainee.

- During the two years after leaving the program, the average annual earnings of members of the treatment group were $20,000, on which they paid taxes of $2,000. During the same period, the average annual earnings of members of the control group were $15,000, on which they paid taxes of $1,500.

- During the two years after leaving the program, the average annual welfare payments and unemployment compensation benefits received by members of the treatment group were $250. During the same period, the average annual welfare payments and unemployment compensation benefits received by members of the control group were $1,250.

a. Using a 5 percent discount rate, a zero decay rate, and a five-year time horizon, compute the present value of the net gain (or loss) from the program from the trainee, non-participant, and social perspectives. In doing this, ignore program impacts on leisure and assume that all benefits and costs accrue at the end of the year in which they occur.

b. Once again ignoring program impacts on leisure, recompute the present value of the net gain (or loss) from the program from the trainee, non-participant, and social perspectives, assuming that at the end of the two-year follow-up period program impacts on earnings and transfer payments begin to decay at the rate of 20 percent each year.

3. Perhaps the most careful effort to measure the effects of compensatory preschool education was the Perry Preschool Project begun in Ypsilanti, Michigan, in 1962. Children, mostly three years old, were randomly assigned to treatment (58 children) and control (65 children) groups between 1962 and 1965. Children in the treatment group received two academic years of schooling before they entered the regular school system at about age five, while children in the control group did not. The project collected information on the children through age 19, an exceptionally long follow-up period. Using information generated by the study, analysts estimated that two years of preschool generated social net benefits (1988 dollars) of $13,124 at a discount rate of 5 percent. (For a more complete account, see W. Steven Barnett, "Benefits of Compensatory Preschool Education." *Journal of Human Resources*, 27(2), 1992, 279–312.)

a. Before seeing results from the project, what would be your main methodological concern about such a long follow-up period? What data would you look at to see if the problem exists?

b.   Benefit categories beyond the age of 19 included crime reduction, earnings increase, and reductions in welfare receipts. If you were designing the study, what data would you collect to help measure these benefits?

4.   Five years ago a community college district established programs in 10 new vocational fields. The district now wants to phase out those programs that are not performing successfully and retain those programs that are performing successfully. To determine which programs to drop and which to retain, the district decides to perform CBAs.

a.   What perspective or perspectives should be used in the studies? Are there any issues concerning standing?

b.   Using a stylized cost–benefit framework table, list the major benefits and costs that are relevant to the district's decision and indicate how each affects different pertinent groups, as well as society as a whole. Try to make your list as comprehensive and complete as possible, while avoiding double-counting.

c.   What sort of evaluation design should the district use in conducting its CBAs? What are the advantages and disadvantages of this design? Is it practical?

d.   Returning to the list of benefits and costs that you developed in part b, indicate which of the benefits and costs on your list can be quantified in monetary terms. How would you treat those benefits and costs that cannot be monetized?

e.   What sort of data would be required to measure those benefits and costs that can be monetized? How might the required data be obtained?

Notes

1. For a detailed review of cost-benefit analyses of social policies, see David L. Weimer and Aidan R. Vining, editors, *Investing in the Disadvantaged: Assessing the Benefits and Costs of Social Policies* (Washington, DC, Georgetown University Press, 2009).

2. This method of diagramming evaluation designs was developed a number of years ago by Donald Campbell and Julian Stanley, *Experimental and Quasi-Experimental Designs for Research* (Chicago, IL: Rand-McNally, 1963).

3. On randomization, see Leslie L. Roos Jr., Noralou P. Roos, and Barbara McKinley, "Implementing Randomization." *Policy Analysis*, 3(4), 1977, 547–59; and Larry L. Orr, *Social Experiments: Evaluating Public Programs with Experimental Methods* (Thousand Oaks, CA: Sage Publications, Inc., 1999).

4. Sometimes some members of the treatment group do not actually receive program services. For example, in the case of a training program, they may take a job before the training course begins. If so, then the comparison is said to estimate the effect of the program on the "intent-to-treat." If all members of the treatment group actually receive program services, then the comparison is said to estimate the effects of the program's "treatment on the treated."

5. Sometimes a problem occurs when some members of the two groups cannot be located for purposes of collecting postprogram information on outcomes or refuse to provide the information. This problem, which can occur with all five of the sample designs listed in Table 14.1 and is known as *sample attrition*, can bias the impact estimates if those who can and cannot be located systematically differ from one another in terms of the postprogram outcome measures. For example, those who can be located may have higher earnings, on average, than those who cannot be located.

6. For discussions of issues and problems that arise in conducting social experiments, see Gary Burtless, "The Case for Randomized Field Trials in Economic and Policy Research." *Journal of Economic Perspectives*, 9(2), 1995, 63–84; James S. Heckman and Jeffrey A. Smith, "Assessing the Case for Social Experiments." *Journal of Economic Perspectives*, 9(2), 1995, 85–110; David H. Greenberg and Stephen Morris, "Large-Scale Social Experimentation in Britain: What Can and Cannot Be Learnt from the Employment Retention and Advancement Demonstration." *Evaluation*, 11(2), 2005, 151–71; and Angus Deaton and Nancy Cartwright, *Understanding and Misunderstanding Randomized Controlled Trials* (Cambridge, MA: NBER Working Paper 22595, 2016).

7. On the sources of variation in nominally similar programs, see Michael J. Weiss, Howard S. Bloom, and Thomas Brock, "A Conceptual Framework for Studying the Sources of Variation in Program Effects." *Journal of Policy Analysis and Management*, 33(3), 2014, 778–808.

8. The name stems from the fact that in the absence of random assignment people select themselves to participate or not participate in a program on the basis of such unobservable characteristics as motivation. If appropriate statistical adjustments cannot be made to control for this – as the text indicates, sometimes this is possible, but often it is not – then sample selection bias results. For further information on the selection problem and econometric techniques that are used to attempt to adjust for it, see William H. Greene, *Econometric Analysis*, 4th edn (New York, NY: Macmillan Publishing Company, 2000); Christopher H. Achen, *Statistical Analysis of Quasi-Experiments* (Berkeley, CA: University of California Press, 1986); and Guido W. Imbens and Jeffrey M. Wooldridge, "Recent Developments in the Econometrics of Program Evaluation." *Journal of Economic Literature*, 47(1), 2009, 5–86.

9. For a survey of the social experiments conducted between 1962 and 1996, see David Greenberg, Mark Shroder, and Matthew Onstott, "The Social Experiment Market." *Journal of Economic Perspectives*, 13(3), 1999, 157–72. For two- to three-page summaries of each of the known 143 social experiments that were completed in the United States by the end of 2003, see David Greenberg and Mark Shroder, *The Digest of Social Experiments*, 3rd edn (Washington, DC: The Urban Institute Press, 2004). For abstracts of more recent social experiments, see David Greenberg and Mark Shroder, editors, *Randomized Social Experiments eJournal*, Social Science Research Network.

10. CBAs have also been used to assess social programs for young people. For example, see Lynn A. Karoly, "Toward Standardization of Benefit–Cost Analyses of Early Childhood Interventions." *Journal of Benefit–Cost Analysis*, 3(1), 2012, 1–45; E. Michael Foster and E. Wayne Holden, "Benefit–Cost Analysis in the Evaluation of Child Welfare Programs." *Focus*, 23(1), 2004, 44–49; Steven Aos, Roxanne Lieb, Jim Mayfield, Marna Miller, and Annie Pennucci, *Benefits and Costs of Prevention and Early Intervention Programs for Youth* (Olympia, WA: Washington State Institute for Public Policy, 2004); and Robert Plotnick, "Using Benefit–Cost Analysis to Assess Child Abuse Prevention and Intervention Programs." *Child Welfare*, 78(3), 1999, 381–407. Further examples appear in David L. Weimer and Aidan R. Vining, editors, *Investing in the Disadvantaged: Assessing the Benefits and Costs of Social Policies*.

11. For summaries of findings from evaluations of E&T programs and methodological issues associated with these evaluations, see Robert J. LaLonde, "The Promise of Public Sector-Sponsored Training Programs." *Journal of Economic Perspectives*, 9(2), 1997, 149–68; Daniel Friedlander, David H. Greenberg, and Philip K. Robins, "Evaluating

Government Training Programs for the Economically Disadvantaged." *Journal of Economic Literature*, 35(4), 1997, 1809–55; James Heckman, Robert LaLonde, and Jeffrey Smith, "The Economics and Econometrics of Active Labor Market Programs," in Orley Ashenfelter and David Card, editors, *Handbook of Labor Economics, Volume 3A* (Amsterdam: North Holland, 1999), 1865–2097; and David H. Greenberg, Charles Michalopoulos, and Philip K. Robins, "A Meta-Analysis of Government Training Programs." *Industrial and Labor Relations Review*, 57(1), 2003, 31–53. For summaries of evaluations of E&T programs specifically targeted at welfare recipients, see Judith M. Gueron and Edward Pauly, *From Welfare to Work* (New York, NY: Russell Sage Foundation, 1991); and Karl Ashworth, Andreas Cebulla, David Greenberg, and Robert Walker, "Meta-Evaluation: Discovering What Works Best in Welfare Provision." *Evaluation*, 10(3), 2004, 193–216.

12. Often the financial records of agencies provide insufficient information for estimating the operating costs of E&T programs and other social programs directed at disadvantaged individuals. Instead, estimates of the hours that staff spends on the program (they may do both program and non-program work) and data on their salaries, fringe benefits, and overhead rates are typically needed. For an overview, see David H. Greenberg and Ute Appenzeller, *Cost Analysis Step by Step: A How-to Guide for Planners and Providers of Welfare-to-Work and Other Employment and Training Programs* (New York, NY: MDRC, 1998). This document discusses cost estimation for ongoing programs, demonstrations, and programs planned for the future. Approaches that have been used to collect needed information on staff hours, which can vary considerably with the circumstances and involve interviews with staff and time diaries, can be found in James C. Ohls and Linda C. Rosenberg. "A 'Building-Up' Approach to Measuring Program Costs." *Journal of Policy Analysis and Management*, 18(3), 1999, 473–80; David Greenberg and Abigail Davis, "Learning from Cost Analyses: An Illustration from the New Deal for Disabled People." *Public Money & Management*, 30(3), 2010, 189–96; and David Greenberg, Johanna Walter, and Genevieve Knight, *The Cost of Services and Incentives in the UK Employment Retention and Advancement (ERA) Demonstration: Preliminary Analysis* (Norwich: Department for Work and Pensions, Working Paper No 64, 2009). Although the literature specifically on cost analysis of social programs is scant, further descriptions of cost analyses can be found as part of descriptions of CBAs.

13. Several recent studies have discussed this problem in some detail and suggested possible ways of addressing the problem, especially by the use of contingent valuation (see Chapter 16). These studies include David L. Weimer and Aiden R. Vining, *Investing in the Disadvantaged: Assessing the Benefits and Costs of Social Policies*; Brian Maskery and Dale Whittington, *Measuring What Works: The Feasibility and Desirability of Additional Cost–Benefit analysis for Sixteen 'Social Programs that Work'* (Chapel Hill, NC:

University of North Carolina, 2007); and Lynn A. Karoly, *Valuing Benefits in Benefit–Cost Studies of Social Programs* (Santa Monica, CA: Rand Corporation, 2008).

14. Many of the topics discussed in this section are also usefully covered in Daniel Fujiwara, *The Department for Work and Pensions Social Cost–Benefit Analysis Framework: Methodologies for Estimating and Incorporating the Wider Social and Economic Impacts of Work in Cost–Benefit Analysis of Employment Programmes*, Working Paper No. 86 (London: Department for Work and Pensions, 2010). The paper contains specific recommendations on how each benefit and costs discussed should be treated in CBA.

15. The supply curve in Figure 14.1 should be viewed as an equivalent variation supply curve – that is, it incorporates substitution, but not income, effects. For reasons discussed in Appendix 3A, this is the appropriate curve for measuring changes in worker surplus resulting from wage changes. However, wage changes may engender substantial income, as well as substitution, effects.

16. The word *leisure*, as commonly used by economists and as used here, refers to all activities that take place outside the labor market. Many of these activities (e.g., child care, home repair, and education) may, of course, be quite productive.

17. Because the hours the recipient is required to work are computed by dividing her welfare grant by the minimum wage (i.e., $h^* = \text{grant}/W^m$), her grant equals $W^m h^*$ a value that in Figure 14.3 is represented by area $W^m a h^* h_0$.

18. Notice that because the supply curve first shifts from S_0 to S_1 and then, in response to this shift the participant adjusts the number of hours she works, the surplus loss is measured using S_1 rather than S_0.

19. Stephen H. Bell and Larry L. Orr, "Is Subsidized Employment Cost Effective for Welfare Recipients? Experimental Evidence from Seven State Demonstrations." *Journal of Human Resources*, 19(1), 1994, 42–61; David H. Greenberg, "The Leisure Bias in Cost–Benefit Analyses of Employment and Training Programs." *Journal of Human Resources*, 32(2), 1997, 413–39; and David H. Greenberg and Philip K. Robins, "Incorporating Nonmarket Time into Benefit–Cost Analyses of Social Programs: An Application to the Self-Sufficiency Project." *Journal of Public Economics*, 92(3), 2007, 766–94.

20. See Daniel Fujiwara, *The Department for Work and Pensions Social Cost–Benefit analysis Framework* (pp. 29–40) for evidence indicating that employment has positive effects on health and well-being. Fujiwara also suggests methods for accounting for some of these benefits in CBA.

21. Based on the existing relative literature and a number of what they call "heroic assumptions," Robert H. Haveman and David L. Weimer ("Public Policy Induced Changes in Employment: Valuation Issues for Benefit–Cost Analysis." *Journal of Benefit–Cost Analysis*, 6(1), 2015, 112–53) have

derived monetary estimates of some of these benefits. Their estimates mainly pertain to an unemployed individual who is hired as a result of the labor needs of a government program or policy, not due to participating in a training program. The following estimates, which are found in table 3 of Haveman and Weimer and are annual, are specifically for an individual who earned $40,000 during the year prior to becoming unemployed, was hired after 15 weeks of unemployment, and avoided 15 additional weeks of unemployment as a result of being hired:

Reduction in treatment cost for depression as a result of being hired	$400
Avoided stigma cost as a result of being hired	$1,600
Children's increased education as a result of parent being hired	$2,800
Avoided loss of human capital as a result of being hired	$12,000

22. As with Figures 14.1, 14.2, and 14.3, the labor supply curve in Figure 14.4(a) should be viewed as an equivalent variation supply curve.

23. As mentioned earlier in the chapter, having as many able-bodied individuals work as possible is considered an important social goal by many US citizens. Thus, even though subsidizing child care may be economically inefficient, it may still be justified if it helps meet this goal. Moreover, it is sometime argued that subsidies are needed to correct market failures in the market for child care that results in a lower quality of services than is socially optimal. For example, there may be information asymmetries because parents have difficulty in judging the quality of child care. In addition, viewing children as third parties, positive externalities may exist in the market for child care if parents are more concerned with convenience and price than with quality. See Suzanne W. Helburn and Barbara R. Bergmann, *America's Child Care Problem: The Way Out* (New York, NY: Palgrave, 2002).

24. This section borrows heavily from David Greenberg, "Conceptual Issues in Cost–Benefit Analysis of Welfare-to-Work Programs." *Contemporary Policy Issues*, 10(4), 1992, 51–63.

25. For a review of what bureaucrats actually maximize, see David L. Weimer and Aidan R. Vining, *Policy Analysis: Concepts and Practice*, 6th edn (New York, NY: Taylor & Francis, 2017).

26. Daniel Fujiwara, *The Department for Work and Pensions Social Cost–Benefit Analysis Framework*, summarizes evidence from a number of studies that indicates that increases in income reduce crime.

27. Jeff Grogger, "Market Wages and Youth Crime." *Journal of Labor Economics*, 16(4), 1998, 756–91.

28. A recent review of studies of public-sector labor displacement finds that these studies suggest that such displacement is fairly high, perhaps on the order of 30–60 percent. David Greenberg, Genevieve Knight, Stefan Speckesser, and Debra Hevenstone, *Improving DWP Assessment of the Relative Costs and Benefits of Employment Programmes* (Sheffield: Department for Work and Pensions Working Paper 100, 2010).

29. The review mentioned in the previous footnote found that most of these studies suggest that private-sector displacement is probably moderate, perhaps well under 20 percent. However, the findings from different studies vary greatly and the study methodologies are subject to important weaknesses. However, results from a recent random assignment experiment found that displacement offset almost the entire impact of a program that offered intensive job counselling to young, educated job seekers in France. See Bruno Crépon, Esther Duflo, Marc Gurgard, Roland Rathelot, and Phillippe Zamora, *Do Labour Market Policies Have Displacement Effects?* Evidence from a Clustered Randomized Experiment, *Quarterly Journal of Economics*, 128(2), 2013, 531–580.

30. David H. Greenberg, Charles Michalopoulos, and Philip K. Robins, "What Happens to the Effects of Government-Funded Training Programs Over Time?" *Journal of Human Resources*, 39(1), 2004, 277–93.

31. David Greenberg, Karl Ashworth, Andreas Cebulla, and Robert Walker, "Do Welfare-to-Work Programmes Work for Long?" *Fiscal Studies*, 25(1), 2004, 27–53.

32. The CBA of the Baltimore Options program provides an interesting example of this sort of forecasting error. A CBA from the participant perspective that was based on 42 months of data found that the net benefits of the program were nearly three times as large as an earlier CBA based on 18 months of data. The entire difference in these findings is attributable to the first study assuming that the program effect on earnings would decline between months 18 and 42, whereas the effect actually grew over these months. Daniel Friedlander, Gregory Hoerz, David Long, and Janet Quint, *Maryland: Final Report on the Employment Initiatives Evaluation* (New York, NY: MDRC, 1985); and Daniel Friedlander, *Maryland: Supplemental Report on the Baltimore Options Program* (New York, NY: MDRC, 1987).

33. See David H. Greenberg, Charles Michalopoulos, and Philip K. Robins, "What Happens to the Effects of Government-Funded Training Programs Over Time?" Greenberg, Michalopoulos, and Robins' findings for random assignment evaluations imply that the growth period may last well over a year. For a summary of the scant earlier evidence, see Friedlander, Greenberg, and Robins, "Evaluating Government Training Programs for the Disadvantaged," p. 1836.

34. David Greenberg, Karl Ashworth, Andreas Cebulla, and Robert Walker, "Do Welfare-to-Work Programmes Work for Long?"

Case 14

Findings from CBAs of Welfare-to-Work Programs

Table 14C.1, which appears at the end of this case, presents summary results from CBAs of 26 welfare-to-work programs.[1] These programs were all targeted at single parents who participated in the Aid for Families with Dependent Children (AFDC) program, which at the time the CBAs were conducted was the major cash welfare program in the United States. Most of the programs were mandatory in the sense that AFDC benefits could be reduced or even terminated if a parent did not cooperate. The CBAs were all conducted by MDRC, a well-known non-profit research firm, and used a similar framework including the classical experimental design with random assignment to treatment and control groups. The estimates in the table, which have been converted to 2016 dollar amounts using the US Consumer Price Index, should be viewed as program impacts on a typical member of the treatment group in each of the listed programs.

The first three columns in the table present estimated benefits and costs from the participant perspective and the next four from the non-participant perspective. Columns A and D, respectively, report total net gains (or losses) from these two perspectives, while columns B, C, E, F, and G provide information on the benefit and cost components that together account for these gains (or losses). For example, column B reports the estimated *net* gain by participants from employment under each program, that is, estimates of the sum of increases in earnings, fringe benefits, and any work-related allowances paid under the program less the sum of tax payments and participant job-required expenditures on child care and transportation. Column C indicates changes in AFDC and other transfer benefits received by participants. Column E presents MDRC's valuations of in-program output. Column F is the sum of tax increases paid by participants, reductions in transfer payments paid to participants, and reductions in transfer program operating costs, all of which may be viewed as benefits to non-participants. Column G shows the government's cost of operating the treatment programs. Finally, column H, which is computed by summing the benefit–cost components reported in columns B, C, E, F, and G, presents the overall CBA results from the perspective of society as a whole.

As can be seen from column H, 15 of the 26 reported estimates indicate overall net gains and 11 imply net losses. Nonetheless, most of the total net gains and losses for either participants or non-participants that are implied by columns A and D are not especially large; all but six are well under $4,000 per program participant in 2016 dollars.

The table distinguishes between five distinct types of welfare-to-work programs. As summarized below, the costs and benefits for different program types vary considerably and are quite relevant to policy.

- Mandatory work experience programs, which assigned welfare recipients to unpaid jobs, appear to be worthy of consideration as a component of a comprehensive welfare-to-work program. These programs were implemented for persons who, after a period of time searching, could not find unsubsidized jobs. The programs are not costly to the government and do little harm to participants. Moreover, society as a whole can reap some benefit from the output produced at work experience jobs.

- Mandatory job-search-first programs require individuals to look for jobs immediately upon being assigned to the program. If work is not found, then they are assigned other activities. Such programs appear worthy of consideration when governments want to reduce their expenditures. The programs tend to be less expensive than mandatory mixed-initial-activity programs and, thus, to have a more salutary effect on government budgets. However, they are unlikely to increase the incomes of those required to participate in them.

- The sorts of mandatory education-first programs that have been tested experimentally – ones that require individuals to participate in GED completion and Adult Basic Education prior to job search – do not appear to offer positive net benefits. They do little to either increase the incomes of participants or save the government money.

- Mandatory mixed-initial-activity programs require individuals to participate initially in either an education or training activity or a job search activity. The first six of these programs that are listed in the table enrolled both short-term and long-term welfare recipients, while the last two enrolled only long-term welfare recipients. Four of the former were cost-beneficial from a societal perspective, but the latter two were not.

- Earnings supplement programs provide individuals with financial incentives or earnings supplements intended to encourage work. The CBA findings suggest that they are an efficient mechanism for transferring income to low-income families because participants gain more than a dollar for every dollar the government spends.

Table 14C.1 *Summary of Cost–Benefit Estimates from MDRC's Evaluations of Selected Welfare-to-Work Experiments (in 2016 dollars)*

	Participant perspective			Non-participant perspective				
	Net present value A = B + C	Changes in income attributable to employment	Changes in transfer payments	Net present value D = E + F + G	Value of in-program output	Changes tax + transfer amounts	Operating costs	Net social gain (or loss) H = A + D
	A	B	C	D	E	F	G	H
Mandatory work experience programs								
Cook County WIN demonstration (*n* = 11,912)	817	335	482	−218	217	−367	−68	599
San Diego (*n* = 3,591)	369	1,325	−956	1,679	487	1,358	−166	2,047
West Virginia CWEP (*n* = 3,694)	−194	−14	−180	1,695	2,085	210	−600	1,501
Mandatory job-search-first programs								
Atlanta LFA NEWWS (*n* = 4,433)	−17	3,601	−3,618	−1,109	0	4,614	−5,723	−1,126
Grand Rapids LFA NEWWS (*n* = 4,554)	−3,412	2,896	−6,308	4,189	0	7,051	−2,862	778
Los Angeles Jobs-First GAIN (*n* = 15,683)	605	5,787	−5,182	3,622	0	5,670	−2,049	4,227
Riverside LFA NEWWS (*n* = 8,322)	−1,911	4,291	−6,201	2,225	0	7,006	−4,781	314
SWIM (San Diego) (*n* = 3,227)	−59	4,025	−4,084	3,093	396	4,710	−2,014	3,034
Mandatory education-first programs								
Atlanta HCD NEWWS (*n* = 4,433)	473	2,827	−2,353	−4,692	0	3,200	−7,892	−4,219
Columbus Integrated NEWWS (*n* = 7,242)	−2,351	3,020	−5,370	351	0	6,375	−6,024	−2,000
Columbus Traditional NEWWS (*n* = 7,242)	−1,694	2,189	−3,883	−929	0	4,384	−5,313	−2,623
Detroit NEWWS (*n* = 4,459)	233	1,992	−1,758	−477	0	2,480	−2,957	−244
Grand Rapids HCD NEWWS (*n* = 4,554)	−2,907	1,458	−4,365	−445	0	4,988	−5,434	−3,352

(continued)

Table 14C.1 (cont.)

	Participant perspective				Non-participant perspective			
	Net present value A = B + C	Changes in income attributable to employment	Changes in transfer payments	Net present value D = E + F + G	Value of in-program output	Changes tax + transfer amounts	Operating costs	Net social gain (or loss) H = A + D
	A	B	C	D	E	F	G	H
Riverside HCD NEWWS (n = 3,135)	−4,387	2,620	−7,006	875	0	7,459	−6,584	−3,512
Mandatory mixed-initial-activity programs								
Butte GAIN (n = 1,234)	2,177	5,483	−3,306	234	143	4,914	−4,823	2,411
Portland NEWWS (n = 4,028)	−1,389	7,581	−8,971	7,541	0	11,667	−4,126	6,151
Riverside GAIN (n = 5,626)	2,520	8,467	−5,947	4,884	10	7,526	−2,652	7,403
San Diego GAIN (n = 8,224)	1,221	4,635	−3,414	1,520	248	4,447	−3,175	2,740
Tulare GAIN (n = 2,248)	2,403	2,604	−201	−3,763	−10	787	−4,540	−1,359
Project Independence (Florida) (n = 18,237)	−689	1,073	−1,762	120	0	2,029	−1,910	−569
Alameda GAIN (n = 1,205)	1,450	4,540	−3,090	−4,943	127	4,225	−9,295	−3,493
Los Angeles GAIN (n = 4,434)	−2,653	952	−3,605	−5,725	−10	3,898	−9,613	−8,378
Earnings supplement programs								
MFIP (Minnesota) (n = 3,208)	12,071	1,411	10,660	−13,040	0	−13,445	405	−969
SSP Applicants (Canada) (n = 2,371)	7,841	5,616	2,225	−691	0	973	−1,663	7,151
SSP Long-Term Recipients (Canada) (n = 4,852)	5,491	2,175	3,315	−2,812	0	−1,336	−1,475	2,679
WRP (Vermont) (n = 5,469)	287	−247	534	−272	0	−610	339	15

Source: Based on appendix table B-2 through appendix table B-16 in David Greenberg, Victoria Deich, and Gayle Hamilton, *Welfare-to-Work Program Benefits and Costs* (New York, NY: MDRC, 2009).

Exercises for Chapter 14 Case Study

1. If you were running a state welfare agency and had to choose one of the programs listed in the table, which table's columns would you particularly focus upon? Why?

2. If you were running a state welfare agency and had to choose one of the programs listed in the table, what information would you like in addition to that provided in the table?

Note

1. A synthesis of the cost–benefit findings that are summarized in the table appears in David Greenberg, Victoria Deich, and Gayle Hamilton, *Welfare-to-Work Program Benefits and Costs* (New York, NY: MDRC, 2009), which also lists the individual reports from which the findings are drawn. These reports provide detailed descriptions of the programs to which the CBA findings pertain, as well as presenting the findings themselves. For a meta-analysis of the findings in the table, as well as those for other welfare-to-work programs, see David Greenberg and Andreas Cebulla, "The Cost-Effectiveness of Welfare-to-Work Programs: A Meta-Analysis." *Public Budgeting & Finance*, 28(2), 2008, 112–45.

15 Valuing Impacts from Observed Behavior: Indirect Market Methods

Generally, estimation of changes in social surplus requires knowledge of entire demand and supply schedules. Chapter 4 discusses direct estimation of demand and supply curves, focusing on the demand curve for the purpose of measuring consumer surplus. It assumes that there is a market demand schedule for the good in question, such as garbage collection or gasoline, and we can observe at least one point on this demand curve. In many applications of CBA, however, the markets for certain "goods," such as human life or pollution, do not exist or are imperfect for reasons discussed in Chapter 3. In such situations it may be impossible to estimate, or inappropriate to use, the market demand (or supply) schedule directly. In the early days of CBA, such goods were treated as "intangible," and their impacts were excluded or analysts reverted to qualitative CBA or multigoal analysis. However, over the past 40 years, economists have devised methods for valuing these impacts, thereby enabling analysts to conduct (comprehensive) CBAs of a wider range of policy alternatives.

In practice, the change in social surplus can often be estimated from knowledge of the impact of a policy (e.g., number of affected persons) and the marginal social benefit or the marginal social cost of one more unit of the affected good or service. In a perfect market, the market price equals both the marginal social cost and the marginal social benefit of an additional unit of a good or service. When a market does not exist or market failure leads to a divergence between market price and marginal social cost, analysts try to obtain estimates of what the market price would be if the relevant good were traded in a market in which the demand schedule represented marginal social benefits and the supply schedule represented marginal social costs. As we discuss in Chapter 5, such an estimate is called a *shadow price*.

When a market for the good of interest does not exist, one of two major methods of estimating shadow prices can be used.[1] This chapter recognizes that although there may not be a market for the good or service of interest, its value (shadow price) may be reflected indirectly in the market for a related good. Through statistical analysis of the related market, we can estimate the value of the nonmarketed good. The second way to estimate a shadow price is to use contingent valuation (survey) or other stated preference methods, which are discussed in the following chapter.

The indirect market methods discussed in this chapter are based on actual behavior. Often, the behavior can be observed by third parties and therefore fits into the conventional category of *revealed preferences*. Nonetheless, surveys are sometimes used to ask individuals about their behavior when it cannot be directly observed. For example, we present a version of the travel cost method as originally developed to rely solely on observed behavior. However, the travel cost method is now more often employed using survey data that asks people about their recent travel. These surveys differ from *stated preference* methods that pose hypothetical choices to respondents involving greater cognitive burdens than questions about their past behaviors.

The chapter begins with a discussion of the market analogy method, which uses information from private-sector markets to value publicly provided goods. It then discusses estimation of shadow prices based on trade-offs, for example, the trade-off between time and wages to value leisure time or the trade-off between salaries and the risk of having a fatal accident to value a statistical life. Next, it discusses the intermediate good method, followed by the asset valuation method. All of these methods are subject to potential estimation biases, including the omitted variables problem and self-selection bias. After discussing these problems, we turn to the hedonic price method, which attempts to overcome them. We then discuss the travel cost method and, finally, the defensive expenditures method. Some of these methods involve estimation of the whole demand or supply schedule, whereas others provide only an estimate of the shadow price. This chapter focuses on methods of estimating shadow prices; Chapter 17 presents and discusses specific estimates of them.

15.1   Market Analogy Method

Governments supply many goods also provided by the private sector. For example, housing, campsites, university education, home care, and adoption services are often provided by both the public and private sectors. The government usually provides these services free or at significantly below market prices. Thus, the actual price paid may not be on the market supply curve and reveals only one point on the demand curve. However, it may be possible to obtain an estimate of the entire demand curve using data from a similar good provided by the private sector.

In some countries, the private-sector market may not be legal. For example, some countries have no legal private-sector adoption services. Nevertheless, analysts may sometimes turn to the *black market* to obtain an estimate of the value of such services.

15.1.1   *Using the Market Price of an Analogous Good as a Shadow Price*

Consider, for example, a local government project that provides housing for 50 families. The local government may charge a nominal rent of $200 per month so that government revenue equals $10,000 per month. Clearly, this expenditure underestimates (gross) benefits because all families would be willing to pay $200 per month or more.

Suppose that comparable units in the private sector charge rent of $500 per month. If we took this market price as the shadow price for the publicly provided units, then the estimated total monthly benefits of publicly provided housing would be $25,000 per month. *Using the market price would be an appropriate estimate of the value of the publicly provided good if it equals the average amount that users of the publicly provided good would be willing to pay.* In the case of government allocation at a lower-than-market price, however, occupants of public units typically have lower-than-average incomes and are probably willing to pay between $200 and $500 per month, that is, somewhere between $10,000 per month and $25,000 per month in aggregate.

The price of comparable private housing units might *underestimate* the value to families in public housing if it were poorly targeted. Specifically, if the public housing units were allocated to moderately well-off people who, in the absence of obtaining publicly provided housing, would have purchased similar or better private-sector units at market prices, then the market price of private housing would be a lower bound for their willingness to pay (WTP) for the public housing. Ironically, from the CBA perspective (and considering only the direct consumption benefits), the more poorly targeted public housing units are, the higher their benefits.

15.1.2   *Using Information about an Analogous Private-Sector Good to Estimate the Demand Curve for a Publicly Provided Good*

Suppose a municipal government wants to measure the gross benefits of a swimming pool that it owns and operates. Currently, the municipality does not charge an admission fee, and the pool receives 300,000 visitors per year, shown as point *a* in Figure 15.1. In a comparable municipality, a privately operated swimming pool charges $5 for admission and receives 100,000 visitors per year (point *b*). If these two municipalities and pools were comparable, it would be reasonable to assume that points *a* and *b* are both on the demand curve. Further, assuming the demand curve is linear implies that it is given (in both communities) by the line *abc* in Figure 15.1.

In these circumstances the consumer surplus for users of the municipal pool is the area under the entire demand curve, which equals $1,125,000 ($7.5 × 300,000/2).

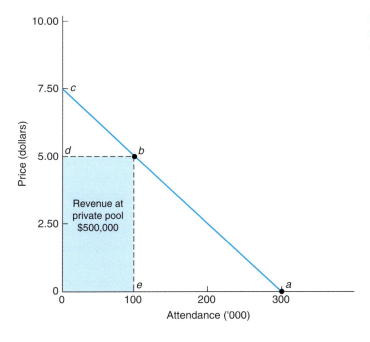

Figure 15.1 Demand curve for visits to a municipal swimming pool.

Using revenues at the private pool ($500,000) would underestimate the benefits of the public pool because it omits the consumer surplus of those willing to pay more than the $5, the area of triangle *cbd*, as well as of those willing to pay something less than $5, but more than $0, the area of triangle *bae*.

In order to regard the observed price and quantity at the private pool as a point on the demand curve for the municipal pool, the pools and their communities should be reasonably similar. For example, the pools should be similar in terms of changing room facilities, hours of business, the friendliness of the staff, and levels of crowding, and the two communities should be similar in terms of population, income, tastes, and availability of other swimming facilities. If these assumptions do not hold, then adjustments should be made along the lines suggested later in the section on hedonic pricing.

15.2   The Trade-Off Method

Economists may use the opportunity cost – the value of what one gives up to get something – as a measure of its value. For example, early CBAs used the after-tax wage as the value of travel time saved by commuters. The basic idea is that if you reduce your travel time by an hour then you can increase your net income by the after-tax wage rate, and vice versa. Put another way, people make trade-offs between time and money wages, and we can use the rate at which they make this trade-off to value time. Similarly, the trade-off people are willing to make between changes in fatality risk and wages can be used to measure the value of a statistical life. Also, analysts can examine the trade-off people are willing to make between cash expenditures and increased safety from air bags, smoke detectors, or other risk-reducing goods and can use this information to impute the value of a statistical life.

15.2.1   *Value of Time Saved*

Many government projects affect people's time, whether it is time spent traveling or in a queue waiting for provision of a government service. In the absence of market imperfections and taxes, the market-clearing wage equals the social value of an additional hour of work, and it equals the opportunity cost of an additional hour of work. If the person would enjoy an additional hour of leisure if he or she worked one less hour, then the wage rate would indicate the value of an additional hour of leisure. Time saved in any other way would also be valued at the wage rate. The value of a government project that saves an hour for a person who earns $20 per hour is worth $20 to that person and to society as a whole.

Setting the value of time saved equal to the wage rate seems straightforward. However, serious problems exist in using the wage rate to value time saved by government projects.

First, wages ignore benefits. As benefits are a form of compensation for work, they should be added to wages. The social value of saving an hour for someone who is working equals his or her before-tax wage plus hourly benefits.

Second, we must take account of taxes. Although it is reasonable to view the value to society of an hour of work as the before-tax wage rate plus benefits, when deciding whether to work, individuals consider their after-tax compensation. Usually, for small changes in hours worked, this equals the after-tax wage rate only, because benefits are usually fixed and do not vary with time worked. Thus, when a government project increases or reduces someone's leisure time its valuation should be based on his or her after-tax wage rate, not the before-tax wage rate plus benefits. However, there is one important caveat: changes in fringe benefits become relevant when they change the availability of benefits. For instance, a part-time worker (typically less than 30 hours per week) may not qualify for important benefits, so that there would be a substantial change in benefits for workers who change part-time to full-time status, or vice versa.

Third, this approach assumes that people do not work while they are traveling or standing in line. In practice, some people multitask: They work and drive or fly at the same time. If they do so, then an hour of travel time saved is worth less than the wage rate. Of course, this does not apply to truck drivers, who are obviously working while they are driving. For them, it does make sense to value their time saved at their before-tax wage rate plus benefits.

Fourth, people are willing to pay different amounts to save an hour doing different things. For example, the value of time saved while traveling may be worth less than the value of an hour saved while waiting in line. Some people like traveling, especially through spectacular scenery, such as along the highway from Banff to Jasper. These people derive consumption benefits from traveling and are willing to pay for the experience of traveling itself. (Consider, for example, the "busman's holiday," say a truck driver choosing to vacation by driving through a scenic region.) In contrast, many people dislike waiting in line or in traffic jams and are willing to pay a lot to avoid it. Thus, the value of time saved depends on what one is doing. Because people generally do not dislike traveling, analysts value an hour of travel time saved for recreational travelers at a fraction (typically between 40 and 50 percent) of the *after-tax wage rate.*

Fifth, the wage rate may not be an appropriate shadow price for time saved because it assumes working hours are flexible. In practice, there are structural rigidities in the labor market. For example, some people involuntarily work overtime and, as a result, are "off their labor supply curve." Also, market failures or government failures, such as minimum wages and the monopoly power of unions, may distort the labor market. Consequently, everyone who wants to work at the market wage may not be able to find work at that wage. Indeed, for some people, such as retirees, no wage rate can be observed.

Finally, firms may not pay their employees the marginal social value of their output. For example, firms with market power may share their profits with employees in the form of higher-than-market wages. Of course, if an industry generated negative (positive) externalities, then the wage rate would exceed (be less than) the marginal social value of an hour saved.

Because of the serious nature of these problems, valuing time saved at the wage rate is only a first approximation to its social value. Later in this chapter, we present better methods for valuing time saved.

The Value of a Statistical Life

Valuing life is a contentious issue. Society often spends fortunes to rescue trapped miners or to give heart transplants to specific individuals. Yet it may not spend money to make obvious gains in mine safety or to reduce the risk of heart disease. In order to allocate resources efficiently in the healthcare sector or to determine the benefits of projects that save lives, analysts require a monetary value of a life saved.

Forgone Earnings: An Inappropriate Method. Early efforts by economists to value life followed a similar method to the one discussed earlier concerning the value of time. Specifically, if one accepts that a person's value to society for one hour equals that person's wage, then one might reason that the value of that person to society for the rest of his or her lifetime equals the present value of his or her future earnings. One would thus conclude that the value of a life saved equals that person's discounted future earnings. This is the *forgone earnings method* of valuing a life saved.[2] It is still used by the courts in some US states and in some other countries to award compensation in cases involving death due to negligence. This method generates a higher value of life for people with higher incomes than for people with lower incomes. On average, it also generates higher values for younger people than for older people and for men than for women.

The forgone earnings method provides unsatisfactory estimates of the value of a life saved for reasons similar to those discussed previously concerning the value of time saved. It assumes full employment, although the method can be adjusted to reflect expected lifetime earnings under average employment expectations. It also assumes people are paid their marginal social product, although often they are not. The lives of full-time homemakers and volunteers who are not paid for their services are unreasonably valued at zero.

Yet the fundamental problem with the forgone earnings method is that it ignores individuals' WTP to reduce the risk of their own deaths. This point was made clearly by Thomas Schelling, who observed, "[t]here is no reason to suppose that a person's future earnings ... bear any particular relation to what he would pay to reduce some likelihood of his own death."[3] Schelling also distinguished between the deaths of identifiable individuals and *statistical deaths*. A safety improvement to a highway, for example, does not lead *ex ante* to the saving of the lives of a few identifiable individuals, but rather to the reduction in the risk of death to all users: It leads to statistical lives saved. *In order to value the benefit of proposed safety improvements, analysts should ascertain how much people are willing to pay for reductions in their risk of death that are of the same magnitude as the reduced risk that would result from the proposed safety improvements.* Such reasoning has led to a series of consumer purchase and labor market studies that have attempted to compute the *value of a statistical life* (VSL).

Simple Consumer Purchase Studies. Suppose that for $1,000 one could buy an optional safety package for a new car that included forward collision warning, automatic breaking, lane departure warning, and other features that reduce the chance of having an accident. These features would increase your survival rate from use of the car from p to $p + \omega$. Would you buy the safety package? This problem is represented as a decision tree in Figure 15.2.

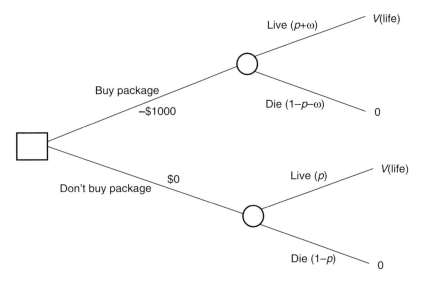

Figure 15.2 Decision tree for safety package purchase.

If a person is indifferent between the two alternatives, then the expected value of the upper-branch alternative (spending the $1,000 more and increasing the probability of surviving by ω) and the expected value of the lower-branch alternative (not spending the $1,000 and surviving with probability p) are equal, that is

$$(p + \omega) \, V \, (\text{life}) - \$1,000 = pV \, (\text{life})$$

$$(p + \omega) \, V \, (\text{life}) - pV \, (\text{life}) = \$1,000$$

$$\omega(V(\text{life}) = \$1,000$$

$$V(\text{life}) = \$1,000 \, / \, \omega$$

If we know that $\omega = 1/10,000$; that is, if 10,000 people buy the safety package, then one statistical life will be saved, then, for a person who is indifferent between buying the airbag or not:

$$V(\text{life}) = \$1,000 \, / \, (1/10,000)$$

$$V(\text{life}) = \$10 \text{ million}$$

This method for estimating the *VSL* has been applied not only to the purchase of the safety package but also to the purchase of other safety-enhancing devices, such as carbon monoxide detectors, walk-in bathtubs, and fire extinguishers.

Simple Labor Market Studies. Simple labor market studies examine the additional salary people require in compensation for exposing themselves to greater risk of death on the job (job fatality risk). Suppose, for example, one type of construction job has a 1/1,000 greater chance of fatal injury in a year than another type of construction job. Further suppose that the riskier job offers a salary that is $11,000/year higher than the safer job. If workers are indifferent between these two types of job, then this implies:

$$(1 / 1,000)V\,(\text{life}) = \$11,000$$

$$V\,(\text{life}) = \$11 \text{ million}$$

In general, if $\$a$ is the amount workers are willing to accept in order to compensate for greater risk, and ω is the change in fatality risk, then the VSL is given by:

$$\text{VSL} = \frac{\$a}{\omega} \tag{15.1}$$

15.2.3   *Problems with Simple Consumer Purchase and Wage–Risk Studies*

One problem with simple consumer purchase and wage–risk studies is that they assume workers have full information concerning the risks – that is, they know ω. For example, in addition to knowing that the chance of dying in a risky job is 1/1,000 higher than in the less-risky job, workers have to know what this means. Evidence that we discuss in Chapter 16 suggests that people suffer from cognitive biases that limit their ability to make rational judgments in such situations. For example, some studies suggest that people overestimate the occurrence of low-probability "bad" events, while other studies suggest that people underestimate such events.[4] When people underestimate the fatality (a bad event) risk of a job, then they will accept a lower risk premium to perform that job, and the VSL will be underestimated.

A second problem is that people who are relatively less risk-averse (more risk-seeking) self-select into riskier jobs. The mean fatality risk in recent VSL studies ranges from about 3 in 100,000 to 22 in 100,000. However, the average US fatality rate for all occupations is about 4 in 100,000.[5] Consequently, risk-averse individuals may be underrepresented in wage-risk studies, which would cause such studies to underestimate the VSL.

A third problem is that researchers may not have an accurate measure of the difference in fatality risk faced by different workers or consumers, the p and the ω. Many US wage–risk studies use aggregated, industry-level data from the Bureau of Labor Statistics. These data do not reflect the difference in risk faced by workers in different occupations within the same industry. For example, a coal miner and a secretary in a coal mining company have quite different fatality risks. Furthermore, ω may be based on currently inaccurate historical data. Suppose that in a consumer purchase study $\$a$ equals $800 and ω equals 0.0002 so that the VSL equals $4 million. Now suppose that there was one more death among 5,000 people, then ω would equal 0.0004 and the VSL would equal $2 million.

The relationship between the WTP for increased safety and the level of safety (fatality risk) is probably convex. The WTP for additional amounts of safety depends on both the base level of safety and the magnitude of the change in the level of safety. A validity problem arises if the level of risk in the consumer purchase or wage–risk study used to obtain the VSL differs substantially from the level of risk applicable to where the policy is being applied.

Other problems with these methods are that they assume markets are efficient and that all other factors that influence prices or wages are held constant. In practice, wage differences may depend partially on the relative bargaining power of unions, on the different characteristics of the different jobs, or on different characteristics (skills) of workers in different jobs. For example, as Adam Smith noted, "[t]he wages of labour vary with the ease or hardship, the cleanliness or dirtiness, the honourableness or dishonourableness of employment."[6] The omitted variables issue, which is illustrated by Exhibit 15.1, is discussed in more detail later in this chapter.

Exhibit 15.1

Are estimates of the value of life that rely on wage premiums that workers receive for working in risky jobs systematically understated? Robert Frank and Cass Sunstein argue that they are understated by 18 to 75 percent *if* they are used to measure WTP for government safety regulations that improve the safety of *all* workers. According to Frank and Sunstein, the reason is that workers who decide to take relatively safe jobs pay for their additional safety by bearing two costs: they lose the wage premium they would receive if they took a more dangerous job and they are lower down in the wage distribution and thus lose status. Both factors affect their WTP for safety, although only the first is reflected in measures of the value of a statistical life that are based on wage premiums. However, a safety regulation that is universally applied reduces risk for everyone without affecting economic position. Thus, workers would be willing to pay more for such a regulation than the amount reflected by wage premiums alone.

Thomas Kniesner and Kip Viscusi take issue with this conclusion for several reasons. They point out that estimates of wage premiums for workplace risk differences are fairly small, on the order of a few hundred dollars a year, and thus are unlikely to have much of an effect on economic status. Kniesner and Viscusi further argue that, even if wage premiums do positively influence status, these gains may be offset because relatively risky jobs are likely to affect feelings of well-being adversely insofar as, by definition, health and safety are lower in such jobs.

Source: Adapted from Robert H. Frank and Cass R. Sunstein, "Cost–Benefit Analysis and Relative Position." *University of Chicago Law Review*, 68(2), 2001, 323–74; and Thomas J. Kniesner and W. Kip Viscusi, "Cost–Benefit Analysis: Why Relative Economic Position Does Not Matter." *Yale Journal on Regulation*, 20(1), 2003, 1–24.

15.3   Intermediate Good Method

Some government projects produce intermediate goods, that is, goods that are used as inputs to some other *downstream* production. For example, a government irrigation project may provide water that farmers use in the production of avocados. If the intermediate good – water – is sold in a well-functioning market, it may be possible to directly estimate the market demand curve for water by using econometric methods. If it is not, we have to impute its value. The intermediate good method estimates the (gross) benefit of a project based on its *value added* to the downstream activity. Specifically, the value of the irrigation project can be measured by the increase in the incomes of avocado farmers. More generally, the intermediate good method measures the annual benefit of a project by the change in the annual incomes of the downstream businesses, thus:

$$\text{Annual Benefit} = \text{Income(with the project)} - \text{Income(without the project)}$$

The total benefit of a project can be computed by discounting these annual benefits over the project's life.

The intermediate good method can be used to value the benefits of education and training programs. Investment in the skills and abilities of human beings improves the stock of *human capital*. Much of the economic successes of Japan and Switzerland, for example, both of which are relatively poor in terms of physical natural resources, can be attributed to their investments in human capital. The intermediate good method measures the annual benefit of human capital programs by comparing the average incomes including benefits of those who have been enrolled in them and the average incomes including benefits of those who have not. The case following Chapter 17 illustrates how to use this method to derive a shadow price for a high school diploma.

One problem with this method is that it assumes that differences in income capture all the benefits of a project. Some intermediate goods, such as college education, may be partially "final" goods. That is, they may have consumption value in addition to having investment value. Some people may enjoy their college education so much that they would pay for it even if it had no impact on their expected earnings. People's WTP for this consumption aspect should also be considered as a benefit of a college education. Also, those with more education may subsequently enjoy better working conditions (as well as higher salaries). Insofar as the intermediate good method excludes these consumption benefits, it underestimates the value of college education. In addition, this method should control for other factors relevant to earnings. For example, the higher income of those with a college education may be partially attributable to greater ability or motivation. Also, some employers may pay those with a college degree more simply because they have better "credentials," even if they do not necessarily have better skills. These latter effects tend to bias upward estimates of the benefit to higher education. Exhibit 15.2 discusses the returns to education in different countries.

Exhibit 15.2

Many studies have used the intermediate good method to value the social benefits from education. These studies usually measure the social benefits from a college education as the difference between the before-tax earnings of college graduates and those whose education stopped after graduating from high school. Some of these studies also estimate the cost of education – tuition fees, tax revenues, donations, and earnings that are forgone while in college. These estimates of benefits and costs can be used to compute the rate of return to different additional amounts of education. George Psacharopoulos and Harry Anthony Patrinos, for example, found that the average worldwide social rate of return to the last year of schooling is 18.9 percent, 13.1 percent, and 10.8 percent, respectively, for primary, secondary, and higher education. The rate of return to private individuals is higher than these estimates because they capture the benefits, whereas the cost is often partially subsidized by the government or donors.

Source: Adapted from George Psacharopoulos and Harry Anthony Patrinos, "Returns to Investment in Education: A Further Update." *Education Economics*, 12(2), 2004, 111–34.

Also, care must be taken in the application of this method to avoid *double-counting*. If the value of an intermediate good has been measured in some other way, then its contribution to the value of downstream production should not be counted as an additional benefit. For example, if the benefits of an irrigation project were estimated based on the estimated demand curve for water, then including the increased income of avocado farmers as an additional benefit would be double-counting – if the market for water is efficient, then the demand curve for water reflects its marginal value in all uses.

15.4   Asset Valuation Method

Government projects often affect the prices of assets such as land, housing, and stocks. The impacts are said to be *capitalized* into the market value of the assets. Observed increases (decreases) in asset values can be used to estimate the benefits (costs) of projects. For example, returning to the irrigation project to provide water to avocado farms, if the farms are the only users of the irrigation water and if the market for farm land is competitive, then the full value of the irrigation project will capitalize into the market value of avocado farms. Using the difference in the value of farms before and after the irrigation project is a relatively quick and easy way to estimate the benefits of a project.

A common application of the asset valuation method uses cross-sectional data on house prices to impute values of particular attributes of houses or of the environment, including negative externalities, such as noise or pollution. For example, the difference in market prices between houses with a view and houses with no view provides an estimate of how much households are willing to pay for a view. The difference between the average price of houses in a neighborhood with a park and the average price of houses in neighborhoods with no park provides an estimate of how much homeowners are willing to pay for a park. Of course, similar to other methods discussed earlier, this method assumes that the houses are similar in all other respects, and that no other factor affects the difference in prices. The section on hedonic prices discusses ways to control for other factors.

Event studies have now become an important method for estimating the costs or benefits to shareholders of new policies or regulations that affect firms.[7] Usually, researchers estimate the *abnormal return* to a security, which is the difference between the return to a security in the presence of an event and the expected return to the security in the absence of the event. These returns are calculated during an *event window*, that is, for the period during which the event is assumed to affect stock prices – often a few days. A main advantage of using stock prices is that new information concerning policy changes is quickly and, in theory, efficiently capitalized into stock prices. Because the return to the security in the absence of the event is unobservable, it is inferred from changes in the prices of other stocks in the market, such as the Dow Jones Index or the FTSE 100. The estimated daily abnormal returns during the event window can be aggregated to obtain the *cumulative abnormal return*, which measures the total return to shareholders that can be attributed to the event. Cumulative abnormal returns provide an estimate of the change in producer surplus due to some new policy.

15.5   Problems with Simple Valuation Methods

The valuation methods discussed earlier in this chapter have several potential limitations, many of which were discussed earlier. This section focuses on the *omitted variable* problem and *self-selection* bias.

15.5.1   *The Omitted Variable Problem*

All of the methods discussed thus far in this chapter implicitly assume that all other explanatory variables are held constant, but this is unlikely in practice. Consider, for example, using the intermediate good method to value irrigation. Ideally, analysts would compare the incomes of farmers if the irrigation project were built with the incomes of the same farmers if the project were not built. In practice, if the project is built, analysts cannot directly observe what the farmers' incomes would have been if it had not been built. One way to infer what their incomes would have been without the project is to use the incomes of the same farmers before the project was built (a before and after design) or the incomes of similar farmers who did not benefit from an irrigation project (a non-experimental comparison group design). The before and after design is reasonable only if all other variables that affect farmers' incomes remain constant, such as weather conditions, crop choices, taxes, and subsidies. If these variables change, then the incomes observed before the project may not be good estimates of what incomes would have been if the project had not been implemented. Similarly, the comparison group design is appropriate only if the comparison group is similar in all important respects to the farmers with irrigation, except for the presence of irrigation.

Salary differences between those with a college degree and those with a high school degree may depend on ability, intelligence, socioeconomic background, and other factors in addition to college attendance. Similarly, in labor market studies of the value of life, differences in wages among jobs may depend on variations in status among jobs, the bargaining power of different unions, or non-fatal accident risk in addition to fatality risk. In simple asset price studies, the price of a house typically depends on factors such as its distance from the central business district and size, as well as whether it has a view. Analysts should take account of all important explanatory variables. If a relevant explanatory variable is omitted from the model, and if it is correlated with the included variable(s) of interest, then the estimated coefficients will be biased, as we discuss in Chapter 4.

Researchers often look for *natural experiments*, in which assignment into treatment and comparison groups is nearly random, to try to control for unmeasured differences.[8] For example, an administrative rule may create a discontinuity in the likelihood of program participation at some cut-off value so that although subjects just above and just below the continuity are essentially the same, some are more likely to be in the program than others. This sort of *regression discontinuity* design has been used to estimate the health effects of the Head Start program.[9] The federal government helped the poorest 300 US counties establish programs, so that those just below the cut-off were much more likely to participate than those just above it.

15.5.2   *Self-Selection Bias*

Another potential problem is self-selection bias. Risk-seeking people tend to self-select themselves for dangerous jobs. Because they like to take risks they may be willing to accept lower salaries than other people in risky jobs. Consequently, we may observe only a relatively small wage premium for dangerous jobs. Because risk-seekers are not representative of society as a whole, the observed wage differential may underestimate the amount that average members of society would be willing to pay to reduce risks and, hence, may lead to underestimation of the value of a statistical life.

The self-selection problem arises whenever different people attach different values to particular attributes. As another example, suppose we want to use differences in house prices to estimate a shadow price for noise. People who are not bothered much by noise, possibly because of hearing disabilities, naturally tend to move into noisy neighborhoods. As a result, the price differential between quiet houses and noisy houses may be quite small, which would lead to an underestimation of the shadow price of noise for the "average" person.

15.6   Hedonic Pricing Method

The *hedonic pricing* method, sometimes called the *hedonic regression method*, offers a potential way to overcome the omitted variables problem and self-selection bias that arise in the relatively simple valuation methods discussed earlier. Most recent wage–risk studies for valuing a statistical life (also called labor market studies) apply the hedonic regression method. It can be used to value an attribute, or a change in an attribute, whenever its value is capitalized into the price of an asset, such as houses or salaries.

15.6.1   *Hedonic Regression*

Suppose, for example, that scenic views can be scaled from 1 to 10 and that we want to estimate the benefits of improving the (quality) "level" of scenic view in an area by one unit. We could estimate the relationship between individual house prices and the level of their scenic views. However, we know that the market value of houses depends on other factors, such as the size of the lot, which is probably correlated with the quality of scenic view. We also suspect that people who live in houses with good scenic views tend to value scenic views more than other people. Consequently, we would have an omitted variables problem and self-selection bias.

The hedonic pricing method attempts to overcome both of these types of problems.[10] It consists of two steps. The first step estimates the relationship between the price of an asset and all of the *attributes* (characteristics) that affect its value.[11] From this it derives the marginal effect of an attribute (e.g., a better scenic view) on the value of the asset, while controlling for other variables that affect the value of the asset. The second step estimates the WTP for the attribute, after controlling for "tastes," which are usually proxied by socioeconomic factors. From this information, we can calculate the change in consumer surplus resulting from projects that improve or worsen the attribute.

Suppose we are interested in determining the hedonic price of a scenic view. The first step estimates the relationship between the price of a house, *P*, and all of its attributes, such as the quality of its scenic view, *VIEW*, its distance from the central business district, *CBD*, its lot size, *SIZE*, and various characteristics of its neighborhood, *NBHD*, such as school quality. A model of the factors affecting house prices can be written as follows:

$$P = f(CBD, SIZE, VIEW, NBHD) \tag{15.2}$$

This equation is called a *hedonic price function* or *implicit price function*.[12] The change in the price of a house that results from a unit change in a particular attribute (i.e., the slope) is called the *hedonic price, implicit price,* or *rent differential* of the attribute. In a well-functioning market, the hedonic price can naturally be interpreted as the additional cost of purchasing a house that is marginally better in terms of a particular attribute. For example, the hedonic price of scenic views, which we denote as r_v, measures the additional cost of buying a house with a slightly better (higher-level) scenic view.[13] Sometimes hedonic prices are referred to as *marginal hedonic prices* or *marginal implicit prices*. Although these terms are technically more correct, we will not use them in order to make the explanation as easy to follow as possible.

Usually analysts assume the hedonic price function has a multiplicative functional form, which implies that house prices increase as the level of scenic view increases but at a decreasing rate. Assuming the hedonic pricing model represented in Equation (15.2) has a multiplicative functional form, we can write:

$$P = \beta_0 CBD^{\beta_1} SIZE^{\beta_2} VIEW^{\beta_3} NBHD^{\beta_4} e^{\epsilon} \tag{15.3}$$

The parameters, β_1, β_2, β_3, and β_4 are elasticities: they measure the proportional change in house prices that results from a proportional change in the associated attribute.[14] We expect $\beta_1 < 0$ because house prices decline with distance to the *CBD*, but β_2, β_3, and $\beta_4 > 0$ because house prices increase with increases in *SIZE*, *VIEW*, and *NBHD*.

The hedonic price of a particular attribute is the slope of Equation (15.2) with respect to that attribute. In principle, it may be a function of all of the variables in the hedonic price equation.[15] For the multiplicative model in Equation (15.3), the hedonic price of scenic views, r_v, is:[16]

$$r_v = \beta_3 \frac{P}{VIEW} > 0 \tag{15.4}$$

In this model, the hedonic price of scenic views depends on the value of the parameter β_3, the price of the house, P, and the view from the house, *VIEW*. Thus, it varies from one observation (house) to another. Note that plotting this hedonic price against the level of scenic view provides a downward-sloping curve, which implies that the marginal value of scenic views declines as the level of the view increases.

The preceding points are illustrated in Figure 15.3. The top panel shows an illustrative hedonic price function with house prices increasing at a decreasing rate as the level of scenic view increases. The slope of this curve, which corresponds to the hedonic price of a scenic view, decreases as the level of the scenic view increases. The bottom panel shows more precisely the relationship between the hedonic price of scenic views (the slope of the curve in the top panel) and the level of scenic view.

In a well-functioning market, utility-maximizing households will purchase houses so that their WTP for a marginal increase in each attribute equals its hedonic price. Consequently, in equilibrium, the hedonic price of an attribute can be interpreted as the willingness of households to pay for a marginal increase in that attribute. The graph of the hedonic price of scenic views, r_v, against the level of scenic view is shown in the lower panel of Figure 15.3. Assuming all households have identical incomes and tastes, this curve can be interpreted as a household inverse demand curve for scenic views.

Yet, households differ in their incomes and taste. Some are willing to pay a considerable amount of money for a scenic view; others are not. This brings us to the second step of the hedonic pricing method. To account for different incomes and tastes, analysts estimate the following willingness-to-pay (inverse demand) function for scenic views:[17]

$$r_v = W(VIEW, Y, Z) \tag{15.5}$$

where r_v is estimated from Equation (15.4), Y is household income, and Z is a vector of household characteristics that reflects tastes (e.g., socioeconomic background, race, age, and family size). Three willingness-to-pay functions, denoted W_1, W_2, and W_3, for three different households are drawn in the lower panel of Figure 15.3.[18] Equilibria occur where these functions intersect the r_v function. When incomes and socioeconomic characteristics differ, the r_v function is the locus of household equilibrium willingnesses to pay for scenic views.

Using the methods described in Chapters 3 and 4, it is straightforward to use Equation (15.5) to calculate the change in consumer surplus to a household due to a

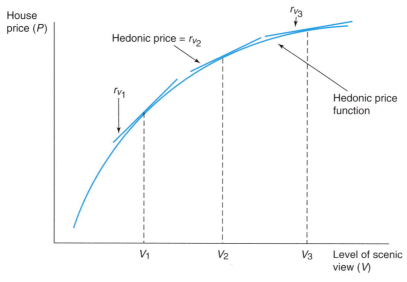

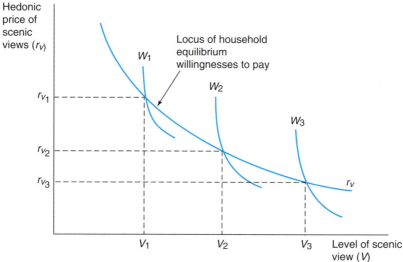

Figure 15.3 The hedonic price method.

change in the level of scenic view. These changes in individual household consumer surplus can be aggregated across all households to obtain the total change in consumer surplus.

15.6.2   *Using Hedonic Models to Determine the VSL*

As we mentioned above, the simple consumer purchase and labor market studies that we described previously may result in biased estimates of the value of a statistical life due to omitted variables. For example, labor market studies that focus on *fatality risk* (the risk of death) often omit potentially relevant variables such as *injury risk* (the risk of non-fatal injury). This problem may be reduced by using the hedonic pricing method and, for example, estimating the following log-log regression model:[19]

$$\ln \text{(wage rate)} = \beta_0 + \beta_1 \ln \text{(fatality risk)} + \beta_2 \ln \text{(injury risk)} + \beta_3 \ln \text{(job tenure)}$$
$$+ \beta_4 \ln \text{(education)} + \beta_5 \ln \text{(age)} + \varepsilon \quad\quad (15.6)$$

This model includes injury risk, job tenure, education, and age in the model as controls for variables potentially affecting wages that would bias the estimated coefficient of β_1 if excluded. Using the procedure demonstrated in the preceding section, the analyst can convert the estimate of β_1 to a hedonic price of fatality risk and then estimate individuals' WTP to avoid fatal risks, thereby controlling for self-selection problems. Most of the empirical estimates of the value of life that are reported in Chapter 17 are obtained from labor market and consumer product studies that employ models similar or analogous to the one described here.

Exhibit 15.3

Dean Uyeno, Stanley Hamilton, and Andrew Biggs used the hedonic pricing method to estimate the cost of airport noise in Vancouver, Canada. They estimated the following hedonic price equation:

$$\ln H = \beta_0 + \beta_1 \text{NEF} + \sum_{j=2}^{k} \beta_k \ln X_j + \varepsilon$$

where, $\ln H$ is the natural log of residential property value, NEF is a measure of noise level (ambient noise levels are in the NEF 15–25 range, "some" to "much" annoyance occurs in the NEF 25–40 range, and "considerable" annoyance occurs above NEFs of 40), the X_j are house characteristics ($j = 2, ..., k$), and ε is an error term.

Their results show that Vancouver International Airport generates noise costs that capitalize into residential house and condominium prices. The estimated coefficient of the noise variable implies that detached houses very close to the airport with NEFs of 40 are 9.75 percent cheaper than houses far from the airport with NEFs of 25.

The estimated noise depreciation sensitivity is broadly consistent with previous studies, leading the authors to conclude that "the similarity of results spanning several decades and several Western countries would seem to suggest a broad and long-lived consensus on the issue (of the impact of airport noise on property values)" (p. 14). In aggregate, the social cost of noise from Vancouver International Airport amounts to about $15 million in 1987 Canadian dollars.

Source: Adapted from Dean Uyeno, Stanley W. Hamilton, and Andrew J. G. Biggs, "Density of Residential Land Use and the Impact of Airport Noise." *Journal of Transport Economics and Policy*, 27(1), 1993, 3–18.

15.6.3   *Problems with Hedonic Models*

In theory, the hedonic pricing method can be used to determine the shadow price of many goods that are not traded in well-developed markets, such as externalities and public goods.[20] It helps to overcome omitted variable and self-selection problems. However, it does not overcome all problems. Here we mention seven problems.

First, people must know and understand the full implications of the externality or public good. For example, in order to use the hedonic pricing method to value pollution, families should know, prior to the purchase of their house, the level of pollution to which it is exposed and should also know the effect of different pollution levels on their health. Similarly, in hedonic wage–risk studies, workers must correctly perceive the actual risks. Second, there must be sufficient variation in the key independent variable of interest. For example, W. P. Jennings and A. Kinderman observe that the rate of occupational fatalities in most industries has fallen roughly 95 percent since 1920 and is now one-third of the rate of accidental deaths in the home.[21] They argue that "the current fatality rates are so low and their individual causes so often random that statistical attempts to measure how fatalities affect wages are unlikely to meet with success." Third, it is important that the hedonic equations, such as Equation (15.3) or Equation (15.6), include correctly measured variables, as opposed to more readily obtainable but incorrect proxies. For example, house values may depend on the quality of construction. As this variable is difficult to determine without inspection, the researcher may use the year of construction as a proxy for quality. In econometrics, this problem is referred to as the *errors in variables* problem. Fourth, if the hedonic pricing model is linear, then the hedonic price of each attribute is constant, which would make it impossible to estimate the inverse demand function, such as Equation (15.5).[22] Fifth, the market should contain many different houses so that families can find an optimal "package," that is, a house with just the right combination of attributes. In other words, there should be sufficient variety so that families can find a house that permits them to reach an equilibrium. This would be a problem if, for example, a family wanted a small, pollution-free house, but all of the houses in pollution-free areas were large. Sixth, there may be multicollinearity problems in the data. To use the same example, if expensive houses were large and located mainly in areas free of pollution, but inexpensive houses were small and located mainly in polluted areas, it would be difficult to estimate separate hedonic prices for pollution and size. Seventh, the method assumes that market prices adjust immediately to changes in attributes and in all other factors that affect demand or supply.

15.7   Travel Cost Method[23]

Most applications of the travel cost method (TCM) have been to value recreational sites. If the "market" for visits to a particular site is geographically extensive, then visitors from different origins bear different travel costs depending on their proximity to the site. The resulting differences in total cost, and the differences in the rates of visits that they induce, provide a basis for estimating a demand curve for the site.

Suppose that we want to estimate the value of a particular recreational site. We expect that the quantity of visits demanded by an individual, q, depends on its price, p, the price of substitutes, p_s, the person's income, Y, and variables that reflect the person's tastes, Z:

$$q = f(p, p_s, Y, Z) \tag{15.7}$$

The clever insight of the TCM is that although admission fees are usually the same for all persons (indeed, they are often zero), the total cost faced by each person varies because of differences in travel costs. Consequently, usage also varies, thereby allowing researchers to make inferences about the demand curve for the site.

The *full price* paid by visitors to a recreational site includes the opportunity cost of time spent traveling and the operating cost of vehicles used to travel (round trip), the cost of accommodations for overnight stays while traveling or visiting, parking fees at the site, and the cost of admission. The sum of all of these costs gives the total cost of a visit to the site. *This total cost is used as an explanatory variable in place of the admission price in a model similar to Equation (15.7).*

Estimating such a model is conceptually straightforward. First, select a random sample of households within the market area of the site. These are the potential visitors. Second, survey these households to determine their numbers of visits to the site over some period of time, their costs involved in visiting the site, their costs of visiting substitute sites, their incomes, and their other characteristics that may affect their demand. Third, specify a functional form for the demand schedule and estimate it using the survey data. For an application of the TCM see Exhibit 15.4.

It is important to emphasize that when total cost replaces price in Equation (15.7), this equation is not the usual demand curve that gives visits as a function of the price of admission. However, as we show next, such models can be used to derive the usual market demand curve and to estimate the average WTP for a visit.

15.7.1   *Zonal Travel Cost Method*

With the *zonal travel cost method*, researchers survey or observe actual visitors at a site, rather than potential visitors. This is often more feasible and less expensive than surveying potential visitors. Also, the level of analysis shifts from the individual (or household) to the area, or zone, of origin of visitors, hence the name *zonal travel cost method*.

The zonal TCM requires the analyst to specify the zones from which users of the site originate. Zones are easily formed by drawing concentric rings or iso-time lines around the site on a map. Ideally, households within a zone should face similar travel costs, as well as have similar values of the other variables that would be included in an individual demand function, including similar prices of substitutes, similar incomes, and similar tastes. If residents from different regions within a zone have quite different travel costs, then the zones should be redrawn. In practice, analysts often use local government jurisdictions as the zones because they facilitate the collection of data and allow for more accurate estimation of travel times.

Australia's Gold Coast beaches are popular with both tourists and local residents. A team of researchers administered onsite questionnaires to 297 people at Surfers Paradise, Narrowneck, Main, and Broad beaches in February (late spring) 2011. The most comprehensive measure of travel costs included onsite expenditures for all respondents. Local residents who walked or bicycled to the beach were assigned no additional costs. Other local residents who drove were assigned time costs and vehicle operating costs based on the engine size of their vehicles. Domestic tourists were assigned time costs as well as either vehicle operating costs or public transportation costs. International tourists were assigned these costs but from the airport at which they arrived in Australia rather than from their residence. All tourists, defined as those who spent one or more nights away from home during the current visit, were assigned accommodation costs. In addition to this most comprehensive measure of travel cost, the researchers constructed less-comprehensive measures to assess the robustness of their analysis.

Local residents (41.9 percent of respondents) were asked about the frequency of their visits to the beach and tourists (42.6 percent domestic and 15.5 percent international) were asked about their prior visits during the past year. Forty percent of local residents visit the beach more than once weekly; just under half of tourists had visited during the prior year.

The analysts employed a zero-truncated negative binomial regression model to estimate the impact of travel costs on the number of annual visits. In these models, the authors rely on results derived by Jeffrey Englin and J. S. Shonkwiler showing that when this functional form is used the average consumer surplus equals the negative inverse of the coefficient of travel cost. The most robust estimates were AU\$16.67 per tourist visit and AU\$10.05 per local visit. With an estimated 7 million tourist visits and 40 million local visits per year, the annual consumer surplus from visits to the beaches exceeds AU\$500 million, suggesting that rather large expenditures on preservation would be economically justified.

Source: Adapted from Fan Zhang, Xiao Hua Wang, Paulo A.L.D. Nunes, and Chunbo Ma, "The Recreational Value of Gold Coast Beaches, Australia: An Application of the Travel Cost Method." *Ecosystem Services*, 11(February), 2015, 106–14; Jeffrey Englin and J. Scott Shonkwiler, "Estimating Social Welfare using Count Data Models: An Application to Long-Run Recreation Demand under Conditions of Endogenous Stratification and Truncation." *Review of Economics and Statistics*, 77(1), 1995, 104–12.

Assuming a constant elasticity functional form leads to the following model:

$$\ln\left(\frac{TV}{POP}\right) = \beta_0 + \beta_1 \ln(\overline{p}) + \beta_2 \ln(\overline{p}_s) + \beta_3 \ln(\overline{Y}) + \beta_4 \overline{Z} + \varepsilon$$

$$(15.8)$$

where, *TV* is the total number of visits from a zone per period; *POP* is the population of the zone; and $\bar{p}$, $\bar{p}_s$, $\bar{Y}$, and $\bar{Z}$ denote the average values of p, p_s, Y, and Z in each zone, respectively. Again, when this equation is estimated, the total opportunity cost of a visit serves as the price.

Note that the quantity demanded is expressed as a visit rate. An alternative specification is to estimate the quantity demanded in terms of the number of visits, V, but to include population, *POP*, on the right-hand side of the regression equation. Although both specifications are plausible, the specification in Equation (15.8) is less likely to involve heteroscedasticity problems (which we discuss in Chapter 4) and is, therefore, more likely to be appropriately estimated by ordinary least squares.

Using estimates of the parameters of Equation (15.8), it is possible to estimate the change in consumer surplus associated with a change in the admission price to a site, the total consumer surplus associated with the site at its current admission fee, and the average consumer surplus per visit to the site. We illustrate how to do this by using the data presented in the first five columns of Table 15.1 for a hypothetical recreational wilderness area. This illustration assumes there are only five relevant zones from which people travel to the recreational site. To avoid unnecessary complications, we assume that demand depends directly only on total cost, not on income, the prices of substitutes, or any other variable.

In this example, the value of time for residents from different zones varies due to different income levels in different zones, as well as different travel times. Zone A is adjacent to the recreational area. Residents from zone A can, on average, pack up their equipment, drive to the site, park, and walk to the entrance in approximately one-half hour. Assuming the opportunity cost of their time is $9.40 per hour and marginal vehicle operating costs are 15 cents/km, their total travel cost is $10 per round trip – 1 hour of total travel time (0.5 hours each way) valued at $9.40 and 4 km of travel (2 km each way) valued at $0.60. Adding the admission fee of $10 per day yields a total cost of $20 per visit. Local residents make 15 visits each year, on average. Zone B is about 30 km away, requiring two hours of total travel time (including driving, parking, walking, and loading

Table 15.1 *Illustration of the Travel Cost Method*

Zone	One-way travel time (hours)	One-way travel distance (km)	Average total cost per person ($)	Average number of visits per person	Consumer surplus per person	Consumer surplus per zone ($ thousands)	Trips per zone (thousands)
A	0.5	2	20	15	525	5,250	150
B	1.0	30	30	13	390	3,900	130
C	2.0	90	65	6	75	1,500	120
D	3.0	140	80	3	15	150	30
E	3.5	150	90	1	0	0	10
Total						10,800	440

and unloading vehicles) for a round trip. Assuming the value of time for these residents is $5.50 per hour and they travel individually, their total cost per visit is $30. Zone B residents make 13 visits per year on average. Zone C is about 90 km away and requires two hours of travel time in each direction. Assuming the value of these residents' time is $10.35 per hour on average, and that their travel costs are shared between two people, the total cost per person is approximately $65 per visit. Zone C residents make six visits per year on average. Zone D residents live on the other side of the metropolitan area and, on average, make three visits each year. Assuming that their average wage rate is $8 per hour and that two persons travel per vehicle, their per-person cost is $80 per visit. Zone E residents have to cross an international border. Although the distance is only slightly farther than from zone D, it takes almost half an hour to get through customs and immigration. The average zone E wage is $8/hour. Assuming two persons per vehicle, the per-person cost is $90 per visit. On average, visitors from zone E make only one visit per year.

The data for average total cost per person visit (TC) and average visits per person (V), which are in columns 4 and 5 of Table 15.1, are represented graphically in Figure 15.4. The equation $TC = 95 - 5V$ fits these data perfectly. (In practice, ordinary least squares would be used to fit a line to data points that would not all lie exactly on the line.) This equation is the "representative" individual's inverse demand curve: it shows how much a typical visitor is willing to pay for a visit to the recreational area (for example, $90 for the first visit, $85 for the second visit, $65 for the sixth visit, and $20 for the fifteenth visit).

Different individuals face different prices (costs) for their visits depending on their zone of origin. It is cheaper for those who live closer. Therefore, individuals' consumer surplus varies according to their zone of origin. The consumer surplus for a particular visit from a particular zone equals the difference between how much someone is willing to pay for that visit, given by the point on the "representative" individual's inverse demand curve, and how much the person actually pays for a visit *from that zone*. As mentioned previously, "representative" visitors are willing to pay $90 for their first visit, $85 for the second, and $65 for their sixth. People from zone C actually pay only $65 for each visit. Consequently, their consumer surplus equals $25 for the first visit, $20 for the second visit, $15 for the third visit, $10 for the fourth visit, $5 for the fifth visit, and $0 for the sixth visit.

The total consumer surplus for someone from zone C is obtained by summing the consumer surpluses associated with each visit across all visits, which amounts to $75. This amount is represented by the area of the shaded triangle in Figure 15.4.[24] Similarly, the consumer surplus is $525 per person for residents of zone A, $390 for residents of zone B, $15 for residents of zone D, and $0 for residents of zone E. These amounts are presented in the sixth column of Table 15.1. Clearly, people who live closer to the recreational site enjoy more consumer surplus from it than people who live farther away.

From this information and knowledge of the populations of each zone, we can calculate the total consumer surplus per year and the average consumer surplus per visit for the site. Suppose zones A, B, D, and E have populations of 10,000 people, while zone C has a population of 20,000 people. The consumer surplus per zone is obtained by multiplying the consumer surplus per person in a zone by the population of that zone,

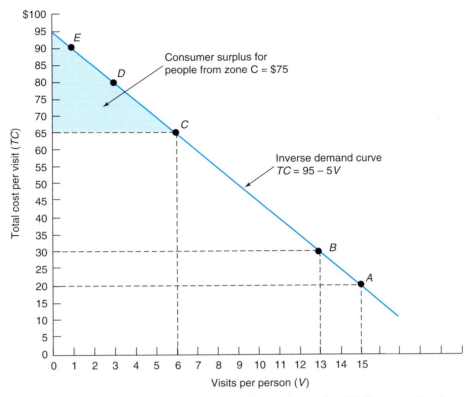

Figure 15.4 "Representative" individual's inverse demand curve for visits to a recreational area as a function of total cost per visit.

as shown in the seventh column in Table 15.1. Adding across all zones yields the total annual consumer surplus for the site of $10.8 million. Adding admission fees of $4.4 million indicates that the annual (gross) benefit of the site to all visitors equals $15.2 million. If the government decided to use the site for some completely different purpose, such as logging, then this would be a measure of the lost annual benefits.

15.7.2   *Estimating the Market Demand Curve for a Public Good Using the Zonal Travel Cost Method*

It is possible to construct the *market demand curve* for a public good from estimation of Equation (15.8) where price is replaced with total cost. That is, we can derive a demand schedule in which the *total* number of visits to the site is a function of the admission price. This curve can then be used to estimate total consumer surplus in the usual way. Unfortunately, because each point on the demand curve has to be estimated separately, precise computation is not straightforward.

For illustrative purposes, we continue with the previous example where $TC = 95 - 5V$. To begin, we know two points on the market demand curve. At the current admission price of $10 there are 440,000 visits, represented by point c in Figure 15.5. Now consider how high admission fees can be raised until demand is choked off (equals zero).

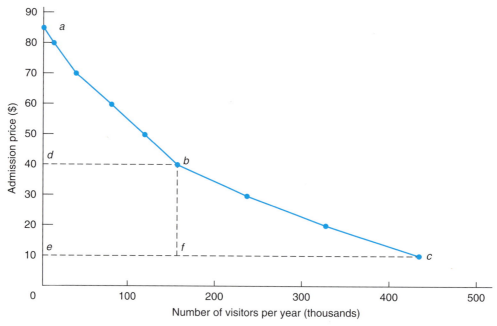

Figure 15.5 The market demand curve for a recreational site derived using the zonal travel cost method.

We know from the representative individual's inverse demand curve ($TC = 95 - 5V$) that the maximum WTP (including all costs) is $95. Subtracting the travel cost of users from zone A (who have the lowest travel cost of $10) implies that the maximum WTP for admission is $95 − $10 = $85. This is the intercept (choke price) of the inverse market demand curve where number of visits is a function of admission price and is represented by point *a* in Figure 15.5.

We can find other points on the market demand curve by assuming that the admission fee is increased or decreased and then predicting the visit rate from each zone at the new price. Suppose, for example, that the admission fee was raised from $10 to $20, so that TC increased by $10 dollars. Because the *individual* demand curve can be written as $V = 19 - 0.2TC$ (the inverse of $TC = 95 - 5V$), a $10 increase in TC would reduce the number of visits per person by two. Thus, if the admission price were $20, then the predicted number of visits would be 13 for zone A, 11 for zone B, 4 for zone C, 1 for zone D, and −1 for zone E. Because negative visits are not possible, we set the number of visits per person for zone E to zero. The total number of visits demanded at the new price is computed by multiplying the predicted visit rate for each zone by its population and summing these products [(13)(10,000) + (11)(10,000) + (4)(20,000) + (1)(10,000) = 330,000]. Thus, at a price of $20 we would expect 330,000 visits. This is a third point on the market demand curve.

With a sufficient number of points, the market demand curve can be sketched to any desired level of accuracy. The market demand curve in Figure 15.5 is computed on the basis of $10 price increments. The annual consumer surplus for the site is the area between the curve and the current admission fee from zero visits to 440,000 visits. Assuming for simplicity that the demand curve is linear between points *a* and *b*, and between points *b* and *c*, we estimate the annual consumer surplus of the site equals $12.6 million, and the annual (gross) benefit of the site equals $17.0 million.[25] Due to the linear approximation and the relatively few points on the demand curve, we slightly overestimate the annual gross benefits, previously calculated as $15.2 million.

15.7.3   *Limitations of the TCM*

The usefulness of the TCM is limited in a number of ways. One limitation is that the TCM provides an estimate of the WTP for the entire site rather than for specific features of a site. As we often wish to value changes in specific features of a site (e.g., improvements in the hiking trails), the basic TCM does not provide the needed information. However, if residents of zones can choose from among a number of alternative recreational sites with different attributes, then it may be possible to use the *hedonic travel cost method* to find attribute prices.[26] This method treats the total cost of visiting a particular site from a particular zone as a function of both the distance from that zone to the site and various attributes of the site. Its application raises a number of issues beyond those previously discussed in the context of the basic hedonic pricing model. Therefore, before attempting to apply the hedonic travel cost method, we recommend consulting other sources.[27]

Measuring the total cost of a visit to the site may be difficult.[28] Perhaps the most obvious problem is the estimation of the opportunity cost of travel time, which we have previously discussed.[29] Even defining and measuring travel costs raises some difficult issues. Some analysts include the time spent at the site, as well as the time spent traveling to and from it, as components of total price. If people from different zones spend the same amount of time at the site, and if the opportunity cost of their time is similar, then it does not matter whether the time spent at the site is included or not – both the height of the demand curve and total price shift by the same amount for each consumer so that estimates of consumer surplus remain unchanged. If, however, people from different zones have different opportunity costs for their time, or if they spend different amounts of time at the site, then including the cost of time spent at the site would change the price facing persons from different zones by different amounts and, thereby, change the slope of the estimated demand curve.

Another problem arises because recreation often requires investment in fairly specialized equipment such as tents, sleeping bags, wet-weather gear, canoes, fishing rods, and even vehicles. The marginal cost of using such equipment should be included in total price. Yet, estimating the marginal cost of using capital goods is usually difficult. As with time spent at the site, however, these costs can be reasonably ignored if they are approximately constant for visitors from different zones.

Multiple-purpose trips also pose an analytical problem. People may visit the recreational site in the morning and go river rafting nearby in the afternoon. Sometimes analysts exclude visitors with multiple purposes from the data. Including visitors with multiple purposes is usually desirable if costs can be appropriately apportioned to the site being valued. If the apportionment is arbitrary, however, then it may be better to exclude multiple users.

A similar problem results because the journey itself may have value. The previous discussion assumes implicitly that the trip is undertaken exclusively to get to the recreation site and travel has no benefit per se. If the journey itself is part of the reason for the visit to the site, then the trip has multiple purposes. Therefore, part of the cost of the trip should be attributed to the journey, not the visit to the recreation site. Not doing so would lead to overestimation of site benefits.

A more fundamental problem is that the travel cost variable may be endogenous, not exogenous. One neighborhood characteristic some people consider when making their residential choices is its proximity to a recreational area. People who expect to make many visits to a recreational area may select a particular neighborhood (zone) partially on account of the low travel time from that neighborhood to the recreational area. If so, the number of trips to a particular recreational area and the price of these trips will be determined simultaneously. Under these circumstances, Equation (15.8) may not be identified, a problem that we discuss in Chapter 4.[30]

Another econometric problem is that the dependent variable in the estimated models is *truncated*. Truncation arises because the sample is drawn from only those who visit the site, not from the larger population that includes people who never visit the site. Application of ordinary least squares to the truncated sample would result in biased coefficients. However, there are more complicated estimation methods that overcome this problem.

There may also be an omitted variables problem. If the price of substitute recreational sites varies across zones or if tastes for recreation varies across zones, then the estimated coefficients may be biased if the model does not control for these variables. As previously discussed, bias results when an excluded variable is correlated with an included variable.

Finally, derivation of the market demand curve assumes that people respond to changes in price regardless of its composition. Thus, for example, people respond to, say, a $5 increase in the admission price in the same way as a $5 increase in travel cost. This presumes that people have a good understanding of the impact of changes in the prices of fuel, tires, and repairs on their marginal travel cost.

15.8   Defensive Expenditures Method[31]

If you live in a smoggy city, then you will probably find that your windows often need cleaning. If you hire someone to clean your windows periodically, the cost of this action in response to the smog is termed a *defensive expenditure* – it is an amount spent to mitigate or even eliminate the effect of a negative externality. Suppose the city passes an ordinance that reduces the level of smog so that your windows do not get as dirty. You would now have to spend less on window cleaners. The reduction in defensive expenditures – the defensive expenditures avoided – has been suggested as a measure of the benefits of this type of city ordinance. In other circumstances, the costs of a policy change might be measured by the increase in defensive expenditures.

This method is an example of a broad class of *production function methods*. In these methods, the level of a public good or externality (e.g., smog) and other goods (window cleaners) are inputs to some production process (window cleaning). If the level of the public good or externality changes, then the levels of the other inputs can be changed so that the quantity of output produced remains the same. For example, when the negative externality of smog is reduced, less labor is required to produce the same number of clean windows. The change in expenditures on the substitute input (window cleaners) is used as a measure of the benefit of reduction of the public good or externality.

Suppose that the demand curve for clean windows is represented by the curve labeled D in Figure 15.6. Let S_0 represent the marginal cost of cleaning windows initially, that is, prior to the new ordinance. The initial equilibrium price and quantity of clean windows are denoted by P_0 and Q_0, respectively. The effect of the new ordinance to restrict smog is to shift the marginal cost curve for clean windows down and to the right from S_0 to S_1: because there is less smog, windows are easier to clean, so more windows can be cleaned for the same price. At the new equilibrium, the price of clean windows is P_1 and the quantity of clean windows is Q_1. The change in consumer surplus is represented by the area of the trapezoid $P_0 abP_1$.

If households continued to consume the same quantity of clean windows after the price shift as they did before the price shift, Q_0, then the benefit of the ordinance would be represented by the rectangle $P_0 acP_1$. This would be the amount by which consumers reduce their defensive expenditure. However, consumers would not maintain their consumption levels at Q_0, but would increase their consumption of clean windows to level Q_1. Individuals would spend area bQ_1Q_0c on the purchase of $Q_1 - Q_0$

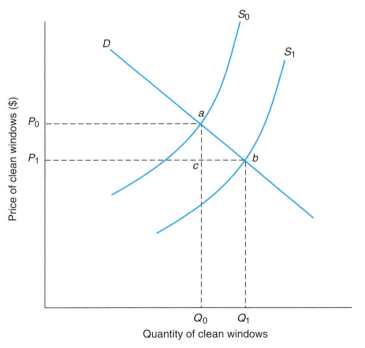

Figure 15.6 The effect of an ordinance reducing smog on expenditures for window cleaning.

additional units of clean windows at a price of P_1. The net change in spending on window cleaning services equals the area of rectangle bQ_1Q_0c minus the area of rectangle P_0acP_1. This net change in spending may be quite small. Indeed, if the demand curve were a constant elasticity demand curve, with an elasticity equal to 1, there would be no change in total expenditure on window cleaning services at all. Yet there are obviously positive benefits to consumers. In general, *the reduced spending on defensive expenditures will underestimate the benefits of cleaner air or whatever benefit is being estimated.*[32]

There are at least four additional problems with the defensive expenditures method. First, it assumes implicitly that individuals quickly adjust to the new equilibrium. It may actually take some time for individuals to adjust their purchases and return to equilibrium. Second, the defensive expenditures may have benefits other than remediating damage. For example, the cleaning necessitated by the smog may result in cleaner windows than one would otherwise achieve. Third, not all of the defensive measures are purchased in markets. Some people clean their own windows, and reductions in their opportunity costs should also be included as benefits. Fourth, a defensive expenditure may not remedy the entire damage so that reductions in this expenditure do not fully measure benefits. For example, expenditures on window cleaning do not "avoid" the whole problem of smog. Smog also leads to dirtier shirts and to health problems. Defensive expenditures spent on these items should also be included. Exhibit 15.5 illustrates that there may be many categories of defensive expenditures. It examines the costs of groundwater degradation and includes five categories of costs, not just the cost of new purchases of bottled water.

Exhibit 15.5

Charles W. Abdalla, Brian A. Roach, and Donald J. Epp measured the costs of groundwater degradation in the small Pennsylvania borough of Perkasie (population 7877) using the defensive expenditures method. They conducted mail and telephone surveys to gather information from a sample of residents on the actions they took in response to trichloroethylene (TCE) contamination of one of the borough's wells between December 1987 and September 1989. They estimated the total costs to the community's residents, including both monetary costs and time expenditures, of each of five defensive actions:

Category of cost	Cost based on value of leisure time equal to minimum wage ($)[a]	Cost based on value of leisure time equal to individual wage rate ($)[a]
Increased purchases of bottled water	11,100	11,100
New purchases of bottled water	17,300	17,300

(continued)

(cont.)

Category of cost	Cost based on value of leisure time equal to minimum wage ($)[a]	Cost based on value of leisure time equal to individual wage rate ($)[a]
Home water treatment systems	4,700	4,700
Hauling water	12,500	34,000
Boiling water	15,600	64,100
Total	61,200	131,200

[a] *Costs in original rounded to nearest hundred dollars.*

Note that the costs of hauling and boiling water are very sensitive to the assumed opportunity cost of leisure. The researchers interpreted these total costs as a lower-bound estimate of the true cost of the contamination to residents because of the generally conservative nature of the defensive expenditures method.

A specific factor suggesting that these defensive expenditures represent a lower bound is that only 43 percent of residents were aware of the TCE contamination despite notification laws. Moreover, not all residents who knew about the contamination took defensive measures. Nevertheless, those who had more information about the contamination, those who perceived the cancer risk due to TCE to be higher, and those who had children between 3 and 17 years old in the household were generally more likely to take defensive action than other residents. Among those who took defensive action, having a child under 3 years of age seemed to be the most important factor influencing the intensity of the defensive actions taken.

Source: Adapted from Charles W. Abdalla, Brian A. Roach, and Donald J. Epp, "Valuing Environmental Quality Changes Using Averting Expenditures: An Application to Groundwater Contamination." *Land Economics*, 68(2), 1992, 163–69.

15.9   Conclusion

This chapter describes the major indirect market methods used in CBA for estimating shadow prices. Some methods are not discussed because we believe that they are too advanced for this book. Perhaps most notably, we have not discussed the use of random utility models or probabilistic choice models to estimate demand, an approach that is important in the transportation area.[33] Also, we do not discuss methods that estimate demand curves by combining survey data with data on observed behavior.[34] Nevertheless, the methods covered here provide a rich set of tools for practical valuation of impacts.

Exercises for Chapter 15

1. Child care services in a small Midwestern city cost $30 per day per child. The high cost of these services is one reason why very few mothers who are on welfare work; given their low potential wages, virtually no welfare mothers are willing to pay these high costs. To combat this problem, the city establishes a new program: in exchange for their welfare benefits, a group of welfare recipients is required to provide child care for the children of other welfare recipients who obtain private-sector employment. The welfare mothers who use these child care services are required to pay a fee of $3 per day per child. These services prove very popular; 1,000 welfare children receive them each day and an additional 500 welfare children are on a waiting list. Do the mothers of the 1,000 children who receive services under the program value these services at $30,000 ($30 × 1,000) a day, $3,000 a day ($3 × 1,000), or at a value that is greater than $3,000 but less than $30,000? Explain.

2. A worker, who is typical in all respects, works for a wage of $50,000 per year in a perfectly safe occupation. Another typical worker does a job requiring exactly the same skills as the first worker, but in a risky occupation with a known death probability of 1 in 1,000 per year, and receives a wage of $58,000 per year. What value of a human life for workers with these characteristics should a cost–benefit analyst use?

3. (Instructor-provided spreadsheet recommended.) Happy Valley is the only available camping area in Rural County. It is owned by the county, which allows free access to campers. Almost all visitors to Happy Valley come from the six towns in the county.

    Rural County is considering leasing Happy Valley for logging, which would require that it be closed to campers. Before approving the lease, the county executive would like to know the magnitude of annual benefits that campers would forgo if Happy Valley were to be closed to the public.

    An analyst for the county has collected data for a travel cost study to estimate the benefits of Happy Valley camping. On five randomly selected days, he recorded the license plates of vehicles parked overnight in the Happy Valley lot. (Because the camping season is 100 days, he assumed that this would constitute a 5 percent sample.) With cooperation from the state motor vehicle department, he was able to find the town of residence of the owner of each vehicle. He also observed a sample of vehicles from which he estimated that each vehicle carried 3.2 persons (1.6 adults), on average. The following table summarizes the data he collected.

Town	Miles from Happy Valley	Population (thousands)	Number of vehicles in sample	Estimated number of visitors for season	Visit rate (visits per 1000 people)
A	22	50.1	146	3,893	77.7
B	34	34.9	85	2,267	65.0
C	48	15.6	22	587	37.6
D	56	89.9	180	4,800	53.4
E	88	98.3	73	1,947	19.8
F	94	60.4	25	666	11.0
Total				14,160	

In order to translate the distance traveled into an estimate of the cost campers faced in using Happy Valley, the analyst made the following assumptions. First, the average operating cost of vehicles is $0.36 per mile. Second, the average speed on county highways is 50 miles per hour. Third, the opportunity cost to adults of travel time is 40 percent of their wage rate; it is zero for children. Fourth, adult campers have the average county wage rate of $9.25 per hour.

The analyst has asked you to help him use this information to estimate the annual benefits accruing to Happy Valley campers. Specifically, assist with the following tasks.

a. Using the preceding information, calculate the travel cost of a vehicle visit (TC) from each of the towns.

b. For the six observations, regress visit rate (VR) on TC and a constant. If you do not have regression software available, plot the points and fit a line by sight. Find the slope of the fitted line.

c. You know that with the current free admission the number of camping visits demanded is 14,160. Find additional points on the demand curve by predicting the reduction in the number of campers from each town as price is increased by $5 increments until demand falls to zero. This is done in three steps at each price: first, use the coefficient of TC from the regression to predict a new VR for each town. Second, multiply the predicted VR of each town by its population to get a predicted number of visitors. Third, sum the visitors from each town to get the total number of predicted visits.

d. Estimate the area under the demand curve as the annual benefits to campers.

Notes

1. When markets do exist but are imperfect due to government intervention, it is necessary to make adjustments to market prices in order to obtain the appropriate shadow prices.

2. The *net output method* of valuing a life subtracts the value of a person's own consumption from his or her forgone earnings. It measures the benefit or cost the individual contributes to or imposes on the rest of society. The courts' use of this method to measure the loss to survivors of someone's death is somewhat arbitrary but perhaps reasonable. However, it is clearly inappropriate to use this method in CBA to value a life saved. Although a typical person's net output will be slightly positive over his or her entire lifetime, it will be negative for a retired person.

3. Thomas C. Schelling, "The Life You Save May Be Your Own," in Robert Dorfman and Nancy S. Dorfman, editors, *Economics of the Environment: Selected Readings*, 3rd edn (New York, NY: W. W. Norton, 1993), pp. 388–408 at p. 402.

4. See, for example, W. Kip Viscusi, "Prospective Reference Theory: Toward an Explanation of the Paradoxes." *Journal of Risk and Uncertainty*, 2(3), 1989, 234–64.

5. Jobs in finance, insurance, real estate, services, retail and government all have fatality rates below 3 in 100,000 according to the US Department of Labor, Bureau of Statistics, Census of Fatal Occupational Injuries, 2002.

6. Adam Smith, *The Wealth of Nations* (New York, NY: Modern Press, 1776, reprinted 1937), p. 12.

7. See, for example, Anthony E. Boardman, Ruth Freedman, and Catherine Eckel, "The Price of Government Ownership: A Study of the Domtar Takeover." *Journal of Public Economics*, 31(3), 1986, 269–85; John C. Ries, "Windfall Profits and Vertical Relationships: Who Gained in the Japanese Auto Industry from VERs?" *Journal of Industrial Economics*, 61(3), 1993, 259–76; Paul H. Malatesta and Rex Thompson, "Government Regulation and Structural Change in the Corporate Acquisitions Market: The Impact of the Williams Act." *Journal of Financial and Quantitative Analysis*, 28(3), 1993, 363–79; Anthony Boardman, Ilan Vertinsky, and Diana Whistler, "Using Information Diffusion Models to Estimate the Impacts of Regulatory Events on Publicly Traded Firms." *Journal of Public Economics*, 63(2), 1997, 283–300.

8. See Thand Dunning, *Natural Experiments in the Social Sciences: A Design-Based Approach* (New York, NY: Cambridge University Press, 2012).

9. Jens Ludwig and Douglas L. Miller, "Does Head Start Improve Children's Life Chances? Evidence from a Regression Discontinuity Design." *Quarterly Journal of Economics*, 122(1), 2007, 159–208.

10. See Sherwin Rosen, "Hedonic Prices and Implicit Markets: Product Differentiation in Pure Competition." *Journal of Political Economy*, 82(1), 1974, 34–55.

11. The basic idea behind hedonic regression was introduced in Kelvin L. Lancaster, "A New Approach to Consumer Theory." *Journal of Political Economy*, 74(1), 1966, 132–57.

12. In general, the hedonic price function can be written: $P = p(C_1, C_2, ..., C_k, N_1, ..., N_m)$, where C ($i = 1, ..., k$) denotes k attributes of the house and N_j ($j = 1, ..., m$) denotes m neighborhood characteristics.

13. Formally,

$$r_v = \frac{\partial P}{\partial VIEW}.$$

14. As we discussed in Chapter 4, in order to estimate the hedonic prices, analysts usually take the natural logarithms, ln, of both sides of Equation (15.3) to obtain the hedonic regression model: $\ln P = \ln\beta_0 + \beta_1\ln(CBD) + C\beta_2\ln(SIZE) + \beta_3\ln(VIEW) + \beta_4\ln(NBHD)$. The parameters of this model, which is linear in logarithms, may be estimated by ordinary least squares.

15. The hedonic price of C_i may be a function of all of the variables in the hedonic price function. For the general hedonic price function presented in note 12, $\partial P/\partial C_i = f(C_1, ..., C_k, N_1, ..., N_m)$.

16. Formally,

$$r_v = \frac{\partial P}{\partial VIEW}$$
$$= \beta_3\beta_0 CBD^{\beta_1} SIZE^{\beta_2} VIEW^{\beta_3 - 1} NBHD^{\beta_4} e^\varepsilon$$
$$= \beta_3 \frac{P}{VIEW}$$

17. The functional form of this model may be linear, multiplicative, or have some other form.

18. These functions indicate households' WTP, holding household characteristics constant.

19. Many researchers estimate linear models of the following form:

wage rate $= \beta_0 + \beta_1$fatality risk $+ \beta_2$injury risk $+ \beta_3$job tenure $+ \beta_4$education $+ \beta_5$age $+ \varepsilon$.

If the dependent variable is the hourly wage rate, fatality risk is measured as the number of deaths per 10,000 workers and $\beta_1 = 0.3$, then researchers estimate the VSL = 0.3 × 2000 hours/year × 10,000 = 6 million. As discussed below, however, linear hedonic models usually have identification problems.

20. The seminal work on this topic, which actually preceded the formal development of the hedonic pricing

method, is Ronald G. Ridker and John A. Henning, "The Determinants of Residential Property Values with Special Reference to Air Pollution." *Review of Economics and Statistics*, 49(2), 1967, 246–57. For a review of studies that have attempted to use the hedonic method to estimate WTP for reductions in particulate matter in air, see V. Kerry Smith and Ju-Chin Huang, "Can Markets Value Air Quality? A Meta-Analysis of Hedonic Property Value Models." *Journal of Political Economy*, 103(1), 1995, 209–27.

21. W. P. Jennings and A. Kinderman, "The Value of a Life: New Evidence of the Relationship between Changes in Occupational Fatalities and Wages of Hourly Workers, 1992–1999." *The Journal of Risk and Insurance*, 70(3), 2003, 549–61.

22. For a discussion concerning identification and estimation of hedonic models, see Ivar Ekeland, James J. Heckman, and Lars Nesheim, "Identification and Estimation of Hedonic Models." *Journal of Political Economy*, 112(1), 2004, S60–109 and John Yinger and Phuong Nguyen-Hoang, "Hedonic Vices: Fixing Inferences about Willingness to Pay in Recent House-Value Studies." *Journal of Benefit–Cost Analysis*, 7(2), 2016, 248–91.

23. This method is often referred to as the Clawson method, or the Knetsch–Clawson method. However, it is now attributed to Harold Hotelling; see Harold Hotelling, "Letter," in *An Economic Study of the Monetary Evaluation of Recreation in the National Parks* (Washington, DC: National Park Service, 1949).

24. Note that computing the area of the triangle using the formula ($95−$65)(6)/2 = $90 provides a slight overestimate of the consumer surplus, while using the formula ($90−$65)(6)/2 = $75 provides the correct answer. In effect, if we treat the intercept as $90 instead of $95, we obtain the correct answer. The problem arises because the number of visits is a discrete variable, while the equation for the inverse demand function is continuous.

25. Area *abd* ≈ $3.6 million, area *dbfe* = $4.8 million, area *bcf* = $4.2 million. Therefore, the total surplus equals $12.6 million. The gross annual benefit also includes the $4.4 million in admission fees for a total of $17 million.

26. Gardner Brown Jr. and Robert Mendelsohn, "The Hedonic Travel Cost Model." *Review of Economics and Statistics*, 66(3), 1984, 427–33.

27. For more detail, see Nancy G. Bockstael, Kenneth E. McConnell, and Ivar Strand, "Recreation," in J. B. Braden and C. D. Kolstad, editors, *Measuring the Demand for Environmental Quality* (Amsterdam: Elsevier, 1991), 227–70; and V. Kerry Smith and Yoshiaki Kaoru, "The Hedonic Travel Cost Model: A View From the Trenches." *Land Economics*, 63(2), 1987, 179–92.

28. Alan Randall, "A Difficulty with the Travel Cost Method." *Land Economics*, 70(1), 1994, 88–96.

29. See also John R. McKean, Donn M. Johnson, and Richard G. Walsh, "Valuing Time in Travel Cost Demand Analysis: An Empirical Investigation." *Land Economics*, 71(1), 1995, 96–105.

30. Also, the travel cost variable may not be independent of the error term, thereby leading to ordinary least squares estimates that are biased and inconsistent.

31. This method is also referred to as the avoided cost method. For a review of the use of this method to measure groundwater values, see Charles Abdalla, "Groundwater Values from Avoidance Cost Studies: Implications for Policy and Future Research." *American Journal of Agricultural Economics*, 76(5), 1994, 1062–67.

32. The accuracy of using changes in defensive expenditures on a substitute to measure the benefits of changes in the levels of externalities or public goods depends on how these goods enter the individual's utility function and on the relationship between these goods and the market for the substitute. For more discussion of this issue, see Paul N. Courant and Richard Porter, "Averting Expenditure and the Cost of Pollution." *Journal of Environmental Economics and Management*, 8(4), 1981, 321–29. Also see Winston Harrington and Paul Portney, "Valuing the Benefits of Health and Safety Regulation." *Journal of Urban Economics*, 22(1), 1987, 101–12.

33. These models are also referred to as qualitative response models. See, for example, G. S. Maddala, *Limited-Dependent and Qualitative Variables in Econometrics* (Cambridge: Cambridge University Press, 1983); and Kenneth Train, *Qualitative Choice Analysis* (Cambridge, MA: MIT Press, 1986).

34. See, for example, David A. Hensher and Mark Bradley, "Using Stated Preference Response Data to Enrich Revealed Preference Data." *Marketing Letters*, 4(2), 1993, 139–52.

16 Contingent Valuation: Using Surveys to Elicit Information about Costs and Benefits

Revealed preference methods facilitate inferences about individuals' valuations of goods by observing their behaviors in markets or analogous situations in which they must make trade-offs between things they value. Analysts generally prefer inferences from revealed preference methods to inferences based on *stated preference methods*, which are normally elicited through surveys. However, there are usually few observable "behavioral traces" relevant to public goods and externalities with missing markets. This is particularly the case for the passive use goods discussed in Chapter 13. In the absence of behavioral traces, analysts very rarely have a viable alternative to asking samples of people about their preferences.

The most common stated preference method is the *contingent valuation method* (CVM) survey, the focus of this chapter.[1] A CVM survey asks a sample of those with standing questions about hypothetical trade-offs that allow analysts to make inferences about how the relevant population would value a change in either the quantity or the quality of a good.[2] Actual or proposed changes in a great number of environmental goods have now been valued using CVM surveys. These surveys comprise over half of the more than 4,000 studies catalogued in the Environmental Valuation Reference Inventory.[3] CVM surveys have also seen extensive use in valuing health and medical interventions.[4] They are now increasingly used to value more complex and abstract goods, such as the preservation of archeological sites and the public goods produced by sports stadiums.[5]

A number of economists remain skeptical of the validity of valuations based on CVM surveys.[6] Nonetheless, their use has become widespread. Indeed, the US federal courts have held that surveys of citizens' valuations enjoy "rebuttable presumption" status in cases involving the assessment of damage to natural resources.[7] A blue-ribbon panel of social scientists convened by the National Oceanic and Atmospheric Administration (NOAA) further legitimized the use of CVM by concluding that it could be the basis for estimating passive use values for inclusion in natural resource damage assessment cases.[8]

In this chapter we first provide an overview of CVM, describe the most common CVMs, and summarize their major strengths and weakness. Second, we consider two generic issues relating to the use of survey instruments that are particularly relevant to CVM in CBA. Third, we review important issues and major criticisms related to CVM use. Fourth, we consider the question: How accurate are CVM estimates? Finally, we present a checklist for analysts preparing or reviewing CVM surveys.

16.1   Overview of Contingent Valuation Methods

All CVM methods feature the following general steps. First, a sample of respondents from the population with standing is identified. Second, these respondents are asked questions about their valuations of changes in the quantity or quality of some good. Third, their responses provide information that enables analysts to estimate the respondents' WTP for desirable changes in the good. Sometimes, however, it is more appropriate to elicit their willingness to accept (WTA) undesirable changes. Initially, we assume a WTP framework. Later, we briefly consider the circumstances under which WTA valuation is appropriate, likely to make a significant difference to valuations, and practical. Fourth, the WTP amounts for the sample are extrapolated to the entire population. If, for instance, the respondents comprise a random sample of the population such that each member of the population had an equal chance of being in the sample, then the average WTP for the sample would be multiplied by the size of the population to arrive at the aggregate WTP.

As CVM surveys are expensive to conduct, analysts may find it necessary to extrapolate the results of existing surveys to different populations. However, the characteristics of these populations may not match those of the population originally sampled. For example, the populations may differ in terms of income, access to alternative goods, or other factors that may be relevant to their demand for changes in the good. Reasonable extrapolation requires that these differences be controlled for statistically.[9] Therefore, analysts increase the chances that their CVM surveys will have use beyond their own CBAs by collecting and reporting information about the characteristics of their samples, including WTP amounts for subsets of the sample, even when such information is unnecessary for their own studies.

The remainder of this section introduces four specific methods that are used to elicit WTP amounts from survey respondents. We first briefly sketch three methods that were commonly used in the past and sometimes used currently: the *open-ended willingness-to-pay* method, the *closed-ended iterative bidding* method, and the *contingent ranking* method. We then turn to the *dichotomous choice, binary choice,* or *referendum* method, which the NOAA blue-ribbon panel recommended for use in most circumstances.[10]

16.1.1   *Direct Elicitation (Non-Referendum) Methods*

Several of the CVMs ask questions about preferences directly. The open-ended willingness-to-pay method and the closed-ended iterative bidding method seek to elicit WTP amounts for each respondent. The contingent ranking method seeks to elicit a preference profile over a set of alternatives for each respondent. These methods contrast with the dichotomous choice method, which is indirect in the sense that it relies on patterns of responses across a large number of respondents to make inferences about the preferences of respondents with particular characteristics.

Open-Ended Willingness-to-Pay Method. The earliest method to be used is the *open-ended willingness-to-pay* approach. Respondents are simply asked to state their maximum WTP for the good, or policy.[11] The question might be asked as follows: "What is the most that you would be prepared to pay in additional federal income taxes to guarantee that the Wildwood wilderness area will remain closed to development?" This method had fallen out of favor as analysts feared unrealistic responses because respondents needed some initial guidance on valuations.[12] Concerns that open-ended questions result in unrealistically large estimates of WTP, however, seem unfounded. Yet a serious problem does appear to be that respondents who have low valuations of the good often state a zero rather than the low value.

Closed-Ended Iterative Bidding Method. In the closed-ended iterative bidding method, respondents are asked whether they would pay a specified amount for the good or policy that has been described to them. If respondents answer affirmatively, then the amount is incrementally increased. The increments continue until the respondent expresses an unwillingness to pay the amount specified. Similarly, if respondents answer negatively to the initial amount specified, the interviewer lowers the amount by increments until the respondent expresses a WTP that amount.

The initial question for determining WTP typically starts with something like the following: "Now suppose the costs to clean the Kristiansand Fjord were divided on [sic] all taxpayers in the whole of Norway by an extra tax in 1986. If this extra tax was 200 kronor for an average taxpayer, would you then be willing to support the proposal?"[13] In this CVM survey the interviewer set the initial price at 200 kronor. If a respondent indicated a willingness to pay this initial price, then the interviewer raised the price by 200 kronor and asked the question again. The interviewer kept going until the respondent gave a negative answer. Similarly, if the initial response was negative, then the interviewer dropped the price by 100-kronor increments and then by 10-kronor increments until the respondent gave a positive response. Although iterative bidding was at one time the most common method in use, it is rarely used now because of considerable evidence that its results are highly sensitive to the initially presented (starting) value.

Contingent Ranking Method. In the contingent ranking, or ranked choice, method, respondents are asked to rank specific feasible combinations of quantities of the good being valued and monetary payments. For example, respondents choose along a continuum that ranges between a low level of water quality at a low tax price and a high level of water quality at a high tax price. The quality–price combinations are ranked from most preferred to least preferred.[14] The rankings provide a basis for estimating each respondent's WTP for various increments of quality. Contingent ranking implies an ordinal ranking procedure in contrast to the iterative bidding procedure, which requires cardinal evaluation. Typically, tasks that require only ordinal information processing, that is, a ranking rather than a precise specification of value, are considerably easier for respondents to perform coherently.[15] This is a valuable attribute in the CVM context where respondents must often process complex information. Of course, unlike either the open-ended WTP method or the closed-ended iterative bidding method, the WTP of interest must be inferred from ordinal rankings rather than directly elicited. Additionally, responses appear to be sensitive to the order in which alternatives are presented to respondents.

16.1.2   *Dichotomous Choice (Referendum) Method*

In the dichotomous choice method, respondents are asked whether they would be willing to pay a particular specified price to obtain a change in the quantity or quality of a good or the adoption of a policy that would induce the change in the quantity or quality of a good.[16] Each respondent receives a single randomly drawn price. Respondents are then asked to state whether they would be willing to pay for the change in the good or policy (e.g., closing the Wildwood wilderness area to development) at that offered price ("yes" means willing to pay and "no" means not willing to pay). Thus, respondents are made a binary "take it or leave it" offer of the same sort that they face in most markets for private goods. The choice situation is also like that faced in a referendum – hence the label referendum method. The dollar amounts, often referred to as *bid prices*, that are presented to respondents vary over a range selected by the analyst.[17] The probability of respondents accepting the offer can then be calculated for each bid price.[18] Declining fractions of acceptances as bid prices increase provides the basis for estimating a demand function, as well as an initial indication that respondents are treating the elicitation as an economic decision.[19]

Figure 16.1 shows the distribution of responses to bid prices in the form of a histogram. Specific bid prices are shown on the horizontal axis ranging from the lowest dollar price offered ($X = \$0$) to the highest price offered ($X = \$100$) in \$5 increments. The vertical axis measures the percentage of respondents who answer "yes" to the bid price offered to them. In this example, almost all of the respondents who are offered the specified outcome at $X = \$0$ state they would accept it. About 75 percent of respondents who are offered the outcome for \$30 indicate that they would accept it at this price. We can interpret the response frequencies as estimates of the probability that a randomly drawn member of the sample of respondents is willing to pay a specific amount. For example, the probability a randomly drawn respondent would pay at least \$30 for the specified outcome is about 0.75.

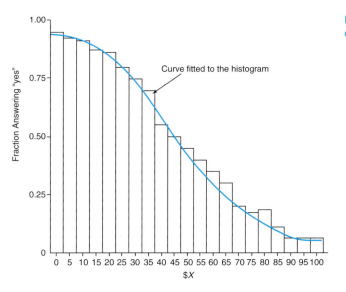

Figure 16.1 Histogram of dichotomous choice responses.

The fitted curve in Figure 16.1 may be viewed as the demand curve of an average member of the sample based on the histogram. The difference between the demand curve in Figure 16.1 and a standard demand curve is that instead of the curve indicating the quantity of a good the individual would be willing to purchase at each price, it indicates the probability that the individual would be willing to pay for the specified outcome at each price.[20] As in the case of a standard demand curve, the area under the curve in Figure 16.1 provides an estimate of the individual's WTP.

If the values of X are evenly spread, then the histogram can be readily used to obtain a rough estimate of the average individual's WTP by applying a simple formula:

$$\text{WTP} = v \sum_{k=0}^{N} \left[\text{Probability of acceptance at price } kv \right]$$

(16.1)

where v is the interval between prices (i.e., the width of the individual bars in the histogram) and N is the number of values of X (i.e., the number of bars). In other words, the area covered by the bars (the approximate WTP for an average member of the sample) can be computed by simply summing the heights of the bars and multiplying by the bar width.

Analysts rarely work directly from the histogram of accepted bids. Methods have evolved – from statistical models of the probability of acceptance to random utility models relating acceptance to the relationship between the bid price and an expression of WTP as a function of demographic characteristics.[21] Corrections are sometimes made to account for the finite range of bid prices[22] and other data limitations.[23] These statistical models can also be used to estimate WTP for each identified group within the sample. *To find the aggregate WTP for the entire population, multiply the mean for each group by the size of that group in the population with standing and then sum across groups.*[24]

Rather than directly estimating WTP as the area under the demand curve in Figure 16.1, a more common practice involves specifying a parametric model of individual choice that takes account of observable differences among respondents. The model begins by specifying WTP_j, the WTP of the jth respondent, as a function of the respondent's income and observable characteristics that may affect WTP, such as education, age, and gender.[25] If questions about relevant knowledge and attitudes are included in the survey instrument, then variables based on the answers to these questions may also be included. When it is reasonable to assume that WTP will be non-negative, that is, no one would view the change in the good being valued as a negative outcome, WTP is typically modeled as an exponential function.

The next step involves specifying a *random utility model* in which acceptance of the bid offered to respondent j, t_j, is treated as a probabilistic function of WTP. For example, the probability that respondent j will accept the bid price might be assumed to be as follows:

$$\text{Prob}\left(\text{accepting bid } t_i\right) = \phi\left(\frac{WTP_j - t_j}{\sigma}\right)$$

(16.2)

where Φ is the cumulative standard normal distribution and σ is a standard deviation. If σ is set to 1, and the coefficients in the WTP function for individual characteristics are estimated with maximum likelihood methods, then the estimation would be equivalent to probit regression if the WTP function is linear in individual characteristics.[26]

These simple models can be modified to take account of problems that may occur around the extreme bid values. The commonly employed WTP functions assume that someone who rejects a bid has some probability of accepting a lower but non-zero bid. However, in some situations, a respondent who rejects a bid may be unwilling to accept any positive bid. For example, bid prices in a CVM to estimate the WTP of smokers for a treatment that would completely remove addiction to cigarettes may be rejected by smokers who would pay something, but not as much as the bid price, as well as by smokers who would pay nothing because they do not believe that they are addicted. If questions about the self-perception of the degree of addiction were to be included in the survey, then the answers could be used to help to distinguish statistically between the two types of rejections to provide a better estimate of the WTP function.[27]

Parametric specifications can be very sensitive to the problem of "fat tails" or unexpectedly high acceptance rates for the largest bid prices.[28] The problem is evident when either the highest bid amount is accepted by more than 20 percent of respondents or the largest bid amounts have very similar acceptance rates that are substantially above zero. Neither case provides adequate information about the bid prices that would choke off demand; the former because the highest bid is too far from the choke price; the latter because the similar acceptance rates do not inform the rate of decline toward the choke price. Arbitrarily dropping respondents from the sample who received the largest bid values only resolves concern about fat tails if doing so does not dramatically change the estimated mean WTP. Somewhat less arbitrary approaches involve dropping respondents who receive bids above their income or, if elicited, their disposable income, or constraining the WTP amounts of respondents to income or disposable income in the statistical estimation.[29] Non-parametric methods, which work directly with the sort of data displayed in Figure 16.1, are typically less sensitive to the fat tail problem.[30]

Because the dichotomous choice method only tells analysts whether a given respondent's valuation is greater or less than the offered amount, sample sizes have to be large in order to achieve reasonable levels of precision – the rule of thumb is at least 500 respondents per elicitation.[31] So, for a survey that values two levels of change in a good, over a thousand respondents would be required. This is a sample size larger than that of the typical public opinion survey.

To gain more information from respondents, some analysts use *double dichotomous choice* (also sometimes called *double-bounded dichotomous choice*), rather than single elicitation questions, in order to reduce the need for large samples. In this version of the method, depending on the answer to the first offer, a follow-up offer is made that is either double (if yes) or half (if no) the first offer. This provides considerably more information than the standard single-offer version. However, there is danger that the respondent's exposure to the first offer may affect the probability that he or she will accept the follow-up offer.[32] Recognizing that follow-up bids provide information to respondents that may change their perceptions of the likely price or quantity of the good being valued, Richard Carson and Theodore Groves have suggested several ways that this information might affect their responses to the second bids.[33] First, those who initially rejected bids may take the lower follow-up bid as an indication that the bid price is negotiable and reject bids that they previously would have accepted. Second, those who initially accepted bids may believe that there is some possibility that the good could be provided at the lower price and reject the higher second bid even though it is below their WTP. Third, in responding to the follow-up bid price, respondents may base their responses not on that price but on some weighted average of the two bid prices they encountered.[34] Whether the greater amount of information generated by the double dichotomous choice method is worth the risk of such response behaviors remains an open research question.

As we discuss in the subsequent section on the strategic response (honesty) problem, a major advantage of a binary choice formulation is that it meets the necessary condition for *incentive compatibility* – that is, the presence of incentives for respondents to give truthful rather than strategic answers. Other methods are not *incentive-compatible*. The possibility that the referendum method is incentive compatible is an important reason that it has become the most commonly used CVM.

16.2   Generic Survey Issues Most Relevant to CV

Before turning specifically to CVM surveys, it is useful to consider some issues relevant to all survey contexts. In considering these generic issues, we focus on two issues that are most germane to CV. The first issue concerns the trade-offs among methods for administering surveys. The second issue is the extent to which the procedures for identifying and reaching respondents leads to an appropriate sample from which to estimate the distribution of attitudes or preferences within the population with standing.

16.2.1   *Survey Administration: In-Person, Telephone, Mail, and Internet*

Currently, there are four major technologies for administering surveys: in-person interviews, telephone interviews, mail questionnaires, and Internet surveys. Each has strengths and weaknesses, and each raises different methodological issues. None of the four procedures is unequivocally superior to the others.

Table 16.1 summarizes the characteristics of the survey administration alternatives. In-person interviews involve interviewers meeting face-to-face with respondents. Especially relevant in the CVM context, face-to-face interaction facilitates the provision of complex information to respondents through the presentation of maps, diagrams, photographs, and other visual aids by the interviewer. The interviewer can also clarify questions and provide additional information and otherwise interact directly with the respondent. This direct contact, however, also involves a high risk of interviewer bias, as respondents may react to the personal characteristics of the interviewer, perhaps slanting answers to gain the interviewer's approval. Unlike telephone interviews, which typically are conducted from a central location, in-person interviews are difficult and costly to monitor. They are particularly expensive for geographically disperse samples, because of the time spent traveling between interviews, and when precautions must be taken to ensure the security of the interviewers. As is the case with mail questionnaires,

Table 16.1 *Survey Administration Alternatives*

	Cost per completed interview	Ease of identifying and reaching respondents	Risk of interviewer bias	Maximum complexity of provided information
In-person	Very high – depends on questionnaire length and geographic spread	Medium – depends on availability of lists and access	High – personal presence, monitoring difficult	Very high – interactive communication and visual aids possible
Telephone	High – depends on questionnaire length and callbacks	Very high – random-digit dialing	Medium – interviewer cues	Low – verbal communication limits complexity of content
Mail	Low – depends on number of follow-ups	High – depends on availability of appropriate lists	Low – uniform presentation	High – visual aids possible
Internet	Low – marginal costs very small	Low – "spamming" restrictions require panels of willing respondents	Low – uniform presentation	Very high – visual aids and interactive questions possible

the capability for identifying a random sample of any population depends on the availability of lists of the individuals, families, or households that make up the population. In many locations, such as cities with guarded apartment buildings or suburbs with gated housing developments, it may be difficult to reach respondents randomly selected to be in the sample.

Telephone interviews are a common method of administering CVM surveys. Telephone interviews cost substantially less than in-person interviews, even with a large number of callbacks to reach persons who were not at home or who used their answering machines to screen calls. They also have the advantage of allowing researchers to draw reasonable random samples through random-digit dialing, obviating the need for address lists in surveys of households. Unfortunately, verbal communication limits the complexity of information that can be provided. It also opens up the possibility of interviewer bias, as respondents react to voice cues and perceptions of the characteristics of the interviewer.

Several trends have made telephone interviews more difficult to implement effectively. One trend is the greater prevalence of telemarketing, often masquerading as surveys. Many people refuse to participate in surveys to avoid unwanted telemarketing solicitations. Others use answering machines and caller identification to screen out calls from strangers. Another trend is the increasing number of individuals who have cut their landlines, which makes it increasingly difficult to draw good random samples through random-digit dialing. Many households also have multiple telephone lines, dedicated to home businesses or teenagers. Cellular telephones are reducing the geographic basis of area codes, making it more difficult to draw samples stratified by location. Dealing with these problems will likely raise the cost and reduce the effectiveness of telephone surveys in the future.

Mail questionnaires, which allow the provision of visual aids to respondents, have the advantage of very low cost. The ease of identifying samples depends on the availability of appropriate lists. Accurate lists also make it easy to identify a sample of respondents and contact them by mail, although response rates are typically low, often requiring multiple mailings to reach acceptable levels. As there are no interviewers, there is no interviewer bias.

As most US adults have become Internet users, the practicality of using the Internet for conducting surveys has increased substantially. Internet surveys have several advantages over the other methods. Because interviewers are not needed, Internet surveys have extremely low marginal costs, potentially lower than those of mail surveys. Unlike mail surveys, the actual data collection can be fully automated and implemented within a very short time frame, an advantage when the CVM survey is intended to inform a pending decision. Like mail surveys, they avoid the risk of interviewer bias and allow for the provision of complex information. Indeed, one can give respondents' access to large quantities of information through interactive menus and other devices. Unfortunately, drawing random samples of populations remains a barrier. Not all members of most populations of interest are Internet users. This is changing, but even when Internet use has become ubiquitous, sampling is complicated by restrictions on spamming, which prevents procedures analogous to random-digit dialing in telephone surveys. On the plus side, survey firms have now developed databases of willing respondents that have become sufficiently large and representative of populations of interest, allowing scientifically valid CVM studies to be administered through the Internet.[35]

16.2.2   *Sample and Non-Response Biases*

The essence of survey research is eliciting information about a population from a relatively small sample drawn from that population. As summarized in Table 16.1, survey administration alternatives differ in terms of the ease with which they facilitate identifying and reaching respondents. How to identify individuals to be sampled from target populations is the topic of *sample design*.[36] The extent to which valid responses are obtained from those identified determines whether the sample design will actually produce data adequate for making valid inferences.

In almost all cases, the sample is selected by a probability mechanism, which produces a *random sample*. In a random sample, each individual has a known probability of being drawn from the population. *Simple random samples* give each individual in the target population the same probability of being sampled. *Stratified samples* give members of particular groups within a population the same probability of being sampled. In either case, knowing the selection probabilities allows researchers to base inferences about the characteristics of the population on the characteristics of the sample.

For CVM purposes, *the relevant target population is usually all individuals with standing who are or would be affected by the policy*. Unfortunately, this heuristic begs the question of who is affected. For many projects it is apparent. Yet often it is not, especially in addressing environmental policies. In some contexts there is congruence between those who bear the cost of policies and those who are affected by them. In other contexts, however, these groups diverge, as when a state or province provides a wilderness area that is valued by people living in other jurisdictions. The greater such divergence, the more problematic it is to choose the correct population.[37]

Several major issues are involved in assessing who is affected. First, all those "users" directly affected by the project should be included. The term *users* is in quotes because we mean it in a specific way. Those who would directly utilize the good in question are, of course, users. But so are individuals who suffer direct negative impacts that they would pay to avoid. For example, nearby residents of a duck hunting reserve who dislike the noise are as much users as the duck hunters. Potential users should also be included. As discussed in Chapter 9, in situations involving uncertainty, the option price that an individual would be willing to pay for a good may differ from his or her expected surplus. So some people who never actually consume the good may value it.

Second, it is important for survey respondents to understand whether they are being asked to estimate WTP just for themselves or as representatives for their whole household. This distinction is important in extrapolating from the sample to the target population.

Third, an explicit decision should be made concerning the inclusion or exclusion of passive use benefits. As Chapter 9 shows, either users or non-users could derive existence value from a project. Conceptually, existence value should be included as a component of benefits. For environmental goods, CVM surveys that either sample non-users or estimate existence values of users typically yield much higher aggregate WTP estimates than do those that include only use benefits.

Fourth, the geographic *spread*, or *reach*, of the sample should be wide enough to capture all affected individuals. There is increasing recognition that decisions concerning the geographic footprint of the relevant market can drive the outcomes of many CBAs, especially if non-users are included.[38] An important sampling question relates to the potential exclusion of some responses. It has been argued that three categories of respondents should be excluded in estimating WTP: first, respondents who reject the whole notion of placing a value on the good in question, or of paying for the good in a certain way; second, respondents who refuse to take the exercise seriously; and third, respondents who clearly demonstrate that they are incapable of understanding the survey.[39] In the direct elicitation methods, all three types of respondents are usually assumed to provide either zero valuations or extremely high valuations. Sometimes such respondents can be directly identified by their answers to specific questions intended to screen them from the sample. Respondents who provide extreme values are known as *outliers*. Outliers are normally handled in CVM by simply eliminating valuations that are above some specified threshold or that are above a specified percentage of the respondent's gross or discretionary income.

An appropriate sampling design can usually eliminate most sample bias if it is fully executed. Yet, bias can still remain if some individuals do not respond to the survey. Non-response bias is a serious problem in almost all survey research. Non-response problems have grown over the last 20 years as the public has been asked to give time to more surveys and has become suspicious of the motives of many who claim to be survey researchers. If non-response is purely random, then it can be dealt with by increasing the sample size. Unfortunately, however, non-response is often not random.

There are two major types of non-response problems: refusal to respond and unavailability to respond. In CVM contexts, the primary approaches for dealing with refusal to respond are to highlight the legitimacy of the exercise (e.g., by stressing government or university affiliations) or to offer various response incentives, such as donations to charities or entries into prize lotteries. Where unavailability biases the sample, researchers typically account for underrepresentation and overrepresentation in the sample when extrapolating to the target population.[40]

Exhibit 16.1

As part of a court case, the plaintiffs conducted a CVM survey to estimate the natural resource damage caused by a mine. The plaintiffs surveyed residents of both the county (Eagle County) and the state (Colorado) in which the mine was located. Based on their surveys, their analysis estimated past damages were $50.8 million and future expected damages would be between $15 million and $45 million. The defendants sampled a much smaller group within Eagle County that they believed had been directly affected by pollution from the mine. The defendants assumed that residents in the rest of Colorado did not bear costs from the mine. Although the per-unit values of both sides were similar (for example, on the value of a day's fishing), the defendants' estimate of total past and future expected damage was approximately $240,000, less than 1 percent of the plaintiffs' estimate. "The discrepancies in these respective aggregate estimates arise from the plaintiff's assumption that … there would be a much larger number of people experiencing gains with the restoration" (p. 605).

Source: Adapted from Raymond J. Kopp and V. Kerry Smith, "Benefit Estimation Goes to Court: The Case of Natural Resource Damage Assessments." *Journal of Policy Analysis and Management*, 8(4), 1989, 593–612.

16.3   Contingent Valuation Issues

CVM surveys raise a number of issues that are more novel and complex than those arising in other survey situations. There are six specific but somewhat overlapping CV-specific issues that warrant discussion. First, best practice requires the specification of some payment vehicle that describes how the bid price would be paid. Second, CVM surveys often involve the problem of *hypotheticality* (this as a catchall word to cover problems of understanding, meaning, context, and familiarity). The issue of hypotheticality is normally more severe when respondents have not previously, and will not, "consume" the good in some way; that is, it tends to be most severe in the valuation of passive use. Third, the issue of *neutrality* in the presentation of information to respondents can arise, particularly for projects that are potentially controversial or partisan. Fourth, for certain elicitation methods, *judgmental biases* may arise in response to certain kinds of questions (including whether the question is framed as willingness to pay or as willingness to accept). Not all these problems necessarily create biases (i.e., a systematic tendency to overvalue or undervalue the goods in question), but all of them raise questions about the validity and reliability of CVM as a procedure. Some specific CVMs appear to be more prone to biases than others. Fifth, it may be more appropriate to use a WTA reference frame rather than a WTP framing. Sixth, CVM raises the potential for biased answers related to *strategic behavior* (misstatements intended to influence some outcome) and the specified payment vehicle.

16.3.1   *Specifying the Payment Vehicle*

CVM elicitations of WTP almost always specify some *payment vehicle*. A payment vehicle describes how the good would be paid for if the policy were to be implemented. Depending on the policy and fiscal context, plausible payment vehicles could include taxes paid into a fund specifically earmarked for the good, increased utility bills, higher income or sales taxes, or higher product prices. *Specifying a payment vehicle, along with reminders that payments reduce the availability of funds for expenditures on other goods, helps ensure that respondents perceive the questions as if they pose real economic choices.* In order to further increase the realism of CVM surveys, analysts ideally try to specify a payment vehicle that is as close as possible to the actual one that would be used.

   A difference in the specified payment vehicle can make a difference to the estimated WTP. For example, researchers found that respondents valued watershed management plans differently depending on whether there was a guarantee that taxes imposed to pay for them would not be used for other purposes.[41] The presence or absence of such a guarantee also affected respondents' valuations of specific attributes of watershed plans.

   There is some disagreement as to whether differences in the WTP of respondents that can be attributed to differences in payment vehicles should be treated as a bias. Kenneth Arrow and others argue that respondents are being asked to value all elements of a project including the method of payment; therefore, respondent preferences about payment methods do not imply bias.[42] Other analysts argue that if a specific payment vehicle, such as a tax increment, introduces "protest" valuations, then such outliers should be excluded from the estimation of aggregate WTP.

16.3.2   *Hypotheticality, Meaning, and Context Problems*

A major concern in CVM design is whether respondents are truly able to understand and place into context the questions they are being asked and can thus accurately value the good or policy in question. The valuation of the supply of many publicly provided goods raises complex and highly contextual issues. CVM questions can be contrasted to many other types of questions for which meaning is not an issue (e.g., "For whom do you intend to vote in the next election?").

Questions of hypotheticality and meaning can be thought of as problems of specifying exactly what the respondent is being asked to value. Understanding the good, or the policy that produces it, is difficult for respondents because they often are not familiar with either. When respondents are presented with questions about goods or projects that they do not understand, attitudes (and responses as expressed in the CVM survey) are unlikely to correspond to the behavior that would occur if the project were actually implemented.[43] When a project (or the good itself) has multiple attributes, these all need to be explained to respondents: "Unless [an attribute is] specified explicitly (and comprehensively), evaluators must guess its value and, hence, what the offer really means. If they guess wrong, then they risk misrepresenting their values."[44]

This problem, however, has to be seen in context. Individuals also differentially value attributes of market goods: Some individuals may value a mountain bike mostly for prestige reasons and others for transportation purposes. The evidence indicates that people find it somewhat difficult to value the attributes of new and unfamiliar products in market contexts.[45] As Richard Carson and his colleagues point out, "Many new products become available each year creating markets in which consumers regularly make purchase decisions … No standard microeconomics text has ever stated that prior experience is a precondition for rational decision-making."[46]

Additional problems arise in CVM if the perceptions of the good by respondents are not independent of the quality or quantity of the information provided. The possible information that could be provided when describing complex goods are unlimited. The quantity and quality of information, however, are limited in practice by the method of survey administration. Several commentators have argued that there is little evidence that hypotheticality per se introduces bias into CV.[47] It is certainly reasonable to deduce that, in the presence of hypotheticality, certain kinds of bias are more likely. The potential for hypotheticality, however, varies enormously across different CBA contexts, so it is difficult to generalize. Unfortunately, CVM is likely to be most useful in contexts in which goods are difficult to define, such as projects involving environmental impacts. When it is difficult to specify potential physical impacts, it is also likely to be difficult for respondents to understand what these impacts mean.

Yet with forethought, hypotheticality and lack of realism can be reduced in a number of ways. *Clearly specifying the project and its impacts increases the likelihood of correspondence between attitudes and behavior; so too does providing explicit detail about the payment vehicle.* Visual aids assist in understanding. One important class of visual aids useful in reducing hypotheticality is known as quality ladders. An example of a quality ladder is described in Exhibit 16.2. Quality ladders help respondents understand both what quality is under the status quo, and what particular increments of quality mean.

Exhibit 16.2

A "water quality ladder" has been used in several CBAs to help respondents understand how differing levels of toxins, dissolved solids, water clarity, and other factors affect water quality. In their CBA of water quality improvements to the Monongahela River, V. Kerry Smith and William Desvousges included a picture of a ladder with a 0-to-10 scale and the following interviewer instructions:

"(*Interviewer: Read the following.*) Generally the better the water quality the better suited the water is for recreation activities and the more likely people will take part in outdoor recreation activities on or near the water. Here is a picture of a ladder that shows various levels of water quality. (*Interviewer: Give respondent water quality ladder.*)

The top of the ladder stands for the best possible quality of water. The bottom of the ladder stands for the worst possible water quality. On the ladder you can see the different levels of the quality of the water. For example: (*Interviewer: Point to each level – E, D, C, B, A – as you read the statements that follow.*)

Level E (*Interviewer: Point.*) is so polluted that it has oil, raw sewage, and other things like trash in it; it has no plant or animal life and smells bad.

Water at level D is okay for boating but not fishing or swimming.

Level C shows where the water is clean enough so that game fish like bass can live in it.

Level B shows where the water is clean enough so that people can swim in it safely.

And at level A, the quality of the water is so good that it would be possible to drink directly from it if you wanted to.

(*Interviewer: Now ask the respondent to use the ladder to rate the water quality in the Monongahela River on a scale of 0 to 10 and to indicate whether the ranking was for a particular site, and if so, to name it.*)"

Source: Adapted from V. Kerry Smith and William H. Desvousges, *Measuring Water Quality Benefits* (Boston, MA: Kluwer Academic, 1986), 87.

Baruch Fischhoff and Lita Furey provide a checklist for evaluating CVM instruments in terms of the likelihood that respondents will understand the questions they are being asked.[48] It requires the analyst to assess the comprehensiveness of information with respect to the good, the specification of the payment vehicle, and the social context. In assessing the adequacy of information about the good, they stress the need to provide information on both substantive and formal components. The substantive aspect of the good deals with why someone might value it (basically its attributes), while the formal aspect of the good concerns how much they value it (once they understand its attributes). The formal components include the magnitude, direction, timing, and, where relevant, certainty of change.

In practice, *the only effective way to minimize hypotheticality and meaning problems in CVM surveys is to devote extensive effort to developing detailed, clear, informative, and highly contextual materials and to pretest these materials extensively on typical respondents.*

16.3.3   *Neutrality*

While the previous section notes that lack of clear meaning does not necessarily pose a bias problem, lack of neutrality is certain to do so. As CBA deals with increasingly controversial and complex topics, the neutrality of the CVM questionnaire becomes an increasingly important issue. Neutrality has come to the fore as litigants in (especially environmental) court cases have conducted their own CVM surveys.

Meaning and neutrality issues often intersect in ways that are difficult to disentangle. For example, Daniel Hagen and colleagues surveyed 1,000 US households by mail concerning the value of preserving the spotted owl.[49] Of the total, 409 questionnaires were returned. Some of the information that respondents were given included the following: "a scientific committee concluded that logging should be banned on some forest lands to prevent the extinction of the Northern Spotted Owl" and "a second group of independent scientists examined this study and agreed with these conclusions." The survey also included the comment that: "the well-being of the northern spotted owl reflects the well-being of the entire old-growth forest eco-system."

In a review of the Hagen et al. study, William McKillop criticized this issue framing. He argues that the survey did not include many relevant facts that respondents should have been told.[50] For example, the "committee of scientists" focused almost exclusively on old-growth habitat for spotted owls and largely ignored the fact that many are found in second-growth timber stands. Respondents were also not told that logging was already prohibited on considerable areas of old-growth timberland, and these acres were likely to increase in the course of normal national forest planning. In sum, McKillop argues that the spotted owl issue was not presented accurately or neutrally to respondents.

There are no simple answers to the neutrality problem. However, an inevitable conclusion is that the analyst has to be especially cautious in interpreting the results of CVM surveys that have been prepared by either parties to litigation or by advocacy groups with an agenda. At a practical level, *neutrality can best be ensured by pretesting the survey instrument with substantive experts who have "no axe to grind" in terms of the specific project that is being considered.* If neutral experts cannot be found, then pretesting with opposing advocates can be an alternative, perhaps enabling researchers to avoid the most serious challenges from those with positions not supported by the results.

16.3.4   *Decision-Making and Judgment Biases*

Although it is reasonable to assume that individuals can make rational judgments about their valuations of goods in most market situations, evidence suggests that in certain circumstances they may not be able to do so readily.[51] This is even more likely to occur in the context of CVM surveys, because judgment rather than decision-making is often involved and because there are not opportunities to learn from mistakes (we discuss the evidence on this issue later in the chapter). More formally, in such circumstances, there is a tendency for individuals to behave as if they are not maximizing utility, especially with respect to choices involving uncertainty. In the context of functioning markets, these behaviors appear as decision-making biases that can result in irrational purchases (or lack of purchases). These decision-making errors can be thought of as a type of market failure.[52] In the context of CV, the term *judgment bias* rather than *decision-making bias* is applicable because the respondent is not actually purchasing the good in question.

Risk-Related Biases. Both decision-making and judgment biases appear to be most serious for activities or projects that would generate small changes in the probabilities of (already) low-probability events that have "catastrophic" costs if they occur (for example, activities that might cause a marginal change in the probability of a nuclear power plant accident).[53] As WTP depends on how likely respondents perceive such events to be, their perception of probabilities and changes in them are important in CVM studies. Fortunately, researchers and analysts rarely rely solely on CVM estimates in such contexts. For example, they can use value-of-life estimates derived from methods in which these biases are less endemic (see Chapter 17).

The major types of judgmental biases to which individuals are particularly prone include:

- *availability bias*, whereby individuals estimate the probabilities of events by the ease with which occurrences can be recalled – more salient instances, such as those covered by the media, are more likely to be recalled;

- *representativeness* or *conjunction bias*, whereby individuals judge the probabilities of events on the basis of their plausibility – people perceive the probability of an event as being higher as more detail is added, even though the detail is irrelevant;

- *optimism bias*, whereby people believe that they can beat the objective odds;

- *anchoring bias*, whereby individuals do not fully update their probability assessments as new information becomes available;

- *hindsight bias*, whereby individuals believe, after an event occurs, that it was more predictable than it actually was;

- *status quo bias*, whereby individuals stick with the status quo even when it is inexpensive to experiment or when the potential benefits from changing are large;

- *probability assessment bias*, whereby people tend either to overestimate or to ignore small probabilities and underestimate large probabilities.

Many of these biases can be explained by the fact that, when dealing with complex information, people tend to use simplifying heuristics, or "rules of thumb." Further, there is quite strong empirical evidence that individuals do not derive their estimates of probabilities in a manner that is consistent with the expected utility hypothesis, which predicts that individuals assess risky outcomes by weighting the utility of each possible outcome by the probability that it will occur.

The most plausible (and researched) conceptual framework for explaining these observed violations of the expected utility hypothesis is *prospect theory*.[54] The axioms of prospect theory are particularly relevant to CVM issues and contexts. They suggest that individuals deviate from expected utility maximization in several predictable ways. Individuals value gains and losses from a reference point rather than valuing net wealth. Moreover, people are risk-averse toward gains and risk-seeking toward losses (known as *loss aversion*) – a loss and a gain of the same size would leave a person who is loss-averse worse off. This may stem from an *endowment effect*, whereby individuals have a greater psychological attachment to things they currently possess.[55]

Several of these effects can be summarized in the prospect theory value function, as shown in Figure 16.2. The vertical axis measures value, and the horizontal axis measures losses and gains. The figure shows three things. First, people start from a reference point from which changes are measured as losses or gains. Second, individuals are risk-averse with respect to potential gains (i.e., they prefer a smaller certain gain over a larger probable gain, when the expected values of the two alternatives are the same). Individuals are also risk-seeking with respect to potential losses (i.e., they prefer a larger probable loss to a smaller certain loss, when the expected values of the two alternatives are the same). This is represented in the figure by the concave gain function and the convex loss function. Third, losses loom larger than gains of equal size. This is represented in the figure as the loss function being steeper than the gain function. In addition to these three attributes of the loss function, prospect theory also allows for the possibility that individuals weigh outcomes with subjective probabilities that suffer from heuristic biases.

The biases suggested by prospect theory are particularly relevant to CVM for a number of reasons. Anchoring via reference points is always a potential problem in CVM elicitations. Even if open-ended questions are used to eliminate starting point bias, payment vehicles and other descriptive detail can introduce anchoring indirectly. Furthermore, detailed descriptions may evoke availability bias. Further, as we discuss later, CVM elicitations can sometimes be plausibly framed as involving either a gain or a loss.

In eliciting WTP for reductions in risks, special attention should be given to communicating risks. Research on risk communication offers some guidance:[56] present all risks in similar formats that do not mix frequencies, percentages, or proportions; provide graphics to help convey probabilities; and present absolute rather than relative risks, because people often have difficulty interpreting the latter. *More generally, CVM surveys should be designed to assess and accommodate the varying levels of numerical and risk literacy of respondents.*

Non-Commitment Bias.[57] It is well recognized in the marketing literature that respondents to surveys tend to overstate their willingness to purchase a product that is described to them.[58] This may be a strategic response problem (an issue discussed later), but could also be a form of anchoring bias (e.g., "this product must be valuable because they are asking me about it and describing it in such detail") in a context in

Value

Losses   Gains

which potential consumers do not engage in any learning. It is likely to be quite uncon-scious. The bias can flourish, of course, because the respondent does not actually have to commit money.

It is difficult to test for non-commitment bias when dealing with passive-use values. An indirect way of testing for the bias is to introduce elements to the survey that encourage respondents to think more carefully about their income and their budget constraints. Michael Kemp and Christopher Maxwell have developed a "top-down disaggregation method" to mitigate non-committment bias.[59] It attempts to do this by raising awareness of budget constraints. After asking respondents to state initially their total WTP, they were questioned specifically about comparative valuations. For example, after respondents were asked about their WTP to avoid a specified oil spill, they were then asked about their valuations of environmental protection versus reduction in crime, homelessness, and other social problems. They were also asked about their valuations for different kinds of environmental protection (wilderness areas versus groundwater qual-ity, rainforest protection, and other environmental goals). At the next level, they were asked to evaluate various kinds of wilderness area protection (reduction in harm from human-caused problems versus natural degradation and other destructive processes). At the end of this top-down disaggregation process, respondents were again asked their WTP. The result was WTP values several hundred times smaller than the WTP values from the initial open-ended questions, suggesting the desirability of asking questions that require respondents to think more carefully about their budget constraints.[60] (There is some caution in regards to the magnitude of these reported differences because of the possibility of starting-point bias discussed below.) For example, asking questions that encourage respondents to think about how much of their income is discretionary may help avoid non-commitment bias.

A less complicated and likely effective approach in dichotomous choice elicitations has been commonly used following research showing that adjusting bid acceptances to reflect respondent certainty provided estimates of WTP closer to those from a revealed preference method.[61] This approach requires a follow-up question to the elicitation that asks respondents who accept bids about the certainty of their acceptance. Only acceptances at face value for which the respondent is "definitely sure" appear to provide adjusted acceptance rates very close to actual purchase rates.[62] *This suggests that analysts should routinely include a certainty question following a dichotomous choice elicitation and convert bid acceptances to bid rejections for respondents who were unsure about their initial acceptances.*

Order Effects. CVM studies have also found important order, or sequence, effects. Consider, for example, a study that asked some respondents to value preserving seals and then whales, while others were asked to value preserving whales and then seals. Seal values were considerably lower when the seal question was asked after the whale question.[63] These findings could be explained by either an income effect, a substitution effect, or a combination of both. The rationale for an income effect is as follows: If someone has expressed a positive WTP to pay for the first good in a sequence of goods, then that person has less income to spend on the second good in the sequence. Critics of CV, however, have observed that it is implausible that the steep declines in WTP as a good moves down in order can be fully explained by income effects because they should be relatively small.[64] However, if the accepted bid for the first good accounts for a substantial fraction of the respondent's discretionary income, it could conceivably leave little disposable income available for accepting a bid for the second good. That is, even if income elasticities for the goods in isolation are small, WTP for the second good may be income constrained.

Substitution effects, such as between seals and whales, could be quite large, and consequently they can be important in CBA, especially in terms of assessing the aggregate impacts of projects because respondents may view one environmental improvement as a substitute for a quite different environmental improvement. If people do engage in extensive substitution, then the net aggregate benefits from a project may be smaller than predicted. For example, if a resident of Chicago agrees to contribute to a project that cleans the air in Chicago and is then offered a project that preserves visibility in the Grand Canyon, the value of the Grand Canyon project may be decreased because of the substitution effect.

The issue of whether substitution effects could account for much of the order inconsistency in CVM surveys of passive use values is still unclear.[65] Critics argue that the phenomenon is explained neither by income nor by substitution effects, but it instead demonstrates that respondents cannot really understand these kinds of questions. Hence, they inevitably engage in judgment heuristics that usually cause them to overstate valuations. Thus, it is uncertain that income and substitution effects provide a complete explanation for order effects.[66] *As the interpretation of order effects remains ambiguous, analysts generally avoid asking respondents to value more than one good.*

Embedding Effects. A fundamental axiom in the standard economic description of preferences is that individuals value more of a good more highly than less of it. This is sometimes referred to as a *scope test*. If CVM respondents' valuations are only slightly higher for large changes in the amount of the good offered than for small changes, then the validity of their responses becomes a concern. However, research indicates that individuals often do not readily distinguish between small and large quantities in their valuations of a good when the different quantities are *embedded* in one another. For example, William Desvousges and colleagues found that different samples of respondents value 2000 migratory birds approximately the same as 200,000 birds, and small oil spills much the same as much larger oil spills (given that these are different samples, it does not directly test whether given individuals prefer more to less).[67] Two additional examples of embedding are described in Exhibit 16.3. It is unlikely that declining marginal utility can explain all or even most of the absence of different valuations for different quantities of goods.

When dealing with passive-use values, embedding is probably the most worrisome problem identified by critics of the use of CVM in CBA. It goes to the very heart of welfare economics. Critics argue that the empirical evidence suggests that in these contexts respondents are not actually expressing their valuations but instead are expressing broad moral attitudes to environmental issues – a "warm glow" or "moral satisfaction."[68] However, Richard Carson and colleagues have argued that most studies that manifest embedding problems, or scope insensitivity, are poorly designed and executed, and well-designed CVM instruments do not manifest the problem.[69] *Nonetheless, although costly because it doubles the required sample size, in valuing changes in non-use goods, analysts should conduct a scope test by randomly splitting their respondents into two subsamples with each valuing a different magnitude of change in the good.* A scope test is also desirable for use goods, like reductions in the risk borne by respondents, although primarily to assess understanding of the change being valued.[70]

Starting Point Bias. As previously indicated, prospect theory identifies anchoring as a common behavioral response to being asked to make complex judgments. A problem arises in CVM when starting values are presented to respondents. The iterative bidding method is particularly prone to this problem because it provides respondents with a specific initial starting "price."[71] Consider, for example, the Kristiansand Fjord study mentioned earlier in the chapter. It was found that a range starting at 200 kronor and progressing to 2,000 kronor produced different valuations than a range starting at 0 kronor and progressing to 2,000 kronor, even when there were no bids between 0 and 200 kronor.[72]

Exhibit 16.3

Daniel Kahneman and Jack L. Knetsch report that residents of Toronto expressed a willingness to pay increased taxes to prevent a drop in fishstocks in all Ontario lakes that was only slightly larger than their expressed WTP to preserve fish stocks in a small area of the province. This is implausible.

The same researchers studied the impact of embedding. They did so by specifying a good: (1) very broadly to one sample of respondents (environmental services that included "preserving wilderness areas, protecting wildlife, providing parks, preparing for disasters, controlling air pollution, insuring water quality, and routine treatment and disposal of industrial wastes"); (2) considerably more narrowly to a second sample of respondents (to improve preparedness for disasters" with a subsequent allocation to go to "the availability of equipment and trained personnel for rescue operations"); and (3) more narrowly still to a third sample ("improve the availability of equipment and trained personnel for rescue operations"). Respondents in each sample were asked to express their willingness to pay for their "good." The differences in WTP among the three samples were not large.

Source: Adapted from Daniel Kahneman and Jack L. Knetsch, "Valuing Public Goods: The Purchase of Moral Satisfaction." *Journal of Environmental Economics and Management*, 22(1), 1992, 57–70. (For a critique of this study, see V. Kerry Smith, "Comment: Arbitrary Values, Good Causes, and Premature Verdicts." *Journal of Environmental Economics and Management*, 22(1), 1992, 71–89.)

The dichotomous choice question format seeks to eliminate starting point bias. It has been argued, however, that "responses to dichotomous choice questions are very strongly influenced by starting-point bias, because respondents are likely to take initial cues of resource value from the solicited contribution amount (e.g., assuming it to be his/her share of the needed contribution)."[73] There is, in fact, some empirical evidence to support the contention that the dichotomous choice method is subject to starting point bias,[74] although WTP estimated from dichotomous choice responses appears to be less affected by the provision of information about the total cost of providing a good or the size of the group receiving it than does WTP estimated from open-ended surveys.[75] Whether or not starting point bias arises from information provided within a single elicitation, it is very likely to arise from information provided in the first of a series of elicitations to the same respondent. *Like the order effect, starting point bias further supports the general practice of one elicitation per respondent.*

16.3.5   *WTP versus WTA*

Standard economic theory predicts similar values of WTP and WTA for goods that are traded in markets. That is, the amount someone is willing to pay to obtain another unit of the good should be close to the amount that the person would have to receive to give up a unit. However, estimates based on either revealed or stated preferences often find substantially larger values for WTA than WTP. The difference tends to be especially large in stated preference studies: studies that compare estimates of WTP and WTA from CVM studies generally find very large differences, with average ratios of five to one or larger, although these differences appear to be falling over time, perhaps because of improvements in the design of CVM studies.[76]

As an illustration, consider the estimates presented in Exhibit 16.4, which compares WTP and WTA for hunting permits estimated from both revealed preference (simulated market) and stated preference (CV) experiments. Although the CVM and simulated market estimates of WTP are quite close, the CVM estimate of WTA is between two and three times as large as the simulated market estimate.

Exhibit 16.4

A wildlife area in Wisconsin is periodically opened to hunting. Hunters require a special permit to participate in these hunts. The permits are issued free to the winners of a lottery. For the 1984 lottery, a large number of applications were received. As a result of the lottery, 150 permits to hunt were issued.

To measure WTA, half of these hunters also received a letter explaining the study and a check made out in their name. To cash these checks, the hunters had to relinquish their permits in this simulated market. The denominations of the checks, which ranged randomly from $18 to $518, corresponded to the dichotomous choice method. The other half of the hunters received a similar letter with a hypothetical payment offer drawn from the same range as the first half. They were asked if they would have been willing to give up their permits for the hypothetical amounts stated in their letters.

To measure WTP, 150 unsuccessful lottery participants were selected at random. Again, 75 received a letter explaining that a hunting permit was available if they paid the amount specified in the letter. The amounts covered the same range as described previously. The other 75 were asked the same question hypothetically. That is, they were asked the CVM question rather than given the opportunity to reveal their preferences through purchases. The following summarizes the results:

	WTP (dollars)	WTA (dollars)
Simulated market	31	153
Contingent valuation	35	420

Note first that the contingent valuation produced an estimate of WTP very close to that revealed in the simulated market. Also note that in the simulated market, WTA was almost five times larger than WTP in the simulated market. Further, the contingent valuation estimate of WTA was almost three times the simulated market estimate.

Source: Adapted from Richard C. Bishop and Thomas A. Heberlein, "The Contingent Valuation Method," in Rebecca L. Johnson and Gary V. Johnson, editors, *Economic Valuation of Natural Resources: Issues, Theory, and Application* (Boulder, CO: Westview Press, 1990), 81–104.

Considerable experimental evidence suggests that individuals demand greater monetary compensation to give up things that they already possess than they are willing to pay to acquire the same exact item. In experiments that actually require people to trade goods for money, as well as in other contexts, it is often found that required WTA amounts range from a ratio of four to 15 times greater than WTP amounts.[77] There is also evidence, however, that as subjects in experiments become more experienced, observed differences between WTP and WTA shrink considerably, usually as a result of decreases in WTA amounts.[78]

The large divergence between the WTP and WTA for tradeable (use) goods appears more consistent with decision framing involving endowment effects like those captured in Figure 16.2 than with conventional consumer theory. That is, the response depends on whether the choice is framed as a paying for a gain or being given compensation for a loss. In the case of non-use goods, however, consumer theory also allows for large differences between WTP and WTA when the non-use goods being valued do not have close substitutes.[79] Thus, large differences between WTP and WTA could result solely from the absence of close substitutes, solely from framing effects, or from both. In contrast to use goods, experimental evidence suggests that experience with non-use goods without close substitutes does not reduce framing effects.[80]

Although larger differences between WTP and WTA can be conceptually valid, CVs that elicit WTA do not pose as direct a trade-off to respondents as does the reminder of the budget constraint in those that elicit WTA. In other words, the absence of a binding budget constraint may reduce the likelihood that the respondent will make an economic response to the elicitation.

Exhibit 16.5

In a project conducted for the National Oceanic and Atmospheric Administration, a distinguished group of researchers used contingent valuation to estimate the monetary value of the natural resource damage caused by the 2010 BP Deepwater Horizon oil spill in the Gulf of Mexico. Rather than attempting to elicit WTA the damage, the researchers elicited WTP for an intervention that would prevent a similar spill. After explaining that 400 new wells like the Deepwater Horizon would be drilled over the next 15 years, and that scientists predict that one of them will have a blowout like that suffered by the Deepwater Horizon, they described how installing a second pipe at each of the new wells would prevent substantial damage from the blowout. Respondents in a national survey were asked about their willingness to pay higher taxes to fund this preventive measure.

The survey included a scope text. Respondents were randomly assigned to two different sets of negative impacts from a new spill based on impacts from the Deepwater Horizon spill. One set included miles of marshland fouled with oil, number of birds killed, and number of lost recreational trips. The other set included these losses as well as deaths of bottlenose dolphins, deep-water coral, snails, young fish, and young sea turtles. Because the survey was administered face-to-face, interviewers were able to show respondents booklets with maps, photos, and summaries of impacts. The summary of the larger set of impacts follows:

Animals		Back to normal
1. Snails and worms	1/3 near well died	10 years
2. Young fish	80 million died	1 years
3. Young sea turtles	8,000 died	20 years
4. Bottlenose dolphins	120 died	20
5. Birds	50,000 died	1 year
6. Deep-water corals	Parts of 120 died	300 years
Plants		
7. Marshes	Oil on 185 miles	3 years
Recreation		
8. Going to the beach	10 million fewer times	1 year

The payment vehicle was a one-time additional federal tax, with the random bid prices set at $15, $65, $135, $265, and $435. The researchers were reassured that respondents were making economic decisions because for both sets of impacts voting for prevention declined as the bid price increased and voting for prevention was systematically higher at each bid price for the larger set of impacts. Follow-up questions asked about perceived effectiveness of the prevention, likelihood of actually having to pay the tax, and acceptance of claims about impacts.

The researchers estimated the mean WTP for the larger set of impacts to be $153 (s.e. $6.87) and the mean WTP for the smaller set of impacts to be $136 (s.e. $6.34). Giving standing to all 112.6 million US households yielded an estimated WTP for the prevention program of $17.2 billion.

Source: Richard C. Bishop, Kevin J. Boyle, Richard T. Carson, David Chapman, W. Michael Hanemann, Barbara Kanninen, Raymond J. Kopp, Jon A. Krosnick, John List, Norman Meade, et al., "Putting a Value on Injuries to Natural Assets: The BP Oil Spill." *Science*, 356(6335), 2017, 253–54.

In eliciting WTAs, some researchers have employed so-called social budget constraints to increase the likelihood that respondents will offer economic responses. For example, researchers seeking to elicit farmers' WTA switching to strains of millet with positive ecological externalities but lower yields preceded the elicitation with the following: "before you answer, please note that *only* a limited number of households in the Kolli Hills would be selected to participate in this scheme, as the amount of funding for the scheme would be limited. Therefore, the smaller the amount of support you would require to participate in the programme, the higher are your chances of being selected."[81]

This particular social budget constraint encourages respondents to think about the trade-off between the amount of compensation and the probability of receiving it. Another approach is to specify a payment source that would otherwise provide local public goods. For example, compensation can be done through reductions in property taxes that would otherwise fund local services.[82] However, a complication arises in dichotomous choice elicitations: rejection could be either because the offered compensation is below WTA or because the respondent sees a reduction in valued services to fund the compensation that offsets enough of the compensation to drive it below WTA.

The perceived problems with WTA, both in terms of endowment effects and inducing economic responses, have led many economists to argue that, even when WTA is the conceptually correct measure, CVs should elicit WTP.[83] However, some critics of attempts to avoid WTA elicitations have argued that stated preferences are preferences and that, if respondents are asked to give up some quantity or quality of a good, then the appropriate formulation is WTA.[84] As WTA reductions in the quantity or quality of non-use goods may be substantially larger in magnitude than the equivalent WTP for increases (even in the absence of endowment effects), a blanket rejection of WTA elicitations is inappropriate. However, *CVs that do elicit WTA should include social budget constraints to increase the likelihood that respondents will provide an economic response.*

As a final point, note that dichotomous choice CVs could adopt either a WTP or WTA format. The former is valid if no one would have to receive compensation to accept the change in the good so that bid rejections can be assumed to be by respondents with WTP between zero and the bid; the latter is valid if no one would pay something to obtain the change in the good so that bid acceptances can be assumed to be by respondents who would actually require positive compensation. In most applications of CV, it is reasonable to assume these sorts of validity: it is unlikely that anyone would require compensation for cleaner air over the Grand Canyon or be willing to pay for a higher risk of an oil spill. However, when a policy that has multiple effects is being valued, it may be less certain that all respondents view it as either desirable or undesirable. In these cases, it is important to ask questions that distinguish between self-perceived winners and losers so that they are not inappropriately pooled into the same elicitation.[85]

16.3.6   *The Strategic Response (Honesty) Problem*

Will respondents answer honestly when asked about their WTP? It is frequently argued that respondents in CVM surveys have incentives to behave *strategically*, that is, to misrepresent their true preferences in order to achieve a more desired outcome than would result if they honestly revealed their preferences. An analogy is often drawn between strategic behavior in CVM studies and free-riding in the provision of public goods. The potential for strategic behavior in CV, however, is actually more varied than the free-riding characterization suggests.[86]

16.3.7   *The Carson and Groves Framework*

Richard Carson and Theodore Groves assess the nature of strategic responses to CVM questions likely to be encountered in the use of the major CVM methods.[87] They begin by making the point that we should not expect respondents' answers necessarily to be consistent with economic theory, and hence appropriate for inclusion in CBA, unless respondents believe that the survey is *consequential* in the sense that it could potentially influence some outcomes about which they care. In contrast, if respondents believe that the survey will have absolutely no influence on outcomes about which they care, then it is *inconsequential*, and economic theory offers no predictions about the nature of responses.

They next note that the design of consequential CVM surveys falls under the theory of *mechanism design*, which deals with the problem of creating rules for collective choice based on signals sent by individuals. Mechanisms that provide incentives for individuals to reveal their preferences truthfully are called *incentive-compatible*.

One of the central theorems of mechanism design is that, in the absence of restrictions on the domain of preferences,[88] mechanisms involving more than binary signals will always be incentive-incompatible.[89] Mechanisms employing binary signals will not always be incentive-compatible, but depending on the specific circumstances of choice, they may be (in other words, a binary signal is a necessary, but not always a sufficient, condition). More complex signals provide an opportunity for individuals to misstate their preferences in order to obtain a more desirable outcome.

As a brief illustration, return to the choice situation presented in Chapter 2. Table 2.2 shows how the mechanism, pair-wise majority rule voting, could result in an intransitive social ordering. Consider a case in which the mechanism is being implemented by first putting X against Y in round one and then, in round two, Z against the winner of round one. Note that the signal sent by the voters in this situation is not binary – it consists of *two* binary signals, one for each round. If the voters send truthful signals about their preferences, then X beats Y in round one and Z beats X in round two, so that the mechanism selects Z as the social choice, which is voter 1's least-preferred outcome. Anticipating this, voter 1 has an incentive to misrepresent her preferences by voting for Y in round one, even though she prefers X over Y, so that Y would win and be put against Z in round two and win. This misrepresentation of preferences in round one would result in Y, an outcome more desirable to voter 1 than the one that resulted from sending a truthful signal about his preferences in round one. Once the voters reach round two, it is as if they are facing a new choice situation in which they send only a binary signal. In this last round, there is no incentive to misrepresent preferences.

One immediate implication of this theorem is that continuous response formats, as used in the open-ended WTP method, or multiple-response formats, as used in the contingent-ranking method, will always be vulnerable to strategic responses that misstate true preferences.

Consider the open-ended WTP method. We can imagine two types of misrepresentation of preferences. First, assume that respondents perceive having to make payments that do not depend on their stated WTPs, that they have true WTPs above their anticipated payments, and that they anticipate that the likelihood of the good being provided depends on the aggregate of stated WTPs. They would then have an incentive to overstate their WTPs, so that the estimated aggregate WTP would be too high. The possibility of such overstatement was widely anticipated by economists. Yet, at least in comparison with the dichotomous choice method, which, as we will discuss, can be incentive-compatible, it does not appear that such overstatement is a major problem in the open-ended WTP method.[90] One explanation is that the assumptions that make overstatement a desirable strategy for respondents may not often hold. For example, respondents may fear that their shares of the cost of providing the good will be a positive function of their stated WTPs and, hence, state WTPs that are smaller than their actual WTP. However, they may also believe that the likelihood of provision depends on the fraction of respondents who state WTPs at or above the average cost of provision, rather than on aggregate WTP. If both of these possibilities hold, then a strategic respondent with a true WTP above the anticipated cost would state a WTP that is only slightly above the anticipated cost – above anticipated cost to increase the chances of provision but as little above as possible to minimize cost share.

Second, now consider respondents with true WTPs that are less than the costs that they anticipate would be imposed on them if the good were to be provided. Assume that they believe that the likelihood of provision depends on aggregate WTP. As they do not want the good provided, they have an incentive to state the smallest possible WTP, usually set to zero for goods researchers believe to be desirable. These strategic responses in the open-ended WTP method should lead to many zeros, and few WTP amounts under the respondents' perceived costs of provision. The larger the fraction of respondents following this strategy, the greater will be the underestimation of aggregate WTP.

As it involves a binary response, the dichotomous choice method *may* be incentive compatible. Carson and Groves note that incentive compatibility requires that payment for the good can be compelled and that the question deals only with a single issue. Table 16.2 summarizes the incentive properties of several circumstances in which the dichotomous choice method has been used.

Using the dichotomous choice method to elicit WTP for a new public (non-excludable) good that will be funded with coercive payments by respondents meets the requirements for incentive compatibility. Respondents have no incentive to vote against their true preferences. Because CVM is often the only way analysts can estimate WTP

Table 16.2 *Incentive Properties of Dichotomous Choice Questions by Type of Good*

Type of good	Incentive property
New public good with coercive payment	Incentive-compatible
New public good with voluntary payment	Not incentive-compatible
Introduction of new private good	Not incentive-compatible
Choice between two new public goods	Incentive-compatible
Choice between an existing and an alternative private good	Incentive-compatible, but choice does not reveal information about quantity demanded

Source: Adapted from Richard T. Carson and Theodore Groves, "Incentive and Informational Properties of Preference Questions." *Environmental and Resource Economics*, 37(1), 2007, p. 192.

for public goods, this is reassuring. Incentive compatibility also holds for comparisons between two mutually exclusive public goods with the same cost. As long as respondents place a positive value on both goods, they have no incentive to misstate their preferred good.

Incentive compatibility is lost in cases in which payment is voluntary because it introduces a second issue, whether to donate or to purchase, into the choice situation. In the case of a public good to be funded by contributions, respondents who place any positive value on the good have an incentive to accept bids above their true WTPs to increase the chances that the good is provided because they do not actually have to make a donation in that amount.[91] Similarly, respondents who have any probability of actually wanting a new private (excludeable) good have an incentive to accept bids above their WTP to increase the chances that it will actually be provided because they can decline to purchase it if they decide that they do not want it. The problem is so severe for new private goods that dichotomous choice CVM has largely been abandoned for this purpose.

Questions that ask respondents to choose between an existing private good and an alternative are incentive compatible as long as only potential users are surveyed. (The question will not be consequential for those who are not potential users.) Answers to the questions, however, do not reveal information about how much of the selected private good will actually be demanded. For example, a town may ask a sample of residents to choose between the existing skating rink, which is available only during daylight hours and has a small entrance fee, and a new skating rink with electric lighting, which would be available evenings and would have a higher entrance fee. The respondents have no incentive to misstate their true preferences over the choices, but the answers do not tell the town about how often residents will use the new facility.

16.3.8   *Conclusion about the Importance of Strategic Responses*

The danger that strategic responses to CVM questions will bias estimates of aggregate WTP cannot be assessed without considering both the elicitation method and the nature of the good being valued. The dichotomous choice method applied to the valuation of changes in public goods to be funded by taxes or other coercive payments can be designed to avoid strategic response bias. It is subject to an upward bias, however, if payments are voluntary. An important reason why the open-ended WTP method is now rarely used, is that it will generally be subject to strategic response bias, most likely leading to aggregate WTP estimates that are too small if payments are coerced and too large if payments are voluntary.

16.4   How Accurate is Contingent Valuation?

It is possible to test the accuracy of CVM WTP estimates in a number of ways.[92] The first method is to compare CVM values to those generated by other indirect methods. CVM values have been found to be approximately the same as those derived from travel cost studies.[93] They have also been found to be reasonably similar to prices derived from hedonic price regressions[94] and to the market prices of substitutes.[95] Wesley Magat and W. Kip Viscusi tested whether respondents' WTP for risk reductions associated with an insecticide and toilet bowl cleaner were consistent with standard economic theory or subject to the kinds of judgment biases described earlier. In general, they did not find strong evidence of bias.[96]

The second type of comparison, one that is more direct, is between respondents' CVM statements and their actual behavior when they participate in experiments that utilize a simulated or constructed market for the good in question.[97] Results from studies that have used experimental techniques to examine CVM accuracy typically suggest that CVM valuations of WTP relying on open-ended and dichotomous choice methods approximate actual market transactions, although there is some tendency for overvaluation.[98] In assessing these experiments, it is useful to keep in mind that the simulated market only approximates the workings of a real market; for example, there is often only one opportunity to buy the good. In addition, the experiments have only been conducted primarily in contexts in which respondents clearly derive use value from the good.

John Loomis has investigated how consistent household CVM valuations are over time. Although not a direct test of accuracy, his investigation is relevant because consistency is a prerequisite for accuracy. He surveyed both visitors and the general public's WTP for recreational, option, existence, and bequest values derived from Mono Lake in California. Identical surveys were administered to the same individuals eight or nine months apart. The results were virtually identical.[99]

Although the available evidence suggests that CVM provides plausible estimates of WTP in use contexts, the plausibility of its estimates of non-use values is more mixed.[100] Obviously, the nature of non-use values makes it much more difficult to elicit WTP from observed behavior, which makes it both more difficult to assess CVM and to replace it. Nonetheless, with sufficient cleverness researchers may eventually be able to find ways to do so. For example, as noted in Chapter 13, voluntary contributions to environmental causes might serve as the basis for estimation. Market-like experiments might also be used.[101] For example, individuals who have expressed WTP for non-use could be given the option of returning none, part, or all of the checks sent to them by experimenters (as described in Exhibit 16.4).

16.5   Heuristics for the Design and Use of CVM Surveys

CVM craft has evolved in a variety of ways over the last 30 years to increase its reliability and validity. As CVM is often the only feasible method for estimating WTP for non-use, its craft will likely continue to evolve. Here, based on the preceding discussion in this chapter, we offer the seven heuristics listed in Table 16.3 for designing CVs and assessing the likely validity of those done by others.

First, design survey instruments to reduce the risk of hypotheticality bias. The survey instrument should provide respondents with sufficient and understandable information to remove their uncertainty about the good being valued. When possible,

Table 16.3 *Seven Heuristics for Doing and Interpreting Contingent Valuations*

1. Design survey instrument to reduce hypotheticality bias
2. Use the dichotomous choice method with one elicitation per respondent
3. Always include budget reminder; consider priming with disposable income question
4. Be more confident in eliciting WTP; use social budget constraints in eliciting WTA
5. Include a spilt-sample scope test (especially for non-use goods)
6. Include a follow-up certainty question to allow adjustment for non-commitment bias
7. Use respondent income or disposable income to address "fat tails"

respondents should have familiarity with the type of choice being posed or given experience with it within the survey.[102]

Second, use the dichotomous choice elicitation format with only one elicitation per respondent. Although it typically requires larger sample sizes than the open-ended or iterative bidding formats or double dichotomous choice, single dichotomous choice elicitation gives respondents a familiar take-it-or-leave-it choice. Further, at least for non-use goods with coercive payments, it satisfies the necessary conditions for incentive compatibility.

Third, include a clear budget reminder in the elicitation question that employs a realistic payment vehicle. Also, consider asking budget-related questions prior to the elicitation to prime respondents for an economic choice.

Fourth, place much greater confidence in elicitations of WTP than WTA. When it is important to have an estimate of WTA because it is the conceptually correct estimate, look for ways to employ social budget constraints to increase the chances that respondents will perceive trade-offs that encourage revelation of minimum WTA.

Fifth, use spilt samples to implement scope tests that estimate WTP for at least two magnitudes of the change being valued. Doing so is especially important in valuing non-use goods where there may be concern about "warm glow" responses. It can also aid assessment of validity for goods, like risk reductions, that respondents may have difficulty understanding.

Sixth, anticipate and adjust for non-commitment bias by following dichotomous choice elicitations with certainty questions and, in WTP elicitations, convert yes responses to the elicitation to no responses for those who are not highly certain about their responses.

Seventh, when bid acceptances show "fat tails," consider shrinking them by using income, or disposable income, as individuals' upper bounds, presenting alternative parametric specifications, or switching to non-parametric methods.

16.6   Conclusion

CVM is now relatively uncontroversial in contexts involving use values, although it may overestimate them. Its accuracy in non-use contexts is more controversial, yet it is in this context where its potential usefulness is likely to be the greatest. Doubts about the accuracy of CVM in non-use contexts stem from the problems of hypotheticality and the attendant judgment biases that appear to flourish in the non-use context. Strategic response bias, on the other hand, does not appear to be a major problem in the use of the dichotomous choice method to value non-use goods with coercive payments, and neutrality bias can be minimized by use of appropriate survey techniques.

Exercises for Chapter 16

1. The construction of a dam that would provide hydroelectric power would result in the loss of two streams: one that is now used for sport fishing, and another that does not support game fish but is part of a wilderness area.

    a. Imagine that a CVM method is used to estimate the social cost of the loss of each of these streams. Would you be equally confident in the two sets of estimates? Why?

    b. Consider two general approaches to asking CVM questions about the streams. The first approach attempts to elicit how much compensation people would require to give up the streams. The second approach attempts to elicit how much people would be willing to pay to keep the streams. Which approach would you recommend? Why?

2. A number of residents of Dullsville have complained to the mayor that the center of town looks shabby compared to the centers of many other nearby towns. At the mayor's request, the Parks Department has put together a proposal for converting the town square parking lot into a sitting park with flower displays – it modeled the design on a similar park in the neighboring town of Flowerville. The annualized cost of installing and maintaining the park, and relocating parking to nearby Short Street, would be about $120,000. With about 40,000 households paying property taxes, the project would cost an average household about $3 per year.

    You have been asked to give advice about conducting a survey to measure the benefits of the project.

    a. The Parks Department proposes conducting a telephone survey. Does this seem like an appropriate survey vehicle?

    b. How might a random sample be drawn for a telephone survey?

    c. Write a statement that could be read by the interviewer to describe the project.

    d. Write questions to implement the open-ended WTP method.

    e. Propose a procedure for implementing the dichotomous choice method.

3. Consider a project that would involve purchasing marginal farmland that
    would then be allowed to return to wetlands capable of supporting migrant
    birds. Researchers designed a survey to implement the dichotomous choice
    method. They reported the following data.

Stated price (annual payment in dollars)	Fraction of respondents accepting stated price (percent)
0	98
5	91
10	82
15	66
20	48
25	32
30	20
35	12
40	6
45	4
50	2

What is the mean WTP for the sampled population?

Notes

1. Most observers attribute the origins of CVM to Robert Davis, "Recreation Planning as an Economic Problem." *Natural Resources Journal*, 3(2), 1963, 239–49.

2. Helpful CVM overviews include Ian J. Bateman and Kenneth G. Willis, editors, *Valuing Environmental Preferences: Theory and Practice of the Contingent Valuation Method in the U.S., EU, and Developing Countries* (Oxford and New York: Oxford University Press, 1999) and Richard Carson, *Contingent Valuation: A Comprehensive Bibliography and History* (Northampton, MA: Edward Elgar Publishing, 2012).

3. The Environmental Valuation Reference Inventory was developed by Environment Canada in collaboration with international experts and organizations, including the US Environmental Protection Agency (www.evri.ca/).

4. Alan Diener, Bernie O'Brien, and Amiram Gafni, "Health Care Contingent Valuation Studies: A Review and Classification of the Literature." *Health Economics*, 7(4), 1998, 313–26 and Pei-Jung Lin, Michael J. Cangelosi, David W. Lee, and Peter J. Neumann, "Willingness to Pay for Diagnostic Technologies: A Review of the Contingent Valuation Literature." *Value In Health*, 16(5), 2013, 797–805.

5. For example, see David Maddison and S. Mourato, "Valuing Different Road Options for Stonehenge." *Conservation and Management of Archeological Sites*, 4(4), 2001, 203–12; Peter C. Boxall, Jeffrey Englin, and Wiktor L. Adamowicz, "Valuing Aboriginal Artifacts: A Combined Revealed-Stated Preference Approach." *Journal of Environmental Economics and Management*, 45(2), 2003 and Bruce K. Johnson and John C. Whitehead, "Value of Public Goods from Sports Stadiums: The CVM Approach." *Contemporary Economic Policy*, 18(1), 2000, 48–58.

6. See, for example, Jerry Hausman, "Contingent Valuation: from Dubious to Hopeless." *Journal of Economic Perspectives*, 26(4), 2012, 43–56 for an especially skeptical view.

7. Raymond J. Kopp, Paul R. Portney, and V. Kerry Smith, "The Economics of Natural Resource Damages after Ohio v. U.S. Dept. of the Interior." *Environmental Law Reporter*, 20(4), 1990, 10,127–131.

8. Kenneth Arrow, Robert Solow, Paul Portney, Edward Leamer, Roy Radner, and Howard Schuman, "Report of the NOAA Panel on Contingent Valuation." *Federal Register*, 58(10), 1993, 4601–14.

9. On this point, see Daniel McFadden and Gregory Leonard, "Issues in the Contingent Valuation of Environmental Goods: Methodologies for Data Collection and Analysis," in J. A. Hausman, editor, *Contingent Valuation: A Critical Assessment* (New York, NY: North-Holland, 1993), 165–208.

10. Arrow et al., "Report of the NOAA Panel on Contingent Valuation," p. 4608.

11. For an example of this approach, see J. C. Horvath, *Southeastern Economic Survey of Wildlife Recreation* (Atlanta, GA: Environmental Research Group, Georgia State University, 1974).

12. One compromise between the open-ended format and the provision of "guidance" that has been used in in-person interviews is the *payment card* with a range of prices. For example, in the Nestucca oil spill CVM survey, respondents were asked to specify the maximum amount their households would pay for programs to prevent oil spills. They were then shown a payment card with dollar amounts ranging from $0 to $5000 and asked to circle the amount closest to their evaluation. Robert Rowe, William D. Schulze, W. Douglas Shaw, David Schenk and Lauraine G. Chestnut, "Contingent Valuation of Natural Resource Damage Due to Nestucca Oil Spill," prepared for the Department of Wildlife, Ministry of the Environment, BC, and Environment Canada, by RCG/Hagler, Bailly Inc., June 1991.

13. James L. Regens, "Measuring Environmental Benefits with Contingent Markets." *Public Administration Review*, 51(4), 1991, 345–52.

14. For an example, see V. Kerry Smith and William H. Desvousges, *Measuring Water Quality Benefits* (Boston, MA: Kluwer Nijhoff Publishing, 1986), chapter 6.

15. Baruch Fischhoff and Louis A. Cox Jr., "Conceptual Framework for Regulatory Benefits Assessment," in Judith D. Bentkover, Vincent T. Covello, and Jeryl Mumpower, editors, *Benefits Assessment: The State of the Art* (Boston, MA: D. Reidel Publishing Co., 1986), 51–84.

16. Introduction of the dichotomous choice method is usually credited to Richard C. Bishop and Thomas A. Heberlein, "Measuring Values of Extramarket Goods: Are Indirect Measures Biased?" *American Journal of Agricultural Economics*, 61(5), 1979, 926–30.

17. Selecting appropriate bid prices is one of the most difficult tasks analysts face in applying the dichotomous choice method. The bid prices must be spaced sufficiently far apart so that they show a range of acceptance rates. Simply spreading bid prices over a very wide range, however, is unsatisfactory because, for a given sample size, statistical efficiency in estimating WTP from the pattern of acceptances is greater for fewer bid prices. This suggests the importance of conducting pre-test surveys to determine an appropriate set of bid prices. (Of course, in any survey study, pre-tests are important for ensuring that respondents understand questions.) See Barbara J. Kanninen, "Bias in Discrete Response Contingent Valuation." *Journal of Environmental Economics and Management*, 28(1), 1995, 114–25.

18. On the technical issues relating to interpreting the function as utility and how to deal with truncation, see W. Michael Hanemann, "Welfare Evaluations in Contingent Valuation Experiments with Discrete Responses." *American Journal of Agricultural Economics*, 66(3), 1984, 332–41.

19. When the number of respondents per bid is small, sampling error may produce acceptance rates that are not monotonically declining as bids increase.

20. The formula for computing the WTP of the average member of the sample can be derived more formally if some additional notation is introduced. (Note that this derivation involves approximating the expected value of WTP.) Assume that the offer prices are 0, v, $2v$, $3v$, …, Nv, where v is the interval between prices, and Nv is the maximum price offered. For example, if the offer prices were 0, $10, $20, $30, …, $200, then $v = \$10$ and $N = 20$. Let $\mathbf{F}[X]$ be the fraction of respondents offered price X who accept the offer – this is the height of the bar in the histogram that sits above X. In order to calculate the expected value of WTP, we require the probability that each offer price is the *maximum* amount that a respondent would be willing to pay. We can approximate this for offer amount $\$kv$ with the expression: $\mathbf{F}[kv] - \mathbf{F}[(k + 1)v]$ for $k = 0, 1, …, N − 1$, which is roughly the probability of a respondent accepting $\$kv$ minus the probability of accepting a larger offer price, $\$(k + 1)v$. The mean WTP (that is, the WTP of the average respondent) is then approximately the sum of the products of maximum payments times their probabilities:

$$\mathbf{E}[WTP] = Nv\mathbf{F}[Nv] + (N-1)v\{\mathbf{F}[(N-1)v]$$
$$-\mathbf{F}[Nv]\} + (N-2)v\{\mathbf{F}[(N-2)v] - \mathbf{F}[(N-1)]\}$$
$$+\cdots+0\{\mathbf{F}[0] - \mathbf{F}[v]\}$$

Collecting terms yields the simple expression:

$$\mathbf{E}[WPT] = v\sum_{k=0}^{N}\mathbf{F}[kv]$$

21. For a treatment of estimation issues, see W. Michael Hanemann and Barbara Kanninen, "The Statistical Analysis of Discrete Response CVM Data," in Ian J. Bateman and Ken G. Willis, editors, *Valuing Environmental Preferences: Theory and Practice of the Contingent Valuation Method in the U.S., EC, and Developing Countries*, 302–441; and Timothy C. Haab and Kenneth E. McConnell, *Valuing Environmental and Natural Resources: The Econometrics of Non-Market Valuation* (Cheltenham: Edward Elgar Publishers, 2002).

22. A complication arises because the statistical model usually assumes an infinite range for x. In practice, surveys use offer prices with a finite range, usually bounded from below at zero. Averaging over this finite range will miss some of the probability assumed by the statistical model. A correction to help account for this truncation bias involves rescaling the distribution to account for the missing areas in the tails of the distribution. See Kevin J. Boyle, Michael

P. Welsh, and Richard C. Bishop, "Validation of Empirical Measures of Welfare Change: Comment." *Land Economics*, 64(1), 1988, 94–98.

23. See Haab and McConnell, *Valuing Environmental and Natural Resources*, for a systematic and comprehensive treatment of the WTP modeling issues.

24. For an overview of the statistical issues in estimating aggregate WTP from such models, see Timothy Park, John B. Loomis, and Michael Creel, "Confidence Intervals for Evaluating Benefits Estimates from Dichotomous Choice Contingent Valuation Studies." *Land Economics*, 67(1), 1991, 64–73.

25. Analysts often assume that the probability of accepting any bid price should go up with income and view a positive relationship between income and WTP as a validity check for the respondent making an economic choice. However, for non-use goods, the income elasticity of WTP need not be positive. See Nicholas E. Flores and Richard T. Carson, "The Relationship Between the Income Elasticities of Demand and Willingness to Pay." *Journal of Environmental Economics and Management*, 33(3), 1997, 287–95.

26. If σ is assumed to be a function of individual characteristics, then Equation 16.2 would be equivalent to a heterogeneous probit.

27. For an illustration of this approach, see David L. Weimer, Aidan R. Vining, and Randall K. Thomas, "Cost–Benefit Analysis Involving Addictive Goods: Contingent Valuation to Estimate Willingness-to-Pay for Smoking Cessation." *Health Economics*, 18(2), 2009, 181–202.

28. George R. Parsons and Kelley Myers, "Fat Tails and Truncated Bids in Contingent Valuation: An Application to an Endangered Shorebird Species." *Ecological Economics*, 129(September), 2016, 210–19; Timothy C. Haab and Kenneth E. McConnell, *Valuing Environmental and Natural Resources*.

29. Hui Li, Robert P. Berrens, Alok K. Bohara, Hank Jenkins-Smith, Carol Silva, and David L. Weimer, "Testing for Budget Constraint Effects in a National Advisory Referendum Survey on the Kyoto Protocol." *Journal of Agricultural and Resource Economics*, 30(2), 2005, 350–66; and Hui Li, Robert P. Berrens, Alok K. Bohara, Hank Jenkins-Smith, Carol Silva, and David L. Weimer, "Exploring the Beta Model Using Proportional Budget Information in a Contingent Valuation Study." *Economics Bulletin*, 17(8), 2005, 1–9.

30. For a clear treatment of the most widely used non-parametric approach, the Turnbull estimator, see Haab and McConnell, *Valuing Environmental and Natural Resources: The Econometrics of Non-Market Valuation*, chapter 3.

31. Michael Hanemann and Barbara Kanninen, "Statistical Analysis of Discrete Response CVM Data," in Ian J. Bateman and Kenneth G. Wells, editors, *Valuing*

Environmental Preferences (New York, NY: Oxford University Press, 1999), 300–441.

32. Joseph A. Herriges and Jason F. Shogren, "Starting Point Bias in Dichotomous Choice Valuation with Follow-Up Questioning." *Journal of Environmental Economics and Management*, 30(1), 1996, 112–31.

33. Richard T. Carson and Theodore Groves, "Incentive and Informational Properties of Preference Questions." *Environmental and Resource Economics*, 37(1), 2007, 181–210.

34. Empirical work supports this weighted averaging explanation; see Anthony C. Burton, Katherine S. Carson, Susan M. Chilton, and W. George Hutchinson, "An Experimental Investigation of Explanations for Inconsistencies in Responses to Second Offers in Double Referenda." *Journal of Environmental Economics and Management*, 46(3), 1996, 472–89.

35. See Robert P. Berrens, Alok K. Bohara, Hank Jenkins-Smith, Carol Silva, and David L. Weimer, "The Advent of Internet Surveys for Political Research: A Comparison of Telephone and Internet Samples." *Political Analysis*, 11(1), 2003, 1–22; and Robert P. Berrens, Alok K. Bohara, Hank C. Jenkins-Smith, Carol L. Silva, and David L. Weimer, "Information and Effort in Contingent Valuation Surveys: Application to Global Climate Change Using National Internet Samples." *Journal of Environmental Economics and Management*, 47(2), 2004, 331–63.

36. For issues specifically relevant to CV, see Steven F. Edwards and Glen D. Anderson, "Overlooked Biases in Contingent Valuation Surveys: Some Considerations." *Land Economics*, 63(2), 1987, 168–78.

37. Richard T. Carson, "Constructed Markets," in John B. Braden and Charles D. Kolstad, editors, *Measuring the Demand for Environmental Quality* (New York, NY: Elsevier Science Publishers, 1991), 152.

38. For an example of an attempt to estimate the extent of a recreational market, see V. Kerry Smith and Raymond J. Kopp, "The Spatial Limits of the Travel Cost Recreational Demand Model." *Land Economics*, 56(1), 1980, 64–72.

39. Desvousges, Smith, and Fisher, "Option Price Estimates for Water Quality Improvements."

40. For a review, see John B. Loomis, "Expanding Contingent Value Sample Estimates to Aggregate Benefit Estimates: Current Practices and Proposed Solutions." *Land Economics*, 63(4), 1987, 396–402.

41. Robert J. Johnston, Stephen K. Swallow, and Thomas F. Weaver, "Estimating Willingness to Pay and Resource Tradeoffs with Different Payment Mechanisms: An Evaluation of a Funding Guarantee for Watershed Management." *Journal of Environmental Economics and Management*, 38(1), 1999, 97–120.

42. See "The Review Panel's Assessment," 180–204.

43. For an extensive discussion of the attitude-behavior nexus, see Robert C. Mitchell and Richard T. Carson, *Using Surveys to Value Public Goods: The Contingent Valuation Method* (Washington, DC: Resource for the Future, 1989), 175–87.

44. Baruch Fischhoff and Lita Furey,"Measuring Values: A Conceptual Framework for Interpreting Transactions with Special Reference to Contingent Valuation of Visibility." *Journal of Risk and Uncertainty*, 1(2), 1988, 147–84, at pp. 179–80.

45. In marketing, a technique called *conjoint analysis* is used to elicit consumer valuations for new, unfamiliar goods. For a review, see Daniel McFadden, "The Choice Theory Approach to Market Research." *Marketing Science*, 5(4), 1986, 275–97.

46. Richard T. Carson, Nicholas E. Flores, and Norman F. Meade, "Contingent Valuation: Controversies and Evidence." *Environmental and Resource Economics*, 19(2), 2001, 173–210, at 178.

47. For a discussion of this point, see Ronald G. Cummings, David S. Brookshire, and William D. Schulze, *Valuing Environmental Goods: An Assessment of the Contingent Valuation Method* (Totawa, NJ: Rowman & Allenhead, 1986) at 43, 253. For the case that hypothetical bias is real and endemic, although variable across locations, see Mariah D. Ehmke, Jayson L. Lusk, and John A. List, "Is Hypothetical Bias a Universal Phenomenon? A Multinational Investigation." *Land Economics*, 84(3), 2008, 489–500.

48. Fischhoff and Furey, "Measuring Values: A Conceptual Framework for Interpreting Transactions with Special Reference to Contingent Valuation of Visibility," table 1, p. 156. Effectively implementing contingent valuation surveys in developing countries is especially difficult. See Dale Whittington, "Improving the Performance of Contingent Valuation Studies in Developing Countries." *Environmental and Resource Economics*, 22(1&2), 2002, 323–67.

49. Daniel A. Hagen, James W. Vincent, and Patrick G. Welle, "The Benefits of Preserving Old-Growth Forests and the Northern Spotted Owl." *Contemporary Policy Issues*, 10(2), 1992, 13–16.

50. William McKillop, "Use of Contingent Valuation in Northern Spotted Owls Studies: A Critique." *Journal of Forestry*, 90(8), 1992, 36–37.

51. For an overview, see David L. Weimer, *Behavioral Economics and Cost–benefit analysis: Benefit Validity when Sovereign Consumers Seem to Make Mistakes* (New York, NY: Cambridge University Press, 2017).

52. See David L. Weimer and Aidan R. Vining, *Policy Analysis: Concepts and Practice*, 6th edn (New York, NY: Taylor & Francis, 2017), 115–24.

53. For an extensive review of this issue and other biases, see Colin F. Camerer and Howard Kunreuther, "Decision Processes for Low Probability Events: Policy Implications." *Journal of Policy Analysis and Management*, 8(4), 1989, 565–92.

54. Daniel Kahneman and Amos Tversky, "Prospect Theory." *Econometrica*, 47(2), 1979, 263–92. Many of the violations of expected utility hypothesis that can be explained by prospect theory can also be explained by assuming people maximize expected utility but employ Bayesian updating of probabilities; see W. Kip Viscusi, "Prospective Reference Theory: Toward an Explanation of the Paradoxes." *Journal of Risk and Uncertainty*, 2(3), 1989, 235–63.

55. Richard H. Thaler, "Towards a Positive Theory of Consumer Choice." *Journal of Economic Behavior and Organization*, 1(1), 1980, 39–60. For some empirical evidence on loss-aversion in housing markets, see David Genesove and Christopher Mayer, "Loss Aversion and Seller Behavior: Evidence from the Housing Market." *Quarterly Journal of Economics*, 116(4), 2001, 1233–60.

56. Vivianne H. M. Visschers, Ree M. Meertens, Wim W. F. Passchier, and Nanne N. K. de Vries, "Probability Information in Risk Communication: A Review of the Research Literature." *Risk Analysis*, 29(2), 2009, 267–87; and Mark Harrison, Dan Rigby, Caroline Vass, Terry Flynn, Jordan Louviere and Katherine Payne, "Risk as an Attribute in Discrete Choice Experiments: A Systematic Review of the Literature." *Patient*, 7(2), 2014, 151–70.

57. It may seem artificial to separate hypotheticality from non-commitment bias. However, as emphasized earlier, hypotheticality does not appear to generate upward or downward bias, whereas, as will be seen, non-commitment does appear to bias valuations upward.

58. See, for example, Linda F. Jamieson and Frank M. Bass, "Adjusting Stated Intention Measures to Predict Trial Purchase of New Products: A Comparison of Models and Methods." *Journal of Marketing Research*, 26(3), 1989, 336–45.

59. Michael A. Kemp and Christopher Maxwell, "Exploring a Budget Context for Contingent Valuation Estimates," 217–65, in Hausman, editor, *Contingent Valuation: A Critical Assessment*.

60. I. J. Bateman and I. H. Langford, "Budget-Constrained, Temporal, and Question-Ordering Effects in Contingent Valuation Studies." *Environment and Planning A*, 29(7), 1997, 1215–28.

61. Patricia A. Champ, Richard C. Bishop, Thomas C. Brown, and Daniel W. McCollum, "Using Donation Mechanisms to Value Nonuse Benefits from Public Goods." *Journal of Environmental Economics and Management*, 33(2), 1997, 151–62.

62. Karen Blumenschein, Glenn C. Blomquist, Magnus Johannesson, Nancy Horn, and Patricia Freeman, "Eliciting Willingness to Pay without Bias: Evidence from a Field Experiment." *Economic Journal*, 118(525), 2008, 114–37.

63. Karl C. Samples and James R. Hollyer, "Contingent Valuation of Wildlife Resources in the Presence of Substitutes and Complements," in Rebecca L. Johnson and Gary V. Johnson, editors, *Economic Valuation of Natural Resources: Issues, Theory, and Application* (Boulder, CO: Westview Press, 1990), 177–92.

64. See Peter A. Diamond, Jerry A. Hausman, Gregory K. Leonard, and Mike Denning, "Does Contingent Valuation Measure Preferences? Experimental Evidence," in Hausman, editor, *Contingent Valuation: A Critical Assessment*, 43–85.

65. See the heated argument between Peter Diamond and Richard Carson, in Hausman, editor, *Contingent Valuation: A Critical Assessment*, 87–89.

66. The case that these effects adequately explain the empirical findings is made in Carson, Flores, and Meade, "Contingent Valuation: Controversies and Evidence," 186–89; see also Richard T. Carson, Nicholas E. Flores, and Michael Hanemann, "Sequencing and Valuing Public Goods." *Journal of Environmental Economics and Management*, 36(3), 1998, 314–23.

67. William H. Desvousges, F. Reed Johnson, Richard W. Dunford, Sara P. Hudson, and K. Nicole Wilson, "Measuring Natural Resources Damages with Contingent Valuation: Tests of Validity and Reliability," in Hausman, editor, *Contingent Valuation: A Critical Assessment*, 91–159.

68. Daniel Kahneman and Jack L. Knetsch, "Valuing Public Goods: The Purchase of Moral Satisfaction." *Journal of Environmental Economics and Management*, 22(1), 1992, 57–70, at 64–68.

69. Carson, Flores, and Meade, "Contingent Valuation: Controversies and Evidence," *Environmental and Resource Economics*.

70. James K. Hammitt and John D. Graham, "Willingness to Pay for Health Protection: Inadequate Sensitivity to Probability?" *Journal of Risk and Uncertainty*, 18(1), 1999, 33–62.

71. Kevin J. Boyle, Richard C. Bishop, and Michael P. Walsh, "Starting Point Bias in Contingent Valuation Bidding Games." *Land Economics*, 16(2), 1985, 188–94.

72. Regens, "Measuring Environmental Benefits with Contingent Markets," 347–48.

73. Walter J. Mead, "Review and Analysis of State-of-the-Art Contingent Valuation Studies," in Hausman, editor, *Contingent Valuation: A Critical Assessment*, 305–32.

74. See Trudy A. Cameron and D. D. Huppert, "Referendum Contingent Valuation Estimates: Sensitivity to the Assignment of Offered Values." *Journal of the American Statistical Association*, 86(416), 1991, 910–18.

75. Alok K. Bohara, Michael McKee, Robert P. Berrens, Hank Jenkins-Smith, Carol L. Silva, and David S. Brookshire, "Effects of Total Cost and Group-Size Information on Willingness to Pay Responses: Open Ended vs. Dichotomous Choice." *Journal of Environmental Economics and Management*, 35(2), 1998, 142–63.

76. Tuba Tunçel and James K. Hammitt, "A New Meta-Analysis on the WTP/WTA Disparity." *Journal of Environmental Economics and Management*, 68(1), 2014, 175–87.

77. Jack Knetsch and J. S. Sinden, "Willingness to Pay and Compensation Demanded: Experimental Evidence of an Unexpected Disparity in Measures of Value." *Quarterly Journal of Economics*, 99(3), 1984, 507–21; Shelby Gerking, Menno De Haan, and William Schulze, "The Marginal Value of Job Safety: A Contingent Valuation Study." *Journal of Risk and Uncertainty*, 1(2), 1988, 185–99; and Wesley Magat and W. Kip Viscusi, *Informational Approaches to Regulation* (Cambridge, MA: MIT Press, 1992).

78. Don L. Coursey, John J. Hovis, and William D. Schulze, "The Disparity between Willingness to Accept and Willingness to Pay Measures of Value." *Quarterly Journal of Economics*, 102(3), 1987, 679–90; Jason F. Shogren, Seung Y. Shin, Dermot J. Hayes, and James B. Kliebenstein, "Resolving the Differences in Willingness to Pay and Willingness to Accept." *American Economic Review*, 84(1), 1994, 255–70; and Wiktor L. Adamowicz, Vinay Bhardwaj, and Bruce McNab, "Experiments on the Difference Between Willingness to Pay and Willingness to Accept." *Land Economics*, 64(4), 1993, 416–27.

79. W. Michael Hanemann, "Willingness to Pay and Willingness to Accept: How Much Can They Differ?" *American Economic Review*, 81(3), 1991, 635–47.

80. Shogren, Shin, Hayes, and Kliebenstein, "Resolving the Differences in Willingness to Pay and Willingness to Accept." Experiments that provide experience with tradeable goods before hypothetical valuations may reduce statements of incoherent preferences. See Todd L. Cherry, Thomas D. Crocker and Jason F. Shogren, "Rationality Spillovers." *Journal of Environmental Economics and Management*, 45(1), 2003, 63–84.

81. Vijesh V. Krishna, Adam G. Drucker, Unai Pascual, Prabhakaran T. Raghu and E.D. Israel Oliver King, "Estimating Compensation Payments for On-Farm Conservation of Agricultural Biodiversity in Developing Countries." *Ecological Economics*, 87(March), 2013, 110–23 at 114.

82. Salvador del Saz-Salazar, Leandro García-Menéndez and María Feo-Valero, "Meeting the Environmental Challenge of Port Growth: A Critical Appraisal of the Contingent Valuation Method and an Application to Valencia Port, Spain." *Ocean and Coastal Management*, 59(April), 2012, 31–39.

83. Arrow et al., "Report of the NOAA Panel on Continent Valuation," 4608.

84. Jack L. Knetsch, Yohanes E. Riyanto and Jichuan Zong, "Gain and Loss Domains and the Choice of Welfare Measure of Positive and Negative Changes." *Journal of Benefit–Cost Analysis*, 3(4), 2012, 1–18.

85. See Devem E. Carlson, Joseph T. Ripberger, Hank C. Jenkins-Smith, Carol L. Silva, Kuhika Gupta, Robert P. Berrens, and Benjamin A. Jones, "Contingent Valuation and the Policymaking Process: An Application to Used Nuclear Fuel in the United States." *Journal of Benefit–Cost Analysis*, 7(3), 2017, 459–87.

86. Mitchell and Carson, *Using Surveys to Value Public Goods: The Contingent Valuation Method*.

87. Carson and Groves, "Incentive and Informational Properties of Preference Questions."

88. On the domain of preferences, see the discussion of Arrow's Possibility Theorem in Chapter 2.

89. Alan Gibbard, "Manipulation of Voting Schemes: A General Result." *Econometrica*, 41(4), 1973, 587–601; and Mark A. Satterthwaite, "Strategy-Proofness and Arrow's Conditions: Existence and Correspondence Theorems for Voting Procedures and Social Welfare Functions." *Journal of Economic Theory*, 10(2), 1975, 187–217.

90. See Kevin J. Boyle, F. Reed Johnson, Daniel W. McCollum, William H. Desvousges, Richard W. Dunford, and Sara P. Hudson, "Valuing Public Goods: Discrete versus Continuous Contingent Valuation Responses." *Land Economics*, 72(3), 1996, 381–96.

91. A number of studies have found a large divergence between WTP as expressed in contingent choice CVM and actual donations. For a review, including a discussion of using follow-up questions on the certainty of donation to adjust contingent donations, see Patricia A. Champ, Richard C. Bishop, Thomas C. Brown, and Daniel W. McCollum, "Using Donation Mechanisms to Value Nonuse Benefits from Public Goods." *Journal of Environmental Economics and Management*, 33(2), 1997, 151–62.

92. For an overview and a listing of relevant studies, see V. K. Smith, "Nonmarket Valuation of Environmental Resources: An Interpretive Appraisal." *Land Economics*, 69(1), 1993, 1–26, at 8–14, and table 1.

93. See William K. Desvousges, V. Kerry Smith, and Matthew P. McGivney, "A Comparison of Alternative Approaches for Estimating Recreation and Related Benefits of Water Quality Improvements," Report to US EPA, Research Triangle Institute, 1983; and Christine Sellar, John R. Stoll, and Jean-Paul Chavas, "Validation of Empirical Measures of Welfare Change: A Comparison of Nonmarket Techniques." *Land Economics*, 61(2), 1985, 156–75. Smith

and Desvousges, *Measuring Water Quality Benefits*, compare CVM to "simple" travel cost methods.

94. David S. Brookshire, Mark A. Thayer, William D. Schulze, and Ralph C. d'Arge, "Valuing Public Goods: A Comparison of Survey and Hedonic Approaches." *American Economic Review*, 72(1), 1982, 165–77.

95. Mark A. Thayer, "Contingent Valuation Techniques for Assessing Environmental Impacts: Further Evidence." *Journal of Environmental Economics and Management*, 8(1), 1981, 27–44.

96. Magat and Viscusi, *Informational Approaches to Regulation*, chapter 7.

97. For a review and new evidence, see Mandy Ryan, Emmanouil Mentzakis, Suthi Jareinpituk, and John Cairns, "External Validity of Contingent Valuation: Comparing Hypothetical and Actual Payments." *Health Economics* (forthcoming). See also, Glenn C. Blomquist, Karen Blumenschein, and Magnus Johannesson, "Eliciting Willingness to Pay without Bias using Follow-up Certainty Statements: Comparisons between Probably/Definitely and a 10-point Certainty Scale." *Environmental and Resource Economics*, 43(4), 2009, 473–502.

98. Coursey, Hovis, and Schulze, "The Disparity Between Willingness to Accept and Willingness to Pay Measures of Value"; Mark Dickie, Ann Fisher, and Shelby Gerking, "Market Transactions and Hypothetical Demand Data: A Comparative Study." *Journal of the American Statistical Society*, 82(398), 1987, 69–75; Craig E. Landry and John A. List, "Using Ex Ante Approaches to Obtain Signals for Value in Contingent Markets: Evidence from the Field." *American Journal of Agricultural Economics*, 89(2), 2007, 420–29.

99. John Loomis, "Test–Retest Reliability of the Contingent Valuation Method: A Comparison of General Population and Visitor Responses." *American Journal of Agricultural Economics*, 71(1), 1989, 76–84.

100. See O. Sarobidy Rakotonarivo, Marije Schaafsma, and Neal Hockley, "A Systematic Review of the Reliability and Validity of Discrete Choice Experiments in Valuing Non-Market Environmental Goods." *Journal of Environmental Management*, 183(Part 1), 2016, 98–109.

101. For a discussion of this possibility, see Douglas M. Larson, "On Measuring Existence Value." *Land Economics*, 69(3), 1993, 377–88.

102. See "Comparison Studies: What Is Accuracy," 71–109, and "reference operating conditions," table 13.1, p. 230, in "Summary and Conclusions," 205–236 in Cummings, Brookshire, and Schulze, *Valuing Environmental Goods: An Assessment of the Contingent Valuation Method.*

Case 16

Using Contingent Valuation to Estimate Benefits from Higher Education

Numerous studies have examined the benefits from and costs of higher education. The major benefit considered in these studies is the increase in earnings that results from additional education, some of which accrues to the individual and some of which accrues to the government as taxes. The major costs that are typically considered are school operating costs (which are covered by tuition, tax subsidies, and donations) and earnings forgone by students as a result of enrollment. This leaves out other potential benefits and costs, many of which occur outside the marketplace and some of which may be of considerable importance to students, other members of society, or both. These include, for example, higher education's effects on the quality of life, child rearing, economic growth, health, crime, and governance.

These sorts of benefits are obviously difficult to estimate by revealed preference methods. For this reason, a study by Glenn Blomquist and four colleagues[1] has attempted to capture them through the contingent valuation method (CVM). The study relied on a carefully designed survey to elicit the willingness of Kentucky residents to pay for a 10 percent expansion of Kentucky's Community and Technical College System (KCTCS). It used a dichotomous choice referendum format and asked the following question:

> Would you vote for the referendum to expand the Kentucky Community and Technical College System by 10% here and now if you were required to pay a one-time $T out of your own household budget?

$T refers to the amount of a one-time tax. Each respondent was asked about one, and only one, of the following values of T, which were randomly varied across respondents: $400, $250, $200, $150, $125, $100, $75, or $25. For those respondents who answered yes, follow-up questions were asked to determine how certain they were that they would actually be willing to pay the stated tax amount. Because the tax is for one time only, it would pay for only the first year of the expansion.

Focus groups were used in designing the survey. To provide context, the survey indicated the number of programs, degrees, diplomas, and certificates, and increases in staff, faculty, and structures that would result from the 10 percent expansion. In addition, questions were asked about the respondents' knowledge of and experience with KCTCS and the sorts of benefits they might receive from the 10 percent expansion. Respondents were also asked to allocate a fixed addition in the state budget among different program areas. This was included to help them think about the opportunity costs involved in the 10 percent expansion. Finally, a series of demographic questions were asked.

The survey was administered in 2007 by a professional survey firm to two samples of Kentucky residents. The larger sample was randomly selected from the telephone white pages. After attaching addresses to the telephone numbers, the survey was mailed to those selected. The response rate was 29 percent. The other much smaller sample was drawn from the Kentucky members of the survey firm's nationally representative web panel. The response rate was 74 percent. Unfortunately, about half the surveys that were returned were unusable because of a wording error in some versions of the survey. Ultimately, there were 1023 usable surveys, 914 from the mail sample and 109 from the web sample. Thus, it is uncertain whether the usable responses are representative of the state's population, although that was certainly the original intent. However, some reassurance is provided by the fact that the demographic characteristics of the high-response web-based sample and the low-response mail-based sample are similar to one another and also to those for Kentucky residents who were surveyed by the US Census Bureau.

After the surveys were returned, it was necessary to determine which respondents would actually be willing to pay the amount of the stated tax. Based on follow-up questions, only those respondents who indicated that they would definitely pay were viewed as true yeses. Both those who indicated they would not be willing to pay and those who indicated they might be willing to pay were treated as answering no. This approach was used to address non-commitment bias resulting from the fact that respondents do not have to commit real money (see Chapter 16), and was based on experiments by Blumenschein and others[2] that indicated that stated willingness-to-pay was similar to that implied by actual expenditure choices (that is, by revealed preferences) only if definite yes answers were treated as true yeses. As indicated in Chapter 16, counting all yes answers, including possible yeses, as true yeses, in contrast, caused willingness-to-pay to be overstated when compared to actual expenditure choices.

Once the survey respondents were divided into those who were and those were not willing to pay for the 10 percent KCTCS expansion, a demand curve for a 10 percent expansion of Kentucky's Community and Technical College System was estimated by using an approach similar to that described for the dichotomous choice method in Chapter 16. The researchers used parametric models to hold constant differences among the survey respondents, including variation in their demographic characteristics, income levels, and previous experience with KCTCS.[3] The key regression finding, which was highly statistically significant, was that for each tax increase of $50, the probability of voting in favor of the 10 percent expansion in KCTCS decreases by about 4 percentage points.

The resulting estimated demand curve implies that about 30 percent of the survey respondents were willing to pay for a 10 percent expansion in KCTCS for a one-time tax of $100, but only around 20 percent were willing to pay for a tax of $200. The mean WTP for the sample of survey respondents is $55.84. In contrast, when those who were definitely willing to pay and those who might be willing to pay were both treated as yeses, the estimated mean willingness was $212.21, an amount almost four times larger. This illustrates the importance of decisions on treating possible non-commitment bias in contingent valuation.

There were 1.66 million households in Kentucky in 2007, the year of the survey. If the research sample is representative of the state's population, then the estimated mean willingness-to-pay of $55.84 implies that the total willingness-to-pay for a 10 percent expansion of KCTCS on part of the state's households is $92.7 million. The researchers interpret this value as the total willingness-to-pay for benefits from KCTCS that are received from community-wide improvements such as higher productivity in the economy, better public health, less crime, improved citizenship, and possibly a more equal income distribution. They refer to such benefits as "education externalities." In addition, they suggest that for those respondents who have attended KCTCS, it may also include their own private benefits. Such benefits include private financial returns to education resulting from higher earnings and, in addition, include private non-market rewards such as human capital imparted to children, productivity in household production, and better health and quality of life.

There is always an issue of precisely what contingent valuation questions are measuring. Less than 1 percent of the respondent sample was taking KCTCS classes at the time of the survey. These persons might view themselves as potentially receiving both market and non-market benefits from an expansion. However, 27 percent had taken courses at KCTCS and 53 percent had a family member who had taken at least one course. Although these persons may well benefit from community-wide improvements resulting from a KCTCS expansion, it is not clear whether most of these persons viewed private financial and non-market benefits from the expansion as also accruing to their families, as their direct future interactions with KCTCS are likely to be limited. Interestingly, however, respondents with a family member who had attended KCTCS had a considerably higher average willingness-to-pay for the 10 percent expansion than respondents without a family member who had attended – $67.32 versus $45.13. This finding is consistent with the possibility that respondents with an attending family member did include private financial and non-market benefits received by their families in valuing the 10 percent expansion.

Exercises for Case

1. A. Why did Blomquist and his colleagues believe that contingent valuation was needed to fully assess the value of a 10 percent expansion of KCTCS?

    B. Did their findings suggest that they were correct?

2. Blomquist and his colleagues predict that willingness-to-pay for a 10 percent expansion of KCTCS would be around $92.7 million. Do you think this is a reasonable estimate? Why or why not?

Notes

1. Glenn C. Blomquist, Paul A. Coomes, Christopher Jepsen, Brandon, C. Koford, and Kenneth R. Troske, "Estimating the Social Value of Higher Education: Willingness to Pay for Community and Technical Colleges." *Journal of Benefit–Cost Analysis*, 5(1), 2014, 3–41.

2. Karen Blumenschein, Glenn C. Blomquist, Magnus Johannesson, Nancy Horn, and Patricia R. Freeman, "Eliciting Willingness to Pay without Bias: Evidence from a Field Experiment." *The Economic Journal*, 118(525), 2008, 114–37 and Karen Blumenschein, Magnus Johannesson, Glenn Blomquist, Bengt Liljas, and Richard O'Conor, "Experimental Results on Expressed Certainty and Hypothetical Bias in Contingent Valuation." *Southern Economic Journal*, 65(1), 1998, 169–77.

3. Because the dependent variable in this regression analysis had a value of either one for yeses or zero for noes, a logit regression was estimated. This regression had the following form: $\Pr(Yes) = 1/(1 + e^{(-X_i\beta)})$, where X_i includes the tax and control variables of the ith respondent and β is a vector of coefficients. As indicated in the text, these control variables included demographic characteristics, income levels, and experience with KCTCS. Mean willingness-to-pay for a 10 percent expansion in KCTCS was estimated by $-(1/b_T)\ln(1 + e^Z)$, where b_T is the coefficient on the tax variable and Z represents the collective effect of the control variables when these variables are evaluated at their means.

17 Shadow Prices from Secondary Sources

Policy analysts typically face time pressure and resource constraints. They naturally wish to do cost–benefit analysis as efficiently as possible and without getting into estimation issues beyond their competence. Anything that legitimately lowers the cost of doing CBA increases the likelihood that any particular CBA will be worth doing, because it increases the chance that a CBA of doing a CBA will be positive.

In order to evaluate existing or proposed policies and projects, analysts require credible measures of the social values of the impacts. As we saw in Chapter 3, where these impacts occur in efficient markets, their value can be estimated from changes in social surplus. Estimating social surplus requires knowledge of the appropriate demand and supply curves. When knowledge of these curves is not readily available, policy analysts have to use the methods described in earlier chapters to value impacts. However, many of these methods are expensive and time-consuming. What else could analysts do? We discuss two situations in more depth.

In the first situation, it is necessary to estimate the demand curve in order to measure consumer surplus. This is relatively easy if the analyst knows one point on the demand curve and can get an estimate of its elasticity or slope at that point. Fortunately, economists have estimated price elasticities of demand, cross-elasticities, and income elasticities for a wide range of specific goods. Peer-reviewed survey articles summarize many of these elasticity estimates.[1] Because these elasticities are based on similar observed price changes, they provide an empirically grounded basis for predicting the responses to proposed price changes. For example, how consumers responded to a price increase for water in New Mexico could be reasonably used to estimate how they will respond to a similar price increase in Arizona. In addition to previous own-price elasticity observations, estimates of cross-price elasticities, which identify changes in the demand for a good that are likely to result from changes in the prices of other goods, are also sometimes available and are frequently useful. For example, are transportation and various forms of communications (such as telecommuting and teleconferencing) complements or substitutes?[2] These cross-elasticities are important to transport planners and policy analysts who are estimating the costs and benefits of transport capital investments, assessing expected consumers' responses to price changes, or forecasting changes in demand for transportation. Existing estimates of various kinds of income elasticities can also be useful, especially when policies have strong distributional effects. Elasticity estimates are scattered widely throughout the academic literature, usually in topic-specific journals. Therefore, analysts often garner and bank them from the relevant economic and policy journals on an ongoing basis.

In the second situation, analysts need to only predict the project's impacts, which we discuss in Chapter 8, and multiply them by the appropriate market prices or shadow prices. Many CBAs involve some impacts that can be valued at current market prices and others that have to be valued using shadow prices. Transportation and infrastructure project analyses, for example, can often use market prices for construction resources (materials, land, labor, and equipment) and ongoing operational costs (labor and maintenance materials), but require shadow prices for the value of lives saved, injuries avoided, crashes avoided, time saved, air quality changes, and noise level changes, to name only a few. In order to obtain a shadow price, some (usually government) analysts may be in a position to conduct their own valuation study using one of the methods discussed in Chapters 15 or 16. However, employing any of these methods is generally time-consuming and resource-intensive. The most straightforward, least-cost approach would be to use a previously estimated shadow price that can be "plugged into" a CBA. Consequently, we refer to such estimates as *plug-ins*. Plug-ins are most common in the evaluation of transportation projects, such as construction of new roads, better road lighting, altered speed limits, or new vehicle safety features. They are also widely used now in a host of other policy arenas including criminal justice, the environment, health, education, employment training, and other social programs. More formally, using plug-ins in a CBA is a form of *benefit transfer*, sometimes called *information transfer*. The literature in this area has expanded considerably in recent years and now includes a variety of benefit transfer methods.[3] In this chapter we only consider the simple transfer of unit values of shadow prices. There are now probably thousands of estimates of unit values and we briefly survey the relevant literature and provide a "best estimate" for some shadow prices commonly used in CBAs. We discuss the value of a statistical life and the value of a life-year, the cost of various kinds of injuries, including those resulting from road crashes, the cost of crime, and the value of time (the cost of forgone time).[4] We also review estimates for impacts that are important in environmental CBAs, such as per-unit values of recreational activities, the value of nature (including specific species and habitats), the value of water and water quality, the cost of noise, the cost of air pollution and the social cost of automobile use. In order to facilitate comparability and for ease of use, we express most of the plug-in values in 2016 US dollars.

Ideally, the characteristics and preferences of the individuals in the population used to estimate a plug-in value are similar to the characteristics of the overall population where the shadow price is being applied. Also, for some plug-ins, the geographical and environmental conditions should be similar. If they are not, they should be adjusted to account for differences. When transferring plug-ins from one country to another, for example, it is important to control for differences in income levels. The final section in this chapter discusses adjusting plug-in values for use in different situations.

Most of the plug-ins discussed in this chapter estimate marginal values. For example, we provide estimates of the marginal social cost of one ton of a particular type of particulate matter pollution or the value of one additional hour saved; we do so because the marginal value is almost always the most useful value for policy purposes. However, in practice, some plug-ins are actually closer to average values. For example, the value of a life saved is the average value in a population consisting of many people with different ages, incomes, and other characteristics. Furthermore, marginal values are unlikely to remain constant as output levels change. For example, the value of time saved is likely to increase non-linearly as the time stuck in traffic increases. Similarly, the marginal cost of a unit of some pollutant is likely to increase with the level of pollution. When marginal costs are not constant over some range, it is not ideal to estimate total costs by simply multiplying the output level by a plug-in estimate of the marginal cost that assumes constancy, but it may be the best that can be done with available analytical resources.

Meta-analyses are helpful for benefit transfer efforts because they summarize large amounts of information from previous studies.[5] Although they synthesize the existing evidence about a particular topic, they do not necessarily provide a summary best estimate. Often, their primary purpose is to explain why different studies obtain different estimates.[6] Thus, they address questions such as: do certain estimation techniques provide larger estimated values than others or do valuations differ according to the characteristics of the populations or the characteristics of the good or service itself? In spite of some limitations, they can be useful when adjusting plug-in values to reflect different circumstances.

17.1   Value of a Statistical Life

Researchers have used a number of different techniques to estimate the value of a statistical life (VSL): WTP for an expected change of one mortality in a population obtained by extrapolating an estimated WTP for a small change in mortality risk. Market-based techniques observe the "price" that people are willing to pay (or accept) in order to decrease (or increase) the risk of a fatality in markets that embody this risk, while contingent valuation methods (CVMs) do so by posing hypothetical choices in surveys. The most widely used market-based techniques are those that examine how much of a wage premium people working at risky jobs must be given to compensate them for the additional fatality risk they bear. The purpose here is to discuss and summarize the empirical estimates of the VSL.

The range in the VSL has varied considerably across studies, even when outlier estimates are discarded or other methodological adjustments are made. More recent estimates of the VSL have trended higher, even after adjusting for inflation. The VSL literature is now vast, so here we only review four quite comprehensive meta-analyses. These analyses were performed by Janusz Mrozek and Laura Taylor, by W. Kip Viscusi and Joseph Aldy, by Ikuho Kochi, Bryan Hubbell, and Randal Kramer, and the most recent by W. Kip Viscusi and Clayton Masterman.[7]

17.1.1   *Mrozek and Taylor VSL Estimates*

Janusz Mrozek and Laura Taylor undertook a meta-analysis of 33 international VSL studies. The explanatory variables in their regression analyses included the study design characteristics (model equation specifications and controls for other risk factors), occupation (dummy variables for occupational attributes), and sample sociodemographic characteristics (blue-collar workers, gender, unionized environment, and actual versus perceived risk levels). They also included variables that reflected the sources of the wage and risk data. The mean VLS was roughly $8.58 million in 2016 US dollars and a regression using their full data set yielded a mean VSL of $8.03 million US dollars.

Mrozek and Taylor are skeptical of VSL estimates from labor market studies that did not control for unobservable but potentially important factors that occur at the industry level. To address this problem, Mrozek and Taylor included industry classification variables in a regression analysis in addition to the usual labor market variables. These industry variables capture the effect of interindustry wage differentials separately from the effect of occupational risks. For instance, a secretary working for an oil firm in an urban area may earn a higher wage than a secretary in the same area working for a non-profit organization, even though their job risk profiles would be very similar. Including these adjustments of studies that did not do so originally yielded a predicted VSL of $3.68 million in 2016 US dollars for the "average worker."

17.1.2   *Viscusi and Aldy VSL Estimates*

In their meta-analysis, W. Kip Viscusi and Joseph Aldy examined 49 wage–risk studies published over 30 years; more than half of the studies were specific to the US labor market. Roughly half of the US labor market studies yielded estimates of the VSL that range between $6.93 million and $16.63 million (2016 US dollars). The median value of the VSL in these studies is nearly $9.7 million.[8] Viscusi and Aldy expressed the most confidence in studies with estimates ranging from $7.4 million to $8.7 million dollars.

Viscusi and Aldy also estimated a number of meta-analysis regressions that replicated models used in previous meta-analyses. They included explanatory variables that measure whether the workplace was unionized, the level of education, income, and the mean risk in the country, the type of risk, and the type of study. They excluded studies that did not include an income measure. Their mean predicted VSL for the US population ranged between $7.6 million and $10.5 million in 2016 dollars. They also note that for most of the regression models the upper bound of the 95 percent confidence interval is roughly twice or more than that of the lower bound of the 95 percent confidence interval.

17.1.3   *Kochi, Hubbell, and Kramer VSL Estimates*

Ikuho Kochi, Bryan Hubbell, and Randall Kramer conducted a meta-analysis on a sample of 31 hedonic wage–risk studies and 14 CVM studies published between 1990 and 2002. They selected studies to minimize bias in computing the mean VSL – for example, they only included studies conducted in high-income countries, and they excluded CVM studies with samples of under 100 and hedonic wage–risk studies that were based entirely on individuals who worked in extremely risky jobs, such as policemen, because they may have risk preferences that are very unrepresentative of the general population. In addition, in computing the mean VSL, they gave greater weight to VSL estimates with greater levels of statistical significance than to other studies. Although this form of selection is common in other kinds of meta-analysis, it apparently had not been done previously in meta-analyses of VSL estimates.

After making these adjustments, Kochi, Hubbell, and Kramer computed a mean VSL of $7.6 million in 2016 US dollars, with a standard deviation of $3.3 million. They find a considerable difference between estimates produced by hedonic wage–risk studies and those resulting from contingent valuation studies, with the former having a mean value of $13.4 million and the latter having a mean value of $3.9 million.

17.1.4   *Viscusi and Masterman VSL Estimates*

Viscusi and Masterman examined both previous VSL meta-analyses and a large number of subsequent studies. They made a serious effort to correct for various potential biases in previous studies, including publication selection bias and significant coefficient bias (two biases that are obviously quite highly correlated). They used two different datasets: a meta-analysis of best estimates of the VSL from 68 studies and a meta-analysis that consisted of the full set of over 1,000 VSL estimates. They also examined various sub-sets of each. Controlling for publication selection bias, they calculate a "preferred mean VSL" of $9.7 million, which is 19 percent less than the raw mean VSL for the whole sample. The US preferred mean VSL using the Census of Fatal Occupational Injuries (CFOI) is $11.5 million, which is only 4 percent less than the overall sample raw mean. Their results yield a bias-adjusted VSL of $9.7 million for the whole sample of countries. They consistently found publication bias, but conclude that the effects of the bias on the VSL are relatively modest. They further conclude that it is feasible to use meta-regression analysis to adjust for publication selection effects, as well as for differences in econometric specification and sample composition.

17.1.5   *Reprise of Estimates of the VSL*

The meta-analyses we review did produce different VSL estimates, but reveal a generally upward trend in valuation over time after correcting for inflation. Mrozek and Taylor are lowest at between $8.03 and $8.58 million; Viscusi and Masterman produce the highest estimates with a preferred mean estimated VSL for the US population of $11.5 million and around $9.5 million for other wealthy countries.[9]

In our view, the best point estimate of the VSL for policy purposes in the US is close to the latest Viscusi and Masterman number at around $11 million, as shown in Table 17.1. The table also summarizes some other plug-in values, which are discussed below.

17.2   Value of a Life-Year

Many health interventions increase life spans by some estimated time period. Using cost–effectiveness terminology, they save life-years. In order to evaluate alternative interventions that save different life-years and cost different amounts, it is useful to have a shadow price for a life-year: the *value of a life-year*, VLY. In CBA the value of a beneficial impact accruing

Table 17.1 *Plug-in Values: VSL, VLY, Injury and Crash Costs, and Vehicle Crashes (in 2016 US dollars)*

Category	Shadow price value	Comments
Value of a statistical life (VSL)	$11 million for US	Based primarily on Viscusi and Masterman (2017). Should adjust for income and risk level
Value of a life-year (VLY)	$515,100 per person per year	Based on a VSL of $11 million, 40-year life expectancy, and a discount rate of 3.5%
Monetary injury costs		
1. Eventually fatal	1. $694,975 per injured person	Based on Rice, MacKenzie, and Associates (1989). Includes monetary costs only, not pain and suffering
2. Hospitalized (non-fatal)	2. $75,020 per injured person	
3. Not-hospitalized (non-fatal)	3. $1,131 per injured person	
4. Average cost of an injury	4. $6,086 per injured person.	
A. Motor vehicle injury	A. $19,817 per injured person	
B. Falls	B. $6,653 per injured person	
C. Firearm injuries	C. $117,909 per injured person	
D. Poisonings	D. $11,036 per injured person	
E. Fire injuries and burns	E. $5,663 per injured person	
F. Drownings and near drownings	F. $142,397 per injured person	
G. Other	G. $2,548 per injured person	
Cost of work-related occupational injuries		
A. Fatal injury	A. $4.6 million per injured worker	Based on Miller and Galbraith (1995). Includes quality-of-life losses
B. Non-fatal injury with compensable lost work	B. $2,943 per injured worker	
C. Non-fatal injury with worker non-compensable lost work	C. $1,218 per injured worker	
D. Non-fatal injury, no lost work	D. $2,274 per injured worker	
E. Average injury cost	E. $23,454 per injured worker	
F. Average motor vehicle work-related injury cost	F. $137,949 per injured worker	

(continued)

Table 17.1 (cont.)

Category	Shadow price value	Comments
Value of one year of work impairment due to injury	$178,586–$277,510 per year	Based on Dillingham, Miller, and Levy (1996)
Social cost of motor vehicle crash injuries		
1. Spinal cord	1. $3.9 million per victim	Based on Zaloshnja, Miller,
2. Brain	2. $1.56 million per victim	Romano, and Spicer (2004).
3. Lower extremity	3. $0.61 million per victim	All means are arithmetic and
4. Upper extremity	4. $0.20 million per victim	do not reflect the distribution
5. Trunk/abdomen	5. $0.38 million per victim	of injury severity within each
6. Other face, head, or neck	6. $0.51 million per victim	body region
7. Minor external	7. $0.01 million per victim	
8. Burn	8. $0.71 million per victim	
Motor vehicle accident costs		
1. PDO (Property damage only)	1. $3,511 per vehicle	Based on Blincoe et al. (2002).
2. AIS 1	2. $20,812 per injured person	Figures reflect per-person
3. AIS 2	3. $218,879 per injured person	costs related to motor vehicle
4. AIS 3	4. $435,391 per injured person	accidents of varying severity.
5. AIS 4	5. $1,013,750 per injured person	AIS, Abbreviated Injury Scale
6. AIS 5	6. $3,329,831 per injured person	
7. AIS 6 (Fatal)	7. $4,664,800 per fatality	

to a person equals that person's willingness to pay for it. Thus, the VLY could, and probably should, be estimated using contingent valuation methods. However, there are few such studies.

Usually, the VLY is derived from an estimate of the VSL. Starting with an individual's VSL, the VLY is the constant annual amount that, over that person's remaining life span, has a discounted value equal to his or her VSL. That is, the VLY is given by:

$$VLY = \frac{VSL}{A(T - a, r)}$$

(17.1)

where $A(T - a, r)$ is the annuity factor based on the expected number of remaining years of life equal to the expected age of death, T, minus the current age, a, and r is the individual's discount rate. Assume the average US person's VSL is $11 million (as indicated in Table 17.1) and has a life expectancy of 40 years. A social discount rate of 3.5 percent yields an estimate of the average VLY of $515,100. We propose this figure as an appropriate estimate of the VLY. Because it is derived from the VSL, it is sometimes referred to as an estimate of the average *value of a statistical life-year*, VSLY. It is higher than previous estimates primarily because it uses a more recent, higher real estimate of the VSL than previous studies.[10]

Rather than deriving the VSY starting with the VSL, one can calculate the VSL for a person aged a as the discounted sum of the value of the remaining life years; specifically:

$$\text{VSL}(a) = \sum_{t=0}^{T-a} \frac{\text{VLY}}{(1+r)^t}$$

(17.2)

where a is current age, T is the expected age at death, and $T - a$ is life expectancy. With VLY constant, this equation implies that VSL declines with age. VSL and VLY cannot both be constant as age increases. Indeed, one might expect the VLY to increase with age. If an individual only has a few more years to live, remaining life-years are scarcer and the person might well be willing to pay more for an additional life-year than when younger. On the other hand, one might expect VSL to decline with age because health status, which is discussed in Chapter 18, tends to worsen with age.

Reflecting these opposing forces, there is considerable discussion in the literature about whether and how the VLY (or the VSL) changes with age. The estimates from wage studies showing lower VSLs for older workers relative to middle-aged workers would more than offset the rise in the VLY as people age.[11] CVM studies suggest that parents have a higher VSL for their children than themselves;[12] one study of the valuation of morbidity (rather than mortality) suggests that parents value the welfare of small children at twice their own welfare, but that the ratio of the difference declines to one as the child approaches adulthood![13] Based on an evaluation of these various studies, one might argue that the VLY starts high, declines to age 18 then rises to middle age and then falls again with increasing age. Nonetheless, the Science Advisory Board of the US Environmental Protection Agency points out that economic theory is inconclusive about the issue, and recent reviews of the empirical literature have differed considerably in their findings and conclusions.[14]

17.3   Cost of Injuries and Crashes

Table 17.1 also summarizes five sets of estimates of the cost of injuries or the cost of crashes in the United States, again reported in 2016 dollars. The first set is based on a major report prepared for Congress by Dorothy Rice, Ellen MacKenzie, and Associates.[15] It provides detailed estimates of the monetary costs of injuries from different causes and for three levels of severity. The second set, produced by Ted Miller and Maury Galbraith, focuses on the cost of occupational injuries.[16] The third set is based on a wage–risk study carried out by Alan Dillingham, Ted Miller, and David Levy that estimated the value of an impaired work year.[17] The fourth set, produced by Eduard Zaloshnja, Ted Miller, Eduardo Romano, and Rebecca Spicer, focused on motor vehicle crash injuries.[18] The fifth set is based on a report that Lawrence Blincoe and colleagues prepared for the National Highway Safety Administration.[19] It provided unit cost estimates for seven categories of motor vehicle crashes with varying levels of personal injury to occupants.

For relatively minor accidents, the cost of a motor vehicle crash per victim is higher than the cost of a personal injury because motor vehicle crashes typically result in additional costs, particularly property damage (vehicle) costs. However, for relatively severe crashes, the cost of pain and suffering from injury is the largest component of crash costs, often greater than half the total.

17.3.1   *Rice and Colleagues' Cost of Injuries Estimates*

Dorothy Rice, Ellen MacKenzie, and their associates focused on the direct monetary cost of injuries. Their estimates incorporated medical and rehabilitation costs and forgone earnings (including an imputed value for household labor). Because these estimates focus on monetary costs, they do not include pain and suffering and other dimensions of unhappiness that people would pay to avoid. Also, these estimates did not include property damage losses and other related social costs, such as court costs. Thus, the study leads to very conservative estimates of the social cost of injuries. However, the methodology and estimates are still widely cited.

17.3.2   *Miller and Galbraith Cost of Occupational Injuries Estimates*

Ted Miller and Maury Galbraith estimated the cost of occupational injuries in the United States using a methodology similar to that of Rice, MacKenzie, and Associates. However, they included a measure of WTP to avoid the disutility associated with injury. Using incidences of injuries reported in the United States, predominantly through state worker's compensation systems, they employ a national accounting framework to estimate the cost of injury for all injuries, for fatal injuries, and for three subclasses of non-fatal injuries (compensable lost work, non-compensable lost work, and non-lost work). As the authors acknowledged, using a top-down accounting method is less accurate than using incidence-based bottom-up estimation techniques.

Their estimated costs include the costs of medical and emergency services (hospital/home care, physician services, rehabilitation services, ancillary items, police, fire/paramedic response, and emergency transportation), wage and household work (lost wages, household work, and fringe benefits), administrative and legal costs (investigation, insurance processing, record keeping, limited litigation costs), workplace disruption (overtime pay, loss of specialized skills, recruitment and training associated with long-term disability), and quality of life (reduced quality of life to workers and their families who bear the nonmonetary losses associated with injury). Quality-of-life losses account for 43 percent of workplace injury costs, and the average cost per occupational injury is $23,454 (2016 US dollars).[20]

17.3.3   *Dillingham and Colleagues' Cost of Injuries Estimates*

One problem with estimating the cost of injuries is that injuries range widely in severity, affect different parts of the body, and cause different levels of pain and disability. Alan Dillingham, Ted Miller, and David Levy attempted to measure the cost of injuries through a wage–risk study, looking at the implied WTP in order to avoid one year of impairment to an individual's work life. They estimated that individuals are willing to pay around $178,286 to $277,510 per year to avoid one year of impairment. However, there is no specific level of severity reported against which to apply this measure. One important assumption is that a work-life shortened by a fatal injury is equivalent to one that is shortened by a non-fatal but permanent total disability. A specific advantage of their estimates is that they are transferable to non-work-related injuries, allowing for the estimation of the WTP for safety improvements in other markets, such as recreational activities.

17.3.4   *Zaloshnja and Colleagues' Cost of Vehicle Crash Injuries Estimates*

Eduard Zaloshnja, Ted Miller, Eduardo Romano, and Rebecca Spicer estimated the social cost of vehicle crash injuries, updating Miller's 1993 estimates.[21] They provide a relatively comprehensive estimate of the social cost of damage to a large spectrum of body parts injured in motor vehicle crashes, such as those to the spinal cord or the brain. Their cost estimates include medical and emergency services, household and workplace productivity losses, insurance and legal costs, property damage, and quality-of-life losses. They supplemented monetary costs by the addition of the WTP to avoid pain and suffering for each type of injury.

Injuries to each body part are also broken down by level of severity, based on the most severe ("maximum") injury sustained by a person according to the Abbreviated Injury Scale (AIS), which is also sometimes referred to as the Maximum Abbreviated Injury Scale (MAIS). This scale ranges from one (minor) to six (fatal); see Table 17.2.[22] The pain and suffering or the lost quality of life for an injury of a particular level of severity is expressed as a fraction of the WTP to avoid a fatal injury, after subtracting the lost human capital.[23] The particular fractions that Miller proposed for each level of severity are also shown in Table 17.2. This approach is not ideal because the selected fractions

Table 17.2 *AIS Classification System, Including Equivalent Proportion of VSL*

AIS code	Injury severity	Fraction of VSL	Description of common injury
PDO	None	0.00	No injury
AIS 1	Minor	0.0020	Superficial abrasion or laceration of skin, sprain, first-degree burn, head trauma with headache or dizziness but no other symptoms
AIS 2	Moderate	0.0155	Significant abrasion or laceration of skin, concussion with less than 15 minutes of lost consciousness, closed fracture with or without dislocation, digit crush/amputation
AIS 3	Serious	0.0575	Major nerve injury, multiple rib fracture without chest collapse, bruise of internal organ, hand/arm or foot crush/amputation
AIS 4	Severe	0.1875	Spleen rupture, leg crush/amputation, concussion with loss of consciousness 15 minutes to 24 hours, chest wall perforation
AIS 5	Critical	0.7625	Permanent spinal cord injury, extensive burns (second or third degree), concussion with severe neurological signs
AIS 6	Fatal	1	Injuries which, if not immediately fatal, ultimately result in death

Source: Adapted from Stephan Hoffer, Frank Berardino, Jack Smith, and Stuart Rubin, *Economic Values for Evaluation of FAA Investment and Regulatory Decisions*, US DOT FAA-APO-98–8, Federal Aviation Administration, June 1998.

are somewhat arbitrary, but many regulatory bodies have adopted it.[24] Table 17.1 also presents the average cost of a motor vehicle crash injury to the spinal cord, brain, lower extremities, upper extremities, trunk/abdomen, and other head/face/neck, as well as minor external injuries, burns, and fatal injuries.

17.3.5   *Blincoe and Colleagues' Cost of Motor Vehicle Crashes Estimates*

Lawrence Blincoe and his colleagues provided fully allocated costs for motor vehicle crashes that include property damage, the costs of emergency and medical services, productivity losses, pain and suffering, and travel time delay to other motorists. They presented estimates of the cost of a crash based on the maximum AIS to an injured person. At the lowest level (property damage only, PDO), there is no personal injury, but there is property damage, insurance administrative costs, and police costs. The figures shown in Table 17.1 are per (maximally) injured person, except for PDO (property damage only) crashes, which are per vehicle.

Transportation economists often distinguish between direct costs, indirect costs, and intangible costs. Direct costs include emergency treatment, initial medical costs (including physician, hospital, prescription costs, and ancillary costs, such as administration costs of processing medical payments to providers), rehabilitation costs, long-term care costs (if required), legal costs, and employer/workplace costs. Other direct costs are property damage to vehicles, cargo, and personal property. Indirect costs include productivity losses due to temporary and permanent disability and decreases in household productivity. Intangible costs relate to pain and suffering or lost quality of life. The individual components of crash costs for each level of severity appear in Table 17.3. These components may be applicable to other settings where injuries occur at similar severity levels.

17.3.6   *Reprise of the Cost of Injuries and Vehicle Crashes*

The study by Rice and colleagues provided estimates of the monetary costs of a wide range of injuries. However, the estimates are not particularly useful as measures of social costs, especially for injuries that eventually prove fatal, as monetary costs are only a fraction of total social costs. If injury costs are underestimated, then the benefits of safety-enhancing road improvements are reduced relative to the benefits of time-saving road improvements. It may thus appear that it is better to be dead than to be stuck in traffic![25] This is usually not the case when the numbers are estimated correctly.

Both the Miller and Galbraith and the Dillingham and colleagues studies focused on the cost of work-related injuries, but using different measures. The Zaloshnja and colleagues study provides comprehensive estimates of injuries sustained in a motor vehicle crash. Blincoe and colleagues adopted a similar methodology to measure the total social cost of an accident.

Table 17.3 *The Cost of Components of Crashes by Level of Severity (2016 US dollars)*

AIS level	PDO	1	2	3	4	5	6 (Fatal)
Medical	0	3,280	21,527	64,057	180,904	458,039	30,441
Emergency	43	133	291	507	1,144	1,173	1,148
Market productivity	0	2,410	34,467	98,444	146,644	604,420	820,244
Household productivity	65	789	10,088	29,035	38,590	205,707	263,893
Insurance admin	161	1,021	9,519	26,029	44,550	93,957	51,142
Workplace costs	70	347	2,691	5,877	6,472	11,285	11,989
Legal costs	0	207	6,863	21,779	46,409	110,020	140,718
QALYs	0	6,138	125,563	176,498	528,287	1,800,474	3,291,656
Property damage	2,046	5,296	5,448	9,367	13,547	13,014	14,154
Travel delay	1,107	1,071	1,165	1,295	1,377	12,603	12,603
Total	**3,492**	**20,692**	**217,622**	**432,888**	**1,007,924**	**3,310,692**	**4,637,988**

Source: Adapted from Lawrence J. Blincoe, Angela G. Seay, Eduard Zaloshnja, Ted R. Miller, Eduardo O. Romano, Stephen Luchter, and Rebecca S. Spicer, *The Economic Impact of Motor Vehicle Crashes 2000,* National Highway Traffic Safety Administration, US Department of Transportation, May 2002, pp. 9 and 62. Available at www.nhtsa.dot.gov.

17.4   Cost of Crime

Many criminal justice and training programs have crime reduction as one of their primary goals and, therefore, benefits. In order to estimate the benefits of crime reduction, it is necessary to estimate the number of crimes of each type that will be avoided during each time period and the social cost of each type of crime. Relatively few studies, however, have examined the cost of crime from a societal perspective and most of them are now quite old. However, in 2010, Kathryn McCollister, Mark French and Hai Fang estimated the social costs of 13 major crimes.[26] They included both the tangible and intangible costs of these crimes when intangible costs are significant. Their estimates represent an important advance for two reasons: first, because a significant proportion of the costs of crimes against the person involve intangible costs, and second, because they examined several categories of crime against the person that have not been previously reported on in a systematic way.

In Table 17.4, we summarize the crime-specific estimates from McCollister and her colleagues for eight of the crime categories that they examined. We also include three earlier studies. Ted Miller, Mark Cohen, and Brian Wiersema estimated the victim costs of crime in a report prepared for the National Justice Institute. Separately, Mark Cohen estimated the cost to the criminal justice system, while Cohen and three colleagues estimated WTP to reduce crime. The earlier sets of estimates did not include prevention costs and the first and the third also did not include criminal justice system costs, except for

Table 17.4 *The Cost of Crime and the Willingness-to-Pay for Crime Reduction (2016 US dollars)*

	Shadow price value				
Crime	Victim cost per incident Based on Miller et al. (1996)	Criminal justice cost per incident Based on Cohen (1998)	Total cost per incident Sum of First Two Columns	Willingness-to-pay per incident Based on Cohen et al. (2004)	 Based on McCollister et al. (2010)
Burglary	2,481	3,596	6,077	34,844	7,391
Armed robbery	33,590	10,774	44,364	97,564	48,394
Serious assaults	42,482	7,178	49,660	323,354	122,409
Rape and sexual assaults	153,998	4,530	158,527	330,323	275,398
Murder	5,156,945	255,060	5,412,005	13,519,558	10,274,594*
Drunk driving, death	5,002,925	NA	NA	NA	NA
Drunk driving, no death	28,283	NA	NA	NA	NA
Arson resulting in death	4,309,186	NA	NA	NA	NA
Arson, no death	58,968	NA	NA	NA	24,137
Child abuse, non-fatal	93,388	NA	NA	NA	NA
Larceny (or attempt)	534	NA	NA	NA	4,040
Motor vehicle theft	NA	NA	NA	NA	12,321
Vandalism	NA	NA	NA	NA	5,559

NA, not available.

* Using the VSL of $11 million as recommended in Table 17.1 yields a VSL estimate of $12,469,942:$11 million plus tangible costs of $1,469,942.

those related to immediate police investigation. The 1996 Miller and colleagues study calculated tangible and intangible victim costs, but did not include crime career costs. Some criminal justice costs, such as immediate police and fire services costs, were included, but legal, adjudication, and corrections costs were not. Cohen and colleagues adopted a more inclusive WTP approach based on contingent valuation.

The McCollister and colleagues study adopted a cost-of-illness approach to estimate the tangible costs of crime. To measure the intangible costs of crime they follow Cohen and use jury awards data from personal injury trials to estimate the dollar value of victims' pain and suffering and psychological distress, or in the case of murder, the VSL.

17.4.1   *Miller and Colleagues' Cost of Crime Estimates*

Ted Miller, Mark Cohen, and Brian Wiersema examined the cost of crime.[27] They focused on victims' costs and ignored society's response to victimizations, including the real costs to the criminal justice system and other social costs, such as fear.

They examined the crimes of rape, robbery, child abuse/neglect, assault, driving while impaired (DWI), arson, larceny, burglary, and motor vehicle theft. They also examined the number of deaths resulting from these crimes and, if not fatal, whether there was injury. They included pain and suffering as well as direct costs. Direct costs included lost productivity, medical/emergency care, mental health care, police/fire services, social victim services, and property damage. The lost quality of life for a fatality was based on a (as we have argued above, very low) VSL of $4.3 million (2016 US dollars). For non-fatal consequences, intangible costs are based on jury awards to crime victims and burn victims. In the case of multiple incidents of crime that victimize a single individual, the estimated intangible costs of that incident are then multiplied by the average number of victimizations. They did not include criminal justice system costs and the cost of actions taken to reduce the risk of becoming a crime victim. These two categories are often two of the largest benefits of avoided crime. Other omitted impacts included expenses for processing insurance or welfare payments to totally disabled victims of crime, long-term effects on earnings resulting from psychological injury, and "second-generation costs," which are described as crimes committed by persons who themselves are victims of crime.

As is often the case in social cost estimates involving personal injury, the intangible costs are the largest component for all crime categories, except for burglary, larceny, and motor vehicle theft, where the likelihood of personal injury is low. The Miller, Cohen, and Wiersema costs are reported per criminal incident in column 1. Their estimates are similar in scale to those from other studies conducted in the past 25 years.

17.4.2   *Cohen Criminal Justice Costs' Estimates*

Mark Cohen used administrative data to estimate criminal justice-related costs. These cost estimates are based on the probability that an offender will be detected and punished.[28] As Table 17.4 indicates, at least in the case of crimes involving a high risk of injury, these cost estimates are generally much smaller than the victim-based cost of crime estimates. However, it makes sense to add these cost estimates to victim costs to get a more comprehensive estimate of the real social cost of crime. Therefore, column 3 of Table 17.4 combines the column 1 and column 2 estimates.

17.4.3   *Cohen and Colleagues' WTP Estimates for Crime Control Programs*

Mark Cohen, Roland Rust, Sara Steen, and Simon Tidd conducted a CVM study with a nationally representative sample of 1,300 households using the dichotomous choice method discussed in Chapter 16.[29] Households were asked if they would be willing to pay a particular price for a program that would reduce a particular crime (e.g., burglaries) by 10 percent. This was then converted into an estimate of total WTP using the methods described in Chapter 16. The resulting dollar figure was then multiplied by the number of households in the USA and divided by the national number of crimes of the type under consideration (e.g., burglaries) that would be prevented by a 10 percent reduction. Thus, the estimates summarized in Table 17.4 represent the total national WTP for a reduction in one crime of each type.

In principle, these estimates should incorporate any reductions in costs that respondents consider in answering the questions – potentially reductions in direct costs, pain and suffering, criminal justice system costs (if respondents considered tax savings from reduced load within the system), costs resulting from actions taken to prevent crime (e.g., time spent locking doors, purchases of alarms, and hiring more police), psychological costs resulting from worry over being a crime victim, and so forth. However, it is difficult to know what respondents actually had in mind when they responded. It should also be kept in mind that respondents probably answered on the basis of their personal judgment about the risk of being a crime victim, rather than the actual risk. For example, if they believed their risk of being murdered is larger than it really is, they may have indicated a larger WTP for a reduction in the murder rate than if they knew the real rate.

The estimates in the fourth column of Table 17.4 are markedly larger than the total cost figures shown for the same crimes in the third column. Moreover, the WTP to reduce murders is considerably larger than the point VSL estimates we earlier suggested using in a CBA. The reasons for the rather large estimates of WTP for crime reduction are not entirely clear. The contingent valuation study from which they were derived was carefully executed. One possible explanation is, as already suggested, that WTP estimates capture some costs, such as crime prevention costs, that are missed by the other cost estimates. A second possible explanation, as also previously suggested, is that individuals tend to inflate the risk of being a crime victim above the actual risk.

17.4.4   *McCollister and Colleagues' Cost of Crime Estimates*

Kathryn McCollister and her colleagues used both the cost-of-illness and the jury compensation methods to estimate the comprehensive social costs of 13 crimes. For comparison purposes, they also reviewed quite a few previous studies that attempted to adopt a societal perspective on the cost of crime. They combine the tangible and intangible cost estimates to calculate a total per-offense societal cost of crime for each crime category. They use a cost-of-illness approach to estimate the tangible costs of crime that include lost productivity for the perpetrator and short-term medical expenses, lost earnings, and property damage/loss for the victim. In order to measure the intangible costs of crime, they followed Cohen and use jury awards data from personal injury trials to estimate the dollar value of victims' pain and suffering and psychological distress. For homicide, they use the VSL.

For those serious crime categories that include a risk-of-homicide cost, their base risk-of-homicide cost was adjusted to avoid double-counting. For crimes that do not include pain-and-suffering costs nor require corrected risk-of-homicide costs, the total social cost estimate equals the tangible cost estimate. (The authors also make available Excel spreadsheets with the relevant formulas and calculations.) To be consistent with using a VSL of approximately $11 million as recommended in Table 17.1, the intangible costs estimated by McCollister and colleagues would have to be increased. This estimation can be readily carried out for murder because the intangible cost equals the VSL. Adding their estimate of the tangible costs of murder ($1,469,942 in 2016 dollars) to the recommended VSL yields a shadow price of $12,469,942.

17.4.5   *Reprise of the Cost of Crime*

As Table 17.4 shows, and not surprisingly, the cost of crime varies widely depending on the nature of the crime. It is clear, though, that crimes with high personal injury rates, especially those resulting in mortality, are much more socially costly than less-violent kinds of criminal activity. We recommend using the most recent and comprehensive study by McCollister and her colleagues as the source for estimates of shadow prices for the social cost of crime.

17.5   Value of Time

Time is a valuable and scarce commodity; as the saying goes, "time is money." Changes in travel time are an important component of many CBAs, most obviously those concerned with transportation. Although it is rarely a dominating cost or benefit category, a change in waiting time can also be an important impact of many non-transportation projects. For example, change in queuing time is an important cost or benefit component of policies that change the level of rationing of goods or that affect the level of access to services, such as changes in motor vehicle registration procedures or access to medical care and social service.

Most of the empirical literature on the opportunity cost of time has been concerned with estimating the opportunity cost or value of travel time. This is normally referred to as the *value of travel time savings* (VTTS), reflecting the fact that many government projects, especially transportation projects, expect to save travel time. The value of saving time in other kinds of activities may differ significantly from the VTTS. For example, people usually experience considerably greater disutility from waiting time than from "pure" travel time.[30] Even the value of travel time saved depends on the travel conditions themselves, for example, whether traffic has just slowed down or is stop-and-go. Often the value of time saved in these different activities or in different conditions is expressed as a multiple of the VTTS.

Time saved actually combines several related but separable dimensions of utility. To begin, one could ask why drivers slow down as traffic flow increases or density increases.[31] Presumably drivers slow down at least partly because they want to prevent or reduce the risk of an accident. Thus, one can think of increases in travel time as reducing the *ex ante* expected cost of an accident. Another way to reduce one's expected private cost of an accident is to buy a larger, sturdier car. So, the VTTS reflects not only the benefits of travel time savings but also the reduced risk of accident. It also reflects the reliability of time savings (the variance of travel time savings).[32] This is one reason why the VTTS is typically estimated to be higher during congested periods, when there is more uncertainty, than under free-flow conditions.

Several authors have reviewed the large empirical literature on VTTS, mostly on a country-specific or regional basis. Typically, these reviews have been commissioned by the governments of individual countries and have led to the adoption of a standard VTTS for use in analyses in that country.[33] In most cases, as we discuss, to simplify analysis, VTTS is expressed as a proportion of the before-tax or after-tax wage rate. This allows analysts to readily estimate travel time costs using local wage rates, although they should be adjusted for income and other factors, as we discuss near the end of this chapter.

Table 17.5 summarizes estimates of the VTTS for road transportation, based on literature reviews carried out by William Waters and by Markus von Wartburg and William Waters.[34] The opportunity cost of travel, and related time, varies considerably based on a variety of factors. Mark Wardman and J. Nicolas Ibanez have estimated how the VTTS varies with the level of congestion.[35] Abrantes and Wardman have estimated the VVTS for other modes, relative to road travel.[36] Von Wartberg and Waters estimate the value of time saved in other activities.

17.5.1   *Waters' Estimates of VTTS*

William G. Waters reviewed estimates of the VTTS from 56 empirical studies conducted between 1974 and 1990. These studies used revealed preference or CVM methods. Revealed preference studies include a wide range of situations: route choice decisions in

Table 17.5 *The Value of Travel and Waiting Time*

Category	Shadow price value	Comments
VTTS for road transportation		
1. Commuting or leisure travel time	1. 50% of the average after-tax wage rate per hour saved	Based on Waters (1996) and von Wartburg and Waters (2004).
2. Travel time paid for by employers	2. 100% of the before-tax wage rate plus benefits per hour saved	
Road transportation congestion		
1. Busy	1. 1.2	Wardman and Ibanez (2012).
2. Light congestion	2. 1.2	
3. Heavy congestion	3. 1.3	
4. Stop–start	4. 1.5	
5. Gridlock	5. 1.8	
Mode (relative to car time)		
1. Bus	1. 1.2	Abrantes and Wardman (2011).
2. Air	2. 1.8	
3. Train	3. 1.1	
Time in other activities		
1. Walking	1. 2 × VTTS	Common convention in many
2. Waiting	2. 2.5 × VTTS	jurisdictions (von Wartburg
3. Congestion	3. 2 × VTTS	and Waters, 2004).

which there are different costs (e.g., toll roads versus non-toll roads), mode choice decisions (bus or car travel versus faster but more costly airline travel), speed choice decisions (in which faster speeds involve higher operating costs), and location choice decisions (hedonic methods that isolate the impact of commuting time on land values). Survey methods have also been used to estimate VTTS because they allow researchers to gather data of direct relevance to determining WTP. As is the standard practice in the VTTS literature, Waters presented the VTTS as a percentage of the after-tax hourly wage rate, rather than as a dollar figure.

Waters found wide variation in estimates from the literature. He aggregated the 32 studies that focus on commuting trips (after eliminating some outliers) and calculated the mean value at 48 percent of the after-tax wage rate with a median of 40 percent. When he used only the 15 studies that were based on North American automobile commuting studies, Waters calculates a mean of 59 percent (54 percent with the elimination of outliers) and a median of 42 percent. The 17 non-North American auto commuting studies generated a mean of 38 percent. Waters concludes that a shadow price of between 40 and 50 percent of the after-tax wage rate is the appropriate VTTS for auto commuting.

17.5.2   *von Wartburg and Waters' VTTS and "Time in Other Activities" Estimates*

Markus von Wartburg and William Waters reviewed more recent advances in the study of the VTTS. They note that the establishment (or elimination) of toll roads is particularly useful for examining the components of VTTS (time saved and reduced variance in time saved). They report considerable heterogeneity of results depending on the parameters of the study designs. They recommend that the VTTS be set at 50 percent of the average after-tax wage rate for commuting or leisure non-work trips and that there should be no distinction based on the reason for these trips (i.e., vacation time saved and commuting time saved should be valued at the same percentage even though some people enjoy traveling in cars on their vacations).[37] The VTTS for business trips in which the time required is paid for by the employer should be valued at 100 percent of the gross (before-tax) wage plus labor-related overheads (e.g., employer-paid benefits); no other adjustments should be made for the socioeconomic characteristics of travelers. Von Wartburg and Waters also suggest that commuting and leisure travel time savings in congested traffic should be weighed at twice the uncongested (free-flow) rate.[38] Finally, they recommend a weighing factor of two times the VTTS for time spent walking and two and one-half times for waiting time.[39] The authors maintain that these multipliers are in line with convention.

17.6   Value of Recreation

The value of various kinds of recreation is important for assessing damage to rural areas, whether this damage is caused by fire or by development. The National Park Service, the Fish and Wildlife Service, the Bureau of Reclamation, and the Forest Service require this information to assess damage. This information is also helpful in assessing the benefits of new recreational opportunities and for determining whether to develop wilderness areas.

Studies that estimate the value of various kinds of recreation generally rely on either the travel cost method or the CVM method. Recreational facilities almost always provide both use benefits and non-use benefits. Within the category of use benefits, we include rivalrous consumption (such as hunting), direct non-rivalrous consumption (such as hiking), and indirect non-rivalrous consumption (such as watching a movie about hiking in the wilderness). Within the category of non-use benefits, we include pure existence value (valuing the "natural order") and altruistic existence value (such as valuing other people's use or non-use value of wilderness).

Reviews of the value of recreational activities have built upon one another over the past 20 years. In 1984, Cindy Sorg and John Loomis conducted an early review of 93 studies.[40] Richard Walsh, Donn Johnson, and John McKean updated and extended their study to incorporate studies through 1988.[41] In 2001, Randall Rosenberger and John Loomis merged the results of two further recent reviews.[42] They focused on recreational activities that are of importance to the Forest Service. Most recently, Pam Kaval and John Loomis extended the survey so that it included the 1967–2003 period and covered 1,239 observations from 593 individual studies.[43]

Kaval and Loomis report the mean net WTP for 30 separate outdoor recreation activities; their results are summarized in Table 17.6. They report their findings by "activity day," which is the typical amount of time pursuing an activity within a 24-hour period. This unit is easily converted to other visitation/participation units (e.g., recreation visitor days, trips, or seasons). Across all recreational activities, the average value of a recreational day is about $59 in 2016 dollars.

17.7   Value of Nature (Specific Species or Habitats)

As interest in the environment has increased, scientists have developed a better understanding of the relationship between the environment, human intervention, and human well-being.[44] However, valuing most environmental impacts is difficult. One reason is that most environmental areas are used for multiple purposes – commercial (e.g., timber and fish), recreation, and other purposes. Moreover, environmental areas can affect the value of neighboring areas. Consequently, there are potential problems of aggregation and double-counting.

This section focuses on valuing aspects of nature and biodiversity: the value of specific species of flora and fauna and, more broadly, of habitats and ecosystems. Studies that value elements of nature most often use the CVM method. Such studies usually incorporate both option price (e.g., for bird-watching and possibly for hunting) and existence value. The option price typically varies according to proximity. For example, Bateman and colleagues found that people living near the Norfolk Broads (a wetland site in eastern England that covers three National Nature Reserves and offers opportunities for bird-watching, sailing, and coarse fishing) were willing to pay about three times as much as people living elsewhere in the UK to preserve these recreational opportunities afforded by the Broads.[45] Some authors have conducted longitudinal studies, which are particularly useful for examining the effects of changes in urban areas on ecosystem services and the value of those services.[46]

Table 17.6 *The Value of Recreational Activities (in 2016 US dollars)*

Backpacking	64.30	Pleasure driving (including sightseeing)	73.10
Bird-watching	36.54	Rock climbing	69.43
Camping	45.89	Rock climbing	69.43
Cross-country skiing	38.73	Scuba diving	39.94
Downhill skiing	41.33	Sightseeing	45.49
Fishing	58.21	Snorkeling	37.41
Boating (non-monatized)	124.54	Snowmobiling	44.79
		Swimming	52.68
General recreation	43.32	Visiting an environmental education center	7.24
Going to the beach	48.67		
Hiking	38.06	Visiting an arboretum	16.70
Horseback riding	22.36	Visiting an aquarium	34.94
Hunting	57.90	Waterskiing	60.50
Motor boating	57.10	Wildlife viewing	52.28
Mountain biking	91.05	Windsurfing	488.07
Off-road vehicle driving	28.28	*Average value of a recreational day*	58.79
Other recreation	60.10		
Picnicking	51.16		

All figures are per activity day.
Source: Adapted from Pam Kaval and John Loomis, "Updated Outdoor Recreation Use Values with Emphasis on National Park Recreation," Final Report to National Park Service, Fort Collins, CO (Colorado State University, Department of Agricultural and Resource Economics: Fort Collins, CO, 2003).

In 1993, Johan Loomis and Douglas White surveyed the value of specific species.[47] They summarized estimates from CVM studies of 18 threatened or endangered species and performed a meta-analysis of these estimates. Respondents to the CVM questions were usually either the residents of an area in which the species was found or visitors to the area or both. Occasionally, however, a national sample was used. The estimates of the public's WTP to preserve an endangered animal species are summarized in Table 17.7. The results are presented on a per-person basis and the amounts pertain either to WTP each year or to willingness to make a single one-time payment. When more than one estimate is available for a single species, the amounts are averaged.

Paulo Nunes and Jeroen van den Bergh also surveyed various measures of biodiversity.[48] As shown in Table 17.7, they find that the existence value of different habitats ranges from $11 to $136 per household per year in 2016 US dollars.

Table 17.7 *The Value of Species, Habitats and Water (in 2016 US dollars)*

Category	Shadow price value	Comments
Specific species		
Annual WTP		
Northern spotted owls	116 per person	Updated from Loomis and White
Grizzly bears	76 per person	(1996)
Whooping cranes	58 per person	
Red-cockaded woodpeckers	22 per person	
Sea otters	48 per person	
Gray whales	43 per person	
Bald eagles	40 per person	
Bighorn sheep	35 per person	
Sea turtles	22 per person	
Squawfish	13 per person	
Striped shiner	10 per person	
Pacific salmon/steelhead	105 per person	
Atlantic salmon	13 per person	
One-time lump sum		
Bald eagle	359 per person	
Humpback whale	287 per person	
Monk seal	199 per person	
Grey wolf	111 per person	
Arctic graying/Cutthroat trout	25 per person	
Existence value of habitats		
Terrestrial	36–136 per household per year	Updated from Nunes and van den
Coastal	12–69 per household per year	Bergh (2001)
Wetland	11–129 per household per year	
Wetland habitats		
Overall	4,410 (236) per hectare per year	Updated from Brander, Florax, and
Woodland	5,040 (315) per hectare per year	Vermaat (2006). Mean values with
Freshwater marsh	5,512 (189) per hectare per year	median values in parentheses
Salt/brackish marsh	4,095 (268) per hectare per year	
Unvegetated sediment	14,174 (551) per hectare per year	
Mangrove	630 (126) per hectare per year	
Water quality improvements		
1. From unusable to boatable	1. 11–79 per year per household	Updated from Luken, Johnson, and
2. From boatable to rough fishing	2. 17–68 per year per household	Kibler (1992)
3. From rough fishing to game fishing	3. 23–56 per year per household	

(continued)

Table 17.7 (cont.)

Category	Shadow price value	Comments
4. From game fishing to superior game fishing	4. 27–47 per year per household	
5. From unusable to superior game fishing	5. 56–203 per year per household	
Water values by use		
Waste disposal	5 (2) per acre-foot	Updated from Frederick, van
Recreation/fish and wildlife	74 (8) per acre-foot	den Berg, and Hanson (1996).
Navigation	225 (15) per acre-foot	Mean values with median values
Hydropower	39 (32) per acre-foot	in parentheses.
Irrigation	116 (62) per acre-foot	
Industrial processing	434 (203) per acre-foot	
Thermoelectric power	52 (45) per acre-foot	
Domestic	320 (149) per acre-foot	

Luke Brander, Raymond Florax, and Jan Vermaat conducted a meta-analysis of 190 studies of the value of wetlands that provided 215 value observations.[49] The studies were from 25 countries, but a little over a half of these studies valued wetlands in North America. A wide variety of methods were used to value wetlands, including the travel cost method, hedonic pricing, and the replacement cost method; but the most important were market prices, which account for nearly 40 percent of the value observations, and CVM, which account for 16 percent. The market price approach simply computed the total revenue obtained from the wetland being valued. Consequently, it ignores the costs of producing the goods and services derived from the wetland and, unlike the CVM studies, misses any non-use value.

17.8   Value of Water and Water Quality

Fresh water is an increasingly scarce necessity. As there generally is no well-functioning market for fresh water in most locations, analysts have to estimate its shadow price. CVM surveys, the market analogy method, the intermediate good method, defensive expenditures, and the travel cost method have all been used to estimate the value of water of different quality levels or the benefits of improvements in water quality for various purposes.[50] Analysts have developed a composite Water Quality Index (WQI) to convey information on water quality on a scale that ranges from 0 to 100. The EPA has used the WQI in a number of RIAs and it is now used by both states and countries and in CVM surveys.[51] Some authors use a three- or five-level water quality ladder (WQL).

The fourth section in Table 17.7 summarizes annual household WTP amounts for water quality improvements for recreational purposes by Ralph Luken, Reed Johnson, and Virginia Kibler.[52] These authors drew on previous studies of the Monongahela River, near Pittsburgh. Luken, Johnson, and Kibler argue for distances of 30 miles as an upper bound in defining the relevant markets for such recreational sites. They also recommend using visitation rates for households within this distance that range from 50 percent for sites with few substitutes to 10 percent for sites with numerous substitutes.

Exhibit 17.1

Ralph Luken wished to estimate the costs and benefits of (technology-based) water pollution standards introduced by the Clean Water Act of 1972. However, there were no existing estimates of WTP for improvements in the water quality of the rivers in question. Therefore, he utilized WTP estimates from existing studies as a basis for his estimates of the value of improvements in water quality.

He initially considered eight existing studies that might provide plug-in values. Five of the existing studies used the contingent valuation method, two studies used the travel cost method, and the eighth study was a user participation study. Luken eliminated five of the studies because their sites were not similar to those he was considering. These five studies dealt with such water systems as those on a large western lake and a western river basin. His sites, in contrast, were generally eastern rivers with local recreation usage. Therefore, he focused on three studies: one on the Charles River in Boston and two on the Monongahela River in Pennsylvania. The Monongahela studies estimated benefits for three levels of improvement in water quality using a three-level WQL (from boating to fishing, from fishing to swimming, and from boating to swimming), whereas the Charles River study only examined improvements in water quality from boating to swimming (i.e., the biggest "jump" in quality). The values as annual WTP per household (2016 dollars) are summarized below:

	Water quality change		
River	Boat–Fish	Fish–Swim	Boat–Swim
Monongahela (contingent valuation)	$58–92	$32–53	$92–148
Monongahela (travel cost)	$18	$23	$42
Charles (contingent valuation)	–	–	$171

Unfortunately, these benefit categories did not directly map into the WQL Luken was using, which covered five quality improvement levels: U, Unusable; B, Boatable; R, Rough fishing; G, Game fishing; and G^*, Superior game fishing. Luken assumed that the travel cost method provided lower-bound estimates (because they include only use valuations) and the contingent valuation estimates provided upper-bound estimates (as they include non-use as well as use valuations). As shown next, he also included estimates to reflect smaller benefit quality benefits (WTP per household per year improvements). His plug-in values for water quality benefits (WTP per household per year in 2016 dollars) follow:

Initial water quality	Final water quality	Lower bound	Upper bound
U	U	$2–7	$21–42
U	B	$12	$81
U	R	$35	$115
U	G	$46	$185
U	G*	$58	$208
B	B	$5–9	$18–35
B	R	$18	$69
B	G	$35	$115
B	G*	$46	$139
R	R	$7–12	$14–30
R	G	$23	$58
R	G*	$35	$81
G	G	$7–14	$12–23
G	G*	$28	$46

Although the purpose of this exhibit is to illustrate the use of secondary sources, it is interesting to note that in using these values, Luken generally found that costs exceed benefits.

Sources: Adapted from Frederick W. Gramlich, "The Demand for Clear Water: The Case of the Charles River," *National Tax Journal*, 30(2), 1977, 183–95; Ralph A. Luken, *Efficiency in Environmental Regulation* (Boston, MA: Kluwer Academic Publishers, 1990), 45–50, 88–90; V. Kerry Smith and William H. Desvousges, *Measuring Water Quality Benefits* (Boston, MA: Kluwer-Nijhoff Publishing, 1986); V. Kerry Smith, William H. Desvousges, and Ann Fisher, "A Comparison of Direct and Indirect Methods for Estimating Environmental Benefits," Working Paper No. 83–W32, Vanderbilt University, Nashville, TN, 1984.

Kenneth Frederick, Tim van den Berg, and Jean Hanson summarize for different uses of water based on a survey of 41 earlier studies.[53] The authors provide estimates of the cost of water in eight uses: waste disposal, recreation/fish and wildlife habitat, navigation, hydropower, irrigation, industrial processing, thermoelectric power generation, and domestic uses. Values are expressed in terms of dollars per acre-foot (one acre-foot equals 325,851 gallons, the volume of water required to cover one acre at a depth of one foot).

Water used for industrial processing and domestic use has the highest mean and median values. However, recreation/fish and wildlife habitat and irrigation account for nearly 80 percent of all the estimates and the highest values of any individual studies. We report both the median and mean values in Table 17.7 due to a lack of weighting in the final estimates. The authors point out that median values may be most applicable to national level assessment and likely reflect normal hydrologic conditions.

The authors note several caveats. Water quality is important in most uses, but this factor is not reflected in the estimates. The timing of rainfall and levels of the water table play a large role in the cost of water, and values vary among regions (as water value is inversely related to availability). They also note that supply and demand conditions change over time (due to seasonal variation, technological changes, and weather conditions), thereby affecting the value of water.

17.9   Cost of Noise

The cost of noise is mostly relevant in the evaluation of road and air transportation projects. The dominant method for estimating the cost of noise is the hedonic pricing method. As discussed in Chapter 15, property values (usually those of private residences) are statistically related to noise. The hedonic method considers variables such as the structural characteristics of the houses (numbers of rooms, square footage), neighborhood characteristics (number of lots or broken windows per block), accessibility characteristics (to downtown or local waterfront) and environmental characteristics. In many circumstances, the level of air pollution is the most important environmental factor. It is especially important to control statistically for air quality because it tends to be quite highly correlated with noise pollution from automobiles.

The US Federal Aviation Agency developed a measure of the level of noise called the Noise Exposure Forecast (NEF) that has been widely used. One NEF is equal to a mean exposure over time to one decibel of noise. Ambient noise is in the 15–25 NEF range, "some" to "much" annoyance occurs in the 25–40 NEF range, and "considerable" annoyance occurs above 40 NEFs. Other commonly used noise measures are the Noise and Number Index (NNI), which is specifically designed to measure aircraft noise, and the Traffic Noise Index (TNI), which measures motor vehicle noise.

The sensitivity of house and other forms of accommodation prices to changes in the noise level is measured by the noise depreciation sensitivity index (NDSI), which is also called the noise sensitivity depreciation index (NSDI) or simply the noise depreciation index (NDI). The NDI represents the percentage reduction in the value of a house that results from a unit increase in the noise level, measured in NEFs.[54] One way to obtain the NDI is to specify a hedonic price function in which the logarithmic price of a house is a linear function of noise and various control variables. The NDI equals the slope of this function with respect to noise multiplied by −100.[55]

In this section, we focus on two reviews of the literature on the empirical cost of noise. Ian Bateman, Brett Day, Ian Lake, and Andrew Lovett reviewed the "noise" studies published between 1970 and approximately the year 2000.[56] Jon Nelson has carried out a more recent meta-analysis of North American airport cost of noise studies.

17.9.1   *Bateman and Colleagues' Estimates of the Cost of Noise*

Perhaps somewhat surprisingly, Ian Bateman and his colleagues found that estimates of the NDI have remained fairly stable over three decades. As Table 17.8 shows, noise pollution has two primary sources – air traffic and road traffic. The best estimate of the NDI for air traffic noise in the US is 0.65 percent.[57] Recall that the NDI measures the percentage change in house prices for a change in ambient noise level of one NEF. In other words, if the noise level increases by one NEF, then the price of an affected house will decreases in value by 0.0065 on average. Thus, houses adjacent to an airport with NEFs of 40 are priced 9.75 percent lower than houses farther from the airport with NEFs of 25. For roadway noise pollution, Bateman and his colleagues suggested that the NDI is 0.64 percent. Becker and Lavee estimated it as a considerably higher 1.2 percent based on Israeli property value evidence.

17.9.2   *Nelson Estimates of the Cost of Noise*

In 2004, Jon Nelson performed a meta-analysis of hedonic pricing studies of airports that produced very similar estimates and similar ranges. Based on a meta-analysis of 20 previous studies containing 33 estimates, Nelson concluded that house prices in North America fall by approximately 0.005–0.006% in response to an increase in aircraft noise of one decibel with a mean value of 0.0058. Nelson notes that high levels of airport noise (above 65 decibels) have fallen substantially because of changes in aircraft engine technology.

The estimated NDIs discussed thus far are mostly for detached houses. Dean Uyeno, Stan Hamilton, and Andrew Biggs have noted that the NDI is likely to differ according to land use.[58] They estimated a hedonic price function where the logarithm of the price of a house is a linear function of noise (in NEFs) and other house quality characteristics. Using Canadian data, they estimated that the appropriate NDI is 0.65 percent for detached houses with NEFs of 25 or higher, but 0.90 percent for condominiums.

Table 17.8 *The Cost of Noise Pollution*

Plug-in category	Shadow price value	Comments
Cost of noise		
Airline noise pollution	0.65 percent reduction in property value per NEF	Based on Schipper (1996), Bateman, Day, Lake, and
Roadway noise pollution	0.64–1.2 percent reduction in property value per NEF	Lovett (2001), Nelson (2004) and Becker and Lavee (2003)
Cost of noise		
Residential properties	0.65 percent reduction in value per NEF	Based on Uyeno, Hamilton,
Condominiums	0.90 percent reduction in value per NEF	and Biggs (1993)
Vacant land	1.66 percent reduction in value per NEF	

17.10 Cost of Air Pollution

Air pollution can result in both health and non-health costs. Health costs include the costs of premature death and the costs of morbidity (illness).[59] Non-health costs include environmental costs, such as those associated with rising sea levels, coastal erosion, river floods, deforestation, retarded plant growth, and reduced agricultural output. Other non-health costs include corrosion to buildings, cars, and materials (such as rubber), as well as loss of views.

Air pollutants are emitted from many sources, especially from motor vehicles, industrial plants, and power plants.[60] Important pollutants are volatile organic compounds (VOCs), nitrogen oxides (NO_x), sulfur oxides (SO_x), carbon oxides (CO_x), and particulate matter of less than 10 microns in diameter (PM_{10}). VOCs combine with NO_x to produce ozone, which is a primary contributor to morbidity. Through chemical reactions SO_x, VOCs, and NO_x produce a particular type of particulate matter, PM_{10}, which causes both premature death and morbidity, especially respiratory diseases. The solution of SO_x and NO_x in cloud and rain droplets causes acid rain, which is known to damage pine and spruce forests and is thought to damage tobacco, wheat, and soya crops. Acid rain also damages buildings, increases the acidification of lakes, and affects fish populations.[61] The accumulation of greenhouse gas emissions, especially, carbon dioxide (CO_2), causes global warming.[62]

Analysts estimate the cost of pollution using two main approaches. One is the hedonic property value method.[63] The more widely used approach is called the *dose response function* or *damage function* approach. A dose response function (or damage function) relates unit increases in a pollutant to various health effects, such as the probability of premature death and increases in different types of important effects such as on visibility, materials deterioration, damage to the natural environment, and health. For example, in the case of health, an increase in a ton of particulate matter might be related to the increased probability of premature death and increases in different types of respiratory problems. These effects would then be weighted by dollar valuations of these effects, which themselves would usually be based on CVM estimates of WTP.

H. Scott Matthews and Lester Lave derived estimates of the cost of key air pollutants based on a number of damage function studies that were conducted in the early and mid-1990s.[64] Table 17.9 summarizes these estimates with the cost figures updated to 2016 dollars. It shows the costs resulting from a one-ton increase in each pollutant. As indicated by the wide ranges between the minimum and maximum values, there is still a great deal of uncertainty related to the actual costs associated with various types of air pollution. As Matthews and Lave point out, much of this uncertainty relates to the damage functions used to obtain the values. For example, it is difficult to isolate the extent to which premature death results from a one-ton increase in particulate matter from increases in premature death due to other pollutants. The wide range of values also occurs because air pollution varies considerably across areas and time. In addition, some studies only consider health effects, while others also incorporate other effects, such as

Table 17.9 *The Social Cost of One Ton of Air Pollutants (in 2016 US dollars)*

Category	Number of studies	Minimum cost	Median cost	Mean cost	Maximum cost
Carbon monoxide (CO)	2	2	890	890	1,796
Nitrogen oxides (NO$_x$)	9	376	1,813	4,790	6,251
Sulfur dioxide (SO$_2$)	10	1,317	3,079	3,421	8,040
Particulate matter (PM$_{10}$)	12	1,625	4,790	7,356	7,713
Volatile organic compound (VOC)	5	274	2,395	2,737	7,527
Global warming potential (in CO$_2$ equiv.)	4	3	24	22	39

Source: Updated from table 1 of Matthews and Lave (2000).

visibility and the natural environment. According to Matthews and Lave, monetization plays a comparatively minor role.

Probably the most important aggregate air pollution cost is the cost of carbon, the major source of global warming. In view of its importance, it is not surprising that there has been considerable effort in recent years to estimate the social cost of carbon emissions. Richard Tol conducted a meta-analysis of 211 estimates of the social cost of carbon from 47 different studies and found that, for peer-reviewed estimates that were based on a 3 percent discount rate, the mean social cost per ton of carbon is $39 in 2016 US dollars, with a median of $31 per ton.[65] After reviewing previous studies and considerable analysis of his own, David Pearce concluded that the marginal social cost of carbon is between $11 and $72 per ton of carbon.[66] Finally, in a less-formal examination of the literature, Ian Parry, Margaret Walls, and Winston Harrington settle on a value of $25 per ton of carbon.[67] They also point out that the social cost of carbon emissions is likely to rise in the future because of growth in the value of world output and because marginal damage will increase as temperature levels rise.

All of the estimates of the current social cost of carbon emissions that appear above, including the mean estimate provided by Mathews and Lave, are roughly of the same magnitude. However, the well-known *Stern Review* contains a much larger estimate of over $300 per ton, which would be equivalent to around $350 in 2016 dollars.[68] William Nordhaus suggests that the major reason for this high estimate is that carbon dioxide emissions have an expected atmospheric life of 100 years or so and, hence, estimates of the cost of emissions are very sensitive to the assumed discount rate.[69] The estimate in the *Stern Review* is based on a low social discount rate of 1 percent, while Chapter 10 of this book, in contrast, suggests a rate of 3.5 percent (and Nordhaus prefers an even higher rate). In addition, the *Stern Review* assumes that the damage of a current emission of carbon will continue into perpetuity. The fairly wide range for the cost of carbon emissions suggested by Pearce is also largely (although not entirely) attributable to discount rate assumptions, with the lower end of the range based on a constant discount rate and the upper end resulting from the use of a time-declining discount rate.

The US Environmental Protection Agency provides estimates of the social cost of carbon and related pollutants.[70] Taking account of larger future marginal costs, it estimates the social cost per metric ton through 2050. Using a 3 percent discount rate, its point estimates in 2016 dollars for 2020 and 2050, respectively, are $50 and $82 per metric ton of carbon dioxide and $1,431 and $2,982 per metric ton of methane, a powerful greenhouse gas.

17.11   Social Costs of Automobiles

Ian Parry, Margaret Walls, and Winston Harrington reviewed numerous studies that estimate negative externalities resulting from the operation of automobiles. Based on this review, they presented "very tentative" assessment of social costs resulting from each mile traveled by lightweight vehicles in the United States.[71] These estimates are shown in Table 17.10.[72] Perhaps surprisingly, the largest item in the table, at approximately 6 cents per mile, is costs that result from congestion, much of which is attributable to wasted time. The second largest item at approximately 4 cents per mile is the cost resulting from accidents. These costs include injuries and property damage, but exclude injuries to the driver and other passengers. Travelers are assumed to internalize these costs because engaging in driving is a voluntary activity. Interestingly, Parry, Walls, and Harrington estimated that the costs associated with global warming that result from driving a mile is less than a penny. This is because a gallon of gasoline contains 0.0024 tons of carbon and they assume that an automobile can drive 21 miles with each gallon, which was the national average at the time of their study. Thus, given their conclusion that the social cost of one ton of carbon is $25, the cost per mile driven works out to 0.28 cents (($0.0024 \times $25)/21) in 2016 dollars. Of course, there are many automobiles in the United States and many of them travel a substantial number of miles each year. Parry, Walls, and Harrington point out that, in aggregate, light-duty vehicles account for about 20 percent of carbon dioxide emissions in the United States.

Table 17.10 *The Social Cost of Automobiles (in 2016 US dollars)*

Plug-in category	Shadow price value (cents per mile)
Greenhouse warming	0.4
Local pollution	2.5
Oil dependency	0.7
Congestion	6.1
Accidents	3.7
SUM	13.4

Source: Adapted from table 2 of Parry, Walls, and Harrington (2007)

17.12 Benefit Transfer

The main premise of this chapter is that analysts or students want to conduct a CBA but will not conduct their own study (or studies) to estimate the shadow prices of all impacts. Instead, they will plug-in an estimate based on previous research. The use of previously estimated shadow prices (of benefits or costs) in the evaluation of new policies, often conducted in different situations, is called *benefit transfer*. Unless one is valuing the benefits of a policy through CVM, all *ex ante* CBAs require benefit transfer for impacts that cannot be appropriately valued with market prices.

Some researchers might begin with the shadow prices recommended in this chapter. However, these estimates are, for the most part, based on US research and, when applied to individuals, they pertain to the average person. When analysts evaluate policies in other countries or projects that affect individuals or groups with different characteristics or tastes, the appropriateness of these estimates comes into question. Shadow prices should be adjusted to reflect the situation and the characteristics of those affected, relative to those upon whom the values were based.[73] Here, we briefly review four sets of factors that one might consider as a basis for adjusting shadow price estimates: (1) differences in socioeconomic and other personal characteristics of the population (e.g., income and age), (2) differences in physical and other characteristics of the jurisdiction (e.g., geographic or climatic characteristics), (3) differences in the characteristics of the project itself (e.g., project quality), and (4) temporal changes.

17.12.1 *Income, Tastes, and Other Socioeconomic Factors*

It is often important to make adjustments because of socioeconomic differences or preference differences among different populations. Perhaps the most important variable that affects WTP is income, which varies across countries and within a country. The willingness to pay for most of the "goods" discussed here, including reductions in mortality risk, time saved, recreation consumed, and environment quality improved, are likely to increase as income increases. Thus, the shadow prices of these goods will be higher in rich countries than in poor countries.

Preferences may also differ from one region to another or from one group to another. People who live near airports may object less than others to aircraft noise; people who live in polluted areas may not value changes in air quality as much as people who live in areas with better air quality; and people who work in dangerous jobs may have greater propensity for risk than the average person. Such differences in preferences affect how much different people are willing to pay for particular policy effects.

Adjusting the VSL for Income and Other Factors. Intuition and empirical analyses suggest that the VSL rises with income: people are willing to pay more to reduce fatality risk as their income rises. The relationship is summarized by the income elasticity of the VSL, E_I, which, for discrete changes in income, is given by:

$$E_I = \frac{\% \Delta \text{VSL}}{\% \Delta I}$$

(17.3)

where %ΔVSL represents the percentage change in VSL and %Δ*I* represents the percentage change in income. This elasticity is called the income elasticity of willingness to pay to reduce mortality risk. It shows how the percentage of income a person is willing to pay to reduce fatality risk varies as income varies. An elasticity less than one (greater than one) implies that as income increases, WTP for a small reduction in fatality risk grows slower (faster) than income and, therefore, individuals are willing to spend a lower (larger) proportion of their income on a risk in fatality risk.

Equation (17.3) provides one possible way to adjust average US estimates of the VSL (or VLY) before they are applied to countries with different levels of income or to groups with incomes higher or lower than average. Let VSL_{US} and VSL_A denote the VSL in the US and in country A, respectively, and let I_{US} and I_A denote the average income in the US and in country A, respectively. Then, we can use the following expression to convert a VSL based on US data to an appropriate figure for country A (in US dollars):[74]

$$VSL_A = VSL_{US} + E_I VSL_{US} (I_A - I_{US})/ I_{US} \tag{17.4}$$

This formulation assumes that the income elasticity of the VSL varies with income; that is, application of Equation (17.3) depends on the initial income. Suppose, instead, that the income elasticity of WTP is constant with respect to income and, for example, $VSL_{US} = \beta_0 I_{US}^{E_I}$ and VSL_A is given by a similar formula. Taking the ratio of the latter to the former yields the following alternative formula for the VSL in a different country:

$$VSL_A = VSL_{US} \left(\frac{I_A}{I_{US}} \right)^{E_I} \tag{17.5}$$

If E_I equals 1, then Equations (17.4) and (17.5) result in the same VSL for country A. If E_I is less (more) than 1, then the non-constant income elasticity formula, Equation (17.4), yields higher (lower) estimates for the VSL in low-income countries than the constant income elasticity formula, Equation (17.5).

The key parameter in both formulas is E_I. There is general agreement that E_I is positive. An important issue is whether it is smaller than, greater than, or equal to 1. Most people would agree that the ordinary income elasticity of demand, which reflects how the *quantity* of mortality risk experienced by an individual changes as income changes, would be greater than one. However, it does not follow that the income elasticity of the WTP is greater than one. Indeed, Nicholas Flores and Richard Carson show that while these two elasticities are related, knowledge of one is insufficient to determine the magnitude or even the sign of the other.[75] A rich person might buy proportionately more safety (have lower fatality risk) than a poorer person, but this does not imply that he is willing to pay proportionately more for a reduction in fatality risk from their respective current levels of fatality risk.[76]

James Hammitt and Lisa Robinson reviewed several CVM studies and meta-analyses and find that estimates of the elasticity of the VSL vary widely and many are less than 1.0.[77] However, most of these studies were conducted in predominately high-income countries and Hammitt and Robinson argue that when they are applied to countries with very low incomes lead to implausibly large VSL estimates. Hammitt and Robinson argue for higher estimates and, in their examples, they use income elasticity estimates of 1.0, 1.5, and 2.0. In the illustrations that follow, we put more weight on Kip Viscusi and Joseph Aldy's meta-analysis than on Hammitt and Robinson and use a central estimate of 0.8, with a range between 0.4 and 1.5.[78] We also present the results for the elasticity equal to 1.

To illustrate how to compute the VSL for another country, consider Canada. Adjusting for purchasing power, Canadian incomes (measured by GDP per capita) have been approximately 82 percent of US incomes over the past 20 years.[79] Therefore, we set $I_{CAN}/I_{US} = 0.82$, and $(I_{CAN} - I_{US})/I_{US} = -0.18$. If the VSL in the United States equals $11 million, then the VSL in Canada equals $9 million (in US $) if the income elasticity equals 1. From Equation (17.4), the VSL in Canada (in US dollars) equals $10.2 million, $9.4 million, or $8.0 million, assuming the income elasticity equals 0.4, 0.8, and 1.5, respectively. If the analyst wants the VSL in Canadian dollars, she would multiply the above estimates by the appropriate exchange rate. For example, in 2016, a US dollar was worth 1.3255 Canadian dollars on average.[80] Therefore, the VSL in Canada in 2016 Canadian dollars equals $15.5 million, $12.5 million, and $10.6 million for income elasticities of 0.4, 0.8, and 1.5, respectively. Using the constant elasticity formula (Equation (17.5)) and converting the resultant estimates to Canadian dollars, the VSL in 2016 Canadian dollars equals $13.5 million, $12.4 million, and $10.8 million for income elasticities of 0.4, 0.8, and 1.5, respectively.[81] Thus, for Canada, there are relatively small differences between the VSL estimates derived using Equations (17.4) and (17.5).

According to the World Bank, GDP per capita equalled $56,116 in the United States in 2015, and $14,451 in China in 2015, the most recent years for which data are available.[82] If the income elasticity equals 1.0, then the estimated VSL in China equals $2.83 million US dollars. It is important to emphasize that this estimate does not suggest that the life of a Chinese person is worth less than that of a US person, but because incomes are so much lower in China, the average Chinese person is willing to pay less in order to reduce fatality risk.

If the income elasticity equals 1.4 or higher, the estimated VSL is negative using Equation (17.4). Therefore, in order to compute the VSL in countries with significantly lower average incomes, it would be more appropriate to use Equation (17.5) with constant elasticity than Equation (17.4). Using this equation yields a "best" estimate of the VSL in China of $3.7 million with an income elasticity of 0.8 with a range between $6.4 million and $1.4 million, corresponding to income elasticities of 0.4 and 1.5.[83]

Social policies often aim at improving the lives of those with low incomes. For example, consider a program aimed at providing health care that improves the quality of life of the homeless. Valuing changes in life quality using the general population VLY would provide implausible magnitudes of benefits. However, if analysts know the earnings of the participants, they can use Equations (17.4) or (17.5) to adjust the VLY. If the participants do not have earnings, then one might impute an income from their likely consumption.[84] The imputation might also take account of the fact that, on average, the homeless have higher mortality risk than the general population.

In theory, the WTP to reduce fatality risk declines as the risk level decreases. Put another way, the WTP increases as the risk level increases, consistent with the idea that one is willing to pay more for a "good" (safety) as it becomes scarcer. Therefore, the VSL should be positively correlated with the level of fatality risk. For example, two countries with comparable wealth may have different base levels of mortality risk because the geography of one of them makes it more susceptible to infectious diseases. Consequently, the VSL would be higher in the more infection-prone country. However, there are at least two problems with adjusting the VSL for the level of fatality risk. First, the appropriate size of the adjustment is unclear. Second, contrary to theory, some studies have found that empirical estimates of the VSL decline as fatality risk increases.[85] More research is needed before adjusting the VSL for the level of fatality risk.

WTP to reduce fatality risk might also vary with an individual's sense of control. M. W. Jones-Lee and colleagues found that the average WTP to reduce death on the London underground is 50 percent higher than on roads.[86] This difference may be due to many factors, including incorrect estimation of the risks, loss of a sense of control, or the method of death (people may think that dying in an underground crash is more traumatic than dying in a car crash). The loss of sense of control may be associated with the feeling that when one gives up control to a train driver or pilot, then that person may not fully internalize the externality associated with one's own death.

Ideally, when estimates of the VSL are applied to other countries or circumstances, they should be adjusted for factors that affect utility like age, attitudes, or culture, not just income. However, it is often impractical to make adjustments for such factors.

Adjusting the VTTS for Income and Other Factors. W. G. Waters examined how estimates of the VTTS vary with income, time (year of study), country, and trip purpose (interurban versus commuting or "other").[87] He finds that VTTS increases with income, but less than proportionately:

$$\text{VTTS}_Y = \left(\frac{Y}{\overline{Y}}\right)^{0.5} \overline{\text{VTTS}}$$

$$(17.6)$$

where VTTS_Y is the VTTS of a traveler with income Y, $\overline{Y}$ is the average income level, and $\overline{\text{VTTS}}$ is the average VTTS. He suggests that a convenient rule of thumb for the relationship is a square root rule. For example, if income goes up fourfold from the average, the VTTS doubles. Using such a rule, the VTTS rises more slowly than does income; it is a normal good, but not a luxury good. Subsequently, von Wartburg and Waters suggested using an income elasticity of 0.75; that is, the exponent in Equation (17.6) would be 0.75, rather than 0.5.[88]

The relationship between VTTS and other variables appears to be weak. Waters found that VTTS increases over time (drifting upward at one percentage point per year) and that interurban travel has a slightly higher value than trips for other purposes. Von Wartburg and Waters suggest using a positive distance elasticity of 0.3.

17.12.2   *Physical and Other Regional Characteristics*

The second set of factors that may affect the transferability of shadow prices are the physical and other characteristics of a region. For example, the impact of air pollution varies widely geographically, depending on population density, climate, and topography. More people are affected in more densely populated areas. Other things held constant, greater precipitation in Vancouver than in Los Angeles means that the morbidity costs of NO_x or particulate matter are lower there.

17.12.3   *Project Differences*

The third set of factors pertains to the similarity between the policy under evaluation and the projects in the studies used to derive the plug-in values. For example, the value of water quality improvement obtained from studies involving small improvements in quality levels may not apply to a proposed policy that would involve a large change in the level of water quality. The magnitude of the error in the generalization depends on the degree of non-linearity in the relationship between water quality improvements and WTP. Additionally, there may be important differences in the price and availability of substitutes which, if not accounted for, can cause biases.[89] In sum, policies or projects under evaluation should ideally be similar to the projects in the studies used to derive the plug-in values in terms of the availability and quality of alternatives.

17.12.4   *Temporal Changes*

The final set of factors arises because valuations may change over time. For example, health costs per vehicle mile traveled are declining over time as heavily polluting vehicles are replaced. Technological change, as well as temporal changes in population characteristics or jurisdictional characteristics, may affect shadow prices. For example, increasing incomes and the declining supply of accessible recreational areas might increase the value of such activities, while increasing congestion at recreational sites might decrease the value of recreational activities. Updating original estimates using the composite CPI or the GDP deflator implies no change in the relative value of a recreational activity.

17.13   Conclusion

By making use of the shadow price values presented in this chapter, analysts can apply CBA to a much wider range of policies than would be feasible if all shadow prices had to be estimated firsthand. Research that produces shadow prices for use in benefit transfer can thus make an important contribution to CBA.

Exercises for Chapter 17

1.   (Instructor-provided spreadsheet recommended.) Suppose a 40-mile stretch of rural road with limited access is used primarily by regional commuters and business travelers to move between two major interstate highways. The legal speed limit on the road is currently 55 miles per hour (mph), and the estimated average speed is 61 mph. Traffic engineers predict that if the speed

limit were raised to 65 mph and enforcement levels were kept constant, the average speed would rise to 70 mph.

Currently, an average of 5,880 vehicles per day use the stretch of road. Approximately half are commuters and half are business travelers. Traffic engineers do not expect that a higher speed limit will attract more vehicles. Vehicles using the road carry, on average, 1.6 people. Traffic engineers predict that raising the speed limit on this stretch of road would result in an additional 52 vehicle crashes involving, on average, 0.1 fatalities annually. They also predict that operating costs would rise by an average of $0.002 per mile per vehicle. The average (before tax) hourly wage in the county in which the majority of users of the road work is $18.30/hour. The average income tax rate is 25 percent. Further assume that the average social cost of an accident (excluding the value of lost lives) is 1.5 percent of the value of a statistical life.

Estimate the annual net benefits of raising the speed limit on the road from 55 mph to 65 mph. In doing this, test the sensitivity of your estimate of annual net benefits to several alternative estimates of the value of time savings, the value of life and the cost of an accident (excluding the value of lost lives) as a fraction of the VSL.

2. Analysts estimate that expanding the capacity of the criminal courts in a city would require about 7,200 additional hours of juror time. The average wage rate in the county is $20/hour. A recent survey by the jury commissioner, however, found that the average wage for those who actually serve on juries under the present system, who are also currently employed, is only $15/hour. The survey also found that about one-third of those who actually serve on juries under the existing system do not hold jobs – for example, they are homemakers, retirees, or unemployed.

    a. What shadow price should the analysts use for an hour of jury time?

    b. About one-fourth of the jurors do not receive wages from their employers while on jury duty. How does this affect your choice of the shadow price?

3. (Instructor-provided spreadsheet recommended.) Assuming that the elasticity of the value of a statistical life with respect to income is between 0.5 and 1.2 and that the value of statistical life in the United States is between $4 million and $13 million, ranges of values of a statistical life for Australia, Portugal, and Brazil are found in the spreadsheet. Data on per-capita income were obtained from the Quick Reference Tables section of the World Bank site: http://siteresources.worldbank.org/DATASTATISTICS/Resources/GNIPC .pdf, using the Atlas method figures. Using the same source of data on per-capita income, calculate ranges of the value of a statistical life for Norway, New Zealand, and Croatia.

Notes

1. For example, see Craig A. Gallet and John A. List, "Cigarette Demand: A Meta-Analysis of Elasticities." *Health Economics*, 12(10), 2003, 821–35; Craig A. Gallet, "Can Price Get the Monkey Off Our Back? A Meta-Analysis of Illicit Drug Demand." *Health Economics*, 23(1), 2014, 55–68; Molly Espey, "Explaining the Variation in Elasticity Estimates of Gasoline Demand in the United States: A Meta-Analysis." *Energy Journal*, 17(3), 1996, 49–60; James A. Espey and Molly Espey, "Turning on the Lights: A Meta-Analysis of Residential Electricity Demand Elasticities." *Journal of Agricultural and Applied Economics*, 36(1), 2004, 65–81; Craig A. Gallet, "The Demand for Alcohol: A Meta-Analysis of Elasticities." *Australian Journal of Agricultural and Resource Economics*, 51(2), 2007, 121–35; Alexander C. Wagenaar, Matthew J. Salois and Kelli A. Komro, "Effects of Beverage Alcohol Price and Tax Levels on Drinking: A Meta-Analysis of 1003 Estimates from 112 Studies." *Addiction*, 104(2), 2009, 179–90; Jasper M. Dalhuisen, Raymond J.G.M. Florax, Henri L.F. De Groot, and Peter Nijkamp, "Price and Income Elasticities of Residential Water Demand: A Meta-Analysis." *Land Economics*, 79(2), 2003, 292–308; Joseph M. Phillips and Ernest P. Goss, "The Effect of State and Local Taxes on Economic Development: A Meta-Analysis." *Southern Economic Journal*, 62(2), 1995, 320–33; and Johan Holmgren, "Meta-Analysis of Public Transport Demand." *Transportation Research Part A: Policy and Practice*, 41(10), 2007, 1021–35.

2. For example, one study suggests that transportation and communications are substitutes; see E. A. Selvanathan and Saroja Selvanathan, "The Demand for Transport and Communication in the United Kingdom and Australia." *Transportation Research-B*, 28(1), 1994, 1–9.

3. See, for example, Robert J. Johnston, John Rolfe, Randall S. Rosenberger, and Roy Brouwer, *Benefit Transfer of Environmental and Resource Values* (New York, NY: Springer, 2015).

4. For our purpose, *value* and *cost* can be used interchangeably, but we stick with common nomenclature – that is, we refer to "the value of life saved (or lost)" and "the cost of injury."

5. See John C. Bergstrom and Laura O. Taylor, "Using Meta-Analysis for Benefits Transfer: Theory and Practice." *Ecological Economics*, 60(2), 2006, 351–60.

6. For example, on gasoline demand, see Martijn Brons, Peter Nijkamp, Eric Pels, and Piet Rietveld, "A Meta-Analysis of the Price Elasticity of Gasoline Demand. A SUR Approach." *Energy Economics*, 30(5), 2008, 2105–22.

7. Ted R. Miller, "Variations Between Countries in Values of Statistical Life." *Journal of Transport Economics and Policy*, 34(2), 2000, 169–88; Janusz R. Mrozek and Laura O. Taylor, "What Determines the Value of Life? A Meta-Analysis."

Journal of Policy Analysis and Management, 21(2), 2002, 253–70; W. Kip Viscusi and Joseph E. Aldy, "The Value of Statistical Life: A Critical Review of Market Estimates Throughout the World." *Journal of Risk and Uncertainty*, 27(1), 2003, 5–76; and Ikuho Kochi, Bryan Hubbell, and Randall Kramer, "An Empirical Bayes Approach to Combining and Comparing Estimates of the Value of a Statistical Life for Environmental Policy Analysis." *Environmental & Resource Economics*, 34, 2006, 385–406; W. Kip Viscusi and Clayton Masterman, "Anchoring Biases in International Estimates of the Value of a Statistical Life." *Journal of Risk and Uncertainty*, 54(2), 2017, 103–28.

8. Based on a meta-analysis of 22 US wage–risk studies, Francois Bellavance and his colleagues obtained a slightly smaller median value of $7.63 million. Francois Bellavance, Georges Dionne, and Martin Lebeau, "The Value of a Statistical Life: A Meta-Analysis with a Mixed Effects Regression Model." Working Paper 06–12. Montreal: Canada Research Chair in Risk Management, 2006.

9. In addition, a recent empirical study in which Viscusi was involved with others found virtually identical values to these for the lower and upper bounds of the VSL. Thomas J. Kniesner, W. Kip Viscusi, Christopher Woock, and James P. Zillak, "Pinning Down the Value of Statistical Life." Discussion Paper No. 3107. Bonn: The Institute for the Study of Labor, 2007.

10. For example, Eduard Zaloshnja, Ted Miller, Eduardo Romano, and Rebecca Spicer suggest the average VLY in the US equals $129,089 based on a VSL of $4.19 million; see Eduard Zaloshnja, Ted Miller, Eduardo Romano, and Rebecca Spicer, "Crash Costs by Body Part Injured, Fracture Involvement, and Threat to Life Severity, United States, 2000." *Accident Analysis and Prevention*, 36(3), 2004, 415–27. Based on a VSL of $3 million, life expectancy of 40 years, and a discount rate of 3 percent, Peter Abelson suggests the VLY for use by public agencies in Australia should be $108,299 in 2016 US dollars; see Peter Abelson, "The Value of Life and Health for Public Policy." *The Economic Record*, 79(Special Issue), 2003, 2–13.

11. For example, Aldy and Viscusi find that workers aged 45–54 and 55–62 have VSLs of 84 percent and 36 percent, respectively, relative to workers aged 35–44 years. This decline with age would more than counter the increase using Equation (17.1) with an age-constant VSL. Joseph E. Aldy and W. Kip Viscusi, "Adjusting the Value of a Statistical Life for Age and Cohort Effects." *The Review of Economics and Statistics*, 90(3), 2008, 573–81.

12. James K. Hammitt and Kevin Haninger, "Valuing Fatal Risks to Children and Adults: Effects of Disease, Latency, and Risk Aversion." *Journal of Risk and Uncertainty*, 40(1), 2010, 57–83.

13. Mark Dickie and Victoria L. Messman, "Parental Altruism and the Value of Avoiding Acute Illness: Are Kids Worth More than Parents?" *Journal of Environmental Economics and Management*, 48(3), 2004, 1146–74.

14. EPA Science Advisory Board, *SAB Advisory on EPAS Issues in Valuing Mortality Risk Reduction* (Washington, DC: U.S. Environmental Protection Agency, 2007); Joseph E. Aldy and W. Kip Viscusi, "Age Differences in the Value of a Statistical Life Revealed Preference Estimates." *Review of Environmental Economics and Policy*, 1(2), 2007, 241–60; and Alan Krupnick, "Mortality Risk Valuation and Age: Stated Preference Evidence." *Review of Environmental Economics and Policy*, 1(2), 2007, 261–82.

15. Dorothy P. Rice, Ellen J. MacKenzie, and Associates, *Costs of Injury in the United States: A Report to Congress* (San Francisco, CA: Institute for Health and Aging, University of California and Injury Prevention Center, The Johns Hopkins University, 1989).

16. Ted R. Miller and Maury Galbraith, "Estimating the Costs of Occupational Injury in the United States." *Accident Analysis and Prevention*, 27(6), 1995, 741–47.

17. Alan E. Dillingham, Ted Miller, and David T. Levy, "A More General and Unified Measure for Valuing Labour Market Risk." *Applied Economics*, 28, 1996, 537–42.

18. Zaloshnja, Miller, Romano, and Spicer, "Crash Costs by Body Part Injured, Fracture Involvement, and Threat to Life Severity, United States, 2000."

19. Lawrence J. Blincoe, Angela G. Seay, Eduard Zaloshnja, Ted R. Miller, Eduardo O. Romano, Stephen Luchter, and Rebecca S. Spicer, *The Economic Impact of Motor Vehicle Crashes 2000*, National Highway Traffic Safety Administration, US Department of Transportation. Available at www.nhtsa.dot.gov.

20. Note the high cost of motor vehicle crashes that cause workplace injuries. Although they account for only 3 percent of workplace injuries, they represent 6 percent of total costs, nearly six times the average cost of $21,040. This is partly explained by the high rate of fatalities from these crashes and by litigation with non-employees over crashes involving multiple vehicles.

21. Ted R. Miller, "Costs and Functional Consequences of U.S. Roadway Crashes." *Accident Analysis and Prevention*, 25(5), 1993, 593–607.

22. There is an AIS 0 category, but we ignore this level because it is very similar to property damage only (PDO).

23. Ted Miller, "Costs and Functional Consequences of U.S. Roadway Crashes."

24. The Federal Aviation Authority, the Office of the Secretary of Transportation for the Department of Transportation, American Road & Transportation Builders

Association, and the Texas Transportation Institute commonly use these fractions of VSL figures to determine the WTP for avoiding an injury caused by an accident.

25. Ascribed by Miller, *Narrowing the Plausible Range around the Value of Life*, 1989, p. 605, to Ezra Hauer (no citation).

26. Kathryn E. McCollister, Michael T. French, and Hai Fang, "The Cost of Crime to Society: New Crime-Specific Estimates for Policy and Program Evaluation." *Drug and Alcohol Dependence*, 108(1), 2010, 98–109.

27. Ted R. Miller, Mark Cohen, and Brian Wiersema, *Victim Costs and Consequences: A New Look*, NCJ 155282, (Washington, DC: National Institute of Justice, 1996).

28. Mark A. Cohen, "The Monetary Value of Saving a High Risk Youth." *Journal of Quantitative Criminology*, 14(1), 1998, 5–33.

29. For a CVM study of the economic value of reducing violent crime in the UK, see Giles Atkinson, Andrew Healey, and Susana Mourato, "Valuing the Costs of Violent Crime: A Stated Preference Approach." *Oxford Economic Papers*, 57(4), 2005, 559–85.

30. Herbert Mohring, John Schroeter, and Paitoon Wiboonchutikula, "The Values of Waiting Time, Travel Time, and a Seat on a Bus." *Rand Journal of Economics*, 18(1), 1987, 40–56.

31. The relationship between speed and flow and between speed and density has been well documented. For example, see Anthony E. Boardman and Lester B. Lave, "Highway Congestion and Congestion Tolls." *Journal of Urban Economics*, 4(3), 1977, 340–59.

32. The value of reliability (VOR) has been estimated as between 50 and 140 percent of the wage rate, a variation larger than for recent estimates of VTTS. See Terence C. Lam and Kenneth A. Small, "The Value of Time and Reliability: Measured from a Value Pricing Experiment." *Transportation Research Part E*, 37(2–3) 2001, 231–51.

33. UK: C. Sharp, "Developments in Transport Policy: The Value of Time Savings and of Accident Prevention." *Journal of Transport Economics and Policy*, 22(2), 1988, 235–38; Mark Wardman, "The Value of Travel Time: A Review of British Evidence." *Journal of Transport Economics and Policy*, 32(3), 1998, 285–316; Canada: J. J. Lawson, *The Value of Passenger Travel Time for Use in Economic Evaluation of Transport Investments* (Ottawa, Ontario: Transport Canada, 1989); New Zealand: Ted Miller, "The Value of Time and the Benefit of Time Saving," presented to the National Roads Board, New Zealand, and the Federal Highway Administration, US Department of Transportation (Washington, DC: Urban Institute, 1989); the Netherlands: H. F. Gunn and C. Rohr, "The 1985–1996 Dutch Value of Time Studies," paper presented at PTRC International Conference on the Value of Time, Wokingham, UK, 1996; Norway: Farideh Ramjerdi, Lars Rand, and Kjartan Saelensminde, *The Norwegian Value*

of Time Study: Some Preliminary Results (Oslo: Institute of Transport Economics); USA: Texas Transportation Institute, "Value of Time and Discomfort Costs, Progress Report on Literature Review and Assessment of Procedures and Data," Technical Memorandum for NCHRP, pp. 7–12; Ted R. Miller, "The Value of Time and the Benefit of Time Saving," Report prepared for the US Department of Transportation; developing countries: John Bates and Stephen Glaister, "The Valuation of Time Savings for Urban Transport Appraisal for Developing Countries: A Review," report prepared for the World Bank, 1990.

34. William G. Waters II, "Values of Travel Time Savings in Road Transportation Project Evaluation." In: David A. Hensher, Jenny King, and Tae Hoon Oum, editors, World Transport Research: Proceedings of the 7th World Conference on Transport Research, vol. 3 (New York, NY: Elsevier, 1996); Markus von Wartburg and William G. Waters II, "Congestion Externalities and the Value of Travel Time Savings." In: Anming Zhang, Anthony E. Boardman, David Gillen, and William G. Waters II, Towards Estimating the Social and Environmental Costs of Transport in Canada: A Report for Transport Canada, chapter 2.

35. Mark Wardman and J. Nicolas Ibanez, "The Congestion Multiplier: Variations in Motorists' Valuations of Travel Time with Traffic Conditions." Transportation Research Part A, 46, 2012, 213–25.

36. Pedro A.L. Abrantes and Mark R. Wardman, "Meta-Analysis of UK Values of Travel Time: An Update." Transportation Research Part A, 45, 2011, 1–17.

37. Richard G. Walsh, Larry D. Sanders, and John R. McKean, "The Consumptive Value of Travel Time on Recreation Trips." Journal of Travel Research, 29(1), 1990, 17–24 found that travelers express a positive WTP for up to three hours of scenic driving in the Rockies on weekends. Carlo Fezzi, Ian Bateman and Silvia Ferrini used utilization of open access versus toll roads to recreation sites and conclude that the VVTS for recreational trips is three-fourths of the wage rate, "Using Revealed Preferences to Estimate the Value of Travel Time to Recreation Sites." Journal of Environmental Economics and Management, 67, 2014, 58–70.

38. See also David A. Hensher, "The Valuation of Commuter Travel Time Savings for Car Drivers: Evaluation Alternative Model Specifications." Transportation, 28(2), 2001, 101–18.

39. See also Mark Wardman, "A Review of British Evidence on Time and Service Quality Valuations." Transportation Research Part E, 37(2), 2001, 107–28. Wardman concluded that the multiplier for waiting time is 1.47 in Great Britain.

40. Cindy F. Sorg and John B. Loomis, Empirical Estimates of Amenity Forest Values: A Comparative Review, General Technical Report RM-107 (Fort Collins, CO: Rocky Mountain Forest and Range Experiment Station, Forest Service, USDA, 1984).

41. Richard G. Walsh, Donn M. Johnson, and John R. McKean, "Benefit Transfer of Outdoor Recreation Demand Studies, 1968–1988." Water Resources Research, 29(3), 1992, 707–13.

42. Randall Rosenberger and John B. Loomis, Benefit Transfer of Outdoor Recreation Use Values: A Technical Report Supporting the Forest Service's Strategic Plan (2000 Revision). General Technical Report RMRS-GTR-72 (Fort Collins, CO: Rocky Mountain Research Station, 2001). This report was based on Doug MacNair, 1993 RPA Recreation Values Database, RPA Program Contract 43-4568-3-1191 (Washington, DC: USDA Forest Service, 1993) and John Loomis, Randall S. Rosenberger, and Ram Shrestha, Updated Estimate of Recreation Values for the RPA Program by Assessment Region and Use of Meta-Analysis for Recreation Benefit Transfer, Final Report RJVA 28-JV7-962 (Fort Collins, CO: Colorado State University, Department of Agricultural and Resource Economics, 1999).

43. Pam Kaval and John Loomis, Updated Outdoor Recreation Use Values with Emphasis on National Park Recreation, Final Report to National Park Service, Fort Collins, CO (Fort Collins, CO: Colorado State University, Department of Agricultural and Resource Economics; 2003).

44. See, for example, the reports produced by the Millennium Ecosystem Assessment (www.millenniumassessment.org/en/index.aspx).

45. I. J. Bateman, K. G. Willis, G. D. Garrod, P. Doktor, I. Langford, and R. K. Turner, "Recreation and Environmental Preservation Value of the Norfolk Broads: A Contingent Valuation Study," Report to the National Rivers Authority, Environmental Appraisal Group, University of East Anglia, 1992.

46. See, for example, Urs P. Kreuter, Heather G. Harris, Marty D. Matlock, and Ronald E. Lacey, "Change in Ecosystem Service Values in the San Antonio Area, Texas." Ecological Economics, 39(3), 2001, 333–46.

47. John B. Loomis and Douglas S. White, "Economic Benefits of Rare and Endangered Species: Summary and Meta-Analysis." Ecological Economics, 18, 1996, 197–206.

48. Paulo A. L. D. Nunes and Jeroen C. J. M. van den Bergh, "Economic Valuation of Biodiversity: Sense or Nonsense?" Ecological Economics, 39(2), 2001, 203–22.

49. Luke M. Brander, Raymond J. G. M. Florax, and Jan E. Vermaat, "The Empirics of Wetland Valuation: A Comprehensive Summary and a Meta-Analysis of the Literature." Environmental & Resource Economics, 33(2), 2006, 223–50.

50. For a CVM survey example, see Jeffrey L. Jordan and Abdelmoneim H. Elnagheeb, "Willingness to Pay for Improvements in Water Drinking Quality." Water Resources Research, 29(2), 1993, 237–45. Charles W. Abdalla, Brian A.

Roach, and Donald J. Epp, "Valuing Environmental Quality Changes Using Averting Expenditures: An Application to Groundwater Contamination." *Land Economics*, 68(2), 1992, 163–69, use both the market analogy method (observations of bottled water expenditures) and defensive expenditures (expenditures incurred in boiling or hauling water or installation of household treatment systems). For a study that estimates the benefits of water quality improvements on river segments using the travel cost method, see V. Kerry Smith and William H. Desvousges, *Measuring Water Quality Benefits* (Boston, MA: Kluwer-Nijhoff Publishing, 1986).

51. Patrick J. Walsh and William J. Wheeler, "Water Quality Indices and Benefit–cost Analysis." *Journal of Benefit–Cost Analysis*, 4(1), 2013, 81–105.

52. Ralph Luken, F. Johnson, and V. Kibler, "Benefits and Costs of Pulp and Paper Effluent Controls Under the Clean Water Act." *Water Resources Research*, 28(3), 1992, 665–74.

53. Kenneth D. Frederick, Tim van den Berg, and Jean Hanson, "Economic Values of Freshwater in the United States," Discussion Paper 97–43 (Washington, DC: Resources for the Future; 1996).

54. Specifically, NSDI = (D/property value) × 100, where D = reduction in property value from a unit increase in noise exposure; that is, $D = -100\,(\partial H/\partial NEF)/H)$, where H represents house prices.

55. NDSI $= -100\,\dfrac{\partial \ln H}{\partial NEF}$. In contrast, the hedonic price of noise or marginal implicit price of noise is the slope of the function relating house prices, H, to noise level, that is, $\dfrac{\partial H}{\partial NEF}$.

56. Ian Bateman, Brett Day, Iain Lake, and Andrew Lovett, "The Effect of Road Traffic on Residential Property Values: A Literature Review and Hedonic Pricing Study," Report to the Scottish Executive Development Department (Edinburgh: Scottish Executive, 2001); Nir Becker and Doron Lavee, "The Benefits and Costs of Noise Reduction." *Journal of Environmental Planning and Management*, 46(1), 2003, 97–111.

57. See Y. J. J. Schipper, "On the Valuation of Aircraft Noise: A Meta-Analysis," unpublished paper, Titenberg Institute, Free University of Amsterdam, 1996.

58. Dean Uyeno, Stanley Hamilton, and Andrew J. G. Biggs, "Density of Residential Land Use and the Impact of Airport Noise." *Journal of Transport Economics and Policy*, 27(1), 1993, 3–18.

59. Dallas Burtraw, Alan Krupnick, Erin Mausur, David Austin, and Deirdre Farrell, "Costs and Benefits of Reducing Air Pollutants Related to Acid Rain." *Contemporary Economic Policy*, 16(4), 1998, 379–400.

60. For more on the sources of emissions in the US, Germany, and the UK, see David W. Pearce and R.

Kerry Turner, *Economics of Natural Resources and the Environment* (Baltimore, MD: The Johns Hopkins University Press, 1990), p. 192. Also see Alan J. Krupnick and Paul R. Portney, "Controlling Urban Air Pollution: A Benefit–Cost Assessment." *Science*, 252(26), 1991, 522–28.

61. Pearce and Turner, *Economics of Natural Resources and the Environment*.

62. Thomas C. Schelling, "Some Economics of Global Warming." *American Economic Review*, 82(1), 1992, 1–14 and Intergovernmental Panel on Climate Change, *Climate Change 2001: Synthesis Report* (Cambridge: Cambridge University Press, 2001).

63. For example see Kenneth Y. Chay and Michael Greenstone, "Does Air Quality Matter? Evidence from the Housing Market." *Journal of Political Economy*, 113(2), 2005, 376–424.

64. H. Scott Matthews and Lester B. Lave, "Applications of Environmental Valuation for Determining Externality Costs." *Environmental Science & Technology*, 34(8), 2000, 1390–95.

65. Richard S. J. Tol, "The Social Cost of Carbon: Trends, Outliers and Catastrophies." *Economics: The Open-Access, Open-Assessment E-Journal*, 2, 2008, 1–22.

66. David Pearce, "The Social Cost of Carbon and Its Policy Implications." *Oxford Review of Economic Policy*, 18(3), 2003, 362–82.

67. Ian W. H. Parry, Margaret Walls, and Winston Harrington, "Automobile Externalities and Policies." *Journal of Economic Literature*, 45(2), 2007, 373–99.

68. Nicholas Stern, *The Economics of Climate Change: The Stern Review* (New York, NY: Cambridge University Press, 2007).

69. William D. Nordhaus, "A Review of the Stern Review on the Economics of Climate Change." *Journal of Economic Literature*, 45(3), 2007, 682–702.

70. US Environmental Protection Agency, *The Social Cost of Carbon* (January 2017), https://19january2017snapshot.epa.gov/climatechange/social-cost-carbon_.html.

71. Ian W. H. Parry, Margaret Walls, and Winston Harrington, "Automobile Externalities and Policies."

72. Parry, Walls, and Winston also discuss costs that cannot be estimated, such as US vulnerability to oil price volatility and military costs associated with protecting access to foreign oil.

73. See Robert J. Johnston, John Rolfe, Randall S. Rosenberger, and Roy Brouwer, *Benefit Transfer of Environmental and Resource Values* (New York, NY: Springer, 2015).

74. From Equation (17.4), $\dfrac{VSL_A - VSL_{US}}{VSL_{US}} = E_I\left(\dfrac{I_A - I_{US}}{I_{US}}\right)$. Rearranging this expression gives Equation (17.5).

75. Nicholas E. Flores and Richard T. Carson, "The Relationship between the Income Elasticities of Demand and Willingness to Pay." *Journal of Environmental Economics and Management*, 33, 1997, 287–95.

76. Adapted from Flores and Carson, p. 294.

77. James K. Hammitt and Lisa A. Robinson, "The Income Elasticity of the Value per Statistical Life: Transferring Estimates between High and Low Income Populations." *Journal of Benefit–Cost Analysis*, 2(1), 2011.

78. In Kip Viscusi and Joseph Aldy, "The Value of Statistical Life: A Critical Review of Market Estimates Throughout the World," the mean elasticities range between 0.51 and 0.61.

79. See the Centre for the Study of Living Standards, table 3 at www.csls.ca/data.asp (accessed June 6, 2017).

80. Source: www.canadianforex.ca/forex-tools/historical-rate-tools/yearly-average-rates (accessed June 6, 2017).

81. Note that we use the exchange rate. Comparisons of countries with less similar consumption patterns would be better based on purchasing power parity (PPP), which is based on expenditures required to buy a specific market basket of goods. A crude but popular version of the PPP is the Big Mac index: the relative prices of a Big Mac in two countries.

82. Foreign exchange amounts are converted to US dollars at purchasing power parity. Source: http://data.worldbank.org/indicator/NY.GDP.PCAP.PP.CD (accessed June 6, 2017).

83. Our estimates are significantly larger than Hammitt and Robinson's estimates because we begin with a larger VSL in the US, larger estimates of income in China, and lower income elasticities.

84. See, for example, Bethany Ackeret, David L. Weimer, Erik A. Ranheim, Lisa Urban, and Elizabeth Jacobs, "Net Benefits of Hospital-Sponsored Health Care for the Homeless: Cost–Benefit Analysis of a Demonstration Project," Robert M. La Follette School of Public Affairs Working Paper No. 2014–010, April 14, 2014.

85. Some studies have found a negative relationship between estimates of the VSL and fatality risk; see, for example, Viscusi and Aldy (2003). This relationship does not imply that willingness-to-pay for risk reduction decreases as risk increases; rather, it comes about because people who value their lives more select safer professions.

86. M. W. Jones-Lee, G. Loomes, S. Jones, P. Rowlatt, M. Spackman, and S. Jones, "Valuation of Deaths from Air Pollution," *NERA and CASPAR*, report prepared for the Department of the Environment, Transport and the Regions and the Department of Trade and Industry, London, 1998.

87. W. G. Waters II, "The Value of Travel Time Savings and the Link with Income: Implications for Public Project Evaluation." *International Journal of Transport Economics*, 12(3), 1994, 243–53.

88. von Wartburg and Waters, "Congestion Externalities."

89. Stephanie Kirchhoff, Bonnie G. Colbey, and Jeffrey T. LaFrance, "Evaluating the Performance of Benefit Transfer: An Empirical Inquiry." *Journal of Environmental Economics and Management*, 33(1), 1997, 75–93.

Case 17

Shadow Pricing a High School Diploma

Educational attainment can benefit society. Most directly, it usually increases the productivity of the educated. It can also provide external benefits to the rest of society by reducing the risks that individuals commit crimes or become dependent on social services. In developed economies, these external benefits are likely to be largest when attainment involves moving beyond secondary schooling. For example, in the United States only 83 percent of individuals overall, and 75 percent of African Americans, earn high school diplomas.[1] Various economic forces have resulted in fewer employment opportunities for those without high school diplomas than for previous generations. Therefore, policies that increase the chances of high school graduation offer potential benefits to society. How can this benefit be monetized?

Analysts at the Washington State Institute for Public Policy (WSIPP) developed a shadow price for a policy-induced high school graduation for use in CBAs of social programs.[2] This case explains and updates the WSIPP methodology, both because the shadow price of a high school diploma has wide application and because it shows how diverse sources of evidence can be used to develop useful shadow prices.[3]

The general approach to developing the shadow price involves a number of steps. First, predict earnings for people with different levels of educational attainment over their working lives. Second, add fringe benefits to earnings to estimate full compensation. Third, adjust for predicted real growth in compensation (wages and fringe benefits). Fourth, take account of mortality risk during the working life. Fifth, specify paths from a high school diploma to higher levels of education. Sixth, separate out the effects of educational attainment and cognitive endowments on earnings. Seventh, discount earnings gains to obtain present values. Eighth, adjust estimates for higher education costs and externalities.

1. Predict Life-Cycle Earnings by Education Level

WSIPP used data from the March Supplement of the Community Population Survey (CPS) for the years 2002 through 2010 to estimate average earnings by age for people with four different levels of education: less than high school diploma, high school diploma, some college (including associates degrees), and a four-year college degree or advanced degree. The model included both age and the square of age as well as indicators for years. After replicating the WSIPP results, we expanded the data set to include years 2011 through 2014 and re-estimated the model.[4] Note that the CPS data include people with no earnings. Therefore, the estimates take account of labor force participation over individuals' working years (ages 18 through 65). We assume zero earnings for ages 18 and 19 for those with some college and zero earnings for ages 18, 19, 20, and 21 for those with a college degree. For each group, we set the age 24 earnings at the real value estimated from the 2014 CPS. Earnings for ages older than 24 are projected forward using the estimated equations. Earnings for years below 24 were also taken for each group from the 2014 CPS.

2.   Add Fringe Benefits to Estimate Total Compensation

The productivity gains from education should be based on total compensation, which is dollar earnings plus the dollar value of fringe benefits. WSIPP derived a ratio of total compensation to wages of 1.4410 as of December 2015 using Bureau of Labor Statistics data on the percent of total compensation paid to civilian workers as wages. Using an estimate of 68.4 percent of compensation paid as wages as of December 2016, we updated the ratio of total earning to wages to be 1.4620 and multiplied wages for each education level by this amount.[5]

3.   Adjust for Predicted Real Growth in Earnings and Fringe Benefits

Both earnings and fringe benefits can be expected to grow in real terms over time. WSIPP analysts estimated growth rates in real earnings and the ratio of total compensation to earnings with time series analyses of annual data over the last six business cycles. We use the WSIPP estimates for the real annual growth rate in earnings: −0.0062 for those without a high school diploma, 0.0053 for those with a high school diploma, 0.0095 for those with some college, and 0.0115 for those with a college degree. We also use the WSIPP estimate of 0.00041 for the annual growth rate in total compensation to earnings ratio.

Figure C17.1 provides projected average real total compensation by age for each of the four education groups. As previously noted, these are averages across all respondents at particular ages and therefore take account of workforce participation. Because of reductions in workforce participation at higher ages for all groups, average earnings eventually decrease even for the higher education groups with predicted positive real growth in wages.

4.   Account for Mortality

Not everyone will live to age 65. Those who die before that age will not realize the full earnings benefits of their education. To take account of mortality, each year of earnings is weighted by the probability of surviving to the next year.[6]

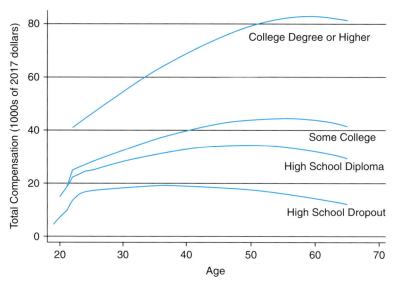

Figure C17.1 Average real compensation by age for four levels of educational attainment.

5.   Discount Compensation Streams

The present value of compensation for each education level is found by discounting the annual compensation amounts from age 18 to 65 using a real discount rate.

6.   Specify Pathways among Educational Levels

Completing high school creates the opportunity to attend college. People who complete high school may or may not go on to higher education. Using the data from the CPS, we estimated that, conditional on earning a high school diploma, 34 percent of people obtain no further formal education, 31 percent obtain some college, and 35 percent go on to earn a bachelor's degree or higher. (WSIPP uses estimates specific to Washington State: 26 percent, 38 percent, and 36 percent, respectively, for the three levels of educational attainment.)

7.   Separate Out Causal Effects

Cognitive, health, and other endowments may make some people more productive than others at any level of education. However, because those who attain a higher level of education tend to be more alike than those who do not, the more productive people might very well have had earnings like those at their education level even if they had not attained it. Consequently, the difference in compensation between two levels of education overstates the causal effect of moving from the lower to the higher level.

WSIPP analysts use estimates made by James Heckman and colleagues to separate out the causal effect of education.[7] We employ the same causal factors for high school graduates, those with some college, and those with higher degrees: 50 percent, 56 percent, and 42 percent, respectively. That is, for example, 42 percent of the increased wages from college graduation relative to no high school diploma would result even without the higher degree. We apply each causal factor to the difference between compensation at the education level and compensation for those who do not graduate from high school. For example, if the mortality-adjusted present value of total compensation for those with a high school diploma were $630,000 and the mortality-adjusted present value of total compensation for those without a high school diploma were $360,000, then the contribution to productivity would be 50 percent of the difference, or $135,000. Further, using the estimate that 34 percent of those who earn a high school diploma do obtain higher education, the contribution to the total gain in productivity from this path would be about $46,000. This would be added to similar gains calculated for those with some college and college degrees.

8. Adjust Estimates for Higher Education Costs and Externalities

Education involves both an opportunity cost for the student and real resource costs for society. We take account of the opportunity cost to students by assuming zero earnings for ages 18 and 19 for those who obtain some college and for ages 18 through 21 for those who obtain a college degree or higher. We calculate the present value of the real resource cost of education by discounting an average annual cost of college of $19,281 for two-year colleges for those with some college and $28,043 for four-year colleges over these age ranges.[8]

Increases in productivity create external benefits that spill over to the rest of society, such as reduced criminalist behavior, improved consumption and fertility efficiency, and intra-family productivity.[9] WSIPP draws on a number of studies to specify a range of external benefits as a fraction of total compensation of 0.13–0.42.[10] WSIPP considers 0.37 to be the modal value.[11] The following table uses this modal value.

Table C17.1 displays estimates of the shadow price of a policy-induced high school diploma in the USA. The top number in each cell is a point estimate using modal values noted above. The second two numbers are the mean and standard deviation from Monte Carlo simulations that each employ 1,000 trials. The simulations introduce uncertainty to the productivity measure by assuming the causal factors are normally distributed with standard deviations equal to those used by WSIPP. In the second and fourth columns, annual two- and four-year college costs depend on plausible random changes in the percentages of students attending lower-cost public schools and higher-cost private schools. In the third and fourth columns, again following WSIPP, the externality factor follows a triangular distribution over the range 0.13–0.42 with the mode at 0.37.

Consider a CBA of an intervention program that is predicted to result in an additional 10 students earning high school diplomas. For a discount rate of 3.5 percent,

Table C17.1 *Shadow Prices for US High School Diploma: Point Estimate and Monte Carlo Mean (Standard Deviation) (1000s of 2017 US dollars)*

Real discount rate	Productivity	Productivity with education costs	Productivity with externalities	Productivity with education costs and externalities
0.030	269	219	368	319
	269	219	352	301
	(43.9)	(44.0)	(60.4)	(60.5)
0.035	239	190	328	279
	241	190	315	264
	(40.1)	(41.3)	(56.3)	(56.5)
0.040	214	166	294	245
	214	164	280	229
	(36.0)	(36.2)	(49.6)	(49.7)
0.045	193	144	264	216
	193	143	252	202
	(33.0)	(33.0)	(46.1)	(46.1)
0.050	174	126	238	208
	173	123	226	190
	(28.0)	(29.3)	(39.9)	(40.1)
0.055	157	110	216	168
	157	108	205	156
	(26.5)	(26.5)	(36.5)	(36.5)
0.060	143	95	196	148
	143	94	186	137
	(24.4)	(24.4)	(33.1)	(33.1)
0.065	130	83	179	131
	130	81	170	121
	(21.3)	(21.5)	(29.2)	(29.4)
0.070	119	72	163	116
	119	71	155	107
	(19.2)	(19.2)	(26.0)	(26.0)

the benefits resulting from these additional diplomas would be predicted to be $2.79 million using the point estimate in column four of $279,000 that takes account of productivity gains, the real resource costs of higher education, and external benefits. An alternative approach, closer to that employed by WSIPP, would be to use the mean from the Monte Carlo simulation of $264,000, yielding predicted benefits of $2.64 million. If one wanted to use the shadow price in a larger Monte Carlo simulation that varied a variety of impacts and shadow prices, then one could draw values of the shadow price from a normal distribution with a mean of $264,000 and a standard deviation of $56,500.

Exercises for Chapter 17 Case Study

1. How would the shadow price of a high school diploma change if the labor force participation rate increased?

2. (Instructor-provided spreadsheet required.) How much would the shadow price of a diploma change if the probabilities of high school graduates obtaining no further education, some college, and college graduation were 26 percent, 38 percent, and 36 percent, respectively, as assumed by WSIPP?

Notes

1. US Department of Education, Office of Elementary and Secondary Education, Consolidated State Performance Report, 2014–15. See Digest of Education Statistics 2016, table 219.46.

2. Washington State Institute for Public Policy, *Benefit–Cost Technical Documentation*, Olympia, Washington, December 2016.

3. Thanks to Falon French and Jordan Krieger for assistance in updating the WSIPP analysis.

4. Following WSIPP, the dependent variable was PEARNVAL from the March Supplement put in 2016 dollars using the implicit price deflator provided by the Bureau of Labor Statistics. The variable MARSUPWT provided probability weights. See equation 4.2 in the WSIPP Benefit–Cost Technical Documentation (December 2016).

5. Bureau of Labor Statistics, *Employer Costs For Employee Compensation – December 2016*, News Release USDL-17–0321, March 17, 2017, table A, p. 2.

6. Elizabeth Arias, "United States Life Tables: 2010." *National Vital Statistics Report*, 63(7), 2014, 1–62.

7. James J. Heckman, John Eric Humphries, and Gregory Veramendi. "The Causal Effects of Education on Earnings and Health." Unpublished Manuscript, Department of Economics, University of Chicago, 2015.

8. Scott A. Ginder, Janice E. Kelly-Reid, and Farrah B. Mann (2016). Postsecondary Institutions and Cost of Attendance in 2015–2016; Degrees and Other Awards Conferred, 2014–15; and 12-Month Enrollment, 2014–15: First look (provisional data). National Center for Education Statistics Report NCES 2016-112rev. Retrieved from https://nces.ed.gov/pubs2016/2016112rev.pdf.

9. Robert H. Haveman and Barbara L. Wolfe, "Schooling and Economic Well-being: The Role of Nonmarket Effects." *Journal of Human Resources*, 19(3), 1984, 377–407.

10. The low estimate comes from Daron Acemoglu and Joshua Angrist, "How Large Are Human Capital Externalities: Evidence from Compulsory Schooling Laws." In: B. Bernanke and K. Rogoff, editors, *NBER Macroeconomics Annual*, 15 (Cambridge, MA: MIT Press, 2000, pp. 9–59); the high estimate comes from Theodore R. Breton, "Schooling and National Income: How Large Are the Externalities? Revised Estimates." *Education Economics*, 18(4), 2010, 455–56.

11. Clive Belfield, Fiona Hollands, and Henry Levin, "What Are the Social and Economic Returns?" (New York, NY: Campaign for Educational Equity, Teachers College, Columbia University, 2011).

18 Cost–Effectiveness Analysis and Cost–Utility Analysis

Cost–effectiveness analysis (CEA) is widely used as an alternative to CBA, especially in policy arenas such as education, health, and defense. It is used in situations with two characteristics. First, the policies being evaluated have one major benefit that analysts or clients are unwilling or unable to monetize. Many public health programs have this characteristic: their major purpose is to save lives (reduce fatality risk) and it may be possible to predict the numbers of statistical lives saved by alternative public health programs, but decision-makers are unwilling to place a monetary (dollar) value on a life saved. In national defense, analysts sometimes deal with intermediate goods with tenuous linkages to individual preferences. For example, the exact contribution of different types of weapon systems to overall national defense is often unclear. However, analysts may be able to compare them in terms of their costs for achieving some objective or their relative effectiveness in promoting some objective. Second, the only cost analysts or decision-makers want to consider is the financial cost of the technology (i.e., the policy alternative) incurred by the government agency that will pay for it, such as the public health plan.

CEA compares (mutually exclusive) alternatives in terms of the ratio of their costs to a single quantified, but not monetized, measure of benefits (effectiveness). For example, alternative highway safety programs may involve different costs and different numbers of lives saved. The cost–effectiveness ratios of the programs would be expressed as the cost per life saved. The alternative program that costs the least per life saved *might* be considered as the most efficient. However, that assessment would generally be incorrect. Consequently, care must be taken in claiming or interpreting cost–effectiveness ratios as comprehensive measures of efficiency. In fact, in order to make a meaningful recommendation, analysts must know the shadow price of the effectiveness measure, such as the value of life or, possibly, the range of the value of life. Thus, even though one might be motivated to use CEA rather than CBA because of unwillingness to monetize the value of life (or some other effectiveness measure), *some* level of monetization is necessary to make recommendations concerning efficiency. Even under these conditions, however, the recommended alternative might not be the most allocatively efficient alternative due to excluded costs and benefits.

Cost–utility analysis (CUA) is most frequently used in the arena of health technology assessment, such as, the evaluation of medicines, medical devices and procedures to improve quality or quantity of life. Alternatives are evaluated in terms of the increase in utility associated with an improvement in the length of life or quality of life, that is, increases in quality-adjusted life-years (QALYs). CUA recognizes that individuals are willing to make trade-offs between their remaining quantity of life and the quality of those life-years. Thus, it serves as a direct proxy for changes in individuals' utilities. In this respect, CUA is a step closer to CBA than is CEA.

The discussion first addresses the following questions: How should cost–effectiveness ratios be computed and used to compare policy alternatives? How should sensitivity analysis be conducted? How should excluded costs or benefits be handled? We then consider cost–utility analysis and the meaning of quality-adjusted life years (QALYs). We describe a number of methods to estimate utility directly and some methods to estimate utility indirectly. However, even with a good estimate of the impact of a policy in terms of QALYs, a policy maker must set a threshold value for a QALY in order to make a decision about the policy. Also, we point out some limitations concerning QALYs and, in particular, its relationship to allocative efficiency. Finally, we ask: can *league tables* be reliably used to compare large numbers of policies?

18.1   Cost–Effectiveness Ratios and Policy Choice

CEA involves computing cost–effectiveness ratios and using them to choose between policy alternatives that promote some degree of efficiency. This section first discusses simple cost–effectiveness ratios and then turns to incremental cost–effectiveness ratios. We stress that it is often helpful to graph the data first.

18.1.1   *Cost–Effectiveness Ratios*

As CEA does not attempt to monetize benefits, it inevitably involves two distinct metrics: costs are measured in dollars, while effectiveness may be measured in a variety of different units. The effectiveness measure could be lives saved, tons of carbon dioxide reduced, or number of children vaccinated. These non-commensurate metrics cannot be added to costs without monetization or some equivalent procedure that "forces" commensurability. Therefore, it is not possible to obtain a single measure of net benefits using costs and a measure of effectiveness. However, it is straightforward to compute the ratio of the two measures, which can be used as a basis for recommending a particular policy alternative from among the considered alternatives. The ratio can be expressed in one of two ways: either as a *cost–effectiveness ratio* (CE ratio) that is computed by dividing the costs of an alternative by the measure of its effectiveness, or as an *effectiveness–cost ratio* (EC ratio), which is computed by dividing the effectiveness measure of an alternative by its costs. The discussion that follows focuses on the cost–effectiveness ratio, which is the more commonly used ratio.

The (simple) cost–effectiveness ratio of an alternative, i, is given by the following formula:

$$CE_i = C_i / E_i \qquad (18.1)$$

where, C_i is the cost of alternative i, and E_i is the number of effectiveness units produced by alternative i relative to the status quo (no new intervention). To illustrate, imagine that

Table 18.1 *Working with Cost–Effectiveness Ratios*

| | Alternatives | | |
Cost and effectiveness	A	B	C
Cost (millions of dollars)	50	150	300
Effectiveness (test score improvement)	10	15	20
CE ratio	5	10	15

a school board is concerned about the achievement test scores of grade 12 students. It is considering three options: Alternative A would cost $50 million and is expected to raise the average test score by 10 points. Alternative B would cost $150 million and is expected to raise the average test score by 15 points. Alternative C would cost $300 million and is expected to raise the average test score by 20 points. Obviously, these alternatives are mutually exclusive.

The first step in conducting a CEA is to display the data in a table, along the lines of Table 18.1, which orders the alternatives from least to most costly. The analyst should immediately examine whether there is any alternative that is *strongly dominated*, that is, it costs the same as another alternative, but is less effective or it has the same level of effectiveness as another alternative, but costs more. No sensible analyst would ever select a strongly dominated alternative and it should be eliminated from further consideration.

The CE ratio appears in the bottom row. *It shows the incremental cost, relative to no intervention, of increasing the effectiveness measure by one unit on average.* The CE ratio of alternative A implies that it costs $5 million to increase the average achievement test score by one unit relative to no new intervention, while alternatives B and C cost $10 million and $15 million per test score increase relative to no new intervention, respectively. Notice that the CE ratio increases as the cost increases. If it did not, then it would indicate that at least one of the lower-cost alternatives is dominated, which we discuss in detail later. In some situations the CE ratio of an alternative is negative, which implies that, if the effect is positive, the alternative is not only more effective than the status quo, but is also less costly. Obviously, such alternatives are preferable to the status quo.

Alternative A, which costs $5 million per average test score improvement, is the most cost-effective alternative. Thus, one tends to be drawn towards it, but it is not necessarily the alternative that represents the greatest allocative efficiency. Suppose, for example, the shadow price of a unit of test score improvement is $25 million, then the net benefit of alternative A would equal $200 million, while the net benefit of alternative B would equal $225 million. The relative allocative efficiency of the alternatives depends on the shadow price of the effectiveness measure. Given that alternative B is more allocatively efficient than alternative A in the above example, some might suggest that they would prefer to replicate alternative A three times rather than adopt alternative B. However, in this illustrative example, this option is not available. If it were, then it should have been included in the original set of alternatives.

18.1.2 *Incremental Cost–Effectiveness Ratios*

In order to make policy recommendations it is useful to compute *incremental CE ratios*. By definition, the incremental CE ratio of project i relative to policy j, denoted $ICER_{ij}$, is given by the following formula:

$$ICER_{ij} = \frac{C_i - C_j}{E_i - E_j}$$

(18.2)

The ICER for alternative A is computed relative to no new program with no incremental effectiveness and no incremental cost. Thus, it equals the CE ratio of alternative A. The ICER of alternative B, the second highest cost alternative, is calculated relative to alternative A; the ICER of alternative C is calculated relative to alternative B. These calculations are summarized in Table 18.2.

Basically, *the ICER measures the incremental cost per unit improvement in effectiveness relative to the next less costly alternative.* More precisely, the ICER shows the incremental cost of an alternative relative to the next less-costly alternative of raising the effectiveness score on average by one unit more than the effectiveness score of the next less-costly alternative. Thus, the ICER of alternative A shows that it costs $5 million to increase the average test scores by one unit relative to the status quo. The ICER of alternative B implies that it costs $20 million more than the cost of alternative A to increase the average effectiveness score by one more unit than 10, the effectiveness of alternative A.

As illustrated in Table 18.2, the ICERs in this example increase as one moves from left to right, that is, as the scale increases from relatively (small) low-cost alternative programs to relatively (large) high-cost alternative programs. If they did not increase, then this would indicate the presence of a dominated alternative, which should be eliminated and the ICERs should then be recomputed.

18.1.3 *Graphing the Data*

It is usually informative to plot the data graphically as Figure 18.1. The cost of an alternative (here measured in $ millions) is shown on the vertical axis and effectiveness (here

Table 18.2 *Computing Incremental Cost–Effectiveness Ratios*

	Alternatives		
Cost and effectiveness	A	B	C
Cost (millions of dollars)	50	150	300
Effectiveness (test score improvement)	10	15	20
CE ratio	5	10	15
$C_i - C_j$	50	100	150
$E_i - E_j$	10	5	5
ICER	5	20	30

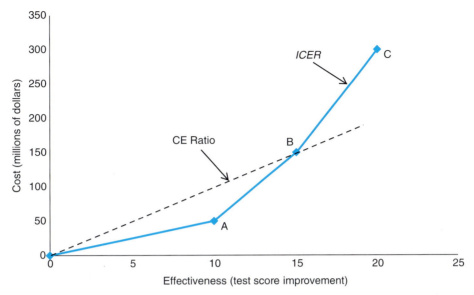

Figure 18.1 Graphical representation of costs and effectiveness.

measured as units of test score improvement) is shown on the horizontal axis. The slope of the dashed line from the origin to alternative B equals the CE ratio of option B. One can see that it increases as cost (or effectiveness) increases.

The solid lines connecting the origin, A, B, and C have slopes equal to their incremental cost–effectiveness ratios; they map out the frontiers of the best possible outcomes – those that push as far to the southeast as possible, where cost is low and effectiveness is high. Any alternative to the northwest of the line connecting the origin and points A, B, and C is a dominated alternative. *A dominated alternative is one that would always have a lower net benefit than one of the alternatives on the frontier, for any possible value of the shadow price of the effectiveness measure.* Thus, a dominated alternative would never be recommended. When identified, they should be eliminated from the table and the ICERs should be recomputed.

Analysts distinguish between strongly dominated alternatives and weakly (or extended) dominated alternatives. As already noted, a strongly dominated alternative has either a cost the same as another alternative but is less effective, or it has the same level of effectiveness as another alternative but higher cost. Diagrammatically, such points are either vertically directly above, or horizontally directly left, of alternatives like A, B, or C that are on the frontier. A weakly dominated alternative lies above the frontier but does not have exactly the same cost or effectiveness as another alternative.

Although it should be possible to identify dominated alternatives from a tabular display of the data, they can sometimes be missed in situations involving a large number of alternatives. Weakly dominated alternatives are especially easy to miss. Graphing the data as in Figure 18.1 allows one to identify the alternatives that lie on the most south-easterly frontier of ICERs and to identify any dominated alternative(s) – those to the northwest of the frontier.

18.1.4   *Making a Recommendation*

Frontiers like the one shown in Figure 18.1 narrow the set of alternatives to consider, but in the absence of information about decision-makers' preferences there is no basis for selecting a particular alternative. In contrast, CBA leads to an unambiguous ranking.[1] In the example presented in Table 18.2, assigning a shadow price to the improvement in average test scores enables an analyst to estimate the net (social) benefit of each alternative and make an unambiguous recommendation (assuming there are no omitted impacts). In the absence of a known shadow price, the analyst can make recommendations that depend on the range of the shadow price of improvement in test scores. The crucial information is contained in the ICERs, displayed in the last row of Table 18.2. One can easily verify that if an average test score improvement (across all students) is valued at less than $5 million, then no policy alternative should be chosen – current policy should not be changed. If an average test score improvement is valued between $5 million and $20 million, then alternative A should be chosen. If the shadow price is between $20 million and $30 million, then alternative B should be selected. If it is more than $30 million, then alternative C should be selected.

Thus, in order to make policy recommendations, CEA generally requires a "threshold" shadow price or a shadow price range. The irony is that CEA is often motivated by an initial unwillingness of decision-makers to monetize the effectiveness measure. If decision-makers really do not want to specify at least a ball-park figure for the shadow price, then they cannot expect CEA to inform a choice that embodies some notion of efficiency.

Cost–benefit analysts naturally look to the academic literature to determine the appropriate shadow price of an effectiveness measure. One might, for example, find from the literature that the social value of an average test score improvement of one point is $35 million and would, therefore, recommend alternative C. In practice, however, a particular government decision-maker might value it at only $7 million and would, therefore, prefer alternative A.

It is important to emphasize that in CEA a weak link may exist between the measure of effectiveness and goods or services that individuals' value. It is quite reasonable to presume that individuals would be willing to pay for reductions in mortality risk that lead to lives saved, an often-used measure of effectiveness. But now consider the "number of addicts treated." This intermediate output may or may not be a good proxy for the final consumption good that individuals value, such as personal sobriety or reductions in street crime. Analysts cannot avoid estimating the value of final consumption goods when doing CBA, even if they must rely on shadow prices from secondary sources or even employ heroic assumptions to construct relevant shadow prices anew. In CEA, however, they may not make an explicit connection between the effectiveness measure used and benefits that individuals value. When analysts use an intermediate output as a measure of effectiveness, they should establish a link between the effectiveness measure and a final consumption good, or at least show that the intermediate output indeed has some value.[2]

Sensitivity Analysis: The Problem of Ratios

Analysts can rarely predict either costs or the other effects of policy alternatives with great certainty. Conveying the level of uncertainty in projected cost–effectiveness ratios provides important information to both other analysts and decision-makers. The methods of sensitivity analysis for CBA presented in Chapter 11 – partial sensitivity analysis, worst- and best-case analysis, and Monte Carlo simulations – also apply to CEA.

The problem posed by ratios, however, makes Monte Carlo simulations particularly attractive in cost–effectiveness analysis. In cost–benefit analysis one adds or subtracts impacts (costs and benefits). If these variables have a multivariate normal distribution with known means, variances and co-variances, then the resulting sum (net benefits) would also be normally distributed with known mean and variance. Thus, it would be possible to obtain estimates of the probability the net benefit is in any specific range. In contrast, dividing one random variable (costs) by another (effectiveness) generally does not produce a CE ratio with a known distribution. Even if the variables have independent normal distributions, the ratio does not necessarily have a normal distribution. Furthermore, the mean cost–effectiveness ratio is not necessarily equal to the ratio of the means of the costs and effectiveness. Figure 18.2 illustrates these properties of cost–effectiveness ratios.

Consider a project that potentially will save lives. Suppose that the cost of the project is normally distributed with an estimated mean of $20 million and standard deviation of $2 million. Further suppose the number of lives saved is also normally distribution with an estimated mean of 10 lives saved and a standard deviation of two lives saved. These estimates might be based on data from similar projects that have been implemented elsewhere. In that case the standard deviations might be a standard error that is a by-product of the estimations. As explained in Chapter 11, the analyst may identify plausible bounds for uncertain parameters and assume particular distributions within the bounds. The Monte Carlo simulation presented in Figure 18.2 involves generating 10,000 pairs of values of cost and lives saved based on draws from their respective independent normal distributions. The top two histograms show the resulting distributions of draws for costs and lives saved separately, with theoretical normal distributions superimposed to demonstrate that the distributions in the histograms are approximately normal. The distribution of the resulting 10,000 cost–effectiveness ratios is displayed in the third histogram. Note that this distribution does not correspond nearly as closely to the normal distribution, again superimposed on the histogram, as with the variables used to construct it. The mean cost–effectiveness ratio of $2.1 million per life saved is higher than $2.0 million per life saved, the ratio of the mean cost to the mean number of lives saved. Furthermore, the distribution is not normal and is not symmetric, but is skewed to the right. In other words, the most likely outcome is a cost–effectiveness ratio slightly below the mean, but with some probability of substantially larger ratios. The distribution of the CE ratios can provide other information, such as the probability of the ratio being above, say, $3 million per life saved (5.6 percent in this example).[3]

The skewness in the distribution of the cost–effectiveness ratio would be even more pronounced if the distribution of effectiveness were spread more evenly over some

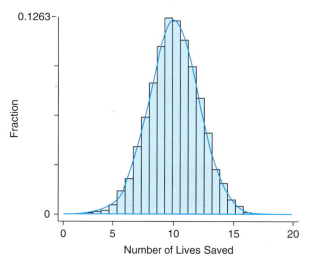

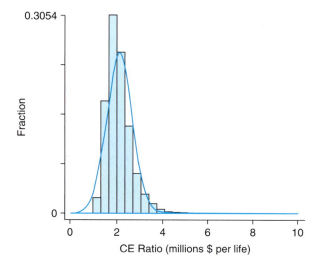

Figure 18.2 Monte Carlo analysis of a cost–effectiveness ratio.

range rather than having a central mode like the normal distribution. Also note that one could compare the distributions of cost–effectiveness ratios for two alternatives by superimposing their Monte Carlo distributions. A thicker left-hand tail, which represents a higher probability of lower CE ratios, would tend to favor that alternative. To make a more systematic comparison, one would need to construct a cumulative distribution for each alternative and, if one cumulative distribution lay consistently to the left of the other, select it as *stochastically dominant*. That is, it would consistently offer higher probabilities of achieving more desirable outcomes.

18.1.6   *Omitted Costs and Benefits*

As should be clear by this point, CBA takes a societal perspective and seeks to include *all* social costs and benefits. For CEA to be a useful guide for a more efficient allocation of resources, it too should take a societal perspective and seek to be as comprehensive as possible in measuring valued impacts. Most fundamentally, it should be based on all social costs, not only budgetary costs, and it should take account of social benefits that arise but are not captured in the effectiveness measure.

The measurement of costs in actual CEA studies varies enormously. When it is conducted for a particular government agency, measured costs usually equal that agency's budgetary costs.[4] For example, a CEA of a new medicine might consider only the cost of the medicine to the particular government agency that would have to pay for it. From a societal perspective, however, the analysis should also include other healthcare system costs, such as the cost of dispensing the medicine (at a pharmacy or elsewhere) and the cost of a health professional to administer the medicine (if applicable). Some healthcare system impacts might be benefits rather than costs. For example, a drug for treating schizophrenia, although expensive, might reduce the time patients spend in hospitals. Typically, CEA does not include costs borne by patients themselves, as well as family or friends, including travel time cost and the cost of unpleasant side effects. Similarly, in the regulatory arena, analysts might measure only the agency cost of enforcing compliance. From a societal perspective, however, firms' costs of complying with the regulations (reduced producer surplus) should also be included. Of course, even when looking at agency costs only, the guiding principle should be opportunity cost, as it is in CBA.

Similar issues arise concerning the inclusion of benefits. For example, regulations that save lives almost always also reduce injuries or illnesses (morbidity).

In order to make recommendations more closely aligned with allocative efficiency, one could compute the following *adjusted CE* ratio, denoted CE*:

$$CE_i^* = \frac{\text{Agency Costs}_i + \text{Other Social Costs}_i - \text{Other Social Benefits}_i}{\text{Effectiveness}_i} \tag{18.3}$$

where, Agency Costs are the costs included in a CEA, Other Social Costs reflect the social costs that were excluded from the CEA, and Other Social Benefits reflect the monetized value of the social benefits, except for the effectiveness measure, that were excluded from the CEA. If effectiveness were also monetized, then this ratio would be an inverted benefit–cost ratio.

One might wonder whether the policy recommendations would change if the omitted social costs and benefits were constant across all alternatives. To address this issue suppose that, in aggregate, the omitted social costs and social benefits for the alternatives shown in Table 18.2 amounted to $20 million. That is, the costs should be raised by $20 million to more accurately reflect omitted impacts. The CE ratios for alternatives A, B, and C increase, but the rank ordering remains the same.[5] For the least-cost alternative the ICER would increase (because it equals the CE ratio), but the ICERs of the other alternatives would be unchanged. Thus, the policy implications change for the smaller projects. Specifically, an analyst would recommend that if an average test score improvement (across all students) is valued at less than $7 million, then no policy alternative should be chosen. If an average test score improvement is valued between $7 million and $20 million, then alternative A should be chosen. However, as before, if the shadow price is between $20 million and $30 million, then alternative B should be selected, and if it is valued more than $30 million, then alternative C should be selected.

Thus, where policy alternatives are reasonably similar in terms of inputs required and the impacts they produce, the omission of some social costs or benefits might not matter, especially if one is likely to choose a relatively large-scale (expensive) option. However, where policy alternatives differ significantly in terms of inputs or outputs, taking omitted social costs or benefits into consideration might change the recommendations. It might also reduce the transparency of the analysis. In such situations moving all the way to CBA with extensive sensitivity analysis is often a better analytical strategy than expanding the scope of measured costs and benefits within a CEA framework.

18.2   Cost–Utility Analysis

Cost–utility analysis (CUA) is useful for evaluating health technologies. In CUA, effectiveness is usually measured in *quality-adjusted life years* (QALYs).[6] The QALY measure combines quantity of life and quality of life. All of the earlier discussion about cost–effectiveness ratios and decision rules continue to apply. Thus, one can think about CUA as a form of CEA that employs a more complex effectiveness measure. In CUA, the CE ratio measures the incremental cost per QALY gained relative to the status quo while the ICER measures the incremental cost per QALY gained relative to the next less costly alternative.

QALYs weight the quantity of life, measured in life years, by the utility derived during those years. Utility varies according to the health status. Worse health states have lower utility than good health states. Utility is scaled between 0, corresponding to death, and 1, which corresponds to perfect health. The utility of having a particular health status, H, is denoted $U(H)$, where $0 \leq U(H) \leq 1$. Utilities should be related to willingness to pay (WTP) values of the health states. The QALYs accruing to a person who has an expected life of y years in health state H equals $U(H)y$. The QALYs accruing to a person who has an expected life of y years in health state H_1 followed by x years in health state H_2 is given by:

$$QALY_s = U(H_1)y + U(H_2)x \qquad (18.4)$$

If decision-makers care only about the effect of a health intervention on the improvement in life years (reduction in death rates), and not the quality of those years, or if they only care about some naturalistic measure of health, such as fractures avoided or reduction in swollen joints, then CEA is a more appropriate evaluation method and CUA is unnecessary. CUA is useful when decision-makers want to evaluate alternative technologies that impact life years (mortality) and the quality of life (morbidity). Consider, for example, three mutually exclusive prenatal programs. Under the current policy, no babies with a particular condition are born alive. Prenatal alternative A will result in five babies being born alive per year, who are expected to live for a certain number of years but with permanent, serious disabilities. Prenatal alternative B will result in only two babies being born alive per year, but they are expected to live for more years and experience only low levels of disability. By knowing the utility associated with the different health statuses, analysts can compute the QALYs of the alternatives. QALYs are also useful when decision-makers want to compare non-mutually exclusive alternatives that have different kinds of outcomes, such as a prevention program and a treatment program. QALY is a common unit of measurement for the outcomes of both types of programs. Thus, QALYs enable comparison of different health technologies that might have quite different effects on health status.

18.2.1   *Utility Weights*

Health economists often use the terms quality of life (QOL), health-related quality of life (HRQoL or HRQOL) and health status. Unfortunately, these terms are often used imprecisely and there is often disagreement on their meanings.[7] Some economists use QOL or HRQoL to refer to health status while others use them to refer to utility. Given the above definition of a QALY, it is essential to distinguish between health status and the utility of a particular health status.

The simplest measure of health status is a unidimensional scale that runs on a continuum from death to perfect health with intermediate points, such as mildly disabled or severely disabled. More recently, health economists have developed multidimensional scales that consider physical, mental, and other dimensions of healthy well-being separately. Analysts can assign numbers to each health state on each dimension and thus one can think about health states H_1 and H_2 as vectors whose components indicate the quality of a particular dimension of health. Construction of a QALY for a health status requires determining the utility of that health status.

In practice, analysts derive preference-based utility weights by administering a questionnaire, interviewing or assembling a panel of medical experts, patients or the general public. For the goal of maximizing allocative efficiency, the most appropriate respondents would be informed members of the general public because they are "society." However, while they (collectively) are generally unbiased, they may be biased against certain conditions, such as those that result from risky behavior or unhealthy lifestyles. Furthermore, members of the general public who have never experienced a particular health state may be unable to make an accurate assessment of what that condition is like. Researchers can provide descriptions of a given health status, but those descriptions might be too short (not provide enough information) or too long (respondents suffer from information overload). Consequently, some researchers argue that researchers should use actual patients that have experienced the condition.[8] Patients are likely to be more knowledgeable than the general public about what it is like to experience a particular health status. However, patients may be more biased than the public concerning their condition, and may act strategically. For example, they might overestimate the severity of their condition because they think it might lead to increased funding. In practice, however, people who experience the status generally reveal a higher utility for it than do those without it.[9] Such differences are consistent with people having a larger WTA to avoid losing health status (the general population) than a WTP to gain it (the patient population).

The advantage of medical experts is that they typically bring relevant experience and knowledge, especially with respect to the physical implications of various health statuses. They also are likely to be sophisticated respondents who can answer more complex questions. Nonetheless, their medically informed assessments may not correspond to the holistic assessments made by patients or members of the general public thinking prospectively about health statuses.[10]

Researchers have used a variety of approaches to assess the utility weights used to construct QALYs.[11] Some methods determine the health status and the associated utility in one step and are referred to as direct approaches. There are also a number of methods that are two-step procedures, first measuring health status through questionnaires administered to patients and then mapping health states into utilities. These methods are sometimes referred to as indirect approaches.

18.2.2   *Direct Utility Weight Estimation Methods*

The health rating (HR) method, the time trade-off (TTO) method, and the standard gamble (SG) method all attempt to estimate utilities directly.

Health Rating Method. Researchers derive a *health rating* (HR) by describing a health state in detail and asking respondents to locate it on a scale that typically runs from 0 (death) to 1 (perfect health). For example, if three intermediate health states described to an individual correspond to "seriously disabled," "moderately disabled," and "minimally disabled," then an individual might assign values of 0.15, 0.45, and 0.90 to these states, respectively. Sometimes researchers provide a visual analog scale and the method is referred to as the health thermometer or feeling thermometer scale. It is often used as a starting point, before other methods.

Unfortunately, respondents often have difficulty assigning realistic numerical values to the various health states. An alternative version of the health rating method uses a bisection process to obviate the need for respondents to provide numerical values. It gives respondents a list of health states from which they are asked to find the one that falls midway between the end points on a visual display, such as a thermometer scale.[12] Respondents are then asked to find the health state that falls midway between the initially placed health state and the upper and lower endpoints, respectively. The process continues until respondents have placed the various health states on the scale. It yields an interval scale for utility, but one without a clear basis in revealed preferences because it is not based on trade-offs. Indeed, the absence of rankings based on a trade-off bring into question their validity and usefulness in CUA.

Time Trade-Off Method. In the *time trade-off* (TTO) method, respondents are asked to compare different combinations of length of life and quality of life.[13] The typical comparison is between a longer life of lower health status and a shorter life with a higher health status. Figure 18.3 illustrates such a comparison. The horizontal axis measures additional years of life (Y), and the vertical axis measures health status (H). Respondents might be asked to compare some status quo point, say R, representing health status H_2 and additional years of life Y_1 with an alternative point, say S, representing health status H_1 and additional years of life Y_2. If a respondent is indifferent between the two points, then he or she is willing to give up $H_2 - H_1$ units of health quality in return for $Y_2 - Y_1$ additional years of life. Assuming that health status H_2 is perfect health and assigning it a utility of 1, the utility assigned to H_1 is then Y_1/Y_2.

For example, imagine that one wanted to assign a utility to the health status of twice-weekly severe lower back pain that prevents strenuous physical activity. The severity and consequences of the back pain would be carefully described to a number of respondents. Then each would be asked to compare living 10 additional years with the back pain to living some number of years in perfect health. If a respondent were indifferent between living 10 years with the back pain and 9 years in perfect health, then

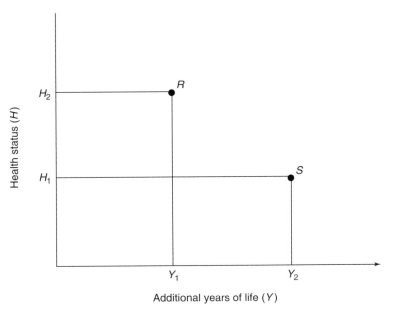

Figure 18.3 Time trade-off example.

the analyst would assign a utility of 9/10 for the health state of twice-weekly severe back pain. Thus, in comparing medical interventions, an additional year of life with back pain would be valued at 0.9 instead of at 1 for an additional year in perfect health.

A complication arises if a respondent views the health status being valued as worse than death. In such cases, they are asked to compare immediate death as one alternative with t_1 additional years of life in the extremely undesirable health status followed by t_2 years in full health as the other. Holding the total of t_1 and t_2 constant, the values that make the respondent indifferent between the alternatives would assign a utility to the extremely undesirable health status of $-t_2/t_1$. The resulting negative value is consistent with the health status being valued as worse than death, which is assigned a utility of 0.

In order for the TTO values to represent valid utilities, a strong assumption must be met: individuals must be willing to give up constant proportions of their remaining life-years to attain an improvement in health status, no matter how many additional life-years remain. For example, if a person expecting to live 10 years with a disability were willing to give up 5 years to attain perfect health, then when the person has only 8 years of expected life, he or she should also be willing to give up 4 of the 8 remaining years to obtain perfect health. The assumption of constant proportional time trade-off implies that the person has a zero marginal rate of time preference. A particularly serious violation of the constant proportions assumption occurs when a person's preferences for life-years in some health status exhibit *maximum endurable time* (MET): there is a limit to the number of years people want to live with the health status.[14] The stringency of the constant proportions assumption suggests caution in interpreting TTO values as utilities. Nonetheless, the TTO method continues to be used to place relative values on health statuses for the construction of QALYs.

Standard Gamble Method. The *standard gamble* (SG) approach is based on the concept of expected value. Respondents are presented with a decision tree like those described in Chapter 11 and are offered a choice between two alternatives.[15] Alternative A has two possible outcomes: either a return to normal health for n additional years (occurring with probability p) or immediate death (occurring with probability $1 - p$). Alternative A might be an operation that has probability $1 - p$ of failure (death), but which, if successful, will return the patient to normal health for n years. Alternative B guarantees the patient n additional years with a specified level of health impairment. This choice is shown in Figure 18.4. The probability p is varied until a respondent is indifferent between alternatives A and B. The p at which a respondent is indifferent can be interpreted as that respondent's utility from alternative B.

For example, consider again the assignment of a utility to the health status of twice-weekly severe lower back pain that prevented strenuous physical activity. There are two approaches to finding the probability of perfect health that would make the respondent indifferent between the gamble and the back pain. Researchers could simply ask the respondent to state the probability. Alternatively, researchers could offer an initial probability, and then raise or lower it until the respondent expresses indifference. The former approach might not work well with respondents who are not used to thinking in terms of probabilities. To minimize this problem, it may be desirable to engage the respondent in some valuations of other health statuses before turning to the current one

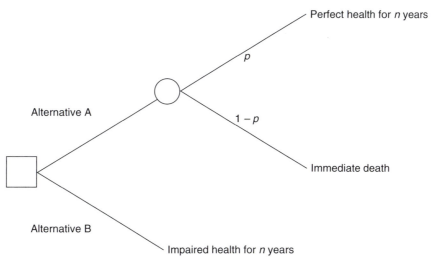

Figure 18.4 The standard gamble method.

of interest. The latter approach risks the sort of starting point bias that was discussed in connection with contingent valuation in Chapter 16. Starting points should be varied across respondents to allow for the possibility of detecting any starting point bias. Suppose that the method used reveals that the respondent is indifferent between the back pain for certain and a gamble with a probability of perfect health of 0.95 and a probability of death of 0.05. The SG method would assign a utility to the health status of lower back pain of 0.95.

The SG method assumes that individuals make rational choices. If they do, then the utilities resulting from the SG method are valid. However, deviations from rational expected utility, such as the judgmental biases discussed in Chapter 16, weaken the validity of the utilities derived from the SG method.

18.2.3   *Indirect Utility Weight Estimation Methods*

Indirect utility assessment methods require two distinct steps. First, through a questionnaire, patients characterize their health state, usually measured over several domains (dimensions). Health analysts have developed a variety of scales to assess variations in health status, whether in relationship to particular diseases, injuries, or mental states, or to health in general. Many, however, including those discussed below are based on generic health classification schemes (i.e., they are not disease-specific). Second, each health state is assigned a utility value. These values are often obtained from one of the direct methods (HR, TTO, or SG). For some states, utilities are imputed following some econometric analysis. The result is a multi-attribute utility function over the various health states.

The Health Utilities Index Mark 2 and 3 (HUI2 and HUI3), and the Short Form Health Survey (SF-36) are widely used generic health status questionnaires. Each of these approaches measures different dimensions of health and then applies different mapping functions to determine utilities.

Health Utility Index (HUI) Method. This method evolved out of a health classification system introduced by George Torrance and colleagues[16] and it was further developed by the McMaster University's Centre for Health Economics and Policy Analysis. Heath Utilities Inc. currently offers several copyrighted versions to researchers.[17] The questionnaires are generic. The Health Utility Index Mark 3 (HUI3), for instance, has eight dimensions (or attributes): vision, hearing, speech, ambulation, dexterity, emotion, cognition, and pain. Each dimension has clearly defined ordinal levels of severity. For example, the levels for pain are "free of pain and discomfort," "mild to moderate pain that prevents no activities," "moderate pain that prevents a few activities," "moderate to severe pain that prevents some activities," and "severe pain that prevents most activities." With either five or six levels for each attribute, this classification system defines 972,000 distinct health states.[18] Health Utilities Inc. provides tables derived from general population surveys and multi-attribute utility scaling that converts each health state into a single utility measure or it can provide a utility measure for each dimension.[19]

Short Form Health Survey (SF-36) Method. The Short Form Health Survey (SF-36) was originated by researchers at the RAND Corporation as part of the Medical Outcomes Study.[20] The SF-36 uses 35 items to construct eight scales: physical functioning, role limitation due to physical problems, bodily pain, general health, vitality, social function, role limitation due to emotional problems, and mental health. The first four of these scales combine to form a summary measure of physical health, and the latter four combine to form a summary measure of mental health. The SF-36 is licensed through Quality Metric Inc.[21] and has been made available in many languages through the International Quality of Life Assessment Project.[22]

Efforts are underway to create a mapping from scales derived from the SF-36 to utilities. For example, John Brazier and his colleagues have created a simplified version of the SF-36, the SF-6D, which reduces the number of scales (dimensions) from eight to six by excluding the general health scale and combining the physical and emotional role limitations into a single index.[23] Each of the six dimensions has five or six levels of response, enabling them to define 18,000 different health states. The researchers next selected 49 representative health states and employed the SG method in interviews with a general population sample of UK respondents. Next they estimated econometric models with utilities as the dependent variable and the various levels on the six dimensions as explanatory variables. The coefficients estimated for the various levels can then be used to assign utilities to any one of the possible health statuses.[24] Researchers who can classify outcomes in terms of the SF-6D scale can thus derive utilities for these outcomes. Of course, the resulting utilities were based on the preferences of the UK general public and might not be appropriate in other national contexts. The estimates have been replicated for around half a dozen countries including Japan, Australia, and Brazil, but so far not for the United States.[25]

EuroQol and Other Methods. Other health status indices have been created and related to population preferences. For example, European researchers organized as the EuroQol association have developed the EQ-5D index to generate cross-national comparisons of health status.[26] Utilities have been assigned to EQ-5D health status through general population surveys using the TTO method.[27]

Exhibit 18.1

Researchers conducted a study comparing various utility elicitation methods for gastroesophageal reflux disease with heartburn. Samples of patients with a history of heartburn were recruited in Germany and Sweden. After asking respondents about the severity of their heartburn in a typical week, the researchers administered the EQ-5D health index and then applied the health rating (HR), time trade-off (TTO), and standard gamble (SG) methods. For example, the SG alternatives were presented as follows:

> Alternative 1 is that you know for certain that you will live for another 10 years in your current health state. During these 10 years, your heartburn as well as symptoms of any other health problems that you may have will be exactly as you have experienced them over the last 12 months. After these 10 years you will die.
>
> Alternative 2 is that there is a treatment that either is successful or fails. If the treatment is successful, you will recover perfect health and remain perfectly healthy during 10 years, that is, the same period of time as in alternative 1. Perfect health means that you are free from all health problems, that is, you are free from heartburn as well as symptoms of any other health problems that you may have. After these 10 years you will die. If treatment fails, you will die immediately. (p. 43)

After giving respondents randomly assigned starting points of either 0.95 or 0.70 for the probability of success, probabilities were raised or lowered until the respondent was indifferent between the alternatives. Over one-third of respondents were unwilling to accept any risk of death for the chance of perfect health (or accept any reduction of years in the TTO method). The mean values from the SG method were 0.92, 0.88, and 0.86 for mild, moderate, and severe heartburn, respectively. The TTO values for the three levels of severity were 0.90, 0.87, and 0.85. In contrast to these relatively high utilities, the HR method produced utilities of 0.75, 0.67, and 0.49, while the EQ-5D based utilities were 0.78, 0.67, and 0.49. Thus, the SG and TTO methods showed much smaller losses in utility from chronic heartburn than the HR or the EQ-5D methods.

Source: Adapted from Bernt Kartman, Gudrun Gatz, and Magnus Johannesson, "Health State Utilities in Gastroesophageal Reflux Disease Patients with Heartburn: A Study in Germany and Sweden." *Medical Decision Making*, 24(1), 2004, 40–52.

18.2.4   *Reprise of Methods to Obtain Utility Weights*

Each of the direct utility assessment methods has its drawbacks. However, the choice-based techniques (TTO and SG) are preferable to the HR method because they are based on trade-offs. Although direct comparisons of the TTO and SG methods generally conclude that they provide similar utilities at least in terms of ordinal rankings,[28] a majority of studies find that the SG method yields higher values for utilities.[29] As mentioned above one reason to prefer the TTO method is that the SG method assumes that individuals make rational choices that are consistent with expected utility theory, which they often do not.

Many researchers prefer indirect utility assessment techniques to direct methods because they are relatively easy and less costly to administer. When using these methods it is usually recommended that analysts use a generic health state classification scheme like those discussed above and map the health states into utilities based on the preferences of the general public. However, there is little information to guide analysts' choice of indirect utility technique. Researchers have begun to compare the utilities and the sensitivity of utilities to changes in health statuses across the various health indexes. For example, a comparison of EQ-5D and SF-6D utilities for liver transplant patients found that the SF-6D does not describe health statuses at the lower end of the utility scale well but is more sensitive than EQ-5D in detecting small changes toward the top of the scale.[30] A comparison of the HUI3, the SF-6D, and the EQ-5D for patients with rheumatological conditions suggested broad agreement, but it also showed a number of specific differences that make the particular choice of index potentially relevant to constructing QALYs.[31] Another study on patients with rheumatoid arthritis found that scores from the HU12, HU13, EQ-5D, and SF-6D yielded significantly different utilities, especially at lower utilities.[32]

18.2.5   *Decision-Making, Review Panels, and Threshold Values*

To make policy recommendations using QALYs, analysts compute ICERs as in any CEA analysis. Suppose that an analyst conducts a study analyzing a new medicine and finds that, relative to a placebo (no medicine), the CE ratio and the ICER equals $400,000 per QALY gained. Before she can make a recommendation, she needs to know the social value of a QALY gained. Chapter 17 suggests that the value of a life-year (VLY) is, on average, about $515,100 in the US. Therefore, in the absence of an alternative medicine, she might recommend adoption of the new technology. However, the new technology might not be adopted because it does not meet the threshold employed by the government agency making the decision.

Many governments have advisory agencies that conduct CEA or CUA analyses of new medical technologies or review analyses conducted by others in order to make policy recommendations concerning the listing of new technologies on government formularies (or benefits schemes). If a drug, for example, is listed on the formulary then government or insurance companies will pay part of the patient's cost of purchasing the drug. These advisory agencies include the National Institute for Health and Clinical Excellence (NICE) in the UK, the CADTH Common Drug Review (CDR) in Canada, the Pharmaceutical Benefits Advisory Committee (PBAC) in Australia, and the Pharmacology and Therapeutics Advisory Committee (PTAC) in New Zealand.[33]

Typically, these review agencies have implicit or explicit thresholds below which a drug would be cost effective and above which it would not. In about 2008, NICE would, in general, consider interventions of £20,000 (approximately $41,000 in 2016 US$) per QALY gained as cost-effective. For ICERs in the range of £20,000–$30,000 per QALY gained, NICE takes other factors into consideration.[34] Governments are not required to adopt the recommendations of their review agencies and often they do not. They may have implicit thresholds, but are reluctant to publically specify them because it would reduce their decision-making flexibility. Whether the advisory agency or government threshold is implicit or not, it is generally considerably lower than the social value of a QALY gained.

One limitation of some CUAs concerns the selection of alternative policies used in the evaluation. CUAs of new drugs often have only two alternatives: the new drug under evaluation and a placebo (no treatment). Studies may not contain head-to-head comparisons with similar drugs, that is, drugs that treat similar conditions or, more formally, are in the same fourth-level Anatomical Therapeutic Classification (ATC) class. Thus, it may often be the case that a new drug is more cost-effective than no drug, but less cost-effective than an existing drug. Another problem is that CUA evaluations rarely control for the effects of multiple comorbidities, that is, where patients suffer from more than one disease or health problem. Finally, and most importantly, CUAs are usually conducted *ex ante* where compliance is relatively high. Rarely are CUAs conducted *ex post*. These problems arise because CUAs are expensive and are often funded by pharmaceutical companies to obtain a listing in a formulary.

18.2.6   *QALYs: Caveats and Use in CBA*

As is evident from Equation (18.4), the construction of QALYs using health status utilities assumes that the utility of being in a particular health state is proportional to the time spent in that state. This strong assumption is equivalent to assuming a zero rate of time preference for QALYs. From an allocative efficiency perspective, it is problematic to discount costs but not to discount QALYs.[35] The reason is that if costs but not QALYs were discounted, the cost–effectiveness ratio of a policy that involves the accrual of costs and QALYs over substantial periods of time would improve if the health expenditure were delayed until the following year.[36] As discussed in Chapter 10, the basic idea that individuals have positive discount rates relating to additional years is widely accepted, although there is some controversy over the appropriate value of the discount rate.[37]

The use of QALYs is not limited to CUA, but can also be used in CBA with a shadow price. The basic procedure would be to monetize QALYs using the value of a life-year. For example, imagine that a public health intervention would save 10 QALYs this year and 20 QALYs next year. If the analyst values a life-year (VLY) at $500,000, then the benefits in the first year of the intervention would be $5 million, and the benefits in the second year would be $10 million. These annual benefits would then be discounted to produce a present value of benefits. As discussed in Chapter 17, however, using a constant VLY is controversial because it implies a VSL that is lower for older people with shorter life expectancies.

More generally, monetized QALYs may differ from WTP in a number of ways.[38] Use of monetized QALYs as an approximation of WTP implicitly assumes that people value health statuses independently of when and how long they experience them as well as independently of their wealth, age, and expected longevity.[39] For example, a 30-year-old may assess a reduced physical capacity for strenuous activities, such as skiing or running, at a much lower utility than would a 70-year-old. For policies that provide general reductions in mortality, analysts commonly use a VSL based on the mean or median for the relevant population even though wealthier and more risk-averse individuals would likely have higher WTP for the risk reductions than would poorer and less risk-averse individuals. Monetizing QALYs involves this simplification when a single VLY based on the VSL is used. It also typically employs mean or median utilities of health states and further assumes that these utilities do not depend on their timing or duration. Consequently, monetizing QALYs generally involves greater uncertainty than monetizing avoided immediate deaths.

18.3   The Use of League Tables

CEA usually compares mutually exclusive projects. By definition, this means that the alternative projects address the same problems, for example, alternative methods of breast cancer screening. Yet, CEA has been used to make rankings *across* policies that have the same broad purpose (e.g., saving lives) but are not necessarily mutually exclusive. *League tables* rank multiple CEAs that share the same cost–effectiveness measure. Tammy Tengs and her colleagues, for example, have developed a league table of 587 interventions intended to avert premature death (i.e., to save lives).[40] They found that, on average, the United States spent about $637,200 per life saved or $61,200 per year of life saved (converted to 2017 dollars). They also asked the question: How many lives would be saved if the same investment were focused on the most cost-effective interventions? They conclude that an additional 60,200 lives could be saved, or about twice as many lives as under the then current allocation. In a similar study, John Morrall III, updating an earlier review he conducted, assessed the cost-effectiveness of 76 regulations issued by the US federal government between 1967 and 2001. He found that the cost–effectiveness ratios differed by six orders of magnitude and that regulations aimed at reducing safety and cardiovascular risks have been much more cost-effective than regulations aimed at reducing cancer risks.[41]

How useful are league tables? Comparisons of mutually exclusive projects inherently control for some of the differences in the measurement of cost and effectiveness. One cannot reasonably make this presumption when comparing studies across different authors, using different data, and somewhat different methodologies. Different studies may measure costs differently, they may omit different costs, and they may differ considerably in scale. These problems also apply to CUA league tables than to other league tables, possibly more so, because different methodologies are used to calculate QALYs and, as discussed earlier, these methodologies do not necessarily produce similar results. Also, in practice, a disproportionate number of CUA studies present their results as "favorable."[42] Other critics have also noted the absence of information on uncertainty in most league tables.[43] Thus, considerable caution is warranted in using league tables as guides for policy choice.

Exhibit 18.2

The Cost–Utility Registry housed in the Center for the Evaluation of Value and Risk in Health at Tufts University provides a comprehensive listing of cost–effectiveness studies in the health area. The registry currently lists approximately 23,000 utilities drawn from CEAs. It thus provides a rich source of information for constructing QALYs for use in CBAs by analysts who do not have the resources to develop their own estimates. More generally, analysts planning to conduct their surveys may find it useful to review studies that used similar methods.

Source: Adapted from CEA Registry, Center for the Evaluation of Value and Risk in Health, Tufts University, www.cearegistry.org

---

18.4   Conclusion: When Is CEA Close to CBA?

CEA can identify the set of alternatives that dominate other alternatives in terms of technical efficiency. Given a specific monetary value (or range) of the effectiveness measure, CEA can provide "reasonable" policy recommendations. These policy recommendations are close to CBA recommendations and may maximize allocative efficiency when the government agency costs are the only opportunity costs of the policy alternatives, when the effectiveness measure captures all of the social benefits, when all of the impacts are short-term, and when the threshold value of the effectiveness measure equals its social value (shadow price).

In practice, these conditions are unlikely to hold. Nonetheless, despite the limitations of CEA as a means of providing a measure of allocative efficiency, it serves a useful function in many circumstances. It is evidence-based and is relatively simple. Bureaucrats and politicians can understand cost per life saved or cost per QALY, for example. Furthermore, they may not care that the cost measure takes a government agency perspective and omits other social costs. Constructing a QALY is more complicated than conducting CEA and often requires strong assumptions. In practice, therefore, decision-makers often request both CEA and CUA when making health technology decisions.

Exercises for Chapter 18

1. A public health department is considering five alternative programs to encourage parents to have their preschool children vaccinated against a communicable disease. The following table shows the cost and number of vaccinations predicted for each program.

Program	Cost ($)	Number of vaccinations
A	20,000	2,000
B	44,000	4,000
C	72,000	6,000
D	104,000	8,000
E	150,000	10,000

   a. Ignoring issues of scale, which program is most cost-effective?

   b. Assuming that the public health department wishes to vaccinate at least 5000 children, which program is most cost-effective?

   c. What is the incremental cost–effectiveness ratio of program D?

   d. If the health department believes that each vaccination provides social benefits equal to $10, then which program should it adopt?

2. Analysts wish to evaluate alternative surgical procedures for spinal cord injuries. The procedures have various probabilities of yielding the following results.

   Full recovery (FR) – the patient regains full mobility and suffers no chronic pain. Full functional recovery (FFR) – the patient regains full mobility but suffers chronic pain that will make it uncomfortable to sit for periods of longer than about an hour and will interfere with sleeping two nights per week, on average. Partial functional recovery (PFR) – the patient regains only restricted movement that will limit mobility to slow-paced walking and will make it difficult to lift objects weighing more than a few pounds. Chronic pain is similar to that suffered under full functional recovery.

   Paraplegia (P) – the patient completely loses use of legs and would, therefore, require a wheelchair or other prosthetic for mobility and suffers chronic pain that interferes with sleeping four nights per week, on average. Aside from loss of the use of his or her legs, the patient would regain control of other lower body functions.

   a. Describe how you would construct a quality-of-life index for these surgical outcomes by offering gambles to respondents. Test your procedure on a classmate, friend, or other willing person.

b. Assume that the index you construct on the basis of your sample of one respondent is representative of the population of patients. Use the index to measure the effectiveness of each of three alternative surgical procedures with the following distributions of outcomes.

	Surgical procedures		
	A	B	C
FR	0.10	0.50	0.40
FFR	0.70	0.20	0.45
PFR	0.15	0.20	0.10
P	0.05	0.10	0.05

c. Imagine that the surgical procedures involved different life expectancies for the various outcomes. Discuss how you might revise your measure of effectiveness to take account of these differences.

3. (Instructor-provided spreadsheet recommended.) Two alternative mosquito control programs have been proposed to reduce the health risks of West Nile disease in a state over the next five years. The costs and effectiveness of each program in each of the next five years are provided in the following table.

	Alternative A		Alternative B	
	QALYs saved	Incremental cost (millions of dollars)	QALYs saved	Incremental cost (millions of dollars)
Year 1	1.0	3.8	0.5	1.0
Year 2	0.5	0.0	0.5	1.0
Year 3	0.3	0.0	0.5	1.0
Year 4	0.1	0.0	0.5	1.0

a. Calculate CE ratios for each program without discounting.

b. Calculate CE ratios discounting cost but not effectiveness assuming a discount rate of 4 percent.

c. Calculate CE ratios discounting both costs and effectiveness at 4 percent.

d. Assume that the uncertainty range for each of the yearly effectiveness estimates is plus or minus 20 percent and the uncertainty in each of the yearly cost estimates is 10 percent. Assuming uniform distributions of errors, produce Monte Carlo distributions of CE ratios for each program and compare them.

Notes

1. Economists have attempted to determine the circumstances under which CEA is consistent with the assumptions of welfare economics that underlie CBA. Overall, strong assumptions are required for consistency. For overviews, see Werner B. F. Brouwer and Marc A. Koopmanshap, "On the Economic Foundations of CEA: Ladies and Gentlemen, Take Your Positions!" *Journal of Health Economics*, 19(4), 2000, 439–59; and Paul Dolan and Richard Edlin, "Is It Really Possible to Build a Bridge Between Cost–Benefit Analysis and Cost–Effectiveness Analysis?" *Journal of Health Economics*, 21(5), 2002, 827–43.

2. See Michael Drummond, Greg L. Stoddart, and George W. Torrance, *Methods for the Economic Evaluations of Health Care Programmes* (Oxford: Oxford University Press, 1987), especially page 76.

3. Monte Carlo simulations can be used to construct cost–effectiveness acceptability curves that give the probability of a particular alternative being optimal for different shadow prices of effect. See Elisabeth Fenwick, Karl Claxton, and Mark Sculpher, "Representing Uncertainty: The Role of Cost–Effectiveness Acceptability Curves." *Health Economics*, 10(8), 2001, 779–87.

4. Karen Gerard found that approximately 90 percent of the health studies she reviewed only looked at direct budgetary costs; see Karen Gerard, "Cost–Utility in Practice: A Policy Maker's Guide to the State of the Art." *Health Policy*, 21(3), 1992, 249–79 at p. 263.

5. The changes in the magnitude of the computed CE ratios may be relevant in using these context-specific CE ratios as a basis for making general comparisons across types of alternatives. See Christopher J. L. Murray, David B. Evans, Arnab Acharya, and Rob M. P. M. Baltussen, "Development of WHO Guidelines on Generalized Cost–Effectiveness Analysis." *Health Economics*, 9(3), 2000, 235–51.

6. Some analysts measure effectiveness by *disability-adjusted life-years* (DALYs), which were developed primarily to quantify the mortality and morbidity burdens of various diseases in populations. See Christopher J. L. Murray and Arnab K. Acharya, "Understanding DALYs." *Journal of Health Economics*, 16(6), 1997, 703–30. For a critique, see Sudhir Anand and Kara Hanson, "Disability-Adjusted Life Years: A Critical Assessment." *Journal of Health Economics*, 16(6), 1997, 685–702.

7. Milad Karimi and John Brazier, "Health, Health-Related Quality of Life, and Quality of Life: What is the Difference?" *PharmacoEconomics*, 34, 2016, 645–49.

8. See, for example, Pirjo Rääsänen, Eija Roine, Harri Sintonen, Virpi Semberg-Konttinen, Olli-Pekka Ryynänen, and Risto Roine, "Use of Quality-Adjusted Life Years for

the Estimation of Effectiveness of Health Care: A Systematic Literature Review." *International Journal of Technology Assessment in Health Care*, 22(2), 2006, 235–41.

9. Peter A Ubel, George Loewenstein, and Christopher Jepson, "Whose Quality of Life? A Commentary Exploring Discrepancies Between Health State Evaluations of Patients and the General Public." *Quality of Life Research*, 12(6), 2003, 599–607.

10. For more discussion about the choice of respondent, see Peter A. Ubel, Jeff Richardson, and Paul Menzel, "Societal Value, the Person Trade-Off, and the Dilemma of Whose Values to Measure for Cost–Effectiveness Analysis." *Health Economics*, 9(2), 2000, 127–36; David L. Sackett and George W. Torrance, "The Utility of Different Health States as Perceived by the General Public." *Journal of Chronic Diseases*, 31(11), 1978, 697–704; Debra Froberg and Robert L. Kane, "Methodology for Measuring Health-State Preferences – IV: Progress and a Research Agenda." *Journal of Clinical Epidemiology*, 42(7), 1989, 775–785; Paul Dolan, "The Measurement of Health-Related Quality of Life for Use in Resource Allocation in Health Care." In: Anthony J. Culyer and Joseph P. Newhouse, editors, *Handbook of Health Economics* 1B (New York, NY: Elsevier, 2000), pp. 1738–39 and 1748; and Rajiv Sharma, Miron Stano, and Mitchell Haas, "Adjusting to Changes in Health: Implications for Cost–Effectiveness Analysis." *Journal of Health Economics*, 23(2), 2004, 335–51.

11. Pirjo Rääsänen, Eija Roine, Harri Sintonen, Virpi Semberg-Konttinen, Olli-Pekka Ryynänen, Risto Roine, "Use of Quality-Adjusted Life Years for the Estimation of Effectiveness of Health Care: A Systematic Literature Review."

12. For an overview of this and the other methods for assessing HRQoL, see Dolan, "The Measurement of Health-Related Quality of Life for Use in Resource Allocation in Health Care."

13. The TTO method was first proposed by G. W. Torrance, W. H. Thomas, and D. L. Sackett, "A Utility Measurement Method for Evaluation of Health Care Programs." *Health Services Research*, 7(2), 1972, 118–33.

14. Paul Dolan and Peep Stalmeier, "The Validity of Time Trade-Off Values in Calculating QALYs: Constant Proportional Time Trade-Off versus the Proportional Heuristic." *Journal of Health Economics*, 22(3), 2003, 445–58.

15. The general SG method was introduced by John von Neumann and Oskar Morgenstern, *Theory of Games and Economic Behavior* (Princeton, NJ: Princeton University Press, 1944).

16. George W. Torrance, Michael H. Boyle, and Sargent P. Horwood, "Application of Multi-Attribute Utility Theory to Measure Social Preferences for Health Status." *Operations Research*, 30(6), 1982, 1043–69.

17. Additional information, including a bibliography of studies that have used the health utilities indices, can be found at www.healthutilities.com.

18. John Horsman, William Furlong, David Feeny, and George Torrance, "The Health Utilities Index (HUI®): Concepts, Measurement Properties, and Applications." *Health Quality and Life Outcomes*, 1(1), 2003, 54–67.

19. It is possible to obtain negative utility values which represent situations worse than death.

20. John E. Ware Jr. and Cathy D. Sherbourne, "The MOS 36-Item Short Form Health Survey: I. Conceptual Framework and Item Selection." *Medical Care*, 30(6), 1992, 473–83.

21. See www.qualitymetric.com/products/descriptions/sflicenses.shtml for additional information.

22. John E. Ware Jr. and Barbara Gandek, "Overview of the SF-36 Health Survey Instrument and the International Quality of Life Assessment (IQOLA) Project." *Journal of Clinical Epidemiology*, 51(11), 1998, 903–12.

23. John Brazier, Jennifer Roberts, and Mark Deverill, "The Estimation of a Preference-Based Measure of Health from the SF-36." *Journal of Health Economics*, 21(2), 2002, 271–92; and John Brazier, Tim Usherwood, Rosemary Harper, and Kate Thomas, "Deriving a Preference-Based Single Index from the UK SF-36 Health Survey." *Journal of Clinical Epidemiology*, 51(11), 1998, 1115–28.

24. John Brazier, Jennifer Roberts, and Mark Deverill, "The Estimation of a Preference-Based Measure of Health from the SF-36," tables 5 and 6.

25. See www.shef.ac.uk/scharr/sections/heds/mvh/sf-6d.

26. Richard Books and EuroQol Group, "EuroQol: The Current State of Play." *Health Policy*, 37(1), 1996, 53–72. For current information about EuroQol and the EQ-5D index, see www.euroqol.org/

27. See, for example, Paul Dolan, "Modelling Valuations for Health States: The Effect of Duration." *Health Policy*, 38(3), 189–203.

28. See, for example, J. L. Read, R. J. Quinn, D. M. Berrick, H. V. Fineberg, and M. C. Weinstein, "Preferences for Health Outcomes: Comparisons of Assessment Methods." *Medical Decision Making*, 4(3), 1984, 315–29; and George W. Torrance, "Social Preferences for Health States: An Empirical Evaluation of Three Measurement Techniques." *Socio-Economic Planning*, 10(2), 1976, 129–36.

29. See, for example, Han Bleichrodt and Magnus Johannesson, "Standard Gamble, Time Trade-Off and Rating Scale: Experimental Results on Ranking Properties of QALYs." *Journal of Health Economics*, 16(2), 1997, 155–75.

30. Louise Longworth and Stirling Bryan, "An Empirical Comparison of EQ-5D and SF-6D in Liver Transplant Patients." *Health Economics*, 12(12), 2003, 1061–67.

31. Barbara Conner-Spady and Maria E. Suarez-Almazor, "Variation in the Estimation of Quality Adjusted Life-Years by Different Preference-Based Instruments." *Medical Care*, 41(7), 2003, 791–801. Also see Jeff Richardson, Munir A. Khan, Angelo Iezzi, and Aimee Maxwell, "Comparing and Explaining differences in the magnitude, content, and sensitivity of utilities predicted by the EQ-5D, SF-6D, HUI 3, 15D, QWB, and AQoL-8D Multiattribute Utility Instruments." *Medical Decision Making*, 35(3), 2015, 276–91.

32. Carlo A. Marra, John M. Esdaile, Daphne Guh, Jacek A. Kopec, John E. Brazier, Barry E. Koehler, Andrew Chalmers and Aslam H. Anis, "A Comparison of Four Indirect Methods of Assessing Utility Values in Rheumatoid Arthritis." *Medical Care*, 42(11), 2004, 1125–31.

33. Steven G. Morgan, Meghan McMahon, Craig Mitton, Elizabeth Roughead, Ray Kirk, Panos Kanavos, and Devidas Menon, "Centralized Drug Review Processes in Australia, Canada, New Zealand, and the United Kingdom." *Health Affairs*, 25(2), 2006, 337–47.

34. See NICE, "Social Value Judgments: Principles for the Development of Nice Guidance," available at www.nice.org.uk/Media/Default/About/what-we-do/Research-and-development/Social-Value-Judgements-principles-for-the-development-of-NICE-guidance.pdf [accessed August 1, 2017].

35. Because of this problem, Abraham Mehrez and Amiran Gafni proposed healthy-years equivalents as an effectiveness measure; see Abraham Mehrez and Amiram Gafni, "Quality-Adjusted Life Years, Utility Theory, and Healthy-Years Equivalents." *Decision Making*, 9, 1989, 142–49. However, HYE is more complex to compute and has not been widely adopted; see A. J. Culyer and Adam Wagstaff, "QALYs versus HYEs." *Journal of Health Economics*, 11(3), 1993, 311–23; and Amiram Gafni, Stephen Birch, and Abraham Mehrez, "Economics, Health and Health Economics: HYEs versus QALYs." *Journal of Health Economics*, 11(3), 1993, 325–29; and Isabel Towers, Anne Spencer and John Brazier, "Healthy Year Equivalents Versus Quality-Adjusted Life Years: The Debate Continues." *Expert Review in Pharmacoeconomics & Outcomes Research*, 5(3), 2005, 245–54.

36. Emmett B. Keeler and Shan Cretin, "Discounting of Life-Saving and Other Nonmonetary Effects." *Management Science*, 29(3), 1983, 300–06. However, this is not a paradox per se because, as we have shown, a CE ratio never tells us whether a project has positive social value and hence, should be implemented – whether this year or next year.

37. Amiram Gafni, "Time in Health: Can We Measure Individuals' 'Pure Time Preference'?" *Medical Decision Making*, 15(1), 1995, 31–37; Donald A. Redelmeier, Daniel N. Heller, and Milton C. Weinstein, "Time Preference in Medical Economics: Science or Religion?" *Medical Decision Making*, 13(3), 1993, 301–03; and Magnus Johannesson, Joseph Pliskin, and Milton C. Weinstein, "A Note on QALYs, Time Trade-off and Discounting." *Medical Decision Making*, 14(2), 1994, 188–93.

38. James K. Hammitt, "QALYs versus WTP." *Risk Analysis*, 22(5), 2002, 985–1001.

39. Lisa A. Robinson and James K. Hammitt, "Skills of the Trade: Valuing Health Risk Reductions in Benefit–Cost Analysis." *Journal of Benefit–Cost Analysis*, 4(1), 2013, 107–30.

40. Tammy O. Tengs, Miriam E. Adams, Joseph S. Pliskin, Dana Gelb-Safran, Joanna E. Seigel, Milton C. Weinstein, and John D. Graham, "Five-Hundred Life-Saving Interventions and Their Cost-Effectiveness." *Risk Analysis*, 15(3), 1995, 369–90. For more on their methodology and policy implications, see Tammy O. Tengs and John D. Graham, "The Opportunity Costs of Haphazard Social Investment in Life-Saving." In: Robert W. Hahn, editor, *Risks, Costs, and Lives Saved: Getting Better Results from Regulation* (New York and Oxford: Oxford University Press; Washington, DC: The AEI Press, 1996).

41. John F. Morrall III, "Saving Lives: A Review of the Record." *Journal of Risk and Uncertainty*, 27(3), 2003, 221–37.

42. Gerard, "Cost–Utility in Practice," 274.

43. Josephine Mauskopf, Frans Rutten, and Warren Schonfeld, "Cost–Effectiveness League Tables: Valuable Guidance for Decision Makers?" *Pharmacoeconomics*, 21(14), 2003, 991–1000.

19 Distributionally Weighted CBA

Government policies, programs, and projects affect some individuals differently from others. Thus, in conducting CBAs, analysts sometimes report – indeed sometimes are required to report – benefits and costs for separate categories of people. The relevant classification of individuals into groups for this purpose usually depends on the specific policy under evaluation. Some common examples of categories include: consumers versus producers versus taxpayers, program participants versus non-participants, citizens (of a nation or a state or a city) versus non-citizens, and high-income groups versus low-income groups.

Once individuals are divided into relevant categories, the first issue that must be decided, as discussed in Chapter 2, is whether each group should be given standing in the CBA. For example, in conducting a CBA of US regulatory policy on acid rain, a decision must be made as to whether standing should be given to Canadians affected by acid rain that results from manufacturing in the United States. Similarly, when evaluating a policy that impacts foreign-based and owned companies, one must decide whether to give standing to foreign shareholders.

Once a decision on standing has been made, costs and benefits can be reported separately for each group with standing. We introduced this idea in Chapter 3 and considered it further in Chapters 5 and 6 in the context of *social accounting ledgers*. In practice, however, it is often difficult to determine and estimate exactly how benefits and costs are distributed across the relevant groups with standing. This is especially true of environmental and other impacts that are not priced in a market, but that must be estimated through hedonic pricing, contingent valuation surveys, or other indirect methods. It is possible, however, to make an approximate estimate if sufficient information is available about how the impacts vary by the demographic groups of interest.[1] If this information is available, how can it be utilized in making a decision concerning the policy being examined?

Throughout this book, we have emphasized use of the Kaldor–Hicks potential compensation test in making such decisions. Using this test, benefits and costs are simply summed across all groups that have standing to determine whether total benefits are larger than total costs and, hence, whether the policy should be adopted. Thus, benefits and costs are assessed from the perspective of society as a whole. In using the Kaldor–Hicks potential compensation test, it does not matter who among those with standing receives the benefits from a government program or who pays the costs ("a dollar is a dollar regardless of who receives or pays it"); all that matters is whether there is a net gain to society as a whole – in other words, whether the program is efficient in terms of potential Pareto improvement.

In making actual policy decisions, however, it is often useful to know the way in which benefits and costs are distributed among various groups. For instance, the distribution across groups can have an influence over whether a policy is politically acceptable. For example, effects on local residents may have more influence than the same amount of funds added to government revenue. Hence, a dollar received or expended by a member of one group may not be treated as equal to a dollar received or expended by a member of another group.

In this chapter, we examine the role of the distribution of benefits and costs among groups in augmenting CBA for decision-making purposes.[2] Those affected by a policy can potentially be divided into groups along many dimensions – income levels, age, gender, race, ethnicity, location, and so forth. This chapter, however, emphasizes CBAs of *policies that have differential effects on groups that differ by income*[3] – for example, projects that are located in underdeveloped regions or programs that are targeted at disadvantaged persons. Many other groupings are correlated with income groups to some extent. Moreover, there is currently great interest in income inequality and, in keeping with this interest, cost–benefit studies have most often focused on the implications of policies for different income groups. Chapter 14 and the case study for that chapter, for example, show that benefits and costs are generally displayed separately for Employment and Training programs participants, who are usually relatively low-income, and for the rest of society or non-participants, who are typically higher-income taxpayers (see Table 14.2 and the case study accompanying Chapter 14). Here we first examine the economic rationale for treating dollars received or expended by various income groups differently in CBA. Second, we consider approaches for doing this in practice.

19.1   Distributional Justifications for Income Transfer Programs

To illustrate differential effects on different income groups, we consider a program that taxes high-income persons in order to provide income transfers to low-income persons. The tax component of this program is illustrated in Figure 19.1. For purposes of discussion, assume that the market represented in this graph is for luxury goods, such as yachts, that are purchased only by high-income individuals. In the absence of the tax, equilibrium in this market would occur at a price of P_1 and a quantity of Q_1. If an excise tax of t is levied on each unit of output, then the supply curve would shift up by this amount as suppliers attempt to pass along to consumers the additional cost on yachts that the tax imposes upon them.

Using the Kaldor–Hicks rule and the same social accounting ledger discussed in Chapter 3, a simple distributional analysis of the costs and benefits associated with this tax would look like this:

	Gains	Losses
Consumers		$A + B$
Producers		$C + D$
Transfer recipients	$A + C$	
Society		$B + D$

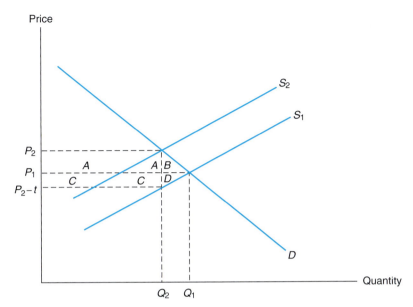

Figure 19.1 An excise tax on a luxury good.
Source: Adapted from Arnold C. Harberger, "On the Use of Distributional Weights in Social Cost–Benefit Analysis." *Journal of Political Economy*, 86(2), 1978, S87–S120; figure 1, p. S89.

Thus, the basic result of the tax would be a deadweight loss equal to areas *B* and *D*. In addition to this deadweight loss, two cost categories that are not displayed on the graph also result from our transfer program:

1. Both the administration of the tax and the administration of the transfers to recipients require the use of real resources.

2. Some of those receiving the transfer will probably work less or stop working entirely; this reduction in output thereby reduces the total goods and services available to society. It is reasonable to infer a reduction because there is considerable evidence that this occurs under existing welfare programs that involve such transfers.[4] Only part of this loss would be offset by the gains in leisure to transfer recipients, as explained in Chapter 14, while the remaining residual is a source of deadweight loss.

It is clear that this program would not pass the Kaldor–Hicks test. It could only be justified on some distributional basis. One would have to argue that giving a low-income person a dollar warrants taking more than a dollar away from a higher-income person. This distributional argument appears to have some force with policymakers because programs such as the Temporary Assistance to Needy Families (TANF) program, the Supplementary Security Income (SSI) program, and the Supplementary Nutrition Assistance Program (SNAP) program, which all transfer income from higher-income to lower-income persons, are all in existence. Hence, society through their political representatives appears to be willing to sacrifice some efficiency in order to provide assistance to low-income groups.

The implication of this willingness to make transfers for CBA is that, in practice, a dollar of benefits received or a dollar of costs incurred by a low-income individual is sometimes given greater weight in assessing government programs than is a dollar of benefits received or a dollar of costs incurred by a higher-income individual. How can this weighting be justified?

19.2   The Case for Treating Low- and High-Income Groups Differently in CBA

There are at least three arguments for giving dollars received by, or paid to, low-income persons greater weight than dollars received or paid by higher-income persons. They are: (1) higher income has diminishing marginal utility; (2) the income distribution should be more equal; (3) a principle analogous to the "one person, one vote" principle for voting should apply in some analyses. We discuss each of these arguments in turn.

19.2.1   *Diminishing Marginal Utility of Income*

The first argument is based on a standard assumption in economics that each additional dollar an individual receives provides less utility than the preceding dollar. A corollary of this assumption is that a dollar received or a dollar of cost incurred by a high-income person has a lower impact on his or her utility than it would on a low-income person's utility. Consequently, the argument suggests, it should count less in a CBA.[5] This argument can be summarized algebraically as follows:

$$\Delta u_l/\Delta y_l > \Delta u_h/\Delta y_h \tag{19.1}$$

where $\Delta u_i/\Delta y_i$ is the marginal private utility of income of individual i, l indicates a low-income person, and h a high-income person.

19.2.2   *The Income Distribution Should Be More Equal*

The second argument for giving dollars received or paid by the poor greater weight in CBA is premised on an assertion that the current income distribution is not as equal as it should be and social welfare would be higher if it were more equal.[6] There are several possible rationales for such an assertion. The first is that a highly unequal distribution of income is more likely to result in civil disorder, crime, and riots and that a reduction in income inequality may reduce these threats to the general social welfare. Second, it can be argued that no one can, or should have to, live below some minimum threshold of income. A base level is required to preserve human dignity. Third, at least some relatively well-off persons will receive utility if the circumstances facing the worse-off members of society at the bottom of the income distribution improve. Certain types of charitable giving, such as contributions to the Salvation Army, provide evidence for the existence of this form of altruism. Finally, it is possible that some persons value greater income equality in and of itself (this is sometimes referred to as "inequality aversion").[7]

If for any of these reasons society prefers greater income equality than currently exists, then a dollar increase in the income of a low-income person would result in a larger increase in the welfare of society in aggregate than would a dollar increase in the income of a high-income person. Note that this conclusion would still hold even if the marginal utility of income were not diminishing and, consequently, a dollar increase in the income of high- and low-income persons resulted in equal increases in the utilities of these persons. Each of the justifications outlined in the previous paragraph suggests that society as a whole (or at least some relatively well-off members of society) becomes better off if those at the bottom of the income distribution gain relative to those in the rest of the distribution.[8] Thus, the first and second arguments are conceptually distinct from one another.

Stated algebraically, the second argument implies that:

$$\Delta SW/\Delta y_l > \Delta SW/\Delta y_h, \text{ even if } \Delta u_l/\Delta y_l = \Delta u_h/\Delta y_h \qquad (19.2)$$

where ΔSW refers to the change in aggregate social welfare and $\Delta SW/\Delta y_i$ is the marginal effect on social welfare of a change in income that is received by individual i.[9]

This argument contradicts the Kaldor–Hicks test quite directly. It claims that some projects or programs that fail the Kaldor–Hicks test should nonetheless be adopted provided they redistribute income in a way that makes the overall income distribution more equal. In other words, some programs that appear inefficient when dollars are treated identically regardless of to whom they accrue, such as one that taxes high-income persons to provide income transfers to lower-income persons, should be undertaken if they increase income equality sufficiently to increase aggregate social welfare. This also implies that some projects that make the income distribution less equal should not be undertaken, even though the Kaldor–Hicks test suggests that they are efficient.

19.2.3   *The "One Person, One Vote" Principle*

This argument begins by acknowledging that the benefits and costs of government programs to consumers are appropriately measured as changes in consumer surplus. However, then it goes on to point out that because high-income persons have more income to spend than low-income persons, the measured impacts of policies on their consumer surplus will typically be larger and, hence, will be of greater consequence in a CBA based strictly on the Kaldor–Hicks rule.

This is illustrated by Figure 19.2, which compares the demand schedules of a typical high-income consumer and a typical low-income consumer for some good. If the good is a *normal good*, that is, if demand for the good increases as income increases, then the demand schedule of the high-income consumer will be to the right of that of the low-income consumer, as the diagram shows. If a government policy increases the price of the good, say from P_1 to P_2, both high- and low-income consumers will bear the cost of that increase in the form of lost consumer surplus. However, the loss suffered by the high-income consumer (areas $A + B$) will be greater than the loss borne by the low-income consumer (area A alone). As a result, such a CBA will give more weight to the impact of the policy on high-income consumers than on low-income consumers.

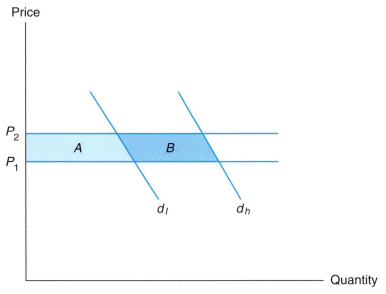

Figure 19.2 Changes in consumer surplus for high- and low-income consumers.

The final part of the argument is analogous to the "one-person, one vote" voting principle: in a democracy, low-income persons should have as much influence over decisions on whether to undertake public projects as high-income persons. In other words, measures of changes in consumer surplus for different persons should be adjusted to what they would be if everyone had the same income.[10] For example, we would count the impact of the price change on the low-income person represented in the diagram at about double what we would count the impact on the high-income person, in effect equalizing the "votes" of the two individuals.[11]

Exhibit 19.1

Whether a dollar of benefits or costs is valued more or less in poor developing countries than in wealthier developed countries has important implications for assessing international environmental agreements. For example, in the absence of distributional weighting, the per-capita benefits of an agreement to reduce global climate change by restricting emissions of fossil fuel would be smaller in a poor country than in a wealthier country. One reason for this is that (as we saw in an earlier chapter) when based on willingness to pay, the value of a statistical life is smaller in the poor country simply because of differences in ability to pay. Without weighting, the per-capita dollar costs of restricting emissions in a poor country (for example, job losses) would also be smaller. Using a CBA framework, Christian Azar found that, compared to a situation in which weighting is not used, the use of weighting greatly reduces emissions that wealthier countries should be allowed to emit relative to those in poor countries. Somewhat similarly, Vaino Nurmi and Heini Atiainen used contingent valuation to estimate the WTP for improved water quality among residents of nine countries that border the Northern Europe and Baltic Sea region and found that the weighted benefits of such a policy are much larger than the unweighted benefits.

Sources: Christian Azar, "Weight Factors in Cost–Benefit Analysis of Climate Change." *Environmental and Resource Economics*, 13(3), 1999, 249–68; and Vaino Nurmi and Heini Ahtiainen, "Distributional Weights in Environmental Valuation and Cost–Benefit Analysis: Theory and Practice," manuscript submitted for publication, 2017.

19.3   Distributional Weights

In principle, different groups can be treated differently in a CBA by using *distributional weights*. Distributional weights are just selected weighting numbers – such as 1, 2, or 1.5 – chosen to attempt to reflect the value placed on each dollar paid out or received by each group. Table 19.1 compares standard and distributionally weighted CBA for two projects affecting two income groups. In standard CBA, as shown in the upper panel of the table, both groups receive an equal weight of 1. In distributionally weighted CBA, Group H

Table 19.1 *Standard versus Distributionally Weighted CBA.*

1. Standard CBA

Projects	Net benefits		Aggregate net benefits
	Group L	Group H	
I	10	50	60
II	20	30	50
Weights	1	1	Selection: Project I

2. Distributionally weighted CBA, when $W_h = 1$ and $W_l = 3$

Projects	Net benefits		Aggregate net benefits
	Group L	Group H	
I	$10 \times 3 = 30$	50	80
II	$20 \times 3 = 60$	30	90
Weights	3	1	Selection: Project II

(the higher-income group) is given a value of 1, while Group L (the lower-income group) is given a value of 3, implying that a dollar received by a member of the low-income group is valued in the CBA at three times that of a dollar received by a member of the high-income group. Given this weighting, as shown in the lower panel, project selection switches from Project I to Project II.

More formally, distributional weights can be incorporated into a CBA through a slight modification of the net present value (*NPV*) formula:

$$NPV = \sum_{j=1}^{m}\left[W_j \sum_{t=0}^{\infty} \frac{B_{t,j} - C_{t,j}}{(1+s)^t} \right]$$

(19.3)

where W_j is the distributional weight for group j, $B_{t,j}$ are the benefits received by group j in period t, $C_{t,j}$ are the costs incurred by group j in period t, m is the number of groups, and s is the social discount rate.

The idea behind this formula is simple. The persons affected by the government policy are divided into as many groups as is considered appropriate, typically on the basis of income. Each group is then given a distributional weight. The *NPV* for each group is first computed and then multiplied by its weight. These weighted *NPV*s are then added together to obtain an overall *NPV*. Note that in CBAs that rely strictly on the Kaldor–Hicks rule, W_j is implicitly set equal to 1 for all groups with standing and W_j is set to 0 for any group that is not given standing.

Exhibit 19.2

Proposed mergers that appear likely to result in price increases are illegal in the United States, but are permitted in Canada if the potential gains in efficiency are deemed sufficient. Viewed somewhat differently, mergers are permitted in Canada if potential gains in producer surplus appear to offset potential losses in consumer surplus resulting from price increases. Thomas Ross and Ralph Winter point out that this formulation gives those receiving either producer or consumer surplus equal distributional weights in Canada. In the United States, the law gives consumer surplus greater weight than producer surplus. Indeed, producer surplus is, in effect, given a weight of zero in the United States. One rationale for the US approach might be that recipients of producer surplus (e.g., corporation stockholders) tend to be wealthier than those getting consumer surplus, but Ross and Winter argue that this need not always be the case (e.g., consider the markets for luxury goods) and, even if it is, distributional weights should be based on the actual wealth or income of individuals, not on whether they happen to be classified as "producers" or "consumers" in the case of a particular merger.

Source: Adapted from Thomas W. Ross and Ralph A. Winter, "The Efficiency Defense in Merger Law: Economic Foundations and Recent Canadian Developments." *Antitrust Law Journal,*72, 2004–05, 471–503.

19.4   Determining Distributional Weights

The difficulty with implementing distributional weights is determining an appropriate weight for each group.[12] The weights should, of course, be consistent with the selected rationale for using them. While there have been attempts to develop distributional weights consistent with each of the three previously presented arguments for using weights, we are not aware of any attempt to base weights on a combination of the three arguments.

19.4.1   *Weights Consistent with Each One of the Three Arguments*

An argument based on the "one person, one vote" analogy suggests an approach that could be used in practice to assign weights. However, it is not commonly used because the information requirements are both substantial and project-specific. The information required to implement it includes the average income level of each relevant group, an estimate of the *income elasticity of demand* for each good affected by the government policy being evaluated (i.e., the percentage change in the quantity demanded of each good that results from a 1 percent increase in income), and an estimate of the market demand curve for each affected good. With this information, the consumer surplus of the average member of each group can be computed. These estimates can, in turn, be used to derive distributional weights for each group that are consistent with the one person, one vote principle.[13]

To develop weights that are consistent with the other two arguments, information is needed on $\Delta u/\Delta y$ (the marginal private utility of income) and $\Delta SW/\Delta y$ (the marginal effect on social welfare of a change in income) for a typical member of each group. There have been attempts to estimate the first of these ratios for different income groups and use these estimates to derive distributional weights.[14] Specifically, the analysts assumed the following isoelastic utility function:

$$U = \frac{y^{1-\eta}}{1-\eta} \quad \text{if } \eta \neq 1$$
$$U = \log y \quad \text{if } \eta = 1 \tag{19.4}$$

where η is the elasticity of the marginal utility with respect to income.

Given this utility function,

$$\Delta u/\Delta y \approx 1/y^\eta \tag{19.5}$$

Setting the distributional weight for the high-income group equal to one, the weight for a lower-income group would be the ratio of the marginal utility of income for the lower-income group to that for the higher-income group:

$$W_l = (\Delta u_l/\Delta y_l)/(\Delta u_h/\Delta y_h) = (y_l/y_h)^\eta \tag{19.6}$$

Obtaining an actual value for W_l obviously requires an estimate of η, the elasticity of the marginal utility of income. A number of such estimates exist. One method to estimate it relies on surveys in which respondents are asked their incomes and to rate their level of happiness on a scale (e.g., very happy, pretty happy, not too happy) and using that as a proxy for utility. Based on this approach and using six surveys of subjective happiness covering over 50 countries including the United States, Richard Layard, Stephen Nickell, and Guy Mayraz estimated six different values for η.[15] Their estimate for the United States is 1.2. Their values for other countries are in a similar range: between 1.19 and 1.34. Daniel Fujiwara compared these estimates to those made by other researchers, who used other data and different methods, and found that most were also in the same range and almost all had values above one.[16]

We illustrate the calculation of W_l, using the 1.2 estimate for η. Consider a government-funded training program that serves individuals from the lowest two income quintiles and which is paid for by taxpayers. According to the US Census Bureau, median household money income in 2015 was $56,832, while the median income of households in the lowest two income quintiles was $22,800. If η equals 1.2, Equation (19.6) implies that $W_l = 3.0$. As we show later in the chapter, there is reason to believe that this weight is somewhat on the high side.[17] For now, it is most important to recognize that weighting is quite sensitive to the exact value of the elasticity estimate. For example, if $\eta = 1$ instead, then $W_l = 2.5$ (the simple ratio of y_l / y_h), but if $\eta = 1.5$, then $W_l = 3.9$. Obviously, there is some uncertainty concerning the value of W_l because it depends on both the assumption about the form of the utility function and the estimate of η. As it should, it also depends on the specific income groups that are being compared. For example, if the participants in our illustrative training program were all drawn from the lowest income quintile, rather than as we actually assumed, the lowest two quintiles, y_l would equal $12,457 and, if $\eta = 1.2$, W_l would equal 6.2.

There has been at least one attempt to develop distributional weights that are consistent with community views on improving *social* welfare, as against being consistent with the argument concerning the diminishing *private* marginal utility of income.[18] In an interesting exploratory analysis, Helen Scarborough and Jeff Bennett used choice modeling (a stated preference approach), which is somewhat akin to the CVM (see Chapter 16). This approach can be used to develop weights that can be used to assess policies, such as environmental policies, that result in redistribution across generations.[19] Their study, which was based on a survey administered across age groups in a small Australian city, implies that benefits that are redistributed from 50-year-olds to newborns should receive a weight of about 2.3, those redistributed from 25-year-olds to newborns a weight of about 1.4, and those redistributed from 50-year-olds to 25-year-olds a weight of around 1.6. Their approach, which is quite complex, and which Scarborough and Bennett admit needs further refinement, could potentially be used to develop weights for assessing policies that redistribute income across income groups, rather than across generations – for example, welfare schemes, health insurance subsidies, and government-funded training programs.

19.4.2   *Obtaining Upper-Bound Values for Distributional Weights*

We pointed out earlier in this chapter that pure transfer programs inevitably fail the Kaldor–Hicks test. However, one can argue that transfer programs can be used as a benchmark by which other types of programs that redistribute income can be assessed.[20] Specifically, the argument is that *if a non-transfer program makes the disadvantaged better off but results in a loss of efficiency, then it should be rejected if a transfer program that results in a smaller loss in efficiency could be used instead.* By the same token, *if a non-transfer program makes the disadvantaged group worse off but results in gains in efficiency, then it should be accepted if there is a transfer program that could compensate the disadvantaged group for their losses without fully offsetting the gains in efficiency from the non-transfer program.*

In order to provide the information required by this approach, Edward Gramlich estimates that it costs taxpayers approximately $1.50–$2.00 to redistribute a dollar to a recipient using a typical transfer program.[21] Gramlich suggests that although these estimates are only approximate and tentative, as long as they are of the right order of magnitude, then it can be argued that distributional weights for the disadvantaged group should never be set above 1.5–2 times the weight for the advantaged.

Consider, for example, a non-transfer program that has a negative unweighted net present value from the societal perspective, although it does make the poor better off. Specifically, assume the program costs the higher-income advantaged group $2.50 for every dollar of benefits received by the lower-income disadvantaged. Gramlich's estimates imply that every dollar received by the disadvantaged group under a transfer program would cost the advantaged group only $1.50–$2.00. Thus, in principle, the transfer program could be used instead to make the disadvantaged group just as well off as under the non-transfer program, but at a lower cost to the advantaged group. It is a less-leaky bucket! Thus, not only does the non-transfer program have a negative unweighted social NPV, but it is also inferior to a simple transfer program for redistributing income to the disadvantaged group.

Now consider a different program that provides the advantaged group with $2.50 of benefits for every dollar of costs incurred by the disadvantaged group. Under these circumstances, each dollar lost under the program by the disadvantaged group could, in principle, be reimbursed to them through a transfer program at a cost to the advantaged group of only $1.50–$2.00. Hence, this program not only has a positive unweighted social NPV, but the disadvantaged group could also be compensated for their losses without completely offsetting the gains in efficiency from the program.

The analysis just presented implies that *distributional weights assigned to some disadvantaged group should not exceed 1.5 or 2 in value when the value for the advantaged group is set at 1.* Larger weights would mean accepting inefficient programs that are also inferior to simple transfer programs for redistributing income and also mean rejection of efficient programs that allow the advantaged group to enjoy net gains even when the disadvantaged group could be fully compensated through income transfers for the losses they bear. Note, however, that this argument is very similar in spirit to the one underlying the Kaldor–Hicks rule. Both are based on the *potential* use of transfer payments to compensate losers under a policy, while leaving winners better off than they would be in the absence of the policy. Nothing, however, requires that these income transfers actually be made.

19.5   A Pragmatic Approach to Weighting

Despite considerable effort to estimate distributional weights, there does not yet appear to be general agreement on an acceptable set of weights, or even on whether weights should be used at all. For example, the government of the United Kingdom now advocates distributional weighting in CBA,[22] but the governments of other countries have not followed. Given the lack of convergence concerning the use of distributional weights, we suggest that their use be limited to only those CBAs where distributional issues involving income distribution are of central concern (for example, CBAs of programs targeted at disadvantaged groups or at impoverished areas within countries, states, or cities) or to CBAs of policies that explicitly treat different income groups differently (for example, a CBA of a plan to store radioactive waste in a low-income area). It may then be possible to use an approach that highlights the importance of the distributional implications associated with the policy being analyzed without requiring that any particular set of distributional weights be selected as the "correct" set.

To illustrate this approach, we return to the CBA of welfare-to-work programs, initially discussed in the case study accompanying Chapter 14. These programs provided various combinations of job search, education, training, financial incentives, and subsidized jobs for welfare recipients. Because these programs were targeted at welfare recipients – an especially disadvantaged low-income group – both their distributional effects and their effects on economic efficiency are relevant. Thus, in principle, CBAs of welfare-to-work programs should take both types of effects into account.

19.5.1   *Displaying Unweighted Cost and Benefit Estimates*

The first step in taking account of both the efficiency and distributional effects of welfare-to-work programs is simply to display unweighted program impacts on society as a whole, as well as on pertinent subgroups. This is shown in the first three columns in Table 19.2. These simply duplicate the total net present value estimates for those programs that were originally reported in the Chapter 14 case study. Column 1 reports these estimates from the perspective of program participants, column 2 from the perspective of non-participants, and column 3 (which is computed by summing the first two columns) from the perspective of society as a whole.

None of the estimates reported in the first three columns of Table 19.2 are weighted. *Regardless of whether distributional weighting is used, unweighted estimates of benefits and costs for society as a whole should always be provided in a CBA. In addition, when distributional considerations are important, benefit and cost estimates for relevant groups should also be provided* if it is feasible to do so.[23]

The unweighted *NPV* estimates reported in the first three columns of Table 19.2 suggest two important conclusions. First, they show that just over half of the reported programs pass the Kaldor–Hicks test. Specifically, 14 of the 26 unweighted *NPV* estimates for society as a whole (column 3) are positive, while 12 are negative. Second, in 5 of the 14 cases that do pass the Kaldor–Hicks test, program participants were made worse off by the tested program, while non-participants – a group who, on

Table 19.2 *Sensitivity of MDRC's Evaluations of Selected Welfare-to-Work Experiments to the Use of Distributional Weights (in 2016 dollars)*

	NPV from participant perspective (1)	NPV from non-participant perspective (2)	Unweighted social NPV [Col 1 + Col 2] (3)	NPV If participant weight = 2 [2 × Col 1 + Col 2] (4)	Estimates of internal weights for participants [Col 2/Col 1] (5)
Mandatory work experience programs					
Cook County WIN Demonstration (*n* = 11,912)	817	−218	599	1,416	NA
San Diego (*n* = 3,591)	369	1,679	2,047	2,416	NA
West Virginia CWEP (*n* = 3,694)	−194	1,695	1,501	1,307	8.74
Mandatory job-search-first programs					
Atlanta LFA NEWWS (*n* = 4,433)	−17	−1,109	−1,126	−1,142	NA
Grand Rapids LFA NEWWS (*n* = 4,554)	−3,412	4,189	778	−2,634	1.23
Los Angeles Jobs-First GAIN (*n* = 15,683)	605	3,622	4,227	4,832	NA
Riverside LFA NEWWS (*n* = 8,322)	−1,911	2,225	314	−1,597	1.16
SWIM (San Diego) (*n* = 3,227)	−59	3,093	3,034	2,975	52.59
Mandatory education-first programs					
Atlanta HCD NEWWS (*n* = 4,433)	473	−4,692	−4,219	−3,745	9.91
Columbus integrated NEWWS (*n* = 7,242)	−2,351	351	−2,000	−4,350	NA
Columbus traditional NEWWS (*n* = 7,242)	−1,694	−929	−2,623	−4,317	NA
Detroit NEWWS (*n* = 4,459)	233	−477	−244	−11	2.05
Grand Rapids HCD NEWWS (*n* = 4,554)	−2,907	−445	−3,352	−6,258	NA
Riverside HCD NEWWS (*n* = 3,135)	−4,387	875	−3,512	−7,899	NA
Mandatory mixed-initial-activity programs					
Butte GAIN (*n* = 1,234)	2,177	234	2,411	4,588	NA

(continued)

Table 19.2 (cont.)

	NPV from participant perspective (1)	NPV from non-participant perspective (2)	Unweighted social NPV [Col 1 + Col 2] (3)	NPV If participant weight = 2 [2 × Col 1 + Col 2] (4)	Estimates of internal weights for participants [Col 2/Col 1] (5)
Portland NEWWS (*n* = 4,028)	−1,389	7,541	6,151	4,762	5.43
Riverside GAIN (*n* = 5,626)	2,520	4,884	7,403	9,923	NA
San Diego GAIN (*n* = 8,224)	1,221	1,520	2,740	3,961	NA
Tulare GAIN (*n* = 2,248)	2,403	−3,763	−1,359	1,044	1.57
Project Independence (Florida) (*n* = 18,237)	−689	120	−569	−1,258	NA
Alameda GAIN (*n* = 1,205)	1,450	−4,943	−3,493	−2,044	3.41
Los Angeles GAIN (*n* = 4,434)	−2,653	−5,725	−8,378	−11,031	NA
Earnings supplement programs					
MFIP (Minnesota) (*n* = 3,208)	12,071	−13,040	−969	11,102	1.08
SSP applicants (Canada) (*n* = 2,371)	7,841	−691	7,151	14,992	NA
SSP long-term recipients (Canada) (*n* = 4,852)	5,491	−2,812	2,679	8,170	NA
WRP (Vermont) (*n* = 5,469)	287	−272	15	301	NA

NA, not applicable.
Source for columns 1–3: Table 14C.1.

average, enjoy substantially higher incomes than participants – were made better off. In 5 of the 12 cases that failed the Kaldor–Hicks test, however, program participants were made better off, while non-participants were made worse off. In these kinds of situations, there is a trade-off between economic efficiency and distributional consider-ations. *It is only when a policy or program change results in a trade-off between efficiency and equality in the income or wealth distribution that distributional weighting is relevant. Distributional weighting is not required in "win–win change" cases (i.e., both efficiency and progressivity improve) or a "lose–lose change" (both efficiency and progressivity decline).*[24] Table 19.2 shows nine win–win change cases, seven lose–lose change cases, and 10 trade-off change cases.

19.5.2   *Conducting Sensitivity Tests*

Column 4 clarifies the degree to which the estimates reported in column 3 of Table 19.2 are sensitive to using distributional weights. In contrast to the unweighted figures shown in column 3, which are implicitly based on the assumption that society values the gains and losses of welfare recipients and non-recipients equally, those shown in column 4 assume that the gains and losses of welfare recipients are valued at twice those of non-recipients: a distributional weight of 2 when non-participants have a weight of 1. The weight of 2 for participants is at the upper bound suggested by Gramlich, but considerably lower than the weight of 3 implied by Layard, Nickell, and Mayraz's findings for the United States.

A comparison of columns 3 and 4 demonstrates, as expected, that this weighting causes changes in the magnitude in all of the social *NPV* estimates. More importantly, however, the comparison also shows that only four of the social *NPV* estimates change their sign. Two of these sign changes are from positive to negative, thereby turning a net social gain into net loss, while the other two are from negative to positive, turning a net social loss into a net gain. The remaining 22 social *NPV*s do not change sign even when a rather large distributional weight is used, suggesting that most of the programs listed in Table 19.2 are not very sensitive to plausible distributional weighting. Although not shown in the table, even if a larger weight of 3 instead of 2 is used, there are only five sign changes with 21 *NPV*s not changing signs.

19.5.3   *Computing Internal Weights*

Column 5 in Table 19.2 is based on the computation of *internal weights*. This is an alternative method to the approach used in column 4 for computing distributional weights. This method works best if there are only two pertinent groups, one of which is relatively disadvantaged (e.g., participants in welfare-to-work programs) and the other relatively advantaged (e.g., non-participants in these programs).

One can derive internal distributional weights by first setting the weight for the advantaged group equal to one and then computing the weight for the disadvantaged group by dividing the estimated *NPV* for the advantaged group by the estimated *NPV* for the disadvantaged group. The idea is similar to that behind the computation of internal rates of return. Rather than somehow selecting weights, one finds the weights at which the program being analyzed would just break even; in other words, the weights at which the *NPV* for society as a whole just equates to zero. Viewed a bit differently, the internal weight for the disadvantaged group indicates the dollars of costs incurred by the advantaged group per dollar of benefits received by the disadvantaged group if the former is made worse off by the program and the latter better off, or the dollars of benefits received by the advantaged group per dollar of costs incurred by the disadvantaged group if the former is made better off and the latter worse off.

In Table 19.2, we compute internal weights for Work/Welfare Demonstration participants by dividing column 2 by column 1. We perform this calculation, however, only when the CBA reveals a trade-off between efficiency and distribution (when column 1 and column 3 are of the opposite sign). In the win–win or lose–lose change cases, there is no trade-off between efficiency and distribution and distributional weighting is not appropriate. As trade-off change cases arose in only 10 of the estimates presented in Table 19.2, only 10 internal weights for program participants are shown in column 5.

Each of these 10 values shows the weight at which the program would just break even. Thus, *if* the "true" weight for participants is actually larger than their internal weight, those programs with positive unweighted (or standard) social *NPV*s would fail to break even once their distributional implications were taken into account, and programs with negative unweighted social *NPV*s would more than break even. However, because the "true" weight for participants is unknown, policy makers would have to make a judgment as to whether dollars of benefits or costs to participants should be given a higher or lower value than that revealed by the computed internal weights. Indeed, a major advantage of internal weighting is that it makes the trade-off between efficiency and distribution explicit for policy makers.

Earlier we argued that a reasonable upper bound value for a distributional weight for the disadvantaged is in the range of 1.5–2. If we use 2 as a benchmark, the three programs in Table 19.2 that have internal weights well in excess of 2 and positive unweighted (standard) social *NPV*s should be adopted, even though they have adverse effects on the income distribution. In contrast, the three programs that have internal weights that exceed 2, but negative unweighted social *NPV*s, cannot be justified, even though they improve the income distribution.

19.6   Conclusion

This chapter focuses on the use of distributional weighting to take account of the fact that many policies have divergent impacts on different income groups. In practice, however, distributional weighting is not often used in CBA,[25] probably because of a lack of consensus on what would be widely accepted weights. One apparent exception is in global-wide studies of climate change where the disparity of incomes among countries is enormous.[26]

Given the absence of consensus on distributional weights, we suggest that the use of distributional weights be limited to policies that meet the following two conditions: (1) they are targeted at the disadvantaged or treat the advantaged and the disadvantaged differently, and (2) they result in reductions in overall social efficiency but make low-income persons better off, or they increase social efficiency but make low-income persons worse off.

There are, in fact, probably relatively few policies that meet both conditions. Those policies that do might be subjected to sensitivity tests based on a plausible range of weights. Or alternatively, internal weights might be computed, thereby providing policy makers with information on which to base their choice of distributional weights. In either case, however, a cogent argument can be made for not allowing the distributional weights for low-income groups to be set much more than 50 (a weight of 1.5) to 100 percent (a weight of 2) above those for higher-income groups.

Exercises for Chapter 19

1. A city is about to build a new sanitation plant. It is considering two sites, one located in a moderately high-income neighborhood and the other in a low-income neighborhood. Indeed, most of the residents in the latter neighborhood live below the poverty line. The city's sanitation engineer insists that "the city needs the new plant and it has to go somewhere." However, he is indifferent as to which neighborhood it is located in. The plant would operate at the same cost and as efficiently in either neighborhood, and about as many people would be affected by the air pollution emitted by the plant. The city hires an economist to study the two sites. The economist finds that the plant would cause a considerably larger fall in average property values in the higher-income neighborhood than in the low-income neighborhood, given the more expensive homes that are located in it. Consistent with this, a contingent valuation study that the economist conducted finds that willingness to pay to avoid the sanitation plant is substantially higher in the higher-income neighborhood than in the low-income neighborhood.

   The residents of the lower-income neighborhood strongly prefer that the plant be built in the higher-income neighborhood. In the face of the economist's findings, what sort of arguments might they make?

2. CBAs have been conducted for six proposed projects. None of these projects are mutually exclusive, and the agency has a sufficient budget to fund those that will make society better off. The following findings from the CBAs are summarized in millions of dollars:

	Net social benefits	Net Group I benefits	Net Group II benefits
Project A	3	3	0
Project B	9	12	−3
Project C	6	18	−12
Project D	−2	−4	3
Project E	−3	−2	−2
Project F	−3	6	−9

   Group I consists of households with annual incomes over $25,000, whereas Group II consists of households with annual incomes under $25,000.

   (a) According to the net benefit rule, which of these projects should be funded?

(b) For which of the projects might distributional considerations be an issue?

(c) Compute internal distributional weights for the projects you selected in part (b). Using these weights, indicate the circumstances under which each project might actually be undertaken.

(d) Recompute social net benefits for the six projects using a distributional weight of 1 for Group I and a distributional weight of 2 for Group II. Using these weight-adjusted net social benefit estimates, indicate the circumstances under which each project might actually be undertaken. In doing this, assume that the distributional weight for Group II is an upper bound – that is, it probably overstates society's true generosity toward low-income households.

Notes

1. For a useful discussion of methods for determining how benefits and costs are distributed across demographic groups, see John B. Loomis, "Incorporating Distributional Issues into Benefit Cost Analysis: Why, How, and Two Empirical Examples Using Non-market Valuation." *Journal of Benefit–Cost Analysis*, 2(1), 2011, Art 5.

2. For a more general discussion of the role of distributional considerations in assessing policy initiatives, see Alphonse G. Holtmann, "Beyond Efficiency: Economics and Distributional Analysis." In: David L. Weimer, editor, *Policy Analysis and Economics* (Boston, MA: Kluwer Academic Publishing, 1991), 45–64; Y. Secret and N. Johnstone, *The Distributional Effects of Environmental Policy* (Northampton, MA: Edward Elgar, 2006); Matthew D. Adler, "Risk Equity: A New Proposal." *Harvard Law Review*, 32, 2008, 1–47; and Vaino Nurmi and Heini Ahtiainen, "Distributional Weights in Environmental Valuation and Cost–benefit Analysis: Theory and Practice," manuscript submitted for publication, 2017.

3. It would be better to distinguish among the persons or families affected by government programs in terms of their wealth (i.e., the value of their stock of assets), rather than in terms of their income (the observed flow of payments they receive in exchange for the labor, capital, and land that they provide the production process). For example, two households may have similar incomes, but if one owns a house and the other does not, their standard of living may be quite different. However, income is normally used instead of wealth in categorizing individuals or families because it is more readily measured.

4. See Robert Moffitt, "Incentive Effects of the U.S. Welfare System: A Review." *Journal of Economic Literature*, 30(1), 1992, 1–61, and the references cited therein.

5. Martin Feldstein's discussion of technical issues in computing distributional weights is premised on this argument. See Martin S. Feldstein, "Distributional Equity and the Optimal Structure of Public Prices." *The American Economic Review*, 62(1), 1972, 32–36.

6. Arnold Harberger's classical examination of distributional weighting ("On the Use of Distributional Weights in Social Cost–Benefit Analysis." *Journal of Political Economy*, 86(2), 1972, S87–S120) can be viewed as a critical assessment of whether this assertion provides a basis for conducting distributionally weighted CBA.

7. These points are discussed in greater detail by Aidan R. Vining and David L. Weimer, "Welfare Economics as the Foundation for Public Policy Analysis: Incomplete and Flawed but Nevertheless Desirable." *The Journal of Socio-Economics*, 21(1), 1992, 25–37. John Rawls, *A Theory of Justice* (Cambridge, MA: Harvard University Press, 1971)

and others have provided a more philosophical basis than the reasons listed here for greater income equality.

8. Modifying Equation (19.1) by allowing for interdependent utility, social welfare would increase if

$$\Delta u_l / \Delta y_l + \Delta u_h / \Delta y_l > \Delta u_h / \Delta y_h$$

where $\Delta u_h / \Delta y_h$ is change in the marginal utility of h attributable to an increase in the income of l. A transfer of income from h to l will be Pareto Optimal if $\Delta u_h / \Delta y_l > /\Delta u_h / \Delta y_h$, that is, if the increase in h's utility from the transfer exceeds h's loss in utility from his or her reduction in income. Note that in this formulation, social welfare can still increase even if the program both fails the Kaldor–Hicks test and is not Pareto Optimal if $\Delta u_l / \Delta y_l$ is sufficiently large. Further elaboration of this model can be found in Larry Orr, "Income Transfers as a Public Good: An Application to AFDC." *American Economic Review*, 66, 1976, 359–71; and Robert J. Brent, "A Cost–Benefit Framework for Evaluating Conditional Cash-Transfer Programs." *Journal of Benefit–Cost Analysis*, 4(2), 2013, 159–80.

9. The first two arguments can be derived more formally by specifying a social welfare function. To illustrate, we specify a very simple social welfare function in which individual utility depends upon income, total social welfare depends upon a linear combination of individual utilities, and the possibility of interdependent utility (i.e., one person's utility being affected by the gains or losses of others) is ignored:

$$SW = f[u_1(y_1) ..., u_i(y_i) ..., u_n(y_n)]$$

where n is the total number of individuals in society. Totally differentiating the social welfare function yields the following expression:

$$dSW = \sum_{i=1}^{n} \left[(\partial SW / \partial u_i)(\partial u_i / \partial y_i) dy_i \right]$$

where dy_i represents the change in income resulting from a government policy. The first argument implies that $\partial u_l / \partial y_l > \partial u_h / \partial y_h$, while the second argument implies that $\partial SW / \partial u_h > \partial SW / \partial u_l$. Thus, together the two arguments imply that $(\partial SW / \partial u_l)(\partial u / \partial y_l) > (\partial SW / \partial u_h)(\partial u / \partial y_h)$.

10. D. W. Pearce, *Cost–Benefit analysis*, 2nd edn (New York, NY: St. Martin's Press, 1983), 64–66. An example of using this approach is found in Richard S. J. Tol, Thomas E. Downing, Samuel Frankhauser, Richard G. Richels, and Joel B. Smith, *Progress in Estimating the Marginal Costs of Greenhouse Gas Emissions*, Working Paper SCG-4 (Hamburg: Centre for Marine and Climate Research, Hamburg University, 2001), www.uni-hamburg.de/wiss. They find that because the countries that are worst affected by global warming are located near the equator and tend to be relatively poor, the costs of global warming from a global perspective appear much worse if aggregation across

countries is based on population size rather than on dollars of income.

11. From the perspective of social choice theory, this is a somewhat naive view of democracy. See William H. Riker, *Liberalism Against Populism* (San Francisco, CA: Freeman, 1982).

12. Although several attempts have been made to develop distributional weights based on political decisions concerning taxes or public expenditures, there has been limited acceptance of any of these weights. Examples of these attempts can be found in Otto Eckstein, "A Survey of the Theory of Public Expenditure Criteria." In: James M. Buchanan, editor, *Public Finances: Needs, Sources and Utilization* (Princeton, NJ: Princeton University Press, 1961), 439–94; Robert H. Haveman, *Water Resource Investment and the Public Interest* (Nashville, TN: Vanderbilt University, 1965); V. C. Nwaneri, "Equity in Cost–Benefit Analysis: A Case Study of the Third London Airport." *Journal of Transport Economics and Policy*, 4(3), 1970, 235–54; and Burton A. Weisbrod, "Income Redistribution Effects and Benefit–cost Analysis." In: S. B. Chase, editor, *Problems in Public Expenditure Analysis* (Washington, DC: The Brookings Institution, 1968), pp. 177–208. In addition, Shlomo Yitzhaki has developed a method for deriving distributional weights from inequality indices commonly used by economists such as the Gini coefficient. He argues that doing this is appropriate because inequality indices are explicitly or implicitly based on a set of axioms concerning distribution and, hence, "by choosing an inequality measure the economist implicitly assumes distributional weights" (p. 326). Thus, Yitzhaki relies on the behavior of economists, rather than that of politicians. See Shlomo Yitzhaki, "Cost–Benefit Analysis and the Distributional Consequences of Government Projects." *National Tax Journal*, 56(2), 2003, 319–36.

13. For an illustration of how this might be done in practice, see Pearce, *Cost–Benefit Analysis*, p. 71.

14. See H.M. Treasury, *Green Book: Appraisal and Evaluation in Central Government* (London: HMSO, 2003); R. Layard, S. Nickell, and G. Mayraz, "The Marginal Utility of Income." *The Journal of Public Economics*, 92, 2008, 1846–57; and Daniel Fujiwara, *The Department for Work and Pensions Social Cost–Benefit Analysis Framework: Methodologies for Estimating and Incorporating the Wider Social and Economic Impacts of Work in Cost–Benefit Analysis of Employment Programmes*, Working Paper No. 86 (UK: Department for Work and Pensions, 2010).

15. R. Layard, S. Nickell, and G. Mayraz, "The Marginal Utility of Income."

16. Daniel Fujiwara, *The Department for Work and Pensions Social Cost–Benefit Analysis Framework*.

17. It would be somewhat lower if income reported by the Census Bureau included in-kind income such as food stamps and excluded taxes because the ratio of y_l/y_h would be smaller, but it does not. However, in computing their estimate of η for the US, Layard, Nickell, and Mayraz appear to have used the same definition of income as the Census Bureau uses.

18. Other research has emphasized the social welfare aspect of distributional weighting. For example, John D. Graham ("Saving Lives through Administrative Law and Economics." *University of Pennsylvania Law Review*, 157, 2008, 395–540) has suggested that unless a regulation designed to save lives "is neutral or yields a net gain for the poor as a group, it should not be promulgated, regardless of its consequences for society as a whole" (p. 519). Doing this is identical to assigning a distributional weight of infinity to the poor. Mathew D. Adler ("Risk Equity: A New Proposal." *Harvard Environmental Law Review*, 32, 2008, 1–47) criticizes using distributional weights in CBA and advocates using what he calls "probabilistic population profile analysis" (PPPA) instead. PPPA involves application of social welfare functions to the utility functions of individuals and, thus far, has not been operationalized, but Adler argues that it is feasible to do so in the foreseeable future. PPPA would not provide distributional weights. Instead, Adler suggests that CBA and PPPA could be used in combination, with CBA indicating whether a policy results in an improvement in economic efficiency and PPPA used to assess the policy's effect on equity.

19. Helen Scarborough and Jeff Bennett, *Cost–Benefit Analysis and Distributional Preferences: A Choice Modelling Approach* (Cheltenham, UK: Edward Elgar Publishing, 2012).

20. This argument was apparently first made by Arnold C. Harberger, "On the Use of Distributional Weights in Social Cost–Benefit Analysis." *Journal of Political Economy*, 86(2), 1978, S87–S120.

21. Edward M. Gramlich, *A Guide to Benefit–Cost Analysis*, 2nd edn (Englewood Cliffs, NJ: Prentice Hall, 1990), 123–27. Gramlich bases his conclusion on his own "simple analysis" and on findings from a general equilibrium computer simulation conducted by Edgar Browning and William Johnson ("The Trade Off between Equality and Efficiency." *Journal of Political Economy*, 92(2), 1984, 175–203). Both analyses are examples of attempts to compute the marginal efficiency cost of redistribution, which is mentioned in Exhibit 3.2.

22. HM Treasury, *Green Book: Appraisal and Evaluation in Central Government*.

23. Scott Farrow ("Incorporating Equity in Regulatory and Benefit–Cost Analysis Using Risk Based Preferences." *Risk Analysis*, 31(6), 2010, 902–07) suggests some interesting idea, such as Lorenz curves, for displaying the relationship between income and net benefits from a project.

24. Shlomo Yitzhaki coined the terms "win–win reforms," "trade-off reforms," and "lose–lose reforms" to distinguish among the three types of reforms described in the text. See Shlomo Yitzhaki, "Cost–benefit analysis and the Distributional Consequences of Government Projects."

25. Matthew Adler, "Cost–Benefit Analysis and Distributional Weights: An Overview," Working Paper EE 13–04, Duke Law School.

26. Vaino Nurmi and Heini Ahtiainen ("Distributional Weights in Environmental Valuation and Cost–Benefit Analysis: Theory and Practice") list a number of these studies. They also point out that many such studies weight on the basis of average income differences among countries, ignoring income disparities within each country, and demonstrate that doing this can sometimes have undesirable effects.

Case 19

The Tulsa IDA Account Program

This case summarizes an ex post CBA of the Tulsa Individual Development Account (IDA) program. The analysis is based on data collected 10 years after the initial random assignment of participants into treatment and control groups and about six years after the program ended.[1] Most relevant to the subject of this chapter, it considers the distributional consequences of the IDA program from participant, government, and donor perspectives. In addition, it uses Monte Carlo simulation to assess uncertainty in the IDA CBA.

To reduce barriers to saving and investment faced by households below 150 percent of the federal poverty guidelines (about $25,000 for a family of four in the late 1990s and about $37,000 currently), the Tulsa IDA program, which was administered by the Community Action Project of Tulsa County (CAPTC), provided subsidies for saving to purchase a home, maintain a current home, obtain post-secondary education, open or run a business, or accumulate assets for retirement. It also provided ancillary training and education. The program contributed up to $750 per year for three years matched at two dollars for each dollar in participants' accounts earmarked for home purchases and matched dollar for dollar for the other designated purposes. Two-thirds of the matching funds, which totaled $853 in 2016 dollars per eligible family, went to either home purchases (43.9 percent) or home maintenance (22.8 percent). The other major use of the matching funds was for retirement (22.2 percent). The remaining matching funds were used for investments in education or businesses. The program evaluation randomly assigned eligible persons to either the treatment group with access to an IDA account or to a control group.[2]

An Overview of the CBA and Distributional Accounting Framework

Table 19C.1 summarizes the anticipated measured impacts of the Tulsa IDA (that is, supposing that program's impacts are in the expected direction). Plus signs (+) indicate anticipated benefits and minus signs (−) expected costs from three distributional perspectives, as well as from the aggregate social perspective. The four columns show benefits and costs from these perspectives: participants, government, private-sector donors to the IDA fund, and society as a whole (the other three perspectives in aggregate). Offsetting items have a neutral sign (0) and no net effect on society. For example, reductions in income taxes (due to housing payment deductions resulting from the positive impact on

Table 19C.1 *Cost–Benefit Analysis and Distributional Perspectives Accounting Framework*

	Participants	Government	Donors	Society (column sum)
Benefit categories				
Impact on income, net of government transfers	+			+
Impact on government transfers payments	−	+		0
Rental value of house for months of impact on ownership	+			+
Impact on appreciation of home	+			+
Impact on equity in home	+			+
Impact on income taxes due to impact on home ownership	+	−		0
Impact on business equity	+			+
Cost categories				
Impact on taxes due to the impact on income	−	+		0
Impact on home purchase expenditures	−			−
Impact on property taxes	−	+		0
Impact on home repair and maintenance expenses	−			−
Impact on investments in business	−			−
Impact on investments in education	−			−
Impact on savings for retirement	−			−
Matching funds expended	+		−	0
IDA operating costs		−	−	−
Total net monetized benefits	+	−	−	?

home ownership) make participants better off and the government worse off by equal amounts (ignoring the marginal excess burden of taxation).

The investments shown in the participant column in Table 19C.1 represent the *total* amounts invested, including amounts invested through matching funds. Thus, from a participant perspective, the costs of the investments with negative signs in the participant column are partially offset by the matching funds that appear in the participant column with a positive sign. The Tulsa IDA encouraged homeownership; those participants who purchased homes received benefits because they no longer had to pay rent and due to appreciation of the home they purchased. These benefits are, of course, at least partially offset by the costs of purchasing and owning a home, which are also shown in Table 19C.1.

The bottom row in Table 19C.1 shows the total net benefits or costs from each perspective, computed as the algebraic sum of each column. These "bottom-line" estimates could be either positive or negative for each group, at least in terms of *monetary* gains and losses. It was anticipated that the total net benefits of participants would be positive if only because their investments would be subsidized. In contrast, it was antici-pated that the government and private-sector donors would incur net costs. Increases in tax receipts and decreases in transfer payments were expected to only partially offset the costs to government of operating costs. Private donors received no monetary benefits from the costs they incurred. The big unknown, as indicated by the "?" at the bottom of the column for society, is whether the total net benefits accruing to participants would be larger or smaller than the total net costs borne by government and donors. The CBA addresses this unknown.

Estimating the Costs and Benefits

The CBA estimates costs and benefit categories on a per-participant basis. In the analy-sis, all members of the treatment and control groups are included, even those for whom benefits and costs are zero. Only by doing so can the various cost and benefit estimates be appropriately compared. The Consumer Price Index (CPI) is used to adjust these estimated values to 2016 prices. Both benefits and costs were discounted using an annual rate of 3.5 percent.

Based on data collected at several points over a 10-year span, the benefits and costs of the program were estimated for a 10-year period. Because program effects were likely to persist for a number of years, this relatively long observation period is important even though participants had only three years to save in their IDAs and up to another six months to use them for matched investments. For example, educational investments are likely to result in income improvements later in life and purchases of home improvements may cause houses to appreciate in value after adjusting for inflation. On the other hand, IDA's impacts could decay over time. Those in the treatment group would have incentives to invest during the three and a half years during which they could receive matching funds. Those in the control group, in contrast, would have no such incentives and, in fact, were supposed to be barred from CAPTC house purchase assistance programs during the operation of the program.[3] However, it was possible that after program operations ceased, but by the end of the observation period, any early impacts of the program would decay as controls caught up to the treatment group. The 10-year observation period allows trends in impacts that persist beyond the three and a half years of program participation to be picked up.

Most of the impact estimates used in the CBA were not close to statistical sig-nificance at conventional levels.[4] With a sample size of 855, the absence of statistical significance occurs because the estimated impacts are typically small relative to the cor-responding control group means.[5] For example, the mean ownership rate for controls is 0.516, but the estimated impact on ownership is only 0.029. Had the estimated impact been twice as large, it still would have been statistically insignificant.

In view of the lack of statistical significance, it is unsurprising that some of the impact estimates are in the opposite direction of those anticipated. The IDA was expected to increase business equity, expenditures on home repairs and maintenance, and savings for retirement, but the signs are negative. Also, monthly income (exclusive of government transfers) was expected to increase, but is negative at ten years. Government transfer payments were expected to decrease, but two of the three estimated impacts are positive. Still, the estimates provide the best quantitative information available about the true impacts of the Tulsa IDA program: the positive sign estimates imply that the true impacts are more likely to be positive than negative, while the negative estimates imply the opposite. They do not indicate that the true impact *is* exactly zero, although a zero value is a possibility.

Based on the point estimates of impacts, the program resulted in an average net benefit of approximately $2,200 per capita for program participants, but a cost of almost $2,870 per capita to government and about $1,650 per capita to donors. (All costs and benefits are in 2016 dollars.) This yields a net cost of $2,320 per capita from the societal perspective: the government and private donors invested a total of $4,520 in the program in terms of expenditures on operating costs and matching funds but participants obtained only $2,200 in benefits. Other than the unexpected increase in transfer payments, the major benefit to participants came from home purchases (mostly from the rental value and appreciation of purchased homes) that more than offset their cost of purchasing a home. From a societal perspective, however, the gains to participants were largely offset by program operating costs.

As discussed in Chapter 19, an extensive literature in economics argues that CBA should recognize the difference in the marginal utility of relatively low-income individuals (such as the Tulsa IDA participants) and relatively high-income individuals (such as taxpayers the IDA donors) by giving each dollar of gain or loss by the former greater weight in the calculation of net benefits. Other considerations discussed in the chapter also imply that weights should be used. As an example, Daniel Fujiwara proposes that the estimated value for net economic benefit per individual should be multiplied by a weight of 2.5.[6] If that weighting is applied to the net gains of participants, then these benefits would increase from $2,200 to $5,500 and would exceed the total losses to the government and private donors. However, as seen in Chapter 19, the appropriate value of the distributional weight, and even whether the dollars of low-income people should be differently weighted at all in a CBA, is controversial.

As discussed in Chapter 19, Edward Gramlich tentatively estimated that it costs taxpayers roughly around $1.50–$2.00 to transfer a dollar to a recipient through a simple transfer program.[7] The results discussed above imply that the IDA cost taxpayers and private donors about $2.05 to transfer $1.00 to participants ($4,520/$2,200). Hence, based on Gramlich's estimate, the program was less efficient than a simple transfer of funds.

The following Monte Carlo simulations take account of uncertainty in the estimated impacts, as implied by the lack of statistical significance, with and without weighting of participant benefits.

Monte Carlo Simulations

In the Monte Carlo simulations, each employing 2000 trials, the original estimates of impacts were replaced with random draws from normal distributions with means equal to the point estimates of the impacts and standard deviations equal to the five-percent

Table 19C.2 *Summary Statistics from the Monte Carlo Simulations with Alternative Weights (Wt)*

	Participants	Government	Donors	Society			
		Unweighted		Wt = 1	Wt = 1.5	Wt = 2	Wt = 3
Mean net benefits from 2,000 trials (2016 dollars)	2,241	−2,858	−1,653	−2,372	−1,146	−23	2,220
Standard deviation of mean (2016 dollars)	2,264	1,677	0	1,536	2,443	3,485	5,673
Probability of positive net benefits (percent)	83.6	4.6	0.0	5.8	32.3	50.4	66.5

confidence intervals implied by the standard errors of the point estimates. Each benefit and cost category estimate was computed as the mean from the 2000 trials, except for operating costs and expenditures on matching funds, which were not varied. Table 19C.2 summarizes the Monte Carlo results for alternative distributional weights of 1.5, 2.0, and 3.0, as well as no weighting.

As expected, with no weighting the social net benefits (column 4) are close to the net benefits calculated using the point estimates of the impacts. Even with the large standard deviation, fewer than 6 percent of the trials yield positive net benefits from the societal perspective. Applying the 1.5 weight to participant net benefits cuts the loss to society by more than half, but only raises the probability of positive net benefits for society to about 32 percent. Social net benefits just about break even when the weight is increased to 2.0, with the probability of positive net benefits reaching 50 percent. Increasing the weight to 3.0 yields positive net benefits of $2,220 per participant with the probability of positive net benefits rising to about 66 percent. Thus, even with the 3.0 weighting, there was about one chance in three that the program would not produce positive net benefits.

Exercises for Chapter 19 Case

1. You are a decision-maker who has to decide whether to adopt the Tulsa IDA program on a permanent basis relying, in part, on the information provided by the CBA described in this case study.

    a. The case study provides results for a range of distributional weights varying between 1 and 3. As a decision-maker would you prefer that those conducting the study had selected one weight and based the reported findings on that weight or, as is actually done, force you to decide on the appropriate weight?

b. As the decision-maker which weight would you select? Why? Based on the weight you selected, what would you conclude about the merits of the program? Note: to the extent you can, base your answers on the information presented in Chapter 19 about the selection of weights.

c. Imagine that participation in the Tulsa IDA had been limited to households with incomes below the federal poverty line, rather than to those with incomes below 150 percent of the poverty line; but the estimates of benefits and cost had been exactly the same as those presented in the case. How would that change your answers to (b)?

Notes

1. Adapted from David H. Greenberg, "A Cost–Benefit Analysis of Tulsa's IDA Program." *Journal of Benefit–Cost Analysis*, 4(3), 2013, 263–300.

2. On program costs see Mark Schreiner, *Program Costs for Individual Development Accounts: Final Figures from CAPTC in Tulsa* (Washington University in Saint Louis, Center for Social Development, 2004); and Mark Schreiner, *What Does an IDA Cost? Some Measures from ADD* (Washington University in Saint Louis, Center for Social Development Research) Report 05–38, 2005. On subsidies paid, see Michal Grinstein-Weiss, Michael W. Sherraden, William Rohe, William G. Gale, Mark Schreiner, and Clinton Key, *Long-Term Follow-Up of Individual Development Accounts: Evidence from the Add Experiment* (Chapel Hill, NC: The University of North Carolina, 2012).

3. They could receive assistance from non-CAPTC sources, however. The time bar on controls seems to have been breached in some instances.

4. The estimated impact on home appreciation is statistically significant at the 10 percent level if a one-tail test is used and the impact on investment in business barely misses statistical significance at this level with a one-tail test. A one-tail test is arguably the appropriate test because both of these estimated impacts are expected to be positive.

5. For instance, for a type I error of 0.10 and a 5 percentage point (or ten percent) impact at a control mean of 0.5, the power is about 0.4. Thus, the ability of the data to detect even a moderate true impact is very weak at even a very low level of statistical significance of 10 percent.

6. Daniel Fujiwara, *The Department for Work and Pensions Social Cost–Benefit Analysis Framework*. DWP Working Paper 86, London: Department for Work and Pensions, 2010. This weight is applicable to typical low income participants in government transfer programs. Of course, participants in the Tulsa IDA program may well have differed from participants in government transfer programs and thus a higher or lower weight may be appropriate.

7. Edward M. Gramlich, *A Guide to Cost–Benefit Analysis*, 2nd edn (Englewood Cliffs, NJ: Prentice Hall, 1990).

20 How Accurate Is CBA?

Chapter 1 emphasizes that CBA can almost always usefully inform public-sector decision-making. In practice, its usefulness depends on its accuracy. One way to examine the accuracy of CBA is to perform analyses of the same project at different times and to compare the accuracy of the results. In Chapter 1 we called such studies *ex ante/ex post* comparisons or *ex ante/in medias res* comparisons. We now return to this topic in more detail.[1]

An *ex ante* CBA informs the decision about whether to proceed with a proposed project. We refer to this time as year 0 or $t = 0$. An *ex post* analysis is performed after all the impacts of the implemented project have been realized. This may take many years, even centuries. Suppose that all impacts have occurred by year T; then an *ex post* analysis is one performed in year t, where $t \geq T$. Although an *ex post* analysis is conducted too late to influence the decision about the particular project, it offers insight into similar projects. An *in medias res* analysis is performed in some year t, where $0 < t < T$. An *in medias res* analysis may provide information about similar projects or about whether to continue or to terminate the as yet uncompleted project. Both *in medias res* and *ex post* analyses are performed in the same way as *ex ante* analysis but they use data actually revealed from the project.

The accuracy of a CBA depends on how well the analyst performs the 10 steps presented in Chapter 1. Errors may occur at any step. The most important errors relate to specifying the impact categories, predicting the impacts, valuing the impacts in *ex ante* CBA, and in measurement error for *in medias res* or *ex post* CBAs. Important errors associated with the other steps, while they can occur frequently enough, should be avoidable by analysts with a good training in CBA. In this chapter, then, we consider only omission errors, forecasting errors, valuation errors, and measurement errors.

In general, these errors decline, but do not necessarily disappear, as observation of the adopted policy reveals data for use in a CBA. Thus, a CBA performed toward the end of a project is more accurate than one performed earlier, but even studies later in the implementation of a project can contain errors. This chapter illustrates some of these errors in CBA by further examining the highway project discussed in Chapter 1, a project that has been the subject of three separate CBAs performed at different times – one *ex ante*, one *in medias res*, and one *ex post*.

The estimates of net benefits differ considerably across the studies. Contrary to what might have been expected, the largest source of the difference was not errors in forecasts or differences in evaluation of intangible benefits, but major differences in the actual construction costs of the project. Thus, the largest errors arose from what many analysts would have thought were the most reliable components of their *ex ante* CBA.

20.1   Sources of Error and Their Effects over Time

Errors in CBA studies may arise for many reasons. They may result from the manager's bureaucratic lens, as we also discussed in Chapter 1.[2] Some errors in CBA studies appear to be disingenuous or strategic, that is, resulting from analyst or decision-maker self-interested behavior. As noted in Exhibit 20.1, firms subject to proposed regulations tend to overestimate compliance costs. There is also considerable evidence that managers tend to systematically overestimate benefits and underestimate costs.[3] Strategic bias of this sort is widespread among managers and is by no means limited to the public sector.[4] For example, Nancy Ryan found that private-sector nuclear power projects experienced "awe-inspiring" cost overruns, some attributable to strategic underestimation of costs.[5] A number of studies have found that firms often reported overly high estimates of compliance costs.[6]

Exhibit 20.1

The US Environmental Protection Agency (EPA) conducts *ex post* assessments of the costs of regulations to help improve the accuracy of *ex ante* predictions of costs in CBAs of proposed regulations. Analysts identify three general sources of error. First, the EPA must rely on firms that would be subject to the proposed rule as a primary source of information about compliance costs. Rather than investing in analyses of all possible compliance alternatives, firms tend to report on one that is plausible but not necessarily the most technically efficient. Firms may also have strategic incentives to overstate costs if they oppose the rule or to understate costs if the rule would provide a competitive advantage. Second, analysts may fail to anticipate technical innovations or low-cost compliance options. For example, the cost of the EPA rule phasing out the use of chlorofluorocarbons was 30 percent less than predicted because the *ex ante* analysis did not anticipate process changes and substitutes that lowered costs. Third, because the rule-making process for major rules requiring CBA typically takes years and may be followed by a long implementation period, there is considerable time for unanticipated exogenous changes to take place. For example, the costs of rules reducing sulfur dioxide emissions were lower than predicted because railroad deregulation reduced the price of low-sulfur coal by reducing the costs of shipping it from mines in Wyoming to East Coast power plants.

Source: Adapted from Elizabeth Kopits, Al McGartland, Cynthia Morgan, Carl Pasurka, Ron Shadbegian, Nathalie B. Simon, David Simpson, and Ann Wolverton, "Retrospective Cost Analyses of EPA Regulations: A Case Study Approach." *Journal of Benefit–Cost Analysis*, 5(2), 2014, 173–93.

When truly independent analysts perform CBAs, as was the case for our highway example, one would not expect to encounter strategic bias. However, as we discussed in Chapter 8, prediction is subject to omission errors and forecasting errors, and monetization is subject to valuation errors. In addition, there may be measurement errors. Exhibit 20.2 summarizes the argument of Steven Popper, Robert Lempert, and Steven Bankes that, due to uncertainty in long-term projects, policy makers should "satisfice" under all possible contingencies, rather than selecting the alternative with the largest expected net social benefits.

Exhibit 20.2

Steven Popper, Robert Lempert, and Steven Bankes are sufficiently concerned about forecasting errors resulting from uncertainty in the case of long-term, complex projects that they are attempting to develop an alternative to conventional cost–benefit analysis. As discussed in Chapter 11, when there is uncertainty about which of several contingencies will be realized, one approach in CBA is to compare alternative policies by first estimating the benefits and costs of each under each contingency, then estimating the expected value for each alternative policy by using predicted probabilities of each contingency being realized, and finally selecting the alternative with the largest net expected values. Popper, Lempert, and Bankes suggest, in contrast to selecting the optimal policy in terms of its net expected value, which under some contingencies may result in outcomes that are unsatisfactory, choosing a policy that yields "satisfactory" outcomes under all possible contingencies, even if this policy has a smaller expected value than another alternative. One reason they promote their approach is that they believe that under many circumstances the probabilities for each contingency cannot be accurately forecast. Thus, they suggest computing what the probability of each possible contingency being realized would have to be to justify selecting one policy alternative over another and then letting policy makers assess whether the actual probabilities are larger or smaller than these estimates.

Source: Adapted from Steven W. Popper, Robert J. Lempert, and Steven C. Bankes, "Shaping the Future." *Scientific American*, 292(4), 2005, 66.

Over time, the net effect of these errors will generally decline and the estimated NPV will converge to the true value. *Ex ante*, the distribution of the present value of net benefits typically has quite a large variance reflecting uncertainty about it. Over time some impacts are realized – nature "rolls the dice" on some impact variable, for example, the initial volume of traffic. Consequently, the distribution of net benefits changes over time. The mean of the distribution may increase or decrease relative to the *ex ante* mean, but it will tend to approach the true value. At the same time, the variance decreases over time, although it never equals zero.

Omission errors certainly decline over time as the full range of project impacts are observed. Similarly, forecasting errors are reduced or eliminated as impacts are realized. Of course, even an *ex post* CBA may contain some forecasting errors due to difficulties associated with predicting the counterfactual events. Valuation errors are also likely to decline over time due to methodological improvements that produce more reliable shadow prices. While measurement errors may not change over time, this type of error is likely to be relatively small. Thus, in aggregate, as *t* increases, the variance of the estimate of the present value of net benefits decreases. The variance never equals zero: uncertainty reduces but is never completely eliminated.

Whether estimates of the present value of net benefits are consistently above or below the "true" value, that is, whether estimators are systematically positively or negatively biased, depends on magnitudes of any biases in omission, forecasting, valuation, or measurement errors. Obtaining and comparing estimates of net benefits at different times provides clues about the magnitude of the different types of errors in a CBA and about the presence of systematic biases. With such knowledge, analysts may be able to provide better information about the precision of their estimates in similar situations.

20.2   Three CBAs of The Coquihalla Highway

The Coquihalla Highway, as described in Chapter 1, is a four-lane road, which was tolled until 2008. It improves access between the interior of British Columbia (BC) and Vancouver. Alternate routes are generally two-lane, with occasional sections of passing lanes. Congestion and traffic safety concerns were important factors in the decision to build the highway. Construction was performed in three phases: Phase I goes from the town of Hope to Merritt, Phase II from Merritt to Kamloops, and Phase III from Merritt to Kelowna.

Three CBAs of the Highway are summarized in Table 20.1.[7] They summarize the benefits and costs of the highway relative to the pre-project status quo (no new highway in this region). The three studies are similar in many respects. All three were performed by independent analysts; they all took a global perspective, that is, everyone had standing, including foreigners; they assumed that there would be tolls at the levels that were implemented initially; and they used a 7.5 percent real social discount rate and a 20-year horizon value. Benefits and costs were expressed as present values in 1984 Canadian dollars, which Table 20.1 converts to 2016 Canadian dollars. One important difference is that the *ex ante* study was performed on the first two phases only, whereas the other two studies were performed on all three phases.

Bill Waters and Shane Meyers (henceforth WM) conducted the first CBA in 1986.[8] This is essentially an *ex ante* study, although Phase I was just opening at that time. The authors used "information and forecasts developed before the highway was built as this is more relevant to assessing the original decision to build the highway."[9] The impact categories, which are listed in Table 20.1, are self-explanatory. Because all three CBAs were performed using a global perspective, there is no impact category for toll revenues, which are all transfers when using this perspective. WM calculated the present value of the net benefit of the project to be $85.2 million (2016 dollars).

Table 20.1 *Three CBAs of the Coquihalla Highway*

	Waters and Meyers Phases I and II *Ex Ante*	Mallery Phases I, II, and III *In Medias Res*	Boardman, Mallery, and Vining Phases I, II, and III *Ex Post*
PROJECT BENEFITS			
Time and operating savings	616.1	885.0	1,908.0
Safety benefits	77.4	109.1	430.4
Reduced congestion on alternative routes	29.9	62.9	120.0
Terminal value after 20 years	113.0	298.0	313.2
Total Benefits	836.4	1,355.0	2,771.6
PROJECT COSTS			
Construction	717.2	1,489.0	1,774.3
Toll collection	17.8	17.8	17.8
Maintenance and snow removal	16.1	120.0	143.9
Total Costs	751.1	1,626.8	1,936.0
NET BENEFITS	85.3	−271.8	835.6

Note: All figures are present values expressed in millions of 2016 Canadian dollars, discounted at 7.5 percent, assuming a project life of 20 years.

Source: Adapted from Anthony E. Boardman, Wendy L. Mallery, and Aidan R. Vining, "Learning from *Ex Ante/Ex Post* Cost–Benefit Comparisons: The Coquihalla Highway Example." *Socio-Economic Planning Sciences*, 28(2), 1994, 69–84, table 2, p. 77. Reprinted with kind permission from Elsevier Science, Ltd., The Boulevard, Langford Lane, Kidlington OX5 19GB, UK.

Wendy L. Mallery (hereafter MLY) conducted the second study in late 1987.[10] At that time, Phases I and II had been completed, but Phase III had not. MLY had access to actual traffic data (for 16 months for Phase I and for one month for Phase II) and published estimates of actual construction costs. Thus, MLY's study is an early *in medias res* CBA. It found negative net benefits of $271.8 million (2016 dollars).

The final study by Anthony E. Boardman, Wendy L. Mallery, and Aidan R. Vining (hereafter BMV) was completed in 1993, although some impacts were estimated earlier.[11] Despite the fact that this study was conducted before the end of the project's life, we follow conventional practice and treat it as an *ex post* CBA. It found positive net benefits of $835.6 million (2016 dollars).

20.2.1   *Omissions*

It could be argued that there were omission errors in all three analyses. None considered the opportunity cost of the land occupied by the highway. This land was owned by the provincial government. Even analysts have a tendency to treat publicly owned land as "free," which, of course, is incorrect. In fact, the land did not have a high opportunity cost, so excluding it did not have a large impact on net present values (*NPVs*).

There has been some controversy over the highway's environmental impacts. Although none of the studies include a separate impact category for environmental damage, the cost of constructing underpasses to allow animals to safely cross underneath the highway, careful timing of the construction activity, and special efforts to repair any encroachment of rivers were included in construction costs. All three analyses assumed implicitly that, after taking these actions, environmental impacts would be negligible. Environmentalists, however, contended that the actual environmental impacts (e.g., wild animal road kills, wildlife and fish habitat destruction) are quite large.

None of the CBAs includes benefits associated with regional development. Such indirect, local benefits are generally viewed in CBA as transfers from other areas, rather than real benefits. Yet, analysis of indirect effects becomes complicated in the presence of *network externalities*. In the years since the construction of the highway, there has been an unexpected economic boom in Kelowna, which is at one end of the route. These positive network externalities or agglomeration effects may be partially attributable to the highway.[12] If so, it would be legitimate to treat part of the regional development benefits as real benefits.

20.2.2   *Forecasting Differences*

Traffic Volume Data for the Coquihalla and Other Routes. Estimates of traffic volume are likely to be the most crucial forecast in a highway CBA because they directly affect many of the benefit categories. Future traffic levels are difficult to predict. Furthermore, they may change over the life of the project as potential users "learn" about the advantages and disadvantages of the highway and alternative routes, as population distributions change, and as consumer tastes change.

WM obtained aggregate annual traffic forecasts by applying traffic growth patterns around the time of their study to a British Columbia Ministry of Transportation forecast for 1986 and allowing for a traffic bulge expected as a result of a major exposition in Vancouver. They then disaggregated the data into different origin-destination groups for three categories of vehicles (trucks, passenger vehicles used for work, and passenger vehicles used for leisure). For each group, they estimated the proportion of diverted, undiverted, and generated traffic.[13] Price-sensitive diversion rates were used to account for the impacts of tolls.

MLY used actual Coquihalla traffic counts from May 1986 (when Phase I opened) to September 1987 (when Phase II opened). For subsequent years, MLY produced three different *NPV*s, assuming a 1, 3, and 5 percent annual traffic growth. The 3 percent rate is used in Table 20.1. Under this assumption, total vehicle traffic (at the toll booth) in the years 2000 and 2005 was projected to be 2.85 million and 3.65 million, respectively. MLY estimated the annual average daily traffic allocations on alternative routes for 1984–1987 based on actual average summer daily traffic counts.[14] This historical information was used to estimate a diversion rate of 30 percent of traffic on Highway 3 to the Coquihalla after the completion of Phase III.

BMV draw on four sources of data: (1) toll booth receipts for the years 1986–1990, which were broken out by the following vehicle classes: motorcycles, passenger vehicles, and trucks with two axles, three axles, four to five axles, or six axles or more;[15] (2) perusal of April 1991 traffic counts at the Coquihalla toll booth and on the Okanagan Connector (Phase III), which showed that completion of Phase III increased Coquihalla traffic by about 40 percent; (3) counters on all alternative routes for 1985–1989 (the summer traffic counts for each highway section were then adjusted to account for seasonality: summer traffic was 1.25–1.9 times the annual average daily traffic); and (4) Ministry of Transportation origin–destination surveys, which suggested that 90 percent of passenger vehicles were leisure travelers, while 10 percent were business travelers. Based on these data, and assuming a 5 percent annual growth rate (after completion of Phase III), BMV projected annual Coquihalla traffic volumes of 4.03 million and 5.14 million vehicles for the years 2000 and 2005, respectively.

It is impossible to determine the accuracy of the traffic volume forecasts of WM's *ex ante* study because they did not present them explicitly, nor did they specify the growth rate. Analysis by backward induction suggests that WM only slightly overestimated initial use, but seriously underestimated future traffic volumes. MLY used actual data for the initial year and then estimated an annual growth rate of 3 percent, while actual growth has been about 5 percent for quite a number of years. WM predicted that the opening of Phase III would increase the traffic base by 20 percent, but it actually increased by about twice as much. BMV's *ex post* study projections for the years 2000 and 2005 are 41 percent higher than MLY's estimates.

Time and Distance Savings on the Coquihalla. One might expect that time and distance savings per trip would not vary by much among the analyses. In fact, they did vary, as shown in Tables 20.2 and 20.3. Differences in distance result from changes in the final design as well as the use of different data to measure distance. Differences in

Table 20.2 *Distance Saved per Coquihalla Trip (Kilometers)*

Trip	Waters and Meyers *Ex Ante*	Mallery *In Medias Res*	Boardman, Mallery, and Vining *Ex Post*
Phase I:			
Hope to Merritt	N/A[a]	87	112
Phases I and II:			
Hope to Kamloops	72	83	107
Phases I and III:			
Hope to Peachland	N/A	77	53

[a]N/A, not available or not applicable.

Source: Anthony E. Boardman, Wendy L. Mallery, and Aidan R. Vining, "Learning from *Ex Ante/Ex Post* Cost-Benefit Comparisons: The Coquihalla Highway Example." *Socio-Economic Planning Sciences*, 28(2), 1994, 69–84, table 3A, p. 79. Reprinted with kind permission from Elsevier Science, Ltd., The Boulevard, Langford Lane, Kidlington OX5 19GB, UK.

Table 20.3 *Time Saved per Coquihalla Trip (Minutes)*

Trip	Waters and Meyers *Ex Ante*	Mallery *In Medias Res*	Boardman, Mallery, and Vining *Ex Post*
Phase I:			
Hope to Merritt	N/A[a]	102	108
Phases I and II:			
Hope to Kamloops	72	89	120
Phases I and III:			
Hope to Peachland	N/A	100	79

[a]N/A, not available or not applicable.
Source: Anthony E. Boardman, Wendy L. Mallery, and Aidan R. Vining, "Learning from *Ex Ante/Ex Post* Cost-Benefit Comparisons: The Coquihalla Highway Example." *Socio-Economic Planning Sciences*, 28(2), 1994, 69–84, table 3B, p. 79. Reprinted with kind permission from Elsevier Science, Ltd., The Boulevard, Langford Lane, Kidlington OX5 19GB, UK.

time saved result from differences in distance saved and different assumptions about the speeds traveled on different routes.

Reduced Congestion on Alternative Routes. WM estimated that, because of the Coquihalla, through traffic on the old routes would save 20 minutes during congested periods. They assumed local traffic would save less time, proportional to the number of cars diverted to the new highway. MLY also used the 20-minute saving. BMV followed a different approach, assuming users of alternative routes would save 2 kilometers per hour in 1986 and 5 kilometers per hour from 1987 onward.

Accident Rates. WM calculated safety benefits resulting from both reduced distance traveled and from traveling on a safer highway. To estimate safety benefits from reduced distances, they multiplied the predicted 130 million vehicle-kilometers saved by the accident rates for fatal, injury, and property-damage-only accidents on two-lane highways as estimated by Radnor Pacquette and Paul Wright.[16] To estimate benefits resulting from a safer road, WM multiplied the estimated 313 million vehicle-kilometers traveled on the Coquihalla by one-third of the accident rate – their estimate of the accident rate reduction that would result from using a four-lane divided highway instead of the existing highway. MLY followed a similar approach but, for benefits resulting from a safer road, the study used the higher accident rate reductions implied by Pacquette and Wright, which ranged from 35 to 50 percent, depending on the severity of accident. BMV obtained accident rate data by severity from the Ministry of Transportation and Infrastructure.

The Coquihalla Highway does save lives. The fatal accident rate of the Coquihalla is about 50 percent lower than on alternate routes, a higher reduction than WM assumed but similar to MLY's estimate. Furthermore, actual fatal accident rates on all routes in

British Columbia are higher than WM or MLY assumed. Consequently, more lives are saved due to reduced distance driving than either WM or MLY predicted. Relative to other routes, the Coquihalla has a lower injury rate but a higher property-damage-only rate. Nonetheless, because both of these types of accident rates are also higher in British Columbia than anticipated, the shorter Coquihalla generates much higher overall safety benefits than projected.[17]

20.2.3   *Valuation Differences*

Values of Saved Vehicle Operating Costs and Time. The three CBAs were similar in terms of how they valued time savings. Specifically, each assumed that business travelers value an hour of their time at the average gross wage for British Columbia hourly and salaried employees, whereas leisure travelers value their time at 25 percent of this rate. All three studies also made similar assumptions about the number of passengers in each vehicle. Based on a perusal of estimates from the ministry, BMV assumed 2.2 passengers per leisure vehicle and 1.2 passengers per business vehicle. The other studies used similar estimates.

The three analyses differed in the estimated gross wage rates and in the vehicle operating costs. Consider, for example, the estimates (all converted to 2016 dollars) pertaining to a trip from Hope to Kamloops. WM estimated vehicle operating cost savings per Coquihalla trip at $14.80 for automobiles and $71.00 for large trucks. Estimated time savings were $17.00, $30.50, and $35.60 per trip for leisure vehicles, business vehicles, and trucks, respectively. MLY calculated vehicle operating cost savings at $20.50 per automobile trip and at $99.00 per truck trip. Time savings were calculated as $13.90 per leisure trip, $41.90 per business-auto trip, and $47.40 per truck trip.[18] BMV's estimates were considerably higher. Based largely on data provided by Trimac Consulting Services, BMV estimated time *and* vehicle operating cost savings at $51.60 per leisure trip, $87.70 per business trip, and $162.10 for a five-axle semitrailer trip.[19]

Value of Safety Benefits. WM valued fatalities, injuries, and property-damage-only accidents at $1.06 million, $23,310, and $4,240, respectively. MLY used slightly higher valuations: saved fatalities, injuries, and property-damage-only accidents were valued at $1.17 million, $25,430, and $4,240, respectively. Since 1984 there has been considerable theoretical and empirical research on this topic. As discussed in Chapter 17, current valuations are considerably higher in real dollars than was thought appropriate in 1984. Based on the most recent research at the time of their study, BMV used $4.66 million for the value of an avoided fatality.

Terminal Value. As discussed in Chapter 9, with a discounting period of 20 years, the terminal value conceptually equals the present value of the net benefits of the project from the twenty-first year to infinity. The obvious difficulty is in making projections that far into the future. Future costs, for example, will depend critically on the actual depreciation rate of the highway, which is partially endogenous insofar as it varies with use.

The method used in all three studies was to base the terminal value on the initial construction cost. WM assumed the terminal value in the twenty-first year was 75 percent of the initial construction costs. MLY used 85 percent of initial construction costs, due partially to the high proportion of Coquihalla construction costs, such as rock cutting and sand blasting, that needed to be done only once. BMV used 75 percent.

20.2.4   *Estimation/Measurement Differences*

Maintenance Expenses. At the time of the *ex ante* study, the Maintenance Services Branch estimated that the cost of annual maintenance and snow removal ranged between $5,300 and $15,890 per lane-kilometer. WM selected a number near the low end of this range but interpreted the figures as per kilometer rather than per lane-kilometer, resulting in an estimate of $5,510 per kilometer. In contrast, MLY estimated $14,830 per lane-kilometer for Phase I, and $10,590 per lane-kilometer for Phases II and III. Because the highway was 80 percent a four-lane highway and 20 percent a six-lane highway, MLY's maintenance and snow removal estimates were far higher than WM's estimates. BMV made a largely unsuccessful attempt to isolate actual maintenance expenses. One problem was that the ministry maintained data by maintenance district, rather than by highway. Ultimately, BMV used an estimate of $12,710 per lane-kilometer, the average of the two figures used by MLY. There was one difference, however, stemming from the record-breaking snowstorms over the 1990–91 winter. To account for the "once in 10-, 20-, or 50-year" snowstorms that can severely affect the Coquihalla, maintenance and snow removal costs were arbitrarily increased in each of two randomly chosen years. Overall, this approach is not entirely satisfactory, but it highlights that, like *ex ante* analyses, *ex post* analyses can suffer from prediction error.

Construction Costs. WM performed their study after Phase I was completed. Consequently, forecasting construction costs was not an issue, but they still encountered measurement problems. Based on the best-available data, WM estimated the present value of construction costs for Phases I and II were equal to $716.4 million.

Soon after completion of the highway, rumors circulated of higher costs. On November 7, 1987, the *Vancouver Sun* published estimates of undiscounted total costs of $1,208 million for Phases I and II and $572 million for Phase III. MLY discounted these estimates to obtain construction costs of $1,076 million for Phases I and II and $411 million for Phase III. BMV's construction cost estimates are based on the MacKay Commission, a commission of inquiry appointed by the British Columbia government when it became publicly known that the Coquihalla had cost much more than originally anticipated.[20] MacKay concluded that "differences between costs and estimates of the Coquihalla Highway … are due to … lack of proper budgeting, monitoring cost-control and reporting systems" (p. xi), and observed "[t]he current method of reporting highway capital spending … by individual contracts, by Electoral Districts, and on an annual basis … has served to disguise the true cost of major projects" (p. xi). MacKay also commented that "The Ministry's cost reporting system for capital works is fragmented and inconsistent" (p. xx). Based on the MacKay Commission report, BMV estimated that the present value of construction costs of the Coquihalla was $1,773 million, which is $286 million higher than MLY. The difference between BMV's estimate and the estimates in the earlier studies probably results mostly from strategic biases.

During BMV's enquiries on actual construction costs, one ministry official estimated that MacKay's total Coquihalla construction cost figures were "out" (underestimated) by as much as 300 percent! Uncertainties undoubtedly remain even after the events. Doubling construction costs would be a rough way of accounting for work that was hidden or lost in general accounts and for increases in indirect ministry overhead costs due to the Coquihalla.

Exhibit 20.3

Richard Anguera conducted both an *in medias res* financial analysis and an *in medias res* cost–benefit analysis of the Channel Tunnel (between England and France). He did not conduct or present an *ex ante* cost–benefit analysis and did not conduct an *ex ante–ex post* CBA comparison, but he had access to many *ex ante* forecasts and was able to make *ex ante–ex post* comparisons. His main conclusions are:

1. *Ex ante* forecasts overestimated the total size and growth of the cross-channel passenger and freight markets. While the Channel Tunnel's market share was predicted accurately, this was only achieved by price-cutting. Eurotunnel's forecasts of freight increased over time, concurrently with cost estimate increases. In fact, its early estimates of freight traffic were lower than actual traffic. In contrast, its passenger traffic forecasts were extremely optimistic – between two and three times the actual traffic.

2. Costs were significantly underestimated: they ended-up being twice the expected amount. The major reason was regulatory risk, mainly attributable to the Independent Safety Authority that had responsibility for the safety design standards. Brent Flyvbjerg, Nils Bruzelius, and Werner Rothengatter (*Megaprojects and Risk: An Anatomy of Ambition*, New York, NY: Cambridge University Presss, 2003) also identified lack of clear ownership and control as another major reason. In addition, and probably not totally unexpectedly, there were unforeseen problems in the works program.

3. According to Anguera, the net social benefit of the Tunnel for the 1987–2003 period was −£10 billion in 2004 pounds, using a real social discount rate of 3.5 percent. While this is a substantial loss, it is important to note that it does not include a terminal value, which is likely large.

4. In terms of distributional implications, the main beneficiaries were users who benefitted from lower prices. The main losers were producers, both the Tunnel operator and ferry operators (competitors). Most of the users' gain was a transfer from producers.

Adapted from Richard Anguera, "The Channel Tunnel – An Ex Post Economic Evaluation." *Transportation Research Part A*, 40(4), 2006, 291–315.

20.3 Overall Underestimation of the Differences among the Studies

Simply looking at the aggregate differences understates the actual differences among the three studies. First, some benefits and costs erred in the same direction, thereby tending to cancel each other. For example, the *ex post* study had higher construction costs but also had higher time and operating savings benefits than the previous studies. Second, some errors offset one another within an impact category. For example, with respect to safety benefits, the Coquihalla accident rate was higher than predicted, but highway ridership and accident rates elsewhere were also higher than forecast.

20.4 Conclusion

Contrasting an *in medias res* or *ex post* analysis with earlier CBAs of the same project provides an opportunity to assess the predictive capability of earlier analyses. This is a critical element in determining the value of *ex ante* CBAs. In the Coquihalla Highway example this exercise was somewhat humbling. *Ex ante* CBA is hard to do precisely.

One comparison study alone cannot tell us everything about the general accuracy of CBA. Are such aggregate prediction errors prevalent in other CBAs? If they are, then it is troubling. One might argue that this particular project raises more problems than is typical, but we think not. This project is *relatively* straightforward; after all, it is a highway, not a high-tech, mega project. Another possibility is that the cost underestimation problem (partly due to regional rather than project-specific budgeting) is specific to "wild and woolly" British Columbia. Again, we do not think so. Several non-British Columbia bureaucrats acknowledge that their agencies routinely hide project budget items in other accounts.

In conclusion, the main lesson illustrated here is the importance of periodically conducting *ex ante/ex post* comparisons. This may seem trivial, but until recently, it has received little attention in the cost–benefit analysis literature. The number of *ex post* CBAs is likely to grow because of President Obama's executive orders (E.O. 13563 and 13610) requiring federal agencies to conduct retrospective analyses to assess the accuracy of predicted costs and benefits of major rules analyzed in prior analyses to determine if continuation of existing rules is economically justified.[21] This chapter provides a template for how to do such comparisons.

Notes

1. The chapter draws upon Anthony E. Boardman, Wendy L. Mallery, and Aidan R. Vining, "Learning from Ex Ante/Ex Post Cost–Benefit Comparisons: The Coquihalla Highway Example." *Socio-Economic Planning Sciences*, 28(2), 1994, 69–84.

2. See Anthony Boardman, Aidan Vining, and W. G. Waters II, "Costs and Benefits Through Bureaucratic Lenses: Example of a Highway Project," *Journal of Policy Analysis and Management*, 12(3), 1993, 532–55.

3. For example, see Bent Flyvbjerg, Mette K. Skamris Holm, and Soren L. Buhl, "How (In)accurate Are Demand Forecasts in Public Works Projects? The Case of Transportation." *Journal of the American Planning Association*, 71(2), 2005, 131–46; and, by the same authors, "Cost Underestimation in Public Works Projects: Error or Lie?" *Journal of the American Planning Association*, 68(3), 2002, 279–95.

4. This bias has been found in a wide range of corporations by Stephen W. Pruitt and Lawrence J. Gitman, "Capital Budgeting Forecast Biases: Evidence from the Fortune 500." *Financial Management*, 16(1), 1987, 46–51. See also Charles R. Schwenk, "The Cognitive Perspective on Strategic Decision Making." *Journal of Management Studies*, 25(1), 1988, 41–55, and J. E. Russo and P. J. Schoemaker, "Managing Overconfidence." *Sloan Management Review*, 33(2), 1992, 7–17.

5. Nancy E. Ryan, "Policy Formation in a Politically Charged Atmosphere: An Empirical Study of Rate-Base Determination for Recently Completed Nuclear Power Plants," paper presented at the 14th Annual APPAM Research Conference, 1992, at p. 3.

6. See studies reviewed in table 1 of Elizabeth Kopits, Al McGartland, Cynthia Morgan, Carl Pasurka, Ron Shadbegian, Nathalie B. Simon, David Simpson, and Ann Wolverton, "Retrospective Cost Analyses of EPA Regulations: A Case Study Approach." *Journal of Benefit–Cost Analysis*, 5(2), 2014, 173–93.

7. For various reasons the summary benefit and cost figures of the *ex ante* CBA in Table 20.1 are not exactly the same as those presented in Table 1.3.

8. W. G. Waters II and Shane J. Meyers, "Benefit–Cost Analysis of a Toll Highway – British Columbia's Coquihalla." *Journal of the Transportation Research Forum*, 28(1), 1987, 435–43.

9. Ibid.

10. Wendy L. Mallery, "A Cost–Benefit Analysis of the Coquihalla Highway," course paper for J. M. Munro, Simon Fraser University, December 1987.

11. Boardman, Mallery, and Vining, "Learning from Ex Ante/Ex Post Cost-Benefit Comparisons." Using a similar approach, Winston Harrington, Richard D. Morgenstern, and Peter Nelson ("On the Accuracy of Regulatory Cost Estimates." *Journal of Policy Analysis and Management*, 19(2), 2000, 297–322) compared *ex ante* cost estimates of the direct cost of regulations with *ex post* estimates of the same regulations and found that the former were overestimated much more often than they were underestimated.

12. A positive network externality arises where the utility one person derives from the consumption of a good increases with the number of other people consuming the good. For example, the benefit of having a cell phone increases with the number of other people who have cell phones that are connected to the same network. In the context of regional development, positive externalities may arise when a region reaches a critical mass, or agglomeration, in terms of the nature, depth, and breadth of its economic activity.

13. Diverted traffic refers to traffic that would have gone on the old routes but now travels on the Coquihalla. Undiverted traffic refers to traffic that continues on the old routes despite the existence of the Coquihalla. Generated traffic refers to traffic that would not have made the trip by road at all without the Coquihalla but now does so because the effective price is lower. These travelers may have gone by air or train or done something completely different.

14. These numbers were then adjusted by the estimated ratio of average summer to average annual traffic.

15. Total traffic data were obtained for 1986–1990. Traffic data by vehicle class were obtained for the period April 1987–March 1991 and estimated for 1986 and part of 1987. The traffic data thus cover three full years of Phase II operation from Hope to Kamloops and a few months of Phase III operation from Hope to Peachland.

16. Radnor J. Pacquette and Paul H. Wright, *Highway Engineering* (New York, NY: Wiley & Sons, 1979), at p. 73.

17. MLY based her projections on Pacquette and Wright (p. 73), who estimated the accident rates on a divided highway are 0.0155, 0.168, and 0.304 (per million vehicle-kilometers) for fatalities, injuries, and property damage only, respectively.

18. MLY used the average April 1986 gross wage for all BC industries for hourly and salaried employees, from the Statistics Canada publication, *Monthly Employment Earnings and Hours*, as the business hourly wage.

19. Trimac Consulting Services Limited, *Operating Costs of Trucks in Canada*, 1986 and 1988 editions, prepared for the Motor Carrier Branch, Surface Transport Administration,

Transport Canada (Ottawa, Ontario: Minister of Supply and Services, 1986, 1988).

20. Douglas L. MacKay, Commissioner, *Report of the Commission Inquiry into the Coquihalla and Related Highway Projects*, Province of British Columbia, December 1987.

21. Randall Lutter, "Regulatory Policy: What Role for Retrospective Analysis and Review?" *Journal of Benefit–Cost Analysis*, 4(1), 2013, 17–38.

Name Index

Subject Index